Hellenic Studies 78

ONE MAN SHOW

Recent Titles in the Hellenic Studies Series

ONE MAN SHOW

POETICS AND PRESENCE
IN THE *ILIAD* AND *ODYSSEY*

by
Katherine Kretler

CENTER FOR HELLENIC STUDIES
Trustees for Harvard University
Washington, DC
Distributed by Harvard University Press
Cambridge, Massachusetts, and London, England
2020

One Man Show: Poetics and Presence in the Iliad *and* Odyssey
By Katherine Kretler
Copyright © 2020 Center for Hellenic Studies, Trustees for Harvard University
All Rights Reserved.
Published by Center for Hellenic Studies, Trustees for Harvard University,
Washington, D.C.
Distributed by Harvard University Press, Cambridge, Massachusetts and
London, England
Printed by Total Printing Systems, Newton, IL
Cover Design: Joni Godlove
Production: Kerri Cox Sullivan

Library of Congress Cataloging-in-Publication Data

Names: Kretler, Katherine L., author.
Title: One man show : poetics and presence in the *Iliad* and *Odyssey* / Katherine
Kretler.
Description: Washington : Center for Hellenic Studies, Trustees for Harvard
University, 2020. | Includes bibliographical references and index.
Identifiers: LCCN 2019021509 | ISBN 9780674980020
Subjects: LCSH: Homer. Iliad. | Homer. Odyssey.
Classification: LCC PA4037 .K716 2019 | DDC 883/.01--dc23
LC record available at https://lccn.loc.gov/2019021509

Contents

Acknowledgements

This book has its origins in my University of Chicago dissertation. I treasure my conversations with my advisors: first, the late David Grene, who demanded that every act of translation be a performance, and then James Redfield, Laura Slatkin and the late Paul Friedrich. Each of these brilliant scholars opened to me doors of reading and thinking and encouraged me to strike out on the path that led to this book.

At Chicago, I benefited greatly from rich discussions that followed workshop presentations within the Committee on Social Thought and the Department of Classics. Thanks to all the students in my *Iliad* seminar at Chicago's Graham School, whose enthusiasm buoyed me in the beginning stages of writing. Many colleagues, friends and students generously critiqued and encouraged individual chapters at various stages: special thanks to Elizabeth Adkins, A. P. David, Lillian Doherty, Nancy Felson, Douglas Frame, Peter Heraty, Ralph Johnson, Gregory Nagy, Mark Payne, and Seth Schein. I would also like to thank the anonymous reader for CHS for many helpful suggestions. Thanks to Jill Curry Robbins for her expertise in shepherding the manuscript through to publication, and also to Raleigh Browne for proofreading assistance.

Thanks to Paul Ballard, Peter Mann, and Oren Riggs, who helped improve the diagrams.

I am grateful that I could call upon Jeremiah Wall's bardic ear for the spoken word and his intolerance for academese; he supported me in innumerable ways.

Thank you to my family for their patient support.

Thank you to Paul Mathai for his skepticism, unstinting encouragement, frank criticisms, and innumerable suggestions at all stages of this project. To the extent that I have gotten something said in this book, it is thanks to him.

Portions of the discussion of Aristotle's *Poetics* in the Introduction, and of the discussion of Phoenix's speech in Chapter 2, also appear in my essay in *Thinking the Greeks: A Volume in Honour of James M. Redfield*, edited by Bruce M. King and Lillian Doherty (Routledge 2018).

Introduction

"Isn't everything that is said by the storytellers and the poets a narrative of what has happened or what is or what is to come?"

"What else?" he said.

Plato *Republic* 392d

This book plumbs the virtues of the Homeric poems as scripts for solo performance. Despite the focus on orality for the last several decades, and on composition *in* performance, we have yet to fully appreciate the Homeric poems as the sophisticated scripts they are. When scholars speak of Homeric performance, they are usually referring to the composition process, or "input." This book turns the focus from the "input" to the "output." Composition *in* performance is, after all, composition *for* performance. Interpreting the poems as scripts changes our perspective in a thoroughgoing manner. Performance is a vehicle of meaning as vital for the one-man show of epic as it is for multi-actor, masked, costumed, staged tragedy. Restoring to the poems their performative nature, moreover, helps get beyond the "meaning" dimension of the poems into the dimension of "presence," to borrow Gumbrecht's terms.[1] It makes something happen.

Part of the book's aim, then, is to do for Homer what scholars have been doing for drama and choral poetry: to bring out the totality of the experience of these works on the stage, as opposed to the page.[2] But the analogy is limited. This is not a "how-to" manual or an effort at historical reconstruction. I cannot emphasize this enough. This approach does not depend upon a particular phase

---

[1] Gumbrecht 2004.

[2] The work of Oliver Taplin, Ruth Padel, David Wiles, and Rush Rehm on tragedy is particularly useful for thinking through the differences, as well as the analogies, between epic and tragic performance. For Pindar, Mullen 1982 is essential, taking on pointed significance for the Homerist in light of David 2006, on the implications of hexameter's origins in dance.

of the development of the Homeric poems or even on particulars of performance style. It is rather a phenomenology of performance, aiming to tune the reader in to the "histrionic sensibility,"[3] the "histrionic force," and the "histrionic patterns and devices"[4] of the poems as solo performances. The focus is on how the text, when performed, sets certain dynamics in motion, not on what a given performance "adds," since performance is not an addition. Precisely how any performer embodied that script is unknowable, and, just as with drama, successful embodiments may have differed widely. I occasionally point out how a gesture,[5] a pause, or the use of a staff[6] would bring these dynamics to fruition. These suggestions make no historical claims, and are heuristic: they illustrate the potential embedded in a script that was, after all, embodied *somehow*.[7] These caveats being made, I hope readers will use not only their mind's eye but their actual bodies to step into their own incarnations of Homer.

The other aim of the book is to show how performance is bound up with all aspects of the poems; the operations of performance form a continuum with such "textual" workings as imagery and background story. Establishing this entails that much of this book is concerned with, for example, background stories that come to light because of a concern with performance.

Some of my readers may more naturally find their way in to the argument through one of these aims or the other; but they are intertwined. Because composition blends with performance, stories must be approached both as traditional compositions and as scripts.

* * *

---

3   Fergusson 1949:250–255 and passim.

4   Goldman 1975:77; Goldman 1985:31.

5   On gestures, proxemics, and the like within the world of the Homeric poems, see Lateiner 1995. Lateiner considers Homeric poetry "a nonmimetic (nontheatrical) medium" (p. 48) and so does not discuss performance. Boegehold (1999: Ch. 3) shows how a gesture by a rhapsode would clarify the meaning of syntactically "incomplete" Homeric sentences. Purves's (2019) treatment of the poetics of gesture in Homer fruitfully analyzes gesture along the lines of formulaic composition. Although Purves does not discuss gesture in performance, her linking of kinesthetic effect and sensibility on the one hand and composition on the other is in many ways companionable with the present study.

6   The evidence from vase painting and from the use of the word ῥαψωιδός ("rhapsode") (Appendix A) motivates an inquiry into how such an object would make a difference in performance (Appendix B). Since it makes no fundamental difference to my readings whether the performer used a stringed instrument, a staff, or nothing at all, I confine discussion of the evidence to the Appendices, while making the occasional observation about the effect a rhapsodic staff would produce.

7   Bölte 1907:573. Goldman's formulation (1985:31; cf. p. 60) is apt: though there are "dozens of ways" to a successful performance, choosing one, "as an actor does," allows one to "illustrate the presence of larger histrionic patterns and devices which make themselves felt—and whose meanings remain substantially the same—over a very wide range of possible local readings." In the context of tragedy, see the stimulating exchange between Wiles (1987) and Goldhill (1989).

Many people who have seen a great performance of a play might resist the infamous assertion found in Aristotle's *Poetics*[8] that one should be able to experience drama fully just by reading or by hearing the plot.[9] But what about epic? In justifying his claim, Aristotle continues: "Besides, tragedy does what it does even without movement, *just like epic*; for through reading it is manifest (φανερά) what sort of thing it is" (1462a11–13). Not only, he seems to say, is enactment even less necessary for epic than for tragedy, but also epic does not need gestures even when it *is* performed—its performance is already so minimal as to be a non-performance.[10]

But—before we delve further into Aristotle's view of Homeric dramatics—on a basic level, a claim that performance is superfluous is even *less*, not more, true for epic than it is for drama. And performance is more crucial to understanding and experiencing epic precisely because epic, as a solo genre, does not "enact" in the same way that drama does, with transactions among multiple bodies and props. As we read a tragedy, we visualize multiple figures spread out in space, entering and exiting our mind's eye, wielding objects, and addressing one another, all of which corresponds more or less to what would be happening on the stage. We do stage it in our mind. But if, as we read epic, we imagine Achilles confronting Agamemnon, Athena behind him, the Achaean camp as the setting, that corresponds to the performance not one bit. Staging Homeric action in our mind's eye while reading diverts our attention from what would be happening in performance. The audience watching Homeric performance sees one man enacting, narrating, embodying: transforming himself and the space around him. The solo performer too "structures attention by means of the ear and the eye simultaneously,"[11] even without choreography or staging as normally conceived. And a large part of what the Homeric script is for, I hope to show in this book, is *that*. That is not to say that spectators do not complete the picture of what is happening in their imaginations, and map epic actions onto the actual space around the performer. Indeed, the script is often geared toward projecting a certain imaginative space, or even objects, within the space of performance; but the performer's body is the *origo* of such a space, its center and its source. The solo performer feeds a "profound

---

[8] δεῖ γὰρ καὶ ἄνευ τοῦ ὁρᾶν οὕτω συνεστάναι τὸν μῦθον ὥστε τὸν ἀκούοντα τὰ πράγματα γινόμενα καὶ φρίττειν καὶ ἐλεεῖν ἐκ τῶν συμβαινόντων (1453b3–6). "One should put the plot together such that, even without seeing, the person who hears the actions as they come about shudders and feels pity at what is happening." Aristotle does not have in mind at this point a dramatic reading or a recitation by a slave (*pace* Halliwell 1998:340–341), a sort of minimalist performance, for he continues, "which very thing someone would experience who is listening to the plot (μῦθον) of the *Oidipous*" (1453b6–7).

[9] Brook 1968:42. As to the grounds for such a reaction, Brook 1968 and Goldman 1975 are excellent guides.

[10] Cf. Plato *Republic* 396c–d.

[11] Mullen 1982:4, on Pindar.

and largely unexplored human appetite"[12] for acting, but does so in a way slightly askew from that of actors in drama, a way that requires its own account.

One can quickly grasp the importance of the performer's bodily presence by looking at the opening of the *Iliad* as a script. This passage will be examined in detail below; for now, simply consider the fact that the first character the performer "becomes" in the poem, in the sense of speaking his words, is Chryses, the priest of Apollo, supplicating the Achaeans to give him his daughter back. As the performer slips into being the priest, we, the audience, slot into place as the Achaeans listening to his plea. We are suddenly put in the physical position not of mere witnesses to a past event, but of being able to *do* something, as it were, about the action of the poem. The performer has already told us that the priest will be refused and that Apollo will then start to kill us. So when we are listening to the performer beg for his daughter's life, we already know it is a bad idea to refuse him, but we do nothing, thereby becoming culpable, as it were, for the plot of the poem, implicated[13] in the story.

That is only the most basic way that performing these lines makes something happen that does not happen when we read it. Yet rarely do readers, including readers interested in the sound of the poetry, try to *envision* the *Iliad* and the *Odyssey* as solo performances, even in such a way as this.

Actually, despite his assertions about reading, and despite the usual interpretation of the *Poetics*, Aristotle understands this very well, and he cannot be blamed for our neglect of performance. First, Aristotle praises Homer precisely as a dramatist. He even singles out the mode of Homeric performance as more conducive to the *thaumaston*, the "to be wondered at," than tragedy (1460a7–11). Why would this be? The short answer is that Homeric performance is an intriguing hybrid between acting and not-acting, for which Aristotle's shorthand is "not seeing the one-doing" (1460a11–17).

Aristotle on Homer as Dramatist

To open the question of what is distinctively "to be wondered at" in Homeric performance, let us turn to the passage in which Aristotle praises Homer as dramatist: the famous discussion of the birth of tragedy (and comedy). Here Aristotle hints at, without detailing, the peculiar semi-embodied presencing of Homeric poetry, and sounds themes that will be taken up throughout the present study.[14]

In this passage, Homer plays a complex role. He is, first, the culmination of the natural activities that brought forth *poiēsis* little by little out of improvisations

---

[12] Goldman 1975:3.
[13] Frontisi-Ducroux 1986a:28.
[14] An expanded version of this argument about Aristotle's account of the birth of tragedy appears in Kretler 2018, where I connect the shape and inner workings of Aristotle's account to the mechanics and imagery of Homeric and choral poetry.

(1448b20–34). Second, he is the font of both tragedy and comedy (1448b34–1449a2). He is an endpoint and a starting point, τέλος and ἀρχή. But how Homer operates in this teleological process is far from clear. This very incongruity and contradiction is an important part of how Aristotle conveys the confounding transformation that occurs in Homeric performance itself.

Aristotle is saying that mimesis has its origins in nature: human beings naturally enjoy mimesis, and we are naturally prone to harmony and rhythm. Nature plays another role as well: before poetry proper exists, people of a certain character imitate certain types of people and their actions (1448b24–27)—and thus *poiēsis* at its very birth is "split according to (the people's) own characters [κατὰ τὰ οἰκεῖα ἤθη]: the more solemn imitate noble actions and the actions of such people, and the cheaper sort imitate the actions of the base."[15] Likewise, after Homer, people each according to their own nature (κατὰ τὴν οἰκείαν φύσιν) become either comedians or tragedians (1449a1–6). But Homer himself confounds this bipartite schema. He is both iambic and heroic, both comic and tragic. Homer, unlike the proto-poets before him *and* the tragedians and comedians who follow him, seems not to have his "own nature" or his "own character." Sandwiched between these two groups of people, he problematizes the very schema of nature that Aristotle is setting up.

That is because he is either a genius or a madman: *euplastos* or *ekstatikos* (1455a34). In Chapter 3, Aristotle had aligned Homer with Sophocles and tragedy in imitating the *spoudaioi* (1448a27), as opposed to Aristophanes. In Chapter 4, with the emphasis on natural processes, we would expect Homer to be put once again with the *semnoteroi* and those disposed toward tragedy; we would expect Homer to be aligned exclusively with those who are attracted by tragedy's "more honorable [ἐντιμότερα] shapes" (1449a7). But Aristotle does not even try to say this; he even tells us that Homer "displayed the gestures/shapes of comedy." Homer controverts the model whereby poets who are better by nature will depict better characters.

Before we try too quickly to resolve these difficulties, we should note that Aristotle has subverted this puzzling account at its very start. For people by nature enjoy *mimēseis* of *all* kinds, not only the noble or base, depending on our own nature. We enjoy seeing "shapes of the most despised beasts" [θηρίων τε μορφὰς τῶν ἀτιμοτάτων] and of corpses (1448b12). Such enjoyment may not be problematic in the case of beasts, but we have to imagine it holds true for people as well: ἀτιμοτάτων ("despised") does not really suit wild animals, and sits uncomfortably with his statement about tragedy's "more honorable" (ἐντιμότερα) shapes.

---

[15] In context, ἤθη indicates the characters of the poets rather than the poetry, but of course the point is that they are similar. Cf. Lucas 1968:75.

If we have a good inner nature, we will be drawn to imitate good people and good actions. But a genius like Homer will imitate all sorts of people, like the poet banned by Socrates in the *Republic*. The better the poet, the more promiscuous or protean the nature.

These kinds of incongruities permeate this passage. Aristotle asserts that some people are drawn toward noble actions, some toward base, and they divide themselves into the encomiasts and blame poets accordingly. Yet immediately he concedes that we can't speak of any such poem prior to Homer. But, he says, "for those beginning from Homer it is possible"—and one expects him to say, possible to see this division between noble and base. But instead, he points to Homer, not as a proto-tragedian as in Chapter 3, but as the author of the *Margites*. This is very odd,[16] but perhaps deliberately so.

There is a similar slippage in what Aristotle says about meter here. At first he claims that iambic meter came along in early blame poetry, fittingly, because people lampooned (ἰάμβιζον) each other in this meter. Poets were divided into those of heroic (hexameter) and those of iambic meter (1448b32). Later, however, Aristotle says that tragedy, from laughable and "satyr-ic" beginnings, became dignified, and only then *changed from tetrameter to iambs*. Here he remarks that iambs are most suited to speech, and so when tragedy moved from being more danced to more spoken, "nature itself found the proper meter" (1449a24). But have we already forgotten that iambs are suited for lampoons? Why does tragedy, when it becomes dignified, switch to the allegedly less dignified meter? And why does tragedy suddenly have its origins in the laughable? Wasn't its origin in serious poets depicting serious people?

Homer would seem to be a promiscuous funnel through which improvisers divided by character flow and eventually become poets divided by nature, no thanks to Homer. Homer's mixed nature problematizes the "natural" development of poetry, and so do other contradictions. It is not so that good people will prefer imitations of good *praxeis*.

How is it that Homer gives birth to both tragedy and comedy? Or is it even true, in Aristotle's account, that he does? After Aristotle claims that Homer was the source for comedy and tragedy, he seems to back up and says that both came about "from an improvisatory beginning" (ἀπ' ἀρχῆς αὐτοσχεδιαστικῆς, 1449a10). In particular, tragedy came about from the instigators of dithyramb, and comedy from the instigators of *phallika*. So how does Homer fit?

Homer's role in the birth of these genres is as dramatizer. He alone made "dramatic *mimēseis*" (1448b37). Aristotle goes on to illustrate this process of dramatization:

---

[16] "It is astonishing that in a passage of this sort Homer should first be mentioned in connexion with the *Margites* and comedy" (Lucas 1968:76, *ad Poetics* 1448b28).

ὥσπερ δὲ καὶ τὰ σπουδαῖα μάλιστα ποιητὴς Ὅμηρος ἦν (μόνος γὰρ οὐχ ὅτι
εὖ ἀλλὰ καὶ <u>μιμήσεις δραματικὰς ἐποίησεν</u>), οὕτως καὶ τὸ τῆς κωμῳδίας
σχῆμα[17] πρῶτος <u>ὑπέδειξεν</u>, οὐ ψόγον ἀλλὰ τὸ γελοῖον <u>δραματοποιήσας·</u>
ὁ γὰρ Μαργίτης ἀνάλογον ἔχει, ὥσπερ Ἰλιὰς καὶ ἡ Ὀδύσσεια πρὸς τὰς
τραγῳδίας, οὕτω καὶ οὗτος πρὸς τὰς κωμῳδίας. παραφανείσης δὲ τῆς
τραγῳδίας καὶ κωμῳδίας οἱ ἐφ' ἑκατέραν τὴν ποίησιν ὁρμῶντες κατὰ
τὴν οἰκείαν φύσιν οἱ μὲν ἀντὶ τῶν ἰάμβων κωμῳδοποιοὶ ἐγένοντο, οἱ
δὲ ἀντὶ τῶν ἐπῶν τραγῳδοδιδάσκαλοι, διὰ τὸ μείζω καὶ ἐντιμότερα τὰ
σχήματα εἶναι ταῦτα ἐκείνων.

Just as Homer was preeminently the poet with respect to *spoudaia*
(not that he alone composed well, but that he alone <u>made dramatic</u>
<u>mimēseis</u>),[18] so too he first <u>demonstrated</u> the *schēma* of comedy, <u>making</u>
<u>dramatic</u> not invective but the laughable. For, just as the *Iliad* and the
Odyssey are analogous to tragedies, so too the *Margites* is analogous
to comedies. And when tragedy and comedy had appeared,[19] people
were attracted to each type of *poiēsis* according to their own nature:
some became makers of comedy instead of lampoons, others became
producers of tragedies instead of epics, on account of these *schēmata*[20]
being greater and more honorable than those.[21]

Aristotle *Poetics* 1448b34–1449a6

[17] τὸ … σχῆμα B: τὰ … σχήματα Π. See Gudeman 1934:128 on 1448b36.

[18] As Gudeman points out, from the use of σπουδαῖα in the previous clause, one would expect μιμήσεις
τραγικάς here and not the more general δραματικάς, since σπουδαῖα are precisely what distinguish
tragedy from comedy. In the *Republic*, of course, Homer is the forefather of tragedy only. For later
writers, the *Odyssey* is a forerunner of comedy (see Gudeman 1934:128 *ad* 1448b35). We do not know
what Aristotle said about the *Odyssey* in *Poetics* Book 2. Another complication is that Π has ἀλλ' ὅτι
for ἀλλὰ, disturbing the construction: my translation (as, it seems, Janko's) follows this reading,
which has the advantage of eliminating the difficulty of Homer "alone" composing well.

[19] παραφανείσης, a "not extremely common" (Else 1957:147n77) compound. Else (1957:146–147n77)
notes that the "sense of παρα- in παραφανείσης is a little harder to define" than the ὑπο- in
ὑπέδειξεν; but "the connotation in our passage is perhaps that of something being caught sight
of, then lost to view again for a time." Else's entire discussion, which harmonizes the conno-
tation of παραφανείσης with that of ὑπέδειξεν, is worth reading. But the verb's usage in the
context of a divine, or quasi-divine, revelation, including in some of the passages Else mentions,
is also worth considering. See e.g. Aristophanes *Frogs* 1361; Cratinus fr. 70 Austin; Philemon fr. 70
Kock; Callimachus *Hymn* 3.214 Pfeiffer; Plato *Gorgias* 527e. Cf. esp. Aristophanes *Ecclesiazusae* 94
with Aristotle *On the Pythagoreans* fr. 191 Rose. It is tempting to take the passive here as passive
in meaning: "once tragedy and comedy had been pointed out, revealed" (i.e. by Homer).

[20] Janko 1987: "because comedy and tragedy are greater and more honourable in their forms
than are lampoon and epic." Else 1957: "because these genres were greater and worthy of more
esteem than the others."

[21] What are the "these" and "those"? Janko 1987 and Else 1957 seem to assume "these" are comedy
and tragedy, whose forms are greater and more honorable than epic and lampoon ("those").

The way this is put, Homer, the maker of dramatic *mimēseis,* indicates some shape(s) of comedy, and then tragedy and comedy suddenly "appear" for people to pursue according to their natures. What Homer indicates, or demonstrates, is the *schēma* or *schēmata* of comedy. Most editors print the singular *schēma,* which they take to mean the form, "the structure, the 'set-up', of comedy, hardly to be distinguished from εἶδος."[22] However, the oldest manuscript has it that Homer indicated the plural *schēmata* of comedy, matching the *schēmata* at the end of the sentence. For some editors,[23] the plural causes difficulty for the abstract meaning "form" with comedy alone, so they read the singular for comedy as opposed to the plural "forms" of tragedy and comedy at the end of the sentence.

But what Homer did is to "make dramatic *mimēseis*" (or "make *mimēseis* dramatic"). He "demonstrated the shapes of comedy." These "shapes" (reading the plural *schēmata*), in the context of the verb ὑπέδειξεν "demonstrated" and δραματοποιήσας "having made dramatic," seem to be gestures. Aristotle uses σχήματα to mean gestures later in the *Poetics* at 1455a29, recommending that the poet work out the plot with gestures as well as diction. Gestures make sense, moreover, because Aristotle is talking precisely about Homer bringing poetry to life as drama. This stronger sense of gestures, or embodied, enacted visual forms, also suits the "revealing" or "epiphany" of tragedy and comedy in the next sentence. Yes, Homer is "revealing" tragedy and comedy in that he is uncovering an already existing dramatic potential,[24] but he does so *by dramatizing.* He is envisioning, gesturing, becoming, enacting. He is being the vessel through which heroes appear. He performs a mimesis of praxis such that the heroes, and then those tragedians and comedians, step into his shoes and put their hands into those gestures (cf. "greater and more honored gestures"). Thus he gives birth to an externalized life: the person who takes over from him, inherits from him, imitates him—the dramatist, and ultimately the actor. And this may be

---

Halliwell limits the phrase to the last pair mentioned: "these" are the tragic, those are the epic. Gudeman (1934:130 *ad* 1449a6) indicates the problem with this and gets around it: "ἐκείνων sc. σχημάτων der nachhomerischen Epen, denn der Übergang von den ἔπη des Homer zur Tragödie von seiten der σεμνότεροι wäre wohl kaum mit διὰ τὸ μείζονα καὶ ἐντιμότερα τὰ σχήματα εἶναι motiviert oder begründet worden, wenn auch A. in c. 26 die Tragödie als Kunstform über das Epos stellt." The word "more honorable" would seem better suited to a contrast between tragedy and comedy, rather than the pairs available by the syntax of the sentence, as though Aristotle is willfully shifting the meaning of "more honorable." "Greater" makes sense in terms of the emphasis on gestures and enactment that I am suggesting: the gestures of tragedy are larger and more demonstrative than those of epic, and so comedy's are larger than lampoon.

[22] Lucas 1968:77 *ad Poetics* 1448b36. Gudeman 1934:128 notes that earlier commentators, who did not have access to the manuscript that has the singular, did not know what to do with the plural.

[23] LSJ however accepts the plural and keeps the abstract meaning "characteristic forms." Similarly for Else (1957:144) the plural is explained by comedy having two different σχήματα: dramatic form and "the substitution of humor for invective."

[24] Halliwell 1987:82.

summarized by the startling, seemingly abrupt remark that tragedy and comedy came about "from an improvisatory beginning," ἀπ' ἀρχῆς αὐτοσχεδιαστικῆς (1449a9–10)—almost as though it is Homer doing the (gestural) improvising.

Only in the next sentence is this "improvisation" specified as that of the leaders (ἐξαρχόντων) of dithyrambs (circular dances) and phallika (processional dances). But Aristotle conceived of the hexameter as a dance meter,[25] so Homeric and dithyrambic/phallic improvisations are not as distinct as they may seem. Homer was no leader of dithyrambs, but he was stepping out from a dance tradition that already had a leader for the dance.

I suggest that Aristotle reinforces what he is saying by enacting it in ring composition (1448b18–49a15):

> **A**   nature as origin [κατὰ φύσιν, 1448b20][26]
> > **B**   primitive song-and-dance (harmonia and rhythm) [κατὰ μικρὸν ... προάγοντες, 1448b22–23]
> > > **C**   improvisations [ἐκ τῶν αὐτοσχεδιασμάτων, 1448b23–24]
> > > > **D**   poetry divided "according to their own characters," solemn vs. cheap; encomia and hymns vs. invective, 1448b24–27
> > > > > **E**   before Homer, 1448b28
> > > > > > **F**   *Margites*, 1448b30
> > > > > > > **G**   lampoon, 1448b31
> > > > > > > > **X**   HOMER MAKES MIMĒSEIS DRAMATIC, 1448b35
> > > > > > > **G′**   comedy, 1448b36
> > > > > > **F′**   *Margites*, 1448b38
> > > > > **E′**   after Homer, 1448a2
> > > > **D′**   poets divide "according to their own natures"; tragedy and comedy replace epic and iambic, 1449a2–6
> > > **C′**   improvisation [αὐτοσχεδιαστική, 1449a9–10]
> > **B′**   primitive song-and-dance (the leaders of dithyramb and *phallika*) [κατὰ μικρὸν ... προαγόντων, 1449a13]
> **A′**   nature as telos [ἐπαύσατο ἐπεὶ ἔσχε τὴν αὐτῆς φύσιν, 1449a15]

The leader stands in the center of the dance and gives birth to tragedy by becoming an actor, using gestures. Or rather, the natural processes of *poiēsis*, divided by character, head toward Homer as their τέλος; once enlivened and given body, they recede again into their divided natures, reaching fulfillment in tragedy and comedy.

---

25 *Metaphysics* 1093a29–b1: see David 2006:96–99.
26 Cf. 1448b5–6, τό τε γὰρ μιμεῖσθαι σύμφυτον τοῖς ἀνθρώποις ἐκ παίδων ἐστὶ ....

This "enlivening" at the center of a ring composition is a well-known high-light of Homeric poetics. It also has a specific potential when used as a solo performance technique; we will examine one particularly elaborate example in Chapter 2 and another in the first Interlude. The solo performer—"Homer"—in the *Poetics'* Aristotelian ring is a point of arrival and a point of departure that gives birth to dramatic action, but he is also where one thing is transformed into another. Once it becomes clear how central this is to Homeric performance, one might ask whether Aristotle is here imitating Homer (as opposed to other varieties of ring composition) all the way down, in a way that would be apparent to anyone who had seen Homer performed.

Contrary to Aristotle's idea about "not seeing the act-or" in Homer (1460a14), and his denigration of spectacle (*opsis*, 1450b18–20), here *Homer is first and foremost a dramatist.* He makes *mimēseis* dramatic, or makes dramatic *mimēseis.* His performance is redolent of epiphany, but also comedy. But how can he be a dramatist, if epic involves "not seeing the one-doing"?

Clearly Aristotle recognized that there is a problem with talking about Homer, and talking about Homer's relation to drama and to the visual. Aristotle did see a virtue particular to Homeric solo performance, as opposed to Homeric *poiēsis* seen solely as composition or as the generous interlarding of narrative with direct discourse. He begins to articulate this virtue in terms of the *alogon*, the *atopon*, and the *thaumaston*, which are better accomplished in Homeric poetry than in tragedy (1460a11–17). He articulates it further through a kind of performance or mimesis of Homeric presencing through ring composition. This may seem to make the *Poetics* too ingenious, but then again, we are talking about Aristotle. If the *Poetics* is a set of lecture notes, it is even more like Homer than is the *Republic*, in that it is a script for performance.[27] In lecture, Aristotle would, for example, have been able to flesh out his discussion by reciting the Homeric passages at length.

* * *

Aristotle's discussion of the dramatic quality of Homer points us toward what is confounding or troubling about Homer from a slightly different angle than that of Socrates in the *Republic*. He hints that Homer is a funnel of identities and characters, and that this has something to do with gesture, and gestural improvisation.

We learn more from Aristotle's imitation, within the constraints of his own genre, of Homeric dramatics than we do from extracting individual pronounce-

---

[27] Aristotle's extant works reflect lectures "which would have been fleshed out ... with examples, jokes, dramatic material—in short, with the oral analogue of some of the 'literary' elements we miss" (Nussbaum 1986:392). One must consider not only what "view" the passage conveys, but what is its pedagogy.

ments. Something about imitation helps him to convey these dual processes, even imitation within a treatise.

Aristotle's ring-shaped treatment alerts us to the relation between drama and poetic structure; between transformation and linear construction; between "becoming" and "making."

Performance, the embodied script, the totality of the poem as a work of art, can be thought of as two intertwined dimensions or axes: first, the fabrication, selection, and assembly of words, lines, images, scenes, episodes—all the way up to emplotment. I will call this the dimension of poetics, in the sense of *poiēsis* or composition/making. This is, roughly speaking, the "meaning" dimension. Second, the actualization and interplay of all of this among the poet/performer ("bard"[28]), narrator, character, and audience: "presence." Presence can be thought of as the opening out of the text into the space and time of the performance—keeping in mind that the "text" need not actually precede performance. If poetics is *poiēsis*, or making, presence is *genesis*, in the sense of "becoming" rather than "origin." An example is how the bard becomes (γίγνεσθαι) a character. The performer transitions from narrator to character; he may appear to merge with a character, to create layers of presence within himself, or to cast his audience into a particular role. "Presence" in the present study[29] includes all the dynamics that solo performance activates, and deploys, among bard, audience, and character, the story-world and the world of performance. The interest in presence comes from the shifting of these dynamics, a "play" of presence rather than a steady "presencing forth." This dimension may be said to exist in written works not meant for performance, such as novels, but in Homeric poetry the interplay is happening in the space of performance. Since the dimension of presence can at least be observed, if not fully experienced, by reading, it is clear that "presence" and "performance" are not coterminous. For instance, Longinus (Ch. 27) notes that "when a writer, narrating about a character, suddenly turns aside and changes into that very character," this is

---

[28] There is no satisfactory term in English for the Homeric performing poet. "Singer" is not right, and "rhapsode," for some readers, connotes a performer who is not a composer. "Poet-performer" is a mouthful; "performer" has the same problems as "rhapsode." "Bard" has its own unfortunate connotations, among them a traditional association with the singers and kitharists Demodokos and Phemius. But since it succinctly connotes poet and performer, I use "bard," alternating with "poet" and "performer," and sometimes, as Plato and Aristotle use the term, "Homer."

[29] This distinction between poetics/*poiēsis* and presence/*genesis* overlaps somewhat with Aristotle's distinction (*Poetics* 1455a22–29) between constructing plots (τοὺς μύθους συνιστάναι) and working them up with diction (τῇ λέξει συναπεργάζεσθαι). This becomes clear in the examples he uses, as I demonstrate in a separate study.

"a sort of outburst of emotion." But one must keep in mind that nothing about the Homeric poems was originally experienced on the page.

Likewise, performance embraces and informs the poems' thematic concerns. That is, performance is intertwined with poetics as well as presence. Ghosts, doubles, repetition, and memory are important thematically because of the guiding performance aesthetics, including the play of presence, and vice versa, in a sort of "virtuous circle." The dimension of "presence" is thus part of the fabric of the poems, not a special effect superimposed upon them by performance.

These two strands or dimensions, poetics and presence, may appear as two to us readers, in part because we have to make an effort to appreciate the performative part of "presence." For a performer, however, there is no separation. Preparing to perform, even for actors working with a written script, involves working through the text at all levels. How much more so for the performer who is also a composer? If acting is "a way of learning to think with the body,"[30] so too the performing poet incarnates the poetic tradition he receives, and composes and recomposes with that same body. For the composer-in-performance, it is not only that a given phrase or episode must succeed with a series of audiences in order to be retained and transmitted to other poets. Performance sits at the very core of the composition process: the poet's horizon *is* the performance.

If the two strands or helices are so intertwined, why note them separately? Because doing so helps to articulate the performance virtues of the script in the first place. Michael Goldman notes a similar relationship between the action of the character and the acting of the actor, and writes that while it is "notoriously difficult to say how acting and action actually work in drama ... we can go a long way toward understanding their operation if we think of them not as separate processes, but as intricately allied."[31]

To take a loose analogy from a related discipline, the linguist David McNeill shows how gestures not only reveal, but actually fuel, thought and speech. "Linguistic forms and gestures participate in a real-time dialectic during discourse and thus propel and shape speech and thought as they occur moment to moment."[32] McNeill speaks of this dialectic as the "dynamic dimension" of language. The present book aims to uncover a somewhat similar real-time dialectic that occurs between poetics and presence, a dialectic that occurs in performance. I find the work on gesture by McNeill and others highly resonant

---

[30] Goldman 1975:89.
[31] Goldman 1985:3. Goldman too resorts to quasi-Aristotelian terms for the related but ambiguous senses of "action," calling the action of the characters *praxis* and that of the actors *poiēsis* (contrary to my terms). My two axes differ from his in large part because of the Homeric performer's moving between narration and direct discourse, rather than enacting a single role. He "becomes" as well as "acts."
[32] McNeill 2005:3.

with and suggestive of composition in and for performance, and his dialectic may serve as a useful analogy for my own interaction between two axes. The analogy is, however, very loose, since this book will only occasionally refer to the effect a given gesture would have, and the dialectic that I am tracing is not between speech and gesture but between poetics and presence.

Performance

"Performance" in Homeric scholarship since Parry has largely been focused on poetics/*poiēsis* rather than presence/*genesis*, i.e. with composition in performance. Composition seen strictly as a linear construction or reconstruction of lines, episodes, or plots[33] would seem to lie somewhat outside the focus of this study, which is pursuing the interplay between poetics and presence. But in reality *poiēsis* cannot be separated so cleanly from presence. In the first place, features of traditional epic poetry that frame it as performance, once "keyed," project a certain image of the performing bard, and of the source of the action he is presenting, even absent any invocation of the Muse. This imputes to him a certain stance or role, and so to this extent belongs to presence.[34] And obviously oral composition is occasioned and shaped by the poet-audience interaction. But virtuosic composition can also fuel presence more dramatically, as Richard Martin notes when he concludes that, since the poet "fully reveals all the possibilities of his own poetic craft only in the extended speech of Achilles," "the effect is to make Achilles sound like a poet."[35] In a study mainly concerned with performance as depicted within the poem (in the story-world; *poiēsis*) Martin also shows how this identification of Achilles with the bard culminates in the narrator's apostrophes to Patroklos.[36]

The Homerist will never produce a thick description of performance context such as Dwight Reynolds's pellucid and poignant *Heroic Poets, Poetic Heroes.* Studying contemporary Egyptian poets of the epic *Sirat Bani Hilal,* Reynolds hears from the residents of al-Bakatush that, for example, they regard the poets as gypsy semi-outsiders who are "not from among us,"[37] in part

---

[33] Even if one considers this linear process as itself proceeding along two axes, combination and selection (Nagy 1996a:50), both of which are appreciated by the audience.

[34] See Foley 2002:91; Bauman 1984:15–24. "Keying" is Goffman's term (Goffman 1974).

[35] Martin 1989:223; cf. 233: "Hektor, whose speech is often reduced or merely summarized by the poet, recedes from view, while Achilles comes closer to us because the poet chooses him as the channel to contact his audience." Achilles is as close to the voice of the poet as we get. But the relationship is more complex than the image of the channel implies.

[36] Martin 1989:236, and on the speech of Achilles, Ch. 4, responding to the seminal studies of Adam Parry (1964) and Friedrich and Redfield (1978). I return to the apostrophes of Patroklos in Chapter 1 and again in Chapter 3, below.

[37] Reynolds 1995:56.

because of ascertainable facts about the poets' ancestors. This divide between the outsider poet families and their patrons figures into the shaping and the impact of the epic itself, such that "a modern epic poet playing *rabab* in front of an Egyptian audience sings of one of the epic heroes disguised as an epic poet playing the *rabab* singing in front of an Egyptian audience."[38] The poets share other characteristics with the poem's heroes, such as the possession of a secret language. Scenes within the epic thus mirror the ongoing performance and allow the poet to comment upon and guide the poet-patron relationship indirectly. All this makes for a considerably more pointed scenario, so far as we can know, than Odysseus reciting among the Phaeacians, or Phemius singing for the suitors. The *mise en abyme*[39] of performance in the Egyptian epic is similar to the *Odyssey*'s Phaeacian episode in general terms. But concrete social and personal facts about the performers and patrons themselves, not abstract narratological or story-world features alone, are key to the charge of the *Sirat Bani Hilal* performance, and nothing like them can be uncovered in the case of Homer.[40] We do not even have external evidence, for example, about precisely who formed the actual audience for the Homeric poems at a given stage of their development.[41] Nevertheless, recent scholarship elaborating the evidence we do

---

[38] Reynolds 1995:73.

[39] *Mise en abyme* in the strict sense refers to "a narrative inserted into another narrative that the inserted component reproduces in whole or in part on a reduced scale" (Létoublon 1983:21–22, following Dällenbach; translation from Loraux, Nagy and Slatkin 2001:377). Létoublon gives as a prime example the dream of Penelope in *Odyssey* 19. Casey Dué's (Dué 2002) "micronarratives" often have a similar mirroring function with respect to the "macronarrative."

[40] But Reynolds's work (esp. Chapter 4 and the chart on p. 164) is of great suggestive value for the study of Homer. To be compared with "becoming the character" in Homer is the movement from prose to poetry in the *Sirat Bani Hilal*: "The critical juncture between prose and poetry is always effected in the same manner: a character within the epic must be emotionally moved to speak. Situations and emotions must reach a confluence that impels a character to stand up and sing: 'and he sang, saying verses which you shall hear, and all who love the beauty of the Prophet, wish God's blessings upon him' ..." (Reynolds 1995:156). Cf. Martin 1989:234.

[41] Internal evidence, however, may offer hints. Doherty (1991:164) writes, "The *implied* audience of the Nekuia, and of the epic as a whole, thus includes women, whether or not women were present in the original external audience for the monumental *Odyssey*. ... What [Samuel Butler] mistook for evidence of authorship is actually evidence for the inclusion of females in the implied audience of the poem." Louden (1997:111–112) suggests the "inclusion of lower-class people among the intended audience," given Eumaeus' importance as an internal audience. Rose (1992:90, 112–114) concludes in part from internal evidence, including even the depiction of Phemius and Demodokos, that the most frequent audience of the *Odyssey* would consist of peasants. At the other end of the social spectrum, Frame (2009:590–599) considers the audience for the "instruction of princes" speech in the *Odyssey*. For Haubold (2000:145–196), a given archaic or classical audience would contrast their own founding people with the λαοί of Homer, with their incompetent leaders, and breathe a collective sigh of relief. But no audience is homogeneous (Scodel 2002:7–16), and different people may have been attuned to different aspects of the poetry. We must, finally, examine our own assumptions about what a given audience is capable of enjoying (Ebbott 2005).

have,[42] especially for the Panathenaia, shows that context makes a substantial difference to our interpretation.[43] Derek Collins, for example, situates rhapsodic competition within the larger Greek cultural practice of poetic "capping," which yields insights into how audiences would have heard individual lines "thrown back at" the speaker.[44]

Attention to the performance of ancient poetry more generally has entailed identifying a social function associated with genre or with a type of occasion. In this view, poetry as *performance*, with a defined social function, predates poetry proper, which is not so delimited.[45] There is no external evidence about the social function the epic is supposed to serve. Although some of the settings (like the Panathenaia) of epic performance are known, Homeric epic is not defined by a ritual or other communal context in the way laments or *hymēnaioi* are;[46] rather it assimilates these genres, synthesizing traditions as it proliferates throughout the Greek world.[47]

Although Homeric epic integrates ritual performances (rather than comprising a ritual in any straightforward fashion), it is nevertheless significant that scholars have often reached for terms such as *epiphany*, *ritual*, *presence*, and *enactment* to describe the extraordinary vividness, or ἐνάργεια, of Homeric poetry.[48] Martin, discussing the intrusion of Achilles' perspective into the Homeric narrator, compares this with other oral traditions in which the hero is conceived of as present for the performance of the epic, or where the performer is possessed by the hero. This kind of language has been criticized[49] as inappropriate for poetry whose performance is not itself ritual.

---

[42] See especially Taplin 1992, Cook 1995, Nagy 2002, Collins 2004, Frame 2009: Ch. 11.

[43] Of particular relevance to the current study, Cook (1995) relates the action of the *Odyssey* to the rituals and themes of the cycle of new-year festivals that includes the Panathenaia; cf. Austin 1975. One nexus of background myths uncovered later in this volume (see Chapters 2 and 4, and Interlude 1) reinforces this aspect of the poem. The themes at the heart of any new-year festival operate on several levels. For epigraphic evidence of rhapsodes at other venues, see West 2010. Skepticism about early performance of the full text of either Homeric poem: Ford 1997b.

[44] Collins 2004; cf. Ford 1997b. Although rhapsodic competition and "capping" are not central to the present study, these practices illuminate certain features of the *Odyssey* explored in Chapter 4.

[45] Ford 2002:9 and passim. This dovetails with the sociolinguistic conception of performance following Bauman (e.g. Bauman 1984), which stresses the culturally specific framing of performance as performance, as well as culturally determined genres of performance or "speech acts" (Bauman 1984:27). This latter is the focus of Martin 1989.

[46] Ford 1997a:400.

[47] Nagy 1979:6–9.

[48] In this they are assisted by the archaic poets themselves. Ford 1992:195, in a discussion of the epithets and diction associated with poets within archaic poetry (here, *thespis aoidē*), writes: "The poet's 'divine human voice' is not an oxymoron or ventriloquism but an epiphany: divine knowledge appears in sound and presents to human senses a world not otherwise apparent. This sound, the body of the poet's voice, is the substance of the heroic world in all its presence; in it the human account of the past and the divine perspective upon it, as far as they can, appear together on earth."

[49] Scodel 2002:12.

Homeric performance may not constitute a ritual. Its mode of mimesis, however, like that of archaic lyric and even tragedy, is not mere imitation but has a share in the reenactment of archetypal situations in the manner of ritual. Dramatic reenactment, in archaic Greece as in other traditional societies, "entails an interaction of myth and ritual."[50] All of this belongs to the realm of "presencing" or *genesis*. Though we cannot trace precisely the bearing of choral and lyric group dynamics upon epic, and the mutual evolution of epic with tragedy, these other genres help account for, and imagine, the intense interplay between performer and audience/group, or performer, audience, and hero.[51] It is in part due to this kind of "ritual context," retaining "the mentality of group performance," that rituals within epic retain their power in a peculiar manner. When a female character like Andromache sings a lament within Homeric poetry, "[i]t is as if the lamenting woman were addressing not only her group but also the audience that is listening to the performer as he re-enacts the woman."[52]

Leave aside for a moment the relation of epic to ritual. It is the case that drama in general, even modern drama, aims at some kind of peculiar presencing in its performance or *representation* that is difficult to attain but much treasured by audiences. Music too, for that matter, partakes of the same strange dynamic: in witnessing a great musical performance, "we understand that ordinary men and their clumsy instruments are transformed by an art of possession."[53] The dimension of presence in Homeric poetry has links with this broader category of dramatic presence, and the even broader category of performative presence. Moreover, as noted above, some of the phenomena falling under the category of "presence" or *genesis* can be observed in texts not composed for performance at all. So even if we did not know anything about the context of Homeric performance, some of these "presence" phenomena would be visible on the page.

Presence/*Genesis*

Indeed, studies not focused on performance have shed light on many of these phenomena. A trail-blazing illumination of Homeric *presence* is Paolo Vivante's *The Epithets in Homer*, which shows how objects as well as characters are made to stand out[54] from the background by means of epithets. Taking into account

---

50 Nagy 1996a:54. We might say that archaic Greek poetry has a share in the "liminal" as well as the "liminoid," in Victor Turner's terms, though debate will continue about what that share is.

51 Even more broadly, on the confluence among rhapsody, prophecy, oratory, and drama from a diachronic perspective, see González 2013.

52 Nagy (1996a:84), in a discussion of the link between "audience" and "group"; Martin 1989:87–88. On the power of lament at the center of a complex dramatic structure, see Chapter 2 below.

53 Brook 1968:42.

54 Vivante 1982 passim, e.g. p. 91.

pragmatic linguistic factors, such as deictic pronouns and the subtleties of particle usage, Egbert Bakker has, in a series of studies, illuminated the mediating stance of the bard "presencing" the past, and precisely that quality of vividness or *enargeia* that has led many scholars to use terms such as "epiphany" of the Homeric poems.[55]

So the bard makes objects and characters in the past present, as it were, by pointing to them; but he also, in moving from one persona to another, makes them present through himself. Now even within his role as narrator, "the 'I' who narrates,"[56] the performer reenacts "Homer," in the act of performing the words "sing to me, Muse." This "I" then "melts," or blends, into the listener, in that the performer now becomes a listener to the Muse's words.[57]

The performer makes characters present through speech and, more generally, through his body. Although he enacts all characters insofar as he speaks their speeches, this enactment varies widely from character to character. Achilles by virtue of his superiority in speaking and thought seems to merge[58] with the poet in an intense fashion—to speak through him or emerge from him.

If the character can speak through the poet, the poet can also use the character as a channel; more dramatically, he may "pivot out" from his usual stance in what Paul Friedrich calls "lyric breakout," or lyric epiphany,

> a metamorphosis of the poet from being a bard telling *about* epic protagonists, to being the otherwise latently or underlyingly lyric poet who is now expressing himself or herself *through* the eyes or voice or gestures of one of the epic protagonists.[59]

Friedrich illustrates how such metamorphosis occurs in several genres, not all of them composed for performance. Deixis, speech-act theory, phonic density—all help us to appreciate the *Iliad* and the *Odyssey* as one-man shows. Friedrich's emphasis on "phonic density," however, points toward the importance of the performer's body. One of Friedrich's examples of "phonic density" is Penelope's reaction to the disguised Odysseus' Cretan tale (*Odyssey* 19.203–213), a lyric poem erupting in "chords of sound and meaning," expressing "the sensitive and haunted woman of Homer's art."[60] The guttural stops, perhaps mimetic of sobbing, become voiced toward the end of the passage, in keeping with a move from crying

---

[55] Bakker 2005:60; Bakker 1993; Bakker 1997a:25–32. Bakker (1997a:32) speaks of the epic text as a transcript, in the context of relating it to regular speech patterns—orality or "vocality"—and to theories of cognition.

[56] Nagy 1996:80.

[57] Frontisi-Ducroux (1986a:18): "Et l'émetteur premier, l'aède, s'efface, apparemment fondu dans l'auditoire, devenu récepteur lui-même, puis réémetteur."

[58] On "mergers," see Nagy 1996a:84, 97.

[59] Friedrich 2001:238–239.

[60] Friedrich 2001:238.

(κλαιούσης 209) to lamenting (γοόωσαν 210, γόοιο 213). It would be pedantic to try to decide whether this is Penelope breaking out through the narrator or the narrator breaking out through Penelope.

As the *Iliad* opening shows, we need to take into account the bodily presence of the performer and the space of performance. Friedrich's meditation on lyric epiphany points us further on this track, since it is only when a performer embodies Penelope's words that phonic density effects a merging between character and performer.

The mere bodily presence of the performer before an audience makes more of a difference to our interpretation than any particular prop or gesture. But bodily presence may also supplement other "presencing" modes. For example, Felson[61] sees the suitors as stand-ins for the members of the audience, some of whom identify with, but eventually distance themselves from, the suitors. Such psychological identification[62] already falls within the realm of presencing, in that it shapes the relation between audience and character, or puts us into the minds and seats of the suitors in a qualified sense. But the identification is also concretely accomplished in space, while the performer speaks as the prophet Theoclymenos:[63] as long as the bard looks at or through the audience as he performs this speech, they are literally in the place of the suitors.

Play

We have already seen hints that the Homeric script produces effects quite beyond the mere representation of a world that is pregiven and that the poet makes present to us. Although he does present this world to us, the bard also plays with his stance with respect to the action of the poem and with the audience's position.

Such sophisticated play is often taken to be typical of modern rather than ancient texts.[64] For instance, Wolfgang Iser describes the play involved in a text as follows: "author, text, and reader are closely interconnected in a relationship that is to be conceived as an ongoing process that produces something that had not existed before."[65] For Iser, this kind of activity is a modern phenomenon, whereas in "closed systems" such as "the cosmos of Greek thought" there

---

[61] Felson 1994:109–10.

[62] See the systematic treatment by Jauss 1974. For identification and related phenomena in drama as opposed to written fiction, see Goldman 1975:119–123; Zamir 2010. Kozak 2017 shows how the audience's relation to the *Iliad*'s characters, especially Hektor, is bound up with the episodic structure (and on a smaller scale, the "beats") of the narrative.

[63] This speech is analyzed below, pp. 40–46.

[64] Létoublon 1983:19. Létoublon is speaking of reflexivity; the play Iser describes is related to, or a form of, such reflexivity.

[65] Budick and Iser 1989:325.

reigns a stagnant "Aristotelian" mimesis, a mimesis that "entails reference to a pregiven 'reality.'" It takes modernity to "puncture" the "closed system" and replace it with "open-endedness," such that "the mimetic component of representation declines and the performative one comes to the fore."[66]

John Herington would rotate 180 degrees the contrast between ancient and modern. Modern poetry and drama

> express the lonely individual's comforting fiction—the structure that he has built for himself (and possibly for a vaguely perceived audience) to stand solid and coherent in an otherwise fluid and inexplicable universe.[67]

Herington contrasts this with the ancient situation, where "a world of heroic and divine myth" is "the common property and theme not only of poetry, not only of tragedy, but of the very audiences, the very society, within which these arts had their being."[68]

Such a shared mythology constitutes an open playground rather than a closed cosmos. Certainly in the *Iliad* and the *Odyssey*, traditional story, shared between poet and audience, is a thing to be used, framed and reframed, ruthlessly examined, and turned inside out. It is in following Homer's lead that Sophocles "has not manipulated myths so much as man-handled them."[69]

Homeric experimentation extends to narrative and theme, where it has inspired musical analogies. Létoublon writes that the *Odyssey* "contains a technique for the exploration of possible narratives, in a sense analogous to Bach's experimentation with keys in the preludes and fugues of *The Well-tempered Clavier*."[70]

The work of Neoanalysis has shown that the Homeric poems do not simply transmit story, they unfold a story in the foreground while opening allusive portals to other stories, portals crucial to the meaning of the entire poem. The poet counts on the audience's knowledge of the tradition to complete the meaning of the poem.[71] It is already in front of this background that Létoublon's

---

[66] Budick and Iser 1989:326, a less subtle account of the supposed "frozenness" of ancient literature than Bakhtin 1981. As Peradotto notes (1990:53n13), "close readers of Homer are far more likely to recognize the *Odyssey* in Bakhtin's characterization of the novel than in his account of epic."

[67] Herington 1985:xi.

[68] Herington 1985:x–xi.

[69] Ringer 1998:212.

[70] Létoublon 2001:376.

[71] Scodel (2002:6) warns against "romanticization of the relation between bard and audience," i.e. postulating audiences who are uniformly ideally conversant with the tradition. It is true that audiences can follow what happens in the epics without extensive knowledge, just as modern readers do. But the meanings generated by allusivity and "traditional referentiality" are not limited to following the plot. One need not imagine homogeneous audiences, only audiences some of whom know the stories being used. For the "ludic" or "puzzle-solving" aspect of the *Iliad*, on analogy with other serial narrative, see Kozak 2017.

Bach-like experimentation goes on: an arrangement and rearrangement of materials in the poetic foreground.

In contrast to Herington and Létoublon, Iser's notion of play emphasizes not the manipulation of themes and plots (poetics) but the manipulation of the roles of author, audience, and text to make something happen (included under the rubric of presence).

We started moving from simple "presencing" in the direction of such play above with examples of the performer or narrator merging with a character. Perhaps the most straightforward case of such play vis-à-vis the audience in Homer involves deictic shifts, such as when the narrator suddenly addresses the audience in the second person. These received considerable attention from the scholiasts and Longinus and recently from narratologists.[72] But they are more playful than the narratologists have it. De Jong discusses the five instances in the *Iliad* when this happens, such as:

> So they fought on in the body of fire, and *you* would not say
> that the sun was ever safe, nor the moon.
>
> *Iliad* 17.366–367

which de Jong analyzes, using her technical vocabulary:

> All five passages contain an optative with ἄν/κεν, which I analyze as follows: I, NF1 [primary narrator-focalizer], tell you, NeFe1 [primary narratee-focalizee], that you certainly would (not) have seen, thought/ said x, (if you had yourself been present at that moment and at that place) ... *Now the external NeFe1, of course, has not been present, but the effect of these five passages is to turn him temporarily into an eyewitness*: in fact, the focalizee here functions as focalizer, yet, of course, as a focalizer who is instructed by the NF1 what to see and think.[73] (my emphasis)

But does the passage really "turn him into an eyewitness"? Is not the audience *usually* in a "witnessing" position, and is not that witnessing being toyed with here? Does the narrator not imply "you would have seen/said this if you were there, *but you were/are not*"? Or is it possible that the two positions of the audience (both there on the battlefield and not there) are held in tension?

The position of the audience inside or outside the poem's action can also be manipulated. In the *Iliad* opening, we are suddenly implicated in the action within the poem. At the other end of the spectrum, the second half of the *Odyssey* lures the audience into imagining they recognize Odysseus more deeply

---

[72] Frontisi-Ducroux 1986a:27–28; de Jong 1987; Richardson 1990:174–178.

[73] De Jong 1987:54–55. Cf. Bakker 2005:63.

than the characters do, but shuts them out when Odysseus and Penelope go to bed and he catalogues for her his adventures—in indirect discourse, such that we cannot hear them.[74] Yet shut out as we are, we can still discern a note of self-censorship[75] in his story. The *Odyssey*, like the Sirens, "deludes [readers] into believing that they are privileged and granted the truth and that a responsible author lies behind the story" only to suddenly deprive us "of our pleasurable and privileged view of the spectacle" portrayed in the poem, as when Athena "vanishes in an unreadable simile."[76]

The *Odyssey*, with its reflexivity and disguises is more conspicuously playful, in the sense of carnivalesque or comic, than the *Iliad*.[77] But both poems manipulate the dynamics existing among bard, audience, and the action within the poem to create an uncertainty as to the audience's "location" with respect to that action and its source. The bard does not stand as an authoritative channel between the past and the present. For much of the time he sets up a process of "joint visualization"[78] with his audience. But the Homeric script also sets up a performance that evokes or hints at the "curious indecisiveness of the playing consciousness which makes it absolutely impossible to decide between belief and non-belief."[79] And, like "the structure of play," the script "absorbs the player into itself," with the player being both the bard and the audience.

Homeric absorption is not something stable, like "transport" or the *thelxis* (spell) that Phemius provided to the suitors. Yet I shall argue that both poems ultimately exploit these shifting dynamics to an end that is in Pucci's sense "readable" or in Doherty's sense "closed." This is in part because of the fact of performance. Performing a script closes some doors and opens others. One has to decide: What is the virtue of this material for me as a performer? But as anyone who has seen a good performance recognizes, that virtue will involve mystery, a sense of "reading" the actor.

This book pursues the play of presence among bard, audience, and characters with a view to the variety of its effects in performance. I trace these

---

[74] David 2006:189–190. Similarly Lowe (2000:147–148) observes: "the stratagem of the bow ... is revealed to the reader only at XXI.4—even though it has evidently been premeditated by the hero since Penelope's announcement at the end of XIX, and by the goddess even longer."

[75] Penelope also "launders her own image" in her own tale (Felson 1994:41). Cf. Doherty 1995:140, 146–147.

[76] Pucci 1995:99, 117.

[77] Pucci's (1995:80) view that "even the strategic situation of Patroclus' wearing the arms of Achilles is hardly exploited by the text" seems extreme, but there is something to it. One would not say that the situation is exploited by the "text" in the way that it is in the *Odyssey*. Pucci's *Odyssey* delights in disguise and indeterminacy for its own sake. But the poet-performer of the *Odyssey* reserves his pyrotechnics for exposing what a limited source of pleasure this is (cf. "Trojan Horse," pp. 96–104 below, and the Cretan Tale to Eumaeus, Chapter 4, in this volume).

[78] Bakker 1993.

[79] Gadamer 1989:104, referring to Huizinga.

dynamics "outward" to incorporate the space of performance, and the "kines-thetics" of performance. I also trace them "inward" to include the background stories that constitute further roles into which performer, audience, and char-acter might step, and further "layers" within the body of the performer. These background stories, that is, do not remain hermetically sealed within the 'story-world' of the poem, any more than the bard represents a story-world that is pre-given to the audience. Rather the back-stories directly affect the performative interplay among bard, audience, Muse, god, and hero.

One way to put it is that, as a character within epic "becomes," or comes under the sway of, another character further in the past, there seems to be a congruent movement, or "becoming," of the character by the bard. Such a continuum between what happens in the world of the poem and what is happening in the performer harmonizes with, for example, Martin's observations on the Patroklos apostrophes or Friedrich's on the sobbing of Penelope. In these instances, the bard so fully "becomes" a character that the character's point of view affects the syntax or the sound of the narration, or he himself does things that the charac-ters do, and vice versa.

At the same time, though this continuum between story-world and performance, and between poetics and presence, makes sense, the effects of the moves within that continuum—like the apostrophes—are often strange and disorienting, rather than merely impressive, epiphanic, or authoritative. In fact, I shall be arguing that such disorientation is often what is aimed at in the passages most virtuosic from a performance point of view. It is as though the performance is aimed at making the audience ask themselves, "Who is this person standing up there performing? And does he really have control of what is going on here?" The play of presence yields a ghostly or uncanny quality to the performance that does not quite come across on the page, and that is also to be distinguished from what transpires in the best dramatic performances.

Plato and Homeric Performance

This haunted quality, this confusion of agency, lies behind the responses to Homer of Plato and Aristotle, two people who saw the Homeric poems performed. Although they are relatively late witnesses, they are the most artic-ulate ones we have,[80] and their responses go much deeper than reportage. I have already suggested that Aristotle reveals more about Homeric dramatics by his imitation, as in his ring composition, than in his overt statements; but this will

---

[80] Herington (1985:13) reviews the problems with Plato as evidence for performance in any time period, but concludes that the poems as scripts call for a histrionic performer such as Ion.

only be fully appreciated when we have seen ring composition at work in Homer (see below, Chapter 2).

In this section, I examine two Homeric examples discussed in Platonic dialogue. As with Aristotle, I do not wish to use Plato as a simple lens by which to interpret Homer; one must after all use Homer to interpret the philosophers, in a sort of virtuous circle. Their responses help flesh out the qualities of the Homeric poems in performance as well as their inner workings.

As we saw above, Aristotle found the mode of Homeric performance, "not seeing the one-doing," more conducive to the *thaumaston*, the "to be wondered at," than tragedy (1460a7–11). It is this quality of "not seeing the actor," as Aristotle put it, the solo performer's occupying a space between acting and not-acting, his ability to occupy various "musical chairs," that is responsible for its charisma and its strangeness.[81]

Aristotle's brief note on the *thaumaston* quality of Homer echoes Plato's elaborate treatment of Homer in the *Republic*. Plato's characters discuss Homer as though he is a ghost, a dead hero, or else a necromancer, someone who traffics in ghosts. The poet is a maker of phantoms (εἴδωλα εἰδωλοποιοῦντα *Republic* 605b; cf. φαντάσματα, 599a). These phantoms interfere with the audience by short-circuiting their souls. The spectator in turn becomes an εἴδωλον, in his involuntary, automaton-like reaction: like a denizen of the underworld, he flits around without a νοῦς (mind; what steers us). Or rather, the poet *qua* maker of phantoms operates upon a part of the soul that, like the souls in Hades, lacks powers of judgment and an internal steering mechanism. The poet is said (605c) to "awaken" (ἐγείρει) and "nourish" (τρέφει) this low part of the soul somewhat as though raising the dead.[82] Plato combines the image of creating εἴδωλα, "images/phantoms," with raising the deadest part of the soul; the poet thus operates on εἴδωλα in his poetry, and on εἴδωλον-like parts of his audience, through one and the same process. Likewise, puppetry ("wonder-making": θαυματοποιία) and shadow-painting, along with "many other tricks" that "do not fall short of γοητεία [magic; necromancy]," are used as an analogy to poetic imitation (602d).

The kind of poet subject to banishment in the *Republic* is "a man, as it seems, capable by his wisdom of becoming παντοδαπόν ['multifarious'] and imitating all things" (398a). This recalls the phrase Plato and Aristotle use elsewhere in

---

[81] I examine Aristotle's treatment of the *thaumaston* in Homer at length in a separate study.
[82] Normally the verb used of raising the dead is ἀνάγω or ἀνίστημι, but see e.g., Aeschylus *Libation Bearers* 495, which has ἐξεγείρῃ.

discussing performance;[83] both philosophers were manifestly impressed by the way Homer "becomes something else."[84]

What precisely do Plato's Socrates, and Aristotle, mean by "becoming the character," and what is so impressive, so disturbing, about it? Why does it inspire analogies to ghosts, necromancers, and puppets? In the remainder of this chapter, let us proceed, not to a "Platonic" or "Aristotelian" reading, but to see why the Homeric poems would inspire such comparisons by these invaluable native (if late) informants. We turn in particular to two Homeric passages treated by Plato, to their "presence" effects and their performative potential.

The *Iliad* Opening

In *Republic* Book 3, Socrates and the young men have just discussed *what* must be said by the poets in the city they are constructing, and are now discussing *how* it must be said.

> "Isn't everything that is said by the storytellers and the poets a narrative of what has happened or what is or what is to come?"
>
> "What else could it be?" he said.
>
> "Now do they not recount either by simple *diēgesis* or by [*diēgesis*] coming about through mimesis or by both?"
>
> "Even with this," he said, "I still need to get a clearer idea."
>
> "I seem," I said, "to be a laughable teacher and unclear: so just like those who are not good at speaking, instead of speaking about the whole, I'll slice off a part and try to make clear to you what I want. Tell me: do you know the first things of the *Iliad*, in which the poet said that Chryses asks Agamemnon to release his daughter, and he is harsh, and he, since he was not succeeding, was cursing the Achaeans to the god?"
>
> "I do."
>
> "You know, then, that up to these lines:
>
> καὶ ἐλίσσετο πάντας Ἀχαιούς,
> Ἀτρεΐδα δὲ μάλιστα δύω, κοσμήτορε λαῶν
>
> the poet himself is speaking <u>and he is not trying to turn our thought elsewhere as if it is someone else speaking other than himself</u>. And the part after that he speaks <u>as though he himself were Chryses</u> and tries

[83] *Republic* 392d–e, Aristotle *Poetics* 1448a21.

[84] Cf. *Poetics* 1455a29; Meijering 1987:15; Nagy 1996a:170, on the third century CE inscription "He became Alexander" above the name of Demetrius the Homeristes. Cf. Bakker 2005:61; Halliwell 2002:18, 52; Schechner 2003:xviii, 197–202. For caveats on, and nuances in, the notion of "becoming," see Zamir 2010.

as hard as he can to make it seem to us that it is not Homer speaking, but the priest, being an old man. And the rest, in fact, just about all the narration, he has made in this way—about the events in Ilium and about those in Ithaka and all the *pathēmata* of the *Odyssey*."

"Very much so," he said.

"So narration is both when he speaks the speeches in each case and when (he speaks) the stuff between the speeches?"

"How could it not be?"

"But when he speaks a speech as if he is someone else, won't we then say that he is likening himself as much as possible in his own speech (*lexis*) to each [character] that he announces on the point of speaking?"

"We'll say that—what else?"

"So: to liken himself to another either in voice or in gesture/form (*schēma*) is to imitate that one to whom one likens oneself?"

"Of course, so ...?"

"In such a mode, as it seems, this one and other poets make their narration through mimesis."

"Very much so."

"If the poet nowhere hid himself, his poetry and narrative as a whole would have come about without imitation. And so that you don't say that you still aren't understanding, I'll show you how it would be. If Homer said that Chryses came bringing ransom for his daughter as a suppliant of the Achaeans, and most especially the kings, and then after this he spoke not as though he'd become Chryses, but still as Homer [μὴ ὡς Χρύσης γενόμενος ἔλεγεν ἀλλ' ἔτι ὡς Ὅμηρος], you realize that it wouldn't be mimesis but simple narrative. And it would be somewhat like this—I'll speak without meter, I'm not poetic: Having come, the priest prayed that the gods grant them to sack Troy and save themselves, and that they release his daughter, taking the ransom and revering the god. And when he himself said these things, the others showed respect and consented, but Agamemnon got angry, telling him to go away now and not to come back again, lest the scepter and fillets of the god not protect him. And before releasing his daughter, he said she would grow old in Argos with him."

Plato *Republic* 392d–393e[85]

In this paraphrase Socrates successfully drains all the life out of the opening of the *Iliad*. He shows us vividly what is lost when one foregoes the dramatic

---

[85] Unless otherwise indicated all translations are my own. For the *Republic*, I have borrowed freely from Bloom.

mode of Homer[86] and banishes this kind of poet from the city. After inducing Adeimantus to say they will only admit the poet who is "the unmixed imitator of the decent" (someone who narrates and only imitates good men, and that just a little), Socrates reminds Adeimantus of the pleasing quality of "the man who is mixed" as a way of warning him of the harshness of what they are doing. We may read "Homer" into "the mixed man" in this sad exchange:

> "However, Adeimantus, the man who is mixed (κεκραμένος) is pleasing, and by far the most pleasing to boys and their teachers, and to the great mob too, is the man opposed to the one you choose."
> "Yes," he said, "he is the most pleasing."
> "But perhaps," I said, "you'd say he didn't fit with our regime, since there is no double man among us or a multi-layered man (πολλαπλοῦς), since each does one thing."
> "No, he doesn't fit."
>
> Plato *Republic* 397d–e

Step by step, Socrates has led his interlocutors to conclude that they cannot admit the performer who is able to "become all sorts of things" (παντοδαπὸν γίγνεσθαι) (398a). In the immediate context, the reasons have to do with "not doing more than one thing." In the city they are founding, everyone must do only one thing: the farmer is a farmer, and not a judge along with his farming (397e).

What is so alarming about "becoming all sorts of things," and what all is entailed in this process, is not fully explicated here. But the example, the opening of the *Iliad*, is well chosen to illustrate precisely what is lost that is "most pleasing" when we rid ourselves of Homer's "becoming something else." This passage—familiar though it is[87]—repays meticulous attention to its performative virtues: to launch the poem, the bard does not merely, as is sometimes said, plunge us into the poem's world, but gives a rapid-fire display of the techniques involved in becoming the character. Much more is at work in the "becoming" process than impersonation ("likening oneself to another") or direct discourse.

> μῆνιν ἄειδε θεὰ Πηληϊάδεω Ἀχιλῆος
> οὐλομένην, ἣ μυρί' Ἀχαιοῖς ἄλγε' ἔθηκε,

---

[86] Contra the usual view that the passage simply illustrates the difference between narrative and represented speech, e.g. Lucas 1968 on Aristotle *Poetics* 1448a20–24: "... it would seem that this distinction was unfamiliar." Even if the distinction is unfamiliar to Adeimantus, the reach of the illustration extends beyond him to Plato's reader. Direct discourse is of course key to the dramatic mode, but much more goes into "becoming Chryses," let alone all the other layering involved. Nor does "creating a fictional voice" (Kosman 1992:52) cover either what Socrates singles out or everything else that goes into the "becoming" in the *Iliad* opening.

[87] See esp. Kullmann 1955; A. Parry 1972; Redfield 1979 (with bibliography in n. 1); Frontisi-Ducroux 1986a:17–18, 47–48; Rabel 1988; Edmunds 2016 (with bibliography).

πολλὰς δ' ἰφθίμους ψυχὰς Ἄϊδι προΐαψεν
ἡρώων, αὐτοὺς δὲ ἑλώρια τεῦχε κύνεσσιν
5 οἰωνοῖσί τε δαῖτα, Διὸς δ' ἐτελείετο βουλή,
ἐξ οὗ δὴ τὰ πρῶτα διαστήτην ἐρίσαντε
Ἀτρεΐδης τε ἄναξ ἀνδρῶν καὶ δῖος Ἀχιλλεύς.
τίς τ' ἄρ σφωε θεῶν ἔριδι ξυνέηκε μάχεσθαι;
Λητοῦς καὶ Διὸς υἱός· ὃ γὰρ βασιλῆϊ χολωθεὶς
10 νοῦσον ἀνὰ στρατὸν ὦρσε κακήν, ὀλέκοντο δὲ λαοί,
οὕνεκα τὸν Χρύσην ἠτίμασεν ἀρητῆρα
Ἀτρεΐδης· ὃ γὰρ ἦλθε θοὰς ἐπὶ νῆας Ἀχαιῶν
λυσόμενός τε θύγατρα φέρων τ' ἀπερείσι' ἄποινα,
στέμματ' ἔχων ἐν χερσὶν ἑκηβόλου Ἀπόλλωνος
15 χρυσέῳ ἀνὰ σκήπτρῳ, καὶ ἐλίσσετο πάντας Ἀχαιούς,
Ἀτρεΐδα δὲ μάλιστα δύω, κοσμήτορε λαῶν·
Ἀτρεΐδαι τε καὶ ἄλλοι ἐϋκνήμιδες Ἀχαιοί,
ὑμῖν μὲν θεοὶ δοῖεν Ὀλύμπια δώματ' ἔχοντες
ἐκπέρσαι Πριάμοιο πόλιν, εὖ δ' οἴκαδ' ἱκέσθαι·
20 παῖδα δ' ἐμοὶ λύσαιτε φίλην, τὰ δ' ἄποινα δέχεσθαι,
ἁζόμενοι Διὸς υἱὸν ἑκηβόλον Ἀπόλλωνα.
ἔνθ' ἄλλοι μὲν πάντες ἐπευφήμησαν Ἀχαιοὶ
αἰδεῖσθαί θ' ἱερῆα καὶ ἀγλαὰ δέχθαι ἄποινα·
ἀλλ' οὐκ Ἀτρεΐδῃ Ἀγαμέμνονι ἥνδανε θυμῷ,
25 ἀλλὰ κακῶς ἀφίει, κρατερὸν δ' ἐπὶ μῦθον ἔτελλε·
μή σε γέρον κοίλῃσιν ἐγὼ παρὰ νηυσὶ κιχείω …

Sing wrath, goddess, the wrath of Achilles, son of Peleus,
baneful, which laid myriad pains on the Achaeans,
and pitched into Hades many strong souls
of heroes, and was preparing them themselves as prey for dogs
and a feast for birds, and the plan of Zeus was being fulfilled,
from the time when, you see, first they stood apart, having
       quarreled,
the son of Atreus, lord of men, and godlike Achilles.
Who was it, after all, of the gods, that brought them together to
       fight?
The son of Leto and Zeus: for he, angered at the king
sent a plague through the army, and the soldiers were dying,
because he dishonored Chryses, the priest—
the son of Atreus, that is. For he came to the swift ships of the
       Achaeans
trying to ransom his daughter, bringing countless ransom,

holding in his hands fillets of far-shooter Apollo
on a golden staff, and he beseeched all the Achaeans,
the Atreidai most of all, marshals of the people:
"Atreidai and the rest of you well-greaved Achaeans,
may the gods who live in Olympian halls grant to you
to sack the city of Priam, and go home safe.
But let my dear child go, and accept this ransom,
revering the son of Zeus, far-shooter Apollo."
Then all the rest of the Achaeans shouted approval—
to revere the priest and accept the splendid ransom:
but not to the son of Atreus, Agamemnon, was it pleasing,
but he sent him off roughly, and dispatched a harsh word:
"I don't want to come across you, old man, by the hollow ships..."

Iliad 1.1–26

Let us take the elements as they arise. To begin the *Iliad*, the performer asks the goddess to sing wrath: the wrath of Achilles, son of Peleus. This wrath is murderous and sent ψυχάς to Hades, independently of the person it inhabits (lines 2–3).[88] Its activity is also connected somehow to the βουλή (plan) of Zeus, as we now learn. Zeus (lines 5–6) may or may not be the origin of strife (ἐρίσαντε, 6) between two leaders, one of whom turns out to be that same Achilles: either he is, or else ἐξ οὗ (line 6) refers to the point at which the singer wants the goddess to start, and the bard leaps from his long description of the wrath back to his request to the goddess. Or the plan starts in motion with the quarrel itself.[89] Or a nice ambiguity is created as to whose wrath is causing whose. This would be in keeping with the rest of the proem, which continues to mix containers and forces in a sort of Klein bottle.

Having plunged his audience into this morass of causes, divine and semi-divine, the bard then begins again (τίς τ᾽ ἄρ) with a question about ἔρις (strife, line 8). Which of the gods flung the two together in ἔρις to fight? The son of Zeus and Leto (line 9): not, now, Zeus himself. Having fixed on this as the answer, he now explains (γάρ) that this god was angered at the king. But since the bard has just evoked the strife between *Achilles* and Agamemnon, the audience may map this anger of Apollo's onto that of Achilles. The jerky wide-angle lens begins to zoom in on the camp. The λαοί (troops) are being killed (line 10); Apollo, or the νοῦσος (plague) he incited throughout the army, now performs the same action as Achilles, or rather Achilles' wrath (line 2)—or even Zeus or his βουλή

---

[88]   On the personification of the wrath, see Redfield 1979:100.
[89]   See Redfield 1979:96–97; Edmunds 2016:9–12.

(plan)[90]—i.e. sending souls of heroes to Hades. The performer continues: because he dishonored Chryses the priest—Atreides did (lines 11–12). Apollo is angry because Atreides dishonored someone; an audience who knows what is coming is increasingly binding Apollo and Achilles together.[91] For "he" came to the swift ships of the Achaeans to get his daughter freed, bringing countless ransom.

Ah, here is "he"—the priest: he enters the visual field, arriving at the ships. He has fillets in his hands, fillets of Apollo who shoots from afar; he represents Apollo, who is not present but operates at a distance (14 ἐκηβόλου Ἀπόλλωνος; drilled home at line 21 as the last words of Chryses' speech). Fillets on a golden scepter: as our mind's eye zooms in on this significant object, we become present at the scene of the priest's arrival; "recognizing" the priest by his attributes,[92] we "arrive" somewhat as the priest does. (And there may be a more concrete sense in which the performer arrives and we come to the scene to see him: if the performer is carrying a staff, as he holds it (up?) it becomes this scepter.[93] The staff, as we focus upon it, is the first thing in our space to transform into that long-ago camp by the ships.) And he supplicated all of the Achaeans, the two Atreidai most of all, marshallers of the host: "Ἀτρεΐδαι τε καὶ ἄλλοι...." A man speaks among us. Strife is about to be sparked.

> Atreidai and the rest of you well-greaved Achaeans,
> may the gods who live in Olympian halls grant to you
> to sack the city of Priam, and go home safe.
> But let my dear child go, and accept this ransom,
> revering the son of Zeus, far-shooter Apollo.
>
> *Iliad* 1.17–21

The performer is speaking to us. We, addressed by the performer-as-Chryses, become the Achaeans in the camp. We are no longer being told a story; we are cast as characters within the poem, faced with a choice in the here and now. This

---

[90] On Zeus' plan as the destruction of the human race, rather than the honoring of Achilles or something else, see Kullmann 1955 and 1956.

[91] On the ritual antagonism and "thematic and formal convergences" between Achilles and Apollo, see Nagy 1979:142–143. As Nagy notes, Burkert "is so struck by the physical resemblances in the traditional representation of the god and the hero ... that he is moved to describe Achilles as a Doppelgänger of Apollo." Here I am talking about the instantiation of this doubling as *layers within the body of the performer*, but the Doppelgänger quality feeds into such layering.

[92] "Like the Greeks, the external audience initially recognizes the priest from his attributes, which he confirms by warning his internal audience of the wrath of Apollo. The sequence puts the external audience in a position close to that of the internal audience" (Scodel 2002:101).

[93] Martin (1989:233–234) notes performance traditions in which a scepter or other object carried by the bard suggests his identity with the principal hero. Here the staff would serve a slightly different, more tangibly "performative" purpose: the first "becoming" of a character, a character who then turns out to be parallel to Achilles in various ways.

choice will determine whether we will die a horrific death. It is a profoundly bad idea to refuse the man before us. We do not intervene, however, because this is only a show.[94]

Someone from another world (the deep past; the world of the poem; a foreign land) has arrived in our midst. There is something behind him, emphasized by the repeated "shooting from afar." If the performer wields a staff, this force from afar is connected to the man before us via his staff: his "golden scepter." When the man speaks, we are plunged into that other world. But there is yet another world *behind* him, a world of forces, including divine forces, already operating through him. Several wrathful figures are evoked, layered onto one another, and then compressed into whatever this man before us represents.

How did he get here, again? Let us take a more detailed look, focusing upon the person of the performer as a portal through which forces are made present.

The man before us in line 1 invoked wrath. Wrath is what he wants the goddess, invisible to us, to sing, through his mouth. The wrath is then said to be a force operating through someone else—Achilles, not the singer. Wrath then is a force operating independently of the bard and Achilles, but through them. Thus is set in motion a play on the identity of the singer that will return again and again: his eerie relation to Achilles. Wrath, μῆνις, a divine resentment that "taps a cosmic power released by the disorder of a basic order,"[95] becomes a social situation, a strife between two men (ἔρις / ἐρίσαντε, 6), becomes an organic condition, χόλος (χωόμενος, 44; χωομένοιο, 46), a liquid seething within the body. μῆνις, an "objective relation, an anger dangerous to someone," descends into χόλος, "a subjective condition, experienced by the angry person."[96] At the same time, the figures, divine and heroic, who are wrathful, angry, or subject to strife bleed into one another.

The first seven lines invoke the goddess to sing the wrath, ending on the vivid line of Atreides and Achilles, names and epithets chiasmically filling the hexameter, standing apart in strife. With line 8 the bard starts over with the question of who brought the two together. They need to be brought together (ξυνέηκε) before they can stand apart (διαστήτην). The question induces the first step backwards in time.

Answer: the son of Leto and Zeus—for he drove a plague (νοῦσος) through the army. If the bard gestures toward the audience as he says νοῦσον ἀνὰ στρατὸν ὦρσε κακήν ("a plague through the troops he drove, evil"), thus "driving" it

---

[94] Alternatively, if members of the audience do react to the priest's speech (like the "other Achaeans," line 22), they are put in their place by Agamemnon, adding dramatic power to that speech. Whatever the audience might do in practice, their presence is key to the script in this opening passage.

[95] Redfield 1979:97.

[96] Redfield 1979:97n5; cf. Redfield 1994:14. On μῆνις, see Watkins 1977; Muellner 1996.

through us with a movement, there is already a subtle transformation of the space of performance, even before the performer speaks as Chryses to us as the Achaeans. Someone is sending something forward to us, or arousing it within us. The performer at once describes a god who incited something in our midst, and also, to whatever degree, himself *embodies* that god, that action. Then there is an explanation (οὕνεκα, 11), and another step back in time: Atreides dishonored τὸν Χρύσην. Why τὸν [this/that] Χρύσην?[97] Does the performer gesture at an absent figure—perhaps behind him, ready to emerge through him? Immediately, another explanation (γάρ, 12): he came to the swift ships of the Achaeans. The performer either does or does not enact this arrival. He might do so with even the hint of a step—really any gesture at all. He came, to get his daughter freed and bringing countless ransom, holding fillets in hand, of far-shooter Apollo—on a golden scepter. If the performer has a staff, it snaps crisply into the place of the priest's scepter. The fact that the scepter is golden (χρυσέῳ) and so echoes the name of Chryses may seem insignificant, but we eventually learn that scepter, priest, priest's daughter (simply called Chryseis), and fatherland all have versions of the same name. Does the staff represent Chryses as Chryses represents Apollo? At any rate, the staff "stands in" for the priest until he arrives more fully into the body of the bard. And he beseeched all of the Achaeans:

Ἀτρεΐδα δὲ μάλιστα δύω, κοσμήτορε λαῶν·
17   Ἀτρεΐδαι τε καὶ ἄλλοι ἐϋκνήμιδες Ἀχαιοί,

And especially the two sons of Atreus, commanders of the people:
Sons of Atreus and other well-greaved Achaeans

What happens in the echo *Atreida/Atreidai* in lines 16–17? Striking as they are, the two instances are already the third and fourth times this word has appeared in line-initial position.[98]

---

[97]   Bakker (1999:5) remarks that we "might want to see some demonstrative force" in some examples of ὁ ἡ τό near the beginning of the *Iliad*, especially τὸν Χρύσην, but like others sees these uses as approximating the Attic article. But Chryses has not yet been mentioned, so the demonstrative force may be to the fore; cf. Chantraine 1953:192. Scodel (2002:101n16) suggests a cognitive reading: the poet "selected 'that man, Chryses, the priest,' from the characters in his memory." I suggest that thinking in terms of performance allows us to preserve the likely original demonstrative force.

[98]   There is a similar "hammerfall" (Redfield 1994:7) of "Atreides" in line-initial position in Achilles' great speech in *Iliad* 9; another link between narrator and Achilles. A suggestive parallel is the echo Ἠετίωνος / Ἠετίων "of Eetion / Eetion" in *Iliad* 6.395–396, in the voice of the narrator, making his way into becoming Hektor and focalizing through him the vision of the approaching Andromache. The narrator registers the approach of Andromache by suddenly having a vivid picture of her father. (It is as though the narrator's sudden vision of Andromache *brings on* his transformation into Hektor.) This is understandable from the perspective of her husband, and also for the narrator looking ahead with dread.

Line 16 particularizes the object in the previous line: the Achaeans, but mostly the Atreidai. Yet, in its anticipation of Chryses' speech in the next line, it also forms a bridge from narration to performing of direct discourse. (Notice that Socrates' quotation stops at line 16, just before the bard "becomes someone else.") Since the line invokes the Atreidai in the dual, it can almost be spoken as a vocative. In the Homeric script there are no stage directions, only opportunities. Line 16 is an opportunity for the performer to make his way into the persona of Chryses by anticipating his words with his own, perhaps with a gesture singling out the two brothers in the audience. Once we hear line 17, we are firmly planted in the position of the Achaean audience. Yet we hear those words of the priest as an echo of words coming from the performer: we hear a rehearsal, and then the real speech; a speech arising out of description; a swivel from telling to doing; a meditation and a praxis; a warmup and the real thing erupting. The staff, the possible gestures, the echoing line-initial Ἀτρεΐδης, and the grammar make possible a gradual entry into the character that blurs the line between recounting and reenacting. It is somewhat akin to the awkward moment familiar from solo performances of our own time, wherein the audience squirms because we are afraid the performer may start talking to *us*.[99]

Once Chryses' speech starts, we are again going forward in time: the description has taken us back to this moment, and from here on we are in the time of the poem's action, moving forward.

So far as direct discourse goes, the first person the performer becomes is a foreigner angry with the king, someone with divine backup from afar. Or rather, he has cause for anger, but he speaks as a suppliant,[100] invoking the divine backup only at the end of his speech.

But the layers of embodiment here complicate the equation of direct discourse and "becoming the character." We are told the rest of the Achaeans acclaimed the priest's request—but not Atreides; he sent him away harshly. Then the performer becomes Agamemnon, and we are now *his* audience, forced to judge him. He insults the scepter of the god, the very pivot by which the performer, and the forces he invoked, emerged into our world—an object whose power we have witnessed.

---

[99] That is, to us *as ourselves individually*—which happens often in standup comedy, because it works. The comedian is obviously, by default, addressing the whole audience directly; likewise the epic performer interacts intensely with his audience as a matter of course. What I am pointing to is the shift as the performer is in the process of becoming Chryses, but is not quite there yet. The standup analogy is not a precise one, but is familiar enough to evoke a useful visceral recollection in many of my readers. Reynolds (1995:167) describes an analogous "element of tension" in Egyptian epic performance, when "no one knows who or what will be the target of the poet's wit."

[100] "The epic itself is constructed around one vital speech-act, supplication" (Martin 1989:147). Cf. Crotty 1994.

When Agamemnon has angrily sent Chryses away, the performer describes Chryses walking beside the sea[101] in silence, "going apart" (35) for his prayer to Apollo. The performer then once again becomes Chryses, insofar as he speaks the prayer. (He may also gesture with his arms in prayer.) The performer-as-priest invokes Apollo to wreak vengeance, and curses the Achaeans (42), enacting the emergence of the *mēnis* he called down in line 1 into speech and gesture. We already know Apollo's reaction: he is angry (9). The priest, then, is calling down the anger of Apollo. But the man before us has *already* invoked wrath—*his* opening gesture was to ask for the unseen muse to *sing* wrath. Now he, as the priest, invokes Apollo. But Apollo is also the leader of the Muse he invoked to initiate everything. It is by assuming his position as a singer leading the Muses that Apollo rounds out Book 1 (1.603), peeking through briefly as someone like the bard. So the dovetailing of the two invocations, each taking place in the body before us, each invoking wrath as an engine of action, is made strange. What exactly is the relation between this man and his character(s)?

The two invocations are not simply variations on a theme, lined up along a horizontal axis for scholars to compare. One can see this by following the course wrath takes through the body of the performer. Rather than standing alongside the priest's invocation in the linear sequence of events, the opening invocation of the Muse brings on what follows. It invokes a song, in effect, to enter the performer so that he can sing it. For the performer himself to "sing wrath," the wrath enters him along with the song. The script dictates that he bring the divine wrath to earth, to internalize it, in order to nurse it bodily like χόλος and release it as someone else.

The performer invokes wrath from the Muse, then first *describes* its effects: sending souls to Hades. Then he backs up into its causes, presenting them one by one, and *bringing it down to earth*[102]—*to the performance space*: the staff, the embodiment of the priest, our becoming the Achaeans. Once he has brought the wrath here and stands before us as the priest, he speaks as a person in the then and there, not the here and now—though now *our* "here and now" has changed. It is anger that has been invoked and internalized, and anger that we know must be released to do its work of killing, for we have been told that is the poem. It is this temporarily confined anger that fuels the emergence of presences being played out before us.

---

[101] Just as Achilles will go to the beach, apart, and pray to his mother (1.349–351): another way the two figures are layered on top of one another through the body of the performer. On Achilles and Chryses, see Rabel 1988.

[102] Redfield (1979:108): "There is ... a shift from theme to plot, from the μῆνις to its causes. In the process the wrath is somewhat 'demystified'; we shift from the more numinous μῆνις to the more mundane ἔρις which underlies ἐρίσαντε. Διίστημι, similarly, is a rather colorless verb ..."

When he is refused, there is a break in the performer's embodiment. He describes the priest's movement into a space apart, for a prayer that we then witness, but, from the description of the scene, are not present for. Once "backstage," as it were, he gives vent to his anger, as he becomes the priest again: both of his entrances into the priest are powered by anger.

He asks "silver-bow" (line 37) to hear him, "you who straddle Chryse"—and here the name of the place recalls his own name, such that he invokes a presence towering *over* him protectively. The "golden" words are spatialized into man (priest), implement (scepter), surrounding space, abducted child. He then widens that protection out to neighboring cities. "If I ever roofed over for you a pleasing temple": here, ἔρεψα ("I roofed," 39) echoes spatially ἀμφιβέβηκας ("you straddle") in 37 and ἀνάσσεις 'you are lord over' in 38: he points, whether with actual gestures or not, to the *roof*, moving from Apollo, as it were, roofing over Chryse (himself/his city) to himself roofing over the house of Apollo. "... or if I ever burned fat thigh bones": gradually the referent of his speech is lowered to the ground, to the altar that sends up its savor, connecting him with the god. Note how the lowering of the referent parallels the bringing down to earth of μῆνις (wrath) by the bard.[103] Finally he prays: "may the Danaans pay for my tears with your missiles." The gradual descent of the actions both describes the priest's past placating gestures and brings on the straddling god's descent to shoot down the mortals below. The performer embodies the priest, who in turn first embodies the god and then "imitates" his action. *Once again we have a conjuring of forces and an embodiment; a rehearsal and an enactment.* Having brought into being several strata of wrathful forces, the bard now taps into the force lying behind the priest. It is a force at once "operating from afar" and lying in wait inside him, from which his actions are bodied forth.

The invocation has its effect, and Apollo descends in anger in the celebrated lines, to which the English translation, unfortunately, cannot do justice.

> βῆ δὲ κατ' Οὐλύμποιο καρήνων χωόμενος κῆρ,
> τόξ' ὤμοισιν ἔχων ἀμφηρεφέα τε φαρέτρην·
> ἔκλαγξαν δ' ἄρ' ὀιστοὶ ἐπ' ὤμων χωομένοιο,
> αὐτοῦ κινηθέντος· ὃ δ' ἤιε νυκτὶ ἐοικώς.
> ἕζετ' ἔπειτ' ἀπάνευθε νεῶν, μετὰ δ' ἰὸν ἕηκε·
> δεινὴ δὲ κλαγγὴ γένετ' ἀργυρέοιο βιοῖο·

---

[103] On the traffic up and down a "vertical axis" in Pindar, see Mullen 1982:86, 138. The lowering of the referent will be actually seen in a performance that gestures subtly at (with hands, eyes, or whatever) the objects. This also makes the speech easier to memorize, such that it is in memorizing the lines that one realizes the kinesthetics. The Homeric poet thinks and composes spatially/kinesthetically more readily, perhaps, than the writer, but not out of mere convenience.

οὐρῆας μὲν πρῶτον ἐπῴχετο καὶ κύνας ἀργούς,
αὐτὰρ ἔπειτ᾽ αὐτοῖσι βέλος ἐχεπευκὲς ἐφιεὶς
βάλλ᾽· αἰεὶ δὲ πυραὶ νεκύων καίοντο θαμειαί.

And he strode down the peaks of Olympus, seething in his heart,
bow on his shoulders, and a lidded quiver:
they clanged—the arrows—on his shoulders as he raged,
his body stirred: and he came like the night.
Then he sat far off from the ships, and let go an arrow.
A terrible clang came forth from the silver bow:
the mules, first of all, he laid into, and the swift dogs,
but then, releasing a piercing arrow at the men themselves
he was shooting them: and pyres thick with corpses ever burned.

Iliad 1.44–52

Once he starts shooting, the burning thighbones invoked by the priest are replaced by the burning corpses of the Achaeans (52).

Achaeans are dying and burning, but Achilles has not been involved at all. But was it not his wrath that was to send souls to Hades (line 2)? Have we just had a dumb show of the actual poem?[104] Logically, from the perspective of plot, we may anticipate the wrath of Achilles as arising out of the current situation. But here is someone who "represents" anger—anger that fuels his presence before us—a persona who "acts from afar" within a recursion of embodied anger. Of anger as a force powering forth presence but also reaching back for an unseen presence to come forward. Wrath, as an external force brought inside, is fecund soil not only for a maker of *plots*, but for a bard who traffics in *presences*.

So when the bodies are burning and the wrath of Achilles has yet to appear, the audience may experience that wrath not only as about to occur, temporally, but also as still one layer further back in that recursion of wrath, spatially: something to be brought forth from the performer in whom that invoked wrath now resides, from *one layer further inside himself*.

There is a Russian-doll quality to this opening, and we have not yet reached the last doll. Rather than the performer opening dolls for us, however, he *is* the dolls.[105] The bard becomes each doll, moreover, in a way that is hard to keep track of. While the uncovering of a Russian doll may be surprising, what is happening is clear. In the *Iliad* opening, however, the layers—the goddess sending the song,

---

[104] See Rabel (1988) on the Chryses episode as "the *Iliad* in miniature," a paradigm "which shapes the form Achilles' wrath will assume" (p. 473). Cf. *Republic* 602d on shadow-painting. See Whitman (1958:201) on the death of Patroklos as a "shadow play" of the death of Achilles, and Chapter 3 in the current volume.

[105] Cf. the statues of the gods inside *silēnoi* to which Alcibiades likens Socrates, *Symposium* 215a-b.

the wrath sending the souls to Hades, the hero embodying wrath, the god whose plan the wrath was, the priest, the god invoked by the priest, the performer himself—collapse and intermingle.

This intermingling makes schematizing difficult but at the same time makes the whole dynamic possible. The performer enacts a quasi-ring composition as he moves from *describing* Achilles, Apollo, and then Chryses, to *embodying* Chryses, Apollo (shooting), and finally Achilles (when he calls the assembly).

[description]   Achilles → Apollo → Chryses
                                             ↓
[embodiment]   Achilles ← Apollo ← Chryses

This broad movement from representation into action, from description into enactment, encapsulates the layered or multidimensional quality of Homeric performance.

Such a movement is seen elsewhere in Homeric ring composition, as we shall see especially in Chapter 2. It is similar to the physician's movement of thought to action described by Aristotle in the *Metaphysics*:[106]

γίγνεται δὲ τὸ ὑγιὲς νοήσαντος οὕτως· ἐπειδὴ τοδὶ ὑγίεια, ἀνάγκη εἰ ὑγιὲς ἔσται τοδὶ ὑπάρξαι, οἷον ὁμαλότητα, εἰ δὲ τοῦτο, θερμότητα· καὶ οὕτως ἀεὶ νοεῖ, ἕως ἂν ἀγάγῃ εἰς τοῦτο ὃ αὐτὸς δύναται ἔσχατον ποιεῖν. εἶτα ἤδη ἡ ἀπὸ τούτου κίνησις ποίησις καλεῖται, ἡ ἐπὶ τὸ ὑγιαίνειν. ὥστε συμβαίνει τρόπον τινὰ τὴν ὑγίειαν ἐξ ὑγιείας γίγνεσθαι καὶ τὴν οἰκίαν ἐξ οἰκίας, <u>τῆς ἄνευ ὕλης τὴν ἔχουσαν ὕλην</u> ...

And the healthy comes about from him thinking in this way: since such-and-such is health, it is necessary that, if there will be health, so-and-so must obtain, for instance homogeneity, and if this, heat: and so he keeps on thinking, until he brings (the thought process) to that which he himself has the power, in the end, to *do* (*poiein*). Then the movement away from this point is called *poiēsis*, *poiēsis* toward becoming healthy. So it follows in a certain way that health comes about from health, and a house from a house; <u>out of that without matter, that which has matter.</u>

Aristotle Metaphysics Z 1032b 6–14

The physician thinks his way back and back until he reaches the last thing, which is the starting point for action. Similarly the bard reaches back through description, backing up in time, until he reaches the starting point for action,

---

[106] We return to this example below, in Interlude 1.

that is, the point at which he springs forward into the body of Chryses—or Chryses enters his body—and *action* begins. The performer, like Aristotle's physician, backtracks into the "wellsprings" of action, something external to himself, which when reached gives him the power to go forward. Only with the *Iliad* 1 bard, he first sets up a world, and within that representation uncannily "finds" something to fuel his continued performance.

What I have uncovered in the *Iliad* opening differs from what Socrates brings to the attention of the young men. When Socrates speaks of a performer "trying as hard as he can to make us believe it is Chryses speaking," he singles out the performer's use of voice and gesture or stance (*schēma*), as well as *lexis* in the sense of how a character would speak. Certain features of performance would sharpen its effect: a confluence between performer's staff and priest's scepter, and the gestures connecting bard, priest, and god. See for yourself. But it is the workings of the script itself, when embodied by a bard before an audience—independent of particular actorly mediations—that produces "presencing" effects such as the emergence of Chryses. To summarize:

1. the sudden casting of the audience into the position of Chryses' addressees, and its use of their stance *qua* audience to involve them in a troubling fashion

2. the invocation of μῆνις (wrath) and its transformation through description and then embodiment (poetics to presence), such that a force invoked into the body of the bard seems to emerge through a character, in a detour around the barrier between story-world and the world of performance

   In this way, μῆνις fuels both the events within the poem and the bard's performance: the emergence into the world of the audience.

3. the threading of the μῆνις through several divine and human characters, producing a "layering" effect

   The bard becomes a container for forces to course through and a mask behind which other figures, of an uncertain metaphysical relationship to one another (what is causing what?) wait to emerge. There is metaphysical confusion, a displacement of the "source of action" outside the body of the bard himself. The source of action "wanders."

All of these dynamics transcend mere "impersonation" and are more threatening to a carefully regulated city such as the young men are creating in speech. So why does Socrates neglect them? Has he, or Plato, simply missed those dynamics, in his description of the opening of the *Iliad*? Has he deliberately left out a full discussion?

The *Republic*, however radically it differs from the *Iliad*, itself recapitulates some of these dynamics. Above we noted how the similarities among bard, priest, and Apollo contributed to the dynamics flowing through the opening of the *Iliad*. Here again, Plato has, rather than explicitly describing such things, carried them into the space of the dialogue in a haunting fashion. Socrates, after transposing the opening of the *Iliad* into deadly narrated prose, virtually coerces Adeimantus into banning the poet, *precisely when he is describing Agamemnon's banishment of the priest of Apollo, Chryses*. This is not only a clue that Plato is not ultimately in earnest about such a ban; it also shows how Plato reveals far more through imitation, and through his transposition of the dynamics of Homeric poetry into the genre of written dialogue, than his characters do in their individual remarks.[107] Indeed, to banish the priest *is* to banish the poet, and the god and hero lying behind both of them.

But Plato imitates Homer here not only by banning the representative of Apollo. The particular way in which Plato uses this passage is itself a Homeric technique. I discuss three instances of this technique later: the Meleager story (Chapter 2), the Trojan Horse story in *Odyssey* 8 (see Chapter 1) and the Cloak Story in *Odyssey* 14 (Chapter 4). All are virtuoso performance moments. In the *Republic*'s "banning" and in these Homeric examples, someone recounts a traditional story, breaking off just before a moment of troubling salience to the current situation. It is extraordinary that in both *Odyssey* passages, the stories told utterly undermine the hero (in each case, he commits vile acts just after the point at which the retelling stops), even though in the first case, Odysseus has requested the story from a bard, and in the second, he himself is telling it. It is, one might say, an anti-epic type scene, one that brings out a psychic split within the hero and within the performer. The workings of the Cloak Story do not seem to have registered with modern readers. But perhaps Plato understood.[108] It would have been much more obvious in performance. It is not surprising that he imitates this sophisticated Odyssean dialectic in a dialogue that owes so much to the *Odyssey*, precisely at the moment of banning Homer.

The *Republic* imitates, as well as probes, the dynamics of Homeric performance.[109] The layered, ghostly or haunted quality that Plato saw in Homeric performance is manifested in his imitation rather than analyzed overtly. And that quality is integral to the script, however it is embodied.

---

[107] This transposition or imitation is the subject of a separate study.

[108] Cf. Nagy (2002:62–63), on Plato's *Critias* and the practice of one rhapsode leaving off for another.

[109] This is obviously true for the *Ion*, as seen below. But the *Republic* has an additional layer of narration to work with, and so is closer than the *Ion* to the complex situation in Homer. For an extraordinary passage linking Plato's thinking about drama with the staging of the Mysteries at Eleusis, see Artaud 1958:50–52.

Theoclymenos

Such imitation is more overt in Plato's *Ion*, where Socrates becomes a rhapsode. In this dialogue the accent is on the comic rather than the ghostly. But the Homeric moment around which the dialogue is designed, the prophecy of Theoclymenos, illustrates precisely the dynamics that Plato saw in Homeric performance.

The *Ion*, being a drama, lacks the layer of narrative that the *Republic* shares with the *Iliad* and *Odyssey*. Nevertheless a shifting of roles similar to that in the *Iliad* opening is at work in the *Ion*, and the way the *Ion* uses Homeric passages brings out their own role-shifting among god, poet, performer, character, and audience.

This is only part of the comedy of the *Ion*, an overtly playful dialogue in which Socrates subverts his own arguments in an egregiously funny way, and the Homeric examples are designed for something other than what they are cited to illustrate. To show Ion the rhapsode that he is only inspired and possesses no art (τέχνη) of his own, Socrates becomes the rhapsode, putting before Ion's eyes his own rhapsodic experience. Socrates invokes scenes that transport Ion—Odysseus making his epiphany to the suitors, Achilles chasing Hektor—and thus transports Ion onto the platform, such that Ion praises Socrates as though he were an epic poet-performer:

> How ἐναργές (clear, palpable) to me, Socrates, is this τεκμήριον (sign) you've spoken: not hiding anything from you I will speak. For, whenever I speak something pitiful, my eyes are full of tears; and when something fearful or δεινόν, my hair stands up under the fear and my heart leaps.

> Plato *Ion* 535c

Socrates asks Ion whether he thinks someone is in his right mind (ἔμφρονα, 535d) who, decked out in a fancy cloak and golden crowns, cries at festival and feast, even though he has lost none of these things and is among 20,000 friends, none of them hurting him. Ion admits he is not at all in his right mind. Socrates asks whether he knows that he does the same to the audience. And now, a few seconds after describing his tears, this shift of focus to the audience prompts Ion to say:

> For I'm looking down, each time, at them, from above, from the platform, them crying and gazing at me awestruck, and συνθαμβοῦντας (astounded) at what's being said. Now I have to pay close attention to

them—because if I see them crying, I will laugh, taking their money, but if they're laughing, I'll cry, losing money!

Plato Ion 535e

Same moment, different Ion: he weeps and laughs at the same time, in different parts of himself.

As Plato elsewhere creates a tension between the poet as dominating shaper and as slave, the *Ion* too has many means of conveying the same tension. This can be seen in the dialogue's treatment of prophecy. Socrates (531b) raises the art of the prophet as something both Homer and Hesiod talk about, something upon which Ion might be expected to expound. When asked whether he or an actual prophet would speak better about passages involving prophecy, Ion admits the prophet is better qualified. Although this is only the first of several arts Socrates holds out hope that Ion might possess, it is crucial in that, by the end of the dialogue, Socrates is congratulating Ion that, although he has no τέχνη, he is inspired by a god: in short, he is just like a prophet after all. The fact that Ion lacks the prophetic art has been used to launch the argument that ends with Ion as a prophet.

The dialogue's use of Homeric examples, while seemingly as facetious as its argument, is more sophisticated. In asking whether Homer speaks correctly of the medical art, Socrates (538c) cites a passage (*Iliad* 11.639–640) in which a slave woman serves a wine concoction to a passive doctor. For chariotry (537a), he cites the grandiose speech of Nestor (*Iliad* 23.335–340), who recalls how in his youth he won all athletic events *except* the chariot race, to his son, who proceeds to cheat his way to second prize. For prophecy he cites two passages. One of them (*Iliad* 12.200–207, cited at 539b–c) is an elaborate description of a bird-sign. The reason this passage is famous is because of what follows it: Hektor's charismatic dismissal of the sign. Yet Socrates stops abruptly just before Hektor responds, "One bird sign is best: to fight for your country." Presumably the point is to prompt the reader to recall Hektor's unforgettable response and to see the nonsense Socrates is making. Each example carries with it an ironic twist, a lesson to the reader, which is left out of the beating being administered to Ion.

The other passage, the prophecy of Theoclymenos (*Odyssey* 20.351–357, *Ion* 539a), is more complicated. The *Odyssey* passage itself is a pyrotechnic display of Homeric poetics[110] as well as performance or "becoming," issuing a devastating critique of the Homeric audience under the guise of a prophecy to the suitors. "No other incident in [Homer] approaches the uncanniness of this,"[111] and its

---

[110] On the prophecy, see especially Benardete 1997:119–120.
[111] Stanford 1996 *ad* 20.351–357.

uncanniness is only fully appreciated in performance. The passage is queerly introduced within the *Ion*, as Socrates ventriloquizes Ion, quoting a hypothetical Ion asking Socrates a comically long question about where in Homer are the passages that concern prophecy. Socrates obliges the ventriloquized Ion, who is by now in fact quite at sea, by quoting Theoclymenos prophesying to the deranged suitors. Socrates quotes only the speech of Theoclymenos, without the troubling context, which is included here:

345	μνηστῆρσι δὲ Παλλὰς Ἀθήνη
	ἄσβεστον γέλω ὦρσε, παρέπλαγξεν δὲ νόημα.
	οἱ δ' ἤδη γναθμοῖσι γελώων ἀλλοτρίοισιν,
	αἱμοφόρυκτα δὲ δὴ κρέα ἤσθιον· ὄσσε δ' ἄρα σφέων
	δακρυόφιν πίμπλαντο, γόον δ' ὠΐετο θυμός.
350	τοῖσι δὲ καὶ μετέειπε Θεοκλύμενος θεοειδής·
	ἆ δειλοί, τί κακὸν τόδε πάσχετε; νυκτὶ μὲν ὑμέων
	εἰλύαται κεφαλαί τε πρόσωπά τε νέρθε τε γοῦνα.
	οἰμωγὴ δὲ δέδηε, δεδάκρυνται δὲ παρειαί,
	αἵματι δ' ἐρράδαται τοῖχοι καλαί τε μεσόδμαι·
355	εἰδώλων δὲ πλέον πρόθυρον, πλείη δὲ καὶ αὐλή,
	ἱεμένων Ἔρεβόσδε ὑπὸ ζόφον· ἠέλιος δὲ
	οὐρανοῦ ἐξαπόλωλε, κακὴ δ' ἐπιδέδρομεν ἀχλύς.

Pallas Athena
stoked unquenchable laughter in them, and deranged their mind.
And they were laughing with the jaws of another,
and they were eating blood-spattered meat, and their eyes
were filling with tears, and their spirit was fixing on lamentation.
And Theoclymenos like a god addressed them:
"Mean creatures, what is this evil you are suffering? In night
are all your heads wrapped, and your faces and your knees
    beneath.
Lamentation blazes forth, and cheeks have tears upon them,
and with blood the walls are spattered and the beautiful columns,
and the door is full of specters, full the courtyard,
running to Erebos under pall: and the sun
is all out of heaven, and mist runs evil in."

Odyssey 20.345–357

Before we turn to the Odyssean context, consider their application to the *Ion* and to Ion himself. Socrates' omission of the introductory lines encourages the reader to interpret the speech as though it is directed at Ion himself.[112] Like the suitors, Ion has undergone a strange combination of tears and laughter (535c–e) at a feast. Like the suitors, he is out of his mind (535b). Ion both recalls this experience—brought on by his performance before an adoring audience—and re-experiences it in the here and now, due to Socrates' rhapsodic skill. His tears and laughter sit ill together, but so does the way his laughter is a response to his audience's tears (535e). Ion describes his experience (535c) in terms recalling the suitors: "my eyes are filling with tears" (δακρύων ἐμπίμπλανταί μου οἱ ὀφθαλμοί). This echoes both Theoclymenos' prophecy, δεδάκρυνται δὲ παρειαί (20.353), and the narrator's description "their eyes were filling with tears" (ὄσσε δ' ἄρα σφέων / δακρυόφιν πίμπλαντο, 20.348–349). The suitors "were laughing with the jaws of another," while their minds "were fixing on lamentation," just as Ion laughs as he tells of something pitiable while his audience, and he himself, weep. If Socrates earlier played rhapsode to Ion's audience, here he takes the role of prophet, diagnosing the hapless Ion, who seats himself in the chairs of the poetry-obsessed suitors. Ion experiences these feelings before an audience of robots whom he "looks down upon" (536e), somewhat as Theoclymenos sees specters, *eidōla*, "running to Erebos."

Plato was interested enough in these resonances to design his dialogue around them. The example is chosen not only because it concerns prophecy but also for the eerie merging among bard, character, and audience, a merging *orchestrated to seem prompted by* the audience's transformation into charmed automata.

The setting of Theoclymenos' vision is the increasingly bestial continuous feast the suitors are conducting at Odysseus' house. The suitors' behavior is of course generally seen as simply justifying their slaughter. But because of Athena's role, and because of scenes such as Theoclymenos' prophecy, there seems to be something more self-reflective at work running alongside that triumphalist vision.[113]

The suitors would seem to need no divine help to bring on their fate, but the way Athena prevents them from restraining their outrage (20.284–286; cf. 266) casts a pall over their stupid insults and their hurling of animal parts. Most disturbingly, Athena's goal being to cause Odysseus further pain, and thus spur him on (20.285–286), he smiles sardonically instead (302 σαρδάνιον μάλα τοῖον, "quite sardonically, *like so* [?]"[114]). In their specter-hood, not only do insults

---

[112] Recall the similar move in the *Republic* whereby a banishment in the poetic world runs underneath the surface of the banishment enacted in the space of the dialogue.

[113] For more on this counter-thread in the *Odyssey*, see below, Chapter 1, "Trojan Horse," and Chapter 4, esp. pp. 254–259.

[114] The suggestion in τοῖον is that the bard is referring to his own expression. Cf. Stanford 1996 *ad loc.*: "implies a gesture indicating intensity here: cp. 15,451 and 23,282." This has an especially strange ring coming just after μείδησε δὲ θυμῷ (line 301): "and he smiled in his spirit"? Or "inwardly" (Russo in Russo, Fernandez-Galiano, and Heubeck 1992 *ad loc.*)? De Jong 2001:500

issue from the suitors' mouths, but also indications of Odysseus' arrival leak out of what they are saying (20.332). If the suitors were beasts before, they are now drained of their *phrenes* to the point where explicit prophecies of their own doom issue from their lips completely disconnected from their actions. They lose sight of their goal, Odysseus' wealth and kingdom, and now only imagine Penelope going off with one of them (336): despite Athena's efforts, an eminently reasonable suggestion. The way they envision it is that Telemachus will be left alone, enjoying himself, eating and drinking, forever after (336–337). And after Telemachus declares that he will not force out an unwilling Penelope, inexplicably, Athena chooses the moment to arouse laughter in the suitors and "blast their mind."

In this vision of Theoclymenos, the suitors have had their being shattered and taken over by something else. Then the narrator is taken over by something as well, and the way this happens ruptures our experience of the bard's vision of the scene: he has suddenly and without warning seen behind the scene. It is not clear whether we are seeing what the narrator sees (347–349) at all, or whether we have already launched into a metaphorical realm unusual for the narrator of this poem.[115] Then Theoclymenos doubles, or takes over, this vision in 351. What he reports has an indefinite relation to what we may or may not have seen. His vision leaps beyond the suitors to the walls and spirals outward as the horror itself spreads uncontrollably from suitors to surroundings.

Theoclymenos' vision is an extension of the narrator's; the line between them is blurry, and the effect is to make strange the voice of the narrator, and the performer. It is as though the performer/narrator is invaded by a strange vision that has no source, before Theoclymenos comes on the scene and he speaks as the prophet. This is due not only to narratological arrangement, and to Theoclymenos' flagrant extraneousness to the plot (he "belongs to another story"[116]), but to things like the narrator's customary avoidance of phrases like "laughing with jaws of another," and to the awkward ethical situation, in which we ourselves are being set up to enjoy a spectacle of violence while the victims of that violence are being systematically de-brained by an authorial goddess.

---

approves "inwardly" even though "the intensifying adverb τοῖον, 'so much', belongs to the character-language (three times narrator text, eight times direct speech)." The fact that τοῖον is typical of character-language (especially given the way it is used in narrator-speech; see LSJ) fits with a bold histrionic interpretation; the performer strangely unmasks Odysseus in order to put his face on. Lateiner 1995:193–195 well describes the baffling nature of this one-of-its-kind smile.

[115] Benardete (1997:119): "This quasi-Biblical prophecy pulls the future into the present: the descent of the suitors into Hades is being prepared. It is a vision without the visible. It turns hearing into sight—'lamentation has flared forth'—and sun and night into metaphors."

[116] Benardete 1997:120. Theoclymenos also, as the Man in the MacIntosh, wanders into Joyce's *Ulysses*. Cf. Gilbert 1955:171–173; Peradotto 2002:12–13.

Part of the power here lies in a consonance and dissonance between visuality and speech. Imagine yourself in the audience for this passage. If it is done right, your hair will stand up, as Ion said earlier (535c), while the performer describes what he is seeing. And what is he looking at? Or past? Or through? You! You, you avid consumers of poetry, are now the suitors,[117] but what I am describing will *contrast* with your orthostatic hair. I see you laughing with the jaws of another, which vision is, when reported, what makes your hair stand straight in the first place. A short-circuiting of causation has been created among bard, characters, and audience, which any spectator, particularly one as intrigued with Homer as Plato, would have noted with relish. As in the *Iliad* opening, the bard has folded the audience into the ongoing story-world. In both passages, he does so by merging with a representative of Apollo,[118] this time a prophet rather than a priest. As for the audience, we become, in the *Iliad* opening, the Achaean masses, ethically superior to Agamemnon but helpless, while in the Theoclymenos scene we play greatly diminished human beings. The merging is enacted by different means and aims at different effects. In both cases we are strangely implicated, but in Theoclymenos' vision, it is our automatic enjoyment of poetry itself that is held up before us. Our eager anticipation of the slaughter is glimpsed, while the fact that we have been set up for such enjoyment is highlighted.

Theoclymenos is ostentatiously introduced (15.223–286) to play a very brief role.[119] And this very fact contributes to the dramatic effect. When the narrator recites the lines about the suitors, how could he not look around at his audience as though they are the suitors? It is the sudden merging of audience with suitors, the sudden "seeing something there" that had not been seen before, that sparks the becoming of Theoclymenos—that brings on the presence of this new figure who has wandered into the world of the story.

If what is being drawn on here is the audience's anticipation of the slaughter, this concurs with Plato's description of the poet's effect upon the lowest part of the soul. Here, however, he does not merely manipulate said part by dangling *eidōla* before it, but weirdly *exposes it to view while he twists it into*

---

[117] Cf. Felson (1994:109) on the suitors as stand-ins for the audience: "Clearly, the entire audience, of whatever age or gender, will gain confidence and solidarity from rebuking the villainous suitors and will experience relief at their destruction. Special beneficiaries are those listeners who identify, even temporarily, with the suitors' plight." On my interpretation this passage rebukes rather than encourages our enjoyment of the slaughter to come.

[118] *Odyssey* 15.225–255, esp. 252. On the figure of the rhapsode and its connection with prophecy more broadly, see González 2013.

[119] The disproportion between Theoclymenos' introduction and his brief appearances plays a part in Reece's theory that, in another version of the *Odyssey*, Odysseus returns disguised as a prophet. See Reece 1994:162–163 with n9 (citing similar theories by Lord and Kirk). If the disproportion is a trace left by a previous version, the *Odyssey* has ingeniously redeployed even this.

the picture of the suitors. The "components" of performer and audience, being manipulated in order to induce enjoyment (laughing with foreign jaws), are spread out for view just as the suitors themselves are being broken down.[120] This recalls the way Socrates and the young men, in the *Republic*, build a city in speech that is partly composed of their own desires. How much they are discovering something new in the city, and how much they are mistaking their own desires for something out there in the world, is blurry. Here in the *Odyssey* a portal suddenly connects the audience's desires, the suitors, the performer, and the characters—and similar "buried" desires are at stake. Where in the *Republic* we are watching these dynamics staged, in the *Odyssey* example we are dramatically seen through.

Precisely how an individual performer would handle the Theoclymenos scene is something for which there is no external evidence (other than Plato's building the *Ion* out of it). What is clear is that the script hands over to the performer, to harness as he will, the audience's latent potential of being seen as characters in the story-world. This fourth-wall breaking[121] finds a startling counterpart in the "frontal face" in vase painting, an unusual occurrence that effects an eerie communication between the figure and the viewer. As Mackay notes, the "frontal face" often belongs to a figure in a state such as drunkenness or extreme grief, or one with a supernatural power to break boundaries, such as Dionysus or a Muse. Frontisi-Ducroux and Mackay each draw richly suggestive analogies between the frontal face in vase painting and apostrophe or the narrator's address of the audience in epic.[122] Apostrophe is a precise parallel for the visual piercing-through on vases. (For further discussion of apostrophe see Chapters 1, 3, and 4 below.) But there is a more general link to the bard's modulating engagement of the audience. When the external audience suddenly slots into place as the internal, or seems to have an effect on the story-world, the bard's normal visual contact slides over into a strange portal between the

---

[120] Compare this situation, where the prophet sees the poetry-loving suitors as laughing with the jaws of another, and thus intrudes into the voice of the narrating bard, with the critique of epic glory in *Odyssey* 8 (see Chapter 1, "Trojan Horse"), where the internal bard induces the hero to weep with the eyes of another, and so to surface through the narrating bard.

[121] How can there be a "fourth wall"? Ibsen this is not. The bard's shuttling between narrator and character makes the term "wall" an overstatement from the start. And one cannot know how any actual performer acknowledged his audience; some performance styles have a more permeable "fourth wall" than others. While the phrase generally refers to modern realistic drama and so carries connotations beyond what I have in mind, I use it because it is well known and gives a general idea to begin with. What I mean by "breaking the fourth wall" becomes clear in further examples, and is tied to the structure of the script, not performance style. The term indicates a striking contact made between bard-as-character and audience, a reaching out to the audience "over the heads" of characters.

[122] Mackay 2001; Frontisi-Ducroux 1986b.

story-world and performance space, with a variety of effects. The effect created here, an uncanny "seeing through," is one that we will meet with again. In the next chapter, a series of moments ringing changes upon the same dynamics will confirm that this play among parties is not a special effect but the stuff of which Homeric poetry is made.

To sum up the play that goes on among bard, audience, and characters: the bard undergoes a strange merging with one of the characters. We the audience are observed by the bard-becoming-Theoclymenos, and our experience is both reflected by that personage (in the speech of the narrator) and seems to bring on the actual speech of Theoclymenos (the full becoming of the character by the bard). The bard seems both to control the situation and to be subject to it, and likewise with us. The chain of causation is in a pretzel similar to the *Iliad* opening, but this time with a much more uncanny effect.

While we cannot reconstruct the performance milieu in which *Odyssey* 20 took shape, the Theoclymenos scene is more or less a *mise en abyme* of the current performance situation, insofar as the suitors are poetry aficionados sitting comfortably at a feast. While the *Odyssey* elsewhere provides vignettes *about* the dangers of poetry—the suitors in *Odyssey* 1, the Sirens, the oblivious Phaeacians, Helen and her drugs—here the script foments the enactment of the dangerous dynamics.

* * *

"Homer"—the Homeric poet-performer—"becomes all sorts of things," but this turns out not to refer to his skill in characterization or the high proportion of direct discourse. If it did, Plato would not have compared him to a magician who summons the dead, or a wandering dead hero. The "becoming" that is peculiar to Homer is an elaborate interplay among the people and actions of the worlds of the poem and the world of performance, and a strange layering of figures within the body of the performer. Plato, rightly understood, shows how the poems are *ekplēktika* 'wonder-producing, powerfully striking': not in that they fully transport us to the there and then, but in that, as it were, we do not know where we are.[123] We do not know from where the action is proceeding. Doors are opened between the world inside the poem and the world outside it, but what takes place at these doors is not mere representation or "presencing," nor is it simply "transport."

---

[123] Freud, in his essay on "The 'Uncanny'" (1955:220), quoting Jentsch (disapprovingly): "so that the *unheimlich* would always, as it were, be something one does not know one's way about in. The better orientated in his environment a person is, the less readily will he get the impression of something uncanny in regard to the objects and events in it." Jentsch's definition brings out the "un-home-y" sense of *unheimlich*, the dis-placement it shares with the ἄτοπον.

Such a play with our bearings can have a variety of effects, including comic effects. These will be explored in the chapter that follows. But what Homeric performance aims at is not so much the vivid, the real, the past, the truth, ethical complexity, pity, fear, meaning, or tradition, as what we would call the uncanny. As Freud noted, literature is not uncanny by virtue of what it represents: ghosts and speaking animals in literature are rarely uncanny. So too with Homeric performed poetry. The *Iliad*'s world has some features of the uncanny—the events of the beginning of the war eerily replay themselves through the events currently unfolding near the war's end—yet the performer does not make present an uncanny world so much as he generates uncanniness through his performance. The performer's body provides one site through which the uncanny can emerge. It is this uncanny or haunted quality of Homeric poetry that most of all comes to light when one envisions the poems as performed, and it is this quality that especially occupied Plato, who saw such performance. And, though Aristotle is ostensibly out to rescue poetry from the daemonic and irrational, he agrees. Of Aristotle's terms for the kind of strangeness at work in the Homeric poems, one he inherited from the sophists, the ἄτοπον (the un-placed, the out of place), is a near calque of *das Unheimliche* and overlaps with it in meaning. The experience of Homeric performance as at once tapping into the sources of human action and estranging itself from them is, perhaps, at the root of its philosophical significance, or of the philosophers' engagement with it. At any rate, this frisson of forces, this vertigo, seems to be what the Homeric script is *for*. And this is precisely what is disturbing, fascinating, and deeply lovable about these poems.

1

The Elements of Poetics and Presence

THE SPECIFIC VIRTUE OF SOLO HOMERIC PERFORMANCE has come into view: namely, the performer's position between representation and action. The bard drifts within the space of half-acting; he does not merely alternate smoothly between narrating and enacting. Epic performance brings characters and objects into presence but also induces uncertainty as to the "whereabouts" of the performer, the characters, and the audience themselves. Are there two separate spheres of action, or are they oddly related?

The scenes I shall examine in this chapter use a wide array of techniques for creating *atopia* and other presence effects. Looking at these relatively less complex passages helps isolate the "elements" of poetics and presence out of which more complex passages (those treated in Chapters 2–4) are formed. But even in these brief scenes the elements are already forming molecules, if not volatile compounds: they do not exist in pure form.

The Elements

Several of these elements have emerged out of the treatment of the opening of the *Iliad*. The body of the bard became a "container" for a multitude of presences through the workings of a shared rage. At the end of the opening there was a play with the fourth wall, whereby the spectators found themselves seated within the world of the poem, implicated in an ethical dilemma that, like them, spanned the inside and outside of the poem. The bard configures space, he tangles lines of causality, he layers figures on top of one another and within himself, and he puts the audience in ethical dilemmas.

A few initial remarks on space, source of action, layering, and background story, and then we will turn to the scenes themselves.

Space

The performer may project the action of the poem's world onto the space of performance, or vice versa. This is distinct from the kind of mapping Jenny Strauss Clay[1] has identified, where the poet is working with a consistent map of the Achaean camp, except when that has consequences for the interaction between poetics and presence.[2]

A basic use of space is putting the audience in the position of characters in the poem, as in the *Iliad* opening. This is not a shift of the narrator's speech into the second person, but simply the bard as a character addressing the audience as the Achaeans. Much more is involved, but the sightline connecting performer with audience is one crucial factor.

Much of the *Iliad* takes place on the battlefield. The performer brings hero after hero forward into presence only for the brief moment when he is killed. Just as the battlefield is a "stage" upon which to display heroic deeds,[3] so too the performance space is configured as the space of heroic action facing death.

In this configuration, the bard raises the dead hero up[4] into the space of performance by embodying him. This basic setup can then be developed—for example, by varying the kinesthetics of the hero's emergence. The performer may create a depth, beneath or behind—a "backstage" out of which characters emerge into presence. But seldom does such a topography remain stable throughout: the variation of spatial configuration, both within scenes and between them, would seem to be a large part of the poet-performer's aim.

In the battlefield scenario, the fourth wall often coincides with the life/death boundary. In addition to his own body, the performer can also configure the space *before* him as a portal for emergence, as in Odysseus' summoning of the dead in *Odyssey* 11. Here the rhapsode's staff (see Appendix B) would take

---

[1]   http://homerstrojantheater.iath.virginia.edu/. See Clay 2011; similarly Minchin 2008. Clay's focus is on the consistency of the map of the Achaean camp and of Troy that the performer has in his memory. For example, the *Iliad*'s "orientation of right and left remains constant throughout and is always seen from the perspective of a narrator situated in the center of the Greek camp facing the Trojan plain" (Clay 2011:45). I will often emphasize the transformation around the space of the performer. Where Clay, like Minchin, emphasizes the mind's eye of the poet in relation to something like a memory palace, I emphasize the body of the performer. For another treatment of spatial representation in the *Iliad*, see Tsagalis 2012a.

[2]   An example is the use of Odysseus' ship in the center of the camp as a space of emergence (see below, p. 66), but the effect of this is independent of claims about a consistent map in the poet's head, since the ship is said to be central within the passage itself.

[3]   On the battlefield as a spectacle for gods and men, see Frontisi-Ducroux 1986a:62–63; as a "stage on which Zeus and Achilles himself witness the rapid and inexorable unfolding of the latter's destiny," Nagler 1974:135.

[4]   On the movement upward, see the analysis of the *aristeiai* below. On the elaborate "proxemics" within the story-world of Homer, see Lateiner 1995:49–56.

on a particular significance. Whereas, in the *Iliad* opening, the staff would nego-
tiate the boundary between present and past, here the staff's conjuring function
comes into the very action of the poem.

But in *Odyssey* 11, the audience also occupies the place of the Phaeacians,
among whom Odysseus is spinning his tale.[5] In other words, how the bard is
configuring his space at any given moment has to be determined by context.

The script's use of space can be broadly divided into scenes that aim
at the emergence of a character and scenes that orchestrate space in a more
complex fashion. The small-scale examples in this chapter clarify the basic
spatial elements that are in play in the more complex scenarios discussed in the
remaining chapters.

Atopia: Problematizing the Source of the Action

Bound up with these manipulations of space is the more abstract exposure of
the workings of composition and performance. This too is metatheatrical; it
reaches full flower in the Cretan Tales (Chapter 4). The bard does this not as
self-display but as yet another mode, or rather aspect, of *atopia*, related to the
spatial: problematizing the source of action, as with the *Iliad* opening. A bard
or rhapsode reciting a script is not *atopos*, nor is an improviser. What would
be *atopos* is a bard who, startled by an object or event he encounters within
the world he is reenacting and/or unspooling, veers off track and transforms
himself in the process. This kind of *atopia* can tend toward the comic[6] or toward
the uncanny. Insofar as the poet, as he performs, is divided from himself, there
is a kinship to Freud repeatedly finding himself in the red-light district, or being
disgusted with the old man in the mirror. Those examples from Freud's essay
"The 'Uncanny,'" show the perspectival nature of these distinctions, because
although uncanny to Freud himself, they are I daresay amusing for his reader.[7]

Layering

A striking pattern that emerges from sustained attention to the dimension of
presence is the layering of one figure on top of another, such that one appears to
"run" the other or emerge from beneath another. Of special note is that a female
is often running a male. In the last example in this chapter ("Trojan Horse"), the
female "takes over" the male through the medium of something like trauma.
This technique, amplified and enriched, takes terrifying form in the Phoenix

---

[5]   For further analysis of the Nekyia in performance, see Appendix B.
[6]   It is apt that the most telling illustrations of performance dynamics should be comic. Metatheater
seems to be endemic to comedy.
[7]   On the inadvertent comedy of Freud's "The 'Uncanny,'" see Royle 2003:13.

speech (Chapter 2). In both of these cases the female's experience of trauma has a rupturing effect upon the male character, whose trauma is related to hers, and she "bursts through" him.[8] The involuntary repetition of trauma is an actorly resource in other ways as well.

The female can burst through the skin not only of the character, but of the bard, in his capacity as performer as well as narrator and plotter. This exemplifies the larger phenomenon of bard/character fusion or "merging." On the one hand, the bard "becomes" a character, donning him as a mask. On the other hand, the character bleeds into, or ruptures through, the bard's mental and physical being.

Background Story

Even stories that lie in the background have an impact on the presence dimension and on performance, and not only in the sense that the poet counts on the audience to "complete the meaning" of the story. Just as characters reenact previous actions, the *Iliad* as a whole makes massive use of background stories, reenacting and "pre-enacting" them in its plot.[9]

This is not just a matter for source criticism (or Neoanalysis) or poetics/composition. It is intertwined with the reenactment that is performance. For example, it is well recognized that the funeral of Patroklos is a kind of rehearsal for the funeral of Achilles, which lies outside the plot of the *Iliad*. Achilles "plays" the dead Patroklos and is in some sense dead already.[10] In the actual funeral of Achilles, outside the scope of the *Iliad*, his mother Thetis plays a major role. But she also, notoriously, "stirs the lament" at Patroklos' funeral at *Iliad* 23.14, without having arrived. So it seems that lines 23.13–14 were taken "bodily from an epic description of Achilles' funeral where the presence of the goddess was

---

8   The tragic in the *Iliad* is, then, both an imagined "futurity in which remembrance does not recuperate" (Slatkin 2007:29) and a perspective or presence buried within the performing poet.

9   Kullmann 1960:227–357, 365–368; Slatkin 2011:87. Kullmann (2001:389–390) writes, "[T]his poetic technique brings out an inner relationship between the events of the *Iliad* and those of the beginning and end of the war. The power of the past and the future on the Iliadic present is especially prominent. *A peculiar background quality is conferred on the individual situations of the Iliad by the events they recall* and the impending doom they portend. *Dramatic composition,* confined to the wrath motif with its tight time-limits yet preserving the structure of grand epic, immediately entails the uncovering of relations between the depicted present on the one hand and the past and future on the other" (my emphases). He notes (p. 390) that these details of past and future are emphasized more in direct speech than in narrative, and so "in the consciousness of men ... thus constituting the inner world of the mind." The use of background stories in the present study extends Kullmann's notion of dramatic *composition* in the direction of performance. Cf. Taplin 1992, Ch. 3, "The Past Beneath the Present." On the performance of Trojan War stories in *Odyssey* 8 according to Homer's "topical poetic" see Ford 1992:112–114. On the relation of narrative repetition to the uncanny more generally, see Brooks 1984:125.

10 See, for example, Redfield 1994:107–108; further discussion in Chapter 3 below.

both necessary and explicit, to use it for Patroclus."[11] Dowden comments: "It is hard to justify the lines and they give the impression of a poet on autopilot who has let the evoked text take over."[12] It could be that the poet has gone "on autopilot." But here we have the mysterious appearance of a goddess at a funeral at which Achilles seems to be already dead, coinciding with a poet evoking a text and letting it "take over." That seems justified.

In this chapter, several scenes use background stories to foment the emergence of a character. This kind of "takeover" by background story, on a grand scale, is explored in Chapters 2–4. This is, in fact, along with the "layering" of figures (characters and performer), the second striking finding of this study: how many moments that are virtuosic from the perspective of presence turn out to harbor multiple strata of background stories. These two phenomena, layering of figures and layering of stories, are related, although one may occur separately from the other.

Other Elements: Structure, Imagery, Ethics

Even the very structure of the poetry, which one might think exemplifies poetics/*poiēsis*, shapes the presence dimension. The bard uses ring composition to "tap" a source of energy or speech, and this results in a deepening of his embodiment of the character by gaining sudden access to his or her memory, or in the emergence of a new force through that character. It must be kept in mind that ring composition in other genres, like Pindar's choreographed poetry, would combine a spatial movement with this "tapping" or "somatizing" of a dead hero.[13] The Homeric bard does this, only making the movement in speech.[14]

---

[11] Kakridis 1949:84, following Sachs.

[12] Dowden 1996:59.

[13] Mullen (1982:65): by dancing out a ring composition with the hero's agon at its center, the young dancers are "thus *somatizing—literally incorporating—the qualities of strength and courage* through which the hero came to be someone whose deeds were deemed worth recounting" (my emphasis).

[14] Some work on Homeric ring composition has sought to reduce its effect to a pragmatic framing like that in everyday speech (Minchin 1995, Nimis 1999), emphasizing the frame at the beginning and end and minimizing the center. I see no reason to shy away from how the rings are actually deployed in Homeric poetry, where there is often a presencing effect at the center similar to that in Pindar, as analyzed by Mullen, as well as in other choral poetry. Ring composition is already highly developed in combination with other poetic devices in the earliest poetry attested in the Indo-European languages (Watkins 1995), indicating it is an inherited feature, and thus had been developing for a very long time indeed. Mary Douglas's impressive demonstration of highly developed ring composition throughout a wide range of ancient literature outside the Indo-European family indicates to me not, as it does to her (Douglas 2007:12), that the advent of writing transforms ring composition into something elaborate, but that it is a feature widespread throughout oral poetics in and (*pace* Watkins 1995:34) outside Indo-European languages. Whether the details of its usage in the Homeric poems are inherited from Indo-European poetics, or are shaped by dance (David 2006:168) or other ritual movements, or are a general

The ring-composition diagrams which appear later in this study signal the links among the various ring structures in the poems, and emphasize the relationship between a ring-structured "path of song" and the "becoming" that takes place in performance. It is this "becoming" at the center of the ring, I believe, that is primary, and that accounts for other, less-embodied forms of vividness in ring structures—that nevertheless are forms of "presencing."

I briefly mention two other phenomena bearing on presence: imagery and ethical issues. Imagery is poetics par excellence, but it figures into how the bard configures and inhabits space. This is true of speech in general—McNeill's idea of the catchment, where "the recurrence of an image in the speaker's thinking will generate recurrent gesture features," comes to mind.[15] But imagery has a special force for performance, whether one is performing a set script, or composing or re-composing in performance. Just as the character's actions foment and are revealed by the doings of the performer, so too the "histrionic imagery"[16] in the text permits the performer to build up everything from a state of mind to a virtual space around and within him. For a performer who composes in performance, gesture forms part of the composition process, as Aristotle[17] recommends to the tragedian. There may well be a feedback loop between speech and gesture;[18] gesture may form a virtual space around the performer that he then reuses in different ways, and elaborates in speech, where it is an "image." Ethical issues seem very abstract, but as we have seen, they can be part of drawing the audience into the poem's world, and they are crucial in creating layers of presence within the bard.

Gesture, though I have just folded it into imagery, has a special force of its own. I mention it here as an optional element, to emphasize that presence effects do not depend on a particular performance choice.[19]

---

development of speech strategies, ring composition is highly refined in the Homeric poems and has an effect that is, as we shall see, of a piece with their being *solo* performances. See below, p. 234 n. 108.

[15] "A catchment is recognized when two or more gesture features recur in at least two (not necessarily consecutive) gestures. The logic is that the recurrence of an image in the speaker's thinking will generate recurrent gesture features ... A catchment is a kind of thread of consistent dynamic visuospatial imagery running through the discourse segment that provides a gesture-based window into discourse cohesion" (McNeill et al. 2001:10–11). Cf. McCullough 2005.

[16] Goldman 1985:102.

[17] *Poetics* 1455a29, ὅσα δὲ δυνατὸν καὶ τοῖς σχήμασιν συναπεργαζόμενον, "as far as possible working it out with gestures."

[18] Gestures do in fact feed back into thinking and speech in everyday life: McNeill 2005; Beilock and Goldin-Meadow 2010; Goldin-Meadow and Beilock 2010. The way this occurs in Homeric performance, however, makes it strange, or draws out the strangeness, in part because of the bridging of self and other, here-and-now and there-and-then, to which the gestures are contributing.

[19] On gesture, and kinesthetic experience more generally, as shaping Homeric composition, see Purves 2019.

All of the above techniques or schemata produce *atopia*, mixing surface and depth, action and representation, bard and character, voluntary and involuntary, turning each of these distinctions inside-out. They are not aimed at realism or vivid narration. They provoke questions in the audience: Who is this person before me? Is he in his right mind? Is he possessed? Am I *in* this drama (as a character)? Is he unfolding this story or subject to it as an automaton?

Brief Scenes of the Elements in Action

Apostrophe: Patroklos

Homeric apostrophes, where the narrator shifts from third-person narration to address a character as "you," activate the dynamics among bard, character, and audience by playing with presence: who, by the structure of the narration, is present with the performer, and who is not? Who exists in the same temporal 'present' as the bard, and who in his past? As with the second-person addresses of the audience mentioned in the introduction, the "device" may be isolated and defined briefly by narratology, but the situation is never that simple. Even if we try to isolate the apostrophe on its own, other elements demand to be taken into account. The Patroklos apostrophe in *Iliad* 16.787 is the masterstroke:[20]

> τρὶς μὲν ἔπειτ' ἐπόρουσε θοῷ ἀτάλαντος Ἄρηϊ
> σμερδαλέα ἰάχων, τρὶς δ' ἐννέα φῶτας ἔπεφνεν.
> ἀλλ' ὅτε δὴ τὸ τέταρτον ἐπέσσυτο δαίμονι ἶσος,
> ἔνθ' ἄρα τοι Πάτροκλε φάνη βιότοιο τελευτή·
> ἤντετο γάρ τοι Φοῖβος ἐνὶ κρατερῇ ὑσμίνῃ
> δεινός· ὃ μὲν τὸν ἰόντα κατὰ κλόνον οὐκ ἐνόησεν,
> ἠέρι γὰρ πολλῇ κεκαλυμμένος ἀντεβόλησε·
> στῆ δ' ὄπιθεν, πλῆξεν δὲ μετάφρενον εὐρέε τ' ὤμω
> χειρὶ καταπρηνεῖ, στρεφεδίνηθεν δέ οἱ ὄσσε.

> Thrice now he sprang, a match for swift Ares,
> with a horrible shout, and thrice nine mortals killed.
> But when at last the fourth time he charged, equal to a
>   daimon,
> just then O for you Patroklos the end of life showed forth.
> For Phoebus confronted you in the thick of battle,
> terrible. He did not notice him coming through the throng.
> For shrouded in thick mist he met him.

---

[20] See Parry 1972:10–15; Frontisi-Ducroux 1986a:21–22; Frontisi-Ducroux 1986b:198–200; Martin 1989:236; Bakker 1997b:25; Mackay 2001. I return to the *Iliad* 16 apostrophes in Chapter 3 below.

And he stood behind, and struck his back and broad shoulders
with a downturned hand, and his eyes spun.

Iliad 16.784–792

This is not a matter of apostrophe alone. To catalogue everything that goes into
the impact of these lines (characterization, diction, deixis, etc.) might be impos-
sible. We are primed by moments such as:

ὣς φάτο λισσόμενος μέγα νήπιος· ἦ γὰρ ἔμελλεν[21]
οἷ αὐτῷ θάνατόν τε κακὸν καὶ κῆρα λιτέσθαι.

So he spoke, begging, a great fool: yes, it was to be
evil death and doom for his very self he begged for.

Iliad 16.46–47

In other words, part of the impact comes from authorial anticipations of
Patroklos' death.[22] Line 16.787 is a variation on moments when a character real-
izes, with authorial awareness, the rest of the plot, or suddenly possesses a poet-
like ability to control the poem. Patroklos is hit from behind and nothing shows
forth at all; he is endowed with the grandeur of φάνη βιότοιο τελευτή, only to
have his eyes spun round to the inside of his head.

The play of the line, "then, O, Patroklos, the end of your life showed forth
for you" shunts among the following configurations, at least:

1. The bard/narrator takes himself to the battlefield and addresses Pa-
   troklos.
2. But he does so in the past tense: is it the already-dead Patroklos being
   addressed?[23]
3. The 'plot-knowledge' aspect aligns Patroklos with the bard—but here
   with a dark falseness.
4. The 'appearance' of his death (false) is only now happening to
   Patroklos, whereas it is part of the bard's intentional plot-making: this
   sharpens the distinction.
5. The rarity of apostrophe, along with the grand phrase, points toward
   an empathy between narrator and character, as though the bard him-

---

[21] Cf. e.g. *Iliad* 11.187, where Patroklos pauses before addressing Eurypylos to apostrophize the
absent leaders of the Danaans: "ah: so you were going to [ὣς ἄρ' ἐμέλλετε]—far from your friends
and fatherland—glut the swift dogs in Troy with your shining fat."

[22] Richardson 1990:137.

[23] Mackay (2001:18): "There is an immediate disruption of our time-sense, for either Patroklos is
among us, his ghost summoned from the distant past to our time and place, or like a double
exposure our narrator is both before us and simultaneously far off in another time and place on
the Trojan plain."

self has just now realized (cf. ἄρα) the death of Patroklos for what it is, which:

- gives the effect of the bard suddenly abdicating control

and/or

- aligns the narrator with Achilles, who stands in the intimate relationship to Patroklos appropriate to such an epiphanic yet despairing remark.

6. This in turn sheds further authorial light on Achilles, and also deepens his role as proximate cause in Patroklos's death (sending him out),[24] and/or puts him alongside Apollo,[25] approaching Patroklos to give him his deathblow.

It is not useful to add all of these together as though they were vectors to get a result such as "vividness" or even affection for the character. But neither does the poet/narrator merge entirely with Achilles, although such merging is clearly responsible for the moment's emotional impact. The effect is rather a sense of vertigo as to the whereabouts of the bard, that very person before us, his intentionality and his *control of* the poem in the here and now. Is this man we see performing before us "inside" or "outside" the poem?

Aristeiai

In a hero's *aristeia*, he is brought forth onto the stage of battle and into the body of the performer. If the shift from narration to speech is the minimal case of "becoming the character," an *aristeia* is "becoming the character" par excellence.

In the *Iliad* opening, wrath, *mēnis*, was instrumental in the transformation of the performer and in the emergence and layering of presence. In the *aristeiai*, *menos* is instilled into the body of the hero, and there is often an extended arming scene in which the armor donned by the hero is described. In the major arming scenes[26] there is an invariable sequence proceeding from greaves to breastplate, sword, shield, helmet, and spear—roughly, from the ground up.

---

[24] Achilles plays a similar role smiling at Antilokhos during Patroklos' funeral games, 23.555–556. Antilokhos being a replacement for Patroklos, and the story of his own death perhaps being in play, is Achilles smiling as though in recognition of this fact? Or does the smile point toward the fact that Antilokhos is objecting to the reassignation of his prize, just as Achilles had done in Book 1? On this latter reading, Antilokhos has just been playing Achilles, and Achilles appreciates the performance.

[25] Cf. the overlay of Achilles upon Apollo in the *Iliad* opening, p. 28 above.

[26] On these see Armstrong 1958; Fenik 1968; Lord 2000:86–92 (who suggests Homeric, medieval Greek, and Yugoslav epic arming scenes may be survivals from ritual); Lord 1995:75–94.

A useful comparandum for these moments comes from a separate perfor-mance tradition, the Indian *kathakali* and the related martial art *kalarippayattu*, as documented in Zarrilli's "What does it mean to 'become the character': power, presence and transcendence in Asian in-body disciplines of practice." Zarrilli, who spent years training in these traditions, shows that the precise movements involved in "becoming a character" are bound up with "psychophysical cultural assumptions which account for the interiority through which he 'becomes the character'," "reaching a state of 'accomplishment' (Skt. *siddhi*) in which the doer and done are one."[27]

No one would suggest that performers of Homer would go through such physical rigors as do *kathakali* actors, or spend a lifetime learning a special language of gestures and control of the breath. But Zarrilli's conceptual frame-work can enrich our notion of what epic performance and "becoming the char-acter" *can* be.[28] Like the *kathakali* actor, the Homeric performer might be seen not as imitating but as "becom[ing] the conduit for the release of the energized life-force":[29] here, *menos*.[30] An as-if movement of forces from below into the body of the performer finds parallels in the way the *kathakali* actor becomes the character, directing their (very real) energy through movement out from a center and back again. Such an energy is not, of course, particular to Indian or epic performance. Michael Goldman speaks of a basic energy of acting that is a "charge of aggression," "the provocative thrust of changing oneself into some-thing other than oneself."[31] These analogies do not show us in advance what is happening in Homeric performance, which has its own dynamics, but they can help envision the possibilities and articulate the relation between what the character does and what the performer is doing.

This kind of presencing of a dead hero for his hour of glory provides the baseline for the extended *aristeiai*. An *aristeia*, however, is not a one-way street from Hades into the body of the bard and the space of performance, as the following examples illustrate.

---

[27] Zarrilli 1990:134, 131.

[28] Cf. Martin 1989:9: "the value of any such analogues lies in their suggestive power."

[29] Zarrilli 1990:137.

[30] "The living man is all one piece; all his processes—metabolic, motoric, affective, and ideational—are aspects of a single functioning. The name of this functioning is *menos*" (Redfield 1994:171).

[31] Goldman 1975:9. For Goldman the concept is quite general, although his examples come mostly from the English tradition, and particularly Shakespeare. It is notable that, even within Shakespeare, Goldman must develop an account of how this energy works that is particular to each play (Goldman 1985).

Diomedes, *Iliad* 4 and 5

Diomedes has the first and (apart from Achilles) most extended *aristeia*. In its triumphalist tone, it is simpler than the *aristeiai* during and after the hellish Battle Books (11–13). The hero comes into the light[32] as glorious, not half-present and horrific, tragic, or ridiculous. Its straightforward ethos makes it a useful backdrop against which to appreciate other moments.

But even Diomedes' *aristeia* is not that simple. First, it is a virtuoso script for comic performance, in the sense of fourth-wall breaking and other shattering of constraints. It is not a simple making-present but a virtuosic play with presence. Second, the emergence of Diomedes is enacted on so many registers as to constitute a symphony, not a note. These two aspects together create a pleasing inconcinnity, through which the Diomedean bard charms and seduces his audience "over the heads" of the "other" characters.

Diomedes takes center stage beginning in Book 4, just before the first actual killing of the poem. The hero "leaps to the earth" from his chariot, and:

> δεινὸν δ' ἔβραχε χαλκὸς ἐπὶ στήθεσσιν ἄνακτος
> ὀρνυμένου· ὑπό κεν ταλασίφρονά περ δέος εἷλεν.
> ὡς δ' ὅτ' ἐν αἰγιαλῷ πολυηχέϊ κῦμα θαλάσσης
> ὄρνυτ' ἐπασσύτερον Ζεφύρου ὕπο κινήσαντος·
> πόντῳ μέν τε πρῶτα κορύσσεται, αὐτὰρ ἔπειτα
> χέρσῳ ῥηγνύμενον μεγάλα βρέμει, ἀμφὶ δέ τ' ἄκρας
> κυρτὸν ἰὸν κορυφοῦται, ἀποπτύει δ' ἁλὸς ἄχνην·
> ὣς τότ' ἐπασσύτεραι Δαναῶν κίνυντο φάλαγγες
> νωλεμέως πόλεμόνδε.

> The bronze roared terribly on the chest of the lord
> as he sprang. Under this, fear would have seized the stout-hearted.
> As when, on the echoing beach, a wave from the sea
> springs up, rushing under Zephyr who moves it:
> on the sea, first it crests [κορύσσεται], but then
> on dry land, breaking, it groans aloud, and on the edges
> arching along it comes to a head [κορυφοῦται], and spits out foam
> > from the sea:
> so then in pursuit the phalanxes of the Danaans were moved
> inexorably to war.

> *Iliad* 4.420–428

---

[32] Cf. Ajax at *Iliad* 17.647, ἐν δὲ φάει καὶ ὄλεσσον, ἐπεί νύ τοι εὔαδεν οὕτως.

In Homeric fashion, the simile begins vis-à-vis Diomedes (ὄρνυτ' in line 423 echoing ὀρνυμένου in 421), and only in the bridge back to the narrative ("so then the phalanxes") points to the mass of the Achaeans.[33]

A moment later, enter Eris:

ἥ τ' ὀλίγη μὲν πρῶτα κορύσσεται, αὐτὰρ ἔπειτα
οὐρανῷ ἐστήριξε κάρη καὶ ἐπὶ χθονὶ βαίνει·
ἥ σφιν καὶ τότε νεῖκος ὁμοίϊον ἔμβαλε μέσσῳ
ἐρχομένη καθ' ὅμιλον ὀφέλλουσα στόνον ἀνδρῶν.

Little at first, <u>she crests</u> [πρῶτα κορύσσεται = the wave, 424] but then
<u>sticks her head</u> [κάρη] <u>in the sky</u> and treads upon the earth.
At that time too <u>she cast</u> leveling *neikos into their midst*
coming through the throng, supporting the groan of men.

Iliad 4.441–445

So far, two images of "cresting": the wave, Diomedes (and the throng?); and Eris, small at first, but piercing the sky with her head, inaugurating the carnage of the *Iliad* as she did the entire war—by casting *neikos* into the midst (444). The imagery so far is that of a force emerging through a surface. The diction particularizes this as a cresting and a coming to a head (κορύσσεται, κορυφοῦται, κορύσσεται again, κάρη). This striking use of κορύσσεται, paired with 445 <u>ὀφέλλουσα</u> στόνον ἀνδρῶν, seems to be an inspired variation on something like the Hesiodic *Shield of Herakles* 148: δεινὴ Ἔρις πεπότητο κορύσσουσα κλόνον ἀνδρῶν, "That horror Eris was on the wing, marshalling [lit., "helmeting"] the turmoil of men."[34] The wording insists upon the puncturing of a surface, and connects Eris closely to the wave that first figured Diomedes' emergence. This imagery culminates in the first bloodshed of the poem, when Antilokhos kills a κορυστήν man, striking right at the κόρυθος φάλος (457–459).

Thus even before Book 5 begins, the poet has erected a strong scaffolding of head, helmet, and "cresting." Now Book 5 opens:

---

[33] As Martin (1997:155) points out, κορύσσεται is more apt when considering its original referent, Diomedes leaping into action; it recovers the etymological sense "put on a helmet" (with crest) from the generalized sense "put on arms." The brief account here buries another layer. The wave spits out foam, foam (in ranks?) being moved, like the Danaans (κίνυντο, 427), rather than moving. Of course, it is ultimately not the wave but Zephyros who is, so to speak, the unmoved mover (κινήσαντος). Cf. 9.1–7, the Achaeans as a glob of washed-up seaweed. More confusion of the source of action.

[34] Assuming, of course, that the line or some variation on it is traditional, so that the relative dating of the Hesiodic poem in which it appears is not important. Martin (1997:154–156) is relating the first simile I mentioned, 4.424–426, to a tradition represented later by Pindar; in making a connection to Hesiod here I am likewise not suggesting priority of either particular passage.

ἔνθ' αὖ Τυδεΐδῃ Διομήδεϊ Παλλὰς Ἀθήνη
δῶκε μένος καὶ θάρσος, ἵν' ἔκδηλος μετὰ πᾶσιν
Ἀργείοισι γένοιτο ἰδὲ κλέος ἐσθλὸν ἄροιτο·
δαῖέ οἱ ἐκ κόρυθός τε καὶ ἀσπίδος ἀκάματον πῦρ
ἀστέρ' ὀπωρινῷ ἐναλίγκιον, ὅς τε μάλιστα
λαμπρὸν παμφαίνῃσι λελουμένος Ὠκεανοῖο·
τοῖόν οἱ πῦρ δαῖεν ἀπὸ κρατός τε καὶ ὤμων,
ὦρσε δέ μιν κατὰ μέσσον ὅθι πλεῖστοι κλονέοντο.

Then in turn Pallas Athena gave to Diomedes son of Tydeus
menos and daring, that he might be conspicuous among all
the Argives and might win noble *kleos*.
For him she kindled unwearying fire out of his helmet (κόρυθος) and
    shield,
like the autumn star, which most of all
glean-glances bright, from his bath in Ocean.
Such was the fire she kindled on him from his head and shoulders,
and rushed him into the midst [cf. 4.444, Eris] where the masses were
    in panic.

                                                              Iliad 5.1–8

Here again we are focused on the helmet, which, rather than bursting out of something itself, is the source of the emanation: fire. The images of emergence form an elaborate chain, from sea to sky to hero's head; from emergence out of the depths to puncturing the sky to instilling *menos* and the consequent emergence of fire from a head like a star from the ocean. This last image *combines* sea, sky, and head as if packing all available forces into the hero's body.

Notice too the emergence of the image itself from simile into narrated action, via the ambiguous action of Eris.

Diomedes will proceed to slaughter vast quantities of humans, but also to fight with the gods. Once Diomedes has fought with Aphrodite and Ares, he has surely, like Eris, punctured some sort of glass ceiling. Once he does, the listener may well wonder what is left for Achilles to do, if this poem is supposed to be about him.[35] But Book 5 is known as Diomedes' *aristeia* not only for these exploits but because of his peculiar appearance.[36] The "descent to earth" from his chariot and the fire from his helmet bring him forward in a quasi-epiphany.

---

[35] Cf. the dumb show before the entrance of Achilles (see above, Introduction, p. 35).
[36] On a hero being more present than others, compare Bakker (1997a:93): "A hero or god who is an agent through a sequence of events is at the same time an active concept through the series of events that constitutes the representation of the epic events in speech, that is, in the consciousness of the speaker and his audience. Such a concept is not merely something experienced on

But what does such an epiphany within the world of the poem have to do with performance, or more broadly with the dimension of presence?

First, the bard is not merely describing action. The imagery surfaces from vehicle into tenor, in parallel with the described cresting action. The bard's imagination is instantiated, dramatized, brought forth one step into the space of performance. The simile of the wave gives way to the semi-invisible puppeteering of Eris, cresting, which gives way to the *menos* instilled in Diomedes by Athena, then flaming out as fire from his helmet and shield, and spilling out both into visible action on the battlefield and into the body of the performer, creating a sense of the depths or layers of motive forces within him.[37]

Second, once it is clear that Diomedes is present on a plane above that of the heroes he is killing, he occupies a position similar to that of the hero-dispatching bard.[38] In this situation, *any* gesture accompanying the *aristeia*—whether at the instilling of *menos*, arming, or slaughter—manifests the killing power shared between Diomedes and bard. Just as in Book 9 the bard is most of all Achilles through their shared creative intelligence, so too in Book 5 the bard is most of all Diomedes.

Third, just as the *mēnis* in the *Iliad* opening threaded through the Muse to the bard to Achilles, Apollo, Chryses, and back again, setting up layers in the bard's body, so too Diomedes in being animated by *menos* figures, embodies, *is* the bard being taken over by another force: a character. Diomedes being run by *menos* is the bard being run by Diomedes.

After Diomedes initiates his rampage, the imagery of cresting and puncturing continues: we see Diomedes through images of bursting out (a river bursting its banks, 5.88), and bursting in (5.136, a hungry lion leaping into a sheepfold[39]). The disorientation of the reversal from out to in finds explicit acknowledgement in lines 85–86, an "aside" to the audience: "You would not recognize the son of Tydeus, which side he was on, whether he kept company with the Trojans or with the Achaeans." Diomedes, in his near-divine power over death, does not quite occupy the space occupied by the others but is somewhere in between, and continuously emerging.

---

the path of speech, but a companion on that path, sometimes for short distances, sometimes for longer stretches, or even all the way through."

[37] One might usefully compare all of these kinds of emergence (image, levels of discourse) that accompany the entrance of the hero into the body of the bard to the emergence of the river Skamander in *Iliad* 21, "this long-dormant creature who only now emerges onto the surface of the narrative, so angered by Achilles' excesses that at last he must penetrate the fabric of the poem" (Nagler 1974:148).

[38] On "Homer the murderer," see Vermeule 1979:97.

[39] A syntactically puzzling simile: one cannot determine who is doing what. See Kirk 1990:70–72.

Once that presence has been brought into the space of performance, other characters, such as Pandaros, can react to it as the puzzling hybrid of divine and human that it is. These other characters, then, step into the shoes of the audience[40] to voice their view of the brilliant hero.

Diomedes, *Iliad* 6: *Peirata* of Performance

Alighting upon terra firma after battling the gods, Diomedes has his celebrated conversation with Glaukos after which they exchange armor. Diomedes asks Glaukos whether he is a god or not; if he *is* a god, "*I* certainly wouldn't fight with the heavenly gods" (6.129) since those who do so don't live long (6.131, 139–140)—ha![41] He then tells Glaukos (and us) a brief, puzzling version of the story of Lykourgos, who chased the nurses of Dionysus and beat them with his ox-goad (6.135). Now, in the beginning of his speech, Diomedes had wondered aloud at the daring of Glaukos, out in front of everyone else, withstanding Diomedes' long-shadowing spear (6.126). Here is an opportunity for Diomedes to let his spear, as he speaks, become the ox-goad of Glaukos, "spearing" the nursemaids until they drop their own ritual implements in terror (6.134). This mimicry would be in line with the playful nature of the entire speech: Diomedes has just done what he is saying, in his sleeve, he would never do—namely, fight with the gods, and with great success too. At the end of his speech, when he beckons Glaukos to come closer, to reach the limits, *peirata*, of destruction, this spear would enact such a boundary physically. The way the spear/goad is used in the speech playfully shifts from one realm to another. If the bard has a staff, he may hold it out to form a boundary between his audience and his own body, and dare the audience to cross over "the *peirata* of destruction" (143). The performer's use of a staff would add a third level, in that the staff "exists" in three time periods: the performance, the battlefield, and the fantastic mountain Nysos. The performer conjures up the playful post-crest Diomedes, who simultaneously conjures up, with his spear, the not so fortunate Lykourgos and his goad.[42]

These multivalent gestures convey the playful high that Diomedes is on following his *aristeia* in Book 5. Diomedes has punctured the glass ceiling holding mortals back from full-on violence against the gods; for him, the real battle is

---

[40] Richardson (1990:111–112): "We are watching Diomedes rout the Trojans and so is Pandaros, and it turns out, as we find in line 95, that we are looking on the slaughter from the same vantage point."

[41] Kirk (1990:183 *ad* 6.129): "A delightful air of self-satisfaction is conveyed by ἔγωγε and by the repetition of θεοῖσιν ἐπουρανίοισιν after ἀθανάτων γε κατ᾽ οὐρανοῦ."

[42] Martin (1989:127–130) treats the Lykourgos story as a projection of the current encounter, but from the perspective of "dueling narratives" between characters, rather than of solo performance.

over, and he cannot but toy with the mere mortals he meets in coming down to earth. It is comic and actorly, not unsettling.[43] In keeping with the comedy, Diomedes shares with the audience a superior perspective and an insider's view of the gods. Both Diomedes and we ourselves have had the mist removed from our eyes. In fact, it is precisely because Athena has removed the mist from Diomedes' eyes that he can see *through* the fourth wall and rhetorically wink at us. The performer, enacting Diomedes' superior viewpoint, may thus conspiratorially acknowledge, play to, or otherwise invade the space of the audience over the heads of the other characters, violating the fourth wall.[44]

The fourth wall or, if you like, the boundary between story-world and the space occupied by the audience, is, in the case of Diomedes and others, coextensive with the boundary of death. The way this can work is complicated by the "metaphysics," so to speak, of the performance. The heroes are dead, and come to life through the performer. The "stage" they occupy through him is sometimes coincident with the battlefield, conceived of as a "space of action." On the other hand, crossing over that border in front of them would mean joining the audience, the world of the living. It is this comic literalism that Diomedes toys with here, goading the nurses, daring Glaukos to cross over, alluding to his recent battle with the gods over Glaukos' head. The comic effect of puncturing a wall during the conversation is situated within the sudden, very extensive, surreal encounter between the two enemies Diomedes and Glaukos, as though they have slipped out of the matrix of action. The two speakers *cross* onto the "other side" (the enemy's) with no danger to their lives. They have entered a strange in-between brought about by the spatialization of performance, the no-man's-land between themselves and the audience. This "in-between" is registered elsewhere more abruptly, as when Diomedes, about to enter his danger-free *aristeia*, into the arc of missiles, prays to Athena, δὸς δέ τέ μ' ἄνδρα ἐλεῖν καὶ ἐς ὁρμὴν ἔγχεος ἐλθεῖν, "grant me to take [kill] the man and [for him?] to come into the rush of a spear" (5.118), which involves "a rather violent

---

[43] Cf. Kirk 1985:172, 176, and 190–191 *ad* 6.128–143, 6.144–151, and 6.234–236.

[44] This is similar to the more overt Aristophanic parabasis, in that a single character "emerges" and in some sense approaches the audience, though obviously it is more subtle, and there is no direct address of the audience as "you." An analogy with which readers may be familiar is August Wilson's *Fences* (Wilson 1986; premiered 1985). The protagonist, Troy Maxson, is scripted such that the actor addresses the audience directly, conspiratorially. (One actor told me that the first time he performed this role for an audience, he suddenly understood he should lean on the stage-front fence as he did so.) He has access to the audience as other characters do not. This has a comic effect, *until* the same access to something beyond the fourth wall transforms into his shattering dialogues with death. In these, compare the scripted use of the baseball bat ("hitting a homerun"/threatening Death) to Diomedes' spear.

change of subject."[45] To clarify the effect specific to solo performance, which aligns the space between enemies with that between performer and audience, just imagine two performers enacting this scene rather than one.

These two aspects of the speech, the multivalent gestures and the shared perspective between Diomedes and audience, work together.[46] As Diomedes reaches the apogee of his *aristeia*, the bard reaches the fullest embodiment of him. There is an obvious call for gestures and use of the staff; the gestures in their playful manner enact the bard's delight at finding himself fully behind the eyes and hands of Diomedes. It is as though a surgeon has for the first time slipped his hand into a virtual reality glove to operate on a faraway patient. The bard is "trying out" his new powers, his powers to connect his will with the body of the character, to imbue him with his own *menos*.[47] These powers are "new" in that this is the first *aristeia* of the poem, but also insofar as this *aristeia* differs from the others in the particular way it punctures reality, and insofar as Diomedes himself is reaching new heights of action. From another perspective, Diomedes, having driven through the plane of the immortals, revels in his full bodying-forth into the bard and into the space of performance, jauntily jabbing his implement at the fourth wall as if to pierce into reality itself.[48]

Agamemnon ... and Eris

The *aristeia* of Agamemnon (11.67–283)[49] is introduced by a full arming scene (11.15–55): the performer, as he narrates the donning of armor, has the opportunity to involve his own body. As with other arming scenes, as the character dons the armor, from bottom (greaves) to top (the spears whose points shine up to heaven), so too does the performer "don" the character as a force rising from below. Alternatively, as *menos* enters the character, so the performer "enters" the character as animating force. The performer may enact the arming in any way; the specifics, as usual, do not matter. In Agamemnon's case, the description sweeps upward from greaves to corselet to shoulders to shield to helmet, and finally, to cap it, two spears whose bronze tips flash far into heaven, where they cause Athena and Hera (one spear per goddess?) to thunder at him in his honor

---

[45] Willcock 1978–1984:232 *ad Iliad* 5.118, who translates the second clause, "and that he may come within spear's throw."

[46] McNeill's concept of the "catchment" captures the bodily transformation in an *aristeia*.

[47] Likewise Odysseus with his sword at the trench, reanimating and directing the ghost speakers (*Odyssey* 11): see Appendix B.

[48] This configuration receives a further twist at 9.48–49 in Diomedes' fantasy of penetrating Troy, together with Sthenelos, until "we discover its limit (τέκμωρ). For we've got where we are with god." That would indeed run him out of available kinesthetic forespace.

[49] On the *aristeia* itself, see esp. Fenik 1986:7–13.

(11.45–46). The upward sweep of the action of arming is here emphasized and transformed by an analogous movement emblazoned on the armor itself. On the corselet, three snakes stretch their heads toward the neck on each side (11.26–28). As with Achilles' shield, the creatures on the corselet seem to be in motion. The shield-strap (11.38–40) also features a snake, one with three heads, twisted around and growing from one neck: ἀμφιστρεφέες ἑνὸς αὐχένος ἐκπεφυυῖαι. An ancient variant reading for ἀμφιστρεφέες ("twisted," Aristarchus' preference) is ἀμφιστεφέες, which would mean their heads were somehow crowned. This is visually akin to the Gorgon in the middle of Agamemnon's shield:

τῇ δ' ἐπὶ μὲν Γοργὼ βλοσυρῶπις ἐστεφάνωτο
δεινὸν δερκομένη

On it bristle-eyed Gorgo was crowned
staring her uncanny stare ...

Iliad 11.36–37

Since the Gorgon is in the center of the shield, ἐστεφάνωτο may simply mean the head was surrounded by the other images, but the listener can hear "crowned" as well.[50] In any case, as with Diomedes, the head is repeatedly emphasized, but rather than the divine light shining from the hero's helmet, the image we are left with is of the snakes, especially their three heads, and the Gorgon head, which, as it were, blots out Agamemnon's.

Diomedes' "bursting out" was prefigured by the image of the goddess Eris who first punctured the heavens with her head and then threw *neikos* into the midst to start the *Iliad*'s battle-scenes. At the opening of the *Iliad*, too, there was a question about *eris*, lowercase e. These may all recall the wedding of Peleus and Thetis where Eris throws the apple "into the midst."[51]

Eris plays an analogous role in the *aristeia* of Agamemnon. But her role here is much more overt and integral to performance, as befits Agamemnon. At the beginning of Book 11, Zeus sends Eris to the ships of the Achaeans, and she stands on the ship of Odysseus, positioned *in the middle* of the line of ships, and shouts her uncanny shout, which endues the Achaeans with great strength: and suddenly war was sweeter than returning home. Now lines 5–9 of Book 11, describing the position of Eris on Odysseus' ship, are the same as *Iliad* 8.222–226, where it is Agamemnon shouting. Eris at 11.9 thus "takes the

---

50 Hainsworth 1993:221 *ad* 11:36–37: "'was set like a wreath'; the image appears to be that of snakes (the Gorgon's hair) encircling the boss." Willcock 1978–1984:297 *ad* 11:36 translates "was put as a crown," simply meaning that the Gorgon head occupied the raised center of the shield.

51 Edmunds 2016:13–14 notes that *eris*, strife, appears at the beginning of the *Iliad*, the *Cypria*, and the *Catalogue of Women*. But of course Eris herself inaugurates the strife in the *Cypria*: see Nagy 1979: Ch. 11.

place of" Agamemnon on the ship. And not for no reason does she do so—for Agamemnon, when he shouts at 11.15, in turn replaces Eris. With this musical chairs prelude complete, the bard enacts the full arming scene.

Eris here is a force working behind Agamemnon, as Apollo, Zeus, and Achilles (not to mention the Muse and the wrath) worked behind Chryses to open Book 1. In these scenes, where the performer "brings forward" a particular character, there is, in the narrative, a divine or semi-divine force at work behind the character. This does not have to be a statement about dual causation in the psychology of Homeric heroes. Instead, the mutual substitutions of goddess and hero can work *in tandem with the performance process*, as the bard is taken over by one hero for an extended period of time. Thus the goddess-hero relationship doubles, without merely emblematizing, that of bard and hero.

A detail on the corselet is telling with regard to Eris—the three snakes:

κυάνεοι δὲ δράκοντες <u>ὀρωρέχατο ποτὶ δειρὴν</u>
τρεῖς ἑκάτερθ' <u>ἴρισσιν</u> ἐοικότες, ἅς τε Κρονίων
<u>ἐν νέφεϊ στήριξε</u>, τέρας μερόπων ἀνθρώπων.

And black-blue serpents <u>had stretched out toward the throat</u>
three from each side, like <u>rainbows</u>, which Kronian Zeus
<u>stuck in the cloud</u>, a portent for mortal men.

Iliad 11.26–28

As mentioned above, the description of Eris at 4.441–445 seems to be a variation upon a line such as *Shield of Herakles* 148: δεινὴ Ἔρις πεπότητο κορύσσουσα κλόνον ἀνδρῶν.[52] Here, if such speculations were permitted, some such line or image as 11.28 may seem to be the inspiration for Eris sticking her head in the sky (ἐστήριξε) in Book 4. I do not mean that one passage comes from the other. But it is as though the composing bard has Eris in mind in describing the corselet. Everything points toward a force rising up from below, as the hero arms and the bard dons his hero. But in Agamemnon's case, the upward sweep swells into phantasmagoric braggadocio.[53]

Not only do the shield's details contribute to the culminating and crowning of the scene, but they serve as a front behind which Agamemnon acts: a Gorgon mask. This contributes to the spatial layering, the sense of surface and depth,

---

[52] "That horror Eris was on the wing, marshalling [lit., "helmeting"] the turmoil of men."
[53] This is so overwrought, and ends in such gross machismo, it verges on the comic. Agamemnon gets the Hera and Athena rejected by Paris; Paris gets Aphrodite. The scholia note the elaborateness of Agamemnon's *aristeia*. A scholiast on 11.17 seems to say that similar qualities in Paris' arming scene are geared toward making him ridiculous. See also Zenodotus on 11.32. But it is mixed with a disturbing quality consistent with the "increasingly hideous" and finally "ghastly" quality of the killings Agamemnon commits, such as his double beheadings (Fenik 1986:8–9).

the theatrical nature of the arming. The bard establishes the character on his surface.[54] The increasingly vivid arming, the snakes that stretch their heads toward his neck—all this could be experienced by an audience as the bard "investing" himself with the *menos* of the great king as he invests his king with the armor. Yet the excessive nature of the imagery brings with it a distancing effect between bard and hero, one oddly coupled with the Gorgon "mask" I have suggested. This distance is consistent with the hideous *aristeia* to follow—which includes not one but two beheadings, perhaps to be connected with the Gorgon. Between arming and *aristeia* comes another angle upon such distance.

After Agamemnon arms, and the two armies begin fighting, a simile likens them to reapers working on the field of "a rich/blessed man" (11.68) marching towards one another as handfuls of wheat and barley fall.

> οἳ δ᾽, ὥς τ᾽ ἀμητῆρες ἐναντίοι ἀλλήλοισιν
> ὄγμον ἐλαύνωσιν ἀνδρὸς μάκαρος κατ᾽ ἄρουραν
> πυρῶν ἢ κριθῶν· τὰ δὲ δράγματα ταρφέα πίπτει·
> ὣς Τρῶες καὶ Ἀχαιοὶ ἐπ᾽ ἀλλήλοισι θορόντες
> δῄουν, οὐδ᾽ ἕτεροι μνώοντ᾽ ὀλοοῖο φόβοιο.
> ἴσας δ᾽ ὑσμίνη κεφαλὰς ἔχεν, οἳ δὲ λύκοι ὣς
> θῦνον· Ἔρις δ᾽ ἄρ᾽ ἔχαιρε πολύστονος εἰσορόωσα·
> οἴη γάρ ῥα θεῶν παρετύγχανε μαρναμένοισιν ...

> And they, as reapers, facing one another
> drive down the line in a rich man's field
> of wheat, or barley. And these cut handfuls fall thick and fast.
> So Trojans and Achaeans springing at each other
> got to cutting. Neither remembered deadly panic.
> The battle held their heads even, and they, like wolves,
> raged. And lo, Eris took pleasure groaning at the sight:
> for she alone of the gods put in an appearance among the fighters ...
> *Iliad* 11.67–74

This is all quite disturbing. On a basic level, the killings are automated and made into a banal repetitive labor. There is also a terrible disconnect: the armies oppose one another like reapers, but disappear into the falling handfuls

---

[54] Diderot describes the actorly process of Mme. Clairon: "As it will happen in dreams, *her head touches the clouds, her hands stretch to grasp the horizon on both sides; she is the informing soul of a huge figure, which is her outward casing, and in which her efforts have enclosed her*. As she lies careless and still on a sofa with folded arms and closed eyes she can, following her memory's dream, hear herself, see herself, judge herself, and judge also the effects she will produce. In such a vision she has a double personality; that of the little Clairon and of the great Agrippina" (Diderot 1963:16–17; my emphasis).

of grain. They are both reaper and reaped. The mechanical quality finds chilling expression in line 72, ἴσας δ' ὑσμίνη κεφαλὰς ἔχεν, "the battle held their heads equal,"[55] as though they are the grain, and as though the abstract "battle," the machine they become as a mass, holds their heads even. Why? To cut a sharper swathe? To transform reapers into crop?

This simile resembles a group of passages in the *Iliad*, elucidated by Laura Slatkin, that trade on the metaphor of "stretching out" and often "stretching out even" to describe both the battle and individual combatants in such a way that, as Slatkin puts it, "individual gains and losses are subsumed in a view of the aggregate."[56] The poem brings out the disturbing quality of such equilibrium imagery in various ways, as in the simile describing the warriors grappling with the body of Patroklos as men stretching out the hide of an ox (*Iliad* 17.389–395) where, in Slatkin's words, the "general image of strained evenness is made hideously specific."[57] Here too, reapers do not simply transform the enemy into crop, but transform into crop themselves just as they step into their role as reapers.

I suggest that the reaping simile in *Iliad* 11 reaps a further disturbing quality in performance, or rather, as one imagines a role for the performer's

---

[55] Close in tone and diction is the gruesome death of the maids, *Odyssey* 22.468–473, who "hold their heads in a row."

ὡς δ' ὅτ' ἂν ἢ κίχλαι τανυσίπτεροι ἠὲ πέλειαι
ἕρκει ἐνιπλήξωσι, τό δ' ἑστήκῃ ἐνὶ θάμνῳ,
αὖλιν ἐσιέμεναι, στυγερὸς δ' ὑπεδέξατο κοῖτος,
ὣς αἵ γ' ἑξείης κεφαλὰς ἔχον, ἀμφὶ δὲ πάσαις
δειρῇσι βρόχοι ἦσαν, ὅπως οἴκτιστα θάνοιεν.
ἤσπαιρον δὲ πόδεσσι μίνυνθά περ οὔ τι μάλα δήν.

As when thrushes or long-winged doves
slam into a snare set up in a thicket,
seeking out shelter, and a chill bed awaits,
so these were holding their heads in a row, and round all
necks were nooses, that they might die most pitifully.
And they were gasping down to their feet; a little; not too long.

There is a question in the *Iliad* 11 passage about the agency of the men: is it the men holding their own heads even, like good hoplites? The parallel with *Odyssey* 22.471 (underlined) could suggest that the battle, i.e., the men, held their heads, rather than the battle, i.e., *something else*, held the men's heads. But although the maids are the subject of ἔχον and provide a grammatical parallel, it is perverse to think that they are the ones holding their heads in a row (unless we are seeing this from Telemachus' viewpoint, in a disturbing free indirect discourse; he would be the one "taking pleasure groaning at the sight" on analogy to the *Iliad* 11 passage). Rather than simplifying we should notice how the bard maximally exploits this image, as well as the κεφαλὰς ἔχον just before the bucolic diaeresis. The simile should also be compared with the simile of the two men disputing, with measuring ropes, over a boundary between fields (*Iliad* 12.421–424; Slatkin 2011:177–178). The disturbing twist in the *Iliad* 11 reaping simile seems to be enabled somehow by the image of disputing with ropes, combining, perhaps, with the image of birds' heads caught in a snare.

[56] Slatkin 2011:174.
[57] Slatkin 2011:170.

body. Reaping grain resembles holding heads in a line not so much as an image—though it does that, too—as in its kinesthetics, or gesture. It is the equation not only of heads and grain, but also of handfuls and the holding of the heads. (The bard returns to such a gesture just a few lines later in the simile of the wood-cutter who is, finally, tired of chopping [11.86–89].[58]) This kinesthetic kinship makes it possible for the bard to—in any way—glide from enacting the reaping (note τὰ δὲ δράγματα ταρφέα πίπτει, line 69, translated above as "and these cut handfuls fall thick and fast"; the bard *demonstrates* the handfuls, whether with a gesture or not) to holding the heads of the grain/cannon-fodder in front of him. And the bard is after all the source of the killings, as he is the source of the heroes surfacing (emphasis on their heads) through him. He stands in a field of so many heroes, summoning them up, most of them, only to dispatch them again. The gesture is thus a strange anticipation of Agamemnon's beheadings.

The reappearance of Eris is equally eerie. Eris suddenly takes the part of the "rich man" of the simile. The rich man was only a pretext for her; she lies behind him as she does everything. In the passage most similar to this one, on the Shield, it is the rich man (βασιλεύς) overseeing the work who rejoices at the scene,

> αὐτὰρ ὄπισθε
> παῖδες δραγμεύοντες ἐν ἀγκαλίδεσσι φέροντες
> ἀσπερχὲς πάρεχον· βασιλεὺς δ' ἐν τοῖσι σιωπῇ
> σκῆπτρον ἔχων ἑστήκει ἐπ' ὄγμου γηθόσυνος κῆρ.

> But behind,
> children grabbing handfuls, carrying them in their arms
> were eagerly presenting them. And the king among them, in silence
> holding his scepter, stood by the row with joy in his heart.
> *Iliad* 18.554–557

The appearance of Eris works like other passages that anticipate the reaction of the audience and criticize it, adding to the sense that people are beholding an actual scene of carnage. But it is also an uncanny *reappearance* of the presence, female and otherworldly, which lies behind the hero whom the performer is currently most closely embodying.[59] We had forgotten her presence once she shouted from the ships and was replaced by Agamemnon: but no

---

58 Note how this simile is introduced by πῖπτε δὲ λαός, "the host of men was falling," 11.85; cf. ταρφέα πίπτει "[the handfuls] fall thick and fast," 11.69.

59 Cf. male actors playing females in tragedy, seen by Zeitlin (1996:364) as "energizing the theatrical resources of the female and concomitantly enervating the male as the price of initiating actor and spectator into new and unsettling modes of feeling, seeing, and knowing." There seems to be an analogous question as to which person lies behind which.

(ἄρ', 11.73), she was behind this scene the entire time, its author and its connoisseur audience. (If there is a parallel *reappearance* of a god, after setting the ball in motion, in the Homeric poems, it is Athena in *Odyssey* 13.) But insofar as she is behind Agamemnon, and he is a "rich man" all too in charge of the carnage, there is a vertiginous sense of Agamemnon, within his own *aristeia*, receding to the sidelines as an appreciative observer of the "work" being done for him.

What is more, this figure of the appreciative observer crystallizes, right in the following lines. Whereas all of the gods are sitting biliously in their respective domiciles, blaming Zeus:

> τῶν μὲν ἄρ' οὐκ ἀλέγιζε πατήρ· ὃ δὲ νόσφι λιασθεὶς
> τῶν ἄλλων ἀπάνευθε καθέζετο <u>κύδεϊ γαίων</u>
> <u>εἰσορόων</u> Τρώων τε πόλιν καὶ νῆας Ἀχαιῶν
> χαλκοῦ τε στεροπήν, <u>ὀλλύντας τ' ὀλλυμένους τε.</u>

> For these the father cared not a whit. But turning aside
> apart from the others he was sitting, <u>exulting</u> in his glory
> <u>looking at</u> the city of the Trojans and ships of Achaeans
> and the flash of bronze, <u>and the killers and the killed.</u>

> *Iliad* 11.80–83

Removed as the gods are, Zeus is even more so. But that does not prevent him from taking pleasure in the carnage, just like Eris—and like us. Thus does the bard build for himself a position apart, from which he can observe his handiwork with pleasure *and* a jaundiced eye.

Why should it be Eris playing such a pivotal role in these two *aristeiai*? Firstly, because of her authorial role (instigating the war as well as this battle) and distance from events; her role behind the hero parallels the bard's. But there is also something about her kinesthetics—her traditional kinesthetics?—that, I now want to suggest, makes her fertile ground for performance.

In the Karlsruhe Paris (see Figure 1, next page), a blasé Eris rises up from behind a hill[60] to observe the judgment of Paris. It is as though she is emerging from within the vase to inspect its two-dimensional surface. She is topmost and *in the middle* (to us), though invisible to the other gods. *They* think themselves clever to realize that all the strings are being pulled by the miniature Eros doing the bidding of Aphrodite, at the very center (despite Hermes trying to distract them by playing with a dog). Meanwhile Eris cannot be bothered to direct her eyes to the Judgment at hand,

---

[60] *LIMC* Eris 8 = Alexandros 12, late fifth century. Cf. her similar position behind a hill on a calyx krater in Leningrad (*LIMC* Eris 7). Figure 1, Badisches Landesmuseum: B36; drawing after A. Furtwängler and K. Reichhold, *Griechische Vasenmalerei: Auswahl hervorragender Vasenbilder* (1902), pl. 30.

Figure 1

which she has ostensibly erupted to observe. What Eris *does*, it seems, is to insert herself, or her surrogate (the apple), where she does not belong. And she does not belong anywhere. She is an inside-out Pandora, dispensing evils by casting them into the middle of feasts or butting in herself. That is why she erupts into the sky, smashes through the surface of a vase, and precipitates out of a simile.

On the vase is a surface that she herself has created; her *prior* intrusion is what has caused the chaos. She emerges from inside the vase to appreciate what, we realize only now, was her own handiwork—which is precisely what was so eerie about her reappearance in *Iliad* 11. The vase, because it is an object with surface and depth, can employ some of the same elements that the bard makes out of his own flesh.[61]

There is one more turn to the musical chairs between Agamemnon and Eris:

αὐτὰρ ἐπεὶ πόσιος καὶ ἐδητύος ἐξ ἔρον ἕντο,
μοῦσ᾽ ἄρ᾽ ἀοιδὸν ἀνῆκεν ἀειδέμεναι κλέα ἀνδρῶν,
οἴμης τῆς τότ᾽ ἄρα κλέος οὐρανὸν εὐρὺν ἵκανε,
νεῖκος Ὀδυσσῆος καὶ Πηλεΐδεω Ἀχιλῆος,
ὥς ποτε δηρίσαντο θεῶν ἐν δαιτὶ θαλείῃ
ἐκπάγλοις ἐπέεσσιν, ἄναξ δ᾽ ἀνδρῶν Ἀγαμέμνων

---

[61] As with the sarcophagi examined below, pp. 223–224.

χαῖρε νόῳ, ὅτ᾽ ἄριστοι Ἀχαιῶν δηριόωντο.
ὣς γάρ οἱ χρείων μυθήσατο Φοῖβος Ἀπόλλων
Πυθοῖ ἐν ἠγαθέῃ, ὅθ᾽ ὑπέρβη λάϊνον οὐδὸν
χρησόμενος· τότε γάρ ῥα κυλίνδετο πήματος ἀρχὴ
Τρωσί τε καὶ Δαναοῖσι Διὸς μεγάλου διὰ βουλάς.

But when they had sent off the desire for food and drink,
the muse inspired the bard to sing the glorious deeds of men,
from the lay whose fame was then reaching wide heaven,
the strife of Odysseus and Achilles son of Peleus,
how once upon a time they came to argue at the rich feast of the
     gods,
with vehement words, and the lord of men Agamemnon
rejoiced in his mind, when the best of the Achaeans were arguing.
For so Phoebus Apollo had foretold to him, prophesying
in sacred Pytho, when he crossed the stone threshold
to consult him: for at that time the beginning of evil was rolling
upon the Trojans and the Danaans through the counsels of great
     Zeus.

Odyssey 8.72–82

This is a vexed passage. Is this a traditional incident being alluded to? Perhaps.[62] But could this scenario also be part of a (traditional) mutual substitution between Agamemnon and Eris? Here Agamemnon, reprising his role as Eris, rejoices in strife at a feast—a feast of the gods (line 76), in fact—just as Eris admires her own handiwork at the wedding of Peleus and Thetis. What else would the dispute be about, if not who is the ἄριστος, just as the goddesses contended to be the καλλίστη? There is even a prophecy from Apollo (lines 79–81), he who (falsely) prophesied at that very wedding feast about the life of Achilles. One cannot imagine Agamemnon himself bothering to go to Delphi in any traditional episode.

There are, of course, several other Homeric episodes that reenact or play on the origins of the Trojan War in the Judgment of Paris. The duel between Paris and Menelaos and the (darkly comic) re-seduction of Helen are just part of this phenomenon. We will look at two more of these in a moment, but it is worth asking why the Judgment of Paris lends itself to this re-play and in particular re-performance, in whatever mode.

---

[62] Nagy 1979:21–23; Nagy 2003:12–19; Hainsworth in Heubeck, West, and Hainsworth 1988:351 *ad Odyssey* 8.75; Danek 1998:142–150. For Scodel (2002:152–154), the tension between their characters means we need not assume a traditional quarrel.

Musical Chairs: The Judgment of Paris and Persuasion of Helen

The dramatic potential of the Judgment of Paris is made clear by connecting a series of ancient depictions of the Judgment to another series depicting the "persuasion of Helen." The Judgment was performed in pantomime in the Roman period. Various features of these scenes make it clear that this is also true of the "persuasion of Helen."[63] For instance, there is a characteristic pillar off to the side upon which someone leans to observe the scene. In some cases (e.g. Figure 2,[64] the Jenkins Vase) the pillar clearly separates the Muses, representing the arts of pantomime, from the performance. If one puts the "judgment" and "persuasion" scenes together, like sequential tableaux vivants,[65] the principal characters—Helen, Muse, Aphrodite, then Hera, Athena, Aphrodite—sit in one another's chairs in such a way as to suggest that the beginning stages of the Trojan War are variations with a rotating cast on a relatively stable tableau. We have referred in passing to this rotation of roles as *musical chairs.* Here on the Jenkins Vase the viewer sees a more literal musical chairs taking place. The shifts operate to throw into question who is the audience, who is causing the scene, who is acting it out, who is inspiring it, who is singing, and who is the judge. The sophisticated play of agent and patient is carefully recorded in the artistic depictions. In some depictions, it is the Muses behind the pillar separating the "plotted" world from the "plotter." In others, Aphrodite distantly observes and manipulates the encounter. In still others, Helen herself seems to be the contemplative figure.

For example, on the Sevso Treasure's Meleager Plate,[66] Paris coolly observes from one end as Hermes delivers an apple to Aphrodite, with Athena and Hera looking on in frustration. Meanwhile, behind a pillar, a mysterious sixth figure avidly takes it all in. This sixth figure is variously identified as Helen and as Eris; no agreement can be reached. But such ambiguity comprises the beauty of the scene and the virtue of it as a pantomime. The two scenes are scenes of decision. But at any given moment, one is unsure who is the force "directing the show," since the same "actors" are involved, but in shifting degrees of responsibility. This would be highlighted by a performance transforming one scene into another, where the Muse of one scene becomes an actor in the next, and vice versa. Three goddesses become three Muses; Helen becomes Aphrodite, or Paris.

What makes this a good set of scenarios to play out in this way is the musical chairs of volition that it enacts. At what point is Helen seduced irreversibly?

---

[63] Balty 2000.

[64] Balty 2000: fig. 3. Figure 2 (Jenkins Vase), after A.-L. Millin, *Mythologische Gallerie* (1836), pl. 159 no. 541.

[65] This is not what Balty argues, but it seems an irresistible implication.

[66] Mango and Bennett 1994: fig. 2-44.

Figure 2

How is one of these scenarios a replay of the other?[67] While the solo performer lacks the "moving parts" of multi-actor pantomime (or tragedy), he is still able to enact one character stepping into the position of another, thereby arriving at the "source of action" and receiving the impetus to act. And this "solo musical chairs" technique, so to speak, is used for the same end, of exploring and entangling the lines of causation.

Helen: Authorial Reenactment

The "persuasion" of Helen is reenacted in *Iliad* 3, to the annoyance of Helen: a moment where the performer, as Helen, expresses disgust with the whole idea of reenactment—performance for those other "characters" on the other level of reality. And this brings Helen forward, as does her weaving scene,[68] or her bard-like naming of the Achaean heroes,[69] as authorial. She is a character who realizes, to her disgust, that she is a character,[70] and as such bleeds comically into

---

[67] See Rehm 2002 for the analogous process in tragedy. For example (p. 31), in Euripides' *Suppliant Women*, Evadne and then Athena occupy the same position (on high), the only time two characters do this in a play in different scenes. Rehm notes that Evadne's position here may echo her hybristic husband's death, climbing a ladder to sack Thebes and being struck down by a thunderbolt. Similarly (p. 97) Athena stands in place of her icon in the center of the orchestra; this moment is similar to the Eris → Agamemnon → Eris substitutions discussed above. Related but distinct is "role doubling," where the tragedian makes use of the fact that the same actor plays two roles (Rehm 2002:31, 133–135, Ch. 4 passim; Ringer 1998:10–11, 47–48, 52, 131–132).

[68] On which see Bergren 1980b; Taplin 1992:97.

[69] Frontisi-Ducroux 1986a:49: Helen is, like Achilles on the kithara, one of the hypostases of the poet, both in her weaving and in her knowing and naming the heroes.

[70] Redfield (1994:133–134): "Some of these actors ... at some moments know part of the fated outcome of the action, but this is curiously irrelevant. They are in the position of characters in a play who are aware that they are characters in a play and have been told how the play comes

the persona of the bard. She interacts directly with the goddess, but for her this is mere harassment. She wearily goes about her role, not as the empty painted vessel of misogynist imagination, but as a jaded performer, or as someone who would rather be back composing her web. She makes one last effort to reclaim the authorial position when she invites Hektor to "sit in the loveseat" (6.354), as Aphrodite had done to her at 3.424 and (as in the visual depictions) at the initial seduction, but in the end she has to take on her usual role. Thus does the bard, embodying her, linger on the brink between authorship and acting. This tale has been told so many times, just as Helen has "acted it out" so many times, that he is, as it were, bored and unimpressed with the divine machinery. So Helen's weariness and annoyance, surfacing through the bard, has a different effect than her authorial weaving or cataloguing, as it threatens to, or toys with, ending the performance, rather than picturing composition from within the story-world.

Menelaos and the Empty Helmet

The reenactment of the initial scene of Seduction, or rather, of its consequences, plays out yet again through Menelaos as well: not in his *aristeia* in Book 17, but in his appearance in Book 13. This scene in Book 13 reenacts a moment from the duel in Book 3 and at the same time draws on other moments in the Helen story, such as the substitution of Deiphobos for Paris and the traditional musical-chairs relationship between Helen and Aphrodite, alluded to above. This conveys a nightmarish, but also comic, effect of uncanny replay. This replay is smoothly integrated into performance: the musical chairs of presence appears, from the audience's perspective, to be set in motion both by associations in the performer's mind and by his intense spatial involvement with the action he himself is reenacting.

> Δηΐπυρον δ' Ἕλενος ξίφεϊ σχεδὸν ἤλασε κόρσην
> Θρηϊκίῳ μεγάλῳ, ἀπὸ δὲ τρυφάλειαν ἄραξεν.
> ἣ μὲν ἀποπλαγχθεῖσα χαμαὶ πέσε, καί τις Ἀχαιῶν
> μαρναμένων μετὰ ποσσὶ κυλινδομένην ἐκόμισσε·
> τὸν δὲ κατ' ὀφθαλμῶν ἐρεβεννὴ νὺξ ἐκάλυψεν.
> Ἀτρεΐδην δ' ἄχος εἷλε βοὴν ἀγαθὸν Μενέλαον·
> βῆ δ' ἐπαπειλήσας Ἑλένῳ ἥρωϊ ἄνακτι
> ὀξὺ δόρυ κραδάων· ὃ δὲ τόξου πῆχυν ἄνειλκε.

---

out. The effect is fascinating precisely because it is self-contradictory ... [T]hey often speak of the fall of Troy as promised or ordained, and they return always with stoic dignity to the enactment of the story in which they find themselves." Cf. Austin 1966:304–305.

τὼ δ’ ἄρ’ ὁμαρτήτην ὃ μὲν ἔγχεϊ ὀξυόεντι
ἵετ’ ἀκοντίσσαι, ὃ δ’ ἀπὸ νευρῆφιν ὀϊστῷ.
Πριαμίδης μὲν ἔπειτα κατὰ στῆθος βάλεν ἰῷ
θώρηκος γύαλον, ἀπὸ δ’ ἔπτατο πικρὸς ὀϊστός.

And Helenos struck Deipyros with his sword near the temple
—with a great, Thracian sword—and broke off the four-phalossed
[helmet].
And it, thrust away, fell to the ground, and somebody among the
Achaeans
fighting picked it up as it rolled at his feet.
As for him, black night covered over his eyes.
And grief seized the son of Atreus, brave Menelaos:
and he went threatening Helenos, hero, lord,
shaking his sharp spear: and he pulled back the arm of the bow.
And there they joined, one with a sharpened spear
aiming to strike, and the other with an arrow from the bowstring.
And the son of Priam struck him in the chest with an arrow
in the hollow of the corselet, but the bitter arrow flew back.

Iliad 13.576–587

This brief encounter is surprisingly complex and depends on the audience's memory of another moment in the poem: the grand finale to the duel of Menelaos and Paris in Book 3. Having failed to kill Paris, Menelaos has in Book 3 got hold of Paris' helmet and (3.370) ἕλκε δ’ ἐπιστρέψας μετ’ ἐϋκνήμιδας Ἀχαιούς, "was dragging [Paris], twisting him about, toward the well-greaved Achaeans," choking him (3.371–372). But Aphrodite slices the helmet-strap and whisks Paris off to Helen in the boudoir (3.375). Paris' disappearing act leaves Menelaos holding the empty helmet (3.376), which he then whirls off in frustration to be taken up by his companions:

ῥῖψ’ ἐπιδινήσας, κόμισαν δ’ ἐρίηρες ἑταῖροι.

He cast it whirling about, and his trusty companions recovered it.

Iliad 3.378

This entire line in Book 3 is *already* a nightmarish replay, including verse-structure echoes, of what he was doing to the helmet while Paris was still in it (3.370). And the rescue of Paris results in the reenactment of the initial "seduction/persuasion" scene, with Aphrodite pulling the strings.

Now in the Book 13 passage, there is some play on names that enhances the musical chairs: the Achaean's name is Deipyros, the Trojan is Helenos (son of Priam: cf. Πριαμίδης, 13.586; cf. 3.356 Πριαμίδαο of Paris). These names are individually unremarkable, but paired, they recall Deiphobos—who steps into the role of Helen's husband when Paris is dead, and who has just been active (13.526–539)—and Helen herself.[71] Helenos, stepping into the role of Aphrodite in Book 3, breaks off the helmet just as she did, which rolls at the feet of an anonymous Achaean (τις Ἀχαιῶν).[72]

Nowhere else in Homer does a single anonymous character *act* in such a way. The closest parallel is in phrases like ὧδε δέ τις εἴπεσκεν Ἀχαιῶν χαλκοχιτώνων, where the effect of the iterative is "here is what someone would be saying in such a situation" or "one and/or another would say ..." (this latter is clear in ὧδε δέ τις εἴπεσκεν Ἀχαιῶν τε <u>Τρώων τε</u>). The τις Ἀχαιῶν who elsewhere watches and gives voice to anxiety has suddenly got himself tripped up by a helmet.

As the anonymous Achaean is odd, so too is his situation in the sentence. Again:

> Δηΐπυρον δ' Ἕλενος ξίφεϊ σχεδὸν ἤλασε κόρσην
> Θρηϊκίῳ μεγάλῳ, ἀπὸ δὲ τρυφάλειαν ἄραξεν.
> ἡ μὲν ἀποπλαγχθεῖσα χαμαὶ πέσε, καί τις Ἀχαιῶν
> μαρναμένων μετὰ ποσσὶ κυλινδομένην ἐκόμισσε·
> τὸν δὲ κατ' ὀφθαλμῶν ἐρεβεννὴ νὺξ ἐκάλυψεν.
> Ἀτρεΐδην δ' ἄχος εἷλε βοὴν ἀγαθὸν Μενέλαον ...

> And Helenos struck Deipyros with his sword in the temple
> —with a great, Thracian sword—and broke off the four-phalossed
>   [helmet].
> And it [ἡ μὲν], thrust away, fell to the ground, and one of the
>   Achaeans
> fighting picked it up as it rolled at his feet.
> As for him [τὸν δὲ] black night covered over his eyes.
> And grief took the son of Atreus, brave Menelaos ...

> *Iliad* 13.576–581

The anonymous Achaean and the rolling helmet intrude into the ἡ μὲν ... τὸν δὲ, almost to the point where an αὐτόν, or some other help for the listener,

---

[71] The killing of Deiphobos by Odysseus and Menelaos is recalled in the *Odyssey* 8 passage discussed below ("Trojan Horse"): in that passage, it is part of a trauma unleavened by humor.

[72] Note the near-ring structure of the action boomeranging from Book 3 (364–454) to Book 13 (576–581): A) Menelaos grieving – B) M. twisting helmet with Paris in it – C) Aphrodite helmet-snap – B') M. whirling helmet; companions pick up – X [repetition of trauma]) replay of seduction – C') helmet-snap II – B") anonymous Achaean picks up rolling helmet – A') M. grieving. It is perhaps significant that the fatal wound preceding the Book 13 action is cruelly un-manning (13.567–569).

is needed to clarify who the τόν is in line 580, who is dead. This is especially so because, although Helenos breaks off Deipyros' helmet, the blow itself is odd. ξίφεϊ σχεδὸν ἤλασε κόρσην (576) seems to be a mashup of σχεδὸν ἤλασεν ἵππους (11.488) and ξίφει ἤλασε κόρσην (5.584). σχεδόν in the former means "drew his horses *near*." While ἤλασε in the context of a weapon conveys *strike*, σχεδόν muddies the waters. It is in Homer occasionally construed with the dative or genitive, but never the accusative as it is here. Perhaps here σχεδόν conveys "at close range," as it does in other combat scenes, but again, σχεδὸν ἤλασεν as a unit simply means "drive near." The blow is far from clearly fatal, so when dark night covers the eyes of τόν, after the intervening business with τις Ἀχαιῶν, the action is murky.

This intervening business is flagrantly extraneous. It is one thing for the helmet to fly off, and the man himself to die. It is another for the helmet to be picked up for no reason by an unnamed party. It is still a third thing for the helmet to roll to that party's feet. The reason is to recall the Book 3 duel. In the Book 3 scene being recalled, Menelaos hurls Paris' helmet off in frustration, and his companions pick it up immediately with no intervening space or time (again, ῥῖψ' ἐπιδινήσας, κόμισαν δ' ἐρίηρες ἑταῖροι, 3.378). By contrast, in Book 13, the bard identifies τις Ἀχαιῶν, intervenes to describe the rolling helmet, and returns to say he "picked it up." The rolling helmet riffs on Menelaos' "whirling" motion, which conveys both frustration and a wind-up, as though to throw a discus as far as possible (itself a vain reenactment of the twisting actions by which he attempts to strangle Paris). The helmet in Book 13 falls to the ground and creates space and time as it goes until it is picked up—and in steps Menelaos. It creates something like a scene of the unconscious.[73] The slow motion is a placeholder for the performer and the audience to recall and re-project Book 3's farce, itself a sendup of the initial seduction,[74] upon the present scene—upon the body of the bard.

The technique here is similar to the *Iliad* opening, where the body of the bard functions as a "container" for the μῆνις. The object rolling is a peculiar action, witnessed not by some hero but by a bystander, someone whose normal

---

[73] I am grateful to Paul Mathai for this formulation "creating the scene of the unconscious," a phrase not meant to conjure any particular psychoanalytic conception, only to indicate vividly the sense of involuntary reenactment of a frustrating, if not traumatic (in any technical sense), event, or the way the poet sets the scene for the strangely mechanical arrival of the relevant party to play his same old role.

[74] A scholiast on 3.451 εἴ που ἐσαθρήσειεν ("in case he might spy out") remarks candidly, γελοίως ζητεῖ τὸν ἀφροδισιάζοντα ("it's hilarious that he's trying to find the guy who's having sex [with Helen]"). The preciseness of ἐσαθρήσειεν (a hapax) is a nice touch, and even helps point forward to Book 13 and the return of the repressed helmet. As long as the bard faces the audience, he cannot but seek out Paris among them.

role is to comment. All this enables the performer, who is narrating at the moment, to step into the shoes of τις Ἀχαιῶν.

The sheer presence of a bard who (unlike written text) wields hands and is not (unlike in drama) holding an actual helmet requires the audience to imagine the empty helmet, without the performer resorting to any particular gesture. And out of the process of filling in these blanks with the empty helmet, recalling the Book 3 helmet, is precipitated poor Menelaos.

The helmet is undeniably comic: Menelaos casts it as far away as possible in Book 3, only for it to show up unwelcome at his very feet. μετὰ ποσσὶ heightens the effect: the helmet rolls into a whirl of feet, tripping them up. The helmet boomerangs back to Menelaos: he can't get rid of it. His grief is not just for Deipyros. The entanglement of bard and audience entails that the helmet boomerang back for them as well, redoubling what is going on *within* the poem. The fact that the bard stages his own "unscripted" reencounter with the helmet as an overlay upon Menelaos' comically nightmarish repetition of his loss, provides just the *atopia* that the epic mode, the mode of "not seeing the actor,"[75] enables. It doubles, overdetermines, the sense of the involuntary.

In the transitional verse (13.580), night covers the eyes of "him" (the unnamed Deipyros). Now pain seizes Menelaos and he springs into action, shaking his spear. As the bard has witnessed the rolling helmet, an activity internal to himself takes place, culminating in the arrival of Menelaos. On the page, there is a mere association of images. But see how it works in performance, *no matter what the performer does.* In the bard, his "recognition" of the helmet brings on the "presence" of the character within the poem who would so recognize it: Menelaos. The metastasis from anonymous Achaean to Menelaos occurs during the line "and murky night covered his eyes," as though to provide the phone booth out of which Superman emerges, the magician's cape. As the visual "stream" becomes murky, a new presence can emerge.

So far we have discussed the effect of the passage in performance regardless of any particular gesture. But given that the performer has a body, what might he do with it? As the unnamed Achaean picks up the helmet, the performer may enact this move in whatever minimal or maximal fashion.[76] As he does, the audience has the chance to *recognize* the moment of the helmet spinning in 3.378 and of Menelaos, foiled again. While the performer, as the anonymous Achaean, looks

---

[75] Aristotle *Poetics* 1460a14: "... there is more room in epic [than in tragedy] for the *alogon*, through which the wonderful especially comes about, because of not looking at the one acting [*ton prattonta*]."

[76] Looking down at the feet or holding the hand in the "I knew him, Horatio" position seems dignified enough for Aristotle, although here, actually stooping somewhat to "pick it up" would be ridiculous enough to suit the ongoing antics. (We do not know what Aristotle may have said about Homeric performance in the *Poetics'* book on comedy. Cf. Marzullo 1980:189.)

at the empty helmet, the audience can project the moment *into the performer's head, and the head of Paris into the empty helmet*; the performer, "remembering" the earlier moment,[77] presto becomes Menelaos. It is choreographed, but it passes for both playful improvisation and magical instantiation of the memories of the characters and of the audience. This passage is playful, or comic, in its relation to the previous moment, however nightmarish it might be for Menelaos himself.

And this is Menelaos' role, to relive in ever more innovative ways the loss of his wife.[78] Through the sparking of memory (Menelaos', the bard's, and the audience's) poetics/*poiēsis* gives way to presence. The found nature of the helmet is crucial to its effect in performance, with or without gestures. Imagining it with gestures, however, better illustrates *why*. The performer gestures to "pick it up," and the thing "found" generates not an idea but a character, reenacting his cuckold role, as he then goes on to do more and more explicitly, and pathetically, through the end of Book 13.[79] "Picking something up" and having something happen can connote improvisation, but it can also convey slipping deeper into the character, as with the skull prompting "I knew him, Horatio ..." There is also an iconic quality to the empty helmet recalling the disappearance of Helen herself (rather than Paris) under the auspices of Aphrodite (cf. Aeschylus *Agamemnon* 416–419).

This use of a helmet is a variation on its central role in (e.g.) the *aristeiai* of Diomedes and Agamemnon. But while this incarnation of Menelaos shares with these *aristeiai* a focus on the helmet, the overall use of space is much different. Agamemnon and Diomedes arise from beneath to take over the body of the bard and then emanate an energy toward the sky. With Menelaos a more ambiguous metastasis occurs, but a richer one in terms of the memory shared

---

[77] Compare too 3.361–363, when Menelaos draws his sword (=13.610) and strikes the *phalos* of Paris' helmet (=13.614) three times, four times, in vain, before his sword breaks and falls out of his hand, followed by a characteristic complaint to Zeus before he begins dragging Paris off by the helmet.

[78] Aeschylus *Agamemnon* 414–426, which itself is likely reenacting in dance, to whatever extent, these events. Cf. Steiner 2001:191–195, esp. 194, "these dreams, ghosts, and *eidōla* have their genesis in the *pothos* that afflicts the grieving individual, and like the statue, too, they leave only more fervent longing in their wake."

[79] Culminating in his slip from exultation to complaint at 13.620–639. The helmet-complex prefigures the empty urn in Sophocles' *Electra*. Ringer's (1998) reading of that moment came to my attention after I had come to my interpretation of "Menelaos." The two moments reward close comparison. This is one of the cases where the *Iliad* seems to take a technique from multi-actor drama with props (cf. the tableaux vivants analogy above)—and adapt it for solo performance. This could be due to the symbiosis between epic and tragedy (Nagy 2009) or to the influence of any early dramatic form. Or perhaps Sophocles took it over from epic, as he did much else; or else the "empty container-of-a-person" is metatheatrically irresistible no matter the genre. On the history and theatricality of the memento mori skull as a prop, see Sofer 2003:89–115.

among bard, audience, and character. Traumatic repetition takes the place of death *in that same nebulous zone.* Here the character seems to come about through the bard penetrating so far into the world of the poem (as Diomedes does in his encounter with Glaukos) as to "discover" a seed of reality that takes over. At the same time, it is something discovered within the space of performance, as it were, that "disrupts" the ongoing plotting that constitutes the poem-world.

Idomeneus and Meriones Backstage

In the examples so far the script outlines a certain use of space. The bard uses the vertical and horizontal dimensions of the space of performance as part of his straddling two worlds, throwing into question the source of the character's action and his own creative performance. But the bard has other ways of imagining space. In the scene between Idomeneus and Meriones in *Iliad* 13,[80] the orchestration of space overshadows the "becoming" of the characters (to the extent that one can separate the two).

At 13.246, Idomeneus, prompted by the disguised Poseidon, is (finally) armed and about to enter the battlefield. Just then he is met by his *therapōn* Meriones, on his way to fetch a spear. Idomeneus, who has been hanging back, castigates Meriones at length, posing various reasons why Meriones could be there before declaring that as for him, he is on fire to fight.

> Μηριόνης δ' ἄρα οἱ θεράπων ἐΰς ἀντεβόλησεν
> ἐγγὺς ἔτι κλισίης· μετὰ γὰρ δόρυ χάλκεον ᾔει
> οἰσόμενος· τὸν δὲ προσέφη σθένος Ἰδομενῆος·
> Μηριόνη Μόλου υἱὲ πόδας ταχὺ φίλταθ' ἑταίρων
> τίπτ' ἦλθες πόλεμόν τε λιπὼν καὶ δηϊοτῆτα;
> ἠέ τι βέβληαι, βέλεος δέ σε τείρει ἀκωκή,
> ἦέ τευ ἀγγελίης μετ' ἔμ' ἤλυθες; οὐδέ τοι αὐτὸς
> ἧσθαι ἐνὶ κλισίῃσι λιλαίομαι, ἀλλὰ μάχεσθαι.

> Meriones—aha—strong companion, encountered him
> still near the tent: for he was going after a bronze spear
> to bring it back. And the strength of Idomeneus addressed him:
> "Meriones, son of Molos, swift of foot, dearest of companions:
> Why have you come, leaving the war and the fight?
> Have you been hit, and the point of a missile is wearing you down,

---

[80]   On this scene in the context of the "poetics of ambush," see Dué and Ebbott 2010, Part I, Essay 2.

or have you come to me with a message from someone? You know—
>   I myself
have no desire to sit by the tents, but to fight!"

Iliad 13.246–253

Meriones—πεπνυμένος—replies that he is going for a spear, since he has broken his own while striking Deiphobos, "in case there is one left in your hut":

> τὸν δ᾽ αὖ Μηριόνης πεπνυμένος ἀντίον ηὔδα·
> Ἰδομενεῦ, Κρητῶν βουληφόρε χαλκοχιτώνων,
> ἔρχομαι εἴ τί τοι ἔγχος ἐνὶ κλισίῃσι λέλειπται
> οἰσόμενος· τό νυ γὰρ κατεάξαμεν ὃ πρὶν ἔχεσκον
> ἀσπίδα Δηϊφόβοιο βαλὼν ὑπερηνορέοντος.

> And in turn shrewd Meriones addressed him in response:
> "Idomeneus, Counsellor of the bronze-clad Cretans!
> I have come in case—you know—some spear is still left in the huts,
> to bring it back. Well this one we broke—that I was carrying before,
> when I hit the shield of haughty Deiphobos."

Iliad 13.254–258

This releases a fabulous tirade by Idomeneus: there is not one, but one and twenty glorious spears standing in his hut—Trojan ones: because he gets them by fighting.

> τὸν δ᾽ αὖτ᾽ Ἰδομενεὺς Κρητῶν ἀγὸς ἀντίον ηὔδα·
> δούρατα δ᾽ αἴ κ᾽ ἐθέλῃσθα καὶ ἓν καὶ εἴκοσι δήεις
> ἑσταότ᾽ ἐν κλισίῃ πρὸς ἐνώπια παμφανόωντα
> Τρώϊα, τὰ κταμένων ἀποαίνυμαι· οὐ γὰρ ὀΐω
> ἀνδρῶν δυσμενέων ἑκὰς ἱστάμενος πολεμίζειν.
> τώ μοι δούρατά τ᾽ ἔστι καὶ ἀσπίδες ὀμφαλόεσσαι
> καὶ κόρυθες καὶ θώρηκες λαμπρὸν γανόωντες.

> And him in turn Idomeneus leader of Cretans addressed to his face:
> "If it's spears you want, one and twenty you shall find
> standing in my hut against the shining wall—
> Trojan ones, which I lift off the men I have killed! For I don't think
> I stand there fighting apart from enemy men!
> That's why I have spears, and bossed shields
> and helmets and corsets, gleaming bright."

Iliad 13.259–265

Ever-πεπνυμένος Meriones, capping him, remarks that he too has many spoils of the Trojans, "but they are not nearby for the taking." He takes the thinly disguised charge of slacking: "No no—ah, I certainly deny I've forgotten my valor," carefully placing himself "in the front [ranks]," right "where *neikos* of war springs up. Well, I suppose some other Achaean may have been oblivious to my fighting, but you *yourself*, I should imagine, know [ἴδμεναι] it":

τὸν δ' αὖ Μηριόνης πεπνυμένος ἀντίον ηὔδα·
καί τοι ἐμοὶ παρά τε κλισίῃ καὶ νηῒ μελαίνῃ
πόλλ' ἔναρα Τρώων· ἀλλ' οὐ σχεδόν ἐστιν ἐλέσθαι.
οὐδὲ γὰρ οὐδ' ἐμέ φημι λελασμένον ἔμμεναι ἀλκῆς,
ἀλλὰ μετὰ πρώτοισι μάχην ἀνὰ κυδιάνειραν
ἵσταμαι, ὁππότε νεῖκος ὀρώρηται πολέμοιο.
ἄλλόν πού τινα μᾶλλον Ἀχαιῶν χαλκοχιτώνων
λήθω μαρνάμενος, σὲ δὲ ἴδμεναι αὐτὸν ὀΐω.

And him in turn shrewd Meriones addressed in response:
"For me, too, you know, in my hut and and black ship
are many spoils of the Trojans: but they aren't nearby for the getting.
No—no I say, I am not oblivious to valor,
but among the foremost through the man-glorying battle
do I take my stand, whenever the struggle of war arises.
Somebody else, I suppose, of the bronze-clad Achaeans
may be oblivious to my fighting, but you yourself have seen me, I wager."
Iliad 13.266–273

Thus does Meriones try to wrangle the stubborn image of himself battling in vain before the oblivious eyes of the Achaeans and shove it before the mind's eye of Idomeneus. Idomeneus balks at the notion that he needs to be told all of this, and launches into a richly imagined scene in which it would become clear who is a coward and who is brave. This would happen, he insists, not if the two of them were actually to venture forth into battle, as they are ever on the point of doing, but if there were to be an assembly of the best "by the ships," right where they are now, "for ambush." Idomeneus casts his mind's eye to such a display of manhood—and in the process, extends and animates his own and Meriones' questionable presence "among the ships," thereby *creating* such a scene—clownishly detailing the behavior of the coward.

τὸν δ' αὖτ' Ἰδομενεὺς Κρητῶν ἀγὸς ἀντίον ηὔδα·
275 οἶδ' ἀρετὴν οἷός ἐσσι· τί σε χρὴ ταῦτα λέγεσθαι;
εἰ γὰρ νῦν παρὰ νηυσὶ λεγοίμεθα πάντες ἄριστοι
ἐς λόχον, ἔνθα μάλιστ' ἀρετὴ διαείδεται ἀνδρῶν,

ἔνθ' ὅ τε δειλὸς ἀνὴρ ὅς τ' ἄλκιμος ἐξεφαάνθη·
τοῦ μὲν γάρ τε κακοῦ τρέπεται χρὼς ἄλλυδις ἄλλη,
280 οὐδέ οἱ ἀτρέμας ἧσθαι ἐρητύετ' ἐν φρεσὶ θυμός,
ἀλλὰ μετοκλάζει καὶ ἐπ' ἀμφοτέρους πόδας ἵζει,
ἐν δέ τέ οἱ κραδίη μεγάλα στέρνοισι πατάσσει
κῆρας ὀϊομένῳ, πάταγος δέ τε γίνετ' ὀδόντων·
τοῦ δ' ἀγαθοῦ οὔτ' ἄρ τρέπεται χρὼς οὔτε τι λίην
285 ταρβεῖ, ἐπειδὰν πρῶτον ἐσίζηται λόχον ἀνδρῶν,
ἀρᾶται δὲ τάχιστα μιγήμεναι ἐν δαῒ λυγρῇ...

And him in turn Idomeneus leader of Cretans addressed to his face:
"I know what you're like for valor: why do you have to retail it?
I wish right now we best men were all gathered by the ships,
for ambush, where most of all the *aretē* of men comes to be
distinguished,
where he that's a coward man and he that's brave manifest
themselves:
for of one—the coward—his skin turns one way and another,
and for him, his spirit can't be constrained, calm, in his *phrenes*,
but he squats around and he sits on one foot then the other,
and in him, his heart in his chest pounds
as he thinks of the *kēres*, and a chatter comes from his teeth:
but, of the brave one, neither does his skin turn nor is he very
panicked, when first he sits in the ambush of men,
and he prays to mix quick in baneful battle..."

Iliad 13.274–286

This conversation between Meriones and Idomeneus creates a space for these two to conduct their own private sizing-up instead of the public performance; a "rehearsal" space for the battle. It is distinct in tone both from the conversation of two enemies in battle and from, for example, Agamemnon's *epipōlēsis* in Book 4. This sharpens the sense of the battlefield as a stage by fleshing out briefly a backstage. It does so even more concretely than Paris and Helen lounging in the boudoir, or Hektor in Troy, or even the ribbing among companions in Book 10's mustering for the council of chiefs. One might say it is the lowbrow version of Helen and Aphrodite's conversation in Book 3.

This dialogue about spears follows upon a most perfunctory arming scene. In replacing a fuller one, it plays with the very notion of an arming scene, and makes explicit what such a scene is all about.[81]

---

[81] In keeping with the gratuitous, set-apart nature of this scene is its excision by analysts.

The "back region" or "backstage," as Goffman writes, is "where the suppressed facts make an appearance":

> It is here that the capacity of a performance to express something beyond itself may be painstakingly fabricated; it is here that illusions and impressions are openly constructed. Here stage props and items of personal front can be stored in a kind of compact collapsing of whole repertoires of actions and characters. Here costumes and other parts of personal front may be adjusted and scrutinized for flaws. Here the team can run through its performance, checking for offending expressions when no audience is present to be affronted by them; here poor members of the team, who are expressively inept, can be schooled or dropped from the performance. Here the performer can relax; he can drop his front, forgo speaking his lines, and step out of character.[82]

The scene we are privy to is not the most remote backstage. Idomeneus points to his tent, lines 260–262, where the twenty-one spears are "standing in the hut against the shining walls," and Meriones counters with his own stash (267–268), further off. But it is clear that the space occupied by the performer in this scene is already one level "behind" the stage of action (the battlefield).

There is a differentiation of levels between the two characters as to who is rehearsing and who relaxing.[83] First Idomeneus says, "I know what you're like for valor: why do you have to retail it?" Thereupon he conjures a performance space *within this "backstage"* area by the ships, 276–286, where "most of all the *aretē* of men comes to be distinguished"—where the coward and the valiant man show themselves, by their skin literally changing color. There is plenty of space for comic gesturing as Idomeneus is ever more inspired, fleshing out the picture by squatting and scooting around, chattering his teeth, as he describes these graphic symptoms. Occupying one sort of backstage gives way to the acting out of another; one backstage cascades into another.

One can see the Goffmanesque nature of this scene. At the same time, it is not a "representation of a battlefield backstage." As this is a performance in itself, it rather draws on these sociological phenomena for effect.[84] And what is that effect? Does it produce the illusion of reality by unveiling the backstage, like candid photography? One thing this scene surely does is to provide an illusion of depth to the story-world—there is a "there" there, beyond the surface the poet normally shows us, and that "there" is not simply within the poet himself.

---

[82] Goffman 1959:112.

[83] Sophocles has taken over this technique and used it for multiple actors in many of his plays. See Ringer 1998, e.g. p. 197.

[84] Contrast Lateiner 1995, which is concerned with such phenomena within the story-world.

But it is important to think beyond world-creation to performance. The quality of this moment as enacted must be grasped, separately from any representation it may remind us of. Idomeneus and Meriones' backstage[85] presents the audience with the spectacle of a person improvising an excuse for not "acting" yet, *not* bodying himself forth, because he had run out of equipment. The audience gains sudden access (as it were) to the bard as a non-actor, creating an awkward stage moment: "he's not acting yet; we aren't supposed to be here yet." Nakedly exposed, the bard works hard to cap himself in the macho dialogue between the characters. Eventually this gives way to full-fledged composition of a scene and enacting it—but, by the character (Idomeneus). Despite the bard's being in a "non-acting" space, the character takes him over anyway—a virtuoso arrangement. But a better formulation is that the performer, exposed in his pre-performance state, puts on a show of composition-and-performance, only to "reveal" thereby his coward self.[86]

Shepherd Similes

The Homeric poet-performer has other ways of "staging" a kind of backstage to the action. Our next example is one of these, opposite in tone and kinesthetics to the Idomeneus-Meriones encounter, and contrasting too with Olympian scenes showing the powers behind the action, yet a startling backstage nonetheless. This is a series of similes in the *Iliad* (4.275, 4.455, 8.559,[87] 13.493; cf. 3.11) that envisions a lone herdsman observing the world. Similes in general provide a sort of backdrop, but not in the performative sense that this series does.

At 4.279 the shepherd is startled by the oncoming storm and begins moving his sheep into shelter; at 4.455 he is there merely to witness the sound or the sight. Such a shepherd is distinct from those in other similes, where he is less of an observer, though this series appears as a development of the others. He is also quite distinct from battle-visitors the bard sometimes welcomes onto the scene, such as one noted above, "You would not recognize the son of Tydeus, which side he was on" (5.85–86). Instead of being beckoned from the audience, the shepherd seems to be one level further *inside* the poem than the mediating bard, particularly in this example:

[85] Why do these two characters in particular enact this backstage? Does it have to do with the reputation Cretans have as liars? Or might the reason be related to their role in the *Odyssey*'s Cretan Tales, where (as I show in Chapter 4) Odysseus makes subtle use of both in improvising his Cretan persona? Note in both the improvisation and the idea of courage being shown in ambush.

[86] As an analogy from modern multi-actor comedy, think of between-scenes stage business where characters are running from one "location" to the next and "happen" to meet on stage, and as they do, they must "perform"—for one another, not quite for us.

[87] See the sensitive reading of Scott 2009:34.

ὡς δ᾽ ὅτε χείμαρροι ποταμοὶ κατ᾽ ὄρεσφι ῥέοντες
ἐς μισγάγκειαν συμβάλλετον ὄβριμον ὕδωρ
κρουνῶν ἐκ μεγάλων κοίλης ἔντοσθε χαράδρης,
τῶν δέ τε τηλόσε δοῦπον ἐν οὔρεσιν ἔκλυε ποιμήν·
ὡς τῶν μισγομένων γένετο ἰαχή τε πόνος τε.

As when rivers in winter flood, flowing down the mountains
force together their weighty water into the churning curve
out of the great springs in the hollow ravine,
and their roar is heard far off in the mountains by the shepherd:
so from the men thus churned, a rising roar and struggle.

Iliad 4.452–456

Here and at 4.277 (cf. 8.557–559) the shepherd is "far away" (τηλόσε, 455): far away from the scene *of the vehicle*. In 4.455 he could actually be witnessing the noise of the battle—from the tenor (the action of the narrative)—rather than a river, as if he is just a little bit too far away from the *actual* noise of the battle, and mistakes it for something else. The shepherd's ambiguous nearness to the action gives him a very odd relation to that action, and to the performer.[88]

This oddness manifests itself clearly when these similes (and in particular the one quoted) are embodied rather than read. The performer does not *become* the shepherd in the strict sense that the shepherd does not speak. But the shepherd as a distant observer already potentially overlaps with the performer's position *qua* narrator. The herdsman is, as Redfield writes, the observer within the *agrou ep' eschatiēn*, the marginal land "beyond the limits of agriculture."[89] This marginal land dominates the world of the similes, a world that perhaps expresses "a substratum of the poet's mind" or the "poetic tradition in which he is at home," because it is itself "an image of the battlefield." If

---

[88] Taplin (1992:111–112) points out that scholars have felt the need to explain the glad shepherd at 8.559, who inhabits the simile of the stars, to which the Trojan campfires are compared. Adam Parry, for example, thought it inappropriate, given that the Trojan fires represent imminent disaster to the Achaeans, while Michael Reeve simply explains that "Homer elaborates his similes without regard to the narrative." Taplin continues: "What neither even considers is that the shepherd is glad because the Trojans are glad, contributing to the simile-picture the same feeling as the watch-fires give the Trojans … The previous seventy lines have been from the Trojan point of view, yet Parry and Reeve both speak as though this never happened, as though the audience is invariably Achaian-minded." I agree with Taplin that the audience is not invariably Achaean-minded. But Taplin's remark brings out the fact that any shepherd on the scene at Troy would, of course, be a Trojan one, and that the shepherd slides seamlessly from the vehicle of the simile into the story-world. It is dark; there are fires, but they look like stars—to poet and to someone on a nearby mountain. The audience may well experience the *gladness* as strange, if not sinister, even though the previous seventy lines have been from the Trojan point of view. Ethics and kinesthetics are related.

[89] Redfield 1994:187–190.

the performer enacts the shepherd, say by looking into the distance, the sense this lends the audience of sudden proximity to the battlefield, or even of an uncertainty as to their proximity, could be quite intense ("What am I hearing?"). The particulars of the gesture are not important; what we need is a person standing before us, with a body that includes ears, onto whom we can project the shepherd.

The shepherd, the "you" when the audience is addressed, and various anonymous viewers of battlefield action[90] are variations on 'witnessing presences' that cannot be subsumed under the category of stand-ins for the audience or bard. In terms of the imaginative space they inhabit, they are as complex as the wide variety of choruses in tragedy. They are a crucial part of the repertoire of the bard, personae whose perspectives on the unfolding action range from the cruelly omniscient to the stunned to the dimly aware, even the nobly unimpressed.[91] These personae are part of the performer's "in-betweenness"—his half-acting; the spine-tingling epic *atopon* that Aristotle tells us arises from "not seeing the actor." The mediation by the performer "between" the Muse (and the poet?) on the one hand and the audience on the other, captured by Plato in the image of the magnet and rings, is not accomplished through a single, stable position "between," like a single ring on the chain (so in that sense Plato's image does a disservice). There are positions that do not range themselves neatly along a single, vertical line between Muse and audience. There are lookouts off to the side horizontally *within* the visualized, reenacted world, such as that of the shepherd, and there are personae whose position in this schema is harder to pinpoint.

Noemon, Son of Phronios, and the Plotting of the Poem

Another, more oblique vantage point on the action of the poem is bodied forth in the person of Noemon in *Odyssey* Book 4 (lines 630–658). Idomeneus and Meriones' comic dialogue about performance brings about a space that is a rehearsal for action, a space that is in that sense the *source* of action. Insofar as it substitutes for a full-fledged arming scene and contemplates that act, the space is a source for presence. Noemon's appearance creates a similar space, this time

---

[90] For example, the unwounded man that Athena leads by the hand (*Iliad* 4.539–542).

[91] With this repertoire in view, one can appreciate more sophisticated scenarios, such as the awkward jostling of personae in Eumaeus' hut at the beginning of *Odyssey* 16 where Odysseus himself occupies the "witnessing" seat. The bard projects onto the reunion of Telemachus and Eumaeus a simile of the reunion of father and son. This projection occupies a precarious relation to (the stunned, disguised) Odysseus' viewpoint, as though he sees he has been replaced. Temporarily the tip of his unconscious iceberg (and disguised physicality) comes into presence in the body of the bard through the simile. As the hero's pangs of regret burst their bounds to power the poetry, so does the disguised Odysseus threaten to burst through the skin of the bard. See below, "The Bard as Trojan Horse."

with regard to the bard's plotting function. In this way he is similar to Athena, whose casual orchestration of the plot, especially in *Odyssey* 1, 5, and 13, works comically to stress the fact that in *this* poem no one of importance is in any real danger—that, in fact, *nothing is happening here* that is not subject to her will. But Noemon is Athena's agent; it is Noemon from whom Athena (2.386), disguised as Telemachus, begs a ship.

The ostensible plot function of Noemon is to get Telemachus off Ithaka to begin his adventure in Book 2, and to provide the suitors with the knowledge that he is gone in Book 4 so that they set their fruitless ambush for him, creating a (however flimsy) sense of danger that Telemachus can then escape. The first thing to note is that this is the entire content of Noemon's character. His very existence and his actions highlight the arbitrariness of his plot function.[92]

The poet has created an Ithaka that is Hades-like in its lack of action and its isolation from the rest of the world. This is in part due to the exigencies of the plot. The poet needs for Telemachus to be stuck on Ithaka until the poem's opening. He needs for the suitors to be courting Penelope without success or failure. Ithaka needs to be kept in a cryogenic state until the arrival of plot-mistress Athena upon the scene. Penelope needs to continually weave and unweave the shroud, and only recently be caught.

Likewise, Odysseus is kept in suspended animation on Ogygia. His return is contingent upon the gods' "remembering" him, but it also has something to do with his own mind. Whereas, for example, the companions "forget" their homecoming among the Lotus-Eaters and otherwise mindlessly lose their day of return, Odysseus does not. His homecoming is also contingent upon his journey to the underworld and his conversation with Teiresias, who alone among the dead has retained his *phrenes* and gives Odysseus instructions about his return.[93]

Noemon son of Phronios is like a comic Teiresias among the mindless denizens of Ithaka stuck in a loop, or a repetition compulsion. And this is crudely, comically embodied in his name and patronymic.[94] The ship that finally, arbitrarily, gets Telemachus off the island, is provided by Mindful, son of Understanding. In his "mindfulness" and his provision of a ship-escort to and

---

[92] Cf. de Jong (2001:114): "The Homeric 'continuity of time' principle ordains that the time which has passed for Telemachus on his trip (four days) has passed for the Suitors, too. The narrator therefore has to motivate why they find out about Telemachus' departure (i) now and (ii) not sooner. For (i) he brings on stage Noemon ... and makes him disclose casually—and innocently—Telemachus' departure. The triviality of Noemon's case ... contrasts with the shattering effect his words have on the Suitors."

[93] Odysseus does not need these instructions; they are superfluous. That renders the underworld scene even more a "mental" event. See Peradotto 1990:60–62.

[94] Compare the comico-pathetic outburst of Odysseus before Laertes: "I am from Wanderville, son of Unsparing Miseryson. And my name is Strife" (*Odyssey* 24.304–305).

from "Pylos," he embodies the poem's continual connection between mind and homecoming, but in a comic fashion. His innocent character is in stark contrast to that other walk-on, Theoclymenos, and does not quite live up to his name. To put it paradoxically, Noemon is a blunt embodiment of the connections between *noos* and *nostos*.[95]

The scene between Noemon and the dumbfounded suitors is saturated with mentality. It is a faceoff between "Mind" (Noemon) and "Antimind" (Antinoos); but the mental imagery goes beyond names. Noemon stumbles upon the suitors entertaining themselves as usual and asks innocently whether "we" know when Telemachus is returning, because he needs to use his ship to fetch a mule; he has twelve mares nursing mules over in Elis. (The fact that Noemon has these horses comically emphasizes his businesslike puncturing of the torpor on Ithaka.)[96]

> Ἀντίνοος δὲ καθῆστο καὶ Εὐρύμαχος θεοειδής,
> ἀρχοὶ μνηστήρων, ἀρετῇ δ' ἔσαν ἔξοχ' ἄριστοι.
> 630 τοῖς δ' υἱὸς Φρονίοιο <u>Νοήμων</u> ἐγγύθεν ἐλθὼν
> Ἀντίνοον μύθοισιν ἀνειρόμενος προσέειπεν·
> Ἀντίνο', ἦ ῥά τι <u>ἴδμεν ἐνὶ φρεσίν</u>, ἦε καὶ οὐκί,
> ὁππότε Τηλέμαχος <u>νεῖτ' ἐκ Πύλου</u> ἠμαθόεντος;
> νῆά μοι οἴχετ' ἄγων· ἐμὲ δὲ χρεὼ γίνεται αὐτῆς
> 635 Ἤλιδ' ἐς εὐρύχορον διαβήμεναι, ἔνθα μοι ἵπποι
> δώδεκα θήλειαι, ὑπὸ δ' ἡμίονοι ταλαεργοὶ
> ἀδμῆτες· τῶν κέν τιν' ἐλασσάμενος δαμασαίμην.

> <u>Antimind</u> was seated there, and godlike Eurymachos,
> leaders of the suitors, and far the best in virtue.
> And to them <u>Mindful</u>, the son of <u>Understanding</u> coming near
> addressed <u>Antimind</u> with words, questioning him:
> "<u>Antimind</u>, <u>do we know</u> at all <u>in our thoughts</u>, or on the other hand,
> not,
> when Telemachus <u>will return from</u> sandy <u>Pylos</u>?
> He went off with my ship. And a need for it has arisen for me
> to cross over to Elis with the wide dancing-floor, where I have horses,
> twelve females, and under them work-sturdy half-asses,
> unbroken: driving out one of these I'd tame it."
>
> *Odyssey* 4.628–637

---

[95] On which connections see Frame 1978 and Frame 2009. On the underworld connotations of Pylos ("Gate"), see Frame 1978:92–93.

[96] This irony here is prepared for in the immediately preceding scene, where Telemachus professes at length to Menelaos that he cannot accept his gift of horses, because of the (heroic?) ruggedness of Ithakan terrain. Rocks be damned, you can always offshore the horse trade.

"Antimind, do we know at all in our *phrenes*, or on the other hand, not, when Telemachus will return from sandy Pylos?" (632–633). The suitors are dumbfounded (οἱ δ' ἀνὰ θυμὸν ἐθάμβεον, 638), reinforcing their status as *phrenes*-less denizens of Hades. Antinoos askes Noemon a series of questions, which eventually focus upon Noemon's will:

645   καί μοι τοῦτ' ἀγόρευσον ἐτήτυμον, <u>ὄφρ' ἐὺ εἰδῶ</u>,
       ἤ σε <u>βίῃ ἀέκοντος</u> ἀπηύρα νῆα μέλαιναν,
       ἦε <u>ἑκών</u> οἱ δῶκας, ἐπεὶ προσπτύξατο μύθῳ.

    And tell me this straight, <u>so that I know it well</u>,
    whether he robbed you of the black ship <u>by force</u>, with you
           <u>unwilling</u>,
    or did you give it to him <u>willingly</u>, when he plied you with a speech?
                             Odyssey 4.645–647

As Adkins notes,[97] although Antinoos may seem to be threatening Noemon here, there are no reprisals taken when Noemon responds that, in fact, he did give the ship to Telemachus ἑκών.

       τὸν δ' υἱὸς <u>Φρονίοιο Νοήμων</u> ἀντίον ηὔδα·
       αὐτὸς <u>ἑκών</u> οἱ δῶκα· τί κεν ῥέξειε καὶ ἄλλος,
650   ὁππότ' ἀνὴρ τοιοῦτος ἔχων μελεδήματα θυμῷ
       αἰτίζῃ; χαλεπόν κεν ἀνήνασθαι δόσιν εἴη.

    And the son of <u>Phronios, Noemon</u>, answered him face to face:
    "I myself gave to him <u>willingly</u>! What would someone else do,
    when such a man with worries in his heart
    is asking? It would be harsh to refuse the gift."
                             Odyssey 4.648–651

All of this flaunts the episode's "mentality" to the point of provoking puzzlement.

But the bard, performing Noemon, takes this flaunting even further. Noemon first answers Antinoos' odd question about whether Telemachus was accompanied by the "choice young men" of Ithaka (isn't that the suitors themselves?) or his own slaves. He then expresses mild puzzlement as to the fact that Mentor ("Intendor") seems to be in two places at once before striding off to his father's house and out of the poem altogether, leaving the suitors aghast:

       κοῦροι δ', οἳ κατὰ δῆμον ἀριστεύουσι μεθ' ἡμέας,
       οἵ οἱ ἕποντ'· ἐν δ' ἀρχὸν ἐγὼ βαίνοντ' <u>ἐνόησα</u>

---

[97] Adkins 1960:25n1.

Μέντορα, ἠὲ θεόν, τῷ δ' αὐτῷ πάντα ἐῴκει.
655 ἀλλὰ τὸ θαυμάζω· ἴδον ἐνθάδε Μέντορα δῖον
χθιζὸν ὑπηοῖον, τότε δ' ἔμβη νηὶ Πύλονδε.
ὣς ἄρα φωνήσας ἀπέβη πρὸς δώματα πατρός,
τοῖσιν δ' ἀμφοτέροισιν ἀγάσσατο θυμὸς ἀγήνωρ.

"Yes, the youth who are the best in town, after us,
that's who went with him: and in the lead I noticed (ἐνόησα)
Mentor boarding—or a god, but he looked in all ways like that very
man.
Well, I wonder about that! I saw right here Mentor divine [δῖον]
yesterday at dawn, and at *that* time he got on a ship for Pylos."
So he spoke, and off he went toward the house of his father,
and the manly heart in the two of them was aghast.

Odyssey 4.652–658

The bilocation of Mentor is never brought up again, and serves the sole purpose of comedy. Not only does the bard post for inspection the divine machinery of the plot, but in particular he highlights the disguise of Athena and her behind-the-scenes machinations. Beyond that, however, is Noemon's offhand curiosity about all of this ("or a god ..."), the way it is tacked on to the end of his speech before he heads for home, and the fact that he himself is but a cog in Athena's—the bard's—wheel, currently being exposed.

There is another curious feature of this passage: the suddenness of the scene change from Sparta to Ithaka at 4.625.[98] This is made all the more strange by the fact that here in Book 4, Menelaos is sending Telemachus off with a mixing bowl, but when we return to Sparta in Book 15, a month has passed and Telemachus still has not departed. Menelaos delivers the same exact speech to him again[99] and once again bestows the same mixing bowl (4.613–619=15.113–119). Here is the scene change:

... πόρεν δέ ἑ Φαίδιμος ἥρως,
Σιδονίων βασιλεύς, ὅθ' ἑὸς δόμος ἀμφεκάλυψε
κεῖσέ με νοστήσαντα· τεῖν δ' ἐθέλω τόδ' ὀπάσσαι.
620 ὣς οἱ μὲν τοιαῦτα πρὸς ἀλλήλους ἀγόρευον,
δαιτυμόνες δ' ἐς δώματ' ἴσαν θείου βασιλῆος.
οἱ δ' ἦγον μὲν μῆλα, φέρον δ' εὐήνορα οἶνον·
σῖτον δέ σφ' ἄλοχοι καλλικρήδεμνοι ἔπεμπον.
ὣς οἱ μὲν περὶ δεῖπνον ἐνὶ μεγάροισι πένοντο.

---

98 See Richardson 1990:117–118; de Jong 2001:113.
99 This is, of course, due to the "continuity of time principle." For discussion, see de Jong 2001:114.

625 <u>μνηστῆρες δὲ πάροιθεν</u> Ὀδυσσῆος μεγάροιο
 δίσκοισιν τέρποντο καὶ αἰγανέῃσιν ἱέντες
 ἐν τυκτῷ δαπέδῳ, ὅθι περ πάρος, ὕβριν ἔχεσκον.
 Ἀντίνοος δὲ καθῆστο καὶ Εὐρύμαχος θεοειδής,
 ἀρχοὶ μνηστήρων, ἀρετῇ δ' ἔσαν ἔξοχ' ἄριστοι.
630 τοῖς δ' υἱὸς Φρονίοιο Νοήμων ἐγγύθεν ἐλθὼν

"... Phaidimos, hero, bestowed it,

King of the Sidonians, when his house covered
me there as I was returning: and I wish to give this to you."
Thus <u>these</u> were addressing such words to one another,
<u>And diners were going into the house</u> of the divine king.
And they were driving <u>flocks</u>, and were bringing wine, good for man:
And their wives with beautiful headdresses were sending bread.
So <u>these</u> were working on the feast <u>in the halls</u>.
And the <u>suitors, in front of</u> the hall of Odysseus
Were having fun throwing their discuses and javelins
On a wrought surface, right where they were before, hybris and all.[100]
But Antinoos was seated along with Eurymachus, godlike,
Leaders of the suitors, and by far the best in virtue.
To them the son of Phronios, Noemon, came near ...

Odyssey 4.617–630

The change of scene is effected as though a camera follows the people inside to the wedding feast chez Menelaos and back out again:[101] only now we are on Ithaka, which it takes us a few moments to realize.[102]

But to use cinematic terms is to assume an audience who, as a reader would, is visualizing the scene completely divorced from the physical presence of the

---

[100] The tacked-on ὕβριν ἔχεσκον has the air of an aside: they were there right where we left them, and, as usual, doing the hybris thing. The fact that they are merely playing heightens the knowing humor. The stupidity and evil of the suitors are, I am here venturing, temporarily seen as part of the arbitrary constraints of the plot. *Pace* de Jong (2001:114), it is far from a simple expression of disapproval. One may also appreciate the spectacle of suitors stacking up outside the door of ... ah, not Menelaos after all.

[101] Cf. de Jong 2001:113. The play on "inside" and "outside" develops soon afterward at 4.677–678, where Medon is able to report the suitors' schemes to Penelope because he "heard their plans, being outside the courtyard: but they, inside, were weaving the plot." This is given body by Penelope, who forestalls Medon's report, at first by addressing him with her complaints, and then suddenly apostrophizing the suitors (686), who have in fact just come into the house (674). This illustrates once more the virtues of "not seeing the actor/the one-doing."

[102] The similar metrical shape of 621 and 625 facilitates the jarring scene shift between Sparta and Ithaka. Notice the other correspondences: the diners are driving livestock into the house, while Noemon wants to go get a mule. The suitors thought Telemachus was among the flocks (μῆλα 622, μήλοισι 640).

bard. With the bard present, what seems to happen is that the space of performance itself is mysteriously transformed. There is a peculiar correlation between the sudden transition from Sparta to Ithaka and the allegedly astonishing transport of Telemachus off Ithaka that forms the subject of discussion on Ithaka. Both involve Noemon son of Phronios: he provides a ship to get Telemachus off Ithaka, and he appears as a strange presence just after the bard has instantly "escorted" the audience back to Ithaka. (The theme of escort is already brought to the fore when Menelaos, about to send Telemachus off, gives him a gift from a previous escort. The shift to Ithaka *takes the place of that sendoff,*[103] which is postponed to Book 15.) The link between mentality and escort, *noos* and *nostos,* is embodied in Noemon, but is instantiated on a higher level. As the bard sweeps the audience back to Ithaka, leaving Telemachus frozen in time for a month at Sparta staring at a mixing bowl, he bodies forth his own plotting mechanism in the weird presence of Noemon.

Now, is this not purely a textual, even literary phenomenon? What does Noemon have to do with performance or presence?

We said above that Idomeneus and Meriones' conversation framed the performance space as a backstage, a zone where "we aren't supposed to be." The shepherd inhabited a space so far inside the world of the poem that he mistakes its action for something else. In Noemon, and in *the atopic transition* between Sparta and Ithaka, the bard has not so much created a space as a perspective. The bard is exposing his plotting function and the arbitrariness, even ridiculousness, of his plot and its constraints. (This would hold, obviously, for a performer who crafted this scene, or any of its details; it would also hold for a purely uncreative performer who nevertheless has the plot in his head and unfolds it before us. This is why it is important for us even today to memorize, rather than recite off the page, to get the effect.) He highlights his ability to transform one space into another before our eyes. He does so "in" a figure whose profession requires him to puncture the isolated torpor of Ithaka on a regular basis, who recognizes the capacity of gods to become human and brushes off the phenomenon of bilocation. The bard enacting him both exposes the operations of the plot and works through them, as though exposing the workings of his mind.

Bodying all of this forth into a character with a comic speech enables the bard to bring it forward *into the space of performance.* It flaunts the fact that there is a single person behind this show, who can after all step forward and speak to us at any time, but who continues to hide himself, however flimsily. As Noemon provides an awkward portal in otherwise-isolated Ithaka, so too does the bard display the porousness, the fabrication, of the world he is creating.

---

[103] Cf. the Idomeneus/Meriones scene taking the place of an arming scene.

This is a performance moment, again, not in the sense that it calls for a particular gesture or manipulates the performance space, but in the sense that it ponders presence or *genesis*, as well as composition or *poiēsis*, during a live performance. It is effective just as it is in Aristophanes and in modern standup comedy. It turns inside out the workings of composition and performance in a way that dovetails with the action of the poem: the bard's escort of his audience is aired out just as the escort to and from Ithaka is demystified and given the name "Thought."

Perhaps there is one more level to this masquerade. According to Proclus' summary of the *Telegony*, after the suitors are buried, Odysseus sacrifices to the Nymphs and "*sails to Elis to inspect his herds*. He is entertained by Polyxenos and receives as a gift a *mixing bowl*, on which are the events surrounding Trophonios and Agamedes and Augeas. Next he sails back to Ithaka and performs the sacrifices mentioned by Teiresias." Meanwhile in *Odyssey* 4, Noemon wants to go to his horses on Elis while Telemachus, departing for Ithaka, is currently receiving a mixing bowl from Menelaos, a mixing bowl he receives once again in Book 15 along with the same description. We would obviously need more of the *Telegony* to use this information, but it would be tempting to see Noemon as effectively a double of Odysseus,[104] showing up in disguise before we first see him on Ogygia. To spectators who catch the reference, the bard gives a glimpse of the bard-like hero Odysseus beginning to peek out of his own body, before he takes it over completely for Books 9–12.

The Bard as Trojan Horse: *Odyssey* 8

Our final brief example, the third song of Demodokos and its aftermath (*Odyssey* 8.499–531)[105] is perhaps the most highly wrought performance moment in all of Homer. Nagy has discussed this moment extensively with respect to its use of "Cyclic" material; it illustrates the various layers in the Homeric tradition, both in its content and its modality (how it continues, but skips ahead from, the first song of Demodokos). In this section, I too am concerned with how the *Odyssey* makes use of Sack of Troy traditions. But I am interested not just in the layers of, or the evolution of, tradition per se, but in the layers of presence within the performer and his immediate environment, and in how these layers of story and presence interact in real time. In addition to illustrating many features of presence (layering; trauma; eruption; female taking over male; ethical realization),

---

[104] As some would make Theoclymenos (see n119 in Introduction above) or Thoas (see page 292 below).

[105] On this passage see Nagy 1979:101; Pucci 1995:221–225; Goldhill 1991:51–54; Segal 1994:119–123; Bakker 1999:13; Nagy 2009:2§302–350; Nagy 2010: Ch. 4.

my treatment of this last example also forms a roadmap to the material in the next chapter.

Comfortably ensconced at the feast with the Phaeacians, but still concealing his identity, Odysseus requests that the bard Demodokos "skip ahead" and sing the *kosmos* of the wooden horse, which Epeios made with Athena, and which "brilliant Odysseus" brought as a trick to the akropolis, filling it with men who sacked Ilion. This sets up an expectation, in an audience that recalls the Cyclops story, that Odysseus will trick the Phaeacians into glorifying him just as he tricked the Cyclops hidden under the ram and just as he tricked the Trojans hidden in the horse. The fact that he is incognito doubles his hiding in the horse within the story, and his anonymous presence among the Phaeacians can be attributed to Odysseus' polytropic cleverness, just like the horse. The masquerade maps onto the bard-as-Odysseus' body, through which he peeks out at us and the Phaeacians, one a knowing and the other an unknowing audience, and this enables the later mapping of the Trojan Horse onto that same body, enclosing it and hiding it. He asks for the *kosmos* (the arrangement? the decoration?) of the horse. In addition to recalling Odysseus' praise of Demodokos for singing the fate of the Achaeans κατὰ κόσμον (8.489), and perhaps linking Demodokos' earlier story with the very artistry of "Epeios" who built the horse,[106] this word *kosmos* perhaps looks forward to the tripartite view the Trojans take of the horse in the story. The Trojans misguidedly decide to leave the horse as a θεῶν θελκτήριον, a "charm for the gods," because they have been consigned to destruction (8.509–511). Odysseus likewise makes a mistake about the horse, and the *thelxis* of the story about it, and is corrected.

Demodokos obliges the hero. The story is related *to us* (the external audience) not in direct discourse, but in an indirect discourse (ἔνθεν ἑλὼν ὡς, 500) that "verges into a discourse mode that seems at first sight to be direct speech, with Demodokos as speaker."[107] Most unusually, it is punctuated more and more with the verb "he sang" as the story continues.

> ὣς φάθ᾽, ὁ δ᾽ ὁρμηθεὶς θεοῦ ἤρχετο, φαῖνε δ᾽ ἀοιδήν,
> 500   ἔνθεν ἑλὼν ὡς οἱ μὲν ἐϋσσέλμων[108] ἐπὶ νηῶν

---

[106] Nagy 2009:2§282.

[107] Bakker 1999:13. Bakker remarks that this, combined with the "immediate deixis of ταῦτα" (521), results in "a curious blend of Demodokos … and Homer. The voice of Demodokos is allowed to intrude into the discourse of the present." That is so, but this effect is then overshadowed by the role of the hero.

[108] Notice how *both* groups of Achaeans are seated in vessels, frozen: we see the first group, allegedly setting sail, at the oars and leave them frozen there—and they aren't going anywhere anyway. Thus are the two groups mapped onto one another. One must not limit the effects of this subtle detail, but it adds to the effect that a third, actually present, group, *the bard and all of us around him*, are seated frozen in place, concealed from outsiders, *waiting for something to emerge*.

βάντες ἀπέπλειον, πῦρ ἐν κλισίῃσι βαλόντες,
Ἀργεῖοι, τοὶ δ' ἤδη ἀγακλυτὸν ἀμφ' Ὀδυσῆα   [cf. 521]
εἴατ' ἐνὶ Τρώων ἀγορῇ κεκαλυμμένοι ἵππῳ·
αὐτοὶ γάρ μιν Τρῶες ἐς ἀκρόπολιν ἐρύσαντο.
505 ὣς ὁ μὲν εἱστήκει, τοὶ δ' ἄκριτα πόλλ' ἀγόρευον
ἥμενοι ἀμφ' αὐτόν· τρίχα δέ σφισιν ἥνδανε βουλή,
ἠὲ διατμῆξαι κοῖλον δόρυ νηλέϊ χαλκῷ,
ἢ κατὰ πετράων βαλέειν ἐρύσαντας ἐπ' ἄκρης,[109]
ἠὲ ἐᾶν μέγ' ἄγαλμα θεῶν θελκτήριον εἶναι,
510 τῇ περ δὴ καὶ ἔπειτα τελευτήσεσθαι ἔμελλεν·
αἶσα γὰρ ἦν ἀπολέσθαι, ἐπὴν πόλις ἀμφικαλύψῃ
δουράτεον μέγαν ἵππον, ὅθ' εἴατο πάντες ἄριστοι
Ἀργεῖοι Τρώεσσι φόνον καὶ κῆρα φέροντες.
ἤειδεν δ' ὡς ἄστυ διέπραθον υἷες Ἀχαιῶν   [and he sang + ὡς]
515 ἱππόθεν ἐκχύμενοι, κοῖλον λόχον ἐκπρολιπόντες.
ἄλλον δ' ἄλλῃ ἄειδε πόλιν κεραϊζέμεν αἰπήν,
              [parenthetical 'he sang' + acc. + inf.]
αὐτὰρ Ὀδυσσῆα προτὶ δώματα Δηϊφόβοιο
βήμεναι, ἠΰτ' Ἄρηα σὺν ἀντιθέῳ Μενελάῳ.
κεῖθι δὴ αἰνότατον πόλεμον φάτο τολμήσαντα
              [ambiguous return to finite verb]
520 νικῆσαι καὶ ἔπειτα διὰ μεγάθυμον Ἀθήνην.
ταῦτ' ἄρ' ἀοιδὸς ἄειδε περικλυτός· αὐτὰρ Ὀδυσσεὺς   [cf. 517]
τήκετο, δάκρυ δ' ἔδευεν ὑπὸ βλεφάροισι παρειάς.
ὡς δὲ γυνὴ κλαίῃσι φίλον πόσιν ἀμφιπεσοῦσα,   [cf. 511]
ὅς τε ἑῆς πρόσθεν πόλιος λαῶν τε πέσῃσιν,
525 ἄστεϊ καὶ τεκέεσσιν ἀμύνων νηλεὲς ἦμαρ·   [cf. 530, 531]
ἡ μὲν τὸν θνήσκοντα καὶ ἀσπαίροντ' ἐσιδοῦσα
ἀμφ' αὐτῷ χυμένη λίγα κωκύει· οἱ δέ τ' ὄπισθε
κόπτοντες δούρεσσι μετάφρενον ἠδὲ καὶ ὤμους
εἴρερον εἰσανάγουσι, πόνον τ' ἐχέμεν καὶ ὀϊζύν·   [present tense]
530 τῆς δ' ἐλεεινοτάτῳ ἄχεϊ φθινύθουσι παρειαί·
ὡς Ὀδυσεὺς ἐλεεινὸν ὑπ' ὀφρύσι δάκρυον εἶβεν.

So he spoke, and he, moved by the god, began, and made the song
      shine forth,
taking it up from when they, on the well-benched ships

---

[109] Compare the similar manner of killing Astyanax. In the *Iliou persis*, it is Odysseus who kills Astyanax. In the *Little Iliad*, it is Neoptolemos. On this song of Demodokos and Cyclic epic, see Nagy 1979:101; Nagy 2010: Ch. 2 passim, esp. 2§328–350.

boarded, were sailing away, casting fire on the huts—
the Argives; but they, round very famous Odysseus
were seated even now in the agora of the Trojans, hidden in the
    horse:
for they themselves, the Trojans, dragged it onto the acropolis.
So it was standing, and they discussed it confusedly
sitting round it. Three ways the plan was pleasing them,
either to slash the hollow wood with pitiless bronze,
or to cast it down the rocks from the height,
or to leave it be, a great icon to charm the gods,
—in this very way it was even then to come out in the end:
for it was their fate to die, when the city covered round
the great wooden horse, when all the best were seated,
the Argives, bearing murder and death to the Trojans.
And he sang how the sons of Achaeans were sacking the town
pouring out from the horse, leaving behind their hollow ambush.
One this way, one that, he sang, was razing the steep city,
but Odysseus toward the halls of Deiphobos
strode, like Ares, with godlike Menelaos.
Just there, at last, he said that, having endured a most terrible war,
he won, then, because of great-hearted Athena.
That, you see, is what the famed singer sang. But Odysseus
melted, and a tear under his eyelids began to wet his cheeks.
As a woman weeps, falling around her dear husband,
who falls before his city and his people,
trying to ward off the pitiless day for town and children:
she, seeing him dying, and gasping,
pouring herself over him shrieks a piercing scream: and they, behind
beating with spears her back and shoulders
lead her into bondage, to have toil and misery:
and her cheeks are melting with most pitiful grief:
so Odysseus shed a piteous tear under his brows.

Odyssey 8.499–531

    In the song, at the point where Odysseus and Menelaos reach the house of Deiphobos and begin their grim mutilations and flinging of infants from towers (pre-echoed by the rejected Trojan plan, 508), Demodokos abruptly ends the song with "just there he [Odysseus?] said that he had won, having endured a most terrible war": the single most lacerating line in the poem, devastating by what it barely papers over. But Odysseus weeps, and the simile comparing him to a woman crying, pouring herself over her Hektor-like husband, and shrieking, shatters through this triumphalism. The simile, in the narrator's voice, continues the story where it left off, as Nagy[110] points out, and we see a woman "casting herself over" (523, πόσιν ἀμφιπεσοῦσα) her expiring husband, in a phrase sonically echoing the city "covering over" the horse (511, πόλις ἀμφικαλύψῃ). The simile then expands to follow the people striking her back and shoulders with spears. It is her "back and shoulders" because this is the perspective of the one at the other end of the spear, driving her into slavery—namely, Odysseus. Yes, Odysseus is being identified with his helpless victim.[111] But this way of putting it flattens the script somewhat. The voice of the performer/narrator standing before us, delivering the simile, is invaded by the memory of Odysseus, his vivid memory of her back and shoulders, and his ongoing performance is shattered by it.

This is perhaps the most confounding of the mergers of the bard and the hero in the *Odyssey*. Odysseus becomes the woman, and this induces a chain reaction: Odysseus erupts out into the speech of the bard as narrator, disrupting the narrative process—that is, the performance itself.

Story and reaction are taking place in an underground fashion. Notice the layering: first[112] Odysseus hidden in the horse, the horse "hidden" in the city; then the dying husband falling (πέσῃσιν), covered by the woman falling over him (ἀμφιπεσοῦσα),[113] covered by—Odysseus. The bard stands over them all and is pierced through by all.

Let us return to Demodokos' song itself as a performance. The part of the story centered on the horse is in a single arc of discourse introduced by ὡς,

---

[110] Nagy 1979:101; Nagy 2009:2§335; cf. Goldhill 1991:53–54. Dué (2002:7) links this passage with Briseis' lament for Patroklos in *Iliad* 19 and comments that Briseis and Odysseus each "become Andromache."

[111] Foley 1978:7, 20. There have been dogged attempts to tame the simile; cf. Hainsworth in Heubeck, West, and Hainsworth 1988:381 *ad Odyssey* 8.523–530. Segal (1994:121) uncharacteristically tries to muffle the effect: "The comparison ... suggests the possibility that this identification with the subject matter of song applies not just to the memory of an actual participant but also to vicarious, imaginary participation. The Odysseus of the *Iliad* never so identifies with the victims on the Trojan side; and, with the exception of the extraordinary scene between Priam and Achilles in *Iliad* 24, there is little in the heroic code that would encourage him to identify with his conquered enemy, especially one of the opposite sex." But Segal has just quoted Briseis' lament for Patroklos, when the other slave women bewail their own circumstances, noting how "the poet's remarkable editorial comment" here "underlines the perspective of the helpless captive woman." Some go to greater lengths: "His weeping indicates ... that Odysseus construes what he hears in relation to some present trouble, that his present unquiet condition, more than the topic of the song, determines his response as an audience" (Walsh 1984:17). These slashings-through of perspective are rare, but we should not blunt their effect by assuring ourselves they cannot be happening. Cf. n118 below.

[112] Unless we count the Achaeans in the ships.

[113] Macleod (1982:4): "... a very fine detail: the mourning wife's gesture re-enacts the husband's death ...." Similarly, Andromache reenacts her husband's fall in *Iliad* 22: cf. Purves 2019:41.

line 500. For this part either the audience can see the performer as Demodokos, or they can have before them the scene at Troy, as though Demodokos has disappeared. Demodokos dwells at excruciating length on the threefold will of the Trojans, as though it could somehow be stopped. As the horrible deliberations go on, Odysseus is hidden in the horse. The line about fate (511) may seem to radically alter what Odysseus thought of the scheme, and to form a little lament as the horse enters the city.[114] When the Achaeans start streaming out, the verb "he sang" begins to punctuate, puncture, the performer's account of the song (514, 516, 521). When we hear the verb of singing, we cannot have Demodokos before us.[115] Moreover, as we have said, the story starts and ends in indirect discourse. The man before us cannot be that man Demodokos. It is not Demodokos who dwells on the deliberations, but Odysseus, *both* a) from his unseeing perspective hidden inside the horse, *hearing* the deliberations, and from his rapidly changing perspective hidden among the internal audience, the Phaeacians; *and* b) from his perspective covertly (to the external audience) governing the syntax of the story. It is this rapidly changing perspective that governs the fitful interruptions of the end of the story by "and he sang" and finally culminates in weeping like the widow.

For the first part of the song, the audience constructs an image that contains another image "inside" it: Odysseus hidden in the horse. Outside the song, the disguised Odysseus listens to the song, clamping down on his own emotions, precisely as, we may recall (*Odyssey* 4.287), he had stifled his own emotions and voice in the horse, and clamped his hand around the mouth of one Antiklos; this gives further body to the drawn-out quality of the deliberations—and to our complicit non-intervention, as in the beginning of the *Iliad*. We anticipate his own reaction as we listen. Odysseus' outpouring tears dovetail with the men streaming out to burn the city; the men pour out, the woman pours onto her husband as his breath goes out ($- \cup \cup - \chi\upsilon\mu\epsilon\nu -$, 515/527); tears are flowing, past and present. For the spectator, the image of the men pouring from the horse is layered on top of the tears flowing from the widow and from the disguised Odysseus. The men suppressing their voices and emotions inside the horse are layered atop Odysseus suppressing himself among the Phaeacians, and his tears within his eyes. Again, this is helped by the fact that the disguise is mapped on the performer's body, and the horse is layered on top of that, concealing the same person. He is listening to a song that is recounting an event he experienced

---

[114] "It is unclear whether this comment is to be taken as part of the reported song, a perhaps more vivid representation of the performance of Demodocus, or whether it is a comment like 'he sang', 'he sang', 'he said', which should not be attributed to Demodocus" (Goldhill 1991:53).

[115] That is, strictly speaking, as Demodokos is in the third person; one can imagine variations in performance.

in two ways: one in the dark and unseeing, and another executing it himself. It is made abundantly clear that he did not see any of it until now; it takes putting it into a song to see it at all. That is, the song does not revive an old grief. It is thus misleading to say that Odysseus' grief seems "as fresh and sharp as if he wept for something immediate and real, rather than a song about the past" or that it is a "transformation of experience into art."[116] Rather his grief lifts into awareness an old, dead experience that was never truly experienced in the first place.

When the horse is hidden in the city (511), the singer's singing is disrupted more and more by the verb "he sang"; the performer here has an opportunity to use these verbs as signs of his own inner turmoil (brought on by Odysseus' emotions working their way to the surface of his disguise, among the Phaeacians, and to the surface of the bard, among us) as he works toward the bitter end of the story. Or rather, the audience will take them as such signs, no matter what the performer does. Moreover, while the first instance of "he sang" introduces another ὡς clause (line 514), the next now shifts into the accusative plus infinitive construction, describing Odysseus and Menelaos going to the house of Deiphobos (line 517). As Odysseus is reminded of his own role in the horror, Demodokos, who had never fully "appeared" in direct discourse, fades from view. The final two lines, "And there he said that he had won," are very fine in their suggestion of a merging between hero and bard. The subject "he" in "he said" seems at first to be Odysseus, especially given the κεῖθι, which seems to mark the shift to a direct view of the action being sung about, and the shift from "singing" to "saying." But in the context of the finite verb "and he sang," "he" seems to be the bard, and this is reinforced by the accusative case of τολμήσαντα.

The story by any measure is one of the most shattering moments in Homer. This fact brings up another layer. For if the bard himself is *really* overcome by performing this moment—I submit it is difficult not to be—and if the external listeners are moved and disturbed as we should be, the lines of causation become even more tangled. The actual bard, the bard within the story, the woman in the story invading the mind of the hero in the outer story who invades the mind of the actual bard before us—the source from which the emotional release finds its way out is indeed mysterious, *or made to appear so.*

From an ethical standpoint, this is the only hint so far that Odysseus has recognized himself, on whatever level, as the doer of questionable acts.[117] And this hint affects how the audience (the Phaeacians, but more importantly *we*) registers the hero. Abstractly, this is an issue of genre; but in terms of live performance, the question is, what kind of an experience are we having? Just

---

[116] Walsh 1984:4.
[117] See below, Chapter 4.

as Theoclymenos, channeling the actual bard, condemns the suitors listening to their own bard—and through them, us—so too, once this inner story and its consequences are over, the audience is left to sort out how to integrate this into the unfolding outer story. Odysseus' outburst of tears and his bursting through the body of the bard eventuates in his self-revelation to the Phaeacians and his takeover of the body of the bard for four books of the poem, as he retails his story. And that story does not seem to register much of this newfound perspective at all.[118] And in fact, the simile leaves precisely *Odysseus'* ethical awareness ambiguous: the Odysseus of story morphs into his victim, but although the victim forces Odysseus up into the body of the narrator, it is left ambiguous as to how much Odysseus registers at all, and how much he registers but keeps suppressed. It is not at all clear that he displays "a hero's magnitude of feeling."[119] Some schema of an unconscious is created in this way that is more subtle than the "return of the repressed" at work.[120] So we, the audience, must sit hiding this inner story inside us throughout the largely triumphal story that the bard-as-Odysseus tells in Books 9–12.[121]

Imagining this moment in performance, spelling out its harnessing of poetics/*poiēsis* in service of presence/*genesis*, makes it impossible to ignore. But readers, who largely dismiss this moment once it is over, are free to experience Books 9–12 as a fairy tale, or at least, an ethically rich story told by a hero who has learned from the events it recounts. Once the hero relinquishes his hold on the body of the bard at the end of that four-hour-long story, the audience has a

---

[118] Likewise with his Cretan Tales. Vermeule (1979:112) writes: "The analogy of grief is in the poet's mind, not in the hero's, for Odysseus is a trained hero, accustomed to the disasters of the weak, and even in his lies about raids in Egypt he automatically slips in the accomplisher's phrase, 'I ruined their lovely fields and took away the women and innocent children,' *nēpia tekna*, xiv.264, xvii.432." The fact that we have to be told to separate the poet's mind from the hero's, and at that, on the evidence of the Cretan persona, indicates something is wrong with the reading, not that we are weak moderns. Foley (1978:2) writes that the simile suggests "how close Odysseus has come to the complete loss of normal social and emotional function which is the due of women enslaved in war ... Once conqueror of Troy, Odysseus now understands the position of its victims; and it is as such a victim, aged, a beggar, and no longer a leader of men, that he reenters Ithaca." Chapter 4 below will examine this question of Odysseus' understanding of war's victims on his reentry to Ithaka.

[119] Walsh 1984:4. Yet in the same sentence Walsh remarks, "there is something uncanny about Odysseus' grief, for he weeps like a woman newly widowed and enslaved."

[120] Odysseus, serving as funnel between widow and Demodokos, seems like Aristotle's picture of Homer, serving as the oddly amoral funnel between primitive poetry and drama (see above, p. 6).

[121] Cf. Goldhill 1991:54: the juxtaposition of the simile and the song "poses the question—but makes any certain answer hard to find—why this song should have been requested by Odysseus or why Odysseus' tears should be the means or the prelude of his recognition." The song and the simile are part of "an elaborate preparation for the first-person narrative of Books 9–12."

new impetus to square this story of the widow we are holding inside of us with the amalgamated bardic hero before us.

While this moment in *Odyssey* 8 is the most potent, and intricate, of the passages examined in this chapter, it has many of the same features. Consider the relationship of Odysseus and the widow to Agamemnon and Eris. One might say that "Trojan Horse" makes the body of the bard into a Russian doll containing Odysseus and, within him, the widow. But this is to make the moment into an object. What happens is that Odysseus takes over the narrator, but we do not realize this until the simile of the woman makes everything clear, and it turns out "she was there all the time." In the case of Agamemnon and Eris, we are warned of Eris' presence beforehand, but her approval of the scene afterwards partakes of the same "so *that* is the ghost in this machine" quality (οὗτος ἐκεῖνος, in Aristotle's terms).

In terms of spatial form or kinesthetics, the emergence of men from horse, widow into Odysseus, Odysseus into bard, Odysseus out of disguise, tears out of eyes, and the various layerings recall Diomedes emerging like a wave, the fire emerging from him, etc. But *Odyssey* 8 does not simply multiply the layers of *Iliad* 5 into a more elaborate *objet d'art*. By situating the same character, Odysseus, in three places—disguised among the Phaeacians, hidden in the horse, and (then) behind the widow, and by orchestrating the story, simile, and the indirect discourse, the script *maps on to the body of the bard* all of these emergences more completely than does *Iliad* 5. Not only that, but because of the involuntary nature of the moment, the layers in Odysseus' memory and consciousness, as well as the layers in the bard's own "ethical" awareness, the emergences happen in real time in a way different from *Iliad* 5. *Iliad* 5, one might say, performs live a preconceived emergence; in *Odyssey* 8 the emergence itself *happens* live. Finally, "Trojan Horse" uses the involuntary reliving of trauma as does "Menelaos" in the service of elaborately spatialized histrionics (presence), but the overall effects produced by the two moments could not be more different.

In the next chapter, we examine the speech of Phoenix in *Iliad* 9. A very similar thing happens there to the body and soul of the bard, with similar elements at work: layering of figures, doubling, artful use of direct versus indirect discourse, traumatic repetition, images of bursting out, women on the point of slavery, rape, and/or the burning of their city. "Trojan Horse" made use of a background story that the audience was familiar with from *Odyssey* 4 and other occasions. This prepares us for a more complex (and indeed layered) use of background stories in the service of presence. In both "Trojan Horse" and in Phoenix's speech, someone requests (Odysseus) or tells (Phoenix) a story about a besieged city that he thinks will serve his purposes, but he is dead wrong. Likewise, the spatial forms that help to fuel a takeover of the bard by a character prepare us for the more elaborately structured spatial forms in our next example. This troubling scene from *Odyssey* 8 is, to a certain extent, a microcosm of Phoenix's speech, and so has provided us with a roadmap.

2

Marpessa, Kleopatra, and Phoenix

> Perhaps it means that at the point where we are we have lost all touch
> with the true theater, since we confine it to the domain of what daily
> thought can reach, the familiar or unfamiliar domain of conscious-
> ness;—and if we address ourselves to the unconscious, it is merely to
> take from it what it has been able to collect (or conceal) of accessible
> everyday experience.
>
> Artaud, *The Theater and Its Double*

The speech of Phoenix in the Embassy to Achilles (*Iliad* 9.434–605), in its sheer scope and intriguing triptych structure, is, on the level of poetics or compo-sition, the most elaborate in the poem by far. But this structure, rather than forming a map or a design on a flat surface, like a piece of paper, rather plays out in the performance, forming layers within the space of performance and within the performer himself.

From one perspective, Phoenix's speech is simply a more complex example of "becoming the character" than those examined in the previous chapter. On another level it transcends that kind of enactment by doubling it. While the performer is becoming Phoenix, Phoenix is becoming another character from the deep, "heroic" past: Kleopatra, wife of Meleager. Phoenix being taken over by Kleopatra is a re-staging within the world of the poem of the very process of becoming the character, rendering visible a process going on all the time in Homeric poetry.

Not to say that the speech thereby becomes a *mise en abyme* for the conve-nience of scholars. The possession of Phoenix by Kleopatra provides the audi-ence with a view of the deep past of the world of the *Iliad* instead of one filtered through reporters of that past. To put this in terms of the audience's experience, we gain—suddenly—access to a whole new realm, or rather realms, of the poem. The *paradeigma* of Meleager suddenly opens up and exposes the memory and the perspective of a minor character within it.

The ecplectic power of the speech comes in part from the fact that Kleopatra's perspective does not harmonize with the *paradeigma*'s purpose, exhorting Achilles to stay and fight. Kleopatra expresses the view of a woman in a city under siege, and the climax of Phoenix's speech is Kleopatra's catalogue of the horrors of the sack of a city. It is as though Phoenix tells a story to shore up his exhortation, is sidetracked to another story-world, and encounters there a character who subverts that purpose and speaks through him. This produces *atopia*, not only in the sense of an objective inconsistency between words and intentions,[1] but in a concrete spatial, bodily sense of one person emerging from within another, one story bursting through another, one force disrupting another. Because Phoenix tells his own story of trauma to begin his speech, the audience sees and hears connections between his own past and the story he tells. The speech effects the emergence of a suppressed *truth* about war as well as an uncanny emergence of trauma, a repressed or suppressed event that forms the highly compressed core of the story.

In that the audience witnesses a strange, foreign force taking over Phoenix, not only truths residing in his own memory, but a dead woman with her own fueling traumas—traumas that exert magnetic force upon the speaker himself—there is here something akin to the uncanny in the sense of ghostly possession and involuntary repetition. The speech thus accords in a general way with images of the poet found in Plato (the poet as a dead hero himself, or as a necromancer of heroes). But, examined in detail as a script, this speech turns out to be a particularly virtuosic enactment of possession. Because of the concrete interplay between the inside and outside of various spaces, as well as of the speaker himself, *atopia* and *unheimlich* convey its sense of spatial confusion better than "uncanny."

The *atopia* spills out, moreover, into the border between the inside and the outside of the poem. For as Phoenix is taken over by the past, he uncontrollably causes the future. Phoenix is taken over not only by Kleopatra and her mother Marpessa; in looking at his audience, Achilles and Patroklos, Phoenix lets them too leak into his story, with disastrous effects, as it were, upon the plot of the poem. This fusion of Phoenix as storyteller with the bard as plotter of the poem brings about the audience's sense of the uncanny with respect to the figure in front of them: the bard appears to have lost control, and the plot to have been disrupted *from within*—one more level of the uncanny.

---

[1]   This, again, in a triple sense: Phoenix's words taken over by Kleopatra (being run by Marpessa, who is the one drawing Phoenix toward Kleopatra), and the bard being taken over by Phoenix (plot-derailment). This sense of *atopia* goes back to the sophists and is used by Socrates in the *Gorgias* (cf. Turner 1993).

Phoenix's speech has invited the closest scholarly scrutiny, mainly focused on explicating its ring structure[2] and, especially, the development of the Meleager story, which occupies the third panel of the speech. Despite the focus on ring structure, however, the story told at the very center of this panel, the story of Marpessa, has been neglected. In part as a result of this, other aspects of the speech have been overlooked: its voicing, its power as a performance script, its layered imagery, and the way the various elements of the speech work together in the flow of performance. The speech is a dramatic weave of emergent voices, inter-nesting images, ambiguously pointed gesture, temporal confusion, re-directed sexuality, and re-possessed intentionality. "Dramatic weave" because these dynamics, though some are customarily seen as "literary" and some as "performative," cannot be understood apart from one another and work toward the same end: toward producing the startling effect of the emergence of a person, and a disturbance of the lines of causality in the plotting and performance of the poem.

In the realm of poetics or *poiēsis*, the extensive web of background stories used in this speech requires a full exploration, first simply to lay out what traditions may be alluded to and what themes they have in common. I then show how these stories are bound up with presence and/or performance. I shall expand the traditional focus from the story of Meleager and the boar hunt to that of his wife Kleopatra and to the stories about Marpessa and Alkyone. These stories, brief as they are, are crucial to understand if one wishes to appreciate the dynamics of enactment, even more important than the story of Meleager.

Nevertheless, the Meleager story itself also holds keys not only to the speech's (and the poem's) composition, and its poetics, but also to the drama of the speech, and what it makes present.

Many scholars who have analyzed this story have focused on determining which forms of this story existed in the tradition before it was taken up by the *Iliad*. They are interested in the development of epic,[3] the Homeric poet's use of his or their sources, and the genres that may lie behind the *Iliad*. Recent treatments build upon the work of Kakridis, who incorporates the modern Greek folk tradition.[4]

---

[2] Gaisser 1969; Lohmann 1970:245–265.

[3] On the Meleager story's development see Bremmer 1988 as well as Grossardt's exhaustive study (2001).

[4] Kakridis 1949 was of course not the first to use "folklore" in connection with Meleager: Heubeck 1984 (orig. pub. 1943) looks back on a long tradition of peeling away the layers to uncover the Ur-form of the ("folk") story and to trace the transformation of old mythical material into an "epic atmosphere," an enterprise that he notes often had contradictory results. Heubeck himself still speaks of an Ur-form.

The central question for these scholars involves Meleager's death. In the usual version told throughout antiquity, his death is caused by a magical object. When Meleager is born, his mother overhears the Fates tracing out the story of the baby's life; the last Fate declares that Meleager will die as soon as a piece of wood then burning in the hearth is destroyed. His mother snatches this brand (*dalos*) from the hearth, extinguishes it, and puts it in a chest for safe-keeping. Time passes, and when Meleager is reaching maturity, the events of the Calydonian boar hunt unfold. Meleager's father Oineus neglects Artemis in a sacrifice, and the angry goddess sends a boar to ravage the fields. Meleager gathers the best young men of the region and hunts down the boar. Meleager kills the boar, and he and his maternal uncles dispute over the boar's head and skin. In the usual account, Meleager gives the spoils to fellow-hunter Atalanta as a love-gift, and the uncles object to giving them to a girl. Meleager kills one or more of his uncles. When his mother, Althaia, hears about this, she whips the *dalos* out of the chest and throws it into the fire, at which point Meleager, out in the field, drops dead.

By contrast, in *Iliad* 9 Meleager's mother does not burn a magic firebrand but rather curses her son, summoning forces from the underworld in a dramatic gesture, thrashing the earth. This is the first major peculiarity in the Homeric account. The next is the blossoming of the family dispute over the spoils into a full-scale war. Meleager withdraws from the battlefield (for reasons initially opaque), and a series of supplicants comes to beg him to return to the fight, offering him gifts, paralleling the currently unfolding situation in Achilles' tent. Finally, his wife, Kleo-patra, whose name when reversed becomes Patro-klos,[5] retails for him the horrors of a city being seized, and Meleager is stirred up and returns to the battlefield. His death is not mentioned, but Phoenix remarks that Meleager "did not receive the gifts." This is an oblique way of hinting at Meleager's death, though the obliquity does not lend Phoenix "tact." Rather the line allows the fatal trajectory of the story, which dramatically undermines Phoenix's entire speech, to leak through to its internal audience, Achilles, and to us. This is particularly apt because in some versions of the story Meleager is killed by Apollo, who is involved in both Patroklos' and Achilles' deaths.[6] By leaving out Meleager's death, this death hovers in the air for the audience when the speech ends, for the audience to connect with the next party they "see": Achilles. This is the third example we have seen so far of the speaker leaving

---

[5]   Howald 1924.

[6]   Contra: Oehler's view (1925:14) that Phoenix simply cannot mention the death because "he would have reminded Achilles of his own early death" is followed by many. For Petzold (1976:156 with n37a) Meleager's death is simply not important: the curse is only relevant in instigating the wrath.

off the end of the story, which countervenes the ostensible reason for the story. Recall Plato's use of the opening of the *Iliad*, just before the banning of the priest of Apollo, and the story of the "Trojan Horse," breaking off just before the atrocities in which Odysseus partook.

Most scholars have it that the *Iliad* must replace the brand by the curse in order to produce the parallel between Meleager and Achilles, just as Atalanta is replaced by a wife whose name echoes Patroklos'. Meleager cannot very well withdraw from the battlefield and receive a series of suppliants if he has died instantly due to the magic brand. Having Althaia curse her son allows the necessary time lag during which the supplications can occur. Thus it is generally assumed that whatever source(s) the *Iliad* drew upon contained the motif of the brand, and not the curse and its consequent withdrawal.[7]

Plot necessity aside, some, like Kakridis, have argued that the curse replaces the magic brand because of the "Ionian poet's"[8] dislike for things magical (or "chaotic"). Griffin diagnoses this avoidance of magic as typical of Homeric rationalization, in contrast to the fantastic epic cycle. He condemns the brand-version thus: "That version, too uncanny for Homeric taste, is memorably told in the Fifth Ode of Bacchylides (37–56). Here her curse is clearly a secondary motif, and it has no apparent effect; a fundamental breach of the nature of such a story."[9] The *Iliad* may well be averse to magic. But the magical or the fairy-tale element[10] has not simply been expunged; it has been replaced with the indirectly supernatural: with, *pace* Griffin's use of the term, the uncanny. The *Iliad* has thus made possible another sort of magic: the magic of dramatic enactment. The magic operates not within the world of the poem but through enactment: from poetics to presence; from depicting magic to performing it.

---

[7] There is not universal agreement. Sachs 1933 argued that a previous epic "Meleagris" included both motifs. Kakridis himself, though he thinks the brand version is older, also posited an earlier epic that included both brand and wrath. Likewise Swain (1988:272) takes the fragments from the *Ehoiai* and *Minyad*, where Meleager is killed by Apollo, as evidence that this mode of death was "as old as Homer, if not older." The problem is obviated by allowing more than one version as source material for the *Iliad*. See Burgess 2017.

[8] When scholars refer to the *Iliad* poet as Ionian, they mean to inscribe him in a world of rational (anti-magical, anti-mythical) thought, by evoking the Ionian "pre-Socratics."

[9] Griffin 1995:135. The aesthetics here and in Griffin 1980 are fleshed out in his remark that "Homer also prefers to get rid of so peasant-like a notion as that of Fates who can be eavesdropped on, filling the story as far as possible with chivalrous warrior motivations." It is a commonplace that Homer avoids magic, but Griffin equates magic and uncanniness, where I distinguish them. Griffin disregards the possibility that Meleager's death is meant to hang over the end of the story, only to fall back down into the plot in Achilles' and Patroklos' own deaths orchestrated by Apollo. Cf. Bannert 1981:69n4. Nagy (1990b:72; cf. Nagy 1979:8) attributes the lack of fantastic elements in Homer, as opposed to the Cyclic epics, to the Panhellenic nature of the Homeric poems.

[10] See Carpenter 1946: Ch. 4.

The Phoenix Speech

Irony

As Phoenix tells it, the Meleager story runs counter to his aim[11] of persuading[12] Achilles to return to battle, and even provides, ironically, the model for how he does return,[13] too late, in grief for Patroklos. Cedric Whitman writes:

> Yet it was Phoenix who drew the pattern, and *sketched the role which Achilles adopts* ... It is in answer to [Phoenix's] speech that Achilles draws most explicitly the distinction between the externals of the case and the inner satisfaction he is seeking: '... I do not need / This honor. But I deem I am honored in Zeus' disposal, / And here by the curving ships it will keep me ...' *The pattern of Meleager, from which old Phoenix tried to dissuade him, appeals to Achilles*: to fight only at the last, and without gifts, with honor only from the 'disposal of Zeus.' *Phoenix achieves not what he intends*; ironically he helps Achilles to know his own intention, and by the time Ajax has spoken, Achilles has embraced the example of Meleager, and states his decision.[14] (my emphasis)

Likewise Lowell Edmunds: "Phoenix conveys messages of which he is apparently unaware ... Achilles is far from persuaded to reenter the fighting. The myth is more useful, one could say, to Homer than to Phoenix":[15]

---

[11] Kakridis notes (1949:13) Meleager would not have lived to enjoy the gifts since he had already been cursed, and links this with the fact that the example "which appears exhortative at first, turns out to be dissuasive in the end." Not only is it not dissuasive (from its ostensible recommendations), it provides the model Achilles chooses to follow. For Kakridis Phoenix is fudging it: "What undoubtedly urges Phoenix *to this hardly suitable introduction* is his desire to influence Achilles strongly at the outset, while preparing him to listen to the story of another hero who was persuaded to abandon his wrath" (my emphasis). This is unsatisfactory; we are meant to see the incoherence.

[12] Lowenstam (1993:94) comments that even Phoenix's *autobiography* "counteracts the old man's message, for, in narrating his own story Phoinix shows that he did not follow the very advice he is giving: as a young man he had refused to yield to his relatives, who were begging him to restore harmony in his family. Although Phoinix certainly does not intend to point out this contradiction, his own story indicates that wisdom comes from experience and not instruction." Scodel (1982:133), agreeing with Bassett that the autobiography is "as close to the sordid and ignominious" as epic can permit, says Phoenix deprecates Achilles' departure by self-parody.

[13] Cf. Cavell (2003:187–188) on Hamlet's sense of being improvised and his sense of theater. For Bouvier (2002:353), nothing warrants the claim that the audience would be bothered by the contradictions in Phoenix's story.

[14] Whitman 1958:191. In the present discussion, the focus is not so much on what happens in the mind of Achilles (though this is relevant) as on what happens to the figure of the poet-performer and his implied control of the plot.

[15] Edmunds 1997:426. For Alden (2000:249) the parallels, including the ascending scale of affection, are a "false trail" that mislead the audience's expectations for the plot and heighten "the impact of what happens instead."

> The tragic implications of the parallelism of the names, as well as of the Meleager analogue as a whole, are intended, but they are intended by Homer for his audience, not by Phoenix for his.

This is to keep the two figures, "Homer" and Phoenix, separate.[16] The collapse of rhetorical levels is, however, part of an orchestrated blending together of the persons of Phoenix, his characters, and the performer. The purpose of the fusion is to provide the pleasure of uncertainty as to who at any given time is "running the show"—the performer, his character Phoenix, or Phoenix's characters—and a sense of one being taken over by others. To explain that the tragic implications are intended by Homer rather than Phoenix is to undo the performative work.

Kleopatra's catalogue, standing out as it does from the speech of Phoenix, gives voice to these contradictions. Kleopatra is urging Meleager to defend their city against would-be sackers: sackers like Achilles. Only by a cynical distortion can the Achaean camp be considered a "city under siege" that needs to be "defended" from the Trojans. All this is transparent to Achilles, and to us listeners. But even if one willfully subscribes to the notion of the Achaeans as defenders, a plea to defend a city from its women being raped and its children dragged off can only truly apply to the Trojans. Kleopatra is particularly worried, we shall see, about rape. But it is precisely a stolen woman who has brought the Achaeans to their knees and forced the current mission to Achilles. Achilles has already seen through the problem. To paraphrase him: "Why are we here in the first place? Isn't it for Helen? Oh, so the sons of Atreus are the only ones who love their wives?" (9.337–341). As though it were not already obvious that Agamemnon cannot make Achilles whole by returning Briseis and piling on seven more women, Phoenix's voicing of Kleopatra's impassioned plea demolishes Phoenix's appeal ("take the gifts") from within. Kleopatra's speech is the culmination of the ironies of Phoenix's rhetoric.

But the impact goes beyond irony and a sense of tragedy. What Kleopatra's speech effects dramatically, and what Phoenix's speech effects dramatically, has gone under the radar. That is strange, because its dramatic power comes in large part from the elaborate structure of the speech and its mythical background, the subject of much scholarly discussion. Within that cluster of background story, what has escaped proper attention is the tightly packed seed of story at the very center of the speech—the digression about Marpessa, Kleopatra's mother.

---

[16] Cf. Chapter 1, n118 above, on Vermeule. A variation of this is to make Phoenix stand in for tradition. For Rose (1992:69), the very fact that Phoenix draws a "simpleminded moral" indicates the unlikelihood that traditional treatments of heroic wrath were critical of "heroic ideology."

Who Is Phoenix?

Phoenix's role in the *Iliad* is almost limited to this one prodigious speech. He appears a few more times, but never again speaks. As an elderly man who gives advice in a long speech, he resembles Nestor, with whom he is paired at 19.311, in a list of Achaeans who stay with Achilles to weep for Patroklos. These two elders are the repository of memories from the previous, more heroic, generation; according to later tradition (Ovid, *Metamorphoses* 8.307), Phoenix himself took part in the Calydonian boar hunt that he recounts in his speech.[17] There is a more pointed link: both Phoenix and Nestor make long, suggestive speeches that result in the tragic dispatch of Patroklos.[18] Nestor openly recommends in Book 11 that Achilles send Patroklos out as a substitute for himself, whereas Phoenix refers obliquely to Patro-klos through the figure of Meleager's wife Kleo-patra, and suggests the plot that is ultimately reversed by Patroklos when he, instead of sending out the Meleager-figure, takes on Meleager's role himself.

This resemblance between Phoenix and Nestor finds an echo in their pairing in visual art, which will be discussed in the following Interlude. But within the Homeric tradition Phoenix has another twin, as it were: Phoenix's speech in *Iliad* 9 resembles in numerous ways that of Eumaeus in *Odyssey* 15.403–484. While Phoenix is foster-father to the protagonist of the *Iliad*, Eumaeus has taken on this role for Telemachus in the absence of Odysseus. The two speeches, delivered to the central hero of each poem, are akin, from structure down to details of allusion and dramatic technique. In Chapter 4, these parallels are presented and the ramifications for the *Iliad* and the *Odyssey* are discussed. The full significance of some details in the present chapter will be uncovered only in the light of that discussion.

Phoenix in the Tradition

Phoenix's scant survival in the canon belies his actual lively presence in ancient literature. He was the subject of plays by Euripides and Sophocles, about which we know little. Euripides is perhaps responsible for the version of his story in which his father Amyntor blinds him, rather than cursing him as in

---

[17] A plus-line at *Iliad* 14.136 attests to the similar place occupied by the two men in the mind of ancient performers or editors. There Poseidon has disguised himself as an old man, and in such cases the god always becomes a specific character. Simply on the basis of, e.g., the dream in Book 2, one expects the old man to be Nestor, but the context prevents this, since the real Nestor is already present. Thus, in most MSS, Poseidon's mortal guise is not named at all, except in the plus-line found in Zenodotus, where the name is Phoenix. Cf. 17.556, where Athena disguises herself as Phoenix.

[18] On Phoenix and Nestor, especially Nestor's speech to Patroklos (*Iliad* 11.656–803), see Lohmann 1970:263–271.

Homer.[19] In Sophocles' *Philoctetes* (344), Neoptolemos tells Philoctetes (whether truthfully or not) that Odysseus and Phoenix came to convince him to come to Troy; thus Phoenix and Odysseus are again paired as ambassadors, this time to Achilles' son. According to Proclus' summary of the *Nostoi*, Phoenix dies on the way home from Troy and is buried by Neoptolemos. Most importantly for the present discussion, in Quintus Smyrnaeus (3.463–489), Phoenix performs a lament for Achilles. It is highly likely that he performed such a lament in the earliest stories of Achilles' funeral, stories which predate the *Iliad*, or rather, which the *Iliad* uses.[20]

Structure of the Speech

The speech falls into three major sections (with a brief appeal to close the speech):

    I. Phoenix's Autobiography (434–495)
    II. Allegory of the Litai (Prayers) (496–523)
    III. Story of Meleager (524–599)
       Short admonition (600–605)

Let us call these "panels" to distinguish them from shorter sections of the speech. The Meleager story is roughly as long as Phoenix's autobiography, with the Litai forming a bridge between the other two panels. Sachs[21] aptly compares this structure to one in *Iliad* 24, where Priam is compared first with Peleus, then with Niobe, while the allegory of the *pithoi* forms the bridge. Both passages are antithetically composed, like the pairs of speeches in Thucydides, with a positive and negative paradigm, to free the mind of the listener so that he or she may judge.

The Autobiography of Phoenix

The first panel of the speech is itself divided into three parts. The first (I) and third (III) concern Phoenix's fatherly relationship to Achilles; these frame the disturbing story of the young Phoenix's familial strife (II). Each of these three smaller parts is structured as a ring, resulting in an overall AXA', AXA', AXA' structure (outline after Gaisser[22]):

---

[19] Or cursing and castrating, as S. West 2001 has it. Cf. Lycophron *Alexandra* 417–423, where Phoenix is blinded by Amyntor but later healed by Cheiron. See Bannert 1981:73n10.

[20] Proclus' summary of the *Aethiopis*, which recounted Achilles' funeral, does not mention Phoenix, but that does not mean he did not appear; Proclus' summary of the *Cypria* neglects to mention Phoenix, but he did appear in that poem (Pausanius 10.26.4). For visual depictions of Phoenix mourning Achilles, see *LIMC* Achilles 866, 867, 883 (all sixth century BCE).

[21] Sachs 1933:24.

[22] Gaisser 1969:16–17, which includes further details on the echoes in diction.

First Panel: Autobiography of Phoenix

I. 434–445
    A. DO NOT LEAVE ME.   437–438
         X. PELEUS SENT ME.   438–443
    A′. DO NOT LEAVE ME.   444–445

II. 445–484
    A. PHOENIX FLEES HIS FATHER.   447–448 φεύγων
         X. WHY HE FLED.   449–477
    A′. PHOENIX FLEES HIS FATHER.   478–480 φεῦγον

III. 485–495
    A. I MADE YOU MY OWN.   485
         X. ACHILLES AS A BABY. 486–494
    A′. I MADE YOU MY OWN.   494–495

ὀψὲ δὲ δὴ μετέειπε γέρων ἱππηλάτα Φοῖνιξ
δάκρυ' ἀναπρήσας· περὶ γὰρ δίε νηυσὶν Ἀχαιῶν·
εἰ μὲν δὴ νόστόν γε μετὰ φρεσὶ φαίδιμ' Ἀχιλλεῦ
435 βάλλεαι, οὐδέ τι πάμπαν ἀμύνειν νηυσὶ θοῆσι
πῦρ ἐθέλεις ἀΐδηλον, ἐπεὶ χόλος ἔμπεσε θυμῷ,
<u>πῶς ἂν ἔπειτ' ἀπὸ σεῖο φίλον τέκος αὖθι λιποίμην</u>   **A DO NOT LEAVE ME**
οἶος; σοὶ δέ μ' <u>ἔπεμπε</u> γέρων ἱππηλάτα Πηλεὺς
    ἤματι τῷ ὅτε σ' ἐκ Φθίης Ἀγαμέμνονι <u>πέμπε</u>
440 νήπιον οὔ πω εἰδόθ' ὁμοιΐου πολέμοιο
οὐδ' ἀγορέων, ἵνα τ' ἄνδρες ἀριπρεπέες τελέθουσι.   **X CENTER**
τοὔνεκά με <u>προέηκε</u> διδασκέμεναι τάδε πάντα,
μύθων τε ῥητῆρ' ἔμεναι πρηκτῆρά τε ἔργων.
<u>ὡς ἂν ἔπειτ' ἀπὸ σεῖο φίλον τέκος οὐκ ἐθέλοιμι</u>   **A′ DO NOT LEAVE ME**
445 <u>λείπεσθ'</u>, οὐδ' εἴ κέν μοι ὑποσταίη θεὸς αὐτὸς ...

After a time, though, the old horseman Phoenix spoke out at last,
bursting with tears: so much did he fear for the ships of the Achaeans:
"If it is homecoming that you, shining Achilles, are revolving in your
        mind,
and you are unwilling to ward off from the swift ships
annihilating fire, since anger has imbued your spirit,
<u>how then should I be left</u> here, <u>apart from you,</u>
        <u>dear child,</u>   **A DO NOT LEAVE ME**
alone? It was for you that the old man, horseman Peleus, <u>was sending</u>
        me
    on that day when he <u>was sending</u> you from Phthia to Agamemnon,

naïve child, not yet knowing anything of leveling war
or assemblies, where men emerge resplendent.   **X CENTER**
That's why he <u>sent</u> me, to teach you all these things,
to be a speaker of words and a doer of deeds.
So I wouldn't be willing, <u>apart from you,</u>
      <u>dear child,</u>   **A′ DO NOT LEAVE ME**
<u>to be abandoned</u>, not even if the god himself should promise..."
                                  Iliad 9.432–445

In the first section of the autobiography, the elderly Phoenix makes an emotional appeal to his foster-child Achilles not to abandon him by leaving Troy. The abandonment is what is at issue here, reinforced by the ring composition. Such a plea papers over the real aim of the Embassy as a whole, that is, for Achilles to return to the battlefield. While Phoenix's fear of abandonment is naturally, effectively pathetic, his plea works quite awkwardly alongside the Embassy's aim of convincing Achilles to return to battle, thus risking his life.[23] The poet has chosen not to keep that discomfiting thought out of Phoenix's speech entirely, for of course that is the thrust of the third panel of the speech, the story of Meleager. Rather the poem allows it to *gradually emerge* that the complaints about abandonment are in the service of this request that he endanger his life, and lets these two rhetorical thrusts fight it out within the same speech without being reconciled.

The center of the first ring (443–448) explains why Achilles should listen to Phoenix: because Achilles' father Peleus sent Phoenix there himself. It also accounts for Phoenix's presence at Troy, and so resembles the centerpiece of the second ring, which accounts for his presence, not at Troy, but in Phthia in Achilles' house.[24] Thus, while the second ring backs up one step along the chain of causation, it too ends up with a center section accounting for the *presence* of Phoenix in a particular place. Note in the first ring ἵνα τ' ἄνδρες ἀριπρεπέες τελέθουσι, "where men emerge resplendent," the vivid coming-forth at the midpoint of the central (X) section of a ring. The audience for this speech is Achilles, and it is his presence before the speaker that *anchors* both locations: both rings account not so much for Phoenix's movement from one place to another as for "why I came to you; why I am *here with you*." The locations are

---

[23] Including Phoenix in the embassy rather than having him quartered with Achilles "allows him to overlook Achilles' belief that if he stays and fights at Troy his life, though glorious, will be short (9.412ff.)" (S. West 2001:14). Transferring him into the embassy for this reason, for West, explains the problematic duals in the episode.

[24] Gaisser rightly begins section "X," the centerpiece, *after* line 438. Peleus "sends" Phoenix in line 438, but the phrase ἤματι τῷ 'on that day' in 439 effectively restarts our vision at a day and a scene unto itself, lending the center section a characteristic flash of vividness.

layered on top of one another in space, while moving backward in time. Both these accounts of presence, Peleus' sending him to Troy, and Amyntor's wrath forcing him to Phthia, partially cover over the immediate issue of his presence in the here and now of Achilles' tent—sent by Agamemnon. On the other hand, that fact leaks out indirectly by the wording of 438–439, "Peleus sent me to you, on that day, when Agamemnon was sending you out of Phthia ..." Leak aside, these first two rings have the effect of replacing that here and now, the tent, with these prior times and locations, which are happier for the relationship of speaker and addressee, of the me and the you of the performer. The first story is only a displacement of time, not place, and so makes a wonderful elision: it is not, after all, Agamemnon that sent me here to you (on this unsavory mission), but Peleus.[25]

Notice too that the first ring's outer sections beg Achilles *not* to leave, while the second ring's outer sections recount how Phoenix did leave his family to become part of Achilles' family. In performance, the very structure of the two rings focuses attention upon the space before the performer as a place *where he has arrived*, a space capable of "containing" several times and places within it, each with clear senses of a center or *origo* at which arrival or departure takes place.

The two sections are connected smoothly[26] by "I wouldn't be willing to be left apart from you, dear child, not even if the god himself should promise to strip away my old age and set me in the bloom of youth, such as when I first left ..." (444–447). The transition to the second section turns into a long run-on sentence that includes much of the trouble at Phoenix's house in Hellas:

```
445   οὐδ᾽ εἴ κέν μοι ὑποσταίη θεὸς αὐτὸς
      γῆρας ἀποξύσας θήσειν νέον ἡβώοντα,
      οἷον ὅτε πρῶτον λίπον Ἑλλάδα καλλιγύναικα
      φεύγων νείκεα πατρὸς Ἀμύντορος Ὀρμενίδαο,
      ὅς μοι παλλακίδος περιχώσατο καλλικόμοιο,
450   τὴν αὐτὸς φιλέεσκεν, ἀτιμάζεσκε δ᾽ ἄκοιτιν
      μητέρ᾽ ἐμήν· ἣ δ᾽ αἰὲν ἐμὲ λισσέσκετο γούνων
      παλλακίδι προμιγῆναι, ἵν᾽ ἐχθήρειε γέροντα.
      τῇ πιθόμην καὶ ἔρεξα· πατὴρ δ᾽ ἐμὸς αὐτίκ᾽ ὀϊσθεὶς
      πολλὰ κατηρᾶτο, στυγερὰς δ᾽ ἐπεκέκλετ᾽ Ἐρινῦς,
```

---

[25] Compare this to the "arrival" of many men on the battlefield: the story of how they came to Troy is told as though they have just arrived, not only at the battlefield on this particular occasion, but also at Troy; the two moments are conflated.

[26] On how the style here reveals the tight connection, within Phoenix's thought process, between his own youth and his role in Achilles' life, see Bannert 1981:72.

455 μή ποτε γούνασιν οἷσιν ἐφέσσεσθαι φίλον υἱὸν
ἐξ ἐμέθεν γεγαῶτα· θεοὶ δ' ἐτέλειον ἐπαρὰς
Ζεύς τε καταχθόνιος καὶ ἐπαινὴ Περσεφόνεια.

Not even if the god himself should promise
to smooth away my old age and set me back in blooming youth,
as when I first left Hellas, with its beautiful women,
fleeing the hatred of my father Amyntor, son of Ormenos,
who got angry with me for his fair-haired concubine,
whom he himself loved, and was dishonoring his own wife,
my mother; who was always taking me by the knees, begging me
to lie with the concubine, so that she would hate the old man.
I yielded to her and did it. And my father immediately suspected,
and called down many curses, and invoked the chill Erinyes,
that never shall there sit on his knees a dear son
begotten from me. And the gods fulfilled the curses,
Zeus of the underworld and dread Persephone.

Iliad 9.445–457

Phoenix's mother was angry that his father Amyntor had taken a concubine and begged her son to sleep with the concubine. Phoenix did the deed (ἔρεξα), incurring his father's wrath. But that is not how the story is told. The poet is backing into the first cause, because he is taking Phoenix's departure as his starting point, and relates first that Amyntor was angry on account of a lovely-haired concubine (449), whom he himself cherished, leaving the fact that Phoenix had slept with her for later, then proceeds to the involvement of the angry mother/wife. The anger of the father comes first, and is explained by events caused in turn by the anger of the mother. As in the opening of the *Iliad*, the explanation of one wrath yields to that of another, which in turn causes yet another, proceeding back up the chain: for the mother wants the concubine not just to despise Amyntor but to hate him (452), which will in turn cause the anger of Amyntor. The chain of hatred is traced back to its first cause—the taking of (or holding on to) a concubine, the same cause that triggers the events of the *Iliad* (Chryseis and then Briseis) and the war (Helen). Phoenix, in the midst of the storm of hatred and anger, is merely obeying. Amyntor goes so far as to curse his son with sterility: "he cursed many times and called upon the chill Erinyes, that never shall there sit on his knees a dear son, begotten from me" (455–456).

Now come the contested lines about Phoenix's impulse to kill his father:

τὸν μὲν ἐγὼ βούλευσα κατακτάμεν ὀξέι χαλκῷ·
ἀλλά τις ἀθανάτων παῦσεν χόλον, ὅς ῥ' ἐνὶ θυμῷ

δήμου θῆκε φάτιν καὶ ὀνείδεα πόλλ' ἀνθρώπων,
ὡς μὴ πατροφόνος μετ' Ἀχαιοῖσιν καλεοίμην.

As for him I planned to slay him with the sharp bronze.
But one of the immortals stopped my wrath, who
set the rumor of the people in my heart, and the many reproaches of
     men,
so that I not be called a patricide among the Achaeans.

Iliad 9.458–461

Phoenix's relatives keep him under house arrest and "supplicating him there, were restraining him in the halls" (αὐτοῦ λισσόμενοι κατερήτυον ἐν μεγάροισι, line 465), slaughtering many animals of all sorts, until on the tenth day Phoenix finally breaks out of the "closely set doors of his chamber," leaps over the court-yard fence, "easily," and goes to Phthia.[27]

ἀλλ' ὅτε δὴ δεκάτη μοι ἐπήλυθε νὺξ ἐρεβεννή,
475 καὶ τότ' ἐγὼ θαλάμοιο θύρας πυκινῶς ἀραρυίας
     ῥήξας ἐξῆλθον, καὶ ὑπέρθορον ἑρκίον αὐλῆς
     ῥεῖα, λαθὼν φύλακάς τ' ἄνδρας δμῳάς τε γυναῖκας.
     φεῦγον ἔπειτ' ἀπάνευθε δι' Ἑλλάδος εὐρυχόροιο,
     Φθίην δ' ἐξικόμην ...

But when the tenth black night came for me,
just then I, bursting the close-fitted doors of the chamber,
went out, and leapt over the fence of the courtyard,
easily, slipping past the guards and the serving-women.
I fled far away, through Hellas with broad dancing-floors,
and came to Phthia ...

Iliad 9.474–479

This house arrest has baffled many scholars. Why should his relatives keep the angry Phoenix in his house? We return to this question when we reach the story of Marpessa.

The first section of the autobiography centered on Peleus sending Phoenix with Achilles; in the second, Phoenix again comes to Achilles, fleeing from his own father. Thus we have a strophe and antistrophe structure, culminating in

---

[27] A thematic web connects Phoenix, Peleus (cf. Mühlestein 1981:85–91, and on the allusion to Akastos on the François Vase, see Stewart 1983), Bellerophon, Euenos/Marpessa, Oinomaos/ Hippodameia, and especially Laodameia and Protesilaos. Outside the Greek tradition, Phoenix's story may be compared with the Biblical Reuben, who slept with his father Jacob's concubine and was denied his first-born privileges: see M. West 1997:373.

the epiphanic epode of the third section, which puts the weft of the rhetorical aim over the warp of these movements of the past and reveals the vivid, static tableau of Phoenix dandling baby Achilles.[28] Amyntor's curse may have been fulfilled, but there has been a double substitution: Phoenix has got a foster father in Peleus (indeed, Peleus treats him as his "only child" [481–482]!), and a foster son in Achilles. In the center of the third ring, Phoenix fondly recalls Achilles sitting contentedly on his lap and burping up wine all over Phoenix's chiton, "in infantile pain" (491). "Thus for you I suffered much, I toiled much, with this in mind—that the gods were not bringing any offspring to fruition out of me; but you, child, Achilles, like the gods, I made you, so you may some time ward off for me unseemly *loigos*. But, Achilles, tame your great *thumos*: it is not fit for you to have a heart without pity: even the gods are pliable ..." (492–497)—with which he launches into the allegory of the Litai. The maximally vivid image of the infant Achilles on Phoenix's knees serves on the face of it as the "cause" of Phoenix's suffering. This third centerpiece deviates from the first two: where the first two account for Phoenix's presence, first at Troy, then in Phthia, the third presents a sort of primal scene that trumps even the tragic melodrama of section two. A good part of its power lies in the way it corresponds to the actual scene unfolding during the delivery of the speech: the post-prandial talk in Achilles' tent. Thus Phoenix invokes the scene at Peleus' *megaron* and layers it on top of the scene in Achilles' tent. The audience, Achilles, is asked to imagine himself once again on the speaker's lap.[29] Thus the strophic structure of the speech gives way to a spatial play of musical chairs, a play ratcheted up as the speech proceeds. Insofar as the performer becomes Phoenix for this very long speech, and Phoenix's words layer such a vivid picture of the past onto the present, the space inhabited by the performer is shaped into an *origo* or a point of arrival, and also a space for the emergence of people from the past.

The Litai

Following the autobiography is the rich allegory of the Litai ("Prayers"), the short central panel (9.496–523) forming a bridge between Phoenix's autobiography

---

[28] See Mullen (1982:90–142) on "epodic arrest" in Pindaric choreography. Section 3 of Phoenix's speech includes many of the features Mullen discusses: a static image, an address to a dead ancestor as "you" (see below on the approach to Achilles as a hero), the arrival at the *archē* of a story, and epiphany. See Gentili (1988:15) on the "strophic structure" of Demodokos' song, "as is clear from the presence of the chorus of dancers": a form that "antedates purely recitational performances in the normalized hexameter form in which the Homeric poems have come down to us."

[29] This placement of the baby Achilles, conjured from the past, tangibly in the intimate space of the speaker, prepares for Phoenix's "lamentation" and "cursing" of Achilles; see below.

and the story of Meleager. The Litai transparently stand in, substitute, for the three Achaeans sent to plead (λίσσεσθαι, 520) with Achilles. Phoenix warns Achilles not to dishonor them, even saying, "do not dishonor our speech / nor feet"[!] (522-523). This last recalls the Litai who, crippled, follow behind ἀρτίπος (solid on her feet) Atē (503-505). The simple interpretation of the passage is that Achilles should listen to the ambassadors, lest he be struck by *atē* and start the cycle all over again. But the allegory is not so circumscribed, and provides a map of the Meleager story to come.

The Litai are at first embodiments of prayers, following in the train of Atē as healing forces:

> ... λισσόμενοι, ὅτε κέν τις ὑπερβήῃ καὶ ἁμάρτῃ.
> καὶ γάρ τε λιταί εἰσι Διὸς κοῦραι μεγάλοιο
> χωλαί τε ῥυσαί τε παραβλῶπές τ' ὀφθαλμώ,
> αἵ ῥά τε καὶ μετόπισθ' ἄτης ἀλέγουσι <u>κιοῦσαι</u>.
> 505 <u>ἡ δ' ἄτη</u> σθεναρή τε καὶ ἀρτίπος, οὕνεκα πάσας
> πολλὸν ὑπεκπροθέει, φθάνει δέ τε πᾶσαν ἐπ' αἶαν
> <u>βλάπτουσ'</u> ἀνθρώπους· αἱ δ' ἐξακέονται ὀπίσσω.
> <u>ὃς μέν</u> τ' αἰδέσεται κούρας Διὸς ἆσσον <u>ἰούσας</u>,
> <u>τὸν δὲ</u> μέγ' ὤνησαν καί τ' ἔκλυον εὐχομένοιο·
> 510 <u>ὃς δέ</u> κ' ἀνήνηται καί τε στερεῶς ἀποείπῃ,
> λίσσονται δ' ἄρα ταί γε Δία Κρονίωνα <u>κιοῦσαι</u>
> <u>τῷ ἄτην</u> ἅμ' ἕπεσθαι, ἵνα <u>βλαφθεὶς</u> ἀποτίσῃ.

> ... supplicating, whenever someone oversteps or goes astray.
> For there are Prayers (Litai), daughters of great Zeus
> lame, wrinkled, eyes looking askance,
> who, you see, are heedful of Atē, <u>coming</u> up behind her.
> <u>But she, Atē,</u> is strong and solid on her feet, so she runs
> out ahead of them all by far, beats them into every land
> <u>damaging</u> human beings: and they go healing behind.
> <u>Whoever</u> reveres the daughters of Zeus <u>as they come</u> near
> <u>him</u> they help, and listen when he prays.
> <u>But whoever</u> refuses and stiffly says no,
> pray they do, yes *they*, <u>coming</u> to Kronian Zeus,
> for Atē to chase <u>that one</u>, so that, <u>damaged</u>, he may pay the price.
>
> *Iliad* 9.501-512

At first the lame, cockeyed shufflers "represent" (embody) prayers and also "represent" someone else (just as the embassy represents Agamemnon); they are certainly not praying on their own behalf. So far, so simple. Then there is an antithesis; first, whoever reveres them when they come near, they help, and they hear him when he prays (ὃς μέν ... τὸν δέ, 508–509). The allegorical sense opens out of strict one-to-one correspondence: do the Litai "come near him" in the sense that he reveres prayers enough to pray (εὐχομένοιο, 509), or in that he has accepted someone else's prayer, such that whenever in future he has need of prayer they "hear" him?

Then, "but whoever refuses them and stiffly denies them, they *pray, oh yes, THEY do,* coming to Zeus son of Kronos, for Atē to accompany that one, that in being hurt he may pay" (511–512). Here the Litai suddenly transform themselves from coming *as* prayers or *representing* prayers allegorically to *performing* them themselves. The language is striking and insistent. Notice how this second pair of phrases begins again in the nominative with ὃς δέ only to break the correspondence, putting the verb of praying which they "represent" into first position with ἄρα,[30] bringing the praying suddenly into view, and most importantly, bringing the Litai themselves forward as agents with ταί γε:

511   λίσσονται δ' ἄρα ταί γε ...

The Litai no longer vacantly represent another but fill with anger and pray for vengeance on their own behalf, suddenly and unexpectedly, to Zeus. Abstract *ainigma* swerves into nightmare: the benign symbols of a fable animate themselves; underneath their humble, placating facade, their unmasked selves desire—and *cause*—the very Ruination it is their day job to repair. Ruin, Atē, is not, it turns out, the initiator but the product of Prayer. Prayers do not smooth over devastation but unleash it in the first place. It is the very incarnation of the uncanny; the symbol bodied forth into the real;[31] effects producing causes. The disturbing cycle is hammered on by the echoes between the two acts of the Litai: κιοῦσαι / ἣ δ' ἄτη (504–505), κιοῦσαι / τῷ ἄτην (511–512); βλάπτουσ' (507), βλαφθείς (512); the repeated "daughters of Zeus" (502, 508) followed by their appeal to Zeus Kronios (511). For the Prayers, representing the Embassy, to take on a sinister life of their own sits ill indeed in ambassador Phoenix's plea to his beloved foster-son. It works beautifully, however, to prepare for the remaining panel of the speech.

In both panels II (Litai) and III (Meleager) there is a loss of control at the center; a sudden emergence of a new agent; an uncanny repetition of the same;

---

[30]   The first full-form ἄρα of Phoenix's speech (cf. 459, 504).

[31]   Cf. Freud 1955:243: "an uncanny effect is often and easily produced when the distinction between imagination and reality is effaced, as when something that we have hitherto regarded as imaginary appears before us in reality, or when a symbol takes over the full functions of the thing it symbolizes, and so on."

the emergence of a female thought to be dormant. Kleopatra should neatly "represent" Patroklos allegorically; the Litai should represent prayers and the pray-ers; both spill out of their respective tales to take the helm and bring about Ruin. And this spilling out takes place within the body of the performer and the space of performance as well.

The Marpessa Story/
Meleager and Kleopatra in the Thalamos

We have summarized the plot of the third (Meleager) panel above. Let us now turn to the digression within it, which brings to a head the speech's pyrotechnics of poetics and presence. Meleager, when he retreats, retreats to his bedroom, and lies by his wife, Kleopatra, as Achilles has retreated to be with Patroklos. This bedroom setting also echoes the "wrath of Paris,"[32] which lasts from Book 3 until Hektor arrives to break up the sad party in Book 6. Meleager and Kleopatra, however, are a diamond formed from the coal of Hektor and Andromache.

Position in Ring Structure

As is clear from Gaisser's outline,[33] adapted below, the Meleager story falls neatly into three sections. The digression about Kleopatra's mother lies at the center of the ring composition which forms the central second section. (I omit details of parts I and III for clarity.)

  I. The War of the Kouretes and the Aetolians. 524–549
  II. Meleager Retires from the Battle. 550–574
      A The Battle Rages. 550–552
         B Meleager's Wrath. 553–555 χόλος
            C He Retires with Kleopatra. 556 κεῖτο
            X Kleopatra's Mother Marpessa. 557–564
            C′ He Retires with Kleopatra. 565 παρκατέλεκτο
         B′ Meleager's Wrath. 565–572 χόλον
      A′ The Battle Rages. 573–574
  III. Meleager Is Persuaded. 574–599 (Catalogue of suppliants, ending with Kleopatra.)

Here is a hyper-literal translation of the Marpessa story (X) with its two proximate framing sections (B C — C′ B′):

---

[32] Kakridis 1949:43–64.
[33] Gaisser 1969:18–19.

ἀλλ' ὅτε δὴ Μελέαγρον ἔδυ χόλος, ὅς τε καὶ ἄλλων

B   οἰδάνει ἐν στήθεσσι νόον πύκα περ φρονεόντων,
ἤτοι ὃ μητρὶ φίλῃ Ἀλθαίῃ χωόμενος κῆρ

C   <u>κεῖτο</u> παρὰ μνηστῇ ἀλόχῳ καλῇ Κλεοπάτρῃ
κούρῃ Μαρπήσσης καλλισφύρου Εὐηνίνης
Ἴδεώ θ', ὃς κάρτιστος ἐπιχθονίων γένετ' ἀνδρῶν
τῶν τότε· καί ῥα ἄνακτος ἐναντίον εἵλετο τόξον

560   **X**   Φοίβου Ἀπόλλωνος καλλισφύρου εἵνεκα νύμφης,
<u>τὴν</u> δὲ τότ' ἐν μεγάροισι πατὴρ καὶ πότνια μήτηρ
Ἀλκυόνην καλέεσκον ἐπώνυμον, οὕνεκ' ἄρ' <u>αὐτῆς</u>
μήτηρ ἀλκυόνος πολυπενθέος οἶτον ἔχουσα
κλαῖ' ὅτε <u>μιν</u> ἑκάεργος ἀνήρπασε Φοῖβος Ἀπόλλων·

C'   τῇ ὅ γε <u>παρκατέλεκτο</u> χόλον θυμαλγέα πέσσων
ἐξ ἀρέων μητρὸς κεχολωμένος, ἥ ῥα θεοῖσι
πόλλ' ἀχέουσ' ἠρᾶτο κασιγνήτοιο φόνοιο,
πολλὰ δὲ καὶ γαῖαν πολυφόρβην χερσὶν ἀλοία

B'   κικλήσκουσ' Ἀΐδην καὶ ἐπαινὴν Περσεφόνειαν
570   πρόχνυ καθεζομένη, δεύοντο δὲ δάκρυσι κόλποι,
παιδὶ δόμεν θάνατον· τῆς δ' ἠεροφοῖτις Ἐρινὺς
ἔκλυεν ἐξ Ἐρέβεσφιν ἀμείλιχον ἦτορ ἔχουσα.

But when *cholos* entered Meleager, which swells up too

B   in the chests of others, even those thinking with close
mind,
yes, he, angered in his heart with his dear mother Althaia,

C   <u>lay down</u> next to his wedded wife, lovely Kleopatra,
daughter of Marpessa of lovely ankles daughter of
Euenos
and of Idas, who was mightiest of men upon the
earth—
those of *that* time. And he took up his bow against
the lord

X   Phoebus Apollo, for the sake of a lovely-ankled
bride,
and <u>her</u>, then, in the halls her father and queenly
mother
called Alkyone as an eponym, seeing that <u>her</u>
mother, with the lot of the mournful *alkyōn*, used
to cry—

that Phoebus Apollo who works from afar raped
her:

C′   by her he lay down, digesting his heart-rending *cholos*,
filled with *cholos* from the curses of his mother, who to the
gods
many times prayed, in grief at the murder of her brother,
many times thrashed the much-nurturing earth with her
hands,

B′   invoking Hades and dread Persephone
sitting and kneeling, and her breasts were wet with tears,
to give her child death: and Erinys who treads the air
heard her out of Erebos with her unyielding heart.

Iliad 9.553–572

Phoenix leaves us hanging with the image of the couple in bed at 565 and backtracks to the mother's lethal curse before moving forward again to the petitioners banging on Meleager's door. So like Patroklos in Achilles' tent, where her story is being told, Kleopatra is a powerful silent presence, until she finally sends Meleager out after all others have failed. As noted above, Phoenix elides the fact that Meleager will now die—a death the audience realizes is immanent, like the death of Achilles after the *Iliad*, and like the substitute death of Patroklos.

Line 565, τῇ ὅ γε παρκατέλεκτο χόλον θυμαλγέα πέσσων, "By her he lay down, digesting his heart-rending anger" (C′), completes a ring begun in 556 (C).[34] In the middle, between the two lines about lying down next to her, the poet suddenly endows this "her," Kleopatra, with a life, in a startling, compressed digression about her mother Marpessa, her father Idas, and her grandfather Euenos.

The lines about lying down (C/C′) are embedded in turn in the wrath of Meleager against his mother (B/B′). Only B′ reveals a connection between his wrath and his mother's curse, leaving his wrath inexplicable for the stretch of time occupied by the digression.[35]

Merging: Three Women

Consider now the Marpessa digression with only its immediate frame:

C   κεῖτο παρὰ μνηστῇ ἀλόχῳ καλῇ Κλεοπάτρῃ
κούρῃ Μαρπήσσης καλλισφύρου Εὐηνίνης
Ἴδεώ θ', ὃς κάρτιστος ἐπιχθονίων γένετ' ἀνδρῶν

---

[34] For another instance of ring composition beginning and ending with a verb meaning "to lie down," this time κεῖμαι, see *Odyssey* 21.10–14 (Nagler 1993:4n8).

[35] We return to the position of the Marpessa story within the ring composition below, page 164.

>   τῶν τότε· καί ῥα ἄνακτος ἐναντίον εἵλετο τόξον
>
> X   Φοίβου Ἀπόλλωνος καλλισφύρου εἵνεκα νύμφης,
>
>   τὴν δὲ τότ' ἐν μεγάροισι πατὴρ καὶ πότνια μήτηρ
>
>   Ἀλκυόνην καλέεσκον ἐπώνυμον, οὕνεκ' ἄρ' <u>αὐτῆς</u>
>
>   μήτηρ ἀλκυόνος πολυπενθέος οἶτον ἔχουσα
>
>   κλαῖ' ὅτε μιν ἑκάεργος ἀνήρπασε Φοῖβος Ἀπόλλων·
>
> C'   τῇ ὅ γε <u>παρκατέλεκτο</u> χόλον θυμαλγέα πέσσων

> C   <u>He lay down</u> next to his wedded wife, lovely Kleopatra,
>
>   daughter of Marpessa of lovely ankles daughter of
>
>   Euenos
>
>   and of Idas, who was mightiest of men upon the
>
>   earth—
>
>   those of *that* time. And he took up his bow against the
>
>   lord
>
> X   Phoebus Apollo, for the sake of a lovely-ankled bride,
>
>   and her, then, in the halls her father and queenly
>
>   mother
>
>   called Alkyone as an eponym, seeing that <u>her</u>
>
>   mother, with the lot of the mournful *alkyōn*, used to
>
>   cry-
>
>   that Phoebus Apollo who works from afar raped her:
>
> C'   by her <u>he lay down</u>, digesting his heart-rending *cholos*.
>
>   *Iliad* 9.556–565

If you are confused, you are in good company.[36] Before sorting through the mythical background, let us note some grammatical elements leading to this

---

[36] Hainsworth 1993:135–137; Levaniouk 1999:119; Scodel 2002:137–138; Bouvier 2002:364n25. Gaisser (1969:19) summarizes: "As a whole ... the section is difficult to follow. This is particularly true in the story of Kleopatra's mother and in the reason for Meleager's wrath against Althaea. In the story of Marpessa and Kleopatra it is difficult for the modern reader to discriminate between the mother and daughter, to determine which was kidnapped and which was called Alkyone. Meleager's wrath against his mother is introduced in 553, but not accounted for until the story of the curse which begins in 565. Furthermore, the reason for Althaea's anger is itself almost unintelligible. She is grieved at the murder of her brother (567), but it is not mentioned that Meleager killed him, or why." Cf. Leaf 1900–1902:1.413 ad *Iliad* 9.563, while defending the single-MS reading οἶκτον against the "very feeble" vulgate reading οἶτον: "But it must be admitted that do what we may it is impossible to make anything but a most confused and clumsy piece of narration out of all this. It has all the air of a fragment of an old Epic interspersed with lines taken from other portions of the original story—aids to the memory, perhaps, of hearers who partly knew a not very common legend, but to us only darkening the obscurity." True, the listeners must have known the legend(s). The question is why the poet would spark these stories in his listeners, and what effects he produces by sparking them in this fashion.

confusion. Particularly bewildering are the pronouns flying by, especially τήν (561), μιν (564), and αὐτῆς (562).[37] Commentators, both ancient and modern, tend to help the reader by glossing each referent, giving the impression that readers have simply missed something. But it is exceptionally difficult to sort out who is doing what to whom. τήν of line 561 seems to refer to the nymph/ bride of 560 on whose behalf Idas fought Apollo. On this reading of τήν, the object of Apollo and Idas' fight *is* the one who is called Alkyone.

She is called Alkyone by her *father and mother*, "because her *mother* used to cry with the lot of the mournful *alkyōn*. ..." This shift of focus from "father and lady mother" (562) to the mother alone (563) implies that the mother of Alkyone has a particular involvement, perhaps even that she was the one raped, rather than Alkyone herself. This shift, that is, affects how we hear the next phrase, "... because Apollo raped her (μιν)." Is the woman who cries the same as the woman who was raped? In other words, does μιν refer to the subject of κλαῖ' or not? It is not clear who is the victim, who is crying, and how many generations are involved.

Some scholars have thought either that it is Marpessa who is nicknamed Alkyone, or that it is her daughter Kleopatra, rather than herself, who is raped.[38] In standard translations, sometimes a third generation appears: it is Marpessa who is raped, but the mother who cries becomes Marpessa's mother, and Marpessa is called Alkyone.[39] Once I thought I had a handle on the possible

[37] On μιν, see Chantraine *Grammaire Homérique* II.154. μιν is primarily anaphoric, but is also used as an indirect reflexive. As Leaf 1900–1902 notes, αὐτῆς in 562 is "used in the weakest possible sense, 'her mother,' a use which can hardly be paralleled in Homer." It does demand a stronger sense. This demand is accentuated by the line-end echo between 560, εἵνεκα νύμφης, and 562 οὕνεκ' ἄρ' αὐτῆς. Students do in fact become exceptionally confused. The pronominal confusion continues outside of the Marpessa digression; see below. Scodel (2002:171) makes somewhat similar sense of the notorious duals of Book 9: "They increase the mystification around Phoenix." Fish (1980) describes a similar process of progressive disorientation induced in a reader by indefinite pronouns.

[38] The confusion is not limited to moderns: the *Etymologicum genuinum* informs us that Alkyone is a φερώνυμον τῆς Μαρπήσσης γυναικὸς τοῦ Μελεάγρου, "eponym of Marpessa, wife of Meleager"— "wrong" on not one but two counts. Cf. Ebel (1972:94–95) wrongly but profoundly: "*Marpessa wailing over the daughter whom Apollo has made away with* reminds us that when Patroclus meets his doom it is Apollo who strikes him from behind and stuns him for the slaughter, and that when Achilles learns his companion has been killed 'he cried out / terribly, aloud, and the lady his mother heard him, / as she sat in the depths of the sea'" (my emphasis). Edmunds (1997:432) speaks of "the excursus on the abduction of Alcyone," though he realizes (pp. 430–431) that it is Marpessa who is abducted and Kleopatra who is named Alcyone. Likewise Levaniouk 2011:316: "When Idas abducts Alkyone from her father..."

[39] Chapman: "Since he had ravisht her, his joy, whom her friends after gave / The surname of Alcyone, because they could not save / Their daughter from Alcyone's Fate." Fitzgerald: "He drew the bow against the Lord Phoibos Apollo over his love, Marpesse, whom her father and gentle mother called Alkyone, since for her sake her mother gave that seabird's forlorn cry when Apollo ravished her." Cf. Gresseth 1964:89–90 on the ambiguous τὴν δὲ in various translators.

permutations, a distinguished scholar informed me I had misread the passage: it was Marpessa's mother who was raped. That is plausible: it involves taking τήν as Marpessa and μιν as referring to the subject of κλαῖεν. After this, another scholar corrected me: Marpessa's mother is the victim, but her grandmother is the one who weeps! On that reading Euenine is a proper name rather than a patronymic, and Marpessa is the daughter of fair-ankled Euenine and Idas. This last interpretation, while grammatically possible, is unlikely to have been heard, given the well-known marriage of Marpessa and Idas, but it confirms the dense ambiguity of the passage. *The poet has made it hard to keep the generations apart.* Is this incidental to the compression of the story—a byproduct of the fact that the story is told so briefly—or is the story compressed in order to produce this fusion?

Survey of the Marpessa Story

The extremely allusive form of the digression indicates, in the first place, that there was at least one story with which Homeric audiences were quite familiar. Marpessa's story was told by Simonides and Bacchylides. Unfortunately, only a summary of Simonides' version and frustratingly thin fragments of Bacchylides' version(s) have survived. These and a few other ancient sources[40] provide more details. Marpessa's basic story is that she is kept locked up by her cruel father Euenos, who challenges her suitors to a chariot race: when they lose, he murders them and nails their skulls to his wall to keep out other prospective suitors. Idas, by all surviving accounts, eventually abducts[41] or rescues Marpessa from her prison. Two sources[42] specify that he does so while she is dancing for Artemis. Euenos chases the pair until he realizes he has lost, at which point he throws himself into a river and dies, giving his name to the river.

Euenos[43] and Marpessa are comparable to, for example, Oinomaos and Hippodameia, the father who guards his daughter against prospective suitors and kills them all until she is rescued by Pelops. The incestuous component in this storyline is not always explicit,[44] but surfaces in Apollodorus (*Epitome* 2.4–9) and the ancient scholia (Σ *Or* 990).

At some point, Apollo rapes Marpessa, and Idas—perhaps already her husband, perhaps not—takes up arms against him. Idas "seized his bow opposite

---

[40] See esp. Bacchylides fr. 20 and 20a, with Maehler's (2004) commentary, Simonides 563 PMG (*apud* Σ B^b *Iliad* 9.557), Σ Pindar *Isthmian* 4.92a, Apollodorus 1.7.7–8. Cf. *LIMC* "Marpessa."

[41] Σ BT on 9.557.

[42] Σ D 9.557; Dositheos *apud* Plutarch *Parallela minora* 40a (*Moralia* 315e).

[43] Euenos, "good with the reins," not tamed (well-reined) himself (εὐήνιος), but in the sense that he bridles his daughter, and defeats her suitors in the chariot race (until he fails to catch Idas).

[44] Cf. Redfield (1995:156): "In one version, Oenomaus wished to marry Hippodameia himself, and this incestuous theme must be seen as latent in all the versions. To marry the daughter is like killing the son, a refusal to let go, to let the next generation take one's place."

the lord / Apollo for the sake of the bride [or 'nymph'] with beautiful ankles," as
our digression has it:

... καί ῥα ἄνακτος ἐναντίον εἵλετο τόξον
Φοίβου Ἀπόλλωνος καλλισφύρου εἵνεκα νύμφης.

Iliad 9.559–560

From the rape, her parents used to call Kleopatra 'Alkyone'.[45] Thus, apart from
the insane father who keeps her to himself, Marpessa's other basic feature
is that she is raped by Apollo. Scholars do not agree on the etymology of her
name: some claim it is non-Greek, others derive it from μάρπτειν, to seize.[46] Her
iconography corresponds with an ample series of depictions of Helen, whose
name can also recall "seizure": both women appear flanked by two men who
grab each arm to pull in opposite directions.[47]

When Idas takes up arms against Apollo, Zeus settles the fight by leaving
the decision to Marpessa. Marpessa chooses a mortal husband, Idas, figuring
that the god Apollo would abandon her when she was old.[48]

The story of Marpessa shares several basic elements with the story of
Meleager and Kleopatra, and with the story of Phoenix and his erotically trou-
bled family. In all three we find the wrath of a parent; erotic attachment in

---

[45] Perhaps in some pre-Homeric version, Kleopatra was the product of the rape, i.e. Apollo's
daughter. Cf. Heyne 1834 *ad* 9.552–560: "Iam in poeta ambiguum est, quo tempore rapta fit
Marpessa; utrum ante nuptias, an iam Idae coniugio habita; nam vs. 557... videri potest declarare
hoc: filiam iam tum, cum mater ab Apolline raperetur, natam esse. Potest tamen illud τότε minus
accurate et laxius dictum esse et est communis narratio, Marpessam puellam ab Ida et Apolline
amatam, raptam et recuperatam esse" ("In the poet it is ambiguous at what point Marpessa was
raped; whether before marriage, or already with Idas as her husband; for vs. 557... might seem
to state this: that the daughter already at that time, when the mother was raped by Apollo, was
born. But it is possible that that τότε is said less accurately and more loosely and it is a common
story that Marpessa as a girl was loved by Idas and Apollo, and was raped and was recovered").
That would make sense of the odd use of αὐτῆς noted above. It would also create a sinister angle
on Meleager's death, as it is she who sends Meleager out, and Apollo who kills him (in the epic
version glimpsed in Hesiod fr. 25 M-W).

[46] "Marpessa," regardless of etymology, may have struck the Greek ear roughly like the now thank-
fully passé American slang "rapable." Eustathius *ad Iliad* 9.557 (van der Valk 1971–1987:2.809)
would extend this to Helen, though the link is less vivid: ὥσπερ Ἑλένη παρὰ τὸ ἑλεῖν διὰ κάλλους,
οὕτω καὶ Μάρπησσα παρὰ τὸ μάρπτειν, ταὐτὸν δέ πως τὸ μάρψειν καὶ τὸ ἑλεῖν, "just as Helen,
from 'to seize' on account of beauty, so too Marpessa from 'to seize,' and *marpsein* and *helein* are
somewhat the same."

[47] See *LIMC* "Marpessa" and "Helene."

[48] Simonides 563 PMG (bT schol.); Σ D 9.557; Apollodorus 1.7.7. Unlike her father, Marpessa accepts
her mortality and chooses the mortal. The iconography neatly folds together her choice with
the rape motif. While the two men fight or try to drag her off, a figure arrives to intervene and
offer her the choice. Sometimes that figure (Iris, Hermes) simply replaces Marpessa on the vase,
producing a new trio representing not rape but the decision, the mortal on one side, the god on
the other, like a balance of scales weighed by the central figure.

conflict with familial affection; confinement followed by dramatically leaving one's home or chamber.

Merging and Layering

What is the function of these shared themes? Sometimes similar motifs are placed in sequence, as variations on a theme.[49] But here the poem has integrated the stories into a more complex structure. The complexity is obvious: here is a story (Meleager and Kleopatra) within a speech (Phoenix's) as opposed to narration. Inside that story is another story (the past of one of the characters, Kleopatra's mother Marpessa), and that story alludes, by way of the nickname Alkyone, to yet another story. Meanwhile, the same speech contains a story about the past of the speaker, and about how that relates to the past of the addressee. Yet while that is a true account, it remains on the level of abstraction. It does not address *why* a poet who was a performer might arrange matters thus, or what effect it might be aiming at.

The pronouns we discussed above are not the only elements lending themselves to ambiguity. It is almost impossible not to hear νύμφης ('bride' or 'nymph', 560) as Kleopatra, who has just been called μνηστῇ ἀλόχῳ (556) and who is lying in the bridal chamber at this very moment with her young (Meleager always dies young) husband: she is a ready-to-hand νύμφη.[50] This impression linking Kleopatra to the νύμφη at the center of the god-mortal dispute would be heightened for an audience familiar with the story that Meleager was killed by Apollo. This story is attested elsewhere in the epic tradition, and many believe it to be pre-Homeric.[51] The speaker leaps so abruptly from the world of the woman raped by Apollo and rescued by Idas back into the world of Meleager

---

[49] See, e.g., Lowenstam 1993 on the wrath theme in the *Iliad*.

[50] "Marpessa is viewed as a maiden (νύμφη 560) and as a mother (μήτηρ 561) almost simultaneously" (Levaniouk 1999:119).

[51] Edmunds 1997:431. Swain (1988:272) writes: "Since the lifeblood of these genealogies [Aetolian=Elean-Pylian and other cycles] lies in the traditions which inform them, it is likely that the traditions themselves had been fixed by the same period and existed earlier. Support for this is offered by the Athenian heroes: with the Attic kings, for example, we know that already existing traditions were harmonized with genealogies which were invented later from the time of the sixth to fourth centuries. Thus Meleager's death in battle at the hands of Apollo in [Hesiod] *Eoiai* fr. 25.12, *Katabasis of Peirithoos* fr. 280.2 M-W, and the *Minyad* (Pausanias 10.31.3 = *Minyas* fr. 5 Kinkel) will not be an extension of the *Iliad* designed to fill in the parallels between Meleager and Achilles which Homer neglected, but part of an already existing epic tradition, that is as old as Homer, if not older." This is sound, though I would caution against Swain's "Thus" and would modify "already existing epic tradition" to "already existing tradition," because the killing of Meleager by Apollo may have been recounted in any number of genres. Kakridis among others believes the story to be post-Homeric. If so, the invention of the motif is perhaps responding to the very superimposing of scenes in this digression.

and Kleopatra that *Meleager* seems to be the mortal fighting Apollo "for the sake of the bride." But the epithet "lovely-ankled" belongs to Marpessa, probably because Idas abducts her from a dance.[52]

We move into this background story on the heels of a very startling line: "angry with his mother Althaia he lay down by his wedded wife" (555). This is one of the story's notoriously bare references. We are given no cause for Meleager's *cholos* until after this, his wife's, background story, and even then it is the barest of hints: Althaia has cursed her son "in pain at the murder of her brother." Of course, according to all attested versions of the story, Meleager has killed his mother's brother(s); the audience could fill in the details. But since Meleager's wrath is introduced so abruptly, the audience will expect an explanation to follow. They are then in fact presented with a hazy background story (557–564) which *does* involve causes for anger, rape, revenge, lament, a wrathful hero fighting Apollo on behalf of a woman, and something to do with a mother (indeed, an indefinite cascade of mothers): but any attempt by a listener to plug Meleager's *cholos* into *this* background story is frustrated. The separateness of the two stories is broken down; they seem to be mingled somehow.

Because of this mingling between stories, line 565, the close of the digression, seems both to sum up the story of Kleopatra and to revert to Meleager's wrath: the *cholos* seems to refer both to the present and the past, to be the *cholos* of both the husband and the wife. Hers is on behalf of her mother, and his is directed against his mother. Both mothers hover in the immediate background. As with the "Trojan Horse" story examined in Chapter 1, a grieving female victim is planted at the heart of a story unfolding on many stages, stages which do not keep themselves apart. Note too the placement of Meleager and Kleopatra in the *thalamos*, the innermost part of the palace, within the city under siege.[53] This plays a kinesthetic role similar to that of the Horse.

---

[52] Marpessa's story was told in choral song, particularly women's or girls'. Cf. Bacchylides *Ode* 20: "Spartan maidens sang the song" of Idas and Marpessa. Willcock 1978–1984 (*ad Iliad* 9.557–564) notes that her story is akin to those comprising the Hesiodic *Catalogue of Women* and the catalogue of heroines in the *Odyssey* 11.235–327. The significance of this will become apparent in "Interlude 1" below. Even if the story was told in catalogue poetry, rather than the "lyric" modes of Bacchylides, it may have been danced out.

[53] There is something of a prototype here of the dynamics of the male and the female in the house in tragedy: "If tragedy … can be defined as the epistemological genre, which continually calls into question what we know and how we think we know it, it often does so by confronting the assumptions of rational thought with those psychological necessities that cannot be denied. … The house has many kinds of secrets that men do not know, and the challenge to male authority over it takes place on several levels—social, cognitive, and psychological. If men enter this domain, assuming their legitimate rights to its custody, only to meet with a welcome they had not foreseen, at the same time they also inevitably fail to lock up, to repress those powerful forces hidden in the recesses of the house. Quite the contrary: tragic process, for the most part conveyed through the catalyzing person and actions of the feminine, puts insistent pressure on

There is a masterful slippage at the end of the background story, when we finally are, it seems, exiting the story of Marpessa and entering once again into Meleager's chamber. For since the story ends, "crying because Apollo raped her" (564), one has to do a double-take in order to realize that the next phrase, "by her he lay down" (565) refers not to Apollo and his victim (whoever she is) but to Meleager and his wife Kleopatra. Again, Apollo and his victim are layered on top of Meleager and Kleopatra.

Equivocation in reference and time (though not so severe) occurs in other Homeric digressions,[54] and scholars assume confusion is a simple byproduct of an allusive style, rather than an effect the performer would strategically deploy.[55]

Against this considerable phalanx of scholarship I suggest that the compression here, along with the temporal and syntactic ambiguities, has a special motivation.[56] As we have begun to see, one effect of the ambiguous pronouns and temporal oscillation is for two poignant figures, Marpessa and Alkyone, to merge into the figure of Kleopatra. The strange merging of these three women into one body effectively animates her, placed as it is just before the line that begins with the pronoun indicating her. In the line "*her* Meleager lay down next to, digesting his spirit-paining anger" (565), all that we have just learned about her is now packed into "her" (τῇ), which is to say into the body that we

---

the façade of the masculine self in order to bring outside that which resides unacknowledged and unrecognized within..." (Zeitlin 1996:355–356).

54 Sachs (1933:24) in her classic account names the Meleager story and other Homeric digressions "Hintergrunderzählungen," "um ihrer nicht spannend erzählten, unplastischen Form." Stylistic features of these stories include "der Mangel an Einheit der Handlung, richtiger an Handlung überhaupt, die nicht-szenische Anordnung, das seltsame zeitliche Hinundherspringen, Umkehrung der zeitlichen Folge, der Mangel an kontinuierlichem Zusammenhang, an Zentriertheit und Plastik; Kürze, Unverhältnismässigkeit, (die nicht affektiv bedingt ist, wie etwa in dem Bericht Achills an Thetis im A 365ff.); Unverständlichkeit, 'abrupte Schlüsse'." She compares these stories to Pindaric poetry; intriguingly, she singles out the "subjective" quality they share with Pindar, as opposed to the "objective" quality of epic—despite their "unexciting" narration and their failure to achieve a "three-dimensional form." The kinship between Homeric passages and lyric is elucidated by Friedrich (2001), who focuses not on digressions but rather on sections of "phonic density" manifesting the possession of the poet by a character in "Lyric Epiphany." Kakridis (1949:11n1) notes that in *paradeigmata* "the stages of the story are told not in chronological order but according to the importance they have for the narrator" but does not speak of the confusion that often results. Cf. Kirk 1962:164–169.

55 If anything is aesthetically motivated, according to scholarly accounting, it is expansion, not compression (Austin 1966): scenes or speeches are expanded in order to emphasize that what is at stake in the scene is significant.

56 The allusion here is more compressed than the allusions to the story of Thetis, traced by Slatkin (1991), but it has a similar resonant quality; both, one might say, form, or are arranged so as to seem to form, fonts for the *Iliad*'s plot, as well as its tragic quality. Dué (2002:4) writes of the "strikingly evocative" compression in the case of Briseis' story, compression that many readers find frustrating. Scodel (2002:127) writes: "compression can itself be a creative force."

picture lying next to Meleager. The line now has the effect of: "*that* is precisely the woman in our hero's [embodied by the performer?] force-field. He is down; what will raise him up?" Thus as he is digesting his *cholos* with his mother, he is lying next to a woman who is not merely an aid to *cholos* digestion (although there may be some sense of funneling off tensions from *cholos* into sex), but a person with a background and a foreground herself. When he first lies down by her in line 556, she is merely his wife. She then acquires a life, a potential life, by means of the backstory: an inner life.[57] She is a felt presence as the story proceeds, as her mother is a felt presence within Kleopatra's mind. Thus does the solo bard populate his scenario with multiple presences.

The memory of rape informs her speech at the end of the Meleager story, when she lists the horrors that happen to a fallen city, the last of which is the rape of its women. The dramatic outburst, which finally rouses Meleager, is "fueled" by the memories of the rape of Marpessa: the story of Marpessa was inside her *phrēn* "all along." (Recall Eris behind Agamemnon, and the widow in "Trojan Horse.") Kleopatra, lying beside Meleager, acts as a container of the fuel that will spur her to speak and her husband to emerge.

This does *not* mean that the 'focalizer'[58] of this digression is Kleopatra alone.[59] We suggested earlier that Marpessa is "lovely-ankled" because she is abducted from the dance. So too fair-waisted Kleopatra in bed; indeed, she is ἐΰζωνος παράκοιτις (590).[60] The epithet makes her present as being in bed, just as with Iphis later in this book in bed with Patroklos (9.667; cf. 366). The epithet, combined with other elements, subtly puts the narrator-performer—Phoenix or the performer or both—behind the eyes and hands of Meleager, somewhat as he entered into the body/soul of Diomedes, or Menelaos, in the last chapter's examples. The erotic element re-funnels the energies of the speaker *toward* the woman lying in bed, just as Meleager's *cholos* is being re-channeled. Later the energy of the speech will be coming *out of* her, when she speaks. Thus the audience can experience the Marpessa digression as focalized through Meleager; it is as though his nearness to Kleopatra prompts the recall of everything lying in

---

57 This is subtly accentuated by the digression being framed by the mother's *curse*, her invocation of underworld forces. Kleopatra too is haunted.

58 This clinical word prunes the lively sense I am trying to get at.

59 If the performer in *any* way embodies the motion of Meleager lying down or reaching for his wife (by simply looking aside or closing his eyes; I don't suggest he actually lie down!), or has been embodying Meleager before the digression, the audience may more fully experience the digression *as the effect of* Meleager's drawing near her.

60 See Lowenstam (1993:23) on "wife" epithets. ἐΰζωνος in his chart is unique, but Lowenstam does not count γυνή as one of his "wife" words. The epithet seems to lend an erotic sense elsewhere (*Iliad* 23.760), and it is used of women as objects of longing (*Iliad* 1.429, Achilles for Briseis; *Aspis* 31) or as abducted into (potentially sexual) slavery.

her background.[61] Meleager comes near his wife, out pours the digression from the narrator; Meleager is not remembering it himself.

The concentrated, violent eroticism of the passage—the way the rapacious Apollo usurps the place of Meleager in the bed via the juxtaposition of stories—adds to the sense that the closeness of Meleager to his wife has brought on this digression as a flood of memories. It is then more attractive to say that the memories, which one thinks will explain Meleager's wrath, but which end up being in the past of his wife, stem not from one or the other character but give body and direction to their intimacy. As with their *cholos*, so with their memories.

The lines enclosing the digression, about the couple lying down together (B / B′) are recalled when Kleopatra comes forth with her catalogue. The line that closes the digression was: "That is who he lay down next to (*par-katelekto*)." At the climax of the story, Kleopatra gives her catalogue of atrocities, her only action in the poem: καί οἱ κατέλεξεν ἅπαντα / κήδε' (lines 591–592). Her utterance thus closes another ring. This is no fluke: καταλέγω, lying-down and telling, is a pun epic makes use of elsewhere of couples talking in bed.[62] Here the combination of physical intimacy and the bursting forth of speech caps off the "ascending scale of affections."

So far, the interaction of themes between the innermost (Kleopatra/ Marpessa) and the proximate (Kleopatra/Meleager) stories, and particularly the manner in which they are nested, prompts the audience to link Meleager's *cholos* with some element in this story of Marpessa, and consequently produces a fusion between the *phrenes* of husband and wife. But there is a like intimacy between Marpessa's story and the personal history of the speaker, Phoenix, himself. So far, the various levels, mergings, redirections, and usurpings have taken place entirely "within" the story-world or on the level of syntax connecting storyworlds. Therefore, although we have seen many features coinciding with the Chapter 1 examples, we have not been speaking explicitly of how this prepares for and pivots out into the performance dimension.

---

[61] Again recall the digression's framing by the curse. The digression is dead material to be tapped, like a dead hero's anger or like Erinys. Cf. below, pages 229–230, on Hektor's touching the ship of Protesilaos.

[62] At *Odyssey* 12.34–35, Circe lies down next to Odysseus, προσέλεκτο, and "asks him about each thing." The hero dutifully lays it all down for her in order (κατὰ μοῖραν κατέλεξα). Helen regales his son with a similar fraught incident of disrobing and cataloguing with Odysseus at *Odyssey* 4.251–256. At *Odyssey* 23.225, Penelope says to Odysseus, νῦν δ', ἐπεὶ ἤδη σήματ' ἀριφραδέα κατέλεξας / εὐνῆς ἡμετέρης, τὴν οὐ βροτὸς ἄλλος ὀπώπει .... Even when it is not this suggestive, extreme disclosure is in the offing: cf. *Odyssey* 15.393–394 (Eumaeus beginning his tale): οὐδέ τί σε χρή, πρὶν ὥρη, καταλέχθαι· ἀνίη καὶ πολὺς ὕπνος, on which see Chapter 4. Is this wordplay at work in the title, of contested date, of the *Catalogue of Women*—the laying out of the lying down of women with gods?

Marpessa and Phoenix

Though we have only sketched Marpessa's story, the resemblance to the story Phoenix has just told about his own youth is manifest.[63] In both, a cruel father prevents his child from having children. In both, that child is kept against his/her will at home with that father until he/she makes a dramatic escape.

As I mentioned, this "house arrest" of Phoenix has proven particularly baffling.[64] It is inexplicable why his relatives restrain Phoenix (464–473) for ten days until he finally breaks out and finds refuge with Peleus. This imprisonment receives a lavish description with only a very loose connection to the story's immediate goals:[65] his relatives, feasting away like Penelope's suitors, guarded him in shifts, keeping the fire burning for nine days. Why are they keeping him there? Indeed, if one is given to psychological realism, one could come up with reasons, but because Phoenix's imprisonment has seemed bizarre to so many, it is tempting to think that Marpessa's imprisonment by her insane father, preventing her marrying and producing children, does not simply echo Phoenix's house arrest, it may even shape it.

A tantalizing fragment of Bacchylides (fr. 20a Maehler) may strengthen this connection between Phoenix and Marpessa. In that poem, a daughter is apparently cursing her father (lines 7–10). A few lines later, Bacchylides is recounting the familiar story of Marpessa. While Snell and Maehler decipher the fragment otherwise,[66] it may be that Marpessa in some version of the story curses her father for keeping her unmarried and childless into old age. We would need the full text of this badly fragmented poem to interpret it properly, but the infamous lines about Phoenix's patricidal impulse may be one more common thread between Phoenix and Marpessa.[67] The Marpessa story as told by Bacchylides should be taken into account in this textual crux.[68]

---

[63] Scholars have noticed how Phoenix's autobiography resonates with the Meleager story (Heubeck 1984; Scodel 1982b), but not how it may relate to the Marpessa digression. Though few would agree with Leaf 1900–1902:1.412 (*ad Iliad* 9.557) that it "grievously interferes with the narrative," some find it barely or vaguely appropriate (Jensen 2002; Rosner 1976).

[64] E.g. Willcock 1978–1984 *ad* 9.445–477; Hainsworth 1993 *ad* 9.447–477; Edwards 1987a:225; Carpenter 1946:171; see S. West 2001:6–7. For Carpenter (p. 172) this detail brings Phoenix into the orbit of the Salmoxis story.

[65] Edwards 1987a:225.

[66] Snell 1952 and Maehler 2004 suggest that the first few lines refer to a different father/daughter pair, perhaps real-life acquaintances of Bacchylides, but the fragment is in such a lacunose state that this is sheer speculation.

[67] Most editors (following Wolf) insert those lines in Book 9 as lines 458–461, just after Amyntor utters his curse and Hades and Persephone fulfill it. But the lines are in fact found only in Plutarch, who states that Aristarchus excised them "φοβηθείς." Some modern editors follow Aristarchus in doing so: for example, Monro omits them from his OCT.

[68] S. West (2001:11) suggests that the patricide lines could come from one of the Cyclic epics, the *Aethiopis* being perhaps more likely than the *Cypria*, since it recounted the funeral of Achilles, in

One could think of other pre-Homeric versions of the Phoenix story that would make sense of the imprisonment. Stephanie West, for example, provides an account as part of her theory that Phoenix has been castrated.[69] While the castration idea itself is compelling,[70] as an explanation of the house arrest it is less convincing. Another idea is that Phoenix is imprisoned in order that his story parallel Meleager's isolation. Since Meleager's withdrawal is itself probably inspired by Achilles', one could appeal directly to Achilles' self-confinement without reference to Meleager at all, and could refer Phoenix's 'supplication' by his kin to the present supplication of Achilles.[71] Considering the complex interrelations among the Marpessa, Phoenix, Meleager, and Achilles stories, it is best to follow Lang[72] who, apropos of another cycle of background myths, describes "a process of reverberation between inherited material influencing the *Iliad* narrative and also the *Iliad* narrative influencing inherited material. Imitation and innovation go hand in hand on a two-way street."

In any case, the Marpessa and Phoenix stories resonate with one another and provide a foundation for a building topos of confinement and eruption/ outburst. Phoenix recalls how he was, in his youth, confined by his father, and then tells the story of a self-confined man who is accompanied by a wife whose mother was confined by her father. The audience of this speech is Achilles, who is in self-confinement: the performance takes place in the space of that confinement, and is meant, ostensibly, to spur its audience *out* of it.[73]

Finally, and perhaps most strikingly, Phoenix's pathetic fears of abandonment in old age echo the choice of Marpessa, marrying the mortal Idas lest she be abandoned in old age by a god, Apollo. His plea to Achilles is, at its root, a plea that he not abandon him, aged as he is. Phoenix seems to be reaching as he speaks for stories about this fear deep in his heart. In the course of recounting the story of "a hero who could be persuaded," Phoenix veers off to the story of the hero's mother-in-law, to whom he is drawn by shared traumas and fears. At the same time, this story sets up Kleopatra's speech expressing her fear of rape.

---

which episode Quintus of Smyrna included Phoenix's autobiographical material.

[69] S. West (2001:12): "If the purposes of Amyntor's friends and relations (464–477) seem unclear, that might correspond to some uncertainty as to whether Phoenix should be regarded as an accident victim or as a continuing threat to his father's welfare. In the immediate aftermath of his injury sympathy might be divided, but while he recovers a decision about his future can be postponed, and (as Penelope's suitors knew) feasting is a good way to pass the time (and wine, for the injured man, the best available painkiller)."

[70] A student in my *Iliad* seminar, Peter Heraty, independently offered this interpretation.

[71] Thus Ebel 1972:87–88.

[72] Lang 1983:140.

[73] Even apart from Marpessa, these stories form four interlaced inner and outer stories: the memories of Phoenix told in the tent of Achilles, with his own unfolding drama, and the memories of Kleopatra, which come to a head in the chamber of the tortured Meleager.

Alkyone

Now we turn from Kleopatra's mother to the other figure in her background, recalled in her nickname "Alkyone." The *Iliad* scholia rightly suggest that this name enters the poem via the Alkyone (daughter of Aiolos) who is the wife of Keux.[74] This Alkyone, like Marpessa, appears at the center of at least two stories of tragic eros, in both of which she is changed into the *alkyōn*, a mythical bird better known to us as the halcyon of "halcyon days." In terms of early sources, one entire poem that would have been of great help, the Hesiodic *Wedding of Keux*, is lost.[75] Other early sources leave better traces. A relatively new papyrus fragment[76] states that the *Catalogue of Women* told the sad tale of Alkyone and Keux, and fragments of this tale are extant (Hesiod fr. 16 and possibly 19 M-W):

Ἀλκυόνην τὴν Αἰόλου ἔγημε Κή[ϋξ ὁ Φωσφό]ρου τοῦ ἀστέρος υἱός. ἄμφω δ' ἦσα[ν ὑπερή]φα[νοι, ἀλ]λήλων δ' ἐρασθέντες ἡ [μὲν .].α̣.[.]κ̣[.] ρυα[.....] Δία κα[λ]εῖ, <ὁ δὲ> αὐτὴν Ἥραν προσηγό[ρε]υεν· ἐφ' [ὧι ὀργι] σθεὶ[ς] ὁ Ζεὺς μετεμόρφωσεν ἀμφοτέρους [εἰς ὄρ]νε[α,] ὡς Ἡσίοδος ἐν Γυναικῶν καταλόγωι.

Keux son of the star [Phosphor]os married Alkyone daughter of Aiolos. Both were [*hypere*]*pha*[*noi*], and being so in love with one [an]other she ... called ... Zeus, [and he] used to address her as Hera.[77] At this Zeus getting angry changed them both into birds, as Hesiod in the catalogue of women.

Hesiod fr. 10d M-W

In this version,[78] she and Keux compare themselves to Zeus and Hera, explicitly because they are so in the thrall of eros; they are changed into birds as a *punishment*. The punishment fits the crime of over-happy, arrogating love: Ζεὺς

---

[74] See also Grossardt 2001:38n129; Hainsworth 1993:136 *ad* 9.563.

[75] Merkelbach and West (1965) present what little can be gleaned of the contents of this poem. It is known to have contained riddles, perhaps told as entertainment at the wedding feast. Merkelbach and West propose that the poem's focus was actually Herakles, adducing the Hesiodic *Shield*, which is only partly about a shield.

[76] Hesiod fr. 10d M-W=Anon. P. Michigan inv. 1447 ii 14–19, ed. Renner. See also fr. 100a, 83–98.

[77] Numerous commentators are struck by the iterative καλέεσκον in the phrase πατὴρ καὶ πότνια μήτηρ / Ἀλκυόνην καλέεσκον ἐπώνυμον (9.561–562). Could it be an echo of the habitual naming in the story of the legendary figure, Alkyone?

[78] Cf. Hesiod fr. 15 M-W (test. from Julian on Hesiod); Apollodorus I.vii.3–4; Σ D *Iliad* 9.562. The *Iliad* here shows familiarity with the mournful quality of the *alkyōn*, and the *Odyssey* with the *kēux* (15.478). On the relation between Alkyone/Keux and Penelope/Odysseus, see Levaniouk 1999. We return to this story in Chapter 4.

δὲ ἀγανακτήσας μετέβαλεν αὐτοὺς εἰς ὄρνεα <u>χωρὶς ἀλλήλων βιοῦντα</u> (Σ *Iliad* 9.562), "Zeus, becoming angry, changed them into birds <u>living apart from one another.</u>"

The other principal variation[79] rearranges the same elements. Keux dies in a shipwreck, and the gods turn Alkyone into a bird out of *compassion* for her unbearable grief. Unfortunately, only Ovid has left us a fully developed example (*Metamorphoses* 11.410–748).[80] His version is extremely baroque; not only does Juno arrange for Morpheus to appear to Alcyone in the form of the dead Ceyx to tell her the news of her husband's death, but when Alcyone walks to the sea in despair, the corpse itself appears on the horizon. At last Alcyone throws herself into the sea and attempts to kiss the corpse with what is now her "hard beak."

Though we have access to a fuller example of this storyline only through Ovid, the shipwreck version is already alluded to by Euripides:

ὄρνις ἃ παρὰ πετρίνας
πόντου δειράδας ἀλκυὼν
ἔλεγον οἶτον ἀείδεις,
εὐξύνετον ξυνετοῖς βοάν,
ὅτι πόσιν κελαδεῖς ἀεὶ μολπαῖς,
ἐγώ σοι παραβάλλομαι
θρήνους, ἄπτερος ὄρνις ...

Bird, you who along the rocky
ridges of the sea, halcyon,
sing your doom as a lament,
a cry easily intelligible to the intelligent,
that you croon to your husband in song for all time,
I set beside you
laments, I a wingless bird...

Iphigenia in Tauris 1089–1095

Note that here she is continually mourning her husband (rather than her eggs). Evidently both versions were circulating by the time of the *Odyssey*.[81]

---

[79] Euripides *Iphigenia in Tauris* 1089–1093; Ovid *Metamorphoses* 11.410 –748; Lucian *Halcyon*; Hyginus fab. 65; Σ Aristophanes *Birds* 250.

[80] As Levaniouk (1999:121) notes, the central elements in Ovid's version are paralleled in Lucian's *Halcyon*.

[81] I refer again to Levaniouk 1999; for more on Keux in the *Odyssey* see below, Chapter 4, "Eumaeus' Autobiography."

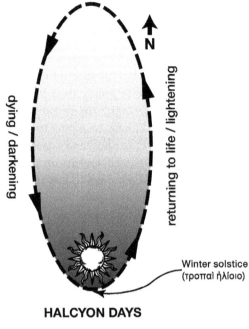

HALCYON DAYS

Figure 3

The theme of the halcyon days, the fourteen[82] days straddling the winter solstice, when winter storms cease in order to ensure the safe brooding of the *alkyōn* on her nest (see Figure 3), is first attested in Simonides (508).[83] Any Greek at any period would be familiar with the halcyon days. While the motif of the halcyon days is better attested than a full-fledged story of Alkyone and Keux, the very notion of the halcyon days implies the broader story.

---

[82] Seven in Ovid and other sources.

[83] Thompson 1936 s.v. Ἀλκυών connects the halcyon days to the Pleiades, one of whom is named Alkyone. He points to a gem and coins that show a bird sitting on a kneeling bull, which he proposes represent the Pleiades, next to Taurus. Thus both Alkyones, the Pleiad and the wife of Keux, are birds. (Cf. *peleiades*, doves.) Aristotle too seems to connect the halcyon days at solstice with the Pleiades in the sky (*History of Animals* 542b). The Pleiades are crucial calendrical markers for the Greeks (Hesiod *Works and Days* 383–387) and for cultures all over the world. Their heliacal and cosmical risings and settings do not coincide with the solstice circa 750 BCE. But there may have been a correspondence much earlier, when the myth came about; that is Thompson's argument. But that does not explain why Aristotle still associates the solstice with the Pleiades. Somewhere in the Cyclic poems (West [2003:150] suggests the *Sack of Ilion*, Bernabé the *Titanomachy*) a connection was drawn between the Pleiades and the sack of a city: the Pleiad Elektra, refusing to watch the sack of Troy, left her place in the sky, making the Pleiads six instead of seven (Σ D *Iliad* 18.486a).

Finally, in some versions Keux appears as the bird κηρύλος, who is thought of as the male counterpart of the *alkyōn*, and *supported by her in his old age.*[84] That idea of support in old age contradicts the version in which the two birds will live in separate habitats.

The myth of the halcyon days surrounding the winter solstice is only alluded to here. No doubt at this point you, dear reader, are skeptical about how much significance such an allusion can bear.[85] Aside from thematic issues I discuss in a moment, a first item to note is the goodness of fit between the halcyon days and ring composition. The unexpected fertility in the midst of death, coinciding with the stopping of the sun before its return journey, is uniquely fitted to the center of a ring composition, which often features flashes of vivid memories from the past, or epiphanic moments. In the case of Nestor's speech before the chariot race in Book 23, the center (formed by a turning-point that is also a tomb) is a point of animation between the less lively first half and a more lively second.[86]

Eros and Mortality

Alkyone's and Marpessa's stories work in counterpoint: each forges a connection between eros and mortality. In Marpessa's case, this theme may already be sounded in the story of her imprisoned youth: Marpessa's father keeps her to himself, perhaps thereby avoiding the idea of his own death. But it becomes more pointed in her dealings with the god and the mortal who carry her off. The Alkyone-Keux and the Marpessa-Idas stories are mirror images: Marpessa chooses the mortal husband because he will support her in old age; in the Keux-Alkyone story, it is the elderly female who supports the male. This makes it more plausible that the poet uses these stories because of their relation to Phoenix's own fears.

As for the relationship of these two women's stories in the far background to the figure in the mid-ground, Kleopatra, no one story of Marpessa or of Alkyone matches the situation of Kleopatra. Rather, the audience's expectations for Kleopatra are orchestrated by the figures set in her background, from which her actions are bodied forth.[87] The love of Alkyone and Keux makes them want to call one another Zeus and Hera: a profoundly bad idea. Marpessa's choice of a mortal husband, in its rare sobriety, is the background against which Kleopatra

---

[84] Alkman 26; Antigonus of Carystus *Historiae Mirabiles* 23 (27); Aelian *On the Nature of Animals* 7.17; Suda s.v. κηρύλος.

[85] On the compressed use of solar bird myths, including the halcyon, in *Odyssey* 19, see once again Levaniouk 1999 and 2011: ch. 17.

[86] I return to the season of the halcyon days below, Interlude 1. Further evidence that this allusion can bear all of the weight I am putting on it is presented in Chapter 4; cf. Levaniouk 2011.

[87] Kleopatra's character in the *Iliad* is almost an amalgam of these figures.

chooses much more poignantly for, in effect, her husband to die *now*.[88] Meleager, responding to his wife's fears of rape, is preceded in a relatively transparent way by Idas, who takes up arms against a raping god: the same god who will (in some versions) kill Meleager, as well as Achilles and Patroklos. Kleopatra is rather given a set of stories compressed in her *phrēn*, and in the audience's as well, as they wonder what it is that will arouse Meleager from his bed.

The rich layering of characters and actions in the Meleager story includes, so far, the narrator's (Phoenix's) past and the semi-legendary but contemporaneous Meleager story; a story deep in the memory of a character from that story (Kleopatra) about her god-raped mother (Marpessa); and another bare allusion to the mythical Alkyone/Halcyon.[89] Thus we have a heroic story in which gods are involved but do not appear, a story in which gods rape humans, and a story in which humans challenge gods and are transformed into animals. But there is another level of characters at work: Hades and Persephone (with their henchwoman Erinys). These characters' stories, like Persephone's, are not told, but they are the ones that will bring the layering effect to full fruition in performance. Curses occur on many levels of the story and, as we shall see, blend with their benign counterparts, supplications. Phoenix's mother supplicates him to sleep with the concubine. Phoenix's father Amyntor calls on the Erinyes (455–456), but it is Hades and Persephone who fulfill the curse (457). Meleager's mother calls on Hades and Persephone (569) and it is the Erinys who hears (572).

Considering the themes of the speech, it is not insignificant that Hades and Persephone are another rape couple—an intergenerational one, causing intrafamily strife like that in Phoenix's family and Marpessa's—who are called upon from their containment in the underworld to exert their powers. Their containment in Hades resembles Marpessa's imprisonment in her own home before her abduction, and then too Apollo's rape of Marpessa echoes Hades' rape of Persephone.[90] The wrath of a mother that follows upon Persephone's rape, the wrath of Demeter, finds a correspondence in the wrath of Phoenix's mother against her husband. Then too the wrath of Althaia against her son on behalf of her brother reverses the terms of Demeter's wrath, against her brother on behalf of her daughter. This affinity of Hades and Persephone (and Demeter) to

---

[88] Contrast Petzold (1976:156–159), who believes the fact that Kleopatra is sending Meleager to his death undermines the notion of the "ascending scale of affections" altogether.

[89] The contrast between the mythical (direct influence of gods) and the less mythical stories figures into Petzold's (1976) quasi-Hegelian attempt to see the beginnings of historical thinking in the Meleager story. That aside, it is true that the stories are of three different types, moving out toward greater involvement of the gods and magic.

[90] As for Idas' abduction of Marpessa, in at least one version he is her great-uncle, and the chariot-abduction image is in play as with Hades and Persephone.

the 'present' cast of characters (as distinct from their affinity to the addressee, Achilles)[91] is moreover emphasized by the way Phoenix orders his tale.

Finally, we note that the myth of Demeter and Persephone is, like the Alkyon, a myth of the changing seasons and the return of fertility.

The abduction of Persephone leaves her as a conjurable force in the underworld; likewise with the tribulations of the Calydonians, who, as dead characters, are invoked by Phoenix. From this perspective, the story lays itself out on three levels: Phoenix, on the top, evokes the stories of Kleopatra and Meleager, and his own past, in an effort to sway Achilles. Within each of those two stories in turn, characters invoke Hades and Persephone. Once Phoenix enters into the Meleager story, he can tap into the deeper powers: Hades and Persephone, but also Marpessa and Euenos, Idas, and the sinister figure of Apollo.

The poet layers the stories such that characters within one level can make magical contact with characters in the level beneath them, through memory or invocation.[92] Phoenix needs to enter fully into the Meleager story, to "enter the soul of Meleager" himself like a bard, to gain access to the body and mind of Kleopatra and the stories and figures one level down. Like the *Iliad* opening or "Trojan Horse," one may imagine this as a series of Russian dolls contained within the bard. In that there are entire worlds involved rather than figures, it also has a "snakes and ladders" schema with a less transparent connection to presence or performance than the *Iliad* opening's "dolls." But there is a connection between nesting of worlds and the nesting of stories within a *phrēn* like a bomb waiting to explode in speech. The upshot of all of this is the eruption of performance. But the connection between physical and mental containment is also drawn, as though in preparation, on the level of imagery.

Images of Containment and Bursting Out

The very compression of the Marpessa story contributes to its startling disruption of the story of Meleager. A whole world is glimpsed and suppressed again for an unstated reason. Since Kleopatra is lying next to Meleager even before the train of supplicants arrives, the audience knows her story has something

---

[91] A. Lord (2000: Ch. 9, esp. 186): "The rape of Persephone in all its forms as a fertility myth underlies all epic tales of this sort [bride-stealing and rescue]"; M. L. Lord 1967; Nagy 1979:80, 84–85. Here we see the collapse of all the levels of story.

[92] An amphora by Exekias (Vatican 344) shows a depth-of-field layering where figures arranged left-to-right in a modified ring-composition occupy different planes; this is shown by the way they make contact with one another (closer versus further hand, etc.). See Mackay, Harrison, and Masters (1999:138–139).

to do with what will send him out. The allusiveness of the story seeds it as an unsolved riddle in the mind of the audience.

The compression of the story on the rhetorical register corresponds to a series of images of containment and emergence in *Iliad* 9, centered on Achilles' withdrawal from battle and the containment of his *thumos*. Within Phoenix's speech itself, there were the various breakouts from physical structures, Phoenix's, Marpessa's, Meleager's, and, prospectively, Achilles'. But Book 9 is full of such images. In some cases they make concrete the major themes of the Book, such as the attempt to spur Achilles out of his tent, and Achilles' annoyance with Odysseus lying and "hiding things in his *phrēn*." In others, they are more arbitrary; these images shape the action of Book 9 into that of containment and emergence.[93] They set the stage for the emergences that take place within the body of the performer and the space of performance by insistently ringing changes on the theme of eruption.[94]

The Achaeans have two problems, the advance of the Trojans and the withdrawal of Achilles. Hektor is threatening to break through the wall and "fall upon" and set fire to the ships. The Achaeans are unable to *contain* the Trojans (234); not even, says Achilles, with the wall and the trench that they have built in his absence will they hold back (ἴσχειν, initial position) the force of Hektor (348–353).

The problem of Achilles is his bodily withdrawal into his tent, but also within that body his pent-up *cholos*, which he is digesting (4.513), just as Meleager digests his (9.565). A series of images of this and other emotions prepares for the climax of Phoenix's speech, in keeping with the Greek conception of emotions as liquids within containers in the body.[95] Emotions are only some of the bodily fluids employed: recall the primal image of Achilles burping up wine on Phoenix's lap (9.491, ἀποβλύζων). He has assumed the care of Achilles' bilious and other eruptions, urging him, "Tame your great *thumos*" (496). Odysseus claims Peleus had told Achilles to contain his *thumos* in his chest (256).

A third cluster of images surrounds Agamemnon's hoarding of loot and the piles of treasure being offered to Achilles. Nestor points out that Agamemnon's tents are "full of wine," a striking image (71), and that Agamemnon still holds the *geras* of Achilles (111). Achilles pushes this hoarding imagery into hyperbole when, with Odysseus' catalogue of offerings hovering, awkwardly extravagant, in the air, he responds that Agamemnon would not persuade his *thumos* even if

---

[93] Cf. Goldhill 1984 on the use of ἐκ in the *Oedipus Tyrannus*.

[94] As usual, no specific "stage directions" need be assumed. The imagery works by constructing the performer as preoccupied by the theme and image, or simply by focusing the audience's mind upon it. In performed poetry, nothing is simply textual. Gradually, however, the various containers are more concretely instantiated in the space around the performer.

[95] On the spatial importance of these ideas in tragedy, see Padel 1992 and 1995.

he offered as much as Orchomenos holds, or "Thebes, where the most posses-sions lie in its halls, Thebes which is hundred-gated, and two hundred men march out of each with horses and chariots, not even if he should give as much as the sand and the dust ..." (381–384). After a few more thoughts Achilles tucks back into the image with relish:

οὐ γὰρ ἐμοὶ ψυχῆς ἀντάξιον οὐδ' ὅσα φασὶν
Ἴλιον ἐκτῆσθαι εὖ ναιόμενον πτολίεθρον
τὸ πρὶν ἐπ' εἰρήνης, πρὶν ἐλθεῖν υἷας Ἀχαιῶν,
οὐδ' ὅσα λάϊνος οὐδὸς ἀφήτορος ἐντὸς ἐέργει
405   Φοίβου Ἀπόλλωνος Πυθοῖ ἔνι πετρηέσσῃ.
ληϊστοὶ μὲν γάρ τε βόες καὶ ἴφια μῆλα,
κτητοὶ δὲ τρίποδές τε καὶ ἵππων ξανθὰ κάρηνα,
ἀνδρὸς δὲ ψυχὴ πάλιν ἐλθεῖν οὔτε λεϊστὴ
οὔθ' ἑλετή, ἐπεὶ ἄρ κεν ἀμείψεται ἕρκος ὀδόντων.

It does not compensate my life—as much as they say
Ilion possessed, well-seated citadel,
before, in peacetime—before the sons of Achaeans came,
not even as much as the stone threshold of the archer
Phoebus Apollo contains within, in rocky Pytho.
For the rustling are cattle and fat flocks,
for the getting are tripods and tawny heads of horses,
but as for a man, his life cannot be rustled back again
nor captured, once, look you, it's passed through the fence of teeth.

Iliad 9.401–409

Thus Achilles transforms the gates of Thebes into the fence of the teeth via the threshold of prophecy. No matter how many hordes of men stream out with horses they cannot balance the one soul pent up behind one's own teeth, he says, explaining to Odysseus that the world is not made up exclusively of loot.[96] This is one of several instances in Book 9 where a *physical, external* restraint and rupture is transformed into the confinement and eruption of *speech and emotion* (or, here, the soul itself).

Hundred-gated Thebes itself expands Achilles' famous complaint, releasing the flood of his reply to Odysseus: "I hate like the gates of Hades that man who hides one thing in his *phrēn* and utters another ..." (312–313). The gates of Hades are one-way trap doors. Likewise Odysseus' mouth. Souls escape the fence of the teeth to pass the gates that never open again; but so too do surprising words "escape the fence of teeth" (4.350). This layers the caginess of Odysseus onto the

---

[96] For the relation between performance and Odysseus counting embarrassing amounts of treasure as equal to a life, see Chapter 4.

hoarding of Agamemnon, and of Hades. Achilles for his part will not hold any words back but speak them all out (309).

Already at the opening of Book 9, a wind simile, these being normally sublime, abruptly ends with the sea vomiting seaweed up onto the beach where the Achaeans are in turmoil. A black wave pours (ἔχευεν, 7) seaweed onto the beach; the simile is meant to describe the divided *thumos* (8) of the Achaeans (cf. Achilles, "stop trying to σύγχει my *thumos*," 612). But they themselves are on the beach, so there is a slight sloshing between tenor and vehicle; the seaweed slops up into their midst to divulge their mucky *thumos* within. This image then flows into the following scene, when Agamemnon sheds (χέων, 14) a tear like a black-watered spring, which pours forth (χέει, 15) its dusky water.

The comic interplay continues. Diomedes conjures up the romantic image of the couple penetrating the city that Achilles will use later on. Let all the others sail away, he and Sthenelos will "find the limit" of Troy (48–49). This sublime metaphor is knocked down by Nestor. Diomedes, he says, you're brave, but "you haven't quite *reached the limit* of words" (56), as if to say, "take the rhetoric down a notch."[97]

Phoenix, we recall, "broke out" from his house arrest. I mentioned this above in conjunction with other escapes from domiciles; but this one intertwines architecture with body and passion:

> ἔνθ' ἐμοὶ οὐκέτι πάμπαν <u>ἐρητύετ'</u> ἐν φρεσὶ θυμὸς
> πατρὸς χωομένοιο κατὰ μέγαρα στρωφᾶσθαι
> ἦ μὲν πολλά ἔται καὶ ἀνεψιοὶ ἀμφὶς ἐόντες
> 465 αὐτοῦ λισσόμενοι <u>κατερήτυον ἐν μεγάροισι</u>

> There my *thumos* in my *phrenes* could no longer be completely
>   <u>constrained</u>
> to reel about the halls of my angry father.
> But my kinsmen and cousins surrounding me
> pleaded and tried to <u>restrain me in the halls</u>
>
> *Iliad* 9.462–465

With his *thumos* as the subject of ἐρητύετ', and ἐν φρεσὶ θυμὸς in between, the additional sense that it is no longer restrained in his *phrenes* is possible. In line 462, ἐν φρεσὶ θυμὸς appears to complete the sense of ἐρητύετ' such that line 463 only adds an additional sense. The *thumos* appears to be constrained both in the *phrenes* and in the halls. The above translation takes ἐρητύετ' with the infinitive as "was constrained to," a sense it has elsewhere in Homer: it would

---

[97] On the ethos here, see Martin 1989:24–25.

be the *thumos* that is no longer constrained to twist itself in the confines of the halls. But later epic authors use this verb with an infinitive in the sense "restrained *from*," which sits well with ἐν φρεσὶ θυμός: the *thumos* is no longer restrained, in the *phrenes*, from roaming the halls at large, where Phoenix is restrained in turn. Only in line 465 does the picture simplify into constraint within the halls: notice -ερήτυ- occupying the same metrical slot as in 462, and the replacement of the *phrenes* with the halls. Finally, he breaks out of the tightly set doors and leaps over the fence to freedom and a loving family.

This coalescence of walls and *phrenes* artfully gears up for the culmination of this series, on the brink of the Marpessa digression. Phoenix brings in Meleager as great-souled but persuadable. The *cholos* that enters Meleager (553) *swells in the chests* even of men whose *noos* is compact (πύκα, 554). Even here the *cholos* enters Meleager at the same time that he enters the city and retires to his chamber with his wife:

550 ὄφρα μὲν οὖν Μελέαγρος ἀρηΐφιλος πολέμιζε,
     τόφρα δὲ Κουρήτεσσι κακῶς ἦν, οὐδὲ δύναντο
     τείχεος ἔκτοσθεν μίμνειν πολέες περ ἐόντες·
     ἀλλ' ὅτε δὴ Μελέαγρον ἔδυ χόλος, ὅς τε καὶ ἄλλων
     οἰδάνει ἐν στήθεσσι νόον πύκα περ φρονεόντων,
555 ἤτοι ὃ μητρὶ φίλῃ Ἀλθαίῃ χωόμενος κῆρ
     κεῖτο παρὰ μνηστῇ ἀλόχῳ καλῇ Κλεοπάτρῃ ...

As long as Ares-loving Meleager was in the fight,
so long it went badly for the Kouretes, and they could not
stay <u>outside</u> the wall, many though they were.
But when *cholos* <u>entered</u> Meleager, which swells up too
in the chests of others, even those thinking with close mind,
yes, he, angered in his heart with his dear mother Althaia,
lay down next to his wedded wife, lovely Kleopatra ...

Iliad 9.550–556

(Note especially ἔκτοσθεν ... ἔδυ ...) The fact that his actual entrance into the city is assumed but elided helps draw the body and the city together.

At the end of the sequence of suppliants, the body and the chamber are superimposed: "not even thus could they persuade the *thumos* in his chest, until when finally the chamber was struck thickly (πύκ', cf. 554 πύκα), and onto the towers the Kouretes were climbing, and they were igniting the great city ..." (587–589). Just after this, Meleager's *thumos* springs up, in response to Kleopatra's speech. But in the passage just quoted the *thumos* seems to respond to the missiles themselves.

We said above that the Achaeans need to contain Achilles' *cholos* and his *thumos*. But it is actually not clear whether their mission is to rouse or to contain his *thumos*, and this ambivalence is manifested in Phoenix's speech. Phoenix tells Achilles, "tame your *thumos*" (δάμασον θυμὸν μέγαν, 496), echoing Peleus' parting advice to Achilles, as just recalled by Odysseus, σὺ δὲ μεγαλήτορα θυμὸν / ἴσχειν ἐν στήθεσσι (255–256). Meleager is supposedly one of the heroes of old who, although angry, are subject to persuasion and gifts (524–526), but when he finally does the right thing, it is because he "yields to his *thumos*" (598) which has been "roused" (595) by Kleopatra's catalogue of horrors. Phoenix has undone his own rhetoric. Achilles' *thumos* is not going to be roused against the Trojans, who have, he now sees, never (yet) done him any wrong. Nor will his *thumos* be roused by the sack of a city; the Achaean wall is only the façade of a city, and Achilles does not care about the Achaeans, whose mission he has come to despise. This very ambivalence about the Achaeans' situation—that one cannot appeal to Achilles to *defend* them—is mirrored in the description of the battle at Calydon just cited:

550 ὄφρα μὲν οὖν Μελέαγρος ἀρηΐφιλος πολέμιζε,
τόφρα δὲ Κουρήτεσσι κακῶς ἦν, οὐδὲ δύναντο
τείχεος ἔκτοσθεν μίμνειν πολέες περ ἐόντες ...

As long as Ares-loving Meleager was in the fight,
so long it went badly for the Kouretes, and they could not
stay outside the wall, many though they were.

Iliad 9.550–552

This makes no sense.[98] The Kouretes are attacking the Aetolians' city wall (Calydon), not the reverse. Remaining outside their wall is what is difficult for the Trojans (e.g., 21.608–609). The description of the Kouretes outside the walls of Calydon, together with all of the other slips and ambiguities, works toward a breaking-point of disorientation, *atopia*. Are the Kouretes attackers or defenders? What about the Achaeans?[99] Does the performer-as-Phoenix aim to restrain Achilles' *thumos*, or to unleash it? Where exactly are we, the audience, in this scenario, and whose side are we on?

---

[98] Hainsworth 1993:134 *ad* 9.552; Willcock 1978–1984:282 *ad* 9.550–552: "Whose wall were the Kouretes unable to stay outside of? They are certainly attacking Kalydon in Phoenix's story ... Does 552 mean that they were previously unable to sustain their position outside the walls of *that* city? ... It seems most likely that the usual story had Meleagros drive the Kouretes within the walls of their own city (so at least Bacchylides V 150); and that Homer had introduced (invented) the attack on Kalydon in order to get the parallel with Achilleus' and the Greeks' present situation. In consequence, he now has two cities successively besieged—a strangely mobile war in Aitolia." Oehler (1925:14–15) proposed that the situation has simply switched in order to better reflect Achilles; he is followed by Willcock and Hainsworth.

[99] Cf. Chapter 3 below on the status of Achilles' tent as a "home."

This thoroughgoing interplay between physical constraint and the constraint of speech and emotion, between the boundary of a wall and that of the body, primes the audience for another kind of interplay, that between theme and performance, through the body of the performer.

Cursing/*Transfert du mal*

The act of cursing, of invoking powers normally contained within the underworld, is one image of containment and eruption that lends itself particularly well to gestures. But, I repeat, the performer need not use any particular gesture to bring the act of cursing into the realm of presence. This emergence of the curse into the space of performance is but the end of a process begun on the level of poetics.

On the simplest level of theme, Hades and Persephone, along with Erinys, are literally otherworldly forces wreaking havoc on the earth. They are, one might say, uncanny. But as Freud said, ghosts are almost never uncanny in literature, just as talking animals are completely normal in fairy tales. The most "Erinys" can do in narrative, or poetics, is to denote an effect or experience that, in real life, would be terrifying. Here is one instance where the literary/poetic and the performative uncanny is built upon a straightforwardly uncanny thematic base.

Althaia thrashes the ground to curse her son, kneeling and weeping:

565 τῇ ὅ γε παρκατέλεκτο χόλον θυμαλγέα πέσσων
ἐξ ἀρέων μητρὸς κεχολωμένος, ἥ ῥα θεοῖσι
πόλλ᾽ ἀχέουσ᾽ ἠρᾶτο κασιγνήτοιο φόνοιο,
πολλὰ δὲ καὶ γαῖαν πολυφόρβην χερσὶν ἀλοία
κικλήσκους᾽ Ἀΐδην καὶ ἐπαινὴν Περσεφόνειαν
570 πρόχνυ καθεζομένη, δεύοντο δὲ δάκρυσι κόλποι,
παιδὶ δόμεν θάνατον ...

by her, he lay down, digesting his heart-rending *cholos*.
filled with *cholos* from the curses of his mother, who (you see) to the
gods
many times prayed, in grief at the murder of her brother,
many times thrashed the much-nurturing earth with her hands,
invoking Hades and dread Persephone
sitting and kneeling, and her breasts were wet with tears,
to give her child death—

Iliad 9.565–571

Althaia's curse, directed toward Hades and Persephone, is immediately (note the mid-verse shift in 571) heard (atopically) down in Erebos by Air-Stalking Erinys. Erinys merely "hears":

> τῆς δ᾽ ἠεροφοῖτις Ἐρινὺς
> ἔκλυεν ἐξ Ἐρέβεσφιν ἀμείλιχον ἦτορ ἔχουσα.
> 573 τῶν δὲ τάχ᾽ ἀμφὶ πύλας ὅμαδος καὶ δοῦπος ὀρώρει
> πύργων βαλλομένων· τὸν δὲ λίσσοντο γέροντες ...

> and Erinys who treads the air
> heard her out of Erebos with her unyielding heart.[100]
> of/from these (?) at once about the gates a roar and boom arose
> of the towers being struck: and him the old men were supplicating ...
> *Iliad* 9.571–574

But something strange happens. The ὅμαδος and δοῦπος that immediately (τάχ᾽) arise (ὀρώρει) around the gates spring from an ambiguous plural source; the towers are being hit (574), we are not told by whom. The way the narrative unfolds, the pounding on the doors in 573 seems to emanate from Erinys in Erebos, no matter how logically it "must" be the enemy warriors' missiles.

The mysterious slide is effected via another ambiguous pronoun, τῶν δέ in 573. The scholarly compulsion to disambiguate continues. Leaf steps in with guidance: the τῶν δέ refers to "the Aitolians. We suddenly return to the main incident, the siege of Kalydon." Indeed; it is more disorienting than any other shift in Homer; the half-line shift from Scheria to Ithaka in the *Odyssey*[101] is sudden enough, but clearer than this. The plural τῶν cannot refer to Erinys, her heart, or Erebos. But ready to hand are the curses and thrashings of the mother, which are not only plural but emphatically so, with repeated line-initial πολλά in 567–568. To over-translate: "from all of this (beating with its otherworldly response) arose the roaring and pounding at the gates—the towers being struck." Of course, if we are literal-minded, we are free to fill in the Aetolians. But the suddenness of the "return to the main incident" seems to be by design. The enemies at the gate are merely the agents of that Erinys with her unmollifiable heart, and her implacable avatar, Althaia. The theme of otherworldly emergence is instantiated on the level of syntax.

---

[100] Notice the thicket of paradoxes. He is digesting his *thumos*-paining *cholos*; she threshes the fodder-rich earth, preventing it from putting forth its fodder so that one could thresh it. Her breasts are wet (δεύοντο), with tears instead of milk which could nurture her son, then "to give her son"—not milk/life (cf. δεύω of milk at 2.471 and 16.643) but death. Erinys who "stalks the air" hears her pleas directed underground. Erinys hears her pleas although she has an unyielding heart.

[101] 13.187. On this and other "abrupt, large-scale shifts of scene," see Peradotto 1990:81. Cf. in Chapter 1 above, "Noemon, son of Phronios."

This beating on the gates then slides over seamlessly into the old men and then the catalogue of others coming to supplicate Meleager. Here again (line 574) a half-line shift transforms the enemy's missiles into the supplications (which will end, in fact, in Meleager's death).

His father, the hapless Oineus, actually shakes the doors.

> πολλὰ δέ μιν λιτάνευε γέρων ἱππηλάτα Οἰνεὺς
> οὐδοῦ ἐπεμβεβαὼς ὑψηρεφέος θαλάμοιο
> σείων κολλητὰς σανίδας γουνούμενος υἱόν·
> πολλὰ δὲ τόν γε κασίγνηται καὶ πότνια μήτηρ
> 585 ἐλλίσσονθ'· ὃ δὲ μᾶλλον ἀναίνετο· πολλὰ δ' ἑταῖροι

> And many times the old man, horseman Oineus, supplicated him,
> mounting[102] the threshold of the high-roofed chamber
> shaking the close-joined doors, imploring his son [by his knees]:
> and many times his sisters and his queenly mother
> supplicated him, but he refused all the more; and again his friends ...
>
> *Iliad* 9.581–585

He supplicates his young son with a violent gesture,[103] and the line-initial πολλά recurs, echoing Althaia's cursing and beating the earth. Althaia herself, as scholars have noticed with dismay, is among the suppliants.[104] And it is her pounding that becomes the missiles that become the more metaphorical beating in which she takes part. The mother's beating uncannily becomes the enemy's pounding becomes the father's shaking, via the unseen (and unembodied) intervention of Erinys. Note how σείων κολλητὰς σανίδας recalls 573 ἀμφὶ πύλας, an otherwise puzzling detail.

Contributing to this uncanniness too is the repetition, or rehearsal, of the cursing outside this particular action sequence. Since Phoenix tells an "oddly

---

[102] οὐδοῦ ἐπεμβεβαὼς in conjunction with ἱππηλάτα may play on δίφρου ἐπεμβεβαὼς (*Shield of Herakles* 195, 324); see next note.

[103] The drink-aspect of his character (note his name) might manifest itself here. A skilled performer could pull it off without sinking into pointless bathos; the drunkenness fuels a full gestural emergence. (For play on a name involving wine, see *Iliad* 13.506–508 where Idomeneus "draws a draft" of Oinomaos' innards: ἤφυσ'.) This would not be the only Homeric example of such a thing: Bowie (2013:223) comments that Odysseus' "Cloak Story" "well characterises one who has been drinking"; see his comments on the entire passage (Bowie 2013:223–230).

[104] Émile Signol uses these dynamics in his painting *Meleager Taking Up Arms* (1830). Signol collapses the various time-frames: the suppliants are in Meleager's chamber, but he, though still deep in thought, is already armed and ready; Althaia, ostensibly one of the suppliants, lurks in the corner with a sinister glare, next to a barely visible firebrand (which is cut off in some reproductions of the painting).

similar"[105] story of parental supplication and curse from his own past, his return to these gestures produces the sense of returning to, and reenacting, the *same traumatic scene.*

The poet insists upon this repetition by how he situates all of these parental scenes: Phoenix's mother and then father, Phoenix as Achilles' foster father, and Meleager's mother and then father. All of these curse/supplication scenes emphasize the knees beyond the natural association of supplication with the knees. Phoenix's mother supplicates him grasping his knees (451). His father Amyntor does not get down on his knees, but curses Phoenix, praying that no son may sit on his knee. Phoenix again mentions knees when he recalls how Achilles would not go into the feast in the hall (compare 487 to 463, the angry Phoenix; the infant Achilles has taken Phoenix's place) "until I, Phoenix, had *seated you on my knees* and satisfied you with meat and holding the wine." Althaia kneels for her curse (570), and Oineus supplicates (γουνούμενος, 583) his son, not grasping his knees, but taking hold of the doors (doorposts?) in place of his son's legs. Then Althaia, back on stage, reprises her cursing role but shifts it to supplication (584–585).

The *transfert du mal* through the mother's thrashing to the enemy fire and the violent supplications, with only a vague sense that it is effected by the unseen and un-narrated agency of Erinys, instantiates the otherworldly force in a way that the description of such a force does not. It produces something like the uncanny. The very action, the very gesture, of cursing *is* what destroys Meleager, rather than causing it by invoking other forces.[106]

Embodying the Curse/Lament

This effect would be heightened in performance. The performer, engaged in speaking this consummately histrionic speech for quite a long time, embodies Phoenix no matter what he does. But in particular, by repeating or continuing the same gesture, in whatever way, the performer would bring the curse forward, from the various pasts of the story-world to the presently unfolding story-world and into the space of performance. Althaia's, and the performer's, ground-thrashing gesture and its noise can be continued, flipping immediately to another space: from Althaia's thrashing-space to the chamber of Meleager.

---

[105] Hainsworth 1993:137; cf. Bouvier 2002:343. Cf. Ebel 1972:94–95: "Althaia beating the ground and summoning the vengeance of the chthonic powers instantly recalls the father of Phoenix who 'called down his curses, and invoked against me the dreaded furies ...'"

[106] This resembles, in small within the story-world, what happens to Phoenix's replication of these gestures with Achilles (see below); rather than being narrated, they spill out to cause something "in the room." Yet saying this is already too simple, because Meleager's Calydon and Achilles' tent are both dimensions of the story-world, and both are "brought forth" into performance.

The gesture itself may even appear to *effect* such sudden shifts in space, since what this particular gesture *does* is puncture the ground of one world to effect the emergence of another. One action does not so much cause another as repeat it or echo it uncontrollably; the lines of causation are tangled.

Performance brings forth visually not only the curses, but all of the imagery of confinement and bursting out. Imagining performance makes clear that what is happening is not limited to linguistic phenomena such as ambiguous shifters. The performer's bodily presence, his incarnation of Phoenix suppli-cating Achilles, takes the imagery and brings it into embodiment. This is true whether he only enacts the stance of supplication through his speech or uses gestures to give body to the curse and to create a space of invocation before him. The performance 'pulls out all the stops': the imagery of confinement and bursting out, the rhetorical compression, the syntactic ambiguity, the merging of characters, the layering of times and actions and realms (story, story within story, story within story within story, space of performance, underworld).[107] Because the performer's body provides a visual *origo* for all of the imagery, gestures, settings, spaces, and figures, he layers and collapses these onto one another, situating his body as the container of some of them and contained by others, and in a way that a written text does not.

The performer, in bringing the action of cursing into the performance space, *brings the curse "forth"* into his very body. In performing the curse, the curse enters him and surfaces through him. The audience may see this as the takeover of the body in front of them, not limited to Phoenix himself. In this way, *something happens in the space of performance that is caused within the world of the poem*, reversing the usual direction of causation.[108]

When the performer enacts this cursing and supplication, he does so for an imagined Achilles seated in the position of the audience. From time to time he addresses Achilles; it is thus Achilles who is in the "you" seat for all of these curses and supplications and any embodiments thereof. In terms of the story as *paradeigma*, the curses and supplications are only leading up to the final act that Achilles is (ostensibly) supposed to emulate: Meleager's being persuaded to "go out." But there is a strange fit between that act and the curses and supplications.

---

[107] Recall (page 54n15 above) McNeill's concept of the catchment for the unity of gestures that accompanies unity of thought and discourse (e.g. McNeill 2001; McNeill 2005; McCullough 2005).

[108] The uncontrolled gestures of supplication and curse, which both repeat and are disjointed from one another, are a more intensely dramatized version of the kind of repetition noted by Nagy 2004, the crescendo of instruction and then the offering to Athena in *Iliad* 6. The "idea of performance as a speech act is especially relevant to cases where we can identify a ritual as the overt referent in a set of reformulated repetitions" (Nagy 2004:145). In the gestures under consideration, ritual is not only the referent, it is as it were leaking into the performance, having an uncanny effect on its addressee and the plot of the poem, and as it were on the performer-as-Phoenix.

Achilles is being beseeched (besieged) by Phoenix and the rest of the embassy to emerge like a demonic force to the rescue.[109] The embassy wants to unleash Achilles' otherworldly power upon the Trojans. In this, he is very much like an angry hero being solicited from his tomb. The ritual approach to Achilles by the embassy encourages this interpretation. The trick is to deflect the anger of the hero onto the proper object. The separateness of realms occupied by Phoenix and his audience is instantiated in the curse itself, but it is given further body by the image of the doorway.

> In each of Phoinix's stories ... there stands a door. Both doors are bolted against suppliants. Both are barriers separating father from son. The one is impenetrable, resisting a father's attempt to force an entrance; the other is forced open with a breaking ...[110]

When the performer embodies Phoenix-as-Oineus (in whatever fashion) he sets up a doorway between himself and his audience, between himself and his foster-son/son: a barrier he desperately wishes to breach.[111]

Outside of the immediate context in Book 9, another tradition may bolster this interpretation of Phoenix's speech as an appeal to the dead. As mentioned above, Phoenix performs a lament for Achilles according to Quintus Smyrnaeus (3.463–489), and the iconographic evidence leads us to suppose that he did so in the *Aethiopis* and its tradition.[112] We saw that Phoenix appeals to Achilles not so much to fight the Trojans as not to abandon *him*. The reproach of the dead for abandoning the living is a common motif of lament throughout the Greek tradition.[113] In particular, Phoenix's reproach for abandoning him and his recalling

---

[109] An analogous phenomenon occurs in Pompeian wall painting. In an elaborate triclinium discussed in the Interlude below, episodes from the *Iliad* are depicted. All are in sequence, except for the Book 9 embassy. Phoenix thus appears in close, ingeniously awkward, proximity to the scene of Priam supplicating Achilles, a scene framed in the poem as a *katabasis*, with Achilles as Hades hoarding the dead son. Both old men are kneeling before Achilles in very similar compositions. Here too Phoenix is "just repeating" the gesture of another infernal pair. Lateiner (1995:38) sees Phoenix, in his own gestures and in those of the Prayers, as an "anticipatory echo" of Priam.

[110] Lynn-George (1988:139), who goes on to compare this with how Achilles and Priam "overcome their insurmountable separation from each other" (140). The door by then transforms into the door on Achilles' tent (which is now a mansion), with its huge bolt. Lynn-George is here speaking of the separation of father and son, but the huge bolt brings home the fact that the mansion is like Hades.

[111] See below, Chapter 3, p. 228, for the development of this "kinesthetic" use of doorways and gates, in terms of the character of Patroklos. There too the suggestion is that Patroklos has been in another realm; in that case the gates are symbolically linked with the gates of Hades.

[112] See page 115n20, above.

[113] Alexiou 2002:183; cf. Andromache's lament, *Iliad* 24.725–726, καδ' δέ με χήρην/ λείπεις ἐν μεγάροισι. In fact, Quintus has Phoenix say "you have left me [κάλλιπες, 3.464] un-defended

---

that he cared for him as a baby in order to have support are traditional motifs in laments of parents for children. To take just one example, from the *Life of Saint Euphrosyne*:

ποῖ πεπόρευσαι, τέκνον; ... τί με τὸν σὸν πενθεῖν καὶ σκυθρωπάζειν γεννήτορα <u>καταλέλοιπας</u>; οὐκ ἐπὶ τοιαύταις ἐλπίσιν ἀνέτρεφον, ἀλλ' ὥστε βακτηρίαν τοῦ γήρως ἔχειν, καὶ τῆς ἀσθενείας παράκλησιν. Οἴ μοι! ... πῶς ἐνέγκω τὴν μόνωσιν;

Where have you gone, my child? ... Why <u>have you deserted</u> me, your father, to grieve for you in sadness? It was not with expectations such as these that I reared you, but to have a staff of support in my old age, and some consolation in my weakness. Alas! ... How can I endure the loneliness?[114]

His appeal to Achilles to "return" would also fall into place in this scheme; this is a highly traditional part of Greek lamentation.[115] An audience accustomed to hearing a lament by Phoenix for the dead Achilles would no doubt be reminded of such a scene while hearing his speech in Book 9, and the gestures of beating the earth would take on even richer significance as drawing Achilles out of the underworld.

To perform a lament or an invocation is to appeal to someone who is, and is not, before you, who does, and does not, exist in the same visual space, on the same plane of causation. In embodying Phoenix "becoming Kleopatra," the performer does not simply double his own "becoming" activity. Nor does he simply repeat the scenario of the *Iliad* opening, addressing his audience as characters within the poem.[116]

The impact of the gestures strikes home, moreover, on a still more profound level. Phoenix is not successful in his surface mission, loosing Achilles upon the

---

pain" and that he had not had any worse pain, even when he left [λιπόμην, 3.467] his fatherland and his parents. Thus, as in his *Iliad* 9 speech, he uses the verb twice at the beginning of his lamentation, though not with the meaning "abandon." In his lamentation he also recalls the baby Achilles sitting on his lap and wetting his tunic (3.473–475).

[114] Alexiou's translation (2002:163) of Jacques Paul Migne 114.316A. Alexiou next quotes a similar, non-literary, example of a mother's lament for her son.

[115] Alexiou 2002:46 and passim.

[116] Bryony Lavery's 2004 play *Frozen*, concerning a serial child-murderer/rapist, provides a vivid analogy. In his first appearance, the actor playing the killer speaks to the audience as though to one of his child victims. Looking directly at a person in the front row, he repeatedly says "Hello" as though speaking to a child, luring the child to respond with "It's rude not to say hello," etc. This goes on at excruciating length, forcing the person through sheer terror to respond with "Hello." This was terrifying not only for that audience member but for the person seated next to him.

Trojans. Rather he unintentionally outlines the plot that will eventually unfold (Achilles sending Patroklos out, Patroklos' own death and thus Achilles' virtual death). The repeated gestures of invocation and curse *embody the actual effect* of his speech, as opposed to its intended effect. Phoenix/the performer's body manifests the speech-act that the speech covers up. *Phoenix in effect curses Achilles rather than supplicating him—or indeed, lamenting him.*[117] This is because he has, as Whitman says, inspired Achilles. But he has done so not only by providing the alternative plot; the multiple curses from his multiple stories have spilled over into the currently unfolding action like effective speech-acts.

Patroklos in the Audience

But Achilles is not the only person in the audience. There is more than one person in the room. Patroklos, particularly as the parallel with Kleopatra plays out, becomes a more salient presence. The audience, in fact, as "overhearers" of Phoenix's speech who never speak, is rather in the position of Patroklos.

As was Kleopatra's, Patroklos' felt presence in the audience is concretely planted earlier, in the well-known passage describing the initial scene at Achilles' tent. Achilles and Patroklos are sitting outside of the tent or perhaps in the entrance. The visitors

> found him delighting his heart in the clear phorminx,
> beautiful, intricate, on it a silver bar—
> this he took from the spoils of Eetion he destroyed.
> With it <u>he</u> was delighting his *thumos*, and was singing, ἄρα, the κλέα
>   ἀνδρῶν.
> And Patroklos, alone, opposite him, was sitting in silence,
> awaiting Aiakides, when he would leave off singing.
> And the two stepped forward, and Odysseus was leading,
> and they stood before him; and astonished, Achilles leapt up

---

[117] Curses are a frequent motif in laments and inscribed epitaphs (Alexiou 2002:178–179). Alexiou notes the example of the *kommos* at Agamemnon's tomb in the *Libation Bearers*, where the wishes of Orestes and the chorus are suddenly joined by the curse of Elektra. "The remote wish has become a curse," Alexiou writes (p. 179). If not only curses, but a sudden shift to a curse, were traditional for the Homeric audience, this would strengthen the connection to Phoenix's lament for Achilles. It would also bolster the idea of the curses within the speech transforming into, in effect, a curse of Achilles, i.e. the speech act itself becoming a curse rather than merely telling about curses. Ebel (1972:95) captures the situation well: "In these passages [the curses of Althaia and Amyntor] Homer turns from the Olympians to the dark gods of the underworld. They cast over the supplication of Phoenix a baleful sense of automatism and vengeance, and in the parable of Meleager suggest a doom that extends beyond the parable itself and that Meleager cannot avert."

phorminx and all, leaving the seat where he was sitting.
In just this way Patroklos, when he saw the men, arose.

Iliad 9.186–195

Why is this scene here at all? Why does the poet have Achilles singing the κλέα ἀνδρῶν when the messengers arrive? Achilles has so distanced himself from the present action that he has turned to the glorious heroes of the past, and is perhaps placing himself in their ranks. And why is Patroklos silent? Patroklos is representative of "*philotēs*"[118]; he is the one who will return Achilles to the community; he is concerned about the Achaeans' current plight (not about entering the ranks of past heroes) and is becoming restive under the maniacal insistence of Achilles that they stay out of battle.

And yet the two lines describing Patroklos waiting (190–191) are nothing short of haunting. As with the Sirens, we desire to hear what Achilles is singing. But at the same time, Patroklos clears a space for the opposite, for a listener who is distant from the story, who does not enter the world of the song, leaving behind the concerns of the present world. Patroklos is the opposite of the Phaeacians entranced by Odysseus. "Waiting for when he would leave off singing"[119] is not what someone does who has fully entered the world of the song.[120] By leaving off what Achilles sang, the bard piques our desire to enter that song, yet at the same time provides us with an image of the seat opposite, occupied by a different sort of listener, preparing us for the speeches of the embassy.

This profound passage frames and affects the audience's experience of Phoenix's speech in particular. Its self-reflexive quality prepares for the more complex interaction between Phoenix and the bard. In terms of the action of the speech, Patroklos here anticipates Kleopatra's silence followed by outburst, just as she anticipates his later action. The image of the silent, devoted listener seated opposite the singing Achilles is burned into our brain; if we ourselves are induced to take such a role, we are also reminded that Patroklos is himself present as well. In Patroklos, "not seeing the actor" is taken to an extreme. Patroklos does not even speak until Book 11, but he is present—*among* us, rather than before us.[121]

The obvious intimacy of the pair overpowers Patroklos' detachment. Although we think of this intimacy as fundamental to the *Iliad* as a whole, it is only now, in this subtle yet dramatic fashion, that it is first revealed. It is

---

[118] Sinos 1980.

[119] Nagy (2002:60) compares this with the technical terms for rhapsodes picking up from one another.

[120] Segal 1994:115.

[121] See Bakker 1997a:173.

Patroklos, not Briseis, to whom Achilles is bonded, a fact further worked out in the speeches of Achilles and Phoenix, culminating in the speech of Kleopatra. (The replacement of lover Atalanta by wife Kleopatra in the Meleager story corresponds to this move.[122]) Kleopatra's fear of rape and her catalogue of horrors pick up on the problematic of Achilles' claim to Briseis as his *alokhos* and at the same time "spear-won." Just as the issue of "who has a claim on Briseis" is boiling to the surface, and along with it Achilles' ferocious critique of heroic society,[123] the role of Briseis is being reassigned to Patroklos. Patroklos is able to locate himself in the story and to hold it in his *phrēn*, as Kleopatra held the story of her mother, until it is time for him to speak.

In the *Oedipus Tyrannus*, when Jocasta overhears the speech of the shepherd, her presence onstage as a bystander ensures that our eyes fall upon her, process the speech through her, and take in the full implications of her exit from the stage.[124] Now in epic, there is only one body performing. But through the vignette framing the Embassy scene, through the imbricating levels of action, through the imagery of release of forces, through the *transfert du mal* of the curse and supplication,[125] through the rising of the curse into the body of the performer, the audience is spurred to imagine and to dread the collateral damage done through the story that exercises an influence upon its audience, not only Achilles but Patroklos.[126]

Attention to Book 9 as a script yields other insights into the inhabiting of performance space. The script layers several times and places on top of one another and invites embodiment in gestures, as we have seen. The bard may not only embody characters' gestures but also flesh out the space he inhabits, by for instance giving spatial recognition by his sightline to the incoming missiles hitting the *thalamos*. Thus any crescendo in gestures can enact the performer's being enclosed in a space threatened from the outside. This enclosing space "represents" spaces in the poem's present (Achilles' tent) and in the mythical past (the *thalamos* of Phoenix, Marpessa, Kleopatra, and Meleager), but it also situates the performer within his own dramatic present. The performer has created for himself a space of transformation, wherein his embodiment of one character is squeezed to the breaking point, and out of the compression comes another.

---

[122] On the question of Atalanta's pre-Homeric status, see Felson and Sale 1983; Most 1983.

[123] See Bruce M. King, "*Iliad* 11.668–762 and Beyond: The Cattle-Raid and the Genre of the *Iliad*" (unpublished manuscript, 2001), PDF file, pp. 12–13.

[124] I owe this analogy and the phrase "collateral damage" to Paul Mathai. Cf. Eurydice's silent response to the news of her son's death and her suicide in the *Antigone*. See below, Chapter 4, on the "seat" occupied by Eumaeus during the second Cretan Tale.

[125] On *transfert du mal* in the story of Patroklos, see Nagy 1979:79–81; Sinos 1980:68.

[126] After Meleager's death, Kleopatra commits suicide. See Interlude 2, below.

In enacting the curses bodily, the performer brought forth that mysterious force one more plane outward into the space of performance, into his body. But in doing so he creates *there* a space for the surfacing of a new force. That is what a curse does. All of these invocations, syntactic shifts, images, gestures, and embodiments culminate in the emergence on the scene of the true Erinys, Kleopatra.

Kleopatra's Catalogue

The performer, already channeling one body, Phoenix, has set up before himself a space for the emergence of further forces. This space he struggles to control through curses, curses he seems uncannily drawn to reenact. Meanwhile, within the story-world there has been a glimpse of this mysterious, compressed history of Kleopatra's family, followed by its immediate suppression, just at the time when Meleager's own emergence is being urged. This history remains compressed within the woman who herself embodies the innermost point of Meleager's withdrawal and return—compressed in her *phrēn*—and forms the spring from which Kleopatra finally speaks out. As Kleopatra acts as the still point at the center of Meleager's world, so Marpessa does for Kleopatra. The center of the ring is reached, and a tidal wave of memory and causality begins to form. Kleopatra becomes present, silent but with a full *phrēn*. The compressed digression 'primes the pump' for Kleopatra's catalogue (591) of the miseries of war (593–594):

590 καὶ τότε δὴ Μελέαγρον ἐΰζωνος παράκοιτις
λίσσετ' ὀδυρομένη, καί οἱ κατέλεξεν ἅπαντα
κήδε', ὅσ' ἀνθρώποισι πέλει τῶν ἄστυ ἁλώῃ·
ἄνδρας μὲν κτείνουσι, πόλιν δέ τε πῦρ ἀμαθύνει,
τέκνα δέ τ' ἄλλοι ἄγουσι βαθυζώνους τε γυναῖκας.
595 τοῦ δ'[127] ὠρίνετο θυμὸς ἀκούοντος κακὰ ἔργα,
βῆ δ' ἰέναι, χροῒ δ' ἔντε' ἐδύσετο παμφανόωντα.

Then it was at last that the fair-sashed wife of Meleager
supplicated him, lamenting, and catalogued (*katelexen*) for him all
the sorrows that arise for people whose city is seized:
The men they slaughter. The city, fire turns to dust.
The children, strangers abduct—and the deep-waisted women.
And his spirit sprang up when he heard the evil deeds,
and he swung out to go, and on his body he put the armor, beaming.

Iliad 9.590–596

---

[127] I have translated this "and his," but the situation is similar to the line-initial τῶν δέ above (line 573). His *thumos* arises "out of this [speech/thought]" or "out of him."

Kleopatra's catalogue emerges despite the narrator, Phoenix—'behind his back.'[128] As mentioned above, only in a house of mirrors are the Achaeans being "besieged." The catalogue can only bolster the idea (nascent in Achilles' speech) of the atrocity being committed upon the Trojan city. In fact, Kleopatra's speech comes to the mind of an ancient scholiast discussing Priam's description (culminating in the enslavement of the women) of what will happen when Hektor is killed (Σ bT 22.61–65).

The catalogue comes forth as *uniquely unintroduced direct speech*.[129] The persona of Kleopatra seems to shove her way through that of Phoenix and to speak at last.[130] It is impossible to prove that we have a new speaker here, but from the perspective of performance it is extremely compelling.[131] The Meleager story—indeed, Phoenix's entire speech—has until now contained no direct discourse: the performer, as he plays Phoenix, does not have to don a double mask at any point, playing Phoenix playing another character. That is reserved for this,[132] the speech's culmination and its undoing.

---

[128] Note how different this is, however, from other such moments: e.g. Agamemnon's speech about Atē (*Iliad* 19.95–133), where the poet uses the paradigm "behind Agamemnon's back to signal to us certain comparisons to which Agamemnon remains oblivious" (Austin 1975:125).

[129] It is possible to perform Althaia's curse too as direct discourse (line 571, παιδὶ δόμεν θάνατον, "give/to give the boy death"), since the infinitive could be construed, i.e. performed, as an infinitive-for-imperative: "give the boy death" instead of "[called on them] to give the boy death." One might be more inclined to do so since the introductory verb is separated from the infinitive clause by descriptions of the mother's gestures and tears, gestures that the performer may enact, thus 'becoming' Althaia just before bringing forth the "give the boy death" clause. This very question of whether to take the infinitive as "infinitive for imperative" (that is, to perform it as the character) or not lies behind Longinus' (27.1) illustration of how the poet suddenly turns and changes into the character for emotional effect (ὅτε περὶ προσώπου διηγούμενος ὁ συγγραφεὺς ἐξαίφνης παρενεχθεὶς εἰς τὸ αὐτὸ πρόσωπον ἀντιμεθίσταται, καὶ ἔστι τὸ τοιοῦτον εἶδος ἐκβολή τις πάθους). Longinus takes *Iliad* 15.346–349, a speech of Hektor, to be unintroduced direct discourse. (Modern editions tend to punctuate the passage such that the speech is introduced.) So too the scholiast on *Iliad* 1.23 interprets an infinitive construction "to revere the priest" as focalized through the Achaeans. Nünlist (2003:65) notes this example as evidence for an ancient awareness of "embedded focalization," but this case is tricky because of the infinitive: i.e. this line too could be performed as direct discourse, dis-embedding the focalization.

[130] An excellent parallel to this moment is "Trojan Horse" (Chapter 1). Compare also when Briseis—the very woman at issue in Book 9, the present raped woman, compared with the past rape of Marpessa and the rape threatening Kleopatra's future—finally speaks at 19.287. See Redfield, "Briseis as a Speaking Sign" (unpublished manuscript, 2004), Microsoft Word file. The emergent, unconcealing, demystifying quality of the speech is deepened when the other women join in: "and with her did th' other Ladies mone, Patroclus' fortunes in pretext, but in sad truth their owne" (Chapman).

[131] On the ritual of pounding the ground to summon underworld forces, see Ferrari 2004:250. Ferrari situates the ritual summoning of Persephone within the rubric of the "anodos of the bride." Repeated summonings of underworld forces culminate in the bodying-forth of the bride, Kleopatra. But I do not want to speculate further about a specific link between ritual and the text.

[132] Oehler (1925:13–14) simply states that this is direct discourse, as the climax of the tension: "Das anaphorische πολλά ... verstärkt den Eindruck der unablässigen Bitten, die doch alle wirkungslos

The very plainness of the catalogue contributes to its slashing effect.[133] What impresses the above-mentioned scholiast in Priam's and Kleopatra's speeches is their *enargeia*, effected not by detail but by its absence.[134] The scholiast points to the lack of adorning epithets:

> [Homer] vividly shows what happens in the sackings of cities, just as in other lines: "the men they kill, and the city..." [9.593]. And although he does not write of the sack of Troy nevertheless he makes clear its sufferings, taking up in turn each cohort suffering something in war: but for the women, the outrage against the body is greater. And δαιμονίως he brings these things into sight, in brief, using diction without elaboration: for he does not say 'high-roofed' or 'well-wrought chambers' or 'daughters with beautiful hair' or 'with beautiful ankles,' but <u>he has traded in the epithets for the calamities of their bodies.</u>
>
> Σ bT *Iliad* 22.61–65

It is an incisive comparison: Kleopatra's speech is perhaps the least adorned in the poem. Its sole epithet, βαθυζώνους, goes straight to the heart of the matter, the threat of rape.[135]

The truth about war is bared in the simplest possible terms.[136] The present tense and the gnomic quality[137] of the utterance, lacking the prophetic specificity of Priam's, heightens the effect of the sudden revelation of universal truth.

---

sind. Wieder tritt die Kampsituation, der Augenblick der grössten Gefahr, in 2 Versen kurz hervor (588f), worauf Kleopatras letzter Versuch, den Meleager zur Hilfe zu bewegen, erzählt wird. Die entscheidenden Worte sind in direkter Rede angeführt: (593f)."

[133] One might fruitfully compare *Odyssey* 9.39–40, with Pazdernik's sensitive reading of the formulaic resonances therein. Odysseus' "terse and dismissive" account (Pazdernik 1995:350) of his destruction of the Cicones (of course, he and his crew also took the "wives" for distribution, 9.41, so that "no one would be without a fair share," 9.42; whatever happens to them?) turns out to be extraordinarily suggestive of the ethical ambiguities of Odysseus' role as sacker of cities.

[134] ἐναργῶς πέφρακε τὰ τῶν πορθήσεων, ὡς καὶ ἐν ἄλλοις· "ἄνδρας μὲν κτείνουσι, πόλιν δέ τε" (Ι 593). καὶ μὴ γράψας δὲ τὴν Ἰλίου πόρθησιν ὅμως ἐδήλωσεν αὐτῆς τὰ παθήματα, πᾶσαν ἡλικίαν τὴν ἐν πολέμῳ τι πάσχουσαν παραλαβών· ταῖς δὲ γυναιξὶν ἡ εἰς τὸ σῶμα ὕβρις μείζων. δαιμονίως δὲ ταῦτα ὑπ' ὄψιν ἤγαγεν ἐν βραχεῖ, χρησάμενος ἅμα καὶ ἀπεριέργως ταῖς λέξεσιν· οὐ γὰρ ὑψορόφους ἢ δαιδαλέους θαλάμους λέγει οὐδὲ θύγατρας καλλικόμους ἢ καλλισφύρους, ἀλλ' ἀπήλλακται τῶν ἐπιθέτων αὐτῷ τὰ δυστυχοῦντα τῶν σωμάτων (Σ bT *Iliad* 22.61–65). On this and other ancient comments on *enargeia*, see Meijering 1987:40–41.

[135] Bouvier 2002:350 argues that Kleopatra here introduces a variation on εὔζωνοι to stress, rather than the beauty of the belts, the quality of their fastening.

[136] The pattern of a truth revealed in direct discourse is seen also in Herodotus, e.g. 3.14.9–10, on which see Gray 2005:301. Gray remarks (p. 294) that Homer's "techniques could usefully be compared with those of Herodotus." Cf. p. 299: it is an "apparent rule" that "stories mainly in narrative mark their crises in direct speech (the revenge of Hermotimus, the revenge of Artayctes, and many others)."

[137] Vermeule 1979:112–113.

It is, then, the collapse of not only two speakers, but three: both Kleopatra and the bard speak through Phoenix, and despite him. The horrors of the sack of a city emerge from Kleopatra's, Phoenix's, and the performer's mouth at once, emerging to confirm the contradictions in Phoenix's ostensibly hortatory tale.

Phoenix, and through him the performer, has veered off[138] within the Meleager story to the black hole that is Marpessa. A performer can convey how Marpessa, as someone imprisoned with an insane father, party to sexual violence, fearing abandonment in old age, draws him like a magnet: the way the gestures of the cursing characters take him over, and the way Kleopatra gives voice to the defenders of the city. The same Marpessa is at the core of her daughter Kleopatra's fears and serves as the taproot for her intervention in the life and death of Meleager, and through him, of Achilles and Patroklos, and the plot of the *Iliad*. "Phoenix" has gone all the way through the story-world of Meleager and come out at the other end, where he is faced with a truth needing to find its way out. That truth emanates both from deep within the story's furthest "phrenetic" reaches, and from outside it altogether, from the bard. This conveys vertigo, a sense of confusion as to the source of action.

Now Kleopatra supplicates her husband, but she does so "mourning," λίσσετ' ὀδυρομένη (591). In this she would be reduplicating Phoenix's "lament" for Achilles that may be being reenacted here. As Nagy notes, the compressed catalogue of Kleopatra contains the same themes as the lamentation of Andromache in *Iliad* 24.725–745. Andromache is actually lamenting Hektor while Kleopatra is only "conjur[ing]" up grief in a "stance of lamentation."[139] But both are, in effect, prospective lamentations for an entire city, not only an individual. In this respect too Kleopatra's nickname Alkyone fits the situation, for birds, including the halycon, are traditionally associated with laments for cities.[140] Although Kleopatra's catalogue may seem too bare to resemble a lament generically, it resembles (especially if one hears the children and women as a single item, resulting in a tripartite scheme) a traditional ballad lamenting the sale of Parga by the British to the Turks in 1817–1819, quoted by Alexiou:

> Women pull their hair and beat their white breasts,
> and old men lament with black dirges.
> Priests strip their churches with tears in their eyes.[141]

---

[138] In fact, performers of epic do sometimes veer off from one tale (or "song pattern") into another by mistake: Lord 2000:120; Foley 1990:359–387; Scodel 2002:17. This feature of Phoenix's speech would seem to harness such a "mistake" for dramatic purposes, somewhat as the Cretan Tales (Chapter 4 below) dramatize the process of developing a tale. This constitutes another way in which Book 9 gives us "a glimpse into the workshop of Homer" (Hainsworth 1993:57).

[139] Nagy 1999:111.

[140] Alexiou 2002:97; Nagy 1999:111n2.

[141] Alexiou 2002:96.

Alexiou also notes, in a ballad from the Pontos, "the sense of tragedy imparted by the sympathetic reaction of nature, and the tension of the dialogue, which is maintained not, as in the literary *thrēnoi*, by sententious appeals, but by *the concentrated ellipse of every superfluous fact*"[142] (my emphasis). This is precisely the quality of Kleopatra's speech noted by the scholiast. In the Pontos ballad, as in other traditional laments, the speaker is a bird (a turtle-dove). The singer of such a ballad does not only allude to birds as lamenting, he or she reenacts the bird's lament.

Kleopatra/Alkyone, then, conjures not only lament for children (the halcyon of the halcyon days) or a husband (Alkyone/Keux), but also lament for cities. This makes further sense of, or gives further body to, the enclosing "kinesthetics" in Phoenix's speech as a whole. Throughout his speech, Phoenix/ the performer constructs around him doors, chambers, walls, and finally the city of Calydon. As we noted, these various structures are layered on top of one another around the performer's body, rather than spread out across the performance space. The final configuration of space is the chamber of Meleager and Kleopatra, within the city of Calydon. The vividness with which Calydon is conjured and "placed" in the space of performance locates the audience in Calydon; Kleopatra thus prospectively laments a city that the performer has created to enclose himself and his audience.[143] Here different performances might alter the space so created. A performer might, through his enactment, circumscribe the "action" strictly to the space occupied by himself and leave the audience out. But the tent of Achilles, having been set up as the dominant structure at the beginning of the episode to enclose performer and audience,[144] would "set the stage" for a performance, and an interpretation, whereby performer and audience are "enclosed" in Calydon as well.

Reanimation: Image, Structure, and Performance

We have sounded out the dynamics in performance of the story of Meleager, focusing on the inner story of Marpessa in the *phrēn* of Kleopatra, which bursts out of the speaking character, Phoenix. We have seen how the story Phoenix tells about his youth orchestrates how we see, hear, and experience the Marpessa story. To say Phoenix's autobiography 'frames' the Marpessa story is too static

---

[142] Alexiou 2002:94.

[143] Compare the effect of Chryses' prayer to Apollo in *Iliad* 1, discussed above, pages 33–34, which vividly places the performer-as-priest back in his home, Chryse, drawing over himself and his people the protection of Apollo's roofed temple and Apollo himself while performing his speech act.

[144] Compare the predominant configuration of Eumaeus' hut in the dialogue between Odysseus and Eumaeus, discussed in Chapter 4 below, page 319.

and textual to capture the dynamics centered in the performer's body. Once the performer has become Phoenix and told us his own story, the Marpessa story is being told by someone with that particular story of his own in his memory, *in his phrēn*. The combined persona spins out one story against the background of the other. He may perform his personal story as coming from his memory, with much material spilling out that is not relevant to his alleged rhetorical goals ("Do not abandon me; you are my son").

Likewise when he begins the Meleager story, much spills out that is irrelevant to the message ("Do/Don't be like Meleager"), but is not irrelevant *to him*. Thus it seems to spill out from his own *phrēn*. The performer deepens his embodiment of Phoenix, suddenly solidifying the audience's sense that the person before us truly is Phoenix, because the chaotic element flows directly from the memory of the speaker: not the memory of the bard, but that of Phoenix.

Marpessa's story forms the center of a ring composition comprising the entire Meleager story; it is most immediately framed by Meleager and Kleopatra lying down together and by Althaia's curse. The Phoenix autobiography frames the Marpessa story as well as the Meleager story as a whole. Framing the entire Embassy is the scene outside Achilles' tent. But the middle panel, the Litai, has its own way of steering the experience of all of these stories as well.

We saw above that Althaia's curse transforms into the missiles striking Meleager's room and the suppliants arriving at his door: curses activated through a final suppliant, Kleopatra. The Litai (Prayers) likewise transform themselves into curses by doing what they do: by supplicating. Curse and supplication wrap around one another like a Möbius strip.

Likewise, Phoenix represents or imitates people who curse and supplicate, and they bleed through his performance, such that Phoenix himself curses/supplicates Achilles. As with the Litai, who move from representing to performing the prayer/curse, there is an uncanny movement from representation to action.

Like the Litai, Phoenix approaches his *supplicandus* at the behest of someone else. Quickly, however, once he has established "contact" with Achilles (panel I, "how I came to you"/"you are my son"), he moves from representing Agamemnon to acting on his own initiative *with his own agenda* (= "do not abandon me").

The cycle of the Litai (see Figure 4) anticipates and maps out the structure of Meleager story. Phoenix approaches the center of the Meleager story, as Meleager approaches Kleopatra, and there taps into a source of energy, the Marpessa digression. This font of energy is something he is drawn to personally and also fuels Kleopatra's outburst.

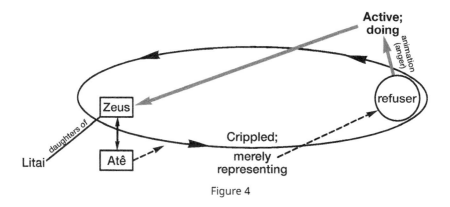

Figure 4

As the Litai spring to life, so too does Kleopatra. As she is animated, she moves from "representing" someone (Kleopatra/Patroklos) to acting through the storyteller to determine that someone's fate, while pivoting out to speak directly to the audience. In both cases a supplication is turned on its head. The Litai now pray for Atē, Ruin; Phoenix now bespeaks the horrors of sacking a city.

Ring composition in the Meleager story, as in the Litai, involves: a) arriving at the center and tapping it as a source; b) "coming to life" at that center. At the center of the Meleager story is Marpessa. Embedded within her story is a reference to the myth of Alkyone, and the halcyon days, the period of rest and fertility at the winter solstice, in the midst of winter storm. At the solstice the sun turns around from its deathward course and returns to bring life to the world again. There is at that turning point a moment of quickening that brings about the reversal.

The Meleager story is at first an ordinary *paradeigma* with terms prearranged to correspond with the situation at hand and dictate a course of action. It then "comes to life" and overthrows its speaker. The Litai parable is a compressed map of its workings, not only its plot but also its drama. The Prayers' animation enacts in small the animation of hero by woman, and bard by hero. Representation becomes action; lines of causality are reversed; spaces and times interfere with one another; plotting is derailed by performance.

Interlude 1

Ring Thinking

Phoenix in *Iliad* 23

A FULL ACCOUNT OF THE THEATRICALITY OR PERFORMABILITY of Phoenix's speech involves features such as structure, image, and mythological background. This Interlude shows how these features carry forward from Book 9 to reappear in the narrative of Phoenix's other major appearance in the poem, in the Funeral Games of Book 23. Somewhat as the second panel of his speech, the Litai parable, mapped the workings of that speech from within, the imagery, mythical allusions, and spatial relations of the Book 23 narrative resonate with his Book 9 speech. These resonant features from Book 23 do more than confirm and deepen some of our findings from the last chapter; they also implicate the character of Phoenix within a nexus of myth and image that appears outside the Homeric poems—especially in visual art. Thus this Interlude expands the mythological discussion outward from figures such as the halcyon to the mythological background of Phoenix himself. Phoenix, like Eris and other figures, has a certain kinesthetics or *schēma* that works in synergy with image and story. It could be that the performativity of Phoenix's Book 9 speech brings into the realm of solo performance dynamics seen elsewhere in story and in art.

Aristotle maps out the movement of thought to action in the *Metaphysics* (Z 1032b 6–14) as follows:

γίγνεται δὲ τὸ ὑγιὲς νοήσαντος οὕτως· ἐπειδὴ τοδὶ ὑγίεια, ἀνάγκη εἰ ὑγιὲς ἔσται τοδὶ ὑπάρξαι, οἷον ὁμαλότητα, εἰ δὲ τοῦτο, θερμότητα· καὶ οὕτως ἀεὶ νοεῖ, ἕως ἂν ἀγάγῃ εἰς τοῦτο ὃ αὐτὸς δύναται ἔσχατον ποιεῖν. εἶτα ἤδη ἡ ἀπὸ τούτου κίνησις ποίησις καλεῖται, ἡ ἐπὶ τὸ ὑγιαίνειν. ὥστε συμβαίνει τρόπον τινὰ τὴν ὑγίειαν ἐξ ὑγιείας γίγνεσθαι καὶ τὴν οἰκίαν ἐξ οἰκίας, τῆς ἄνευ ὕλης τὴν ἔχουσαν ὕλην ...

Aristotle *Met.* Z 1032b

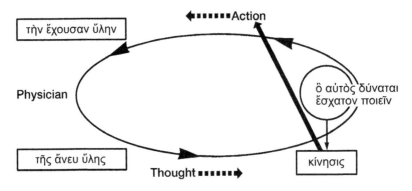

Figure 5

And the healthy comes about from him thinking in this way: since such-and-such is health, it is necessary that, if there will be health, so-and-so must obtain, for instance homogeneity, and if this, heat: and so he keeps on thinking, until he brings (the thought process) to that which he himself has the power, in the end, to *do* (*poiein*). Then the movement away from this point is called *poiēsis*, *poiēsis* toward becoming healthy. So it follows in a certain way that health comes about from health, and a house from a house; <u>out of that without matter, that which has matter.</u>

In the Introduction, this passage was used to help imagine the opening of the *Iliad*, the bard's movement from thought to action when bodying forth Chryses (in another speech, please note, protesting the abduction of a woman).

Aristotle's process (see Figure 5) is a smooth cycle, but the *Iliad* uses a similar schema both for the Litai and for Phoenix's speech as a whole to enact the entrance of a new, disturbing force. The Litai move from representation to action, being activated and "becoming themselves" via the disturbance of refusal and suddenly speaking vengeful prayers on their own behalf (see Figure 4). Phoenix thinks to calm Achilles' *thumos* by using a canned story, but instead, via a central moment, provokes a force within that story to spring to life through himself.

Phoenix in *Iliad* 23: Another Ring

The ring structure itself may suggest a cosmology of eternal return, or it could suggest ending and renewal. We can but look to observe whether the concluding mood is hopeful or grim. The point is that the rhetorical form does not impose any particular mood for the ending.

The general impression is that the ring is a literary form that is good
for reflecting on, and for establishing a long view.

Mary Douglas, *Thinking in Circles*, p. 41

The other significant[1] appearance of Phoenix in the *Iliad* is at the funeral games
for Patroklos in Book 23. Achilles stations him at the turning-point of the chariot
race "to remember the courses, and report back the truth":

> σήμηνε δὲ τέρματ' Ἀχιλλεὺς
> τηλόθεν ἐν λείῳ πεδίῳ· παρὰ δὲ σκοπὸν εἷσεν
> 360 ἀντίθεον Φοίνικα ὀπάονα πατρὸς ἑοῖο,
> ὡς μεμνέῳτο δρόμους καὶ ἀληθείην ἀποείποι.

> And Achilles marked out the end-point
> far off on the smooth plain: and near it he seated as a lookout
> godlike Phoenix, companion of his own father,
> so he could remember the courses and report back the truth.

Iliad 23.358–361

Phoenix is positioned at the midpoint as lookout or judge (*skopos*), yet he
will not be called upon to render judgment after the race and instead vanishes
from the poem.[2] This is odd, because his judgment is precisely what is needed in
the ensuing dispute between Menelaos and Antilokhos. Instead, Achilles himself
judges each event, rendering Phoenix superfluous. Why then does Phoenix
appear in the games at all? As discussed above, it is likely that he had a tradi-
tional role in the Funeral Games for Achilles (as he did in lamenting Achilles),
so to the extent that those games served as a model for these,[3] his appearance
would be expected. Yet his role here in Book 23 turns out to be tailored to crys-
tallize his speech in Book 9, much as the Litai mapped it out in advance.

The chariot race is nearly overshadowed by the famous speech that
precedes it, Nestor's advice to his son Antilokhos (23.306–348). The speech's ring
composition itself embodies a chariot race.[4] It is abstracted in time and place
up to the center of the ring, the elaborate description of the turning-post, and
then moves into the concrete. In the first half, Nestor is pessimistic; then, as if

---

[1] He appears also at 14.136a (plus-line in Zenodotus; cf. page 114n17, above), 16.196 (leading one of
the five Phthian contingents), 17.555, 561 (Athena disguised as Phoenix appearing to Menelaos),
and 19.311 (list of *basileis* who stay to weep with Achilles).

[2] Aristotle himself links arguments to or from the principles to races that proceed from the judges
to the end, or the reverse: *Nicomachean Ethics* 1095a33–1095b2.

[3] Kakridis 1949:65–83; Frame 2009:171n69, 216n117.

[4] Lohmann 1970:15–18. (Only after Nestor's speech is Phoenix stationed at the turning-post, so
Lohmann does not discuss him.)

gaining momentum from coming out of the turn, he suddenly becomes wildly hopeful about Antilokhos' chances, "even if the others had Arion!" The turning-post, *sēma*, animates Nestor even though he is only going around it in speech. As we have seen, Phoenix's rendition of the Meleager story is a masterpiece of ring composition, with the *mise en abyme* of Marpessa at its center and the speech of Kleopatra as its eerie culmination. Phoenix was identifying with and speaking as a dead heroine.

What stands as the midpoint of the chariot race, where Phoenix is stationed as a *skopos*, is itself a *sēma*, both a generalized marker (23.326) and a tomb (23.331). Nagy[5] brings out the significance of *sēma* and *noos* in Nestor's speech and in the race itself, and connects this with the fact that "the turning points of chariot racecourses at the pan-Hellenic Games were conventionally identified with the tombs of heroes."[6] In one instance, Taraxippos, "upsetter of horses," was thought to be active from his tomb.[7] The chariot race is an ideal model for ring-composition, for disturbance by dead heroes at the center is precisely what we found in Phoenix's speech.

There is another "phoenix" present at the chariot race, and this one helps interpret the other. As the racers are coming down the home stretch, one horse emerges as the leader: the *phoenix* horse with the moonlike white *sēma* on its forehead:

ὃς τὸ μὲν ἄλλο τόσον φοῖνιξ ἦν, ἐν δὲ μετώπῳ
λευκὸν σῆμα τέτυκτο περίτροχον ἠΰτε μήνη.

who for the rest of him was *phoenix*, but on his forehead
was rendered a white sign (*sēma*), *peritrochos* [round; revolving] like
the moon.

Iliad 23.454–455

The Homeric use of *phoenix* in the adjectival sense "reddish" to refer to the dye[8] or the tree, is limited to this one line. The *phoenix* horse rounding the turn is similar to, or duplicates in miniature, the neighboring scene at the turning-post: Phoenix stationed by a *sēma*. The word περίτροχος (Homeric hapax) used to describe the white *sēma* on the horse recalls the *sēma* at the turning point. LSJ offers only "circular," but the verbs περιτρέχω and περιτροχάω mean basically "run around," and if περίτροχος is used of the sun and moon and of a hat,

---

5   Nagy 1990a:202–222.

6   Nagy 1990a:215, citing Sinos 1980:53n6.

7   Pausanias 6.20.15–19; Nagy 1990a:215, 1990b:210.

8   Van den Broek 1971:51–66. Its pairing here with the white moon-*sēma* may recall the simile describing Menelaos' wound at *Iliad* 4.141, the woman dying ivory with *phoenix*.

it bears both "running around" and "circular" meanings. On vase paintings of chariots racing around tombs—in particular, Achilles dragging Hektor around Patroklos' tomb—the tomb is sometimes portrayed as a white, egg-shaped object protruding from the ground.[9]

What is the significance of this *phoenix* horse with its white *sēma* like the moon? This conjunction of the moon and *phoenix* brings to mind *phoenix*'s associations with the sun: that is, the solar phoenix-bird, who returns from the East at the end of an era to retrieve or replace his dead father (or to resurrect himself from his own ashes).[10] This link turns out to have broad implications.

In the immediate context, the link sheds light on the drawn-out contest over who can discern the first appearance of the leading horse. Idomeneus, at the sight of that horse, asks if he is the only one to αὐγάζομαι the horses (23.458), sparking a drawn-out dispute with Ajax son of Oileus. Richardson notes that this is the only occurrence of this verb in Homer, and cites West's remark on *Works and Days* 478: "I suppose the essential idea is 'fix the gaze on' a particular object."[11] But this rare verb, almost entirely poetic, cannot but recall αὐγή, a ray of the sun, in line with the solar imagery.[12]

Spotting the return of the sun is entirely appropriate in the context of a phoenix-bird. And the chariot race itself has solar connotations. The sun, of course, was thought to travel in a chariot, and the sun's daily return from the underworld was linked with chariot racing around a tomb, and with human beings "returning to light and life." This is succinctly illustrated by Pindar, *Nemean* 7.19–20, ἀφνεὸς πενιχρός τε θανάτου παρά σᾶμα νέονται, "Both rich and poor return by going past the *sēma* of death."[13]

The same motif of return to life around the turning-point of a racecourse appears in the second stasimon of Euripides' *Herakles* 655–662, when the old men wish that excellence would be compensated by a "double youth," whereby after death virtuous men would run "a double course [δισσοὺς διαύλους] back to the rays of the sun."[14] This "double course" would be, according to the chorus, a "clear sign of excellence" (φανερὸν χαρακτῆρ' ἀρετᾶς, 659) by which one could

---

[9] E.g. the famous Boston Hydria, Boston 63.473.

[10] On the phoenix-bird, see Detienne 1977:29–36 and van den Broek 1971.

[11] Richardson 1993:221 *ad Iliad* 23.458.

[12] With this conjunction of sun and moon compare the forces at work near the end of the *Odyssey* (Austin 1975). *Works and Days* 478, the only other use of the verb in early epic, is sandwiched between mentions of spring and the winter solstice. Cf. Frame's (1978:88) remark on Augeias: "The name Augeias is related to the noun *augē*, which in turn suggests the 'radiance' of the sun. It is clear that this figure was originally connected, or even identical, with the sun itself." See also Frame 2009:49–50.

[13] On which see Nagy 1990a:219.

[14] The old men are, of course, currently being embodied by younger ones. On the choral associations of this passage see Martin 2007:51–54.

recognize the bad and the good (665–666); but, they continue, "now, there is no clear boundary-marker [ὅρος] from the gods for the good and the bad, but a lifetime, whirling around [εἰλισσόμενος], builds up wealth only" (669–672). Martin notes that the "highly marked verb" ἐλίσσω is connected with a boundary-marker in the chariot race in Book 23 (line 309; to which add 466) as well. But the two passages also share an emphasis (indeed, a strange emphasis) on a clear sign that distinguishes one man from another as they come whirling around the turn.[15]

The race in Book 23 does not only exemplify the connection between chariot racing and the chariot of the sun. Rather it is exceptionally infused with imagery and diction associated with the sun and the sun's "return," with its connotations of rejuvenation and reanimation[16]—quite apart from the phoenix-bird. So it should not be surprising to find a further instance of solar imagery. The chariot race is introduced with a speech from Nestor to his son guiding him through the race. The very name "Nestor," according to Frame's analysis linking it to IE *nes-, cognate with *nostos*, has the significance of "bringing back to light and life." Frame places Nestor in the context of solar imagery, or solar cult,[17] such that, for example, Nestor's story of his cattle raid (*Iliad* 11.671–707) would go back to a story about retrieving the cattle of the sun, and "Pylos" would recall the gates of the sun at the edge of the world.[18]

The verbal root *nes- occurs also in *noos*, mind. Frame sees "return to light and life" and "mind" as deeply connected in a pattern repeated in the *Iliad* and *Odyssey*. The fruit of this connection is seen most clearly in the journey of Parmenides, which is both drawn ("escorted," πέμπον) by horses and taking place in Parmenides' mind. Nestor himself is strongly associated with νόος/ νοέω throughout the *Iliad*, especially in the present passage. Given Nestor's significance, and the chariot race's associations with the sun, the phoenix-bird is quite at home in this passage.

---

[15] Notable too is the theme, shared between the *Herakles* chorus and the Book 23 chariot race, of youth versus age. While the *Herakles* chorus is lamenting their lost youth and celebrating the young Herakles, while wishing for a double youth for the virtuous, the *Iliad*'s race stages two contests of youth versus age on top of one another: Menelaos versus Antilokhos, in the race, and Idomeneus versus Ajax (who jeers that Idomeneus is not the youngest, and "your eyes do not see the sharpest out of your head," 476–477), competing to catch sight of the winning team. This theme is of a piece with the theme of reanimation at the turning-point, or point of judgment.

[16] In addition to the evidence that follows, Nagy (1990a:220) points out that σῆμα is a cognate of Skt. *dhya-*, which he links through Indic *dhīyas* to concepts of reincarnation, somewhat as Frame links νόος / IE *nes- to "return from light and life" (see below). Nagy suggests for the chariot race a connotation of reincarnation, even without bringing in the Phoenix at the center, standing by the σῆμα.

[17] Frame 1978:21.

[18] Frame 1978:87–95. After discussing (pp. 58–62) the "gates of day and night" in Parmenides and Hesiod and in the Telepylos episode (*Odyssey* 10.81–86), Frame discusses (pp. 92–93) Nestor's home Pylos, noting that Herakles wounds Hades *en Pulōi en nekuessin*, *Odyssey* 5.397.

Other details support a "return to light and life" interpretation of the race. Aside from the tomb itself, representing a "death" from which the heroes return (to Nes-tor), there is a repeated emphasis on it as the *termata* (309, 323, 333, 358). Nestor is said to have "told the *peirata* [limits] of each thing" to his son (350). The race is concerned with ends and limits.

The chariot race, moreover, like the other funeral games narrated in Book 23, draws upon the traditional stories of the returns (*nostoi*) of the heroes from Troy (and the fates of those who do not make it home),[19] just as its counterpoint in Whitman's ring-compositional scheme, Book 2, echoed the war's beginnings. Within this "nostos" frame or subtext, Nestor in instructing Antilokhos would be reenacting his role as one who returns the people to light and life, from the *peirata* and the *termata* embodied by the tomb; their salvation would be seen in the celestial horse driven by the winner.

Yet Antilokhos will not return at all, but will meet his death while saving his father, Nestor himself. Nestor's instructions to his son about "limits" take on eerie overtones fully at home in Book 23.[20] Antilokhos' death in the *Aethiopis* at the hands of Memnon will bring on Achilles' own actual death in avenging him, as Patroklos, in Achilles' armor, has brought on Achilles' metaphorical death in the *Iliad*. Antilokhos is in short Achilles' Patroklos-replacement,[21] a relationship mentioned in the *Odyssey*.[22] At the end of the chariot race, Antilokhos refuses to give his prize to Menelaos, in a line rich with resonance (23.552). τὴν δ' ἐγὼ οὐ δώσω, "her [the mare] I will not give up," he says, and let someone try me, whoever wants to fight me with his hands. The speech recalls Agamemnon's refusal to hand over Chryseis, τὴν δ' ἐγὼ οὐ λύσω ("her I shall not release," 1.29), which instigated the plot of the *Iliad* by replaying the stealing of a female.[23] Poor Menelaos is again on the point of replaying the loss of a female (here, a mare rather than a woman) to a beautiful youth,[24] but for the intervention of Achilles.

Antilokhos' words recall also Achilles' own threatening words at 1.298-303. Achilles' response to Antilokhos' threat here in Book 23 is to smile, "delighting in Antilokhos, because he was his dear companion (*hetairos*)" (23.555-556).

[19] See, e.g., Whitman 1958:263-264; Kullmann 1960:336-355; Richardson 1993:202, 249; Frame 2009: 170-172, 205-216.
[20] Cf. Nagy 1990a:208-212.
[21] This is stated explicitly by Philostratus (*Imagines* II.7), explaining that Menelaos arranged that Antilokhos, the youngest Achaean, be the one to deliver the news of Patroklos' death in order that Achilles be distracted by touching Antilokhos and crying. Of course, in terms of the development of the tradition, Patroklos may be designed as a premonition of Antilokhos.
[22] *Odyssey* 24.78-79; cf. Nestor's speech at *Odyssey* 3.103-119.
[23] Cf. Frontisi-Ducroux 1986a:50; Martin 1989:188-189.
[24] Cf. above, Chapter 1, "Menelaos and the Empty Helmet."

Richardson, noting that this is the only time Achilles smiles, remarks that Achilles "knows ... what it means to be deprived of one's prize" and takes the passage to be a "a sign that they both share the same nobility of character."[25] No: the smile is another eerie recognition of Antilokhos' future role, replacing Patroklos as Achilles' "dear companion," and, like Patroklos, dying. The authorial, unrattled Achilles smiles just as the authorial Zeus smiles upon awakening (15.47) and issuing his long speech calmly "predicting" the tragic remainder of the *Iliad*, including the death of Patroklos. All this results in a chain-reaction exchange of prizes whereby all are satisfied. Another *Iliad* is averted, but an *Aethiopis*, with the death of Achilles, is set in motion. Antilokhos' death, then, is at stake in Book 23, layered atop Patroklos' funeral.

So the chariot race in itself is infused with imagery of return to life and light, given its odd vocabulary, the speech of Nestor, the undercurrent of *nostos* stories. But Nestor, as we began to see, is not the only solar figure here.

The phoenix-bird has further features in common with the Phoenix/phoenix under consideration. The early literary evidence is scanty,[26] but it is clear that the Hesiodic tradition alluded to the phoenix as a familiar theme. While the preponderance of artistic depictions of the bird appears much later, in a Christian context, the phoenix was clearly better known to Greeks of the archaic and classical periods than the extant number of allusions would suggest. We cannot say which features of the bird were familiar at a given stage of the *Iliad*'s development, but several are fundamental. The phoenix-bird is a fabulously long-lived creature associated with the sun. He is born from the ashes of his predecessor or otherwise comes to replace him at his death, or else regenerates himself at his own death. At any given time, there is only one. The lifespan of the phoenix is associated with various astronomical systems and cycles. His long life was already proverbial for Hesiod; he appears in a riddle with various creatures whose lifespans are multiples of one another and of human beings.[27] According to Herodotus (2.73), he appears at Heliopolis once every five hundred years, when his father dies. Thus, the phoenix-bird, like Nestor (*Iliad* 1.250–252, *Odyssey* 3.245–246),[28] lives a certain number of "generations of men."

Besides being associated with a return/resurrection at the end of a long era, the phoenix-bird is also pictured as the escort of the sun in its daily course to the underworld and back.[29]

---

[25] Richardson 1993:229, *ad* 23.555–556.
[26] For a survey of the phoenix in classical and Christian traditions, see van den Broek 1971. According to him (pp. 393–394), there are only nine extant mentions of the bird (in Greek or Latin) before the first century CE.
[27] Van den Broek 1971: Ch. 5; on Hesiod fr. 304 M-W, see pp. 76–112.
[28] On Nestor's longevity ("sole survivor from a former era") see Frame 1978:113–114.
[29] Van den Broek 1971:261–304.

Figure 6

The Egyptian solar bird *benu*, with a solar disk over his head, is probably the same Egyptian bird mentioned by Herodotus,[30] which he says is the "phoenix." The *benu* accompanies the dead on their journey to the afterlife, for instance, in the barge of the sun (see Figure 6).[31] The bird is pictured standing on or next to tombs[32] or on an upright mummy.[33] It is tempting to link this quality to Phoenix stationed by the tomb. In the last mentioned example, admittedly a late and unusual one, on a mural painting in the temple of Isis in Pompeii, the bird's head bears a uraeus with a *solar disk and a lunar crescent.*

The phoenix-bird, like the sun itself, is an overseer of human beings:[34] a judge like Phoenix, the *skopos* who is to report back the truth about the *dromoi*.[35]

---

[30]   Or his source, Hecataeus.

[31]   Figure 6 photo by Flickr user kairoinfo4u. See also in van den Broek 1971, which gives the caption (p. 425): "Mural painting in tomb of Irenifer. Del el Medineh; 19th dynasty (ca. 1345–1200 BC). "

[32]   See van den Broek (1971:Pl. I, 2): "*benu* in willow tree next to grave of Osiris." Mural painting in tomb of royal scribe. Van den Broek says "probably second century B.C."

[33]   Tran 1964 Pl. X, 2. Bird with uraeus with solar disk and lunar crescent, perched on an open sarcophagus with Osiris mummy, first century CE. Cf. van den Broek 1971:242 and n4.

[34]   Cf. van den Broek 1971: Ch. 7, "The Phoenix as Bird of the Sun," sect. 2, "Escort of the Sun."

[35]   Tombs and *skopoi* are linked in the *Iliad*. At 2.791–792, Iris disguises herself as Polites, who sat as a *skopos* on a burial mound. At 24.799, after the Trojans heap up Hektor's burial-mound (σῆμα), *skopoi* seat themselves "around": ῥίμφα δὲ σῆμ' ἔχεαν, περὶ δὲ σκοποὶ εἵατο πάντῃ. Here perhaps the *skopoi* were seated *on* the mound facing outward in various directions.

The sun is the *skopos* par excellence: Demeter addresses Helios as θεῶν σκοπὸν ἠδὲ καὶ ἀνδρῶν (*Homeric Hymn to Demeter* 62), standing in front of his horses. The phoenix as escort of the chariot of the sun is akin to the chariot race in general and the *phoenix* horse in particular. At the Eastern extreme, the phoenix is reborn on his own tomb, nest, or pyre, or his father's egg. This self-reanimation differs from rescue by a solar hero/deity (cf. Frame on Nes-tor), but the similarity is clear.

Enough has been said to make plausible an association between Phoenix standing by the *sēma*, the *phoenix* horse with its moon *sēma*,[36] and the phoenix-bird. It is best not to limit the harmonic resonances, but here are some interpretive paths:

1. Phoenix, at the turning point (cf. τροπαὶ Ἠελίοιο, the solstice point; see below Chapter 4), which is a tomb, like the phoenix-bird perched on the tomb, now returns—like the sun (cf. αὐγάζομαι) from solstice or from the underworld.[37]

2. The subtext of Book 23 being the Returns (*nostoi*) of the heroes, Phoenix turns into a horse as escort of heroes back home, just as the phoenix-bird escorts his dead father (cf. Herodotus) or the sun itself. Phoenix here is a (transitive) returner of heroes (cf. Nestor) rather than (intransitive) the returning sun (cf. esp. Parmenides 1).

[36] Cf. Herodotus on the Epaphus/Apis bull, 3.27–29. Like the phoenix, the bull appears only after a long interval, at which time the Egyptians hold festivals. Like the phoenix-horse, Apis is identified by *sēmeia*, among which is a white square (or as a variant reading has it, a triangle) on its forehead and an eagle on its back. The Apis bull is born from a lightning bolt striking a cow who is no longer able to conceive offspring "into her belly." Does the Apis bull, then, arise from her ashes? Herodotus tells the story of another solar cow, the one made by Mycerinus in which he buried his daughter (2.129–134). This cow, exhumed every year to see the sun in accordance with the daughter's wishes, is covered with a φοινικέῳ εἴματι, with her head and neck covered with gold. Between her horns is a "golden imitation of the circle of the sun." Given Egyptian proclivities to solar headgear, all this would be unremarkable, except that Herodotus associates these creatures with, respectively, an appearance after a long interval of years, and an annual reanimation through a sighting of the sun. One is tempted to take into account Mycerinus' rape of his daughter (and only child) here. Note his pathetic attempts at annual reanimation, followed by comical attempts at immortality through abolishing the difference between night and day.

[37] Carpenter's (1946) theory that Phoenix's autobiography slots him into the Salmoxis myth came to my attention after I had drawn the connection between Phoenix and the phoenix bird. Carpenter adduces the fact that Phoenix rules over the Dolopians in Phthia, in which Halos is located, and Herodotus situates at Halos a story that Carpenter links to the Salmoxis cult (p. 122–123). He also cites the odd feasting during Phoenix's house arrest as parallel to the "town banquet hall from which the victim is led out with pomp and sacrificial ceremony to his death." The link to the Salmoxis story seems to me tenuous. But since the Salmoxis/hibernating bear myth complex is basically a solstice/rebirth myth, it is strange that Carpenter does not mention the phoenix bird in his discussion of Phoenix (1946:170–172).

3. Taking more literally the moon *sēma* as an image, there is a movement from the indexical (*sēma* as marker) to the symbolic, or a movement from the more to the less bodily; Phoenix disappears from the poem into a *phoenix* horse that is hard to discern and has a distinguishing moon-spot (eclipse).

4. There is a conjunction or eclipse with some more enigmatic meaning.

Connections with Phoenix's speech in Book 9 present themselves. Even Phoenix's remark at 9.445, "Not even if the god himself should promise / to smooth away my old age and set me back in blooming youth," looks different. Griffin[38] believes these lines to be the source of the lines in the *Nostoi* (fr. 6) where Medea (herself of solar descent) magically rejuvenates the elderly Aeson.

Most conspicuous is the reference at the center of the Meleager story to the ἀλκυών, the halcyon bird. We noted that this was a timely myth at the middle of a ring composition, because it concerns the endpoint of the sun's annual travels (winter solstice), when it stands still before returning to bring life back to the world. This annual cycle complements the sun's nightly journey to the underworld, accompanied by the phoenix. On a still larger scale, the cosmos, through the phoenix, renews itself after a number of years. Thus both birds, the halcyon and the phoenix, achieve rebirth out of a deathly turning point (Hades/winter/pyre/tomb/corpse): the reemergence of the sun.[39]

This solar emergence at the center on the level of theme corresponded, then, to the ring structure with its central figure, embedded like a Russian doll, and compressed into a narrow space. Theme and structure (*poiēsis*) effected a "burst of energy" in the speaker, Phoenix. This "burst of energy" is often seen in ring composition, most notably in Nestor's chariot race speech, whose muted, cautious first half swerves inexplicably into unbridled optimism in the home stretch, pivoting on the description of the turning point (see Figure 7, next page).

But the burst of energy in Phoenix's speech was disturbing as well as enlivening, not so much the sun "disturbing" its course and coming back, as an angry hero rising from his tomb, like Taraxippos, to upset the rhetorical horses. This

---

[38] Griffin 1977:42. For Griffin, this is further evidence of the Cycle admitting "miracles of a sort Homer does not." But it is striking that the *Nostoi* or its tradition made this link; or else, that both epics draw on a traditional description of magical rejuvenation. Lucian *Navigium* 44–45 uses ἀποξύω in the context of a fantasy of living one thousand years by means of a magic ring, a fantasy containing a reference to the phoenix-bird and "shedding old age." ἀποξύω is used by the person making fun of such a fantasy, to say he forgot the ring to "scrape off the vast quantities of snot" (i.e., drivel), clearly responding to the fantasizer's ἀποδυόμενον τὸ γῆρας. The latter is what a snake does; the "stripping" is what magic does.

[39] Gresseth (1964:93–94) connects Alkyone/halcyon and the phoenix-bird but does not make a connection to the Homeric character Phoenix.

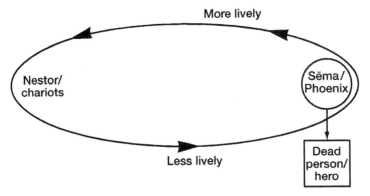

Figure 7

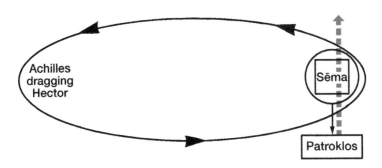

Figure 8

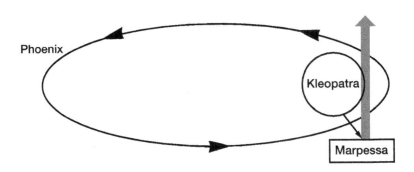

Figure 9

aspect of mourning and of hero cult is active in the poem. When Achilles drags Hektor around Patroklos' tomb (24.14–18), it seems to be a vain effort to bring Patroklos back (see Figure 8). And in the well-known vase paintings depicting the scene, he does come back: Patroklos' psyche flies out from his white, egg-shaped tomb, fully armed.[40]

In this scene, it is Patroklos. In Phoenix's speech, it is his counterpart Kleopatra who is raised to the surface, fueled by her mother's story at the center of the ring.[41] A combination of necromancy and memory brought Phoenix to the center and from there brought Kleopatra to the surface. Phoenix, like Parmenides and like Nestor (and Aristotle's physician), went on a ring journey through his memory (see Figure 9). But it was Kleopatra's memory, the stories in her *phrēn*, that raised her to the surface for her speech and that roused Meleager from his bed. Kleopatra finally threw Phoenix's rhetoric off course.

Phoenix, like a bard, acted to "escort" dead heroes into the space of performance and back to life. (Another escort of heroes who resurrects them and is connected with the phoenix is Nausikaa, whom Odysseus compares to the phoenix [palm] on Delos [*Odyssey* 6.162–163][42] and who, he says, "lifed" him [8.468] during his sojourn with the otherworldly escorts the Phaeacians.) Phoenix's position in Book 23 at the tomb and his duty to "remember the courses and report back the truth" (ὡς μεμνέῳτο δρόμους καὶ ἀληθείην ἀποείποι) recalls his necromantic memory-work in Book 9. This emphasis on memory dovetails with the link between *noos* and *nostos* as explicated by Frame. The tomb's obvious memorial function is played upon when Nestor tells Antilokhos that the man with slower horses turns around the *termata* keeping his eyes on it, nor does it escape (λήθει, 23.323) him, and proceeds to reveal the nature of the turning-point as a tomb, saying first "I shall give you an exact sign (σῆμα), and it shall not escape you (λήσει)" (23.326). In fact the only other instance of the word "truth" (ἀληθείη) in the *Iliad* (24.407) is when Priam is asking the disguised psychopomp Hermes for the truth about his dead son's corpse.

With these connections in mind, let us turn again to Marpessa, Kleopatra's mother. Marpessa's father Euenos ("well-reined") defeated her suitors one by one in deadly chariot races. His name closely resembles Euenios, the name belonging to a figure Herodotus (9.92.2–95) describes as a prophet and guardian of solar sheep, as Geryon or the Sun's daughters guard the solar cattle.[43]

---

[40] This Book 24 scene nightmarishly reenacts the chariot race in Book 23, but it also bookends the passage in Book 23 (lines 13–14) where Achilles leads the Achaeans in driving their horses around Patroklos' corpse three times.

[41] On Patro-klos' name as a *sēma*, see Sinos 1980:48–49; Nagy 1990a:216.

[42] On the ramifications of this allusion to the phoenix on Delos see Ahl and Roisman 1996:53–58.

[43] The story in Herodotus has "elements of sun mythology as preserved in an actual cult to Helios" (Frame 1978:43–44).

Once we go down that path, we are not dismayed to find that Idas, who rescues Marpessa from Apollo, is known as a raider of cattle and also that he and his brother Lynkeus are cousins of the Dioskouroi, the Divine Twins.[44] It is Idas and Lynkeus who kill Kastor and present Polydeukes with the choice of sacrificing half of his immortality to bring Kastor back to life. Idas and Lynkeus (the Apharidae) are also objects of cult (Pausanias 4.27.6).

The prophetic nature of Phoenix's speech in Book 9 is in keeping with the solar imagery.[45] He selects a *paradeigma* that mirrors what has gone on so far (the embassy: the first two parties in the sequence of suppliants to Meleager), but goes beyond it, planting the seed of the tragic Patroklos plot. In this he is similar to Circe[46] in the *Odyssey*, a prophetic solar figure wrapped up in ring composition (cf. her name). As the solar Circe gives Odysseus guidance as to how to get safely out of the underworld, Phoenix is attempting to get Achilles out—and his tent, at least by Book 24, is a kind of underworld. We will

---

[44] In some versions, the Dioskouroi steal cattle from the Apharidae. On the Dioskouroi and their relation to the Vedic twins the Nasatya ("they who bring back to life and light"), see Frame 1978:140–142; Frame 2009:21, 72. Levaniouk (1999:128–129), in the context of discussing the dense links between the halcyon and the *pēnelopes*, who "come from the limits of the earth," remarks that the diction of the *Iliad* passage suggests Apollo carried Marpessa to the streams of Okeanos. Cf. Levaniouk 2011: Ch. 17.

[45] See Frame 1978:38–53 on Circe (including p. 44, on Euenios), and p. 92, on Melampus.

[46] Phoenix's autobiography would not in itself suggest solar connections. Yet many details slot into such an interpretation. Aside from the motif of "taking over for one's father"—in Phoenix's case, like Oedipus, in bed and as a would-be patricide—Phoenix escapes from a house resembling Night and Day in *Theogony* 744–757 and other solar locations (*Iliad* 9.464–473):

ἦ μὲν πολλὰ ἔται καὶ ἀνεψιοὶ ἀμφὶς ἐόντες	
465 αὐτοῦ λισσόμενοι κατερήτυον ἐν μεγάροισι,	= *Odyssey* 9.31 (Circe)
πολλὰ δὲ ἴφια μῆλα καὶ εἰλίποδας ἕλικας βοῦς	cf. *Odyssey* 9.46 (Ciconians)
ἔσφαζον, πολλοὶ δὲ σύες θαλέθοντες ἀλοιφῇ	
εὑόμενοι τανύοντο διὰ φλογὸς Ἡφαίστοιο,	
πολλὸν δ' ἐκ κεράμων μέθυ πίνετο τοῖο γέροντος.	cf. *Odyssey* 9.45 (Ciconians)
470 εἰνάνυχες δέ μοι ἀμφ' αὐτῷ παρὰ νύκτας ἴαυον·	
οἳ μὲν ἀμειβόμενοι φυλακὰς ἔχον, οὐδέ ποτ' ἔσβη	cf. *Theogony* 749
πῦρ, ἕτερον μὲν ὑπ' αἰθούσῃ εὐερκέος αὐλῆς,	cf. *Theogony* 752–753
ἄλλο δ' ἐνὶ προδόμῳ, πρόσθεν θαλάμοιο θυράων.	

But my kinsmen and cousins surrounding me
pleaded and tried to restrain me in the halls;
many fat sheep and rolling-gaited, spiral-horned cattle
they were slaughtering, and many pigs, blooming with fat,
being singed, were stretched over the flame of Hephaistos,
and much drink out of jars was drunk—the old man's.
For nine nights they slept alongside me, by night;
they kept watch, exchanging shifts, and never was extinguished
the fire, one under the portico of the walled courtyard,
and one in the hall, in front of the bedroom doors.

examine further evidence for the return of Achilles as a reanimation in the next chapter.

Given all this, it is surprising that no extant ancient commentator tells us all about a relationship between Phoenix and the phoenix-bird, and of those two with Nestor. Then again, perhaps the Phoenix/Nestor/chariot/sun complex is a relic, lingering from a tradition—only in the case of Phoenix, not an Indo-European one! On such a reading, the individual elements, like the lines about "escaping from death" in the *Odyssey*, would remain despite their having been unmoored from the original sun-worship context.[47] But the phoenix-bird is most certainly not a relic, but a living tradition; and there is other evidence that we must now consider.

Phoenix in Visual Art

Although no ancient writer does so, ancient wall painting may preserve further evidence for an interpretation of Phoenix along the lines sketched in the previous pages. If this evidence is deemed relevant, it would bolster the idea that the symbolic complex under discussion is not merely a relic. Any attempt to relate the artistic evidence to the previous discussion is fraught with problems, and certainly stretches beyond the bounds of my expertise. But after I had analyzed the Phoenix speech and his role in Book 23, two specimens of ancient wall painting seemed to offer visual correlations to some of my analysis. I pivot out here into visual art to stimulate readers to think in three dimensions. It could be that some ancient listeners (and spectators) were better attuned to the spatial aspect of Phoenix in the *Iliad* and its broader tradition, in the way I have discussed, and that this found rich expression in the way they decorated their surroundings.[48]

---

[47] Frame, in *Hippota Nestor* (2009), revises his earlier view (Frame 1978) that Nestor's name had no meaning for the Homeric poets. But the later work still distinguishes earlier and later stages of Greek epic in terms of the meaning of *nes-, which as "return *from death to life*" did not "survive into the Homeric era" (p. 39), *asmenos* in the *Odyssey*'s lines about return from death (no longer understood as a verb), and the traditional refrain about "return to life." But Frame notes that classical Greek *asmenos* still occurs "in the context of a 'return to the light'" (Frame 2009:42n78). Since the Homeric poems may have taken shape during New Year festivals such as the Panathenaia, a context that features a turn of the sun is not so remote. Cf. Cook 1995: Ch. 5, and see below, pages 192–193 (on the calendar of the *Iliad* and the halcyon myth) and 304–305 (on the winter solstice in *Odyssey* 15).

[48] I do not mean to suggest a close connection here between either of these works and what an audience member of the solo *Iliad* performer would witness. Rather these works seem to reflect on the role of Nestor and Phoenix in *Iliad* 23, and traditions related to it, in a way that bears upon Phoenix's pivotal position and the parallels between his own mythology and Nestor's. What we see in *Iliad* 23 in turn finds more histrionic expression in Phoenix's *Iliad* 9 speech.

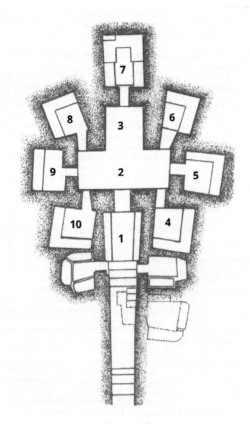

Figure 10

Nestor and Phoenix are depicted mirroring or facing one another in various visual media.[49] This is no surprise: they are obviously similar characters, apart from any particular "return" or "sun" significance, and apart from their roles in the chariot race. Nevertheless a few visual examples do point toward this particular complex of symbols.

In some of the examples where Nestor and Phoenix are paired, they are observing the funeral games of Patroklos: most notably, the sacrifice of Trojan prisoners upon the tomb of Patroklos. For example, on a volute crater from Canosa from about 340/330 BCE,[50] they are hovering over the sacrifice observing

[49] Phoenix is depicted as Nestor's companion, facing him, or else positioned opposite him, at many important events: *LIMC* Nestor 1064, listing entries 15, 19, 25–27, 29 (which must be an error for 28), 34.

[50] *LIMC* Nestor 26; for bibliography, see *LIMC* Achilles 487. Höckmann (1982:84), following Furt-wangler, interprets Nestor and Phoenix on this vase as occupying Achilles' tent. She suggests

Figure 11

it from the upper tier of a three-tiered vase painting, and turn to one another to discuss the matter. Although the two are set apart in their own tent-like space, they share this upper register with several gods.

The François Tomb, an Etruscan tomb whose frescoes date from 330–310 BCE, roughly the same date as the volute crater, is a tomb of extraordinary proportions with an elaborate decorative program (see Figure 10).[51] Once again Phoenix and Nestor (named in the inscriptions) face one another, this time on opposite sides of a door to one of the burial chambers (see Figure 11).

Behind each figure a large palm seems as though it is growing from each head. Here too, moreover, the sacrifice of Trojans occupies a significant place in the tomb. The sacrifice is depicted along a wall leading up to the focal door of the entire tomb, opposite another wall depicting an important event from Etruscan history, portraying it as an event akin to the sacrifice of prisoners.

This is part of an elaborate system of mirrors in the tomb's decoration. Phoenix and Nestor face each other beside the door to Chamber 9, while two other figures face each other beside the door to Chamber 5 on the other side of the atrium. Directly across from Nestor is a figure labeled "Vel Saties," presumably a historical figure, and perhaps the inhabitant of Chamber 5.[52] Vel Saties stands next to a small figure, a child or a dwarf, who is holding a bird. Some scholars interpret this small figure as performing haruspicy. Unfortunately, the

---

this scene is not meant to be simultaneous with the sacrifice; rather, perhaps the painting draws on a version in which Nestor told Phoenix about the gruesome sacrifice in Achilles' tent. Höckmann however would separate the figures in the tomb from the sacrifice around the corner.

[51] The plan of the tomb in Figure 10 is by Louis-garden, used under the CC BY-SA 3.0 license. The nineteenth-century reconstruction by Carlo Ruspi in Figure 11 is also featured in Buranelli 1987: 180. A 3-D tour of the tomb is available at http://www.canino.info/inserti/monografie/etruschi/tomba_francois/tomba_francois_1.htm.

[52] Rebuffat and Rebuffat (1978) make a case for Vel Saties being a historical ancestor of the individual who commissioned the tomb, rather than this individual himself.

figure directly across the atrium from Phoenix has been lost; but here, as with the Trojan prisoners and the Etruscan slaughter, characters from the *Iliad* are set opposite actual Etruscans. And not just any *Iliad* characters, but ones traditionally associated, in the poem and in visual art, with Book 23's funeral games and, in art, with the sacrifice of Trojan prisoners.

What then is the significance of the two elderly Achaeans facing the two dead Etruscan inhabitants of the tomb? One interpretation is that "Phoenix" is an eponymous figure of the Phoenicians, while Nestor represents the ancestor or founder-figure of the Etruscans. In support of this interpretation, Coarelli speculates that the palm (phoenix) behind Phoenix is a sign that Phoenix is simply an eponym of the Phoenicians or more particularly, since they had close ties to the Etruscans, the Carthaginians.[53] Nestor would then be the ancestor of Vel Saties, while Phoenix would be an ancestor of the putative Carthaginian pictured facing him. In objection to this it is pointed out[54] that *both* Phoenix and Nestor have palms[55] behind their heads. At any rate, the two appear in the vicinity of the sacrifice of Trojan prisoners, in accord with the tradition linking the two elders with the sacrifice.

Unlike in the other examples, Phoenix and Nestor do not observe or preside over the sacrifice of Trojans, which is nevertheless depicted around the corner. What are they doing here opposite Vel Saties and his cryptic companion? If Vel Saties represents the family buried in this tomb, his position opposite Phoenix and Nestor suggests that, rather than simply mirroring him, they are escorting him into the afterlife or otherwise mediating, like the Etruscan Underworld figures seen among the Trojan captives, the tomb-dwellers' dealings with death.[56] It is admittedly puzzling for this interpretation that Phoenix and Nestor are not either heraldically surrounding the door of Chamber 7, the visual focal

---

[53] Coarelli 1983:58–59.

[54] Buranelli 1987:101.

[55] I note that another palm is depicted in the *dromos* of the tomb, with a serpent. On the association between the phoenix *bird* and the palm (phoenix), see van den Broek (1971:52–60, 183), for whom the link is a late development, via Lactantius inspired by Ovid. Hubaux and Leroy (1939:103–104) list longevity and notional asexuality among the features common to tree and bird. (For example, note Aristotle fr. 246: palms are ἄνορχοι and therefore called eunuchs.) This last is interesting in light of Phoenix's sterility. Hubaux and Leroy's comparisons are dismissed by van den Broek (1971:54n2), despite his discussion later (357–389) of the sexuality of the phoenix bird. Van den Broek does not discuss the Iliadic Phoenix. Thierry Petit (personal communication, 2015) suggests that the phoenix (palm) may be the origin of the tree of life motif in Near Eastern art. For Höckmann (1982:87) the palm is a general allusion to Troy.

[56] The Nestor-Phoenix pairing is not only, I am offering here, an ennobling "complementary analog" or "resonating gloss" for the Etruscans across from them (Brilliant 1984:34; cf. Rebuffat and Rebuffat 1978). The artist, as Brilliant puts it on the same page, "deliberately blended this diverse cultural and ethnic material to create a new narrative cycle of death and transportation." Phoenix and Nestor act as more than mirrors within that project.

point of the tomb, or surrounding the entrance to the tomb, the doorway leading from the "tablinum" into the atrium. Nevertheless, the François Tomb and the chariot race in the funeral games of Book 23 seem to ask to be read together somehow, rather than Phoenix and Nestor serving as more generic figures of wisdom. It would admittedly be easier to do so if they flanked the door of Chamber 7, which might be thought of as the central tomb (*sēma*) seen from the *dromos*. Still, they do occupy such a "turning-point" position vis-à-vis Vel Saties and his companion.

The door near Vel Saties originally bore a painting that disintegrated while being transported. Art historians note the strong symbolism of the door and of the "epiphanic" quality of the figure on it.[57] The figure on this door is thought to have been female. Perhaps then Vel Saties had a portrait of himself placed next to the door to his wife's chamber, on the door of which she was painted. Thus the door was both the site where she crossed into death and where she appeared in an epiphany after her death.

Both because of the fragmentary nature of the evidence and because the tomb's paintings seem designed to be suggestive, a simple, totalizing reading is not attractive. What has emerged, however, is a relationship between Phoenix and Nestor and the inhabitants of the tomb, and a relationship to the tomb itself as a liminal space. If one thinks of the painted figure on Chamber 5 as beginning a loop roughly like the chariot race,[58] Phoenix and Nestor would preside over the midpoint, at which there was, indeed, a tomb. If the painted figure instead provides the turning point, Phoenix and Nestor would stand at the beginning and end of that race. Unfortunately for this latter interpretation, the two should be switched so that Nestor could guide the beginning and Phoenix judge the end (assuming a counterclockwise race as in the *Iliad*). Perhaps Vel Saties reserved Chamber 9 for himself, so that he and his wife could visit one another in this reciprocal fashion, while being painted next to one another as well.

At any rate, however we interpret the details, the François Tomb appears to indicate that the associations between Nes-tor and "rescue from death,"[59] as well as a strong association between Phoenix and Nestor and of the pair to the funeral games, remained alive among the Etruscans of the late fourth century, *Iliad* connoisseurs with a voracious appetite for elegant visual art inspired by it and by associated traditions.

---

[57] Maggiani 1983:78.
[58] Mycenaean and Dark Age tombs did, of course, contain horse burials, some of which are thought of as chariot teams, but I am not suggesting anything corresponding to this for the François Tomb.
[59] This may be strengthened by the palms over their heads; see above n55.

There is another exceptionally large-scale work that merits attention in this regard. This work is manifestly concerned with the structure of the *Iliad*, and highlights the chariot race in the games for Patroklos. The House of Octavius Quartius (Pompeii II.2.2) is an opulent house with an enormous garden, stretching out over nearly the whole of Insula II.2 (see Figure 12).[60] The triclinium (or *oecus*) is strategically oriented toward the garden, which stretches out from its south door. The two primary friezes in this room depict episodes from the Herakles cycle (the upper frieze) and the *Iliad* (the lower frieze). The lower, smaller frieze begins to the west of the south door with Apollo, instigating with his arrows the plague of *Iliad* 1. Proceeding north, after a doorway, we have the Teichomachia, followed by the Battle at the Ships (Book 15: Ajax and Hektor are shown). Proceeding clockwise onto the north wall, there are some "Phrygians" (inscription), followed by Patroklos on the rampage with Achilles' horses, trampling over corpses (Book 16). Following this is Thetis and Achilles with the Shield (Book 18) and a chariot guided by Automedon dragging the corpse of Hektor.

Turning the corner onto the East wall, the viewer sees a large expanse depicting the funeral games of Patroklos, the beginning of which is damaged. The chariot race takes up the most space here, followed by small figures of a discobolus and two boxers. Following this is Achilles supplicated by Priam,[61] and then two figures identified as "Priam and a Trojan, perhaps the herald Ideus."[62] One would expect the episodes to end here or else proceed to the funeral of Hektor, but we have instead Achilles and Phoenix.[63] (I mentioned this vignette above because Phoenix is here kneeling before Achilles just as Priam had done two vignettes to the left.) Then follows a solitary pensive figure, presumably Achilles alone outside his tent. Turning the corner to the south wall, there is an embassy to Achilles. This is presumably the embassy of Book 9, but from what I can see it could also be the heralds dispatched in Book 1. In other words, the lower frieze depicts the principal events of the *Iliad* in order—except for the embassy, and in particular Phoenix and Achilles.

The larger, upper frieze depicts two sequences of events, both of which begin at the north wall and proceed south, ending at the garden doorway. The eastern sequence features the deeds of Herakles and Telamon. It proceeds from the rescue of Hesione through her restoration to her father Laomedon, Herakles killing Laomedon, the wedding of Hesione and Telamon presided over by Herakles, Herakles with a bow, and finally, Herakles investing the young Priam,

---

[60] Drawing after Knox 2015: 174, with additions and modifications.
[61] Pugliese Carratelli 1990:88, fig. 71.
[62] Pugliese Carratelli 1990:88.
[63] See Pugliese Carratelli 1990:89, fig. 73. These two figures are framed by a tent, although the figure following it to the right, presumably Achilles again, seems to have a shield hanging on a wall behind him.

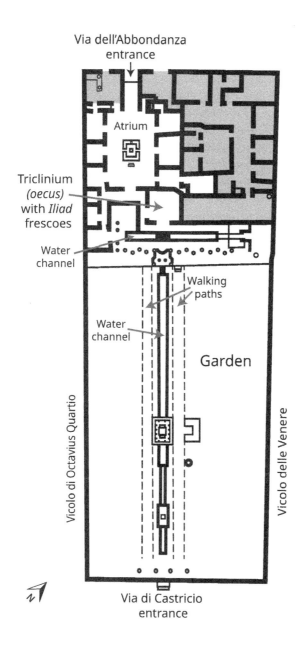

Via dell'Abbondanza
entrance

Atrium

Triclinium
(oecus)
with *Iliad*
frescoes

Water
channel

Walking
paths

Water
channel

Garden

Vicolo di Octavius Quartio

Vicolo delle Venere

Via di Castricio
entrance

Figure 12

brother of Hesione, with royal power. The western sequence depicts the events of Herakles' death. Beginning from the north wall, Herakles fights Nessos; proceeding to the west wall Nessos gives Deianeira poison, Herakles on the pyre is assisted by Philoctetes, and finally, on the south wall, a very fragmentary image presumably[64] showed Herakles being escorted to Olympus. Thus whoever is sitting at the north end of the room is "embraced by the frieze of Hercules"— by these two sequences that culminate in the two scenes straddling the passage into the garden, scenes of mortals crossing into royal status, on the one side, and immortality, on the other: "two models of political-moral promotion supported by the current Stoic philosophy. The waterway that runs through the garden is placed along the axis of the South door of the *oecus*: the green and the water of the garden reward those who, having absorbed the moralistic lesson, pass from the darkness inside into the light outside."[65] This passage from darkness into light is however quite literally undermined by the panel beneath. Most pointedly, the young Priam on the upper frieze on the south wall faces the corpse of Hektor being dragged on the lower frieze on the south wall, and is also in the neighborhood of his aged self ransoming his son's body. The *oecus* has a tinge of the tragic sense that infused the François Tomb.

Why is Phoenix out of place in the otherwise chronological sequence? Keeping in mind the other evidence linking Phoenix and Nestor to the funeral games, it is tempting to think that Phoenix here occupies the would-be "turning-point" of the chariot race that dominates the wall to the left.[66] If so, Phoenix is doing several things at once. He is reprising Priam's supplication just to his left,[67] while occupying spatially his position at the turning-point of the chariot race, and reprising his Book 9 role, supplicating Achilles to "go out of his chamber" toward (à la Meleager) his death.

In this richly stimulating room, Phoenix and Nestor do not, as they do in the François Tomb, flank the symbolically loaded doorway to the garden. Nevertheless, the Book 23 schema seems to be operating here too. Phoenix

---

[64] Pugliese Carratelli 1990:86. Thierry Petit (personal communication, 2015) points out the relevance of Herakles' apotheosis in a chariot to the symbolic complex of the chariot and reanimation. Perhaps the damaged panel depicted just this? It would certainly be in keeping with the proliferation of chariot scenes. Herakles on the pyre, followed by his apotheosis, resembles the phoenix bird; this scene roughly faces Phoenix and Achilles on the opposite wall.

[65] Pugliese Carratelli 1990:86.

[66] Does the damage at the other end of the chariot race leave room for Nestor?

[67] See page 154n109 above. The gestural/proxemic analogy between Phoenix and Priam may have been even more obvious to someone who had seen the *Iliad* performed. By this I mean the literal gestural enactment, however this is done. For another perspective on the parallel between Phoenix and Priam in terms of enactment, see Taplin 1992:80. According to Taplin's scheme, the bed made up for Priam in Book 24 parallels that made for Phoenix in Book 9—closing the first and third days of performance respectively.

Figure 13

presides over the exit of Achilles toward his death in close proximity to the south exit to the garden, an exit that already, from the two sequences in the upper frieze, bears clear significance as a passage into blessedness, even immortality. Yet the garden on the other side is no generic Elysium (see Figure 13[68]).

The long, narrow garden is bisected by a channel, ending just before the south limit of the property in a circular fountain and a couple of planters (?).

[68] Photo by Wikimedia Commons user Magistermercator, reproduced under the CC BY-SA 3.0 license. See Price and Van Buren 1935, Plate 12 for a reconstruction of the original garden plantings.

One who strolls in this garden walks south, turns around, and comes north again, returning into the *oecus*. Such a person is not only reaping the rewards of whatever Stoic lesson is on offer in the upper frieze; he or she also *reenacts the chariot race* depicted on the lower frieze.

What would one give to be a guest of the Homer enthusiast who commissioned this house, to dine in its triclinium and take in these scenes—surely this room hosted some form of Homeric performance—and afterward to stroll around the garden, pondering the painting? Here, spread out over the heads of the diners, would seem to be the performer's very path of song, an ecphrasis in reverse, or a literalization of the performer's mnemonic loci. If the circling Muses could serve Mnemosyne, why not seated diners—actual occupants of couches, rather than ones in the poem?[69] But the path here would seem to go astray: why did the host have Phoenix painted in this way? Does the host associate the south doorway with death? Was he aiming, at the endpoint of our feast and its stories, for a space in which we might feel ourselves to reenact them?

Conclusion: The Speech of Phoenix and Its Contexts

Phoenix's appearance in the chariot race in Book 23 turns out to be closely attuned to his speech in Book 9. There is a surprising confluence among drama, structure, and theme: the importance at the speech's center of a silent dead figure who is animated through the person of Phoenix in the second half of the ring, its dramatic change after this turn—as in the speech of Nestor guiding Antilokhos—as though something has changed in the mind of the speaker in tandem with that strange emergence of another figure. The themes associated with Nestor and Phoenix—solar cycles of day and year, solar birds, *noos*, the underworld, patricide (phoenix-bird), bursting out of gates—figured into Phoenix's speech. These images, along with the imagery of containment/bursting out, imprisonment and rescue, were all related within a web embracing plot and imagery (poetics), on the one hand, and embodiment, instantiation and performance (presence), on the other.[70]

---

[69] Jenny Strauss Clay (Clay 2011:110–115; cf. Clay 1994) recalls the story of Simonides reconstructing the positions of banqueters after they have been killed and connects it to the "*dais* of death" dealt out to the suitors of the *Odyssey*. Clay (p. 113) notes that "the poet provides us with three circuits around the great hall." She further relates the "path of song" to the use of various forms of loci (both actual places in the story, and the artificial use of loci such as in a memory palace) by storytellers and orators.

[70] The distinction between poetics and presence bears some relationship to that between *noos* and *nostos* as discussed by Frame (1978). Which term corresponds to which depends on one's point of view. Poetics as plot bears a resemblance to *nostos* as journey. But *nostos* as a reemergence can be compared with presence, an emergence into the body of the performer.

If the plots (poetics) of the *Iliad* and *Odyssey* are organized around the return from "death" of their respective heroes, there is a corresponding reanimation on the level of presence. We have seen one of the best examples of this in the script of *Iliad* 9, the speech of Phoenix, and we shall see further examples in the following chapters. The power of the script derives in part from themes and images, and especially the theme/gesture of cursing that culminates in the emergence of Kleopatra. This becoming, this 'carnation' of the character by the bard, belongs in the realm of the 'reincarnation' or rescue from death that goes on in *noos/nostos*. Epic acting takes its place within this reanimation.

In case all this seems too complex, perhaps that is only natural. It may be that to talk about Alkyone and Phoenix is to enter the realm of riddles. Above I mentioned that one of the only things known about the *Wedding of Keux* is that riddles were told.[71] And let us look again at the Euripides passage mentioned above,[72] sung by a chorus of *captive* Greek girls in the East, yearning to return west to Greece (cf. the *nostoi* of heroes in Book 23). Note the presence of Apollo and Artemis, and *phoenix* as palm; we return to this grouping in Chapter 4.

> ὄρνις ἅ παρὰ πετρίνας
> 1090 πόντου δειράδας ἀλκυὼν
> ἔλεγον οἶτον ἀείδεις,
> εὐξύνετον ξυνετοῖς βοάν,
> ὅτι πόσιν κελαδεῖς ἀεὶ μολπαῖς,
> ἐγώ σοι παραβάλλομαι
> 1095 θρήνους, ἄπτερος ὄρνις,
> ποθοῦσ' Ἑλλάνων ἀγόρους,
> ποθοῦσ' Ἄρτεμιν λοχίαν
> ἅ παρὰ Κύνθιον ὄχθον οἰ-
> κεῖ ποίνικά θ' ἁβροκόμαν
> 1100 δάφναν τ' εὐερνέα καὶ
> γλαυκᾶς θαλλὸν ἱερὸν ἐλαί-
> ας, Λατοῦς ὠδῖνι φίλον,
> λίμναν θ' εἱλίσσουσαν ὕδωρ
> κύκλιον ἔνθα κύκνος μελωι-
> 1105 δὸς Μούσας θεραπεύει.
>
> Bird, you who along the rocky
> ridges of the sea, halcyon,
> sing your doom as a lament,

---

[71] See above page 138n74. Frame (2009, encapsulated at pp. 599–600) argues that secrecy character-izes the sections of the Homeric poems associated with Nestor or the Neleids.
[72] See above Chapter 2, n78.

a cry easily intelligible to the intelligent,
that you croon to your husband in song for all time,
I set beside you
laments, I a wingless bird,
longing for the gatherings of Hellenes,
longing for Artemis of childbirth
who has her home by the Kynthian hill
and the phoenix, lavish-leaved
and the laurel, sprouting
and the sacred shoot of grey olive,
dear to the child of Leto's pangs,
and the lake, whirling its water
in circles, where the swan, singing,
serves the Muses.

Euripides, *Iphigenia in Tauris* 1089–1105

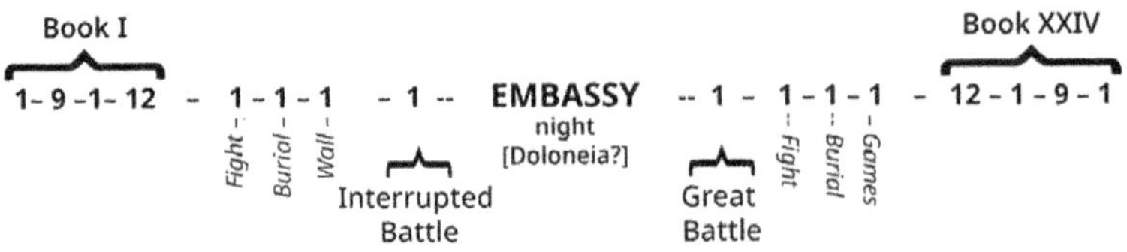

Figure 14

One last piece of evidence ties Phoenix's speech to a solar-lunar cycle that is also ring-compositional: the location of the speech in the poem, in the exact chronological center.

The calendar of the poem (Figure 14, after Whitman 1958:257) is carefully set out in a symmetrical scheme. This symmetry is centered on a different point from that in Whitman's ring-composition map of the poem by theme, but is just as striking. This calendar reflects the poem's accounting in multiples of 3 and 9,[73] but also ensures that there is a month preceding and following the night of the Embassy. As a result, the Embassy may be thought of as occurring during the same phase of the moon as the beginning and end of the poem, as a new moon or full moon. This would accord with the *phoenix* horse and his moon,

---

[73] Fenno 2007; Whitman 1958:257.

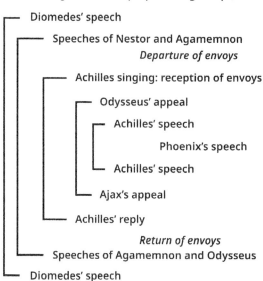

Agamemnon's proposal to give up (dark-watered spring)
Diomedes' speech
    Speeches of Nestor and Agamemnon
        Departure of envoys
        Achilles singing: reception of envoys
            Odysseus' appeal
                Achilles' speech
                    Phoenix's speech
                Achilles' speech
            Ajax's appeal
        Achilles' reply
        Return of envoys
    Speeches of Agamemnon and Odysseus
Diomedes' speech

Figure 15

and bring the *Iliad* into line with the *Odyssey*'s solar and lunar cycles.[74] The main point is that Book 9 is at the center of the calendrical ring, flanked by four days before and after it, days which themselves form a ring within the ring.[75] "All the meaning is to be found there."[76]

Within Book 9, Phoenix's speech occupies the central position, as Whitman's better-known chart shows (see Figure 15, adapted from Whitman[77]).

Phoenix's speech is, as we saw, divided into three panels: the autobiography, the Litai, and the Meleager story. Within the Meleager story (not the central panel), there are three sections. In the central section, Meleager is embedded in

---

[74] Austin 1975; Nagy 1990a:225; Frame 1978; Levaniouk 2008:28–35. Regarding the Doloneia's (*Iliad* 10's) contested status in this scheme, perhaps it "extends" this central night to extraordinary length just as does the winter solstice operating in the *Odyssey*. See below, Chapter 4.

[75] Compare Otterlo 1948 and Douglas 2007:101–124, esp. Fig. 12, showing Night 4 (the Embassy) as the mid-turn of the minor ring of eight days, which in turn forms the mid-turn of the major ring, Fig. 13, and Table 8.

[76] Douglas 2007:109.

[77] Whitman 1958:281; cf. the relevant section of his full fold-out chart. The discussion of ring composition here also appears in Kretler 2018.

the recesses of his house with Kleopatra. And within that central section, point-edly ensconced in the center of ring composition, was the story of Kleopatra's mother Marpessa.

I. The War of the Kouretes and the Aetolians. 524–549
II. Meleager Retires from the Battle. 550–574
    A The Battle Rages. 550–552
        B Meleager's Wrath. 553–555 χόλος
            C He Retires with Kleopatra. 556 κεῖτο
               X Kleopatra's Mother. 557–564
            C′ He Retires with Kleopatra. 565 παρκατέλεκτο
        B′ Meleager's Wrath. 565–572 χόλον
    A′ The Battle Rages. 573–574
III. Meleager Is Persuaded. 574–599. (Catalogue of suppliants.)

The allusion to Alkyone was vital to understanding the speech as a whole. This triple- or quadruple-embedding in ring composition (a ring-composition largely built upon numbers of days, and day-and-night alternations) strengthens the links between Alkyone and Phoenix and their solar associations. Recall, finally, that the myth of Alkyone is a myth not about a single point in time, but about a series of days straddling the winter solstice. There is a poetics of the nightingale in Homer; but there is also a poetics of the halcyon.[78]

The next chapter uncovers an instance of emergence at the center at the geographical turning point rather than the chronological center of the poem. At the end of Book 15, the Trojans finally reach the Achaean wall and threaten to burn their ships, as is contemplated in the speeches in Book 9 and imagined in the fire raining down on Meleager's chamber. The disaster imagined via the Meleager story is finally happening. While the plot features the reemergence of the Patroklos-Achilles pair (followed by the *aristeia* and death of Patroklos), this is coupled with the emergence of yet another dead hero and his wife. Once again, a performative (presence) uncanniness is built atop an uncanny thematic (poetics) foundation: this time not an act of cursing but a return from death.

---

[78] Nagy 1990a:36–37. The nightingale (*Odyssey* 19) and the halcyon (*Iliad* 9) lament their children. They both are entangled with the thought of a woman (Penelope/Kleopatra), not only thematizing her grief but trying to represent the levels of her consciousness. The halcyon in *Iliad* 9 points to a similar depth within a woman that the nightingale does for Penelope. Levaniouk connects the poetics of the halcyon to that of the nightingale (Levaniouk 1999; Levaniouk 2011: Ch. 17).

3

Half-Burnt

The Wife of Protesilaos In and Out of the *Iliad*

The most passionate advocacies for the art of poetry in sophisticated late periods, such as the period of Horace, turn upon the function of poetry as keeping alive, across the abysses of death and of the difference between persons, the human image. ... Now I think you make a generational error ... by viewing poetry as having as its function the continuity of the image of the poetic writer. Poetry traditionally, and in my view fundamentally, deals in the continuity of the image not of the poet but of the poet's *beloved*.

Grossman and Halliday, "The Winter Conversations," in
The Sighted Singer, pp. 6 and 12

Just so at the sacramental drinking of the wine, unfamiliar, uncanny guests were present beside the friends and family who had been invited. ... Thus, one encountered the sacred through that which is uncanny.

Burkert, *Homo Necans*, p. 230, on the Anthesteria

> illic Phylacides iucundae coniugis heros
>   non potuit caecis immemor esse locis,
> sed cupidus falsis attingere gaudia palmis
>   Thessalus antiquam venerat umbra domum.
> illic quidquid ero, semper tua dicar imago:
>   traicit et fati litora magnus amor.[1]

Propertius 1.19.7–12

---

[1] "There the hero Phylacides could not be unmindful of his lovely wife in the blind places, but wanting to touch his bliss with illusory palms, the Thessalian came, a shade, to his old home. There, whatever I will be, I will always be called your image: even the shores of death great love thrusts through."

The last chapter examined a speech that aimed to break Achilles out of his withdrawal and spur him back onto the battlefield. Achilles was to return to battle before it was too late to get gifts, unlike Meleager, who lay in his chamber until the person dearest to him, his wife Kleopatra, recited to him the disasters about to befall her and the rest of Calydon. Now we are drawing near the moment in Book 16 when Patroklos steps into Kleopatra's role and begs Achilles to fight. Instead of going out himself, of course, Achilles agrees to send Patroklos out in his armor to drive the Trojans away from the ships: a half-measure, neither returning nor remaining completely withdrawn. The act, then, forms a pendant to the story of Meleager both in this straightforward way and in more subtle ways that will shortly become apparent. Yet the moment is puzzling, if one thinks in terms of plot or Achilles' intentions.[2]

We will deepen our understanding of this moment, along with the drama leading up to it and falling out from it, by analyzing it from the perspective of performance or presence. But it is not an instance of "becoming the character" like the speech of Phoenix; it is something more complex. Its kinesthetics are more dispersed, and grapple more directly with absence, longing, and action at a distance, instead of with bringing something buried into vigorous presence. Once again a background story, previously neglected, foments a set of poetic and performative effects. The background materials I excavate in this chapter are deployed even more delicately than those in play in the Phoenix speech, almost forming a meditation upon performance at the same time that they fuel it.

On the face of it, Book 16 resembles the *aristeiai* of Diomedes and Agamemnon; it is after all the *aristeia* of Patroklos, complete with arming scene.[3] Yet the script here is not simple: Book 16 dramatizes not only the emergence of Patroklos but also a strange partial emergence of Achilles—the emergence of

---

[2] Redfield (1994:59): "We can thus define fiction as the outcome of a hypothetical inquiry into the intermediate causes of action ..." and p. 106: "Surely Achilles makes errors, and surely Achilles suffers; but the poet has not been at pains to construct a clear relation of cause and effect." Nimis (1987:40): "Achilles' actions in Book 16 are, in fact, quite inexplicable in terms of his stated 'intentions.' It is difficult to see how sending out Patroklos will profit Achilles at all in reestablishing his lost honor. If Patroklos beats back Hector, how will the Greeks be forced to give Achilles back his due honor? If Achilles now feels that his ends have been accomplished, why does he not return himself? We could state the problem in Riffaterre's terms by saying that in Book 16, the significance of the poem, which can be identified thematically with the *Dios boulē*, the 'plan of Zeus' to honor Achilles, begins to contradict the meaning of Achilles' actions; that is, the portrayal of Achilles begins to become 'ungrammatical.'" See also Scott 2009:156–157.

[3] Taplin (1992:291) sees the book division between 15 and 16 as arbitrarily disruptive: "The thinking behind the far less telling division at 16.1 is not hard to see: 'Aristarchos' wanted to turn a single book into a 'Patrokleia' (as with Diomedes in book 5)." One would not want to end a performance session after Book 15; the reason, however, is that one would miss the transmogrification of space and consciousness that does in fact occur at the book division. On this book division, see also Heiden 1996, Nagy 2002:62–65.

Patroklos as Achilles' double.[4] The plot of the *Iliad* as a whole, of course, may be thought of as the withdrawal and emergence of Achilles, or withdrawal, devastation, and return.[5] Though Achilles does eventually have his own massively elaborated arming scene, there is no single moment of emergence, but an unfolding over several books. Achilles makes several appearances verging on the epiphanic, viewed from within the world of the poem, including when he shouts at the trench and twelve people automatically drop dead (18.230).[6] From the perspective of the Achilles plot, the dispatch and death of Patroklos is only a substitute epiphany.

In this study I am concerned with what happens in the world of the poem insofar as it strikes against "presencing" to create a spark. There are, for example, moments when the bard draws a spark of "presence" or "becoming" from the flint of composition or poetics that prompt the audience to ask: Where is this action coming from? Is this performer inside or outside the poem?

One such moment, one within the "becoming," or emergence, of Achilles, was examined in Chapter 1: the apostrophes to Patroklos leading up to his death. Through the apostrophes, the bard is taken over by Achilles and seems to lose control of the unfolding plot. (These apostrophes, and especially the first, will be enlivened further by a closer look at how they function in the drama: see below.) One might also single out Achilles' speech in Book 9, a speech whose superior insights and verbal pyrotechnics lift Achilles to the level of the performing poet, effacing the distinction between bard and character.[7] The apostrophes, the epiphany at the trench, and the famous speech are part of a larger arc, an arc that includes the extraordinary scene in Books 15–16.

But this scene is something beyond the emergence of a character: it is the orchestration of an uncanny space. At the juncture between Books 15 and 16, a more subtle space of transformation is created where the body of the performer is less central to that transformation, where characters from the past haunt the present in multiple ways without entirely taking it over. The focus of this process is the stern of a ship, which is transformed into a stage and a portal in time and space. And the dimensions of the created space expand outward.

Nevertheless, the poet-performer here draws on ingredients familiar from the previous chapter, elements we can use to get our bearings for this more complex histrionic path. This includes a background story that involves eros and death, the overlaying of the space of present action with an alternative space,

---

[4] Nagler 1974:135–138.

[5] A. Lord 2000: Ch. 9; M. L. Lord 1967; Nagler 1974: Ch. 5 (who describes three interlocking withdrawal-devastation-return cycles); Nagy 1979:69–93.

[6] M. L. Lord 1967:247. On the shout, see Griffin 1980:38–39. They die "by their own chariots and weapons," but the superhuman is there, even if muted compared with warriors' shouts in other epics; cf. A. Lord 2000:196.

[7] See the Introduction above, p. 13n35 and n36.

the gradual approach to a "source of energy" for the emergence of a character, and characters who are taken over by figures from the past. As with the themes in Phoenix's speech (e.g., the repeated cursing), the background material here provides especially fertile thematic ground for the "coming forth" of the character. In the Interlude following this chapter, I make the case for a connection between this background material and that in Phoenix's speech, and speculate about a possible source for this connection.

The role of this background material—even its existence—has not been sufficiently recognized. I thus begin by showing how this story, the story of Protesilaos, works in the background of the poem in a general way, and then turn to how the story bodies itself forth. I shall first examine thematic resonances between the Protesilaos story and the unfolding drama. I then turn to the way space is reconceived as well as transformed in performance. This discussion of space in turn frames a closer examination of the theme of substitution and the way this theme surfaces into the level of performance. As the discussion proceeds, I bring the embodied performance into the argument more openly, suggesting how the "kinesthetics" of the background story operates in performance. In the light of this interpretation, one may detect stirrings of this performative impetus in the books leading up to Book 15.

The Leap

Protesilaos was, of course, the first of the Achaeans to leap from his ship onto Trojan soil and to die. This is alluded to in his name[8] and mentioned in the Catalogue of Ships:

> τῶν αὖ Πρωτεσίλαος ἀρήϊος ἡγεμόνευε
> ζωὸς ἐών· τότε δ' ἤδη ἔχεν κάτα γαῖα μέλαινα.
> τοῦ δὲ καὶ ἀμφιδρυφὴς ἄλοχος Φυλάκη ἐλέλειπτο
> καὶ δόμος ἡμιτελής· τὸν δ' ἔκτανε Δάρδανος ἀνὴρ
> νηὸς <u>ἀποθρῴσκοντα</u> πολὺ πρώτιστον Ἀχαιῶν.

> Of these Protesilaos like Ares was the leader,
> while he was alive: but at that time already the black earth held him down.
> And his lacerated wife had been left in Phylake
> and his house, half-complete: a Dardanian man killed him
> <u>as he was leaping from</u> his ship far the first of the Achaeans.
>
> *Iliad* 2.698–702

---

[8] Nagy 2001a:xxvi n18; Nagy 1979:70; Eustathius ad *Iliad* 2.700–702 (van der Valk 1971–1987:I.506).

Figure 16

As Eustathius notes, death comes to Protesilaos in mid-air, as he leaps in a present participle.[9] Later, at least, on his cult statue at Elaious, a copy of a copy of which now dominates a gallery at the Metropolitan Museum in New York[10] (see Figure 16), he is forever about to leap from his ship to his death, his canonical mid-action pose. This much of his story is clearly alluded to in the *Iliad* as a familiar one.

Less well recognized is the way that Protesilaos' leap and death continue to haunt the *Iliad* beyond the Catalogue. In Book 15, Protesilaos' ship becomes the focal point of intense drama when Hektor is at last about to set fire to the

---

[9]   Van der Valk 1971–1987:I.508.
[10]   Richter 1928–1929. See also n24 below.

ships.[11] Ajax with his long spear is striding from ship to ship (15.676, μακρὰ βιβάσθων), which is envisioned in the simile of the trick rider as a leaping (θρώσκων, 684). This leaping, taking place on the Achaean ships on the Trojan beach, and ending at Protesilaos' ship, recalls Protesilaos' initiatory leap (2.702, ἀποθρώσκοντα). To oppose him, Hektor makes straight for a single black-prowed ship (15.693). After presenting Hektor's swoop with an eagle simile, the narrator reveals that Hektor was guided in this by a shove of Zeus' big hand (694–695), an eerie intervention. The narrator pauses to describe what "you would say," along with the thoughts of the opposing warriors:

> φαίης κ' ἀκμῆτας καὶ ἀτειρέας ἀλλήλοισιν
> ἄντεσθ' ἐν πολέμῳ, ὡς ἐσσυμένως ἐμάχοντο.
> τοῖσι δὲ μαρναμένοισιν ὅδ' ἦν νόος· ἤτοι Ἀχαιοὶ
> οὐκ ἔφασαν φεύξεσθαι ὑπὲκ κακοῦ, ἀλλ' ὀλέεσθαι,
> Τρωσὶν δ' ἤλπετο θυμὸς ἐνὶ στήθεσσιν ἑκάστου
> νῆας ἐνιπρήσειν κτενέειν θ' ἥρωας Ἀχαιούς.
> οἳ μὲν τὰ φρονέοντες ἐφέστασαν ἀλλήλοισιν·

> You would say that tireless and unwearied they opposed
> one another in war, from how they rushed for each other in the fight.
> And for those battling, here was the thinking: the Achaeans
> said that they would not escape from under the evil, but would
> > perish,
> and the spirit in the chest of each Trojan expected
> they would burn the ships and kill the Achaean heroes.
> Thinking such things they stood up to one another ...
> > > *Iliad* 15.697–703

All three parties, Achaeans, Trojans, and we the audience, are mistaken; the narrator's comment seems to stretch the opposed forces to the breaking point in presenting these mistaken impressions on all sides. This slow-motion action[12] reaches its climax when in a vivid, cinematic gesture Hektor finally lays hold of the stern of that one particular ship:

[11] As has been repeatedly forecast since Book 9. Nagy (1979:335–336) links Hektor's firing of the ships to Zeus' flash (*selas*) of lightning at 8.76 (Zeus looks forward to Hektor's fire using the same word at 15.600); cf. Whitman 1958:133. Hektor's firing completes the loop that is the Will of Zeus: a deviation from the steady onward march of the plot. The loops and rings I discuss here are thus inscribed within this larger circle. The firing of Protesilaos' ship has been made the nexus of many threads. On the fire as accomplishing the ἐξαίσιον (extraordinary) prayer of Thetis to Zeus (15.598), see Slatkin 1991:104.

[12] Leaf (1902:1) complains about "the great retardation of action" beginning with Book 13 and continuing to the end of Book 15. For an appreciation of this dramatic retardation, see Taplin 1992:18; Scott 2009:130–145.

Ἕκτωρ δὲ πρυμνῆς νεὸς ἥψατο ποντοπόροιο
καλῆς ὠκυάλου, ἣ Πρωτεσίλαον ἔνεικεν
ἐς Τροίην, οὐδ' αὖτις ἀπήγαγε πατρίδα γαῖαν.
<u>τοῦ περ δὴ</u> περὶ νηὸς Ἀχαιοί τε Τρῶές τε
δῄουν ἀλλήλους αὐτοσχεδόν.

But Hektor got hold of the stern of the sea-coursing ship
graceful, seaswift, which carried Protesilaos
to Troy, but did not bring him back again to his fatherland.
<u>This was the very man</u> round whose ship the Achaeans and Trojans
were slaughtering one another hand-to-hand.

Iliad 15.704–708

Hektor's grasp seems to inspire the memory of the ship's former captain.[13] The sudden proximity to this object seems to release from the performer the description not only of Protesilaos but of his sad fate: this very ship would not bring him back again to his fatherland.[14] Note the connotations of ἥψατο (704): Hektor "grasps" the stern of the ship, but the word also means "kindle," and shortly, at the other end of the Patroklos–Achilles encounter, Hektor will help do just that to this ship (16.112–124). The verb collapses the two moments, a neat encapsulation of the series of collapses and substitutions that comprise this scene and its sequel.[15] Ajax and Hektor are frozen in place for all of 16.1–102, while the fatal conversation unfolds. As others have noted,[16] line 102 of Book 16, Αἴας δ' οὐκέτ' ἔμιμνε· βιάζετο γὰρ βελέεσσι, repeats 15.727. Notice too that while Hektor's grasp of the stern brings on the transformation at the beginning of Book 16, the stern is once again the focus of the fire at 16.124, followed by a startling mid-line shift back to Achilles,[17] stirring up Patroklos.

Ajax has manifestly stepped into Protesilaos' role as he leaps onto his ship, reprising the very pose of Protesilaos in his moment of glory, frozen into his cult

---

[13] "By a sudden inspiration," as Janko 1994:304 remarks *ad* 693–695.
[14] The sense of this phrase is echoed (Schibli 1983, at line 5 in his text) in what appears to be a parody of the Protesilaos story (Schibli 1983:2), the *Galeomuomachia*.
[15] In Philostratus' *Heroikos* 47, we hear that Patroklos died "grasping [ἁπτόμενον] the wall," perhaps an intertextual thickening of these two layered moments; there is a shared kinesthetics between Hektor at his apogee, having penetrated the Achaean wall, grasping Protesilaos' ship and facing Ajax, and a moment later Patroklos facing Achilles (perhaps on his own ship), only to be sent out to Protesilaos' ship, and thence to the apogee of his own success, short of the Trojan Wall.
[16] West 2011:314. West (2011:315) also notes that 16.120 repeats 15.467, "where the castration metaphor is especially apt to the severed sinew of the bowstring."
[17] Notice the construction ὡς τὴν μὲν πρυμνὴν πῦρ ἄμφεπεν· αὐτὰρ Ἀχιλλεὺς, bringing out the quasi-magical effect of the fire on the stern, which as it were transfers its energy to Achilles, and from Achilles to Patroklos. Only after Achilles' first line does he acknowledge (16.127) that he sees the fire.

statue (again, Figure 16). There is a sense of a return to the beginning of the war, of things shifting and replaying themselves ("around the ship *of that very man ...*" τοῦ περ δὴ[18]), perhaps even a sense that Ajax has been possessed by Protesilaos; Protesilaos has somehow entered the unfolding drama.[19] In the tradition seen in the *Cypria*, it is Hektor who kills Protesilaos, so it requires little imagination to see Ajax facing Hektor, on Protesilaos' ship, as a replica or reenactment of that earlier moment.[20] It is as though Zeus, with his big hand, is guiding the puppets back into proper position so that a new beginning can spring forth, a beginning not of the war itself but of something else.

This duel at the ship of Protesilaos is the scene that sets up Patroklos' tears at the beginning of Book 16: the scene suddenly shifts to Achilles and Patroklos, and they finally have the conversation that sends Patroklos out to his death. But Protesilaos' ship frames that fatal conversation at both ends, since it is there, when Patroklos emerges (16.286), that his first encounter takes place. Protesilaos' ship signifies the initiation of action, and his leap the necessary death of one fighter at the beginning of action, a quasi-sacrifice. These themes frame and make sense of the intervention of Patroklos; it is not difficult to see how the "leap" story plays in the background of the action.[21]

---

[18] Recall the use of τὴν and αὐτῆς in Phoenix's speech to layer one character over another. Recall too the "fate" line within "Trojan Horse" (Chapter 1 above), τῇ περ δὴ καὶ ἔπειτα τελευτήσεσθαι ἔμελλεν, *Odyssey* 8.510. The Trojan Horse's entrance into Troy is the point diametrically opposed to Hektor reaching the ship of Protesilaos: the nadir and peak of Trojan fortunes.

[19] Ajax is also stepping into a reenactment of his own duel with Hektor (Book 7). This duel in turn is part of a cluster of reenactments of the beginning of the war (Finkelberg 2002). Finkelberg convincingly links Hektor's invocation of a tomb that will soon cover his opponent with the tomb and shrine of Protesilaos. She further links the Hektor–Ajax duel with the Achilles–Kyknos encounter in the *Cypria*; but in the *Cypria*, of course, Hektor kills Protesilaos. The repetitions proliferate.

[20] The Catalogue entry mentions only a "Dardanian man," which led Aristarchus to condemn the "Neoteroi" who, not understanding that "Dardanian" is different from "Trojan," filled in Hektor as the killer (Severyns 1928:19–20, 118, 303). But as Currie (2015:292) remarks, this description's vagueness "may be attributable to the focalization" in lines 700–702: "all that matters to Protesilaus' widow left in Phylace is that a Dardanian man killed him." Kullmann (1960:111 with n4, 184–185) sets out the case against Hektor being the killer of Protesilaos in the *Cypria*, despite Proclus' summary (p. 105.1 ed. Allen). In doing so Kullmann points to the phrase "Dardanian man" at 16.807 being the "transparent source" of the phrase in the Catalogue. This is, if anything, backwards. This very phrase at 16.807, moreover, confuses the distinction between "Dardanian" and "Trojan," since the "Dardanian" Euphorbos' father Panthoos is one of the Trojan elders at 3.146 (West 2011:327). On this question see further Stanley 1993:290; Burgess 2001:64.

[21] With Protesilaos' leap compare Odysseus' leap, *Odyssey* 24.538: another "end which is also a beginning" (Purves 2019: Ch. 3).

The Couple

Returning to the catalogue entry (2.698–702), recall the bare mention of the widow left behind in Protesilaos' "half-built" (ἡμιτελής) house, an ἀμφιδρυφής widow, "torn on both [cheeks]" (in mourning). That is all the audience hears of his wife in the *Iliad*. But a fully developed love story about the couple was exceedingly popular in later tradition, and there is no way to know when such a story came into existence.[22] Euripides wrote a *Protesilaos*, of which fragments are extant;[23] the *Cypria* at least alluded to the story, since it gave the wife a name and probably told some version of her suicide.[24] But full versions happen to survive only in much later texts, in Lucian, Apollodorus, Philostratus' *Heroikos*, Ovid's *Heroides*, Propertius, Catullus, and others, as well as in visual art, most impressively on Roman sarcophagi, which often recall Euripidean tragedy.[25] Most scholars have concluded that the later tradition takes this bare suggestion from the Catalogue of Ships about the half-built house and torn cheeks (a "genre scene"), and fleshes it out into a romance.

[22] Grossardt 2001:49; Jouan 1966:330.

[23] For a full reconstruction of Euripides' *Protesilaos*, see Jouan 1966:317–366. This play was familiar to the makers of Roman sarcophagi and their clients. One can understand the appeal, for the dead couple inhabiting the Velletri or Protesilaos sarcophagus, of posthumously fleshing out the plum roles projected around them.

[24] Pausanius 4.2.7: full discussion below. Jouan (1966:330) doubts Séchan's view that the *Cypria* told a full version of the story, but agrees that it told of the widow's suicide, at least. The resurrection might have appeared in the *Cypria*, but is "in any case ancient," derived probably from ritual (Jouan 1966:332). For Burkert, Herodotus' story of Artauktes using the Protesilaos sanctuary for orgies "presupposes some kind of custom or at least a fantasy of a sacred marriage in the temple of Protesilaos. In that case, Protesilaos' tomb and Laodameia's fatal night of love would not merely stand within a novelistic context"; these stories and Laodameia's relation to her statue presuppose a ritual such as is reflected in the Lenaia-vases where a woman dances before a statue until the statue comes to life (Burkert 1983:245). The orgies themselves are not evidence that Herodotus (or Artauktes) knew the love story, but the "miracle that confronted the sinner," as Burkert puts it, the pickled fish come back to life, combined with the sexual activity, does suggest the story. See Boedeker 1988:39. On the fish as a sign indicating Protesilaos' power to exact retribution, see Nagy 1987:210, 212. In inscribed works, Protesilaos appears alone on coins from the early fifth century BCE (in his canonical pose on his ship), and in the company of other warriors, including Achilles, beginning with a late-Corinthian pyxis, 575–550 BCE. Burkert puts the orgy story in the context of Bacchic rituals, which he believes to be very ancient. The earliest inscribed work associated with the couple may be a fifth-century Etruscan gem (LIMC "Protesilaos" 9), inscribed "Laor" or "Laod." Canciani (LIMC) disputes the view that this inscription is modern. Figures on uninscribed works have been tentatively identified as Protesilaos, including (highly doubtful) a late geometric crater fragment at Athens (LIMC 12).

[25] On the development of the story, Fulkerson 2002 and Lyne 1998 are essential; Maclean and Aitken (2001:l–lvi) provide a concise treatment. Sarcophagi: 1) Vatican, Galleria dei Candelabri, inv. 2465: Zanker and Ewald 2004:94, 393–396 with bibliography; 2) Santa Chiara in Naples: Zanker and Ewald 2004:95, figs. 85 and 86; 3) Velletri, Archaeological Museum: Lawrence 1965; Zanker and Ewald 2004:23, fig. 21.

And it is a supernatural, deeply romantic story, the kind of thing for which, we are often assured, the Homeric poet has no use.[26] But the previous chapter brought into focus some of those love stories, including that of Marpessa and Idas, which the *Iliad* puts to quite intensive use. Not to mention the fact that Achilles and Patroklos have already found themselves mirrored by Meleager and Kleopatra. So: what if the story of Protesilaos and his wife, too, were kindled in the audience's minds by the barest of references, just as surely as if I were to utter the words "Lear" or "Ophelia" or "Danny Boy"? Let us presume that the Homeric audience was just as familiar with this story as, for example, an Athenian fresh from Euripides or a Roman husband shopping for a sarcophagus.[27] What would come to the mind of such a listener?

The passionate devotion between Protesilaos and his wife allowed them briefly to overcome death. The dead Protesilaos returns from Hades for one last visit with his wife, either because one of them persuades the gods,[28] or because his eros lifts him to the surface.[29] (Some versions present, instead, a vision of the live man.[30]) After this visit, the wife kills herself, either on her own initiative or because Protesilaos convinces her to join him. In some versions, he arrives before the news of his death, so that when they are first reunited, she believes she is embracing a live human being, and although he hesitates, he eventually has to tell her he is dead. At some point, either before or after the visit, the wife makes a statue of Protesilaos. This statue she worships with offerings or tries to animate by means of Bacchic ritual. Most pathetically, she also tries to sleep with it. A servant, observing this, believes that she has taken a real lover; when her father intervenes and discovers the statue, he burns it on a pyre in disgust. Deprived of this surrogate object, the widow throws herself on the same pyre with the statue or kills herself some other way. At any rate, in all versions, she kills herself.

---

[26] See, e.g., Griffin 1977. On love stories as "latently present throughout" early Greek poetry, see Redfield 1995:159.

[27] See, e.g., Figure 17 below (= Lawrence 1965:plate 47 fig. 6).

[28] Usually the gods of the underworld are specified. Protesilaos does the praying (or lawyering) according to, e.g., Lucian and the Aristides scholia; his wife does so in Hyginus. The gods are in some versions moved to act by the wife's pitiful caressing of the statue, rather than by any articulate supplication.

[29] Propertius 1.19.

[30] Ovid *Heroides* 13; Jouan (1966:320–321) suggests the presence of this motif, in addition to that of the ghost, in Euripides' *Protesilaos*. Jouan also compares Propertius 1.19.9–10 (see epigraph to this chapter), where Protesilaos comes as an *umbra* with *falsis palmis*.

Rising Up Again: Protesilaos And Achilles

That may be, but does the *Iliad* know of Protesilaos' resurrection? The answer seems to be yes. An initial piece of evidence is found in the Catalogue of Ships.

The *Iliad* figures the return of Achilles into battle not only as a withdrawal and return, but more specifically as a figurative resurrection, an *anastasis*.[31] In the Catalogue, the poet remarks that Achilles was lying in grief by his ships, but that he would soon "rise up again" (τάχα δ' ἀνστήσεσθαι ἔμελλεν, 2.694). This line in itself need not, of course, carry connotations of resurrection. But immediately following it are three catalogue entries in a rhyming relationship to it that illuminate its significance. Immediately after Achilles comes Protesilaos,[32] whose catalogue entry we discussed above. Protesilaos is in turn followed by Eumelos, son of the resurrected Alcestis, who volunteered to die for her husband Admetus.

Following Eumelos is the absent Philoctetes, whose catalogue entry closes with the refrain, τάχα δὲ μνήσεσθαι ἔμελλον, "but quickly they were going to remember him" (2.724), echoing closely the line in Achilles' own catalogue entry, τάχα δ' ἀνστήσεσθαι ἔμελλεν. Memory, the means by which Philoctetes is retrieved from Lemnos, often serves metaphorically as a kind of resurrection in Greek poetry, notably when the gods "remember" Odysseus and retrieve him from the death-realm called Calypso. In the Protesilaos story, too, it is Protesilaos' inability to forget his wife that enables his return from the underworld.[33] The schema is then:

---

[31] See esp. 18.304–305 and 18.358; also 15.235, where Zeus declares the Achaeans will ἀναπνεύσωσι πόνοιο. ἀνίστημι is used of "raising the dead" (24.551). Cf. also n5 above.

[32] Once it is accepted that the *Iliad* knew of Protesilaos' resurrection stories, it is interesting to compare a line from Protesilaos' catalogue entry, 2.699, τότε δ' ἤδη ἔχεν κάτα γαῖα μέλαινα, "by that time the black earth already held him down," with 3.243, τοὺς δ' ἤδη κάτεχεν φυσίζοος αἶα, "the life-nourishing earth already held them down," describing the Dioskouroi. The phrase is also used of the Dioskouroi at *Odyssey* 11.301, along with the story of their alternating life-death state. The earth "holds down" others besides those who come up again, but not with ἤδη and the past tense. It does so in Homer mostly in the future tense, in predictions about the enemy (16.629) or Achilles about himself (18.332); cf. Athena on the suitors (*Odyssey* 13.427, 15.31). The exception is Ajax (*Odyssey* 11.549).

[33] For example, the poem quoted at the beginning of the present chapter, *coniugis heros / non potuit caecis immemor esse locis* ("The hero could not be unmindful of his wife in the blind places"), Propertius 1.19.7–8. The Protesilaos and Philoctetes entries are linked also by the lines:

οὐδὲ μὲν οὐδ' οἳ ἄναρχοι ἔσαν, πόθεόν γε μὲν ἀρχόν·
ἀλλά σφεας κόσμησε Ποδάρκης ὄζος Ἄρηος

Nor were they leaderless, longing as they were for their leader:
But Podarkes, scion of Ares, marshalled them (2.703–704; cf. 726–727)

Since this "longing for the leader" occurs in both, one hesitates to attribute specifically erotic longing to the phrase, but the presence of Protesilaos' love story in the *Iliad* makes plausible an allusion to the erotic aspect of his story in his catalogue entry. Nagy (2001a:xxvii n20)

> Achilles
> > Protesilaos
> > Eumelos, son of Alcestis
> Philoctetes

—that is, two stories of actual resurrection framed by two metaphorical ones. Eustathius remarks (*ad* 695–710),[34] καὶ ὅρα ὅτι μετὰ τὸν ὡσανεὶ κείμενον, ὡς προείρηται, Ἀχιλλέα τὸν ὡς ἀληθῶς κείμενον Πρωτεσίλαον ὁ ποιητὴς παρέθετο, "Observe that after the one who is 'as-if' lying down, as mentioned previously, Achilles, the poet puts next to him the one truly lying down, Protesilaos." (There is more to say about the connection between Alcestis, dying in place of Admetus, and Patroklos, but in this chapter we are concerned with Protesilaos.)[35] So the *Iliad* not only incorporates the return of Protesilaos from Hades; it also links this return with the metaphorical reanimation of Achilles.

To return to the action in Book 15 and 16: the audience sees Protesilaos' ship, there is a moment of desperation on the part of Ajax (playing Protesilaos), and the camera suddenly shifts to Patroklos and his tears. "The usual arrival sequence is abandoned: we are not told what [Achilles] was doing when [Patroklos] found him, and [Patroklos'] speechless tears replace his expected utterance, provoking [Achilles] to speak first."[36]

Patroklos has not, it would seem, observed the action at Protesilaos' ship. "Achilleus and Patroklos are unaware how desperate a stage has been reached in

---

links the connotations here to the conventional eroticism of the cult hero more generally: "On a deeper level ... the reference implies the emotional response of native worshippers who are 'yearning' for their local cult hero in all his immanent beauty; we may compare the application of ποθέω to Patroklos at his funeral, *Iliad* 23.16." Cf. Vernant (1991:102): "Funereal *pothos* and erotic *pothos* correspond exactly."

[34] Van der Valk 1971–1987:I.503.

[35] The very associations among the various couples crossing the barrier of death were themselves a traditional trope (e.g., Phaedrus' speech in the *Symposium* linking Achilles-Patroklos, Orpheus-Eurydice, and Alcestis-Admetus); the Catalogue sequence would be the first extant instance. Lucian, at *Dialogues of the Dead* 23, puts these associations into the mouth of Protesilaos, using the precedents of Alcestis and Orpheus to justify his own reanimation. Depictions of the reanimated spouse in visual art are subject to debate as to which story they represent: the couple on the front left of the Velletri sarcophagus (LIMC Protesilaos 21; good reproductions in Lawrence 1965), usually identified as Protesilaus and Laodamia [using the Latin spellings here], has also been seen as Alcestis and Admetus (who certainly appear on the right, with Heracles). Both couples reunite through a door, which for Lawrence represents the gate of Hades (and which would give access to the actual dead). These two couples flank the enthroned Pluto and Persephone, another death-spanning couple (cf. pages 142–143 above on the superimposition of Marpessa, Kleopatra, and Persephone). This is inverted in the Catalogue, where these two human couples are "flanked" by Philoctetes and Achilles. On these four catalogue entries as a unit, see Stanley 1993:20–21.

[36] West 2011:312.

Aias' battle against Hektor. ..."[37] The narrator does not describe Patroklos' tears as a response to the battle at the ship, but *we* have just been witnessing it, and Patroklos now surfaces with an emotional response—as though he has seen the ship, or slipped into our position.[38] Still, it is striking that Patroklos makes no mention of the urgent situation at Protesilaos' ship and catalogues instead the Achaean injuries. This adds to the impression that the two are strangely removed from the action, yet close to it at the same time. This simultaneous distance and nearness resonates with the themes of the substitute and the ghost, which are at work in the Protesilaos-wife and in the Achilles-Patroklos stories.

When all signs point toward Achilles finally rising up and emerging from withdrawal to save the Achaeans, Patroklos comes out as his substitute, or Doppelgänger. His is a rising-up-again, but also a death. As often in both Homeric poems, although various spaces have connotations of death, there is no consistent one-to-one correspondence. Achilles' hut is a quasi-death realm, eventually fully transmogrified into Hades' palace in Book 24,[39] and clearly the emergence from that realm is a movement from death to life. Yet Patroklos goes out of it to his death.

How should we formulate what happens when we hear the name of Protesilaos, see his ship, and then witness the tears of Patroklos, stepping into our shoes, and his conversation with Achilles? I would not wish to circumscribe the effects. Just as a simile would not be Homeric if tenor and vehicle were aligned in every detail, so too we should not press for tight analogy, but open ourselves to the resonances.

The theme of eros inducing resurrection and suicide—penetrations of the boundary of death from either side—figures in many ways into the presentation of Achilles' return, and into what is here in its place, the substitute-death of Patroklos. Everything that follows, Patroklos' quasi-sacrifice[40] and Achilles' quasi-suicide[41] in response (expressing his wish to die, killing someone in his own armor, etc.), is compressed into this episode taking place under, and narratively framed by, Protesilaos' ship. The stories of Protesilaos and his wife are part of this compression. I do not mean to suggest that the Protesilaos story contributed this or that element to the *Iliad*. Many of these likely stem from or are inspired by the "Memnonis"[42]—some version of the story of Memnon's

---

[37] Taplin 1992:178.
[38] Cf. Chapter 2 above, page 157.
[39] See, for example, Nagler 1974:184–185; Crane 1988:35–38; Stanley 1993:237–239.
[40] Lord 2000:197; Nagy 1979:292; Sinos 1980:55; Lowenstam 1981.
[41] Or, as Lowenstam (1981:175–176) would have it, self-sacrifice.
[42] Kakridis 1949; Schoeck 1961; Schadewaldt 1965; Slatkin 1991. Useful brief discussions of Neoanalysis include Schein 1984:25–28, Edwards 1991:15–19, and Edmunds 2016:4–8. Edwards' (1991) commentary on Books 17–18 makes generous use of the "Memnon-theory"—briefly, the

killing of Antilokhos, and Achilles' death while avenging him. Here I am focused in the first place upon how framing the tragedy of Patroklos by allusion to Protesilaos affects the audience's experience of Achilles and Patroklos. The story of Patroklos is strongly demarcated by the presence of Protesilaos' ship; it comes right into the narrative, unlike (say) Memnon. On the other hand, the story of Protesilaos may not only frame the narrative but also suffuse the story in several ways. So although the Protesilaos story may not form the warp or weft for Book 16 in the way that the Memnon story does, it both frames the whole and complements the Memnon story. Textually speaking, the Protesilaos story could be thought of as an additional thread in the weave, or as an embroidery on top of a Memnonis subtext, or as a filter through which we experience the Memnon subtext as well as the main events of the *Iliad*. Insofar as the Neoanalysts have not accounted for the presence of Protesilaos in a satisfying way, I propose to bracket the Memnon theory to a large extent in exploring the way the Protesilaos story functions in the text and in the performance.

Protesilaos' wife kills herself because she cannot live without her husband. As is well recognized, Patroklos' death replays in advance, so to speak, the death of Achilles. More poignantly, Patroklos' death seems to bring on Achilles' death already within the *Iliad*. Patroklos' death starts a chain reaction leading eventually to Achilles' actual death, but it also entails Achilles' immediate death. And so, when Achilles learns (from Antilokhos!) of Patroklos' death in Book 18, Thetis and the Nereids come to mourn (not console) Achilles. This scene recalls, or rather replays, the story of their mourning him when he is actually dead.[43] Even a scholar who denies that the Memnon story is known to the *Iliad* remarks that Thetis' accompaniment by the Nereids reflects their lament for Achilles (an event reported in the *Odyssey*).[44] Achilles goes to avenge Patroklos knowing it

---

theory that the death of Antilokhos in the *Aethiopis* (e.g. Schadewaldt) or its tradition (most later scholars) is the model for Patroklos' death in the *Iliad*—throughout; for Book 16 a brief summary appears at Janko 1994:312–313. Bouvier helpfully surveys Neoanalytic theory focused on Patroklos and Book 16 and adds his own convincing argument about Antilokhos and Patroklos (especially Bouvier 2002:379–401). I myself find the theory compelling, and compatible with the present argument. The role of many other traditions, such as that found in *Gilgamesh* (e.g. Lord 2000:197; West 1997:336–347), would also have to be considered for a fuller account of the workings of this episode.

[43] On Achilles' mourning as a miming of Patroklos' death, see for example Pucci 1995:169–172; Kakridis 1949:65–75; Sinos 1980:71–73. As Burgess (2001:92) notes, the painter of a sixth-century Corinthian vase and a hydria has "also linked the story of the *Iliad* to myth about the death of Achilles" and "evokes the death of Achilles while he is still alive."

[44] West 2013:344. The idea that Achilles' lament for Patroklos is in effect a ghostly replay of his own death is, then, not dependent on embracing any version of the Memnon-theory. For Burgess (1997), the lack of a one-to-one mapping of the story of Achilles, Memnon, and Antilokhos onto the story of Achilles, Hektor, and Patroklos (the fact that Patroklos "plays" both Antilokhos and Achilles) undermines the theory. It is true that the theory is complex—see for example Schoeck

means his own death. He is explicit in his wish to die (18.98, αὐτίκα τεθναίην). This may not have been the case in the Memnon-story, where Achilles merely defies an oracle in avenging his friend.

Achilles' insatiable manipulation of the corpses of Patroklos and Hektor (which, in the latter case, the gods step forward to limit) bears a family resemblance to the wife's manhandling of her husband's statue which her father puts an end to by fire. Achilles' contact with Patroklos' corpse occurs throughout the rest of the poem. At 19.4–5, Thetis finds Achilles Πατρόκλῳ περικείμενον ὃν φίλον υἱὸν / κλαίοντα λιγέως ("lying round Patroklos / crying shrilly"). One ancient scholiast, deeply struck by this word περικείμενον, "lying *round,*" remarks:

περικείμενον· περιπεπλεγμένον·... μονονουχὶ δὲ διὰ τῆς μεταφορᾶς τὸν τῷ νεκρῷ προσηλωμένον ἐδήλωσεν. ἐπὶ δὲ τῆς γυναικὸς "ἀμφ' αὐτῷ χυμένη" φησί. δαιμονίως δὲ ἀμφότερα καὶ λίαν μιμητικῶς.[45]

περικείμενον: interwoven: ... Through the metaphor he has all but shown us the one nailing himself to the corpse. And in the case of the wife he says "ἀμφ' αὐτῷ χυμένη" [pouring herself around him]. Both are δαιμονίως and extremely mimetic.

Notice that the passage that provided the last example in Chapter 1 ("Trojan Horse"), the wife "pouring" herself over her husband, comes to the mind of the scholiast. Later Achilles, laying his man-slaughtering hands on Patroklos' corpse (23.18), speaks to him "even in Hades," and then stretches out Hektor's corpse beside the bier, the bed, of the dead Patroklos (23.25), as though trying to replace him. After the funeral, Achilles cannot sleep, but tosses and turns this way and that (24.5), crying, remembering his dear companion, longing for his manhood and his good μένος, every exploit they shared, all the pains he suffered with him. The memory of these things causes him to lie now on his side, his back, his front. Suddenly he stands upright and whirls around on the beach. He has still not satisfied himself with manipulating the bodies and drags Hektor's corpse around Patroklos' tomb, three rounds at a time, pausing to rest each time. It is this that draws the ire of the gods, and particularly Apollo, who complains (24.46–49) that Achilles' grief has gone beyond standard operating procedure for mortals and that he should have done with it.

1961:16—but understanding the ways that the characters mirror and "play" one another only adds to the pleasure. The lack of a one-to-one mapping contributes to the frenzy of substitutions that reaches its climax at 16.173–178; see below.

[45] Erbse 1969–1988:4.573.

It would seem that the widow's father in Euripides' *Protesilaos* made a simi-larly calculating speech to his grieving daughter, which included such *bons mots* as:

πέπονθεν οἷα καὶ σὲ καὶ πάντας μένει.[46]

He has suffered such things as await you and everybody.

Euripides *Protesilaos* fr. 649

and:

οὐ θαῦμ' ἔλεξας θνητὸν ὄντα δυστυχεῖν.

You've not said anything spectacular, that being mortal he has
suffered misfortune.

Euripides *Protesilaos* fr. 651

and finally (in threatening to burn the statue and urging his daughter to remarry):

κοινὸν γὰρ εἶναι χρῆν γυναικεῖον λέχος.

For a womanly bed must be shared.

Euripides, *Protesilaos* fr. 653

To this his daughter perhaps replied:

οὐκ ἂν προδοίην καίπερ ἄψυχον φίλον.

I wouldn't abandon the beloved, though he/it be deprived of life.

Euripides *Protesilaos* fr. 655

The statue, an image of Protesilaos, could even influence the way Achilles makes an image—this time of himself—out of Patroklos, as he arms him to resemble himself, and then of Hektor, an image which he then kills, as the wife kills herself when the image is destroyed.[47] Achilles' dream of Patroklos, his reaching out to grasp his image that cannot hold him in return, may or may

---

[46] On all of these fragments, see Jouan 1966:323.
[47] Fulkerson (2002) argues that Ovid *Heroides* 13 innovates in having the wife forge a statue (here of wax) of Protesilaus before, rather than after, his death, and that the poem is thereby suggesting that the wax statue acts as a magic effigy, which when burned will kill Protesilaus: in making the statue the wife causes, rather than compensates herself for, her husband's death. It is unclear whether Ovid's is the only version to order the events in this way (Jouan 1966 on Euripides *Protesilaos* puts the building of the statue at least before the visitation of the ghost, if not before the death). Of course Achilles makes an image out of Patroklos—an image of himself—while he is still alive, and so causes his death and in essence his own. This could be influenced by a prior version in which Protesilaos' wife made her image while her husband was still alive. Alternatively, the voodoo-doll coincidence between Ovid and the *Iliad* is simply due to both

not recall the wife's commingling with the statue, or her vision of the ghost visiting her for so short a time. Achilles begs Patroklos to stand closer to him: "embracing each other, even for a little while, we could take our fill of deadly mourning" (23.97–98). Something similar could be said of Patroklos' request that their bones be mixed in the single golden amphora given to Achilles by Thetis.[48] Achilles' dragging the corpse of Hektor is explicitly characterized by Hekabe (24.756) as an attempt to reanimate Patroklos.

Of course, many of these motifs might be found in other stories of passionate grief, or stories connected with hero cult, in which lament figured prominently. Some may have appeared in both the Memnon story and that of Protesilaos and his wife. The point is not to collapse the two levels, background and foreground, via their similarities into some sort of single conglomeration of meaning, or to use one as the key to the other. The similarities between the stories of Protesilaos and his wife, and Achilles and Patroklos, should not be appreciated from afar as a table with two columns. Rather, the poem *frames* the shared motifs, and shapes how they are experienced, alerting the listener to similarities that would not come to mind without that framing. The ship of Protesilaos overhangs these motifs such that they all fall into one Protesilaian undercurrent[49] that runs through the rest of the poem but gushes to the surface here at the end of Book 15 and the beginning of Book 16 in a powerful set of images. Perhaps even the "torn cheeks" of Protesilaos' wife may come to mind later, in the startling wish Achilles expresses to Thetis, not only that he win noble *kleos*, but also that he:

> καί τινα Τρωϊάδων καὶ Δαρδανίδων βαθυκόλπων
> ἀμφοτέρῃσιν χερσὶ παρειάων ἀπαλάων
> δάκρυ' ὀμορξαμένην ἀδινὸν στοναχῆσαι ἐφείην ...

> drive one of the Trojan women and the deep-bosomed Dardanians,
> with both hands on her soft cheeks
> wiping her tears, to wail in heaves ...

> *Iliad* 18.122–124

---

drawing upon a finite set of actions belonging to the same themes. It is also conceivable that the demonically clever Ovid has altered the story to mirror the *Iliad*'s use of it.

[48] 23.91–92.

[49] Cf. Kullmann 1984 on the wounding of Diomedes in the foot by Paris (11.369–400), a passage using motifs appearing in other battle scenes but fundamentally inspired by Achilles' death. I stress that, in the case under discussion, Protesilaos' name is mentioned, and his ship forms a turning point of the action of the poem, whereas other Neoanalytic arguments depend on the similarity of motifs. The objection, that is, raised to some Neoanalytic claims (that similarities are a matter of multiforms rather than the use or echo of a particular story) does not apply. Again, that is not to say that any given motif is imported from a story of Protesilaos.

House and Ship

If the theme of resurrection is active in the foreground and in the background, we must add that, in the case of Protesilaos, there is no resurrection without the wife. In all surviving versions, Protesilaos' return from the dead goes hand in hand with his passionate erotic attachment to his wife, and hers to him. But where is she in the *Iliad*?[50] Any audience familiar with the story will cast their mind's eye over the sea to her when they "see" Ajax facing Hektor on Protesilaos' ship. And just as they do, the scene is transformed to Patroklos and Achilles, "at home" in their tent, and a conversation about home. The audience will expect her, as she and Protesilaos longed for one another. She will not appear, but another couple, an image of them, takes their place. Her presence, however, also seems to be signaled within the framing of the episode itself.

As I mentioned, when Patroklos finally emerges, his first encounter takes place at Protesilaos' ship. The poetic choice to stage the action at that ship is accounted for well enough by the story of Protesilaos' leap, as was the case with Ajax's leap in Book 15. Patroklos sacrifices himself as did Protesilaos; Protesilaos' initial leap corresponds to Patroklos initiating the return of the Myrmidons and eventually of Achilles.

But that explanation is incomplete, for a detail there strongly suggests the wife at home. When Patroklos puts out the fire, the poet comments:

ἡμιδαὴς δ' ἄρα νηῦς λίπετ' αὐτόθι

Half-burnt, you see, the ship was left on the spot.

Iliad 16.294

The Homeric hapax ἡμιδαής, "half-burnt," along with the ship in the nominative being left behind, λίπετ', echo (again) two details from the catalogue vignette:

τοῦ δὲ καὶ ἀμφιδρυφὴς ἄλοχος Φυλάκῃ ἐλέλειπτο
καὶ δόμος ἡμιτελής.

And his lacerated wife had been left in Phylake
and his house, half-complete.

Iliad 2.700–701

---

50   Kullmann (1960:274): "Über die Frau des Protesilaos berichtet die Ilias naturgemäß nichts: das liegt für sie zu weit vom Thema ab." Kullmann seems to have excluded the story in part because he did not consider it part of the Trojan War cycle. The Neoanalytic Memnon-theory may also have obstructed his view. In any case, Kullmann's view that Protesilaos' wife "liegt zu weit vom Thema ab," I suggest, prevented his recognition of a key to the *Iliad*'s structure and narrative background—even though the wife appears in the *Cypria*.

ἡμιτελής is another Homeric hapax, and again we have "left behind," in the passive (ἐλέλειπτο). It is gratifying to discover that Eustathius pointed out this connection long ago:[51]

εἰ δὲ καὶ <u>ἡμιδαὴς</u> ἐκείνη ἔμεινεν, εἴη ἂν ὅμοιόν τι τοῦτο πρὸς τὸν τοῦ ἥρωος δόμον, ὃς χηρωθείσης τῆς γυναικὸς <u>ἡμιτελὴς</u> ἐλείφθη, ὡς τοῦ Πρωτεσιλάου πεσόντος, καθὰ μετ' ὀλίγα δηλωθήσεται, ἢ καὶ ἀμφιδρυφὴς ἐπὶ τῷ τοῦ ἀνδρὸς θανάτῳ γέγονε. καὶ τοῦτο μὲν τοιοῦτον.

And also if that [ship] remained <u>half-burnt</u>, this would be something similar to the house of the hero, which, when his wife was widowed, was left <u>half-finished</u>, when Protesilaos fell, just as will be made clear shortly after, who also became torn on both sides [καί linking her and the house?] at the death of her husband. This too is like that.

Eustathius, Commentary on *Iliad* 2.695–710

The epithet in one sense closes the door that was opened with the reference to Protesilaos at the end of Book 15, but also reminds us that Patroklos, in extinguishing the fire and leaving the ship half-burnt, will now launch out on the excessive part of his mission, leaving Achilles "at home" with his own action halfway initiated. It would be an exaggeration to say that we see the ship of Protesilaos transformed into the house of his wife, and that now we have the "wife," Patroklos—though he has taken on the role of Protesilaos and gone out first. But because the two spaces are both formed around the solo performer, something akin to such a transformation occurs. The ship of Protesilaos itself even appears as an image or sign of him, here threatened with burning like his statue, as its transformation into the house recalls the wife's self-destruction by fire.[52] Protesilaos' ship is already figured as a double of Achilles' ship, setting off the action; its metaphoric nature is at least double.

---

[51] Again, I.503 van der Valk. Di Benedetto (1998:111–112), in a list of phrases found only in connection with a given character, notes that these words referring to Protesilaos, ἡμιτελής 2.701 and ἡμιδαής 16.294, are the only two adjectives in archaic Greek epic composed of ἡμι- and a bisyllabic element ending in -ης with the accent on the last syllable, and notes that they are both found with λείπω in the passive, but does not pursue the matter. Is it possible the half-finished house is also alluded to at 13.679–683, where Hektor drives on "where he *first leapt* at the gates and the wall ... where the ships of Ajax and Protesilaos were ... and over them the wall had been built lowest to the ground"? That way both the vulnerable spot of the wall and the ship reached by Hektor would be linked directly to the Protesilaos story.

[52] In the *Galeomuomachia*'s parody, the line about the wife with her torn cheeks (*Iliad* 2.700) is precisely echoed (Schibli 1983, restored text line 7, τοῦ δὲ καὶ ἀμφιδρυφὴς ἄλοχ<ος> οἴκο`ι´ ἐλέλειπτο). It is immediately followed with a description of their *thalamos* (line 8), in a phrase Schibli restores as [τρ]ωγιδίωι ἐν θαλάμωι, "in their nibbled (half-nibbled?) *thalamos*." Schibli remarks, "In sum, τρωγίδιος, jestingly preceding the lofty and dignified sounding θάλαμος,

Does the half-burnt ship become the half-built house? The epithet super-imposes the two locations, house and ship, Thessaly and Troy. It is the story of Protesilaos that makes possible this transport in space as well as time (going back to the original leap). The role of Protesilaos and his ship is not simple, but overdetermined;[53] this overdetermination extends into spatial dimensions as well as pointing temporally to the beginning of the war. These dimensions shape and are shaped by performance dynamics.

Domesticity

How does this connection between house and ship affect the episode that is framed by the ship? It is with the battle at Protesilaos' ship hanging, and a reminder that Protesilaos would not return home again, that the poet suddenly shifts attention to Patroklos and Achilles. In Book 16, the audience is presented with Achilles and Patroklos as a "domestic" pair. This image of domesticity is enhanced in multiple ways, and it is far from straightforward: Aristotle might label it *atopon*.

Achilles, seeing Patroklos weeping, pictures him, in the first words of his speech, as a little girl clinging to her mother's dress and asking to be picked up (16.7–10).[54] After this domestic simile the first question that occurs to Achilles is whether there is news from home—but "they say" that both their fathers,

---

describes the mousehole of Squeaky's wife as a 'little-nibble chamber' (θάλαμος may at the same time correspond to the δόμος ἡμιτελής of Protesilaos' wife in B 701 ...)." For a mouse, nibbling may be building or destroying, so perhaps this parodist, so enmeshed in Homeric diction and the Protesilaos story, has made the connection. This is reinforced by the fact that these lines of the parody, echoing the catalogue, follow closely upon the line about his fatherland not welcoming him home again (line 5), the line found in the *Iliad* in Book 15. The *Galeomuomachia* brings together these *symbolon*-like pieces that are set at a distance in the *Iliad*. At any rate, this shows what an impression these Homeric lines made on the parodist, and they are intriguingly combined with other aspects of the story. For a different application of the notion of *symbola* to Homeric poetry (in particular similes), see Bergren 1980a.

53 Slatkin (1991:7) speaks of the *Iliad*'s "superbly overdetermined economy" in its shaping and being shaped by the mythology of Thetis.

54 Taplin (1992:177): "In extreme contrast [to the battle scene ending Book 15], an intimate and emotional atmosphere is immediately established (reinforced by the mother–daughter simile at 16.7ff.), unlike anything yet encountered in the poem, except perhaps Hektor and Andromache." Gaca 2008 sees the simile as depicting the plight of, note, a city being sacked; see also the response by Porter (2010). In contrast, for Scott (2009:169) this is the first of three similes that "remove any note of threat and create a picture of normal, day-to-day life." For what it is worth, Maximus of Tyre was capable of describing (however facetiously) this weeping as itself "erotic": ἐρωτικὸν δὲ καὶ τὸ τυχεῖν ἐθέλοντα ἐξουσίας πρὸς μάχην δακρῦσαι ὡς οὐκ ἀνεξομένου τοῦ ἐραστοῦ: "It is a lover's ploy too to win the permission to fight that he so desires by crying in a way that his lover won't be able to resist" (*Oration* 18.8.34–36; trans. Trapp 1997:167). Is there also a play on Achilles' simile in Maximus' ἀνεξομένου?

Menoitios and Peleus, are still alive: those ones we would grieve if they were dead (13–16). This is strangely detached, and effectively so: Achilles affects to be so far removed from the ships that he is "at home"; yet he is interested in news from his home on the other side of the sea as from a distant place.[55] The unhurried way in which Achilles' speech unfolds as he studies the face of Patroklos[56] both adds to the sense of being wrenched away from the space of the battlefield and re-grounds the performer's center of consciousness, his origo as a performer, in Achilles. Achilles, like the bard, is neither here nor there. The scene in Book 16 mirrors the half-built house back in Phylake, where the drama of Protesilaos' wife turns upon bad news from the other side of the sea. Only after mentioning their fathers at home does Achilles suggest that Patroklos might be grieving for the Argives. His last line, "Tell me, so that we both know," occurs twice in mother-child dialogue, when Thetis asks Achilles first about the loss of Briseis (1.363), and then, of Patroklos himself (18.74).

But this line is surely not only "typical of parent–child interviews—an apt resonance here."[57] Rather, as Ledbetter[58] has shown, Achilles' speech at the opening of Book 16 emphatically reenacts the earlier tearful encounter between mother and son, with Achilles playing Thetis and Patroklos playing Achilles— what we are calling musical chairs. So while Book 15 ends with Ajax reenacting Protesilaos' leap, initiating the war, the first speech in Book 16 draws from the first book of the poem. Bringing the Memnon-theory into the mix complicates matters, for the Thetis–Achilles conversation, on that theory, already recalls an earlier tradition of her warning him.[59] But this in turn may be related to the initial leap of Protesilaos (see below), so rather than a nexus of many threads, we may have here one thread knotted up.

---

[55] Still another thread in the nexus of the opening here is the echo of this question about fathers within Achilles' lament for Patroklos in *Iliad* 19. There Achilles pointedly contrasts the death of Patroklos with that of his father: "I would not suffer any greater evil, not even if I were to learn of my father's death" (19.321–322). As Pucci (1993:270) writes, "This devaluation of his family ties before Patroclos seems to feminize Achilles and make of him a mirror image of Briseis," whose lament Achilles follows. Achilles then pictures the aged Peleus waiting for the news of Achilles' own death and shedding a tear, echoing the tear shed by the girl in Achilles' simile (τέρεν κατὰ δάκρυον εἴβει, 16.11, 19.323) and elsewhere used of female characters. "We could read in that feminine transfer the sign of his fully emotional suspension to his unique destiny of death" (Pucci 1993:270).

[56] On the unfolding drama of this speech in performance, as Achilles responds to the reacting face of Patroklos, see Bölte 1907:574–575.

[57] Janko 1994:317 *ad* 16.19: Demeter uses a variant of it with Persephone (*Homeric Hymn to Demeter* 394).

[58] Ledbetter 1993; cf. Bouvier 2002:408–409.

[59] Or as Schoeck would have it, the opening of Book 16 is a new beginning of a phase for those parts of the *Iliad* that "stand under the aspect of the mother-warning" (Schoeck 1961:89).

Patroklos here stepping into Achilles' Book 1 role, weeping to a mother, can be seen to anticipate or flag his stepping into the role of Achilles in his replay of the Achilles–Memnon story later in Book 16.[60] Better, Achilles' simile reflects, from a distance, on the role that his friend is about to play. If Achilles' simile and the replay of *Iliad* 1 prepares for the later role-playing in Book 16, this in turn is prepared and framed by the scene at Protesilaos' ship. But with a difference: the Protesilaos story itself contains the theme of the ghost and the substitute, and the effect of a death on a distant beloved, so that the acts of substitution are experienced within this frame.

But all of this is experienced not as a set of stories layered on top of one another, as in a series of friezes running atop another series, but rather as a transformation of the body of the bard. If Achilles' simile reflects on the events to come, pondering them from a strange distance, what immediately follows this speech deepens this effect. For here is the first of the apostrophes to Patroklos in Book 16. The effect of this first apostrophe is manifold; but it is shaped and amplified by the shift from the ship of Protesilaos to the ship of Achilles. It is shaped by this shift just as powerfully as the last apostrophe is shaped by Patroklos' imminent death. The bard, in becoming Achilles, 'seeing' Patroklos and using the simile, indicates not just the 'special relationship' between the bard and Achilles, as we see in Book 9, but also the special relationship between Achilles and Patroklos, and as it were the bard and Patroklos. The simile and the drawn-out attention to how Patroklos looks go so far in setting Patroklos before the performer that the apostrophe comes forth from the mouth of the narrator, who remains in Achilles' shoes after his speech. This sudden transport of the bard into Achilles can also be experienced as a transport of Achilles forward into the time of the audience—forward into the body of the bard, in our time— since he addresses Patroklos in the past tense. So while in his speech Achilles intimately addresses a Patroklos who is in fact before him, the apostrophe in effect means that "he can't really be there": it is the dead Achilles recalling this episode. So the apostrophe puts Achilles in the underworld, as we remarked in Chapter 1: but he is also being reanimated. He is, then, already a ghost: the apostrophe, set in the context of the Protesilaos imagery and the other poetic effects we have noted, crowns these effects and puts Achilles forward as haunted and

---

60 Such flagging is similar to the exchange of armor, as characterized by Schoeck (1961:16: "It is as if Homer wanted to clarify his procedure with the exchange of arms"), or the echoing of language between Patroklos and Antilokhos that points out the permutation of roles (Bouvier 2002:397) rather than simply enacting it. One should also mention, as Bouvier (2002:398) points out, that Patroklos' tears at 16.2–3 are echoed in Antilokhos' tears at 18.16–17, as each arrives to give bad news to Achilles; Antilokhos is here stepping into the role of Patroklos in more ways than one, as Patroklos' death has just replayed in advance his own. This is one more loop in the knot that is the opening of Book 16.

haunting at that moment.[61] Yet just prior to this he is querying Patroklos as though he were the one with instant access to news from over the sea. Here Protesilaos appears not only to frame the ongoing action, indicating its meaning through the "sign" of his ship, and to steer its plot, but to enter into the body of the performer-as-Achilles.[62]

This combination of the pair's distance from and nearness to the threatened ship, as well as the ambiguous distance of Achilles and Patroklos to each other, is a kind of zooming in on the Achaean camp as a city, the building of the wall, and the eventual transmogrification of Achilles' tent into a palace. (This theme appears in Phoenix's speech, discussed in the last chapter, when Phoenix pretends that the Achaean camp constituted a "home" to be defended.) After the initial exchange between Achilles and Patroklos, Achilles retrieves a cup from a chest that Thetis sent with him on his departure for the war, as though he is at home sending Patroklos off.[63] This "domestication" is crystallized in the mounting surreal series of similes bringing out the domesticity of the Myrmidon camp, of Achilles' tent, and eventually of Achilles himself bereft of Patroklos. After Achilles compares Patroklos to a little girl, this series includes the simile of a man *building a wall* for his home (16.212–214), and continues with the simile of the wasps who "have their homes on the road" (16.261), houses that stupid children disturb, "making a common evil for many."

The culmination of this image, linking Achilles with "home" and with burning, thus bringing to completion the magical effect Trojan fire has had on him through the ship of Protesilaos, is the simile of fire destroying homes at 17.737–739, its development at 18.207–214, 18.219–221, wherein an island village lights fires in the hope that people will come to save them, and finally Achilles' shield flashing at 19.375 like the flash of fire from the mountains that appears to sailors being swept by winds away from their loved ones.[64] However often animals' homes are devastated by hunters and other animals in similes throughout the poem, this series concentrates our attention upon the

---

[61] The moment takes its place beside Achilles' conversation with the already-dead Patroklos (22.381–390) wherein "Achilles speaks as if he were already among the dead, alone with the dead Patroclus" (Redfield 1994:108).

[62] The bard then takes over the action of the cult-hero himself, entering into the action of the poem rather than, as Protesilaos does in Herodotus, intervening in reality to take vengeance on Artauktes and indicate a message to Herodotus' audience (Nagy 1987; Nagy 1990a:268–273). Insofar, however, as the action in Book 16 is the turn in the tragedy, perhaps Protesilaos can be seen here too as exacting a kind of retribution.

[63] This chest is full of wind-protecting cloaks and blankets (16.221–224), as though what is to be faced, for both the then-departing Achilles and the now-departing Patroklos, is the chill of the winds. Achilles for an instant is lent the fond naivete of a mother—or a new wife.

[64] On this simile, see Nagy 1979:338–343. Nagy (1979:340) links the simile to the tomb that encloses Achilles and Patroklos (*Odyssey* 24.80–84).

Myrmidon camp as a domestic space and then, once Patroklos has died, zooms in laser-like upon Achilles himself, who, ostensibly coming to the rescue as the defender hoped for in the simile (18.213), instead has actual fire shooting out of his own head (19.381): "Help me: help *me*. My house is burning."

In fact, Ajax sounds this "home front" theme in the stirring speech that closes Book 15, immediately before the fatal conversation:

> οὐ μέν τι σχεδόν ἐστι πόλις πύργοις ἀραρυῖα,
> ἦ κ' ἀπαμυναίμεσθ' ἑτεραλκέα δῆμον ἔχοντες ...

> It's not like there is a city close by, fitted with towers
> Where we could defend ourselves with a *heteralkea* people ...[65]
> *Iliad* 15.737–738

The epithet ἑτεραλκής focuses upon the pivot point, and resonates with the fact that Hektor has now reached the point furthest from the city; the limit is now being reached that will trigger "outside" intervention from Achilles. ἑτεραλκής is used elsewhere[66] of victory going to the other side; the sentence as a whole points toward the change in perspective in the Patroklos and Achilles scene that follows. The Achaeans have no *polis* or *dēmos* close by: but of course it is Patroklos and Achilles who immediately respond to this need and (as if) this speech; the couple are thus framed as such a *dēmos*, a home front that is yet ἑτεραλκής, an *unheimlich* home.[67]

Substitutions

The replacement of Protesilaos and his wife by Achilles and Patroklos is part of a complex web of substitutions of one character for another or for a group. Some are part of the mythic background, some are part of the action of the poem.

---

[65] Some scholiasts on this passage try to explain the literal meaning of ἑτεραλκέα; another remarks simply (and movingly) πάντα δὲ εἰρωνικῶς.

[66] *Iliad* 7.26, 8.171, 16.362, 17.627.

[67] Cf. Lynn-George (1988:140–152) on "the *heimlich*/*unheimlich* structure of this homeless home which is the tent of Achilles" in Book 9 (p. 145), a "tent of words" or "chamber of echoes" (146). Within the imagery connecting the camp to a polis one should include the simile, describing the Trojans attacking the Achaean wall, of the ship overcome by waves at *Iliad* 15.381–384. Martin (1997:158–159) connects the unusual diction used of the ship's hull (τοίχων, which in Homer normally means "walls") to Theognis' lines (673–676) on the ship of state: "it could be that the simile makes use of an emotionally intense song-moment in which one can lament the total loss of civil order in a *polis*." The ship simile is followed, as Martin says, by its reification, when the Trojans pour over the wall to threaten the actual Achaean ships. There is a loose analogy here to the action in Book 9, when Phoenix's conceit finds embodiment in the conflation of Meleager's chamber and city with Achilles' tent and the space of performance, and Kleopatra's speech laments a city now to some extent shared by the audience, internal and external.

Even those that seem tamely informative, however, come out into the dramatic proceedings in Book 16.

We learn in the Catalogue (2.703–709) that Protesilaos has been replaced by his brother, whose name, Podarkes, is Achilles' epithet; indeed, Achilles is ποδάρκης immediately before this in his own Catalogue entry (2.688). Podarkes gets his name from his father Iphikles, whose swiftness was superhuman,[68] whereas swiftness of death is actually more salient to Achilles, ὠκύμορος ("swift-fated").

As Protesilaos is a sacrifice for the entire fleet,[69] so is Achilles himself a sacrifice for the cosmic order, the substitute for the child Thetis never had with Zeus.[70] By one account Protesilaos is even a substitute *for Achilles*. Thetis warns Achilles not to be the first to leap from his ship since whoever does so will die;[71] Protesilaos, in taking the lead, thus takes Achilles' place,[72] as Patroklos does in the *Iliad*. Philostratus' *Heroikos* recounts a dialogue between a skeptic called "Phoenix"[73] and the gardener in the sanctuary of Protesilaos. In this work, which revels in the details of Protesilaos' erotic resurrection, Achilles and Protesilaos appear as rivals. The *Dardanos anēr* ("Dardanian man," 2.701) who kills Protesilaos provides another link, since that phrase is used of Euphorbos when he helps to kill Patroklos-playing-Achilles.[74]

---

[68] See Janko 1994:134 *ad* 13.698. His swiftness is known to the *Iliad*: 23.636.

[69] So Jouan (1966:317), comparing Protesilaos with Iphigeneia. Protesilaos may also be compared with such heroes as Archemoros. See Burkert 1983:40, on διαβατήρια, and 245, on Protesilaos.

[70] Slatkin 1991.

[71] This story of the prophecy is not attested until Apollodorus *Epitome* 3.29, but may have appeared in the *Cypria* (West 2013:114). That Protesilaos is first to land and to die we have already seen is pre-Homeric. If the prophecy Patroklos, echoing Nestor at 11.794–795, inquires about at 16.36–37 were to allude to that story, rather than to some other warning by Thetis or to her general tendency to give these warnings, this would add to the ongoing echoes of Protesilaos' story. Notice the diction of Patroklos' inquiry: "But if you are keeping clear of some prophecy in your mind, one your mother has explained to you from Zeus, then send me forth at once [πρόες], and send the rest of the army [λαὸν] with me": there may be a reminiscence of Protesilaos' name, as Patroklos takes the place of Protesilaos. Rather than any individual story carrying weight here, the sheer number of examples lends credence to the idea that this substitution pattern is part of what goes into any myth about Protesilaos (and Podarkes).

[72] Boedeker 1988:36.

[73] He is a Phoenician. But he is never given another name. Cf. Chapters 2 and 4 on Phoenix and Phoenissa.

[74] At 16.807. These are the only two instances of this phrase. Meanwhile Euphorbos is described in the same terms as Achilles (16.808–809): Lowenstam 1981:121; Nickel 2002. In the *Cypria*, it is Hektor who kills Protesilaos; I suggested above that the *Iliad* knew such a story and restages it. See above n19. Janko (1994:414) explains how Euphorbos and Paris can be both Dardan and noble Trojan: "Euphorbos" is a pastoral name; Paris was exposed and reared as a shepherd on Ida. That would perhaps not apply to Hektor. On Euphorbus as a double of Paris, such that his role in the killing of Patroklos recalls Paris' in the killing of Achilles, see Mühlestein 1987:78–89. Contra Mühlestein: Nickel 2002.

I have not yet discussed the name of Protesilaos' wife. It enters the discussion here because of its role in the play of substitution. In the *Cypria*, her name is Polydora, whereas in most later accounts she is Laodameia, daughter of Akastos.[75] Now Achilles has a (half-)sister named Polydora. She is mentioned only as the mother of Menesthios,[76] who stands in Achilles' place in the quasi-catalogue of ships immediately following the decision to send Patroklos out. Thus, Protesilaos' brother Podarkes shares Achilles' epithet, and Achilles' sister Polydora bears the same name as Protesilaos' wife in the *Cypria*. Achilles has stepped into the role of Protesilaos, to the extent that the burning of Protesilaos' ship has been equated with the burning of Achilles' own ship. Yet his place is now taken by someone (Menesthios) who is given a mother, Polydora—who shares the name of Protesilaos' wife.

The orgy of substitution in this catalogic passage recalls, in its themes of substitution and replacement, the sequence in the Catalogue of Ships we discussed above. And it is playing alongside, as an accompaniment, the primary substitutions of Patroklos for Achilles, and Patroklos-Achilles for Protesilaos-wife. Yet it ratchets up the substitutions into the bizarre, as though the poet-performer is feverishly turning over in his mind the act of substitution being undertaken by Patroklos.[77] This is yet another way in which the bard is taken over by Achilles, anxious about his act in acceding to Patroklos' request. Here emerges the connection between the themes of substitution and compensation, as grappled with by Achilles,[78] and the substitution that occurs in performance.

Perhaps this sister Polydora is invented just for this moment, as another reminder of Protesilaos; perhaps not.[79] Whatever may be her connection to

---

[75] It may be relevant to the development of the myth that Achilles' father Peleus narrowly escapes sleeping with the wife of Akastos.

[76] 16.173–178.

[77] This orgy is adumbrated in a geographical musical chairs (13.693–700) involving the two substitute leaders, Podarkes (in for Protesilaos) and Medon (in for Philoctetes: 2.727). (Thoas is in for Meleager, but Meleager never went to Troy, and Achilles' troops led by Patroklos will form the fourth.) There Podarkes and Medon are leading the Phthioi, whom one would assume are from Phthia, Achilles' kingdom (though the matter is complicated: see Janko 1994:133 *ad* 13.685–688, including the observation that "here the Phthioi are ruled by Podarkes, Akhilleus' epithet"). Even more puzzling, Medon, the Philoctetes substitute, bastard son of Oileus so half-brother of Ajax, is now said to live "in Phylake," land of Protesilaos and Podarkes, because he had killed a man (a story repeated in 15.335, where Phylake is also mentioned: cf. the "prison" or "safeguarding" implications of the name). In this Book 13 passage, then, three of the four "resurrection" entries in the catalogue of ships have shifted properties. Protesilaos' substitute Podarkes and Philoctetes' substitute Medon "move" to Achilles' territory (Phthioi), while Medon in a subsidiary clause occupies the seat of Protesilaos and Podarkes (Phylake). On the proliferation of doubles in tragedy, including in Euripides' *Protesilaos*, see Steiner 2001:193. For Briseis as substitute, see Dué 2002: chs. 2 and 3.

[78] Bruce M. King, "*Iliad* 11.668–762 and Beyond: The Cattle-Raid and the Genre of the *Iliad*" (unpublished manuscript, 2001), PDF file.

[79] She also appears in *Catalogue of Women* fr. 213 M-W.

Achilles, in the *Cypria*, according to Pausanias, Polydora, wife of Protesilaos, is the daughter of Meleager and Kleopatra, and thus the granddaughter of Marpessa and Idas:

> The poet of the *Cypria* says that Protesilaos' ... wife was called Polydora, and was the daughter of Meleager, the son of Oineus. If this is true, these very three women, beginning the count from Marpessa, upon their husbands dying first, all killed themselves.
>
> Pausanias 4.2.7

Back in Book 9, Meleager was put forward as an example for Achilles not to follow; yet the parallels between the two heroes were clear, and the tragic trajectory of the rest of the poem was outlined, even initiated in the Meleager story. There would be a largely involuntary replay of the Meleager story. Patroklos would obviously play Kleopatra, cued by their names and their initially silent but intimate role, but that shoe had not actually dropped—Patroklos had not confronted Achilles—until this moment in Book 16. Now is when Patroklos is speaking to Achilles as Kleopatra, long silent, spoke at last to Meleager,[80] sending him to his death. Patroklos will fail where Kleopatra succeeded, and will take the role of Meleager himself. *The moment when Patroklos is making his Kleopatra-like speech is framed by a story involving Kleopatra's daughter.* In both cases, we think he is the woman (the wife of Meleager, then of Protesilaos), but he turns out to be the man.[81]

From Source of the Poem to Source of Action

Already it is clear that Achilles and Patroklos "become" Protesilaos and—let us call her by her more popular name—Laodameia. This is true not necessarily in the sense that their story has been woven, tailored, or embroidered to resemble that tale; it could be true in the minimal sense that the action in Book 16 is framed by this outlandish love story. However, it is possible that the Achilles-Patroklos story was altered to fit with Protesilaos. The ship's epithet

---

[80] Nagler (1974:135) links Patroklos' stepping into this suppliant role, Kleopatra's role, to the Achilles' simile likening him to a girl. It is probably too nice to connect this to Kleopatra's daughter, but this would be one reason for why the simile presents a mother and a daughter rather than a mother and a boy (as would suit Ledbetter's argument).

[81] This reversal redoubles, or overlaps, the reversal in which Achilles comforting Patroklos plays the role of Thetis comforting Achilles (Ledbetter 1993). Compare the reversal of roles noted by Schein (1984:107) in Achilles' four parent–child similes, in which he positions himself as a parent to Patroklos (older) and Agamemnon (higher status). The silent Patroklos of Book 9 is reminiscent of the curiously evocative "palinopt" figure in vase painting identified by Mackay, Harrison, and Masters (1999), where "the perception of one margin of a traditional scene already predicts the arrangement of the other in more or less of mirror-image" (Mackay et al. 1999:141).

"half-burnt" might be the most striking example of this, but we have considered other themes above, such as the creation of a substitute and reanimation, that begin to make their way into the performance. If we had the *Cypria*, we would have a better idea of precisely what our text owes to the Memnon story, as opposed to the Protesilaos story.

These questions of *Quellen* are pertinent, as in the case of Marpessa and Phoenix, and they are indeed related to the workings of presence and performance. So now that we have cleaned up the grammatical situation—that is, the background story along with some of its implications for the audience's experience of the performance—we can examine the virtues of the passage as a script more freely. The question is how the script deploys background myth in tandem with other techniques to produce certain effects of presence: the sense of the bard taken over by a character, or, as with Phoenix, a character animated "from elsewhere." In other words, we are concerned not so much with the source of the text as, in this chapter as with the previous one, the (as-if) source of action—though for a performing poet these are not really separable.

Having the Protesilaos story in the background, and as a tangible backdrop (the ship), the unfolding tragedy of Achilles and Patroklos seems to be psychagogically "being run from elsewhere." Achilles and Patroklos are not moving under their own volition, or from motives bound up with the plot; they are playing out roles in a different story.

This is different from, but related to, their reprising of roles from earlier stories about Achilles, Memnon, and Antilokhos, or for that matter Achilles and Thetis. The Protesilaos story bears the theme of the visiting ghost and magic substitution right in the heart of the story. While an audience who knows the story of Memnon and Antilokhos can experience the events in Book 16 and following as a replay in advance, the ship of Protesilaos touches off the theme of the ghost and configures the events to follow as a ghostly replay. But there is a more directly performative way in which the Protesilaos story "ghosts" the *Iliad*. The first apostrophe to Patroklos was one glimpse of this. But these eerie kinesthetics are set up much earlier: to this we now turn.

Patroklos' Circuit and Reemergence

While Achilles vows to Ajax not to emerge and fight until the fire reaches his own ships (9.650–653), the half-measure he takes in sending Patroklos out, and triggering the tragedy, is (as it were; see above) in response to the fire reaching the ship of Protesilaos. In fact, earlier in Book 15 the poem reinforces the expectation that the turning point would be Achilles' own ship. At 15.63–64, Zeus has wrenched back his awful control of the plot, and predicts/vows that the

Achaeans will "fall among the ships of Peleid Achilles." So the ship of Protesilaos substitutes for the ship of Achilles.[82] But let us not dispose of this by saying Achilles sends out a substitute of himself because the fire has reached the substitute for his ship. It is not so abstract.

Although Phoenix's speech had inspired or anticipated the tragedy of Patroklos, this plot is actually set in motion when Achilles, *standing on his ship* (11.600), notices the Achaean rout and calls Patroklos from the tent. This is where Patroklos gives his chilling reply, "What do you need from me?"[83] (his first words in the entire poem), and Achilles sends him out to see what is happening (anticipating his later dispatch in Book 16). When we return to Achilles in Book 16, it is possible that the audience is to think of him as still standing on his ship, waiting for the news. (This can also be simply indicated by gesture and eye-direction.[84]) This spatial orientation, however embodied, is of a piece with the notion that "the battleground … is but a stage on which Zeus and Achilles himself witness the rapid and inexorable unfolding of the latter's destiny (11.597–604)," as Nagler puts it,[85] except that Achilles' role in this unfolding is far from clear, in part because the plot is invaded by other persons from other plots. In any case, the action in Book 16 *does* follow close upon a speech by a man standing on a ship—Ajax, alone on *Protesilaos'* ship, lamenting the fact that there are no nearby allies. Patroklos' interaction with Achilles in Book 16, the prelude to his *aristeia*, is framed on both ends by Protesilaos' ship, as we saw. But his Book 11–16 circuit, in which he visits Nestor, receives the suggestion to don Achilles' armor, and encounters Eurypylos, is also framed by a man standing on a ship: Achilles in Book 11, and Ajax at the end of Book 15 (followed by Achilles in 16).

The Protesilaos story lends itself to such concrete expression; there is a "kinesthetics" to the story just as there is for Eris, as discussed in Chapter 1.[86] The hero's most striking aspect is his leap, which appears on the cult statue and from there on coins and visual art. The Vatican Protesilaos sarcophagus (see Figure 17, next page),[87] though late and heavily influenced by Euripides, provides unexpected help in seeing what the *Iliad* has done in its own, mini-

---

[82] Schoeck (1961:49–52) argues that Protesilaos' ship represents the corpse of Achilles as though the scene around the ship in Books 15 and 16 is somehow a variation of the traditional battle over Achilles' corpse. This particular argument seems to rest on weak evidence.

[83] Taplin 1992:175: answer = "your life." See Lynn-George 1988:128–129; Bouvier 2002:371–372.

[84] Cf. 16.8, 10: Achilles addresses the just-arrived Patroklos as a girl wanting to be picked up.

[85] Nagler 1974:134–135.

[86] I find suggestive along similar lines Muellner's argument that a series of vase paintings portraying Achilles veiled is evidence for a traditional multiform in the representation of Achilles, a representation that would not necessarily be limited to a particular genre (Muellner 2012).

[87] Figure 17 (Vatican sarcophagus) photo by Flickr user Egisto Sani; see also Lawrence 1965: fig. 6.

Figure 17 (left half)

malist, medium. The sarcophagus is framed at both ends by ships: Protesilaos first leaping off his ship to his death on the left, and finally boarding the boat of Charon at the extreme right. For Protesilaos, his ship was the boundary between life and death, and this is what makes his cult statue so powerful. His ship's edge represents death as well as the initiation of action, and makes an ideal beginning and ending for a quasi-ring composition—as appears on the sarcophagus and also in the *Iliad* when Hektor reaches it—as well as an evocative cult statue pedestal. While on the sarcophagus the ship at one end is echoed by the boat of Charon at the other, here in the *Iliad* the ship of Protesilaos is replaced by the ship of that lord of the dead manqué, Achilles, who will reprise this role more explicitly in Book 24. (On the Alcestis sarcophagus, Museo Chiaramonti, the place of Charon is taken by Hades on his throne.) The pairing of the ship of Protesilaos with Charon's boat and the house of Hades on the sarcophagi spreads out in linear space a transformation embodied in space and time by a solo performer in the *Iliad*.

Both a sarcophagus and a Homeric bard are ideal media for representing the boundary between life and death, or rather, for mediating that crossing. The house on the tragic stage often represents the House of Death. But the sarcophagus and the Homeric bard are by nature containers of the dead, and they each exploit this nature in various concrete ways. We have seen that the performer uses his own body as a kind of gateway for the dead to emerge. This emergence operates hand in hand with other kinds of emergence at other levels of the text, such as the emergence of Patroklos and/or Achilles from their tent or their camp.

The circuit that Patroklos completes between being dispatched by Achilles in Book 11 and his second dispatch, to his death, in Book 16, is so full of imagery

Figure 17 (right half)

of the death realm, not to speak of the carnage of the Battle Books, that it might be called a *katabasis* in the same sense as Priam's visit to Achilles. Now it is virtually impossible to map the various spaces of the *Iliad* in terms of a life vs. death dichotomy, and so such readings will not convince those who require a one-to-one allegorical reading.[88] For example, if the gates of the Achaean wall manned by Lapiths in Book 11 function as gates of Hades,[89] a skeptic may well wonder whether the gates of Troy can equally well serve this function.[90] The answer is yes: "the connection between Hades and its gates was so strong that the mere mention of gates could evoke associations of death,"[91] and in each case the impending death (of Asios and Patroklos, respectively) and other contextual details complete the picture. Again, if Achilles' withdrawal and return are bound up in the symbolism of a *katabasis*, how is it that, when he returns to the battle, he is "already dead" and the Nereids perform a quasi-funeral for him? The answer is that this is simply how this poem is: using traditional patterns, but not subject to systematic "this is that" allegorical reading. Similarly, only in Book 24 does Achilles' tent transmogrify into the house of Hades, but, as we have

---

[88] Cf. the objections to the Memnon-theory expressed by Burgess (n44 above).

[89] Lowenstam (1981:42–43), on the five references to gates in the Asios episode: "These references may not appear to be surprising since the battle is, of course, taking place around the Achaean Wall. On the other hand, Asios' attack may have been situated at the gates by the poet (and his tradition) precisely because of the connotations of gates. The collocation of references to gates and the theme of impending death suggests that the gates through which Asios will enter to meet his death provide an emotional coloring reminiscent of the gates of Hades."

[90] Lowenstam (1981:68n1): "A particularized epithet of Hades is πυλάρταο (Θ 367, N 415, λ 277). When Pylartes ("Gate-closer") is disposed of (Π 696), the gates of Troy (mentioned in Π 698) appear highly vulnerable. When Patroklos reaches the gates of Troy, he enters the gates of Hades."

[91] Lowenstam 1981:36; bibliography on Pylos-gates-death at 43n29.

seen, the Achaeans make a procession to supplicate him in Book 9 somewhat as though he were a (dead) hero of cult.

Lowenstam's reading of the gates may suggest that the Achaean wall and trench form a kind of Hell. Indeed the wall, based somehow upon the τύμβον... ἕνα ... ἄκριτον (translated by Kirk as "one communal mound,"[92] 7.336–337) has an uncertain relationship to the burnt corpses: are they still in the τύμβος and thus part of the wall? At any rate, it is from the hellish fight around the wall that Patroklos is—finally—emerging when he meets Achilles in Book 16. But Patroklos himself has not witnessed the battle firsthand. More accurately, while we the audience are emerging from the action of battle, Patroklos is emerging from his encounter with Eurypylos. As Lowenstam argues, "Eurypylos" strongly connotes the gates of Hades.[93] Patroklos is with Eurypylos for all of Books 12–14 and part of Book 15, as the audience discovers when he is still there tending his thigh-wound at 15.390. It is from those "gates" that he emerges at 16.1, just as we, the audience, emerge from the scene at Protesilaos' ship.

It is strange to find that Patroklos has been at the hut of Eurypylos so long, as though frozen in time, but stranger still that even when he is not with Eurypylos he spends most of his time in doorways (or tent-openings). Thus in Book 11 he runs out of the tent, "like Ares, and this was the beginning of his evil" (11.604), only to appear suddenly at Nestor's tent and stand impressively in the doorway, "a mortal equal to a god" (θύρῃσιν ἐφίστατο ἰσόθεος φώς, 11.644). Nestor leads him in by the hand and bids him to be seated (ἐς δ' ἄγε χειρὸς ἑλών, κατὰ δ' ἑδριάασθαι ἄνωγε, 11.646). He refuses a seat (11.648), and thus stands frozen in (or near) the doorway throughout Nestor's entire speech (11.656–803). In the course of this (lengthy as usual) speech, Nestor tells a story about when he went with Odysseus to recruit Achilles and Patroklos, and Peleus poured wine and prepared the meat. Within this embarrassingly contrived *mise en abyme* of the present situation, some musical chairs takes place, and *Nestor himself makes a sudden appearance in the doorway* (11.776, note the half-line break):

σφῶϊ μὲν ἀμφὶ βοὸς ἕπετον κρέα, νῶϊ δ' ἔπειτα
στῆμεν ἐνὶ προθύροισι· ταφὼν δ' ἀνόρουσεν Ἀχιλλεύς,
ἐς δ' ἄγε χειρὸς ἑλών, κατὰ δ' ἑδριάασθαι ἄνωγε ...   [= 11.646]

---

[92] Kirk 1990:279. Having explained the complex historical and textual problems here, Kirk seems to assume in his note on lines 336–337 that the corpses are to be read as collected, as in the later echo of this passage at 436, but then also that the mound is "undiscriminated" (ἄκριτον) "in relation to individual corpses."

[93] Lowenstam 1981:36, 66n72. He shows, moreover, that the details of Patroklos' treatment of Eurypylos (cutting his thigh with a *machaira*, etc.) suggest sacrifice. Lowenstam posits an early version of the Patroklos story as a literal human sacrifice, in keeping with *therapōn* as stemming from human sacrifice in Hittite tradition.

> You two were round the ox, tending to it, and we two then
> stood in the doorway: and amazed, Achilles rose up
> and led us in by the hand, and bid us be seated ...

Iliad 11.776–778

It is in the context of this rehearsal of the previous visit to Peleus that Nestor delivers the fatal recommendation that Achilles send Patroklos out in Achilles' armor (11.794–803).

Without a response to this sermon, Patroklos runs off, but immediately happens upon Wide-Gate himself (11.809), who, despite his dire thigh-wound, has a mind still intact (νόος γε μὲν ἔμπεδος ἦεν, 11.813), like Teiresias among the dead (*Odyssey* 10.493–495), and is consulted by Patroklos as such. The long time Patroklos sits tending to Eurypylos (thus reprising Nestor tending to Machaon, though Patroklos, unlike Nestor, tells stories to cheer his patient, 15.393) is emphasized (15.390–393) and framed by references to Eurypylos and his shelter, lest the audience forget (12.1–2; 15.392). His circuit resembles Hektor's Book 6 farewell sojourn in Troy, itself enclosed within encounters at the gates, only Patroklos is, as it were, frozen at the "gate" until he suddenly reappears beside Achilles in Book 16.[94]

This striking spatial configuration could be interpreted as some sort of "liminal" condition prior to his death, such that he spends Books 11–15 at the gates of Hades before going to this death—sent by Nes-tor, playing his ironic role as with his son in Book 23.[95] When Patroklos finally speaks his fateful speech, he ends with the words of Nestor (16.36–45, 11.794–803), words that provoke from the narrator the observation that, great childlike fool, he was begging for his own death. These words are "ghosting," as it were, words that Nestor already framed by rehearsing an earlier scene in which he takes up a pose in imitation of Patroklos, framed by a doorway. Pylian Nestor himself has a strong traditional association with gates, and perhaps this scene takes its inspiration from that—after all, it is in this same scene that Nestor tells the story of leading the Pylians, as Frame argues, not simply to victory but back to life.[96]

---

[94] Recall again the palinopt figure in vase painting described by Mackay, Harrison, and Masters 1999. The marginal makes his way to the focal point.

[95] See Interlude 1. As King remarks, "it is with the wounding of Makhaon and with Akhilleus' consequent sending-forth of Patroklos that the *Iliad* ventures into previously unexplored and unexpected complexities of plot and signification" (Bruce M. King, "*Iliad* 11.668–762 and Beyond: The Cattle-Raid and the Genre of the *Iliad*" [unpublished manuscript, 2001], PDF file). The strange kinesthetics of the performance here and Patroklos' ghosting of Nestor's words are bound up with these complexities and, I think, reinforce King's larger point about the poem's distancing itself from Nestor.

[96] Frame 1978:92–94. Nestor is in that story enacting his traditional role, as explicated by Frame. The fact that he is sending Patroklos to his death here is again part of the poem's distancing itself from the ideal that Nestor represents, as King argues.

Figure 18

Later, in fact, when Patroklos is actually in this liminal state between life and death, as a ghost, he complains to Achilles that he is trying to pass through the gates of Hades (23.71) and is wandering through the wide-gated house of Hades, ἀν' εὐρυπυλὲς Ἄιδος δῶ (23.74), the only instance of this epithet in the *Iliad*.[97] (Note too the doubling of this image in Iris' visit to the winds, standing on their stone threshold, 23.201–202, and especially her refusal to take a seat, οὐχ ἕδος, a unique echo of Patroklos' refusal at 11.648.)

But it also sets up kinesthetically—or *schēma*-tically, in terms of stance and gesture—Patroklos' emergence through the body of the bard, and finally, fully, through the door into the space of performance for his *aristeia* and death. Compare again the Protesilaos (Figure 17) and Velletri (Figure 18)[98] sarcophagi, where scenes of the dead emerging through doorways (as though from inside the sarcophagus, the corpse) to reunite with the living are framed by Protesilaos' ship and the boat of Charon (or the house of Hades). The bard both is the gate and emerges through it. While Patroklos lingers frozen at the gate of the bard's body, through the kinesthetic imaginings of the Gate, the two men on ships framing Patroklos' sojourn create a space for emergence (see Figure 19: "Patroklos' Frozen Circuit," drawn by Oren Riggs). The performer can easily embody Achilles

---

[97] Richardson 1993:173 *ad* 23.74 notes the contradiction between these two descriptions. Could this be furthering the sense of disorientation?

[98] Figure 18 (Velletri sarcophagus) photo, detail of Gibon Art / Alamy Stock Photo.

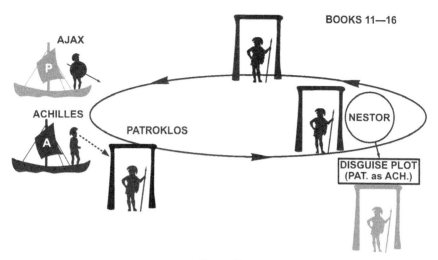

Figure 19

standing on the ship in Book 11 by looking down at the mass of battle, just as the authorial Helen does in Book 3, and by calling Patroklos out of the hut, directing his voice downward (this is indirect discourse, but the performer can gesture all the same). As Patroklos, the performer might call upward as he asks, "What do you need of me?" Similarly, in Book 15, whenever and however he embodied Ajax on the ship (please, not actually leaping), he could indicate his position by looking down at his invisible opponents.[99]

The Ship: Action at a Distance

When Hektor then lays hold of the ship, I do not see how any performer would not embody this gesture, whether subtly or broadly. This concrete gesture would breathe new life into the following lines about Protesilaos and his own doomed journey, which come as Janko says "as if by sudden inspiration." The very proximity, the physical contact in performance with this invisible object, primed by moments when he seems to stand upon it as someone else, seems to give birth *in the performer-narrator* to the memory of Protesilaos and his sad fate.

At that moment there is a slippage in the chain of causation, as things unfold somewhat as if Protesilaos' ship *were* the ship of Achilles. But let us not resort to the level of the text and speak of a slippage of the signified under the

[99] The "anchoring" of the plot at these pivotal ships, which then are harnessed into a space of transformation, would perhaps be enhanced in a performance in which the performer stood on a raised platform, as rhapsodes do in vase painting. Or rather, it might occur to a poet who performed on a platform to use it to draw a connection to certain characters and to use them for presencing effects.

signifier, or some such thing. It is rather more concrete and enjoyable than that. Once the performer as-if lays hands on the ship, gesture or no, he 'receives' this new story, as registered by speaking the lines about the ship (15.704–708) that did not take Protesilaos home again: lines apropos of Achilles, and, we soon find, of Patroklos too. Now, shunted suddenly to that ship as the leaping Ajax, he speaks Ajax's speech, with its reference to the polis and its odd use of *heteralkea*, putting us on the lookout for a "home front." Then, suddenly, the performer as narrator informs us that Patroklos was standing by Achilles crying, and utters the simile of the dark spring (16.3–4).

The vividness and studied quality of the simile brings about a shift: the bard now stands before the weeping Patroklos, gazing upon his face, his body thus in the position of Achilles. As the performer becomes Achilles, he is strangely distant, as though he had not seen anything that we just saw, gently (or in whatever tone) asking Patroklos about whether there is any "news from Phthia." This violently wrenches us out of the previous violent action, which we have left so abruptly. At once the encounter at Protesilaos' ship seems to cause the appearance of Achilles and Patroklos—*and to have nothing to do with it.* Hektor's grasp fills the bard with the memory of Protesilaos, which induces the becoming, the reanimating, of Achilles, *both* in terms of his partial emergence (through a substitute) into battle, returning through an image of himself, *and* in terms of his occupation of the performer's body. The performer has already set Achilles up as standing on his own ship (11.600). Touching Protesilaos' ship, however enacted, induces the becoming of Achilles, the inhabitant of a space that has now been set up as the equivalent to Protesilaos' ship, the pivot point for the action, and its initiating source. But now as Achilles, he suddenly slips into the role of the dead occupier of that ship (Protesilaos).[100] They are at the same time transported into an oddly removed "home." Patroklos' tears, at once seemingly caused by the action at the ship and utterly unconnected with it, convey to the audience the effect of action at a distance. But this is just what the performer does in touching his invisible object: as he does so, the space around him shifts.

It would be ham-handed to force this orchestration of objects and characters in space into the rubric of "becoming the character." But it does use some of the same ingredients, and isolating these helps to grasp the complex play with presence. When the bard grasps the ship as Hektor, as with Menelaos and the

---

[100] Thus, though the performer may be orchestrating the action using a full picture of the Achaean camp as with a memory palace, as Clay (2011) convincingly argues, he simultaneously manipulates his own surroundings in a way more directly instantiated in performance. In the present instance, while Clay (2011:84–87) shows how the poet tracks the action around Protesilaos' and Achilles' ships within the camp, I am discussing a transformation of one space into another around the body of the performer.

helmet (see Chapter 1), an object in the world of the poem induces a "becoming" in the performer (along with other effects). The ship, like the helmet, is empty of its former inhabitant. Hektor has reached the apogee of his heroic action, and the bard embodies the intensity of Hektor's contact by remembering Protesilaos, bringing on a total recall of the beginning of the war as well as the beginning of the *Iliad*. Hektor's heroic reach pierces through the world of the battlefield to the world of domestic suffering and also to the unfolding performance.

Seeing the animation of Achilles as a reaction to Hektor's broaching reach brings out an unexpected parallel to the appearance of Eris flanking both sides of the "becoming" of Agamemnon (11.1–73; see Chapter 1 above). Recall that Eris appears at the beginning, in a relation of "musical chairs" with Agamemnon, to animate him, and then oddly reappears afterward to oversee with pleasure the work that was after all inspired by her. Remarkably, this sequence too is centered on a ship, as Eris stands on Odysseus' ship to shout. She is, both at the beginning, on the ship, and at the end, taking the place of the ἀνὴρ μάκαρος 'blessed/wealthy man' of the farming simile, an overseer, standing above the action. So too is Achilles. Like Eris, atop his ship in 11.600, he sets Patroklos' circuit in motion. At the end of the cycle, there is an eerie sense that Achilles is "behind" Patroklos as Eris is Agamemnon, but here the analogy's crudeness starts to become obvious.

What is this space that is constructed for the ship of Protesilaos? A character, laying hands on the ship, gives birth to bardic memory, and also induces a virtuosic presencing. This performance effect is in keeping with the kind of space in which the stern is thematically a boundary between life and death: that is, for Protesilaos, dying as he leaps off of it. So the life/death boundary coincides with the "becoming" boundary, as in the first examples of Chapter 1, the *aristeiai*. The performer reaches into the beyond for a new motivation and a new plot, but involuntarily. He is induced to become Achilles and Patroklos; they are induced to play out their suicidal roles. This is registered in the apostrophes, first when a half-present Achilles reacts on his own and through the narrator to Patroklos' strange, disconnected weeping, and then, as Book 16 proceeds, when the narrator, focalizing Patroklos' imminent death through the absent Achilles, reacts to that death as though he has inadvertently let it happen.

Like the *sēma* in the chariot-race speech of Nestor, and like Kleopatra in Phoenix's speech, the ship of Protesilaos is also an end-point for action, a goal that, when reached, ignites new ideas and a new presencing effect in the performer. (Recall too Aristotle's ring-compositional image, where *thought* backs up to a certain point, and then gives way to *action*.) Unlike those moments, however, this one does not take place at the center of a speech. Instead Protesilaos' ship forms the turning point of the action of the entire *Iliad*. It is also the furthest point reached by Hektor, the turning point in his "chariot race" ending in his death. The bard uses Hektor as the vehicle for his own processes of memory and enactment.

Half

That the ship is envisioned as a kind of transitional space, a space for linear progression to pivot out into a new dimension (Friedrich), a space in which dead people rise up to inhabit live ones, is consonant with its being "half-burnt." Half-burnt objects were used to communicate with the dead and in curses, drawing up power from the underworld.[101]

The ramifications of "half-complete" (ἡμιτελής) are similar, only for dead rather than living practitioners. In Lucian's *Cataplus*, the dead Megapenthes uses the fact that his house is half-built to bargain with Plouton and Persephone for his return to life.[102] This is no doubt a parody of the Protesilaos story (see Lucian's *Dialogues of the Dead* 27.1, where Protesilaos specifically mentions his half-built house to Aiakos). But the principle is well known from hero cult (and modern ghost stories): the dead person returns to tend to unfinished business.[103]

The image of being half in one realm and half in another also matches the state of mind of Achilles, straddling two plots or two intentions. Taplin writes:

---

[101] *Semusti cineres* (half-burnt ashes [of human corpses, most commentators have it]) were found in the walls of the dying Germanicus' room along with curse-tablets and other items "by which it is believed that souls are consigned to the lower spirits" (Tacitus *Annales* 2.69). Noy (2000:193) connects the magical use of half-burnt corpses here and elsewhere to the ambiguous status of the soul of the half-burnt deceased. The obscurity of Tacitus' wording here, along with the fact that human remains appear earlier on the list of things discovered, is pointed out by Goodyear (1981:410), who tentatively refers to "partially burnt animal/human remains." Did half-burnt sacrifices, or other half-burnt objects, have such a power? Most animal sacrifices to the gods were after all half, or partially, burnt before the rest was eaten. For wooden objects, recall Althaia's use of a firebrand, seized from the fire and stored away for years, to kill her son Meleager (in the more popular version of the story). This seems to be a perversion of the usual use of half-burnt wood, in the form of an ember, to revivify a fire the next day. Perhaps cases such as the Derveni papyrus, found "half-burnt over a grave around 330 B.C." (Kirk, Raven, and Schofield 1983:30) belong somewhere in this category, unless it is simply "luck" (Papadopoulou 2014:ix) that it was not completely burnt. Graf (2014:75n31) suggests that the unburnt part of the papyrus was perhaps protected by the hand of the deceased on the pyre. A suggestive analogy is Theocritus *Idyll* 2.132–133, following the use of fire in love-magic. In Hippocrates' *Epidemics* 2.6.29 a half-burnt substance sparks animation in the form of pregnancy.

[102] ἡμιτελὴς γὰρ ὁ δόμος καταλέλειπται, "For the house is left behind half-complete" (Lucian *Cataplus* 8).

[103] Notice that it is a half-built living space, a *container* for a wandering psyche, which operates in this animating fashion. Likewise the ship, the vehicle *containing* the wandering living, reaches the faraway shore. In its half-burnt state it spans the distance to death as well as back to the other shore and the wife. Cf. Superman's need for a phone booth.

"He did, however, concede to Aias that he would not fight until Hektor threatened his own ships with fire. Now Patroklos' plea ... tips the balance so that the undertaking to Aias is half-fulfilled and half-evaded."[104]

A half-burnt object straddles the realm of the living and the dead. In the realm of love, the soul splits itself between two lovers. Aristophanes' speech in Plato's *Symposium* elaborates a comic variation on this theme, where the lovers are two halves of one body. The "half-soul" is particularly appropriate to songs or poems of farewell (so-called *propemptika*).[105] These poems wish for the safe return of the beloved just as Achilles prays to Zeus (16.233–248) upon Patroklos' departure (cf. esp. ἀσκηθής μοι, 247). Bringing such love-*symbolon* imagery into this moment may appear to make the poetry too overdetermined. But this very motif of the single spirit in two bodies appears just at the moment of Patroklos' departure, although it is Patroklos and the charioteer who are described as ἕνα θυμὸν ἔχοντες, "having a single spirit" (16.219). This same formula appears at 15.710 just after the elaborate invocation of Protesilaos' ship. There it is applied to the opposing armies, who "did not wait for the rushes of arrows and of javelins, but they standing nearby and having one *thumos* fought with sharp double-axes and battle-axes ..."[106] This description is framed by Hektor's grasping the ship (704, 716). "Having a single spirit" is not a common formula in the *Iliad*. Besides these two instances, the only other (17.267) describes the Achaeans around the dead Patroklos.

Thus, the two epithets form two halves of a whole—half-complete house, half-destroyed ship, one on each side of the sea—and each envisions the kind of object that permits travel between realms.[107] This is a good place for a shape-shifting bard (the man whom Plato easily associates with the wandering, dead hero and the magician) to bring his characters to light and to create confusion about his own source of action. In the image of Protesilaos and Achilles on their ships, the poet has created a figure—or a Gestus, in Brecht's sense—of being

---

[104] Taplin 1992:177. For a similar evocation of the action of Achilles being partially begun see Nagler 1974:136 with n8.

[105] Nisbet and Hubbard 1970:48.

[106] Janko (1994:305) explains, "οἵ γ' denotes both sides, but ἕνα θυμὸν ἔχοντες ... means that each side is 'of one mind'." But the oneness is startling.

[107] If some statue portraying Protesilaos leaping from his ship were present in his shrine at Elaious already in the Homeric period, it is striking that he already "leaps" across the Hellespont, in that the ship is placed on the other side of the Hellespont from the site of his landing and death. The trees in his shrine, according to late evidence (Pliny *Natural History* 16.88, Quintus of Smyrna *Posthomerica* 7.408; Boedeker 1988:37) grow until they can "look" across the sea—to Troy, rather than his wife—and then wither and die. His shrine accomplishes something like what his ghost does: so when Hektor touches his ship, if the poet has in mind the ship-statue, that statue provides an extra 'model' for the casting through space that occurs when Protesilaos dies and returns to his wife.

stuck between worlds, a space for himself to most fully realize his play between life and death, between lover and beloved, between action and spectatorship, narrator and character, in the poem and out. The ship itself, as a transitional space and as a source for "action at a distance," which when fired sets off action on an equivalent stage at a certain remove, prepares the ground for the series of substitutions and false images that follows, and for the eerie equation between the death of Patroklos and the death of Achilles.

Like the ship, these substitutions are made of the warp of poetics, or *poiēsis*, and the weft of presence, or *genesis* in the sense of becoming. Some of them seem tamely "poietic": the mere information, for example, that Menesthios substituted for Achilles. Others are entirely on the level of presencing or becoming: the poet "substitutes for" Achilles. But for most of these substitutions it is not easy to separate the two dimensions. And this is because substitution is the very business of the Homeric performer.

The analogy to the chariot-race speech of Nestor, where the performer more deeply "becomes" Nestor when he envisions approaching the turning point (which is a *sēma*, a tomb), prompts the observation that Protesilaos on his ship, on his cult statue, may have served a similar function in ritual, as worshipers processed to the statue and away from it again. Though speculative in the extreme, this—or something like it—seems to me a satisfying approximation to the workings of ring composition in Homer, if not some sort of counterpart in an earlier stage of the tradition.[108] It also recalls the journey of the sun to the winter solstice point, and the burst of fertility there, as embodied in the myth of Alkyone.[109]

The script at the juncture of Books 15 and 16 has some of the same performative virtues as other passages we have seen, including the speech of Phoenix. It also involves similar themes: a structure threatened with fire, sacrifice, and

---

[108] Ring composition in the limited sense of beginning and ending a poem with similar elements is "extraordinarily widespread" in Indo-European poetry (Watkins 1995:34). It structures many books of the Hebrew Bible, and a broad spectrum of ancient literature, in a thoroughgoing manner (Douglas 2007). Douglas (1999) found a different, but analogous, pattern in Leviticus, where the structure of the book reenacts the structure of the Tabernacle. Rather than picturing a static structure, though, Leviticus gives the reader a "virtual tour" (Rendsburg 2008:177) of the tabernacle, following a path into the Holy of Holies and back out again. Cf. Nagy's (1990a:209) "semiotic" treatment of the chariot race, and his diagram there. One can imagine such processions and other movements (on dance, see David 2006:168) shaping Homeric composition as they do choral composition (only less directly). Other spatial paradigms such as weaving (which has already been linked with archaic poetics), or a scroll with episodes painted on it (as with Pabuji epic from Rajasthan: Smith 1991) may also play a role. On the analogies between narrative and painted ring composition, see Mackay, Harrison, and Masters 1999.

[109] If ring composition as it occurs in Homeric poetry has been influenced by choral strophic turns and returns, solar imagery such as Alcman's association of the sun with the choral leader Agido (*PMG* 1 lines 40–41) is relevant.

an exceedingly uxorious husband.[110] But as a package it has an entirely different quality. One can see this difference as a matter of poetics with a corresponding effect in presence. Meleager's physical intimacy with Kleopatra, along with her mother's rape, fomented her takeover of the body of Phoenix and the bard. Protesilaos' ghostly intercourse with their daughter across the sea and away among the living conjured a delicate play among longing, death, resurrection, distance, memory, creation, destruction, and spanning of realms. Phoenix, in his speech, marshals and unfolds numerous figures and spaces, and also creates a space of emergence in the performance of the repeated curses. But to a great extent these containers and the figures bursting out of them are nested within one another inside the body of the bard. In contrast, here in the scene overshadowed by the ship of Protesilaos, along with its prelude and its aftershocks, the disparate and dispersed kinesthetics, the imagery of the gate, the turning-point, the ship, the house, the sea of separation, the mental and physical frenzy of substitutions, and the dimension added by death and resurrection, orchestrate a play of presence that the bard, shall we say, could only half embody.

---

[110] It even involves a substitute self-object containing the "life" of the hero: the statue of Protesilaos, both in cult and in his desperate widow's bed, bears comparison with the brand containing the life of Meleager (though this is in turn replaced by the curse in the *Iliad* version).

Interlude 2

A Source for the *Iliad*'s Structure

NOW THAT WE HAVE DRAWN OUT THE PERFORMATIVE VIRTUES of the *Iliad*'s use of the Protesilaos story, let us pivot around and look again at the question of sources and intertextuality. What are we to make of the genealogical connections among the female figures in the background: Marpessa, her daughter Kleopatra, and her granddaughter Polydora? As Pausanias[1] remarks, one after the other all kill themselves when their husbands die.

The possibility certainly exists that some clever person, the author of the *Cypria* or someone else, noticed the connections between the two couples, Protesilaos and his wife and Meleager and Kleopatra, saw how the *Iliad* used them to structure its plot, and made one woman the daughter of the other as a midrash on the *Iliad*. But the connection between Kleopatra and her daughter seems too deeply enmeshed in the structure of the *Iliad* to be a later invention. *Iliad* 9 shows detailed knowledge of Marpessa's story. Both the Catalogue of Ships and the plotting of Books 15 and 16 show familiarity with stories of Protesilaos' leap, death and return to life and used them in developing the figure of Achilles and his plot. These stories of Protesilaos' death and return from Hades are inseparable from the love story of Protesilaos and his wife. Once this is admitted, their story takes its place beside the story of Meleager and Kleopatra both as a background against which the tragic story of Achilles and Patroklos plays out and as an inspiration for the shaping of that story.

The existence of a tradition that Protesilaos' wife Polydora (or Laodameia) was the daughter of Kleopatra, who was the daughter of Marpessa, strongly suggests that these two love stories (Meleager/Kleopatra; Protesilaos/Polydora) were not put together for the first time by the poet or poets of the *Iliad*. It is rather as if at some point in the development of the *Iliad*, a poet was inspired by catalogue

---

[1] Pausanias 4.2.7; see page 221 above.

poetry relating the genealogy of Marpessa, her daughter, and her granddaughter, and used them to structure the *Iliad*. This is a more elegant solution to the genealogy's relation to the *Iliad* than the midrashic one suggested above, according to which a later author noticed the role of the women in the plotting of the *Iliad* and invented a genealogy to suit it.

Such a genealogical tradition could have been found in any number of poems, including the Hesiodic *Catalogue of Women* itself, any earlier version of it, or one of the local traditions that served as its source. While scholars continue to disagree about the dating of the poem from which our *Catalogue* fragments derive, the Nekyia in the *Odyssey* shows familiarity with some version of the *Catalogue of Women*, and it is argued that the Aeolid section of the *Catalogue*, or a close relative, served as a source for the catalogue of heroines of *Odyssey* 11.[2] What I am suggesting is that the *Catalogue*, or a similar genealogical tradition, served not only as a source for catalogic sections, such as *Odyssey* 11's heroines or Zeus' list of conquests in *Iliad* 14, but also as an inspiration for the shaping of the *Iliad*'s plot.

In fact, the stories of Alkyone and Keux, as well as the stories centered at Pleuron and Calydon (i.e., Meleager), would have been found in the very same section, the Aeolids, which is considered a source of *Odyssey* 11. The story of Alkyone (herself a daughter of Aiolos) and Keux was indeed told in the *Catalogue* (fr. 10d M-W). The stories of Marpessa, Kleopatra, and Polydora may have followed closely upon the story of Alkyone in this poem. Apollodorus' *Bibliotheke* may follow the same order of families as the *Catalogue*.[3] If so, it is significant that Apollodorus places the story of Alkyone and Keux (1.7.4) just before the account of her sisters Kanake and then Kalyke, mother of Endymion, father of Aitolos, who sired Pleuron and Calydon. Pleuron is the ancestor both of Marpessa, mother of Kleopatra, and of Althaia, mother of Meleager (Marpessa's father Euenos is the brother of Thestios, the father of Althaia; Kleopatra and Meleager are thus second cousins).[4] While Marpessa's name does not appear in the meager fragments, Althaia's does (fr. 26 M-W). West leaves room for Kleopatra and Marpessa in his genealogical tables[5] showing the structure of the *Catalogue*, despite the absence of their names from the extant fragments. If the *Iliad* poet had some such genealogical poetry[6] at his disposal, the connection between Alkyone and

---

[2] West 1985a:32. Cf. Merkelbach 1951; Page 1955.

[3] West (1985a:35) remarks that recent papyri reinforce this view of Apollodoros and the *Catalogue*.

[4] Cf. Hainsworth 1993:134–135 and his stemmata. On the shared name between Idas' father and Althaia's brother, see Hainsworth 1993:131, 136.

[5] West 1985a:174.

[6] Despite the probability that the *Catalogue of Women* contained the line Marpessa–Kleopatra–Polydora, I hesitate to single out that particular poem as it appears in the extant fragments. If, as Irwin (2008) argues, the gods in the *Catalogue* stand in for elite males, the story of Idas and Apollo fits somewhat awkwardly; but for that matter so would the *Odyssey*'s Nekyia (Irwin 2008:41). But perhaps both the Nekyia and the *Catalogue* incorporate women's traditions: see Doherty 1995, 2008.

the story of Calydon, and so Meleager, would be natural, as would the direct line Marpessa-Kleopatra-Polydora.

Of course, any poem (or, indeed, non-poetic tradition) that told the story of the three women would have served this purpose. This would include the *Cypria* tradition. Given Pausanias' wording, the *Cypria* may not have told all these stories in detail, but only included the fact that Polydora was the daughter of Kleopatra. Severyns' remark[7] that their genealogy creates a link between the *Cypria* and the *Minyad*, in which Meleager's story was told, is intriguing; but perhaps such a link, rather than being peculiar to those poems, is interacting with or based on genealogical poetry. While Pausanias' testimony on the *Cypria* is invaluable because it gives us the genealogical connection, a poem such as the Hesiodic *Catalogue* is a more attractive possibility, both because these stories would find a plausible home in such a work and because it may help to connect (genealogically) the name of Alkyone to the trio of Marpessa-Kleopatra-Polydora.

The use of erotic scenarios, and even romantic stories, to constitute not only the background (Helen) but the structure and the very fabric of his story of war might seem to be an innovation of the poet of the *Iliad*. The combination of erotic story and war is quite traditional: witness Hesiod's *Theogony* and also the *Catalogue of Women*, which ends in the strange montage of the beginning of the Trojan War and the twilight of the heroic age. And the use of erotic tales to structure or frame an individual battle scene is found elsewhere in Homer: for example, the duel between Menelaos and Paris and its postlude, recalling Paris' earlier abduction of Helen. Protesilaos' story is used to frame and deepen the scene at the beginning of Book 16. This framing, however, we now see taking its place in a broader structure: the use of the genealogical stories not only to frame a single episode but to connect the scene in Achilles' tent in Book 9 with the reappearance of Achilles and Patroklos "at home" in Book 16. This connection can be seen as an expansion of the catalogue form. This would be another example, besides ring composition, where the deep structure shapes turning points in the plot as well as virtuosic performance moments.

In the very relationship of Book 16 to the Catalogue of Ships perhaps there is an indication of how the *Iliad* may be using other catalogue poetry—or of the mutual formation of epic narrative and catalogue. Rather than a genre scene, the Catalogue contains a vivid image that points to a larger story. This might remind one of an image in a memory palace, or better, a tally (*symbolon*) bearing half the story and, for those who know, traces of the other half. The shared mythological background between Books 9 and 16 falls into place in the overall structure of the *Iliad*, a structure that makes systematic use of background story. Book 9 and Book 16 correspond with one another in the *Iliad*'s master-ring

---

[7] Severyns 1928:303.

composition (rather than the calendrical ring) as elucidated by Whitman's "Geometric Structure" chart,[8] where 9 and 16 form the innermost ring around the center. On that chart, Whitman labels the common theme of these two books abstractly as "Heroic Absolute vs. Commitment." But the Marpessa-Kleopatra-Polydora link means that Books 9 and 16 share a mythical background just as do other pairs in Whitman's scheme: Books 2 (where events echo the departure for war) and 23 (where events reflect the stories of the returns from war), and Books 3–7 (which Whitman labels Montage of Early Years of the War) and Books 18–22 (Montage of the Fall of Troy).

Whether the use of these women's stories is traditional or innovative, one should not be diverted by *Quellenforschung* from observing the particular effects achieved by the placing of these stories *in the background*—not "suppressing them," because there is not a wholesale rejection, but rather the strategic deployment of an erotic tale as background. Although the poet relegates other erotic stories, including heterosexual ones (for example, Meleager's love for Atalanta)[9] to extra-poetic space, he does so not out of any kind of epic distaste for those stories.[10] Rather the contrary: to draw out the harmonics, so to speak,

---

[8] Whitman 1958.

[9] Felson and Sale 1983. Griffin (1977:40) writes that the Homeric poems avoid "romantic" elements just as they do the "miraculous" or magical, on which see above, Chapter 2. Nagy (1990b:72n99) attributes the Homeric poems' avoidance of both elements to Panhellenism: both types of story reflect localized interests, since miraculous stories reflect local cult, and love stories lead to conceptions of heroes, a theme in genealogical poetry promoting the localized aristocrats connected with these heroes.

[10] It should be noted, however, that this is how some scholars have taken the absence of an explicit statement in Homer that Patroklos and Achilles are lovers (Janko 1994 *ad* 16.97–100, following Dover). See also Friedrich (1977:283): "Achilles grew up with Patroclus, and addressed him with a quasi-kinship term for respected, older persons (*ētheios*)—indeed, Achilles acts toward Patroclus as though the latter were a sort of structural elder brother." Friedrich disputes the notion that Achilles and Patroklos are lovers against the assertions of "psychoanalytically oriented scholars." The present argument is not psychoanalytic but structural and thematic, concerned with how the poet has framed Book 16 mythologically. For one interpreter, "An erotic interpretation of the *Iliad*—however philologically inappropriate it might be—can be explained in historical terms as the effect of a perspective that merged the actual text of the Homeric poem with its eroticized reinterpretations" (Fantuzzi 2012:3). I agree that the poem offers "no explicit evidence" that the two were "bound by an erotic bond, or were anything more than exemplary good friends" (Fantuzzi 2012:3). Nevertheless, the Protesilaos story is deployed in such a way as to accomplish—among other things—an eroticizing, however delicate, of the ongoing story. The *Iliad* is, to a certain extent, already a complication of and meditation upon the "elegiac love-in-death fantasizing" that for Fantuzzi (2012:253) is a later working-up of a "martial" bare-bones *Iliad*. Cf. Halperin 1990: whereas Halperin shows that the Achilles–Patroklos relationship, like that of Gilgamesh and Enkidu, and David and Jonathan, is compared with relations of kinship and conjugality to "make the friendship between the main characters into an image of sociality" (Halperin 1990:85), I am making sense of the fact that the Achilles–Patroklos relationship is connected in particular with stories of married couples in the background of the plot—not only that of Meleager and Kleopatra (cf. Halperin 1990:84) but also Protesilaos and his wife.

of the tune he is singing—to spark his histrionic performance, he deploys these stories in the background by such means as are discussed Chapter 2. δεινὴ δ' ἡ κευθομένη ἔμφασις.[11] The love story running behind Book 16 and the rest of the poem is powerful *because* it is in the background, and seems to "run the characters from elsewhere." The very mysteriousness of the force it exerts, the "ungrammaticality" it introduces into the story, is crucial to the sense of tragedy and to the virtues of the poem in performance. As Slatkin writes, "What becomes instrumental in this mode of composition is not only what the poet articulates by way of bringing a given myth (with its associated themes) into play, in relation to his narrative, but also what is left unsaid; for his audience would hear this as well."[12]

As for the highly compressed story of Marpessa (and Alkyone) looming behind the story of Kleopatra, one may interpret the compression of that story and its time-delayed release into the speech of Kleopatra in terms of the erotics of the passage in which it is embedded and also in terms of Kleopatra's mind. Our interpretation, however, focused upon the speaker, Phoenix: the speech erupting from Kleopatra, motivated by the story of her mother Marpessa, seemed to burst out of him involuntarily. Yet at the same time Marpessa bore a strange resemblance to Phoenix himself, as though we were given a view here of associations in Phoenix's memory, associations that hijack his speech and fuel a contrary message about the sack of a city.

In the case of Meleager and Kleopatra as a model for Patroklos and Achilles, the story looms over the *Iliad* in an obvious fashion, since it is used outright as a *paradeigma* for Achilles. Much of the tragic effect of the *Iliad* comes from the way the Meleager story looks forward to an intervention of Patroklos that does not occur until a massive delay has pushed the paradeigmatic story into the background. Likewise, the tragic events of Books 15 and 16, centered around Protesilaos' ship, gain depth from the story of love and death playing *underneath* the figures of Achilles and Patroklos. In this latter case, the tale of Protesilaos and his wife and their genealogical connection to Kleopatra lurked within the deep structure, rather than being invoked outright as a *paradeigma*. That is, at least in part, why scholars such as Kullmann have failed to recognize their role in the *Iliad*, while they could not deny the role of Meleager and Kleopatra. Yet if the *Iliad* was capable of using one married couple as a paradigm for Achilles and Patroklos, it was surely capable of using another. The rewards for the Homeric

---

[11] "There is strange power in the hidden impression/significance": Demetrius *On Style* 261.

[12] Slatkin 2011:20. Cf. Slatkin 1991:101–102: the use of the Thetis myth is "the definitive instance of the potency of myths in Homeric epic that exert their influence on the subject matter of the poems yet do not 'surface' (using Watkins' term), because of the constraints of the genre. Nevertheless, the poem reveals them, through evocative diction, oblique reference, even conspicuous omission."

audience of recognizing this particular couple are hard to overestimate. The story adds to the deepening sense of tragedy, and, like the Meleager story, works by setting up expectations that are then reversed. It opens up interpretive trajectories that cannot be circumscribed, as the audience's knowledge of the themes connected with Protesilaos—love, return from death, fashioning a substitute, boundless grief, and suicide—is drawn on just at the dawning of Patroklos' *aristeia* and his death.

4

The Living Instrument

Odyssey 13–15 in Performance

The actor ... must make his own inner being 'an instrument capable of playing any tune,' as it is often put.

Francis Fergusson, *The Idea of a Theater*, pp. 252–253

Turning our focus from the *Iliad* to the *Odyssey*, it seems plausible that the distinct virtue of the *Odyssey* in performance is somehow bound up with this poem's conspicuous self-awareness: Odysseus' consciousness of himself as a quasi-bard, the thematic concern with storytelling, deception, disguise, poetry, and the like.[1] But what does all this have to do with performance—not as a theme, but in the flesh? Odysseus spends Books 9–12 telling his story to the Phaeacians; for several hours the performer merges seamlessly with the hero as we do with the Phaeacians.[2] The hero then spends most of the second half of the poem in disguise; as the performer remains largely hidden behind his characters, so too does Odysseus. The hero is moreover in the Cretan Tales a composer, concocting elaborate lies on the spot.

But the Cretan Tales are not simply a realistic depiction of clever lying, or a mirror held up to the composing bard. To be sure, the tales do lend themselves to analysis as compositions (poetics/*poiēsis*). And, as did Chapters 2 and 3, this chapter deals with the ingredients of tales, with how they are put together—in

---

[1] From the vast bibliography on the *Odyssey*'s self-consciousness or reflexivity, I have found the following particularly useful: Létoublon 1983; Goldhill 1991; Felson 1994; Segal 1983 and 1994; Doherty 1991 and 1995; Slatkin 1996; Louden 1997; Danek 1998. Its "exuberant passion for bravura narrative acrobatics": Lowe 2000:129.

[2] With the exception of the "intermezzo" of Book 11, which "remind[s] the external audience that the internal audience exists" (Doherty 1991:150).

this case, the first two Cretan Tales—and will once again be bringing into play neglected background stories. But the motivating question is, as usual: What are the tales, and Books 13–15 more generally, good for in performance? What does the exchange of tales between Odysseus and Eumaeus allow to happen (presence/*genesis*) through the solo performer who enacts them? How does the composition of the tales, the reenactment of their composition, and the actions that form their content, relate to the action that is the action of the performer?

The multi-dimensional quality of Books 13–15 stems from the fact that Odysseus' return takes place on several levels. On Phaeacia, Odysseus merges with the bard, and we with the Phaeacians, connoisseurs of epic. Their role as audience to the primal epic scene—the tale from the mouth of the last returning hero at the close of the heroic age—is bound up with their role as "painless escorts," their possession of magic autopilot ships. These ships, and other features of their existence, endow the Phaeacians with mythological over-tones as escorts of the dead.[3] It is when he is finished with his epic tale that the Phaeacians deliver him to Ithaka in a state "most like to death"—which is pointedly also a rebirth, both of the hero and of the epic itself.[4] As Odysseus emerges from "death," so too does he cross over from the Otherworld and the Adventures to homely Ithaka, from the idyllic world of games and epic connois-seurship to the post-heroic world of Telemachus and the suitors.

What has not been fully realized is that these crossings manifest them-selves in the performance of Books 13–15. Scholars emphasize the realism[5] of Ithaka, but that is in service of a *thaumaston* of a different sort from that of the Phaeacians and Odysseus' deathlike voyage in their ship. On Ithaka, as the hero returns to life and reality, the bard "becomes" the hero like never before. The two had merged in Books 9–12 as Odysseus played the bard, a raconteur of the past. But now performer and hero merge into one *improviser*. It is as though the hero has never acted before in his life! Odysseus does not merely surface into the body of the performer, as in the *Iliad*'s *aristeiai*, or even as in his takeover in Books 9–12. Emerging from death, and from the fantasy-world of Phaeacia, he steps out bodily into the live space of performance, all but obliterating the fourth wall—for now, it is made to appear, he (the hero-bard amalgam) is getting his materials from beyond it.[6] The *unheimlich* home that greets Odysseus on his arrival gives on to the dynamic space we and the bard share; Odysseus' bewilderment overlaps with a freer give and take with space on the part of the

---

[3]   Cook 1992.
[4]   Segal 1962 and 1967; Newton 1984.
[5]   E.g. Redfield 1994:37; Segal 1994: Ch. 8.
[6]   Cf. Rehm (2002: Ch. 2) on *nostos* and performance space in tragedy. On the "fourth wall," see above page 45n121.

244

bard.[7] As Odysseus launches into the improvisations of the first Cretan Tale, we have an unprecedented view of the inner workings of composition. With this privileged proximity, the audience watches as objects in the space we share with the bard give rise to lies. The "layers" in the performing bard become peculiarly clear, to the extent that Odysseus does not "become" the Cretan so much as the persona is pieced together before our eyes.

Focusing on performance brings out yet another previously neglected background story, or rather, what turns out to be a cluster of stories: the story of Idomeneus and associated myths. But this tale differs from other background stories in that we watch its disparate pieces being picked up for bricolage over the course of several hours, as though events in the poem and within the mind of the hero are guiding its creation. We see the wellsprings of this bricolage in the anxieties and strategies of the hero. We see him slipping into this role due to fears of what he will find at home, at the same time that he tries to wrangle the story in order to craft a role for himself. While elsewhere the poem "incorporates an explicit awareness of the creative tension of composition, an awareness of the existence of possibilities that could become other songs; and this implies a claim that alternative treatments have been rejected,"[8] here the poem, sharing out its plotting function among hero, goddess, and slave, goes very far down the path of another *nostos* story, or cluster of stories, as a way of creating layers of meaning but also layers in the performer.

The comic, monologic "liveness" of the first improvisational encounter with Athena in Book 13 sets the stage for a profound dialogue in Books 14 and 15. Once it is seen as a dialogue for solo performance, the relatively neglected[9] Eumaeus episode becomes, from being "waiting books,"[10] the most dynamic episode of the poem, perhaps even surpassing the hearthside interview between husband and wife.[11] Odysseus does not simply test the loyalty of Eumaeus, prove his own worthiness, or lie his way into the next stage of his homecoming. Rather the plot is hatched from elements emerging in their dialogue—elements that develop the subplot of Idomeneus.[12] The hero has come so far out into the space of performance that we are slotted into the "you" seat and can see him through the eyes of Eumaeus.

---

[7] Lateiner (1995:56) writes that the second half of the *Odyssey* "revels in the intricacies" of spatial manipulation, even though, as I noted earlier, he is not interested in performance.

[8] Slatkin 1996:228.

[9] Segal 1994:164; Lowe 2000:133–134; Gainsford 2003:58; Bowie 2013:1.

[10] Stewart 1976:87.

[11] Fenik 1974:155 is typical: the Eumaeus episode is an anticipatory doublet of the more important conversation with Penelope; cf. Austin 1975:205.

[12] Compare this to Penelope's arrival at the stratagem of the bow contest; the idea mysteriously arises from their conversation by a process opaque to the audience. Cf. Felson 1994:18; Levaniouk 2011: Ch. 14.

What is scripted here is not a top-down seduction of slave by master or a reestablishment of intimacy or proper roles. It is a dialogue in which Odysseus comes face-to-face with his slave as a slave. Thanks to solo performance, there is a revolution within the performer; the consciousness of Eumaeus seems to eclipse that of his bardlike master. The merging between the bard and Odysseus is ruptured, as we see one layer further into the bard, where Eumaeus was waiting in ambush. Eumaeus is no longer simply a 'living instrument,' subject to a superior mind. Somewhat like an improvising musician whose hands find a melody by playing, the bard seems to find, through his own instrument, not only speech but a speaker.

Much like *Odyssey* 8's "Trojan Horse" story, the dialogue with Eumaeus complicates, interrogates, our view of the hero and our own bloodthirsty impatience for his revenge and the regaining of his kingdom.

The return and revenge of Odysseus, in disguise to "test" the hospitality of the suitors, has fruitfully been seen as a "theoxeny,"[13] a story-type in which a disguised god tests the hospitality of mortals, the paradigm being Philemon and Baucis. This is part of the mythical register that underwrites Odysseus' restoration of order out of chaos, a reinstatement of hierarchies, a reestablishment of rapport, or even, for the most optimistic readers, a re-invention of his own personality.[14] Within this scheme, Odysseus is testing the loyalty of Eumaeus or proving his own worthiness. But running underneath this "centripetal" drive toward order is the "centrifugal"[15] tendency of the plot and its hero, as glimpsed in the allusions within the Cretan Tales to alternative stories of Odysseus, stories that throw into question the finality of the *Odyssey*'s "and so to bed."

This chapter contributes to the insights gained through attention to extra-Odyssean stories by fleshing out the role of Idomeneus traditions and the significance of Eumaeus as a wisdom figure, both of which shape not only the background but the masterplot, thereby undermining the theoxeny plot. The slave, who could have been a mere instrument, surprises us and the hero when he forces the hero to confront the reality of slavery from the slave's perspective, releasing the hero's monopoly on the body of the bard. What emerges is not an aristocratic suppression of the unpleasantness of slavery, or Bakhtinian polyphony, but an ethical upheaval fomented through the medium of solo performance. Rather than plots competing within a text, a transformation takes place through performance that spans hero and performer. The hero returns to life and the bard to a liveness that brings on an ethical quickening of hero and audience alike.

---

[13] Kearns 1982; Louden 1999.
[14] Stewart 1976:105.
[15] Bakhtin's terms, adapted by Peradotto (1990:53–58) for the *Odyssey*.

ἀλλοειδέα φαινέσκετο πάντα:
Seeing Something as Something Else

In Books 9–12, Odysseus was absorbed into the body of the bard by his long occupation of it. Now in Book 13, Athena, who showed herself the plotter of the poem in Book 5, resurfaces to instigate events on Ithaka. She does so in a subtle fashion, by prompting Odysseus to begin weaving a certain Cretan identity for himself. But first she plots something else.[16]

ὣς ἔφαθ', οἱ δ' ἔδδεισαν, ἑτοιμάσσαντο δὲ ταύρους.
185   ὣς οἱ μέν ῥ' εὔχοντο Ποσειδάωνι ἄνακτι
δήμου Φαιήκων ἡγήτορες ἠδὲ μέδοντες,
ἑσταότες περὶ βωμόν.[17] ὁ δ' ἔγρετο δῖος Ὀδυσσεὺς
εὕδων ἐν γαίῃ πατρωΐῃ, οὐδέ μιν ἔγνω,
ἤδη δὴν ἀπεών· περὶ γὰρ θεὸς ἠέρα χεῦε
190   Παλλὰς Ἀθηναίη, κούρη Διός, ὄφρα μιν αὐτὸν
ἄγνωστον τεύξειεν ἕκαστά τε μυθήσαιτο,
μή μιν πρὶν ἄλοχος γνοίη ἀστοί τε φίλοι τε,
πρὶν πᾶσαν μνηστῆρας ὑπερβασίην ἀποτῖσαι.
τοὔνεκ' ἄρ' ἀλλοειδέα φαινέσκετο πάντα ἄνακτι,
195   ἀτραπιτοί τε διηνεκέες λιμένες τε πάνορμοι
πέτραι τ' ἠλίβατοι καὶ δένδρεα τηλεθάοντα.
στῆ δ' ἄρ' ἀναΐξας καί ῥ' εἴσιδε πατρίδα γαῖαν·
ᾤμωξέν τ' ἄρ' ἔπειτα καὶ ὢ πεπλήγετο μηρὼ
χερσὶ καταπρηνέσσ', ὀλοφυρόμενος δὲ προσηύδα·

So he spoke, and they took fright, and readied the bulls.
So there they were, praying to lord Poseidon,
the leaders and counselors of the Phaeacian people,
standing round the altar. And he awakened, brilliant Odysseus,
sleeping in the land of his fathers, and he did not recognize it,
being away so long: for the goddess was pouring a mist round,
Pallas Athena, daughter of Zeus, that she might make him himself
unrecognizable and tell him everything,

---

[16] Athena's actions here exemplify her role as manipulator of, rather than participant in, the plot, a role finding expression elsewhere in the phrase ἔνθ' αὖτ' ἀλλ' ἐνόησε, which, as Bakker (1997a:181–183) explains, "effects an episode boundary in the tale, rather than an interaction between two protagonists."

[17] This startling mid-line scene change disorients the audience, mirroring the impact of his environment upon Odysseus himself. The repeated ἄρα manifests the strangeness, but also lifts the veil on Odysseus: here he is, after all this!

lest his wife recognize him beforehand, and the townspeople and his
loved ones,
before he wreaked vengeance on the suitors for all their
transgression.
That is why, you see, everything kept appearing otherwise [*alloeidēs*]
to the lord,
far-reaching paths, all-compassing harbors,
rocks steep to climb, trees in bloom.
He shot straight up and lo, laid eyes on his fatherland:
and then did he ever wail! and struck his thighs
with flats of hands, and cried out, lamenting ...

Odyssey 13.184–199

Poseidon has turned the Phaeacian ship to stone, cutting off the Phaeacian traffic between fantasy and reality, their painless escort service that verges on escort to or from death. Alkinoos' father's prophecy has come true, and they can no longer obliviously entertain both undisguised gods and returning heroes. The epic heroes are all returned. The Phaeacians will hear no other stories of Troy but those that have made their way into the repertoire of Demodokos.

So, as this door closes, Odysseus is waking up in a new world indeed. But just as that world might be settling into something like "life," or "post-epic," or "reality," Athena shows up to make everything incessantly (φαινέσκετο) manifest itself as otherwise, ἀλλοειδέα. The *heimlich* will be *unheimlich*. This well encapsulates the poetics—or the performativities—of the authorial bard. As with the love story of Protesilaos and Laodameia running beneath the *Iliad*'s tragedy, so too on Ithaka things will not be quite what they seem. There is not mere overlay of the fabulous upon the realistic, but intrusion and interference. Here that interference, that sense of one plot derailing another, will indeed be iterative. The ostensible reason for this is that the background story is seeded within the consciousness of Odysseus himself. In Book 13, he seizes on the basic plot, both because of his fears and as a front for his actions, and only gradually works out its implications. But the real reason is Athena's, the bard's. It makes for a better performance.

The practical or plot reason for the mist is to disorient Odysseus and prevent him from running home before he is prepared, to keep him from being recognized prematurely. One cannot have recognition scenes without un-recognition. But that is not how it is put. Athena sheds a mist all around

ὄφρα μιν αὐτὸν
ἄγνωστον τεύξειεν ἕκαστά τε μυθήσαιτο,
μή μιν πρὶν ἄλοχος γνοίη...

> to make him
> unrecognizable [see below] and to tell him everything,
> lest his wife recognize him beforehand...
>
> *Odyssey* 13.190–192

So while the purpose of the mist may be to prevent Odysseus from being *recognized*, what it actually does is to make Odysseus unrecognizing, as emerges in lines 194–196.[18] (ἄγνωστον has both active and passive connotations in archaic poetry.) This play between vision and knowledge, active and passive, inside and out, mirrors the shifting dynamics among bard, goddess, hero, and slave. We watch plotlines being generated outside, traveling inside for incubation, and being transformed by an unexpected source of intelligence, a source "one layer deeper inside"[19] the bard than we knew existed. The disorientation and reorientation of Odysseus through the device of the mist contributes to the kinesthetics of return, to the "home" constituted by the performance space.

Cretan Tale 1:
To Athena Disguised as a Young Prince

For objects of transformation, use things that shouldn't be there.

The Second City Almanac of Improvisation

ὣς εἰπὼν τρίποδας περικαλλέας ἠδὲ λέβητας
ἠρίθμει καὶ χρυσὸν ὑφαντά τε εἵματα καλά.
τῶν μὲν ἄρ' οὔ τι πόθει· ὁ δ' ὀδύρετο πατρίδα γαῖαν
ἑρπύζων παρὰ θῖνα πολυφλοίσβοιο θαλάσσης,
πόλλ' ὀλοφυρόμενος. σχεδόθεν δέ οἱ ἦλθεν Ἀθήνη,
ἀνδρὶ δέμας ἐϊκυῖα νέῳ, ἐπιβώτορι μήλων,
παναπάλῳ, οἷοί τε ἀνάκτων παῖδες ἔασι,
δίπτυχον ἀμφ' ὤμοισιν ἔχουσ' εὐεργέα λώπην·
ποσσὶ δ' ὑπὸ λιπαροῖσι πέδιλ' ἔχε, χερσὶ δ' ἄκοντα.

Having said that, he began to count the lovely tripods and cauldrons
and the gold and the fine woven garments.
And lo, not a one of them was missing! And he was bewailing his
    fatherland
creeping along the shore of the churning sea,

---

[18] Pucci 1995:100; Goldhill 1991:6–7; David 2006:195.
[19] This is the equivalent, for the internal "landscape" of the bard, of the shepherd, who appears one layer deeper inside the *poem-world* than the audience knew existed (see above, page 87).

> grieving heavily. And along came Athena next to him,
> in form like a young man, a shepherd of flocks,
> delicate—such as the children of lords are—
> wearing a well-worked double-layered cloak around her shoulders,
> and sandals on her sleek feet and a javelin in her hands.
>
> *Odyssey* 13.217–225

Face to face with a noble youth who could very well be his own son, Odysseus lights upon a Cretan identity for himself. Why Crete?[20] Among other factors, Cretans are traditional liars, and Crete is far enough[21] away. (In this, Odysseus responds to Athena's prompt τηλόθεν εἰλήλουθας [237].) But the persona is no generic liar. Through the series of tales, the Cretan progresses[22] from 1) the hostile compatriot of Idomeneus, who has killed Idomeneus' son, to 2) a co-commander with Idomeneus, to 3) Idomeneus' younger brother "Aethon." It is as though his identity converges upon Idomeneus himself with each pass. Why this affiliation with Idomeneus in particular? Certain details have given rise to the theory that in a previous version of the *Odyssey*, Telemachus travels to Crete and meets his father in the house of Idomeneus, where he has been waiting out a storm, and that the Cretan Tales contain traces of this earlier version.[23]

Another approach to the question is taken by Haft,[24] who notes that Odysseus and Idomeneus are associated in the *Iliad* and share certain traits. Odysseus in the *Odyssey*, moreover, has aged and now resembles the Idomeneus of the *Iliad* even more: for example, he can no longer sprint. But for Haft, Odysseus has modeled his Cretan persona not on Idomeneus himself, but on his *therapōn* Meriones. Odysseus claims to be a Cretan leader ambivalently subordinate to Idomeneus, just like the Meriones of the *Iliad*.[25] Odysseus and Meriones share characteristics even outside of the Cretan persona. Like Odysseus, Meriones is good in the ambush and an excellent bowman. The boar's-tusk helmet lent to Odysseus by Meriones for the Doloneia was passed from Odysseus' grandfather

---

[20] Concise summary of various theories at Tsagalis 2012b:314n19.

[21] Walcot 1977:10–11.

[22] Haft (1984:305) provides a table charting the progression. Cf. de Jong 2001:596–597.

[23] Woodhouse 1930; Reece 1994. Zenodotus reads Κρήτην for Σπάρτην at *Odyssey* 1.93 and 1.285, and Idomeneus for Menelaos in the latter passage (on these readings, found in the scholia to *Odyssey* 3.313, see S. West 1981; Tsagalis 2012b:316); the poet shows detailed knowledge of Cretan geography (Reece 1994:165). Summary of the evidence for a "Cretan *Odyssey*" at Tsagalis 2012b:314–316; see also Levaniouk 2012; Martin 2005; Nagy 2017.

[24] Haft 1984:294–299.

[25] See also Federico 1999:280–288. Lowenstam (1981:135–137), following van Brock's (1959) interpretation of *therapōn* as "ritual substitute," suggests that Odysseus is here informing the goddess that he will not be "sacrificed": he will not serve as a *therapōn*.

Autolycus down to Meriones.[26] Most strikingly, Meriones wins ten double-axes in the archery contest in the funeral games for Patroklos (*Iliad* 23.851, 882) while Odysseus shoots his arrow through twelve double-axes in the bow contest (*Odyssey* 21.421–423).[27]

Given these curious links between Odysseus and Meriones, no further motivation for Odysseus' Cretan persona may seem necessary. But it is somewhat puzzling if the purpose is simply to make the persona more credible[28] or admirable.

The Cretan identity bears a relationship to the Tales' internal audiences (Athena, Eumaeus, Penelope), scenarios, and ambient objects, that one can observe as Odysseus improvises it in real time.[29] (Recall that the backstage improvisation in *Iliad* 13 features Idomeneus and Meriones.) Close attention to the improvisation process points to a deeper significance for the stories behind the persona: it is not only a matter of verisimilitude or general rhetorical purpose. Nor is the Cretan persona chosen primarily to "deauthorize" alternative stories of Odysseus' return, stories that may have included a Cretan episode.[30]

In the first Cretan Tale, to Athena dressed as a young prince, Odysseus says that he has *killed the son of Idomeneus*. This is a highly specific detail; here is no generic murderer on the run.[31]

Now there are two major branches to the Idomeneus traditions. In the first, Idomeneus kills his own son. Faced with a violent storm on his way home

---

[26] *Iliad* 10.260–271; Meriones also lends him a bow. Haft 1984:296; Clay 1983:96–101; Petegorsky 1982:200. Haft and Clay note that Plutarch (*Marcellus* 20.3) mentions weapons dedicated to Meriones and Odysseus.

[27] Haft 1984:296. The name "Meriones" (which the ancients connected with μηρός, "thigh") may also have resonance with the image of Odysseus' thighs, which increasingly become the focus of attention, reaching a climax when Eurykleia grasps them in the bathing scene (see Lowenstam 1981:138).

[28] Haft 1984:298. The detailed links do not figure into Haft's overall reading of the Tales (299–309) as disguises that also enact self-revelation and re-creation.

[29] It is as though we were given the perspective of the interrogation room in the film "The Usual Suspects" instead of watching the events transpire as the protagonist narrates them. Just this constitutes the "Saturday Night Live" parody of "The Usual Suspects," where the liar constructs his tale out of objects placed for his convenience from left to right. This illustrates one source of humor in the Cretan Tales. (In "The Usual Suspects," we watch events of a crime unfold as narrated by one of a gang of criminals. At the end of the film, we slip into the interrogation room where the narrator has been telling the story to the police. Unbeknownst to the police and to us, the narrator has constructed the story as a bricoleur, using random objects in the room, and no part of the story actually took place.)

[30] Danek 1998; Marks 2003 and 2008; Tsagalis 2012b.

[31] Reece (1994:163–164) compares this to Theoclymenos' situation and uses it as evidence that Theoclymenos is a doublet of Odysseus, even though the exile-for-homicide theme is common, as he himself admits (Reece 1994:164n10; cf. de Jong 2001:329). But the victim's identity here sets this story apart.

from Troy, Idomeneus vows to Poseidon to sacrifice the first thing he sees; this turns out to be his son.[32] (This tradition varies: he either kills his son or intends to kill him.[33]) When he kills his son, the horrified Cretans send Idomeneus into exile (where he has further adventures). If the listener does recall some such Idomeneus tale, the Cretan Tales reward that listener by converging on an Idomenean identity for Odysseus until his real identity is finally revealed (in an episode that, as it happens, includes an abortive mock-Oedipal struggle with his son, when Telemachus is a bit too eager to assert his βίη in the bow-contest).[34]

Here already in the first Cretan Tale appear the themes of: 1) an aging man returning from the Trojan War; 2) the first thing he encounters (13.228, ὦ φίλ', ἐπεί σε πρῶτα κιχάνω τῷδ' ἐνὶ χώρῳ) being someone very like his own son (the son of a lord, *wanax*: cf. line 194 where *wanax* denotes Odysseus);[35] and 3) that son-figure representing either a threat or salvation.[36] Faced with such circumstances, Odysseus concocts a story wherein 4) *he kills the son of Idomeneus*, and, as a result, 5) is on the run.

Although numerous characteristics of Idomeneus and Meriones have been brought to bear on the Cretan Tales, scholars tend to neglect the stories

[32] Servius *ad Aeneid* 3.121, 3.401, and 11.264; Mythographi Vaticani I.192, II.254. On this story and related stories in the folk tradition, see Frazer's Appendix XII to Apollodorus, "The Vow of Idomeneus."

[33] In at least one version (eventually fleshed out by Fénelon and adopted by Mozart's librettist Varesco; see Starobinski 2002) appears the detail that Idomeneus must keep the vow secret from his son. Cf. 13.254–255, οὐδ' ὅ γ' ἀληθέα εἶπε, πάλιν δ' ὅ γε λάζετο μῦθον / αἰεὶ ἐνὶ στήθεσσι νόον πολυκερδέα νωμῶν, "nor did he, of course, tell the truth, but being who he was, he tamped down his speech, wielding the wily mind in his chest."

[34] 21.113–129. Of course, in the *Telegony*'s version (cf. Apollodorus *Epitome* 7.36; Oppian *Halieutica* 2.497–505; Parthenius *Erotica Pathemata* 3), Odysseus *is* killed by his son: Telegonos. This is not the time to review the controversy over whether Teiresias' prophecy that death would come to Odysseus ἐξ ἁλὸς (*Odyssey* 11.134–135) refers to that story. But the allegedly unhomeric spirit (e.g. Hansen 1977:45) of the story is not evidence that it is *post*-Homeric. It is clear that the *Odyssey* alludes to and recasts such "unhomeric" stories without telling them outright (Danek 1998; Marks 2003; Marks 2008; Tsagalis 2012b; Sacks 2012). It is conceivable that the confrontation on the beach in Book 13 looks forward to a confrontation with Telegonos on Ithaka, and/or "backward" to a meeting with Telemachus on Crete. This by no means precludes the argument about Odysseus and Idomeneus. If it was in the repertoire, one would also have to find room in the account for Odysseus killing his own son Euryalus (cf. Ahl and Roisman 1996:163–164), but again, we are here talking about the son of Idomeneus.

[35] The "noble youth" is the first of Reece 1993's list of conventional elements in a Homeric hospitality scene, and the second motif within Louden 1999's "extended narrative pattern" that largely constitutes the *Odyssey* (the other two major instances being Hermes on Aiaia and Nausikaa on Scheria). Cf. Cook 1995:153 (Peisistratus, Nausikaa, Athena-as-youth). The poet has here varied that fundamental structure in a specific direction to make use of the Idomeneus story.

[36] See the "First thing you meet" motif in Thompson 1966, and again Frazer's Appendix XII to Apollodorus.

of Idomeneus' homecoming that are attested later in Greek tradition and that may have been told in the *Nostoi*.[37] One reason (aside from their late attestation) scholars have assumed that stories of Idomeneus' disastrous homecoming are post-Homeric is that at *Odyssey* 3.191-192 Nestor remarks that "the sea did not rob Idomeneus of any companion." This does not[38] imply a happy homecoming, especially as Nestor bothers to say that he has this information secondhand and that he is uninformed (ἀπευθής) about further details (3.184-187).

Having isolated key details that recall the Idomeneus story, let us see how the tale unfolds in time. The audience knows that the Tale's audience, the implied body standing in their midst facing the performer, is a slick well-dressed son-of-a-lord type (13.223 οἷοί τε ἀνάκτων παῖδες ἔασι); it is this figure that the performer/hero must contend with on the spot—along with the enormous pile of treasure given him by the Phaeacians.

The performer, perhaps registering the suggestion at the end of Athena's speech (13.249 τήν περ τηλοῦ φασὶν…) by pretending to get an idea (255 αἰεὶ ἐνὶ στήθεσσι νόον πολυκερδέα νωμῶν) comes out with the Cretan locale (256–257, ἐν Κρήτῃ εὐρείῃ, / τηλοῦ ὑπὲρ πόντου) and remarks that in fact he *has* heard of Ithaka, and that "now I've come here myself! / with these χρήματα" (257-258; note the enjambment). Now "these χρήματα" were carefully counted by Odysseus in lines 217-218, after he expressed deep concern for his treasure, which seems to exceed concern for his own safety. In that speech he refers to "these χρήματα" twice (203, "Where am I going to take all these χρήματα here?" [πῆ δὴ χρήματα πολλὰ φέρω τάδε]; 215, "Come now, let me count τὰ χρήματ' and look at them"). The counting of the treasure is said to serve the purpose of characterization.[39] Given Odysseus' profit-mindedness, it is odd that anyone comments on this passage at all—though it does unveil that character rather vividly. Besides characterization, there is a specifically performative aim in

---

[37] Lowenstam (1981:135-137) notes the D-scholiast's (on 13.259) mention of Idomeneus' story, but favors Meriones rather than Idomeneus as the model for the Cretan persona, remarking that "ν 265-6 preclude Idomeneus from real consideration." Federico (1999, esp. 291-299) infers from certain details the pre-Homeric existence of the Idomeneus traditions. He believes that power struggles among Cretan cities, rather than dramatic purposes, lie behind the poem's use of these traditions.

[38] *Pace* Gantz (1993:697) and Haft (1984:299). For Federico (1999:299) this remark about the safe return *with all his companions* (as opposed to Odysseus) is anti-Odyssean and represents the official Knossian version of the story, while competing traditions are marked as false by their placement in the Cretan Tales. For Marks (2008: Ch. 5) Nestor's report is part of the *Odyssey's* attempt to "de-authorize stories in which Odysseus is indirectly responsible for the … seduction of [the Achaeans'] wives."

[39] E.g., Hoekstra in Heubeck and Hoekstra 1989:177 *ad Odyssey* 13.218 says the poet is here "individualizing the old folk-tale hero." De Jong (2001:318) notes the central role of the treasure throughout lines 120-371.

the emphasis on the goods, the repeated deixis,[40] and the actual counting. The performer, as it were, *sets the loot before him*. The χρήματα now occupy a tangible spot in space and can be used as an invisible prop.

With the arrival of the young man, the χρήματα (a fabulously massive pile of tripods, cauldrons, gold, and garments) become an embarrassment for Odysseus that must be explained.[41] The performer-as-Odysseus, enacting his realization of what he must now accomplish in his lie, can now refer to them with alarm. The enjambment of the goods adds to the comic potential, as the performer strings his tale together bit by bit, slightly pausing if he wishes[42] before the enjambed χρήμασι σὺν τοίσδεσσι (258), "with these-here χρήματα," as if realizing that this inconvenient heap of treasure must now be somehow incorporated into the story that he is presently concocting.

To distill the distinct virtue of the Tale's (and the Tales') comic liveness, compare the way they spring to life before the audience's eyes to the virtuosic intellectual discourses in the heart of Shaw's *Man and Superman*. The effect of the latter comes from the gradual unmooring of the actors' brains from any scripted action until their display of memory becomes a display, as it were, of their own wit over and above Shaw's. This wit is not simply bogus: it is a rare actor who would take on such a role. But the overall effect is the comic "coming forward" of the actors out of anything resembling a play to settle comfortably into their chairs and simply enjoy one another's intellectual companionship. Such a coming forward is not entirely modern: it is akin to, while distinct from, Aristophanes' *parabaseis*, where a character "steps aside" from the action to harangue the audience. In *Man and Superman*, however, while the characters come unmoored from the script, they do not thereby emerge into the audience's world. Rather, by virtue both of their unmooring (no longer caged actors parroting Shaw's words) and of their sheer intellectual superiority, the actors come out of the play but remain aloof from the audience. The audience has rather to approach *them*, as awkward dinner guests who linger, like Aristodemus, to listen in on an elite conversation.

The charm of χρήμασι σὺν τοίσδεσσι in 258 comes from the performer-as-Odysseus, pleased with himself for coming up with the Cretan bit, being confronted with this invisible pile that the audience is now projecting into that spot that he had "forgotten about" in his initial greeting. As with *Man*

---

[40] De Jong (2001:324–325) notes the conspicuous use of deictic pronouns throughout this dialogue and remarks, "This brings it close to drama." It is drama; the question is, what is the deixis good for in the performance?

[41] Cf. Austin 1975:203.

[42] Daitz 1991 argues for a pause at the end of each hexameter line, with the length of the pause determined by the presence or absence of enjambment (p. 156). Cf. Danek and Hagel 1995:11–12. Of course, the pause itself can be used, or lengthened, for artistic purposes.

and *Superman*, the performer is unmoored from the script;[43] but here his path has been blocked, and he must now forge ahead using the obstacles in front of him. That is, the comedy stems both from the classic "hand in the cookie jar" moment and also from a split in the performer: the part who has composed (or recomposed or even simply recounted) all of this, and the part who has to deal with the mess created by previous moments and some inconvenient, now-materialized-by-himself objects. The inconvenience sets him scrambling, and his next words (13.258–259) are λιπὼν δ᾽ ἔτι παισὶ τοσαῦτα / φεύγω ("and having left so much [i.e. as much as you see here] for my children / I am now in flight"). This irrelevant detail is perhaps, on a superficial level, designed to prevent the young interlocutor from thinking Odysseus an out-and-out pirate. But keep in mind, the interlocutor looks like the son of a *wanax*, and has just explained that this is Ithaka, making it ever more likely to Odysseus that *this is, in fact, his son*. Thus his leaving "just as much at home for his children" can be registered as an attempt to deflect criticism (by someone who may be his child) of a long abandonment of his children spent—as it now appears—amassing treasure. All of this can easily be registered by the bard-as-hero as he pieces together his story, focusing sharply upon his invisible interlocutor and sizing him up.

Having established that 1) he is a Cretan 2) in flight 3) with his goods—leaving behind some for his children, of course—he backs into the previous cause: why is he in exile? For the same reason that Idomeneus had to go into exile:[44] because he killed the son of Idomeneus!

This son is someone with swift feet (Orsilochos πόδας ὠκύν), a champion runner.

> λιπὼν δ᾽ ἔτι παισὶ τοσαῦτα
> φεύγω, ἐπεὶ φίλον υἷα κατέκτανον Ἰδομενῆος,
> Ὀρσίλοχον πόδας ὠκύν, ὃς ἐν Κρήτῃ εὐρείῃ
> ἀνέρας ἀλφηστὰς νίκα ταχέεσσι πόδεσσιν...

> And—leaving so much for my children—
> I am on the run, after I killed the dear son of Idomeneus,
> Orsilochos, swift-footed, who in wide Crete
> would win out over bread-eating men with his swift feet...
>
> *Odyssey* 13.258–261

---

[43] As throughout this study, I do not mean a written "script" or even a completely fixed text, but a scenario or routine that is being unfolded. Obviously here and in Shaw there is no actual unmooring, but the impression of a strange loosening of the performer from a pre-planned performance.

[44] The D-scholia on 13.259 φεύγω briefly recount Idomeneus' travels, without mentioning his exile. Cf. Lowenstam 1981:135; Federico 1999:294.

Although the epithet "swift in his feet" can be heard as inspired by Odysseus' rivalry with Achilles, he killed someone very like the figure standing just before him, the young son of an island lord with emphatically shining feet.[45] Here too the performer may easily "look" at the figure to register the source of this detail as he speaks.

His name, Orsilochos, "instigator of the strategem," fits the story "altogether too neatly."[46] One sees the wheels turning to produce the name: and this is typical of the new world when Odysseus reaches Ithaka. While in the *Iliad* (and even in the *Odyssey*) heroes often had significant names, that is because they belonged to a certain realm: the heroic world, fairy tale, myth, or whatever. Now, on the brink of the post-heroic world, one sees vividly the process of forming the name rather than seeing the world already made.[47]

The name Orsilochos adds an element of comedy and a subtle confusion of causation. Walcot comments that the name fits the story ironically, since Orsilochos is the victim and not the instigator of the stratagem. But the composing Odysseus is gazing at a young man who has given rise to the character and to the lie as a whole, and is the "instigator of the stratagem" in this sense. A hall of mirrors emerges, where the chain of causation has gotten lost. Odysseus reaches for a name to represent his interlocutor in his Cretan projection, and comes up with a name describing that very moment: the "young man," the invisible Athena and his/her ghostly projection on Crete, gives rise to the ambush that is the Cretan Tale and the ambush within it.[48]

He killed him because—because "he wanted to deprive me of all this loot—Trojan loot!" (note τῆς ληΐδος, *this* loot: he points to the very same loot over which he has already murdered one young prince very like his interlocutor):

οὕνεκά με στερέσαι τῆς ληΐδος ἤθελε πάσης
Τρωϊάδος, τῆς εἵνεκ' ἐγὼ πάθον ἄλγεα θυμῷ
ἀνδρῶν τε πτολέμους ἀλεγεινά τε κύματα πείρων
οὕνεκ' ἄρ' οὐχ ᾧ πατρὶ χαριζόμενος θεράπευον ...

---

[45] Recall the description of Athena (13.222–225):
ἀνδρὶ δέμας ἐϊκυῖα νέῳ, ἐπιβώτορι μήλων,
παναπάλῳ, οἷοί τε ἀνάκτων παῖδες ἔασι,
δίπτυχον ἀμφ' ὤμοισιν ἔχουσ' εὐεργέα λώπην·
ποσσὶ δ' ὑπὸ λιπαροῖσι πέδιλ' ἔχε, χερσὶ δ' ἄκοντα.

[46] Walcot 1977:10.

[47] This does not mean that the name Orsilochos does not already exist in the tradition prior to the composition of this passage (as Willcock 1977 claims of other names), perhaps even as the son of Idomeneus; the poem dramatizes the invention of such a name.

[48] "Orsilochos" might also be heard as "ambush-jumper." Odysseus has been ambushed by the "young man," who then provokes the counter-ambush.

Because he wanted to deprive me of all this loot—
Trojan loot! Because of which I suffered pains in my heart
and went through the wars of men and painful waves—
because, see, I would not please his father, serving as his *therapōn* ...
Odyssey 13.262–265

Again, a new idea, hit upon and released in enjambment (/ Τρωϊάδος),
taken in part from the last two lines of Athena's speech (καὶ ἐς Τροίην) and
in part from the "performer's" most recently hit-upon idea about Idomeneus.
The bard-as-Odysseus is now straddling the line between explaining "all this
χρήματα," now newly configured as Trojan loot (ληΐδος), and warning off the
figure before him by projecting upon this already-invisible scene another,
Cretan one, in which the same characters (loot-bearer, youth) and props (*this*
loot) recur. This has all happened before, on Crete, and it did not end well for
the young man.

The bard-as-Odysseus now backs himself into a self-portrait as an unknown
leader, a possessor of Trojan loot, bound to no one, a leader of his own men.
He does so via a peculiar (unparalleled in Homer)[49] triplicate causal clause
οὔνεκα ... εἵνεκα ... οὔνεκα compressed into four lines (13.262–265). This yields
a tone of desperate self-assertion, as the performer, as it were, casts about him
for his next step back in the causal sequence. That the loot is looming very
large can be seen by the τῆς εἵνεκ' clause. It is because of this loot that he has
suffered pains—the phrase πάθον ἄλγεα θυμῷ at 263 recalls 13.90, heard just
a few minutes before, and the following line 13.264 echoes 13.91: ἀνδρῶν τε
πτολέμους ἀλεγεινά τε κύματα πείρων. While Odysseus was sleeping through
his magical transport at the beginning of Book 13, this stately phraseology[50]
was used to summarize the whole of Odysseus' adventures as he is meta-
phorically reborn to his old life. There the phrase recalls the beginning of the
Odyssey: it is a beginning (or "proem") for the poem as well as its midpoint.
Just a few minutes later, all of that epic suffering has been boiled down to one
thing: "this loot."[51] And indeed, although no causal connection exists between

---

[49] The closest parallels in early hexameter are *Homeric Hymn to Aphrodite* 198–199 οὔνεκα/ἕνεκα, *Homeric Hymn to Apollo* 374/377; cf. *Odyssey* 11.544/549.

[50] This phrase, as Seth Schein reminds me, is also used at *Iliad* 24.8 by Achilles of the suffering he shared with Patroklos, perhaps implying solemn traditional associations (funerary? as *Odyssey* 13.91 summarizes the hero at his moment of "as-if" death). It also occurs at *Odyssey* 8.183.

[51] "As far as this pseudo-Cretan is concerned, the Trojan War was a drawn-out pirate raid and no sacred principle was at stake [...]. Odysseus declares in his first lie that his dignity and his prop-erty are so tied together that any attempt either to disgrace or rob him will involve a fight to the death, and he is prepared to kill and get away with it" (Benardete 1997:108–109).

the loot and Odysseus' suffering,[52] we are now privileged to see that Odysseus is almost more concerned about it than his own life. The line gives new meaning to the Phaeacian tale, told so that he may receive escort, but also wealth.

The humor here arises from the combination of at least two things:

1. The desperate Odysseus scrambling to explain why he is standing there not knowing where he is, with a massive pile of tripods, cauldrons, etc., and arriving at an account for the loot that makes it the *raison d'être* for all of his adventures. This overloading of the loot with significance seems to be an overcompensation for his being in such a rush to account for it, but ...

2. In a very rare instance where we the audience see Odysseus without other characters present, the man is at pains to do nothing before he totes up his winnings.

We the audience observe him using his own concupiscence as a tool to dig himself out. He hurtles out toward related mythology of return (Idomeneus) and comes to rest on the bedrock of his profiteering mind.[53]

The treasure in fact has no relation to his suffering, but he gives it this significance, as though a life of suffering is compensated for by a sufficient amount of booty. And it is used to similar comic effect after Athena reveals Ithaka to Odysseus. Odysseus kisses the earth in gratitude and, praying to the cave-dwelling nymphs, daughters of Zeus, offers to give them gifts if "the *loot-grabbing* daughter of Zeus kindly allows me to live and enhances my dear son" (360, a nice actorly line). Athena in effect tells him "never mind all that, softy, right now let's stuff these χρήματα into a corner of the cave" (362–365). The would-be offering to the nymphs is crammed into their cave merely to hide it from enemies. Odysseus and Athena flaunt their superiority to religious folderol[54] just after the bard has mesmerized the audience with his description of the cave of the nymphs. At the same time, Athena/the bard flaunts her authorial function. The performer becoming her steps back from his embodiment of Odysseus, and

---

[52] The fact that Odysseus got this particular cache not by pillage but by exploiting his own and—let's face it—others' pain through *mythologeuein* is brought out by this false assertion. Odysseus lost the actual plunder in the course of adventures bringing epic fame to him and death to his companions, only to have this trove handed to him in the course of delivering his story.

[53] Cf. Athena's remark κερδαλέος 291 ... κέρδε᾽ 297; νόον πολυκερδέα, 255; Segal 1994:182. Such is Odysseus' character; but is this particular scene with Trojan loot one more link to Idomeneus? The scholia on Callimachus' *Hymn to Zeus* explain the proverb "all Cretans are liars" with reference to Idomeneus' appropriating the greater share of Trojan spoils for himself (and presumably lying about it); see Martin 2005:12 (PDF version).

[54] Again, Clay 1983:235. This sets up the contrast between the Cretan persona and Eumaeus in the following episode. One expects that the "enlightened" Athena and Odysseus will be aligned with the bard, looking down upon pious Eumaeus.

finds a perspective within the poem superior to the hero's, and more authorial. She has so much influence over the plot that each and every thing is foregone; all that is left is playing it out.[55] As for the goods, she herself is responsible for them anyway, as is repeatedly stressed.[56] As a mask for the bard, Athena says, Yes, I created these things; now let's sweep them away for a scene change.

This theme of how much treasure a human life is worth will make a powerful reappearance later in the Ithakan narrative, from just the same perspective—the splitting of the self observable in a one-man performance. (Recall too that it is henchman Odysseus who catalogues the treasures Agamemnon offers Achilles as recompense for a woman and for the risk of his own life.)

Yet the effect extends beyond this splitting. The loot is a remainder from that other world, the world of fairy tale. It is not only a nuisance but a metaphysical, or generic, embarrassment. The performer may perform some stage business with his invisible prop that conveys the awkwardness: he has crossed from one genre over to the next, and yet there is still this *thing stubbornly sitting there* from the world of fairy tale. That is, the performance works on two registers, as Odysseus explaining the loot to those who might steal it, and as the performer conveying himself—with a bit of trouble—from one set of generic expectations to the next.[57]

---

[55] Cf. 13.362–365, 373, 376, where Athena urges him not to worry about the 'that,' but just to think about the 'how.' Cf. Reinhardt 1997:224 on 13.404ff.: "I do not know of any more charming transformation of a poetic plan into poetic dialogue." See also Austin 1975:240.

[56] 13.121, 304–305; de Jong (2001:319): this is "intended to prepare for Athena's leading role as Odysseus' helper in the ensuing scene."

[57] As imaginary "transitional" objects the loot recalls the spear of Diomedes in *Iliad* 6.126 discussed in Chapter 1. That scene adds another layer, since the performer may use an actual staff to bring the spear into our presence. Note that each hero is coming down from some rarified air his interlocutor cannot be expected to comprehend (for Diomedes, combat with the gods). Similar modes in similar contexts, quite different comic effects.

Given all this, it is odd that the loot may be the only real element in the tale. "Thirteen tripod-cauldrons, dating from the ninth to eighth centuries"—one for each Phaeacian king—"were found in a cave of the Nymphs at Polis Bay" (Hoekstra in Heubeck and Hoekstra 1989:177 *ad* 13.217–218). Whether the cave was the site of a hero cult for Odysseus within any time period associated with the *Odyssey* remains an open question. (A similar question arises for the *nekyomanteia* in Epiros.) Either a) the *Odyssey* is playing on such a cult, or b) worshippers of the Nymphs, or Odysseus, or someone else took the hint from the poem and put the tripods there. On the first possibility, the tripods are offerings for the hero from his worshippers, crossing the line from human to heroized dead. The *Odyssey* would then be replacing this boundary-crossing with another: from the *au-delà* of the Phaeacians, Escorts of the Dead, to the here-and-now. This would be another way that the poem plays upon the identity of the audience with those strange people: the hero would be embarrassed by the real gift of a sort we could have given him as though it were the airy figment from a world that simply stands for escort between worlds. The tripods obtrude themselves between us and the performer, despite their invisibility, instead of embodying our effort to reach over to that other shore. On the level of presence, the prop induces a comic splitting of the performer and fuels the tour de force of the

To return to our tale, one element does emerge from this "because-because-because" process that Odysseus can use: the companions.

τὸν μὲν ἐγὼ κατιόντα βάλον χαλκήρεϊ δουρὶ
ἀγρόθεν, ἐγγὺς ὁδοῖο λοχησάμενος σὺν ἑταίρῳ·
νὺξ δὲ μάλα δνοφερὴ κάτεχ’ οὐρανόν, οὐδέ τις ἡμέας
ἀνθρώπων ἐνόησε, λάθον δέ ἑ θυμὸν ἀπούρας.
αὐτὰρ ἐπεὶ δὴ τόν γε κατέκτανον ὀξέϊ χαλκῷ ...

Him I shot with a bronze spear as he came down
from the field, in ambush near the road with a companion;
and night imbued the sky with gloom, and no
human being noticed us, but I robbed him of life all unseen.
Well, once I'd killed *him* with the sharp bronze ...

Odyssey 13.267–271

He shot him "coming down" (267), as Athena has just come down to beach level. Why "with a companion"?

As he speaks, the performer may with a simple gesture incorporate the scene of the killing, projecting it onto the performance space (and of course, onto the "here and now" of the story-world, the Ithakan shore). He may gesture in the distance as he mentions his companion, hinting to his interlocutor that he is not alone, unarmed though he may appear. Not only that, but he could kill the young man without anyone finding out. One by one he imagines potential gaps in the front he is setting up, and fills them. A skilled performer may play it as though he himself is improvising, even when the routine has been performed many times and the general shape has been set;[58] the merging with Odysseus suddenly deepens under "new" conditions (Ithaka / a space for a more radical improvisation than the usual composition in performance).

He has now spent lines 259–271 (thirteen lines of a thirty-one-line speech) describing how he dispatched a young prince. Now he must say how he got here, and why he is alone with all of this treasure. He begged some Phoenicians (standing in for the Phaeacians) to take him to "Pylos or Elis." But they were driven off course "much against their will—and they did not want to deceive me" (277).

This last detail comes out of nowhere. It sits ill with the portrayal of the Phoenicians, in the second Cretan Tale and in Eumaeus' life-story, as greedy, lying

---

first Cretan Tale. For more on the tripods, see Malkin 1998:94–119. For χρήματα as indicating treasure in a hero's sanctuary, see Herodotus 9.116, 120; Nagy 1987:308.

[58] Of course, during the development of this scene, the poet(s) was/were more or less improvising—virtuosically improvising an as-if improvisation—but to a lesser extent than the hero, to the extent that the scene has a definite goal and looks forward and backward to other scenes.

murderers: clearly, the stereotype that the *Odyssey* is working with.[59] But the audience has just witnessed Odysseus' own *undisguised* remarks (13.209–211), when he was alone, about the—so he suspected!—faithless Phaeacians. Now that he has learned from the "young man" where he is, his fictional detail about the faithful Phoenicians (277) sounds like Odysseus explaining to *himself* what happened with the Phaeacians and inserting it into the story as the information sinks in.[60] These tensions create a comic "liveness," and a sense of penetrating the mask.

Odysseus lets slip another concern, this one completely irrelevant: "nor did we have any remembrance of dinner, much as we needed to get some" (279–280). In this remark one sees the insertion into the story of the current pressing state of his belly: Odysseus always has food on the brain.[61] The tale is not quite under the control of its teller. On the one hand, he makes full use of the materials at hand, bricoleur-style; on the other, the result is not as polished as his tales, well-fueled by food, to the Phaeacians. The audience is free to interpret the inconvenient hunger as issuing from the performer's own γαστήρ or from his character's, and a variety of actorly styles may exploit this ambiguity.[62]

Odysseus goes on to say that they all disembarked and fell asleep on the beach. And "then sweet sleep came on me, worn out as I was, and they taking my goods from the hollow ship set them down, just where I myself was lying on the sand. And they went off for Sidonia: but I was left, grieving at heart" (13.282–286).[63] End of Tale 1. Left hanging is just why any self-respecting Phoenician, having conveyed the tale-teller to the wrong location, would bother to unload the amazing treasure that now lies before the speaker.

---

[59] Winter (1995:248): "... as noted by Carpenter, the pointed references to seagoing Phoenicians who kept to their bargain and did not rob him of his personal goods effectively underscore expectations to the contrary," citing Carpenter 1958. Winter sums up the image of the Phoenicians in the second Cretan Tale: "These traits go beyond mere description to serve a moralizing subtext, the underlying message of which is that hunger for commercial profit leads to the breaking of higher laws of social honor, punishable by divine retribution." She notes that the Phoenicians are "not above trafficking in humans as well" (p. 249), arguing that they serve as a foil for Odysseus' own "just" form of *mētis*. But Odysseus' family partakes in precisely this human traffic, a fact whose significance will soon become apparent.

[60] De Jong 2001:327.

[61] Pucci 1995:169–172. To put it this way implies humor, as I believe may be at work here. But see Rose 1992:108. While we know Odysseus will eventually eat, hunger may be no laughing matter for the audience.

[62] Perhaps the very variety of ways a scene can be exploited may lead to its being preserved or even developed in the first place. To borrow Nagy's use of the term (Nagy 1996a: Ch. 1; cf. Zumthor 1990:203–205), the *mouvance* that is seeded within a given scenario, script, or routine and issued as a de facto challenge to the next performer manifests itself as variance in gesture, tone, pace, etc., rather than or alongside a variation in diction. The reason it survives in the tradition is because of its fertility: because of what one can *do* with it, each time.

[63] Note that Eumaeus uses these same last words in his autobiography, 15.481. Of course Eumaeus is not present for this first Cretan Tale; nevertheless this anticipates a pattern.

The story is simple but still begins to collapse towards its end. Why should they have left Odysseus behind with all his treasures intact? Unscrupulous enough not to convey the hero to his stipulated destination of Pylos or Elis, they did not attempt to trick Odysseus initially (277) and went to the bother of leaving treasures as well as passenger in Ithaca. Remarkable Phoenicians these. 'Good' Phoenicians are the exception and, therefore, less tractable material to accommodate a lie.[64]

Thus the performer designs a scene, complete with treasure and Athena-as-prince, and then, becoming Odysseus, concocts a lie out of elements in his visual field, along with his worst fears (as embodied in traditional Idomeneus elements) and realizations that he has been wrong (about the Phaeacians).

As a composition, it has coherence, but the liar does not manage to incorporate everything seamlessly, and that is the poem's cunning. The loot stubbornly sits there mocking his "courteous Phoenicians" story, and all Athena can do is smile (287).[65] Odysseus is known for his wiliness, but his lying has exposed rather than protected him. If we have been going into this *nostos* with the idea that *polymētis* Odysseus will restore order, wreaking justice through his wits, just as he alone has "escaped from death," this is our first clue that we have been put on the wrong track.

Instead of an Odysseus in full possession of his *noos* and *phrenes*, surrounded by mere shadows, *eidōla*, of human beings, he is briefly revealed as split: the performance takes its cues from the environment but at the same time reveals underlying anxieties, resulting in a comic hodgepodge. This is not what we would expect from an initiate, bringer of enlightenment, or a wrathful god-hero about to conduct a theoxeny, and not what we would expect having listened to Books 9–12 and the voyage of Book 13.[66]

Aside from these considerations of character, genre, and masterplot, there is the audience's kinesthetic sense. The Odysseus who tells the Tale to Alkinoos is fully merged with the performer (since the first-person tale is so long), and to that extent transparently before us as we blend with the Phaeacians. But he is also aloof from his audience, in that he does not refer directly to them as he tells his story, plunging into the world of his adventures. Here in the first Cretan Tale the performer pre-seeds the environment with invisible stage properties and then brings the character forward into that shared imaginary

---

[64] Walcot 1977:9.

[65] And affectionately caress him (χειρί τέ μιν κατέρεξεν, 288). "In both poems these words describe a stronger character caressing a weaker and dependent loved one" (Levine 1982:102).

[66] That is not to say that the audience would suddenly regard Odysseus as a lesser being than his traditional self. On the contrary, the performer, as it were, struggling to overcome the obstacles he has placed in his own path, might create a certain charismatic or winning aura that would enfold the hero within it. But a seed has been planted that bears fruit later.

space. The bard as Odysseus then continuously refers to and wrestles with his physical surroundings, which are given such tangibility as to become "inconvenient" to the storyteller. The comic pleasure involves both the performer's physical contact—through eye, gesture, and moment-to-moment shifting of the tale—with the environment he shares with us, and his simultaneous "out-of-placeness" to that "real" environment: to borrow the term Aristotle[67] uses precisely of the dispatch of Odysseus in Book 13, his *atopia*.

An instructive parallel is Doug Wright's one-man play *I Am My Own Wife*.[68] To open the play, the performer (playing an East German transvestite) emerges suddenly from backstage with no warning the play is beginning, walks out on the bare stage like a performer who has hastily opened the wrong stage door, or even the woman he is playing back in East Berlin who suddenly found herself with an audience. Surprised to see us,[69] she scurries back through the door and closes it, as though it were all a mistake. But no: she reemerges with a prop: a phonograph. She is delighted to have someone to *show this treasure to*, across the gap of ages and spaces. This sequence 1) characterizes the in fact troubled and troubling elderly persona, living a painful life of continuous self-creation in the teeth of the Stasi, and 2) creates an instant intimacy through its manipulation of space, gesture, and prop, as well as an instant sense of the 'reality' of the character, the 'slippage' between character and performer.

I recount this example because it alerts us to the performative vertigo of a bard playing an Odysseus awakening alone on Ithaka and dealing with what he finds there. Though he utters the same lines as he does on arriving at Scheria and the Cyclops' island,[70] the "interface," the fourth-wall situation, is different. *Through the vehicle of lying* the bard steps out through the world of epic, as his character has just exited the strange world where he has become the bard of his own story, to address and engage with the prop-filled world that comes to meet him and that now begins more and more to impinge upon him *as a performer and storyteller*.

Where the Phaiakis enacted the transmission of story, the first Cretan Tale enacts the storytelling process from another angle.[71] The un-epic Tale and the

---

[67] *Poetics* 1460a26–b5.

[68] Wright 2004.

[69] This "surprised to see the audience" trope is a common way of opening a modern solo performance. Nilaja Sun opens her one-woman show *No Child ...* (Sun 2008; premiered 2006) by emerging as a janitor sweeping the stage, preoccupied and surprised to see us. I do not mean to suggest that Book 13, let alone Odysseus' first tale, would have opened a performance session, but rather to emphasize the way in which the performer "steps forward" here.

[70] 13.200–202 = 6.119–121; 13.201–202 = 9.175–176.

[71] This is not to say that the tale told to the Phaeacians cannot be appreciated by an audience for its creative strategies and omissions, or, for example, for the way it reuses Argonautic myth (Clay 2002:81–83) or responds to its audience.

un-bardlike Odysseus (gathering his lie from his immediate surroundings[72] and anxieties as much as the tradition) seem to reveal a split between performer and hero. Yet it seems to take us more intimately into the composition process—so far that we are no longer just an enraptured audience. The illusion that the poem-world is impinging on the creative process itself may lend that world an extra solidity, but a bard at the mercy of his own material is hardly the same as 'realism.'

Cretan Tale 2:
To Eumaeus

Acting is in many ways unique in its difficulties because the artist has to use the treacherous, changeable and mysterious material of himself as his medium. He is called upon to be completely involved while distanced—detached without detachment. He must be sincere, he must be insincere: he must practise how to be insincere with sincerity and how to lie truthfully ...

Peter Brook, *The Empty Space*[73]

The loot safely stowed away, Odysseus approaches Eumaeus' hut. With the introduction of Eumaeus and the second Cretan Tale, we enter a new realm: the world of slavery. This is the very world that looms on the outer edges of Odysseus' Cretan Tales, the fate his Cretan persona manages to squeak out of again and again. Eumaeus was not so fortunate.

Careful attention to the second Cretan Tale and the encounter with Eumaeus will result in a view of slavery in the *Odyssey* that undermines a triumphalist reading. I mentioned above the reading of the second half of the poem as the violent setting-right of disorder by the righteous king. The various recognitions are certainties in the realm of cognition that accompany the realignments of the cosmos.[74] The good slaves are sorted out from the bad, and the bad dispatched with various modes of torture. Scholars are divided between, to use Doherty's terms,[75] a "celebratory" interpretation, wherein the reader applauds Odysseus' restoration and holds up Penelope as Odysseus' equal, and an "oppositional" reading intended to inoculate us from the aristocratic ideology.[76]

---

[72] Of course, a given poet may have incorporated elements from his surroundings. But not like this.
[73] Brook 1968:117.
[74] Austin 1975.
[75] Doherty 1995:12.
[76] Thalmann 1998; Murnaghan 1987.

The *Odyssey* certainly presents "good" and "bad" slaves:[77] Eumaeus, Philoitios, and Dolios are loyal to Odysseus and help defeat the suitors, while Melanthios is swaggering and unpleasant—and is relieved of his testicles. Such stock types likely arose from an ideology that sorts out good and bad from the perspective of the master class. And the poet does create a desire in the audience for Odysseus' victory, thus placing Odysseus, his nice helpers, and the audience all on the same side: that of *dikē*.

The *Iliad*'s heroes treat women as loot to be distributed according to rank, to perpetuate hierarchies and solidify the Männerbund. That system, whether it is fictional or a trace of a prehistoric society or a reflection of the outgoing class of initiated *kouroi*,[78] is radically thrown into question by the protagonist of the poem, who separates himself from it and becomes a scandal to his mates. Nevertheless readers continue to attribute the system, and passive acquiescence to or even vigorous advocacy of said system, not only to the "Homeric world," but also to the audience, or to the Homeric poet or his tradition. Chapter 2 showed how proper attention to the drama of Phoenix's speech makes that reading untenable, as though more evidence were needed after the speech of Achilles.[79]

The *Odyssey* is often seen as simpler in its ethical horizon,[80] as defending the old aristocracy against encroaching polis-life without the *Iliad*'s tragic depth or irony. Odysseus the rightful king returns to clear out the corrupt suitors as well as the female slaves whose sexual "betrayal" undermines his honor. To a great extent, the poem sustains such a triumphalist interpretation; otherwise it would not be so common.

Yet there are moments and scenes that yank the rug out from under such a listener. Just as the Phoenix speech produces an ethical disorientation alongside a play with the speaker's persona, temporality, and the source of action, so too

---

[77] Thalmann 1998: Ch. 2; de Jong 2001:341; Segal 1994:167. Perhaps however Philoitios is meant to be a free man (Ahl and Roisman 1996:167, noting 20.222-225).

[78] Sinos (1980:15) likens Achilles to the Kouros figure worshipped "by an analogous group of worshippers, such as initiates." The epic tradition contains "vestiges of cult." This suggests, but stops short of claiming, that the *Iliad* is in some way linked with such worship.

[79] Adam Parry 1964.

[80] See Doherty 1995:13. Lowe (2000:150–151), comparing Books 22–24 of the two poems: "Cheekily, the *Odyssey* seeks to cap the *Iliad*'s one-on-one showdown by vastly increasing the odds against him: the fatalistic tone of *Iliad* XXII, where the hero's victory is never in doubt and sympathy lies more with his victim, gives way to a comforting sense of moral certainty and triumph over the odds ... Again [in Book 24] the *Odyssey* seeks to improve on the *Iliad* by multiplying numbers and satisfying the sense of justice; again we feel the humane complexities get somewhat blunted in the process." A triumphalist interpretation works hand in hand with the claim that the poem is replacing the "trickster" Odysseus of tradition with its own version, "deauthorizing" other traditions (e.g. Danek 1998; Marks 2003 and 2008). But see, e.g., Farron 1979–1980; Fajardo-Acosta 1990; Rose 1992; Benardete 1997; Clay 2002; Newton 2009; Schein 2016: Ch. 4 (esp. p. 54).

the *Odyssey*'s ethical disorientation works in conjunction with other kinds of disorientation.

These moments of "ethical disorientation" go well beyond "inadvertent" disclosure of the harsh reality of slavery in Odysseus' kingdom.[81]

While many scholars would avoid discussing the intentions of the Homeric poet(s), they use such a concept both explicitly and implicitly. "The *Odyssey shows an interest in idealizing* the life led in the countryside by dependent laborers, partly to portray it as poor but honest in contrast with the suitors' dissolute life at Odysseus' house in town. Nevertheless, we get occasional glimpses of how harsh it could be."[82] That is, the *Odyssey* sloppily, unintentionally reveals some things about slavery—things that are contrary to its aristocratic ideology.

Likewise Nagler:[83] the poem exposes the problematic nature of Odysseus' violence, but only because it cannot help it. Nagler rightly sees the execution of the slave women as "disgraceful," remarking that Odysseus "does not even respond to [Telemachus'] report about the problematic execution (22.481)," but does not explain why the poem should make it so. The history of the bow (21.11–41) awkwardly raises the theme of violence against *xeinoi*, noting that Herakles killed Iphitos even though he was his guest-friend in his own house, and draws connections between Odysseus and the family-slaughtering Herakles in a way that emphasizes Odysseus' violence toward his own community. Yet Nagler, extracting these red flags from the *Odyssey*, does not conclude that it is the *Odyssey* raising the flags.[84] If something ugly is exposed, the exposure was not intentional: rather there is some underlying reality, e.g., slavery in the eighth century, which the text is simultaneously exhibiting and incompetently

---

81 E.g., Thalmann 1998:57.

82 Thalmann 1998:57; my emphasis.

83 Nagler 1993. Cf. Nagler (1990:345): although the poem "rouses a twinge of horror for him as killer," "[t]he complexity and allusiveness of references between proem and narrative, domestic and exotic, surely means the poet is dealing with something he cannot or does not want to confront directly, which is obviously that Odysseus (the 'savior of the *oikos*' ...) has to kill his own retainers."

84 Nagler (1993:5): "to put Odysseus against this background [of Herakles] is to say, among other things, that he is specially sanctioned to use normally illicit forms of violence." But Herakles is among the most appalling of heroes and commits heinous crimes in his own household. Schein (2016:44) notes that Herakles belongs to the generation of heroes that Hesiod associates with "great violence" (*Works and Days* 148). Feeney (1991:160) remarks, on comparisons of Aeneas to Hercules: "Recent attempts to redeem Aeneas' violence from any suspicion of anxiety miss the point of the identification with Hercules. Hercules' outsize power and his unassimilable nature are his hallmark from the very beginning of the tradition, and these characteristics become a way of reflecting upon the unassimilable nature of the divine, and the arbitrary nature of divine power, which may always manifest itself to humans as mere violence." This corrects the "redemptive" reading but at the same time associates Aeneas with "the unassimilable nature of the divine." In the case of Odysseus and Herakles, the matter seems to be more troubling but less unassimilable, indeed all too similar (see below).

disguising. But why not elide the ugliness altogether? It is as though the poem had found its material, slavery, too recalcitrant to fully master.

Jane Austen, one might say, "could not entirely keep out" the fact that her heroines' haute couture and idleness derived from the spoils of slavery. But what is transpiring, really? Did Austen in giving us glimpses of the slave economy mean it to undermine the entire elite and middle class way of life? The heroine of *Mansfield Park*, Fanny Price, asks about the slave trade and is met by a "dead silence," a silence Edward Said would foist upon Austen herself. But why bring up the silence, if one wanted to quiet the issue oneself? Susan Fraiman is right: "Austen deliberately invokes the dumbness of Mansfield Park concerning its own barbarity precisely because she means to rebuke it."[85]

In the *Odyssey*, the glimpses of ugliness are just the tip of the iceberg when it comes to the ethical disorientation and reorientation of the poem. So while "glimpses" might be seen as obstinate realia extruding into a poem intended to cover them over, many moments are not plausibly accounted for in this way. It is more plausible to let both the "glimpses" and the forceful shakeups take their place within a major thrust of the poem. In the case of the allusion to Herakles during Penelope's contemplation of the bow, it is, as Seth Schein has shown, part of a group of allusions that "challenge interpreters to make sense of complex—even contradictory—versions of stories and raise ethical questions about the poem's dominant values."[86]

Leaving open the question of intentionality, the point is that, rather than chalk up the moments of exposure to a forfeited or ill-executed intention, one can let the moments take their place alongside more elaborate poetic structures, such that the poem enacts through its characters the suppression and emergence of such ugliness, very much, as perhaps my reader has by now realized, as in the speech of Phoenix. That this happens in the *Odyssey*'s second half will not surprise an audience of the *Iliad* who has seen Odysseus thrash the unaristocratic

---

[85] Said 1993:96; Fraiman 1995:812. (Fraiman's argument here is more complex, since the slave trade in the Austen passage is in turn offering a "convenient metaphor" for the "casual import and export of Fanny Price." Her whole essay is a valuable stimulus for students of the *Odyssey*.)

[86] Schein 2016:44. Cf. pp. 50–51: "Clearly the poem expects its audiences and readers to approve of the slaughter of the Suitors, and in the end Odysseus and Telemachos get away with killing them all, thanks to the assistance and approval of the gods. On the other hand... Odysseus' slaughter of the Suitors is introduced by the story of Herakles killing a guest in his own halls, at his own table, and stealing the guest's property in violation of the divinely sanctioned norms of guest-friendship. According to Odysseus, Herakles offered himself in the Land of the Dead as a model for Odysseus, but in Book 8 Odysseus had already declined to associate himself as an archer with Herakles, because this hero of earlier times had competed with his bow against the gods. Yet... one of the first things said in the poem about Odysseus as an archer is that he poisons his arrows, which makes Odysseus resemble Herakles in a behaviour which, as Athene/Mentes implies, is disapproved of by the gods." On this last passage, see Clay 2002:77–78.

Thersites nearly to death for saying what Achilles has just said (*Iliad* 2.212–269).[87] When the *Iliad* goes on to say that the Achaeans laughed delightedly at such actions (*Iliad* 2.270), that is nearly always taken as "just the facts" reportage of "the Achaean attitude toward non-elite speech" (which in turn is blurred into the "dominant ideology" of eighth-century reality).[88] Yet there is no reason for an audience not to take the episode as a rebuke to themselves, particularly those who have, as someone still usually does, taken pleasure in the beating. Likewise in *Iliad* 9 Achilles has it right: Odysseus is the one who keeps the truth stifled within himself, and this "suppressing" motif is often made explicit (e.g., *Odyssey* 13.254). The poet of *Iliad* 9 was keenly attuned to such suppression and emergence and used them to dramatic effect (see Chapter 2 above).

The *Odyssey*, just like the *Iliad*, establishes a world in order to shatter our expectations once we have entered it. That world, for the *Odyssey*, is one in which the just avenger comes to slaughter the evil people, and in which we are supposed to enjoy it. That is a world not of any particular era or location, poised at the birth of the polis in Euboia, Athens, or Ionia, or colonization, but of the comic mode.[89] The nostalgia for the good king, the restoration of old bonds, the recognitions: these are all there,[90] but they also form the backdrop for a drama counter to this.

Such an interpretation has in common with Peradotto's reading of the dual tendencies of the *Odyssey* and its hero—centripetal and centrifugal—an identification of the two separate voices, one could say, of the poem. Similarly for Pucci the text continually renders vain our attempts at interpretation. In brief, where the post-structuralists see two voices fighting it out on an equal footing,[91] I see one voice emerging out from under the other. This sometimes has the effect of uncovering a rock-solid truth rather than of carnivalesque polyvocality for the sake of itself. In that the emerging voice is of lower status, my performance-oriented reading complements Rose's description, from a Marxist perspective, of the *Odyssey*'s ambivalence or double-voiced quality with respect to inherited kingship and class conflict. The voice of the wandering poet, for Rose, is identified with the wandering king in disguise; there is a nostalgic layer to the poem, including an insistence on inherited monarchy, but the poet's voice speaks convincingly for the "hunger-haunted peasant" and ultimately "pit[s] poor against rich" and "calls into question the full range of assumptions underlying

---

[87]   See Whitman 1958:161, 261–264; Thalmann 1988; Rose 1988; Ford 1992:87; Rose 1997:162–164.

[88]   Rose 1997:163.

[89]   Or, if you like, the mode of *theoxenia*.

[90]   Cf. Redfield 1990:331.

[91]   Clay, while distancing herself from a post-structuralist account, writes, "One could argue that the poet from the start consistently and strikingly evokes two images of Odysseus, images familiar to his audience, and, by repeated reinforcement, keeps them both in front of us" (Clay 2002:78). Two images of Odysseus do not necessitate "two voices" in the poem.

the social hierarchy of his own time."[92] While this class-conscious dialectic is, like the tension between the Homeric and extra-Homeric Odysseus, readable on the page, performance (not a concern for these authors) makes possible a dialectic movement that unfolds not only between characters or classes, but within the solo poet-performer.

To return to the drama: already in Odysseus' approach to Eumaeus' house in the opening of Book 14 the relationship between the two men is put in the form of an *ainigma*, alerting a keen listener that she might find something in Eumaeus other than Uncle Remus. The abstraction and enigmatic syntax disrupt the sense that here, at long last, we are to enter the real Greek world. Landing on Ithaka, Odysseus at first encounters a world unrecognizable to him, where he has direct contact with the gods and where the real remnants of his fantastic voyage are brusquely stowed by the goddess into a fantastically-described hiding place. With the departure of the goddess and the hiding of the Phaeacian treasure, we may expect to enter a world that is not only humbler in the social sense but also more human. Our hero is planning the destruction of the suitors, which we know will succeed; he will be operating upon inert matter, bad people without his divine clout and worldly-wise *mētis*. Athena goes off on other business to close Book 13. But:

αὐτὰρ ὁ ἐκ λιμένος προσέβη τρηχεῖαν ἀταρπὸν
χῶρον ἀν' ὑλήεντα δι' ἄκριας, ᾗ οἱ Ἀθήνη
πέφραδε δῖον ὑφορβόν, ὅ οἱ βιότοιο μάλιστα
κήδετο οἰκήων, οὓς κτήσατο δῖος Ὀδυσσεύς.

But he set out upon a rough path from the harbor
up the wooded country through the hills, where Athena to him
pointed out the <u>divine</u> swineherd, [who most
cared for his substance, of all the domestics—see below] whom
    <u>divine</u> Odysseus had acquired.

Odyssey 14.1–4

In line 3 is the first occurrence (of 18) of the phrase δῖον ὑφορβόν, "divine swineherd." Scholars have debated the connotations of this phrase, some going so far as to call it parodic or "mock-epic," others attributing it to the author's affection for this character.[93] (The parodic or mock-heroic reading of Eumaeus is

---

92 Rose 1992: Ch. 2; quotations from p. 119. While I agree that the poem itself has these features, and that attention to performance highlights them further, I do not, as Rose does, see the poem's dialectic as necessarily arising within a precisely defined political moment.

93 See Reece (1993:154) for bibliography on the "parodic" view of the Eumaeus episode; he believes "heroic" language in it is relatively insignificant. On the affection for Eumaeus, see especially Louden 1997.

not limited to this epithet.) But it is the suitors, in fact, who use epithets sarcastically (17.375). Here it is found in a sentence that ends with δῖος Ὀδυσσεύς, δῖος being one of Odysseus' most common epithets. She, Athena (the hyper-literal translation shows the tangled syntax and the enjambment):

> πέφραδε <u>δῖον</u> ὑφορβόν, ὅ οἱ βιότοιο μάλιστα
> κήδετο οἰκήων, οὓς κτήσατο <u>δῖος</u> Ὀδυσσεύς.

> pointed out the <u>divine</u> swineherd, who most of his *biotos*
> had care of the domestics, whom <u>divine</u> Odysseus acquired.
>
> *Odyssey* 14.3–4

As to the word *biotos* (line 3), "substance; means of life," it is also used in Homer in the sense of "life" *tout court*, such that Eumaeus cares for Odysseus' life.[94] More to the point, these lines have an almost Heraclitean syntactic ambiguity.[95] The sentence is arranged to slide from *biotos*, something perhaps owned by Odysseus, to the servants or domestics (οἰκήων) being what Odysseus has come to own. As both βιότοιο and οἰκήων are in the genitive, a listener may hear κήδετο (cared) as governing one and then the other, or both (note the caesura), unlike in my translation.[96]

κήδετο οἰκήων, however unlikely as a syntactic unit here, seems to be a play on the formulaic phrase οἴκου κήδεσθαι, which occurs twice at the beginning of the line (*Odyssey* 19.23, 19.161; cf. 23.8), such that lines 3–4 take a formula referring to the house and household, and apply it more specifically to its people, putting it thus after another word already referring to "substance." This word βιότοιο, even more than οἰκήων, refers not only to that which Odysseus holds but what holds him: that which sustains his very life and on which he is dependent. Phonically, enclosed between the master and slave who are both, somehow, δῖος,[97] there also seems to be a play between κήδετο (cared for) and κτήσατο (purchased) in line 4, opening the first and fourth feet of the hexameter.[98] Such

---

94 Cf. Slatkin 2011:193–194 on the hiding of *bios* at Hesiod *Works and Days* 42. Wordplay between βιός, bow, and βίοτος at *Odyssey* 19.577–580 = 21.75–78: Ahl and Roisman 1996:237.

95 E.g., fr. 12 ποταμοῖσι τοῖσιν αὐτοῖσιν ἐμβαίνουσιν ἕτερα καὶ ἕτερα ὕδατα ἐπιρρεῖ, where one may (and does) hear ἐμβαίνουσιν as a verb, until one reaches the end of the sentence. The sentence flows over us and becomes a different sentence, though it is we who are changing.

96 A similar ambiguity occurs when Penelope bids Eurykleia, νίψον σοῖο ἄνακτος ὁμήλικα (19.358). "For a fraction of a second, before ὁμήλικα joins the other members of its clause, we hear a construction that leads us to think Penelope has somehow penetrated Odysseus' disguise and is revealing his secret" (Russo in Russo, Fernandez-Galiano, and Heubeck 1992:94 *ad* 19.358). Thanks to Seth Schein for the comparison.

97 Segal 1994:167. Bowie (2013:19) notes that the "use of such epithets of a herdsman acts as a challenge to the aristocratic monopoly on such terms elsewhere."

98 Accentuated perhaps by οἰ<u>κή</u>ων. This wordplay, though subtler, should be compared with the multiple punning on "wandering" and "truth" that follows in Book 14 (see below, page 310).

chiasmus and phonic play call attention to or perceptually cue the semantic ambiguity or obscurity, in a way paralleled, as Watkins demonstrated, elsewhere in Indo-European poetics.[99] It may even be semantically cued by the "rough track" of line 1.[100] Perhaps the way the riddle unfolds from one line to the next reflects the practice of relay competition among poet-performers.[101] The lines elegantly encapsulate the situation of a dependent of Odysseus having care for what he depends on: his stuff of life. What may not seem paradoxical—a possession that cares for one's life—is exposed as such.[102] It raises questions of agency, what that *biotos* amounts to, and who is in charge of whom: *dios huphorbos, dios Odysseus.*[103]

Now this is also the situation *within the performer*: his possession of or being possessed by his character; the character in control of his lies or inadvertently leaking irrelevancies. The master-slave relationship takes its place beside the anxieties about performance that are expressed by Platonic characters.[104] If the slave is a "living instrument" (Aristotle *Politics* 1253b), so too is the body, or the being, of the performer.

<blockquote>

5   τὸν δ' ἄρ' ἐνὶ προδόμῳ εὗρ' ἥμενον, ἔνθα οἱ αὐλὴ

       ὑψηλὴ δέδμητο, περισκέπτῳ ἐνὶ χώρῳ,

       καλή τε μεγάλη τε, περίδρομος· ἥν ῥα συβώτης

       αὐτὸς δείμαθ' ὕεσσιν ἀποιχομένοιο ἄνακτος,

       νόσφιν δεσποίνης καὶ Λαέρταο γέροντος,

10   ῥυτοῖσιν λάεσσι καὶ ἐθρίγκωσεν ἀχέρδῳ·

       σταυροὺς δ' ἐκτὸς ἔλασσε διαμπερὲς ἔνθα καὶ ἔνθα,

       πυκνοὺς καὶ θαμέας, τὸ μέλαν δρυὸς ἀμφικεάσσας·

</blockquote>

---

[99] Watkins (1995:101–102), on a passage (the proem to Hesiod's *Works and Days*) similar enough to the present passage to be suggestive. See Watkins 1995 passim.

[100] Heath (1985:249) similarly suggests that Hesiod warns his audience about the subtlety of the hawk-nightingale *ainos* in a somewhat similar fashion, with φρονέουσι καὶ αὐτοῖς (*Works and Days* 202).

[101] See Collins (2004:184–191) for a discussion, using the *Certamen*, of enjambment and other techniques of verse-capping among rhapsodes. The riddling nature of the verses is in keeping with this practice. (Cf. Collins' discussion of the *Certamen*'s (102–103) ἀμφίβολοι γνῶμαι, "ambiguous sentences.") Obviously I do not mean that these particular verses are the actual product of such capping (i.e. a new rhapsode took over at line 4), only that they are reminiscent of the practice of competitive composers-in-performance and suggest the kind of skill learned in such competition.

[102] Cf. 13.405, ὅς τοι ὑῶν ἐπίουρος, ὁμῶς δέ τοι ἤπια οἶδε, with Stanford's (1996) note *ad* 13.404–405.

[103] Just these two phrases end two successive lines (17.506–507) in a more conspicuously striking passage in which the narrator refers to *dios Odysseus* and then Penelope summons the *dios huphorbos*: see Scodel 2002:157–160. For Scodel, the epithet is a "puzzle" that is part of the poet's "narrative teasing" in the second half of the poem, a puzzle solved when Eumaeus' royal birth is revealed, and when he fights alongside Odysseus.

[104] This intra-performer reading becomes more attractive in the light of the performer's "becoming" Eumaeus, as examined below.

271

ἔντοσθεν δ' αὐλῆς συφεοὺς δυοκαίδεκα ποίει
πλησίον ἀλλήλων, εὐνὰς συσίν· ἐν δὲ ἑκάστῳ
15 πεντήκοντα σύες χαμαιευνάδες ἐρχατόωντο...

Him—voilà—he came across sitting on the porch, where his court
had been built high, with a view all around,
fine and grand, encircling it: which, note, the swineherd
himself built for his pigs while the lord was absent,
apart from the mistress and old man Laertes,
with stones he'd hauled, and he topped it with prickly pear:
and outside he drove stakes all along, here, and here,
thick and fast, splitting apart the black of the oak:
but inside the court he made twelve sties
near one another, beds for pigs: and in each
fifty ground-bedding pigs were penned...

Odyssey 14.5–15

The description of Eumaeus' house and his pigsties, however humble, has
much in common with some of the fantastic locations of the Tale to Alkinoos.
Powell notes that Odysseus wends his way along a rough path through wood-
land, as on Circe's island, and:

> He comes to a court 'visible from all around' (14.6) (a phrase used else-
> where to describe Circe's court: 10.426). Within are 12 sties (cf. the
> 12 daughters and sons of Aeolus, the 12 kings over whom Alcinous
> presides), 50 sows in each (as many as the cattle and sheep in each of
> Helius' herds: 12.130). The boars, which number 360 (cf. the 350 cattle
> and 350 sheep of Helius), sleep outside. Like Helius' herds, however,
> their number, through the suitors' depredations, has lately declined
> (14.17) ... Circe, in her own way a swineherd too ...[105]

The swineherd Circe has, Wizard of Oz–style, found her human counterpart
on the farm.[106] Rather than literally turning men into pigs, however, Eumaeus
takes care of the pig-substance, substance which sustains the life of swinish

---

[105] Powell 1977:37 (Powell translates differently the difficult phrase περισκέπτῳ ἐνὶ χώρῳ.).

[106] De Jong (2001:343): "Whereas Circe's watchdogs are wild animals behaving like domestic dogs
(10.212–219), Eumaeus' domestic dogs 'resemble wild animals' (21), a circumstance which adds
to the danger facing Odysseus." Eumaeus' compound is an echo, in the "low-mimetic mode,"
of Alkinoos' palace (Segal 1994:166). On Eumaeus' pigsties and the Cyclops' pens, see de Jong
2001:238. Eumaeus' house is also similar to Priam's palace. Although Monro (1901:20 *ad* 14.13–16)
saw this as "almost a parody of the description of Priam's palace," the parallel seems rather to
ennoble the description (Bowie 2013:20).

men. Likewise, the suitors' threat to Eumaeus at 21.363–364, that "swiftly the swift dogs will eat you among the pigs / alone from the people, whom you used to feed/nurture," (τάχ' αὖ σ' ἐφ' ὕεσσι κύνες ταχέες κατέδονται / οἶον ἀπ' ἀνθρώπων, οὓς ἔτρεφες ...) confuses the dogs, pigs, and people, and sets up Eumaeus as a Circe-esque foster-father for the whole compound. That the male pigs, one killed each day to feed the suitors, now number 360, may be ominous in the context of the *Odyssey*'s concern with days and the coming around of the year, the moment of Odysseus' return. Alternatively, the number, a bit too perfect, considering it should be diminishing each day, may suggest (like Penelope's web) the stoppage of time on Ithaka in the absence of Good King Odysseus. The absolute separation of male and female pigs that Eumaeus has established, the paragon of regimented sexuality,[107] seems to mock the licentious scene that Odysseus will find at his house, the scene that will make him bark like a bitch over her pups (20.14–16). In this sense Eumaeus is an anti-Circe. The scene in which the dogs threaten to attack Odysseus inverts the beginning of the Circe episode where the wolves and lions, rather than attacking Odysseus' men, fawn on them "as when dogs fawn about their master coming from a feast, for he always brings sweets for their *thumos*" (10.216–217). The Märchen Circe episode thrusts its head up within the rustic reality of a swineherd making sandals and dogs that do not recognize Odysseus.

Eumaeus, however, is not merely a realistic Circe, or a multiform of Alkinoos as an ideal listener.[108] His homely realism[109] is a trap: his mythical dimensions will shortly be revealed, and he will not only listen to and comply with the bard-like hero's plotting. Eumaeus stands within the solar themes that pervade the *Odyssey*, but not only as a helper or certifier.

There seems to be a link between the riddling lines at the opening of Book 14, about possession, caring, and slaves, and Eumaeus' connections with Circe. Perhaps Eumaeus will prove some combination of "helper" and "obstacle" analogous to Circe, who un-mans Odysseus' men and counsels Odysseus through the underworld. Perhaps slavery constitutes another world of adventure through which our hero must find his way, just as he did the enchanting world of sex, drugs, song, and death. It is striking that Thalmann emphasizes the paradoxical language employed by Aristotle in his discussion of slavery in the *Politics* and

---

[107] Cf. Austin 1975:166–167.

[108] For Louden (1999:52), Eumaeus and Alkinoos are multiforms of the same figure, the male that serves as conduit between Odysseus and the powerful female. These structural parallels reinforce the idea of the encounter with Eumaeus as a stage toward a more important encounter, but also obscure the links between Eumaeus and Circe.

[109] The usual view, e.g. Segal (1994:177): "Eumaeus has the transparent simplicity of the completely straightforward, honest man."

again in the *Ethics*: the contradiction in a being at once instrument and human.[110] By lending Eumaeus the equipment of a sorceress who deprives men of agency, and by the episode's enigmatic opening, the poet is already raising questions of agency, setting the stage for a dramatic confrontation that surpasses, in its rich stew of politics and performance, the prose discussion of Aristotle.

The Cretan Tale that Odysseus tells Eumaeus (14.192–379) is much longer than the first Tale to Athena, and its speaker seems to have gained control. Its length and its relatively straightforward structure allow the audience (us and Eumaeus) to consider the speaker and the way he reacts to previous remarks made by Eumaeus, in whose "seat" we now sit. Many events in this Tale are cobbled together out of episodes from the Tale to Alkinoos.[111] Control is asserted in the leisurely opening, a wish for enough food and drink to sit for a year (recall the 360 boars forming part of Odysseus' *biotos*) telling his tale—and still, he says, he would not get through all the κήδεα (cares) that the gods have inflicted on him. Again he claims to be a Cretan, this time by birth (he uses the phrase γένος εὔχομαι twice in quick succession [199, 204]). He is the son of a rich man (200): now inheritance, not pillage, is the source of wealth. Once again, however, he is cheated of his riches: this time because he is the son of a concubine, and the legitimate sons cut him out when they are dividing the ζωή (208–210). Not skipping a beat, he marries a woman from πολυκλήρων folk (κλήρων [211] occupies the same position in the line as κλήρους [209], lending a jaunty tone to the lying).

He obtains the woman specifically by his own ἀρετή, "for I was no vain idler or war-shirker" (14.212–213). This detail may be just another boast building up his persona, but it jars with what Eumaeus has just said at line 64: that if Odysseus returned, he would *give* Eumaeus a wife and property. Relevant here too is Eumaeus' famous remark:

ἥμισυ γάρ τ' ἀρετῆς ἀποαίνυται εὐρύοπα Ζεὺς
ἀνέρος, εὖτ' ἄν μιν κατὰ δούλιον ἦμαρ ἕλησιν.

---

[110] Thalmann 1998:36. The tradition of enigmatic language surrounding slavery does not stop with Aristotle. A similarly paradoxical passage featuring an *oikonomos* (who squanders rather than preserves his master's *biotos*) is found in Luke 16, where Jesus unaccountably recommends, "Make to yourselves friends out of the mammon of unrighteousness," a passage the late Rev. Peter Gomes called an "odd, paradoxical and remarkable text" and (playfully?) counted among those he would rather were not in the Bible at all (oral presentation, September 2007). For Gomes, the "rather simple-minded solution" presented in the parable—where the text "seems as if it is saying, If you are going to serve Mammon, this is the way to do it"—suggests that the steward needed a new life and a new job. The language in *Odyssey* 14, Aristotle, and Luke, perhaps all part of a wisdom tradition about slavery, signals, "there is something deeply wrong here, and I am not telling you the whole story."

[111] See, for example, Danek 1998:285; de Jong 2001:327, 353–354.

> Half, you see, of virtue wide-seeing Zeus robs
> from a man, when the day of slavery takes him.
>
> *Odyssey* 17.322–323

While this proverbial-sounding utterance (whose purport is surely to oppose the idea of natural slavery) is in context directed at the household maids, it has a particular application in the Cretan Tale. Odysseus' Cretan boasts not simply of a resilience, but of a virtue (as evidenced by obtaining a wife) which Eumaeus has just said he specifically lacks. Eumaeus lives in the tragic world of reality, in which ἀρετή can be robbed and goodness should be but is not rewarded:[112] in which one must work hard and hope for the best. The stranger rebukes this attitude and holds up his fictional wife as the reward of an unrobbed virtue for Eumaeus to admire. Immediately after this latent insult he utters the cryptic lines:

> ἀλλ' ἔμπης καλάμην γέ σ' ὀΐομαι εἰσορόωντα
> γινώσκειν· ἦ γάρ με δύη ἔχει ἤλιθα πολλή.
>
> But still, you, I think, looking at the straw,
> recognize it: ah, heaping misery has hold of me.
>
> *Odyssey* 14.214–215

This comment raises suspicions that Odysseus is asking Eumaeus to recognize him through his disguise, or that the performer winks through him at us, who know he is "really" Odysseus.[113] But from this nice gesture at intimacy, he abruptly resumes his broad, arrogant boasting:

> ἦ μὲν δὴ θάρσος μοι Ἄρης τ' ἔδοσαν καὶ Ἀθήνη
> καὶ ῥηξηνορίην· ὁπότε κρίνοιμι λόχονδε
> ἄνδρας ἀριστῆας, κακὰ δυσμενέεσσι φυτεύων,
> οὔ ποτέ μοι θάνατον προτιόσσετο θυμὸς ἀγήνωρ,
> ἀλλὰ πολὺ πρώτιστος ἐπάλμενος ἔγχει ἔλεσκον
> ἀνδρῶν δυσμενέων ὅτε μοι εἴξειε πόδεσσι.

---

[112] Contrast readers for whom Eumaeus falls squarely into the *Odyssey*'s "optimistic," comic mode: he has it pretty good, is content with his good master, and so on. "Eumaeus is the ideal servant, the good slave, utterly devoted to his master's welfare. In this role of the happy slave, he justifies and reaffirms the status quo. In his case the existing social order works. It is humane, decent, and just; and under it a good and simple man prospers and finds the rewards of industry, honesty, and fidelity" (Segal 1994:167; cf. 176–177). Nagler (1996:152) writes that, unlike the *Iliad*, which acknowledges the awfulness of slavery, "This is not the perspective of the *Odyssey*, where once captured, Eumaios and Eurycleia are happily patriated, and domesticity is fully restored and valued."

[113] This should be added to the passages used by Roisman 1990.

Oh yes Ares and Athena gave me daring,
and man-crushing strength: whenever I am choosing for the ambush
men who are best, sowing evils for enemies,
never does death my spirit manly foresee for me,
but leaping far the foremost I'd take with my spear
men, enemies, whoever yielded to me with his feet.

Odyssey 14.216–221

Note that he defies death "whenever I am *choosing men for* the ambush" rather than "whenever I am sitting in an ambush."[114] And "choosing for the ambush/ the best men" is his aim, recruiting Eumaeus for his ambush against the suitors. The speaker is poised between boasting and seeking an alliance. Ambush is a theme taken over from Cretan Tale 1,[115] where Odysseus plucks it from the immediate situation, to intimidate his unknown interlocutor. Here his partner is known, and rather than testing Eumaeus he leans in to recruit him. Eumaeus will require no hard sell.

τοῖος ἔα ἐν πολέμῳ· ἔργον δέ μοι οὐ φίλον ἔσκεν
οὐδ' οἰκωφελίη, ἥ τε τρέφει ἀγλαὰ τέκνα,
ἀλλά μοι αἰεὶ νῆες ἐπήρετμοι φίλαι ἦσαν
225   καὶ πόλεμοι καὶ ἄκοντες ἐΰξεστοι καὶ ὀϊστοί,
λυγρά, τά τ' ἄλλοισίν γε καταριγηλὰ πέλονται.
αὐτὰρ ἐμοὶ τὰ φίλ' ἔσκε τά που θεὸς ἐν φρεσὶ θῆκεν·
ἄλλος γάρ τ' ἄλλοισιν ἀνὴρ ἐπιτέρπεται ἔργοις.
πρὶν μὲν γὰρ Τροίης ἐπιβήμεναι υἶας Ἀχαιῶν
230   εἰνάκις ἀνδράσιν ἦρξα καὶ ὠκυπόροισι νέεσσιν
ἄνδρας ἐς ἀλλοδαπούς, καί μοι μάλα τύγχανε πολλά.
τῶν ἐξαιρεύμην μενοεικέα, πολλὰ δ' ὀπίσσω
λάγχανον· αἶψα δὲ οἶκος ὀφέλλετο, καί ῥα ἔπειτα
δεινός τ' αἰδοῖός τε μετὰ Κρήτεσσι τετύγμην.

That's how I was in war. As for work, it never did please me,
nor the growing of the household, which nurtures shining children.
But for me, oared ships were always dear,
and wars, and sharp javelins and arrows,
baneful things, that come as a shudder to others.

---

[114] Contrast Idomeneus' speech (Chapter 1, pp. 84–85 above): in ambush itself the virtuous will stand out from the cowards.

[115] Of course, ambush is a typical Odyssean motif. But for an audience listening to the Cretan Tales in order, the second tale can be heard as an "improvement" upon the first, and so on. An audience can appreciate the improvements as developments rather than variants.

Well, these things were dear to me, that I guess a god put in my head;
different <u>men</u>, you know, like different kinds of "work"!
Before the sons of the Achaeans landed at Troy,
nine times I led <u>men</u> and sea-coursing ships
against <u>men</u> of other lands, and many things fell in my lap.
Of these I picked out what suited me, and a lot, later,
fell to my lot. And pretty quick my household grew, and then you bet
I got myself feared and revered among the Cretans.

Odyssey 14.222–234

Odysseus claims "work was not dear to me, nor οἰκωφελίη (household increase, 223), but nevertheless by leading men out against ἀλλοδαπούς men, many things fell into my lap, and I took what I wanted, and divided up the rest later. *And my* <u>οἶκος ὀφέλλετο</u> [*my household increased*]." This not only sets up a persona that is "gruff and manly,"[116] it is a direct response to what Eumaeus says at 14.65 (cf. 15.372), just after he speaks of how a slave works hard:

θεὸς δ' ἐπὶ ἔργον ἀέξῃ,
ὡς καὶ ἐμοὶ τόδε ἔργον ἀέξεται, ᾧ ἐπιμίμνω

and god fosters his work even more,
as even in my case this work is fostered, in which I persist.

Odyssey 14.65–66

Odysseus, that is, creates a persona diametrically opposed to the Hesiodic point of view of Eumaeus. This persona is stuck in the world of the bronze men, or of the heroes,[117] where Eumaeus has accepted the realities of the iron age. The way the script unfolds allows the audience to see how this freewheeling looter persona indulges both his own whim and the whim of the *composing* Odysseus, heedless of his listener and all of his god-fostered *erga*—*erga* being kept faithfully for him by that listener: "Well, these things were dear to me that I guess god put in my *phrenes*. Hey, one guy likes some *erga*, another guy likes others!" (227–228). This play on *erga* catapults the persona further out of the orbit of his companion, as he has just acknowledged he doesn't like work *at all*: now he goes so far as to call his looting "work," just a different kind from his

---

[116] Walcot (1977:12), citing Pitt-Rivers, thinks that the persona corresponds to modern men "forced to leave home in search of work" rather than to "professional beggars"; Odysseus pretends to the former status, denying the latter.

[117] Notice the tedious repetition of ἀνήρ or ἀνήρ-compounds in lines 217, 218, 219, 221, 228, 230, 231 (underlined; translation arranged to emphasize the "man" at line-end and line-beginning). King 1999, situating the Cretan persona within the wisdom tradition represented by Hesiod (p. 75), argues that the persona is a caricature of Odysseus' counter-type, the Iliadic hero (p. 83).

companion's.[118] In other words, just as Odysseus launches into his anti-Hesiodic picaresque, as though he were Perses, looking at Eumaeus, the script in 227–228 allows for a play with his audience. The performer may here acknowledge that what he is saying is uncompanionable, only to fall over himself in justifying it so that he can continue.

This works on several levels. The audience has just heard Eumaeus' speech, and can appreciate how he must be reacting, especially if the performer enacts Odysseus' speech as a moment-by-moment response *to that reaction* of Eumaeus, as exemplified in 227–228.[119] The audience knows, moreover, that Odysseus did sack at least two cities (Troy and the Kikones, the latter being the model for the attack on Egypt in the Tale),[120] slaughtered their men and carried off their women. The performer has already in Book 8 used to excruciating effect the moment of striking the "back and shoulders" of a woman pouring herself onto her dying husband (see Chapter 1, above). There Odysseus wanted Demodokos to drive the Trojan story to its slamming conclusion, and was repaid by having the tears of the woman at whose back he—it would appear—shoved his spear rise up before and into his eyes. If we listeners are in the mood for pirate tales, we are getting them, but with a nagging awareness that the person in whose seat we are sitting, Eumaeus, has quite a different point of view. We are divided in two.

This unease, the question of *whether we are supposed to be enjoying the story* at any given moment, is crystallized within the performer's stance. On the one hand he acknowledges a different perspective (227–228), one embodied in the person he is looking at (us/Eumaeus); on the other hand he cannot stop himself. Line 227, τά που θεὸς ἐν φρεσὶ θῆκεν, "this I guess a god put into my head," just as the speech is becoming outrageous to its listener, can be experienced on two levels: as coming from the stranger, acknowledging his difference from Eumaeus, and as the composing Odysseus—if we can keep him separate from the performer bodily before us—acknowledging to us behind Eumaeus' back that some god has put it in his head *to say this*. In the latter, the persona has taken

---

[118] Cf. *Works and Days* 146 on the so-called "work" of the Bronze Men. I was alerted to Hesiod's ironic use of the word by Laura Slatkin. Perhaps the ironic use of the word *ergon* is part of the tradition of meditating on it: on which see Slatkin 2011:188–213.

[119] Cf. Bölte (1907:572) on the speech of Apollo to Achilles in *Iliad* 22.8–13. On "Have you not yet recognized that I am a god?" he comments: "Woraus schliesst Apollon das? Denn ein Schluss liegt vor, das besagt νύ. Er kann es nur *aus den Mienen Achills* schliessen, der allerdings recht verblüfft dareinschauen mag, als sich ihm plötzlich der Gott enthüllt ... Nach einer äusseren Veranlassung der Frage zu suchen, ist nicht unbedingt nötig; die Anwesenheit Achills in diesem abgelegenen Teil der Ebene würde sie allein schon erklären. Aber nachdem wir bereits einen Beweis dafür gehabt haben, dass der Dichter die Szene dramatisch vor sich sieht, liegt doch auch hier die Annahme recht nahe, dass eine Bewegung Achills die Frage veranlasst." This is one of the few appreciations of the actorly art of the performing poet, the potential of the script.

[120] King 1999:76–77; Fenik 1974:159.

over the body of the performer-as-Odysseus; the god puts an idea into *phrenes* shared by composer and actor, out of which it is now flowing as speech. "I don't act, I only react," says the psychopath. This has a thrill of its own, but one that comes from cutting *off* our pleasure in pirate tales. It is the frisson of uncertainty as to whether the body before us is in control of his own performance: Are we still watching the reenactment of a just king using his wits to restore his kingdom? Or is something skidding off the road here?

Our hero continues. He borrows another line from Eumaeus' earlier speech about Helen, and alters it to blame Zeus instead of Helen for the war (235–236, ἀλλ᾽ ὅτε δὴ τήν γε στυγερὴν ὁδὸν εὐρύοπα Ζεὺς / ἐφράσαθ᾽, ἣ πολλῶν ἀνδρῶν ὑπὸ γούνατ᾽ ἔλυσε, "but when at last wide-seeing Zeus pointed the hateful way which loosened the knees of many men," recalling 69–70, ἀλλ᾽ ὄλεθ᾽ ὡς ὤφελλ᾽ Ἑλένης ἀπὸ φῦλον ὀλέσθαι / πρόχνυ, ἐπεὶ πολλῶν ἀνδρῶν ὑπὸ γούνατ᾽ ἔλυσε, "but he died, as the tribe of Helen should have died—on its knees! since she loosened the knees of many men"). A vague "they" ordered Idomeneus and him to go to the war, and there was "no device [μῆχος]" (238–239) he could find for avoiding it. This picks up and adapts Eumaeus' disapproval of the war, putting the persona suddenly again on the same side as Eumaeus, but also recalls the extra-Homeric draft-dodging Odysseus, whose μῆχος, pretending to be mad, was foiled when the baby Telemachus was placed in front of his plow.[121] The persona is flung out into a still more distant orbit. Now he is out of step with God-fearing Eumaeus but also with the reliable henchman familiar from the *Iliad* and the *Odyssey*.

But instead of being thereby hurled out of all recognition, he lands in the realm of Odysseus: the Other Odysseus familiar from stories outside of Homer. The body before us is in this way revealed to have yet another layer; we are reaching an inner core, as the extra-Homeric Odysseus, normally more or less suppressed, leaks out of the performer.[122] There is then a dramatic virtue to the fact that the *Odyssey*'s suppression of the extra-Odyssean Odysseus is only partial; the suppression is being used to concretely dramatic as well as broadly thematic[123] ends. The merging between the performer and Odysseus from Books

---

[121] Cf. Ahl and Roisman 1996:162; Benardete 1997:113. This trick was carried out by Palamedes, who becomes important shortly. For Scodel (2002:15) this story is likely behind *Iliad* 4.350–355, when Odysseus responding to Agamemnon's rebuke calls himself the "dear father of Telemachus," but the allusion "works by negation" and implies that the story is not true.

[122] Note again the difference from the reading of (for example) Marks 2003, whereby the *Odyssey* earnestly tries, and fails, to suppress the ignoble, extra-Homeric Odysseus. So too Scodel (2002:14–16): "the *Iliad* no longer works" if the audience pursues these intertexts so far that Achilles or Odysseus "become the Achilles and Odysseus of the stories from outside the epic" (p. 16).

[123] As Sacks (2012) puts it, the poem seems to insist on the "paradox inherent in the tension between what it takes to get home and what it takes to stay there."

Chapter 4

5–12 is given a twist as these allusions seem to spill out casually from his—the bard's? Odysseus'?—memory as ingredients of the new story. He continues:

μῆνα γὰρ οἶον ἔμεινα τεταρπόμενος τεκέεσσι
κουριδίῃ τ' ἀλόχῳ καὶ κτήμασιν· αὐτὰρ ἔπειτα
Αἴγυπτόνδε με θυμὸς ἀνώγει ναυτίλλεσθαι

For a month, only, I stayed, enjoying my children
and my wedded wife and possessions. But then
my *thumos* urged me to sail for Egypt

Odyssey 14.244–246

After the war the Cretan could not abide his wife and children (whom to be sure he "enjoyed") more than a month ("only") before his *thumos* urged him out again, this time to Egypt. But this is also true of the real Odysseus, as represented both in the extra-Homeric traditions[124] and within the *Odyssey* itself. These lines form a comic "stepping out" from the current situation in anticipation of the further adventures.[125] The bard may play the lines as though Odysseus is impatient to get through the slaughter and family reunion so that he can get back to his escapades; this effect may come through to the extent the "Cretan" expresses enthusiasm for the adventures. This lends a mildly supernatural quality to Odysseus and an unstable, comic effect, as the bard and Odysseus merge in imagining new future adventures.

The attack on Egypt (14.245–284) is modeled on the Cicones episode from Book 9 but modified slightly. In Book 9 (lines 39–41) Odysseus takes credit for killing the men and seizing the women; here he blames his men, who "yielded to hybris" (262) and acted against his orders. While Odysseus may here be (finally) reining in his tale out of regard for his enslaved audience,[126] the modification is also a cover-up. Again there are two layers, the city-sacker hiding behind the

---

[124] Danek (1998:285): "Bestimmte Charakterzüge des 'Kreters' lassen an den 'alten' Odysseus der vorhomerischen Tradition, besonders an die ungezügelte Abenteuerlust denken; die Angabe, er habe sich nach der Rückkehr von Troia sofort zu neuen Abenteuern aufgemacht, evoziert Versionen, in denen Odysseus bald nach seiner Heimkehr Ithaka wieder verliess."

[125] Benardete (1997:113): "Odysseus, it seems, is looking forward to a short stay in Ithaca before he ventures forth once more; but Athena would not have had to hold back the dawn, after the killing of the suitors, if he really had so much time. Penelope will have him home, we suspect, for one day."

[126] On the differences between the Book 9 and Book 14 stories Emlyn-Jones (1986:6–7) comments: "In 14 Odysseus … is at pains to project himself, not as a major Homeric hero engaged in a military operation, but as someone involved in an exploit which gets out of hand. This is surely calculated to appeal to Eumaeus no less than Odysseus' action in supplicating the Egyptian King at 276ff., and the pointed reference to Zeus Xenios in 283 drives the point home." Cf. King 1999:76–77. But, on the ambiguities of the seemingly hardheaded Cicones episode, see Pazdernik 1995.

moderate commander. Likewise the Egyptian episode becomes a cover for Calypso (in the seven-year stay in Egypt), and his year with the wily Phoenician covers the Circe episode. This Cretan is not a man to be taken in by feminine wiles, divine or otherwise. But how is Eumaeus supposed to be taking the man's narrow escape from slavery and *his abandonment of all of his men to that fate*? Some would like the stranger's narrow escapes (three of them!) from slavery to be an occasion for Eumaeus to extend his sympathies, since this was "so much like his own experience of life."[127] So close; yet one escaped. And the other is (in reality) now his slave.

The stranger's success with the Egyptian king once again picks up an earlier extraordinary utterance of Eumaeus. Eumaeus had said, gliding from a remark on the suitors' disregard for the gods' vigilance and mercy to a general statement:

> οὐ μὲν σχέτλια ἔργα θεοὶ μάκαρες φιλέουσιν,
> ἀλλὰ δίκην τίουσι καὶ αἴσιμα ἔργ᾽ ἀνθρώπων.
> 85 καὶ μὲν δυσμενέες καὶ ἀνάρσιοι, οἵ τ᾽ ἐπὶ γαίης
> ἀλλοτρίης βῶσιν καί σφιν Ζεὺς ληΐδα δώῃ,
> πλησάμενοι δέ τε νῆας ἔβαν οἰκόνδε νέεσθαι,
> καὶ μὲν τοῖς ὄπιδος κρατερὸν δέος ἐν φρεσὶ πίπτει.
> οἵδε δέ τοι ἴσασι, θεοῦ δέ τιν᾽ ἔκλυον αὐδήν,
> 90 <u>κείνου</u> λυγρὸν ὄλεθρον, ὅ τ᾽ οὐκ ἐθέλουσι δικαίως
> μνᾶσθαι οὐδὲ νέεσθαι ἐπὶ σφέτερ᾽, ἀλλὰ ἔκηλοι
> κτήματα δαρδάπτουσιν ὑπέρβιον, οὐδ᾽ ἔπι φειδώ.

Odyssey 14.83–92

"The gods do not like σχέτλια ἔργα, but they honor δίκη and the αἴσιμα ἔργα of men—and yet," (καὶ μὲν, 85) he says wistfully, "evil-minded, unhinged people, who go to the land of another—even to them Zeus gives loot.[128] And filling up their ships they go back home, and yet," (καὶ μὲν, 88) he says, turning the screw, as though considering more deeply, "on these people's *phrenes* falls a powerful fear of the Watch.[129] *These* people, mark you, *know*—and they have heard some voice of god—the λυγρὸν ὄλεθρον of that one ... that they are not willing to woo properly or to go back to their own, but at their ease they arrogantly devour the possessions ...."

Here Eumaeus, maintaining an innocent facade, oddly slides from a) the people who fill their ships and go home, to b) the people on whose hearts falls

---

[127] Walcot 1977:14; cf. Rose 1980:289 ("both have endured long wandering or permanent exile"); Segal 1994:173–174, 177; King 1999:75; Austin 1975:204; Louden 1997:111. Tsagalis (2012b:323): "as Eumaeus ... is a compromised elite, so also is Odysseus' Cretan persona."

[128] Notice how this papers over the rape and pillage.

[129] Contrast line 82, on the suitors, οὐκ ὄπιδα φρονέοντες ἐνὶ φρεσὶν οὐδ᾽ ἐλεητύν.

a powerful fear, to c) the people who have heard the λυγρὸν ὄλεθρον of that one. As soon as he utters "of that one," one realizes the identity of "that one" (Odysseus) with the "filler of ships."[130] It is a buried jab at Odysseus: its utter inappropriateness to the suitors, who were the initial occasion for the speech, suggests a performance where Eumaeus takes the measure of his companion as he speaks and ends up making the seemingly offhand remark about looters.

These reflections of Eumaeus presently serve as a seed for Odysseus' response in Cretan Tale 2. Now the notorious looter caps the description of his successful supplication of the Egyptian king with the remark that the king was looking out for the μῆνις of Zeus, ξεινίου, ὅς τε μάλιστα νεμεσσᾶται κακὰ ἔργα, "xeinios [of strangers], who especially takes vengence for evil deeds" (283–284). That is the only conceivable reason the king protected him since, as he admits (283), everyone hated him. "Odysseus," man of hate, peeks out, and the line reeks all the more of coverup. Zeus has nemesis for evil deeds, and yet does not punish Odysseus for doing what Eumaeus said evil people do; rather, he gave him loot anyway (in the form of gifts, to be sure) for his troubles—just as Eumaeus admits Zeus sometimes does.[131] Odysseus sits in Egypt for an idyllic seven years mysteriously raking in gifts which "everyone gave" (cf. the Phaeacians). This wealth fantasy is interrupted by the gobbling Phoenician evildoer. This fellow, curiously Circean, seduces the Cretan into staying with him in his exotic eastern locale for one year. Suddenly, when the year turns back around,[132] the man without provocation decides to lure the Cretan into a journey to Libya, where he plans to sell him as a slave. The lack of causation in this story ("Zeus put it in my head"; the man deciding after a year to sell him; him following "though he suspected it, by necessity") gives the impression of cobbling together elements from the previous Tale to Alkinoos, and the audience watches a yarn being spun (or scraps tacked together) rather than being swept up into a story-world. This is the second time the Cretan is threatened with slavery and escapes.

Next comes the Thesprotian episode (14.314–338), which includes another moment when Odysseus appears to be reaching out for the recognition of Eumaeus.[133] The Thesprotian king told the Cretan that Odysseus was off to Dodona, to consult the god about whether to return openly or in secret (330). The hall of mirrors reaches a climax when Odysseus says: "There I asked about

---

[130] Cf. 14.122 and the conversation between Penelope and the disguised Athena, 4.832–837; on "that one" in these passages see Goldhill 1991:28, 38.

[131] It is Zeus *xeinios* whose wrath the Egyptian king fears, not (as might be expected) Zeus *hikēsios* (of the suppliant)—a nod to the present situation with Eumaeus, and recalling Eumaeus' avowal (14.57–58) that *xeinoi* come from Zeus.

[132] Notice in passing the emphasis on the year, in the context of an Eastern location, and a Φοῖνιξ who is like Circe.

[133] Roisman 1990:225.

Odysseus. And that one was saying that he hosted and loved him as he went to his fatherland ...." Here a simple use of gestures can map the Cretan's conversation with the Thesprotian king onto Odysseus' conversation with Eumaeus (and us).[134] Aside from another moment of suspense, we are free to take this as an attempt to flatter Eumaeus, who can recognize himself in the Thesprotian king: both the person whom "I" asked about Odysseus and the one who "loved and entertained"—Odysseus!—on his way home as he is.[135] The element of possessions from Tale 1 returns, as the Thesprotian king is seized by a sudden, Croesus-like desire to exhibit to the stranger the heaps of treasure that he is keeping for Odysseus. This adds nothing to verisimilitude, but perhaps serves as a further incentive for Eumaeus to join the cause in what he must be realizing is Odysseus' return. It also, however, directly responds to Eumaeus' catalogue of Odysseus' possessions in 14.99–104. That catalogue, while it seemed merely touching at the time, now takes on added dimension, as the catalogue of fictional loot in Thesprotia, of questionable provenance, is added to the list of possible offenses against Eumaeus' principle that one should not go to another land and take things.

The Thesprotian episode is a final reminder of the extra-Homeric Odysseus,[136] who travels to Thesprotia and marries the queen. This is a final opportunity to perform a double reading on the performer's body in front of us; to see the mention of this adventure either as an overflow from the performer's knowledge of and enthusiasm for these stories, or as Odysseus looking forward to these adventures himself; if we see both, there is a merging between narrator and character once again.

At last, for a third and final time evil sailors try to sell the Cretan into slavery, and a third time he escapes, hiding in a thicket on Ithaka in a scene reminiscent of the olive tree on Scheria from the end of Book 5. A third time the gods single him out for salvation ("the gods kept me hidden," 357), and deliver him to Eumaeus' *stathmos*—the home of a "man who knows: and now, a dispensation for me yet to live" (359).

Ending solidly on a flattering, rapport-building sentiment, landing the speaker back in his seat opposite Eumaeus, the tale has meandered through a variety of attitudes and responses to his companion. Sitting as we are in Eumaeus' seat, we are invited, even *induced by our position* to notice and weigh how the echoes of Eumaeus' speech are incorporated into the tale. The passages

---

[134] Cf. the similar musical-chairs hospitality in *Iliad* 11; see above page 226.

[135] In this musical-chairs play the scene anticipates Eumaeus' turning of the tables on Odysseus, on which see below.

[136] For Danek (1998:286), the episode recalls an alternative homecoming in which Thesprotia was the penultimate stop; see also Ahl and Roisman 1996:163–164. On Odysseus' post-homecoming adventures in Thesprotia, see Marks 2003:221–222; Marks 2008: Ch. 4.

that verbally echo Eumaeus' claims about the value of hard work and the fear of the Watch go beyond "testing" Eumaeus into scoffing at his very words as naively pious[137] and even, with his assertions about *aretē* gaining him a wife, taunting him with his slavery.

In fact, the oft-cited "function" of the Cretan Tales, testing the various interlocutors, and arousing their sympathy and assistance, is in this case superfluous.[138] Eumaeus' first words (14.37–47) express grief for his absent master. That speech too is notable for the way it deploys the speaker's developing vision of his interlocutor and a curious combination of mental association with that developing vision. Again this process is bodied forth in enjambment. Eumaeus slides uncannily[139] from saying the dogs attacking the stranger would be a shame on him, to saying that would be just one more grief the gods had given him, "for I sit grieving and in pain over my godlike lord" (40–41), "and I raise fatty pigs for others / to eat," to a remark about his absent master both connected and disconnected from the remark about "feeding pigs for others to eat": "but that one, hoping, probably, for food, wanders to the country and city of foreign men."

Here the performer playing Eumaeus curiously emphasizes the theme of eating. "Curiously," because the theme of food is made to arise simultaneously through "inner-directed" and "outer-directed" routes. First, along the inner route, it arises as if by mental association from the present near-ravaging of the stranger by dogs' teeth, "in" through a seemingly self-directed thought about how many griefs the gods have given "me," Eumaeus, to a recollection of how he sits grieving for his master, and by the way also raises pigs for others → to eat → and that one (my master) must also be on the lookout for food. On the other hand, the outer route: the very flimsiness of the steps in Eumaeus' thinking here, along with the fact that *he is looking at Odysseus*, encourages a performance whereby the stranger's appearance draws Eumaeus both toward the theme of hunger and toward the theme of his absent master *being hungry*.

The very tension between sheer mental association and the visual recognition of hunger can be played a variety of ways. There are a variety of actorly courses for the performer to take as he makes his way through the tape-marks

---

[137] On this piety, cf. Clay (1983:235), discussing the apostrophes. For Clay the addressee *of the poem* is a man like the pious Eumaeus, the only character the poet calls 'you,' but Homer is beyond the piety of Eumaeus and the *mētis* of Odysseus. While this is attractive, one can reach a similar judgment about the poet via a reading like the present one, which shows how the superiority of Eumaeus to Odysseus emerges in the course of the poem.

[138] As with Laertes: Gainsford (2003:48) writes that the cruelty of the testing makes it seem it is being done not for Odysseus but for the sake of the audience or "for the sake of the formalized significative effect of the recognition scene." This is to back too far away from the words. No doubt there is an inherited pattern in which the returning hero tests loyalties. But there is more going on, which can be fleshed out by attending to performance.

[139] We are given no grounds, this early on, to think it is cannily.

in the script of Books 14 and 15, and no doubt the general "routine" invites developments of the script to enhance the performance. Some of these ways will convey more of a recognition on the part of Eumaeus, others less.

Another way of seeing the tales besides as "tests" is represented by Stanford, namely:

> to make the most of this poignant scene between the long-absent lord and his most loyal servant, and to show how skilfully Odysseus can control and guide another's thoughts. The whole episode will seem long, perhaps even tedious, to modern readers unless they discern its subtle characterization and ingenious handling, and feel the suspense of wondering when Odysseus will reveal himself.[140]

But the scene is not "poignant," except perhaps due to the obliviousness of the master to his slave. As for Odysseus' control of another's thoughts, we have seen that Odysseus responds detail for detail to Eumaeus' earlier speeches, perhaps in an effort to contradict him, but that one should hesitate before declaring him successful. In fact the "leakage" of extra-Homeric stories into this second Cretan Tale may tilt toward the opposite effect: that of a narrator not quite in tune with his (inner, and perhaps outer) audience, and disturbingly so. "Perverse"[141] is not too strong a word.

But the chief problem with standard readings is not their characterization of Odysseus or Eumaeus, but rather their inattention to performance. As a script the tale is an opportunity not only for characterization but for providing the audience with a sense of uncertainty as to the source of action: the merging between bard and character, the alternating obliviousness and responsiveness to the audience, and not least the split in us produced by the fact that, while "Odysseus" is speaking, we are sitting in Eumaeus' seat. All of this is not a matter of characterization. It is rather what can happen in performance by means of the layers of space and presence involved. It is what can happen, and what must happen, if a performance is to captivate its audience as well as catalyze the Western ethical and aesthetic tradition.

First, the performer and we audience members inhabit one space, Odysseus and Eumaeus another; still another space is the normal situation of epic, where the performer inhabits the space of his characters to a certain extent as a Hermes-like mediator, and we are invited partially into that space. In the first two Cretan Tales the performer seems to come forward, in that, although he

---

[140] Stanford 1996:221 *ad* 14.115.

[141] Benardete (1997:113), on the Egyptian king's awe at the wrath of Zeus (14.283–284) in the Cretan Tale to Eumaeus: "The criminal Odysseus claims the protection of Zeus who watches over strangers. This is perverse."

is reprising his role as hero-narrator from Books 9–12, he seems to gather his materials from the space we share with him. Then he seems to craft his story, at once oblivious and responsive to his audience, whose position is taken by us. This increased "presence" of the narrator in "our" space corresponds to the return of the hero. The contentious way of putting this is that the answer to the question, "Why does Odysseus have to lie so much to get home?" is not "because he has to test loyalties and thread his way in to the center" or "because he's Odysseus; he's a liar," but because it is part of the *Odyssey*'s movement from narrating past action to wrestling with the present. This act—the performer, as it were, wrenching himself out of the epic narrator position, as his character lands in Ithaka—ratchets up the play with the dynamics of performance.

Second, the performer's Hermes-like flow between character and narrator in performance can be mapped onto the performer's bodily control of his character or lack thereof. One can see a lack of control in the first two Cretan Tales. In the Tale to Laertes, where Odysseus lies to his aged father seemingly to no purpose, this lack of control reaches a climax. It is dramatically effective in that episode, near the end of the poem, for both the performer and Odysseus to be unable to stop lying: neither can give up the role. A variety of interpretations of this dramatic scaffolding are possible, both by the actor and by the audience, resulting in a spectrum from uncanny possession to ironic, comic metatheater.

The tales must be read for their dramatic virtues rather than their psychological truisms.

Eumaeus' Response: The Aetolian

Eumaeus reacts to this Cretan Tale with an almost[142] completely neglected speech:

> ἆ δειλὲ ξείνων, ἦ μοι μάλα θυμὸν ὄρινας
> ταῦτα ἕκαστα λέγων, ὅσα δὴ πάθες ἠδ' ὅσ' ἀλήθης.
> ἀλλὰ τά γ' οὐ κατὰ κόσμον ὀΐομαι, οὐδέ με πείσεις
> εἰπὼν ἀμφ' Ὀδυσῆϊ· τί σε χρὴ τοῖον ἐόντα
> 365   μαψιδίως ψεύδεσθαι; ἐγὼ δ' εὖ οἶδα καὶ αὐτὸς
> νόστον ἐμοῖο ἄνακτος, ὅτ' ἤχθετο πᾶσι θεοῖσι
> πάγχυ μάλ', ὅττι μιν οὔ τι μετὰ Τρώεσσι δάμασσαν
> ἠὲ φίλων ἐν χερσίν, ἐπεὶ πόλεμον τολύπευσε.
> τῶ κέν οἱ τύμβον μὲν ἐποίησαν Παναχαιοί,
> 370   ἠδέ κε καὶ ᾧ παιδὶ μέγα κλέος ἤρατ' ὀπίσσω

---

[142] See especially Marks 2003.

νῦν δέ μιν ἀκλειῶς ἅρπυιαι ἀνηρείψαντο.
αὐτὰρ ἐγὼ παρ' ὕεσσιν ἀπότροπος· οὐδὲ πόλινδε
ἔρχομαι, εἰ μή πού τι περίφρων Πηνελόπεια
ἐλθέμεν ὀτρύνῃσιν, ὅτ' ἀγγελίη ποθὲν ἔλθοι.
375 ἀλλ' οἱ μὲν τὰ ἕκαστα παρήμενοι ἐξερέουσιν,
ἠμὲν οἳ ἄχνυνται δὴν οἰχομένοιο ἄνακτος,
ἠδ' οἳ χαίρουσιν βίοτον νήποινον ἔδοντες·
ἀλλ' ἐμοὶ οὐ φίλον ἐστὶ μεταλλῆσαι καὶ ἐρέσθαι,
ἐξ οὗ δή μ' Αἰτωλὸς ἀνὴρ ἐξήπαφε μύθῳ,
380 ὅς ῥ' ἄνδρα κτείνας, πολλὴν ἐπὶ γαῖαν ἀληθείς,
ἦλθεν ἐμὰ πρὸς δώματ'· ἐγὼ δέ μιν ἀμφαγάπαζον.
φῆ δέ μιν ἐν Κρήτεσσι παρ' Ἰδομενῆϊ ἰδέσθαι
νῆας ἀκειόμενον, τάς οἱ ξυνέαξαν ἄελλαι·
καὶ φάτ' ἐλεύσεσθαι ἢ ἐς θέρος ἢ ἐς ὀπώρην,
385 πολλὰ χρήματ' ἄγοντα, σὺν ἀντιθέοις ἑτάροισι.
καὶ σύ, γέρον πολυπενθές, ἐπεί σέ μοι ἤγαγε δαίμων,
μήτε τί μοι ψεύδεσσι χαρίζεο μήτε τι θέλγε·
οὐ γὰρ τοὔνεκ' ἐγώ σ' αἰδέσσομαι οὐδὲ φιλήσω,
ἀλλὰ Δία ξένιον δείσας αὐτόν τ' ἐλεαίρων.

Odyssey 14.361–389

This speech is once again a masterpiece of transitions, of suggestive brico-lage. Although Eumaeus claims to be moved ("Ah, wretch among strangers, you have really stirred my heart / telling each of these things, as many as you've suffered and as much as you've wandered," 361–362), he does not believe what the Cretan has said about Odysseus, and he is slightly disgusted with him for lying so extravagantly. He knows the truth about his absent master: he is thoroughly detested by the gods (366–367) and has been snatched away by harpies ingloriously (ἀκλειῶς). The truth about Odysseus is that there will never be any news about him.

Then, ostensibly, Eumaeus starts to talk about himself: he is *apotropos* (outcast, but also, that which one turns out of one's presence as polluted, such as a scapegoat; or that which averts evil) among the swine (372). But then he turns back again, as though spontaneously, to the subject of news of Odysseus, this time by another route. "Never to the city do I go ... unless, I suppose (πού τι), *periphrōn* (!) Penelope stirs me to come—whenever a message comes from somewhere" (372–374). But he no longer takes pleasure in these meetings at the palace, which in his view have degenerated into gatherings of gossips and freeloaders, "some grieving deeply for the absent lord, others having a terrific time devouring his *biotos* unpunished" (376–377).

> But I am no longer fond of questioning and inquiring,
> <u>ever since the time when</u> an Aetolian man led me on with a speech,
> 380   who, mark you, had killed a man, had wandered over the earth,
> and came to my house, and I embraced him with affection.[143]
> He said that he had seen him among the Cretans at Idomeneus' place,
> repairing ships, which the winds had smashed.
> And he said [he] would return either in summer or at harvest,
> 385   bringing a lot of money, with his godlike companions.
> And you, much-suffering old man, since a daimon brought you to me,
> don't try to ingratiate yourself with me, charm me (θέλγε) with your
>   lies:
> not for that will I respect you and treat you kindly,
> but fearing Zeus Xenios and pitying you-yourself (αὐτόν:[144] him?).
>
>   *Odyssey* 14.378–389

Our initial expectations for the Ithakan episode were that Odysseus, returning from the world of Iliadic war and of fantastic adventure, would operate on an elevated plane compared with that inhabited by the Ithakans he would manipulate and/or slaughter. We, the audience, would likewise command a superior perspective. If so far we have been given an inkling that Eumaeus would not quite fit into this schema, suddenly all these expectations are jolted.

Who is this Aetolian? How is it that he knew the story of the lie Odysseus has just told, and even *invented before our eyes out of a miscellany of materials*, about Odysseus repairing ships in Crete with Idomeneus? How is it that this Aetolian, who had killed a man and done a lot of wandering, so resembles the Cretan persona from Tale 1? Instead of being taken in by clever Odysseus, either Eumaeus has hosted a liar who so far exceeds Odysseus that he has anticipated the hero's own lies, and certainly deserves his own poem, or else Eumaeus himself has created this masterpiece on the spot. (The artfulness of the narrative seems to be signaled in its imposing introductory phrase ἐξ οὗ δή, recalling *Iliad* 1.6.)[145]

This moment can be played in a number of ways. Eumaeus may maintain a bumpkinly persona, recalling the incident and mourning his master all the more. Or he may register his dawning awareness of Odysseus, his acceptance of

---

[143] ἀμφαγάπαζον is stronger than "hosted kindly." It is used of parents and children, and especially of Demeter and Persephone once the latter has told the former "the whole truth" (*Hymn to Demeter* 437; cf. 440, 291). But it is also used of men "embracing their own evil" (*Works and Days* 58), that is, woman, that slipshod jar of deceptions called Pandora. Such was the Aetolian.

[144] Cf. the pregnant use of αὐτῆς at *Iliad* 9.562 (see above, Ch. 2, page 128).

[145] Marks 2003:215n5.

being "chosen for ambush" (cf. 14.217), and his understanding of the stranger's tale of Odysseus consulting the oracle about whether to return "in the open or undercover" (330). A sly acknowledgement of his guest's mendacity may come across in line 362, ὅσα δὴ πάθες ἠδ' ὅσ' ἀλήθης, which may play on "deception" (ἀπάτη, ἀπατάω) and "truth."[146] (Compare 379–380, where deception [different word, ἤπαφε] appears with ἀληθείς [aorist participle].)

Eumaeus moves, whether artfully or artlessly, from sitting among the pigs, to being summoned by Penelope "whenever" a message should come "from wherever" (373–374), to one particular messenger who has told just the Cretan story we were, perhaps, supposed to be impressed by when it came out of Odysseus' mouth. The creation of this Aetolian, and the way Eumaeus moves toward him in his story, is the structural equivalent for Eumaeus of Penelope's celebrated bed test (23.174–180).[147] When Penelope casually mentions moving the bed, the horrifying implication for Odysseus is that "someone has been here before me." Here too, "someone has been here before me," someone who not only charmed Eumaeus such that he embraced him, but also seems to have stopped him from going to listen to the messengers plying Penelope with stories. Note that Penelope's reason for performing the test is her fear that some schemer would come and beguile her with words (23.216–217).[148]

To this Odysseus reacts with some annoyance: "Well! that is some unbelieving spirit in your chest, such that not even when I swore did I lead you on or persuade you!" (391–392). Yet he does not proceed to bare all in anger as he will with Penelope. Thus, this moment, in its ironies and performance potential, surpasses the bed test, where Odysseus' indignant response is transparent and is the final "clarifying" act of their exchange of signs. The script of the Aetolian moment is richer than that of the bed-trick in that it leaves more of its meaning to be completed by the performer.

The options open to the performer are not something to enumerate definitively, but we can sketch the script's dramatic potential. Before the performer

---

[146] Eumaeus uses a similar phrase to begin his autobiography at 15.401, on which see below. Cf. also 14.125–127, where Eumaeus, picking up Odysseus' last word at 14.118, ἀλήθην, "I wandered," links wandering (ἀλητεύων, ἀλῆται) with not telling the truth (ἀληθέα); Goldhill 1991:38; Segal 1994:179–183. Other wordplay concerning "truth": Watkins 1995:101 on Hesiod *Works and Days* 10.

[147] Recall again the general expectation of a recognition scene between Eumaeus and Odysseus: A. B. Lord 2000:180.

[148] It is the dramatic virtue of the "Aetolian moment" that indicates it is not merely a reference to an alternative Cretan *Odyssey*, to be condemned because not conforming to the Panhellenic *Odyssey* (Marks 2003). In some sense it may be true that "the rumor reported by Eumaeus in 14.379–385 makes sense only if Odysseus did actually pass from Crete in an earlier version of his *nostos*" (Tsagalis 2012b:317, citing West 1981:171). But the very nonsensical or, as I would put it, shocking quality of the rumor makes dramatic sense, whether the audience attributes the rumor to Eumaeus' cunning or not or (as I would prefer) is left in doubt.

speaks as Odysseus, he has a choice of how to register the astonishing informa-
tion about the Aetolian.[149] One strong possibility is to end the speech of Eumaeus
on a firm note of refusal to be taken in (387 μήτε τί μοι ψεύδεσσι χαρίζεο μήτε
τι θέλγε), mixed with resolve to fulfill his duty to Zeus Xenios (389), regardless
of his slightly dubious companion, and then to make the transition to being-
Odysseus by letting a look of complete wide-eyed bafflement dawn over one's
face. One may mix this with an attempt to cover that bafflement, even turning
away from the audience to regain composure or as if to say, "And who is *that*
guy?—he's not part of this poem!" One may even simply emit a blank stare for
an awkward moment and allow the audience to "become" Odysseus to fill in the
silence—that is, to think through the implications of the Aetolian as they dawn
on the performer's face. There is no reason the hexameter must keep marching
steadily on in the face of such a beautifully scripted opportunity.[150] The script
virtually begs the performer to flesh out the silence here for the audience.

What is comic here is not only the moment within the world of the poem—
Odysseus ambiguously out-foxed by the swineherd—but also outside of that
world. In the silence, the bard straddles Odysseus and Eumaeus, but also
himself and Odysseus. He has the opportunity, seen in many one-man and one-
woman shows, to be split between two levels of knowledge—and for the seem-
ingly lower-level character to trump the higher, resulting in a bafflement regis-
tered at once as "in" the higher character and in the performer identified with
that character. This is difficult both to describe and to pull off successfully.[151]
A blank stare before line 390 (introducing Odysseus' speech) works differently

---

[149] That a performer would do so is indicated too by the fact that Odysseus incorporates an "Aetolian"
into his Cloak Story that immediately follows; see below. Any pause before he launches into this
story will give the audience a chance to "see the wheels turning" in his mind as he picks up the
ingredients for his bricolage. Such between-speech head-scratching would be expected for an
audience used to performers capping one another, although just here it seems unlikely that a
new performer would take over as the speaker changes, both because of the speeches' length
and because some of the dynamics within a single performer would be lost. The script here may
be inspired by relay delivery, rather than scripting an actual rhapsodic hand-off.

[150] See n42 above.

[151] That is why there are professional standup comics and solo performers, as well as profes-
sional singers of a charismatic stamp. The movement from being, at root, one character, to
being another is clearly illustrated by solo song lyrics involving two characters, one of whom
addresses the other only to be taken over by him. For a familiar contemporary example, Jimi
Hendrix's "Hey Joe" clearly registers such a shift in 'voice' not on the page but in performance.
Hendrix does not modulate the timbre of his voice. Rather the energy of the song (instantiated
in volume, "gestures" on the guitar, etc.) drifts, such that the song more and more seems to be
coming from the homicidal Joe, rather than from Joe's alarmed companion, who begins the song.
As Hendrix becomes Joe, so does the bard become Eumaeus, a movement not completed until
Eumaeus' autobiography. Like the *Odyssey*, "Hey Joe" would have been banned from Socrates'
interlocutors' ideal city, for its untraceable causes inducing the possession by "Joe." A similar,
but less disturbing, possession comes about in Sappho's poem to Aphrodite (although as with

from one after it, because the audience may "read" the stare more easily as coming from the performer rather than the character. I suggested above that the audience is free to "read" the performer's presence into Cretan Tale 2, as *his* repertoire of extra-Odyssean tales provides fodder for his ever-expanding Cretan Tales. Such "reading" would be natural for an audience accustomed to a bard developing the *Odyssey* as a work in progress, a work that includes an Odysseus who develops the Cretan Tales over the course of the poem. An Aetolian has come in and out-barded the bard, being familiar with the story repertoire and getting in first.[152]

Other effects are possible too. We do not give the poem its due if we reduce these effects to an exposure of Odysseus behind his disguise within the realm of the story, which is what the parallel to the bed-trick might suggest. And yet these other effects do coexist with such an "exposure of the character." The whole concatenation of dynamics here manifests a bard "brought up short" by his material—like Odysseus, but in the performer's own world—rather than taking on his characters' emotions or even being possessed by them.

To speak of physical realizations of the moment is fraught but worth the risk. On the one hand, different effects may be suggested by different gestures, facial expressions, and eye contact. On the other, there may be no one-to-one correspondence between a given acting choice and a given effect. The speech is full of shifts in the stance or σχῆμα of the speaker, his deepening knowledge, and the story he is weaving, shifts in the implied space of performance and in the mental state of the performer.[153]

The Aetolian moment combines poetics and presence, story-world and space of performance such that they reinforce one another. Within the poem-world, a mysterious character lying his way around the Mediterranean[154] has anticipated Odysseus; on the axis of presence, Eumaeus has been "hiding" deeper within the performer than we realized. The audience had thought that the performer "was" Odysseus, but he has laid a trap for us. If we got a glimpse of ourselves in this trap during Cretan Tale 2 and the Aetolian moment, the trap will snap shut in Eumaeus' autobiography.[155]

Hendrix the music may have made all the difference). Contrast the Protean Anna Deveare Smith (imitative of "all sorts"), less disturbing from a *Republic* perspective.

[152] There is also a potential for a higher-stakes performance which would be more difficult: that Odysseus is suddenly felt to be fictional: "Then who am I?" This would be even more vertiginous, more charismatic, than the "baffled bard" interpretation.

[153] Bölte 1907:573.

[154] See the next section, on the role of this figure in the Nauplios story.

[155] Minchin 1992 discusses how Eumaeus' story surprises the audience in a general way, because it turns out Eumaeus is noble by birth.

The Cloak Story

In the story Odysseus tells Eumaeus in 14.462–506,[156] he takes up Eumaeus' "Aetolian" character and weaves it into a tale of his own.[157] He, the Cretan, was shivering in an ambush one cold night—much like the "evil" rainy night they are currently sheltering from[158]—and to help him (the Cretan) out, Odysseus tricked someone else into giving him his cloak, by pretending to have had a prophetic dream. The fellow tricked into running off leaving his cloak behind is "Thoas, son of Andraimon," that is, "Speedy, son of Man-blood" (line 499). This character is a well-known (traditional) Aetolian. As with Idomeneus in the Cretan Tales, scholars take various positions on why this character is chosen for this story. Marks maintains that Thoas is "in a sense Odysseus' double,"[159] much as Haft claims for Meriones. This is true, and Odysseus and Diomedes (whose cannibal father Tydeus is Aetolian), a traditional "trickster" pair, perhaps only form the tip of the iceberg of a mythical Creto-Ithaco-Aetolian cartel, which gravitates toward lies, ambushes, and mob-style murders. Thoas is also associated with Idomeneus, in a passage (*Iliad* 13.216–239) where Thoas himself does not appear, but Poseidon appears to Idomeneus in the guise of Thoas.[160] The *Iliad*, then, associates Thoas not only with disguise, but with a god in disguise, and with Idomeneus. Elsewhere in the tradition, Thoas is directly linked with Odysseus and disguise. In the *Little Iliad*, it is Thoas who disguises Odysseus for his spying mission. "Lest, being recognized, he be killed, he persuaded Thoas the son of Andraimon to whip/beat him with violent blows to make him unrecognizable."[161] *This episode, just like the Cloak Story,*

---

[156] Particularly instructive on the Cloak Story are Nagy 1979:235–238; Lowe 2000:145–147; Marks 2003.

[157] Brennan (1987:3) notes that the adjective form of Aitolios is used only here, and that the only mention of Thoas in the *Odyssey* is in the cloak story, and concludes: "Odysseus, therefore, is almost certainly exploiting Eumaeus' deception by the Aetolian; the Thoas-story can be regarded as a sort of 'ethnic joke' which makes the swineherd drop his guard." Marks (2003:214) notes that Thoas and this Aetolian are the only Aetolians in the *Odyssey*. For Marks (p. 222 and passim), the lying Aetolian is a mouthpiece through which the *Odyssey* signals to the audience that certain stories are untrustworthy.

[158] A gesture taking in both settings could make clear that Odysseus is taking his cue from his surroundings to weave the ambush story—and perhaps enjoying his own cleverness in doing so.

[159] Marks 2003:212.

[160] This itself raises intertextual questions that cannot be dealt with here. The connections between *Iliad* and *Odyssey* here as elsewhere are so entangled that we suspect mutual interaction such as Pucci 1995 describes. Marks (2003:212) comments that this connection in *Iliad* 13 shows the influence of the geography of the Catalogue of Ships on the narrative. The Catalogue order is Ithaka, Aetolia, Crete.

[161] OCT *Ilias Parva* VIII (Σ Lycophron *Alexandra* 780); fuller version in Bernabé fr. 7, n. 9. For Marks (2003:212) the *Odyssey* is here *fending off* extra-Odyssean traditions about Odysseus.

takes place under the wall of Troy (contrast *Odyssey* 4.244, where according to Helen Odysseus beats himself).[162]

All of these themes are in play in the Cloak Story. It is Thoas' cloak that "Odysseus" gives the Cretan Stranger, and it is just such a situation that the Stranger asks explicitly to be repeated. Eumaeus takes the hint, drily[163] complimenting him on the perfection of his *ainos* (14.508), a story with a hidden meaning,[164] and gives Odysseus a cloak before retiring to sleep with the pigs. But the hints are not limited to the cloak. How far are we to take the echo of Eumaeus' Aetolian?

Odysseus reprises the Aetolian's role *as messenger*: Eumaeus said that the Aetolian wanderer *brought false messages about Odysseus* to him and *to Penelope*. Thoas *likewise bears a false message in the Cloak Story, this time to Agamemnon*. There is a complex interplay among tradition, the currently unfolding drama, and its instantiation in performance. Its salience to the broader plot is that the disguised Odysseus is currently asking Eumaeus to put him into the role of *messenger to Penelope*. Eumaeus, for all that he claims to be hardened against further lies about Odysseus, steps squarely into the role of go-between,[165] even praising the stranger's seductive powers to Penelope and comparing him to a bard.[166]

Given the stranger's Cretan identity, and his convergence upon the identity of Idomeneus, it is uncanny that in the story of Idomeneus a similar agent is at work upon the queen, Idomeneus' wife Meda. This is the other story of Idomeneus' unhappy homecoming besides the one in which he sacrifices his son. In this story, Nauplios is avenging his son Palamedes' death, a murder *orchestrated, of course, by none other than Odysseus*. When his son is killed, Nauplios goes to Troy to accuse his killers before the army; this comes to naught, as those responsible are the leading heroes, and the army wants to please them.[167] Nauplios arranges for a seducer (or more than one) to sail around the Mediterranean systematically leading astray the wives of the Achaean heroes.[168] He succeeds with the

---

[162] According to one story, Odysseus takes refuge with Thoas in Aetolia after the slaughter of the suitors, marries his daughter, fathers a child, and dies (Apollodorus *Epitome* 7.40; see Marks 2003:217).

[163] See the sensitive reading of King 1999:91n65.

[164] Marks 2003:216 and n18. For Marks, Eumaeus appreciates the poetic justice of the victim being an Aetolian, and that is the "special meaning" he acknowledges.

[165] Felson (1994:22): "Eumaios arranges the interview at the hearth by shuttling back and forth between Penelope and the stranger, as if arranging a tryst."

[166] 17.513–520. The extravagant simile comparing the Stranger to a bard begins with "a man gazing upon a bard," inviting Penelope to take the role of the one gazing. Despite Eumaeus' aversion to charming strangers, he praises the Stranger precisely because "he would charm you."

[167] Σ *Orestes* 432; the story was probably told in Aeschylus' *Palamedes* and Sophocles' *Nauplios Katapleon* and/or *Nauplios Pyrkaeus* (Gantz 1993:606–607).

[168] Lycophron 1216–1224; Apollodorus *Epitome* 6.9.

wives of the Aetolian cartel mentioned above: Diomedes' wife Aegialeia, who falls in bed with Kometes, son of Diomedes' friend Sthenelos,[169] and Idomeneus' wife Meda.[170] He is also responsible for Klytemnestra's affair with Aigisthos. Conspicuously missing from this list of conquests is Penelope, wife of the man *who was the real target* of Nauplios' wrath.[171]

From later accounts,[172] it would seem that the way the seducer led the Achaean wives astray was by telling them stories, whether true or false, about their husbands' wartime infidelities. This is an issue that the *Odyssey* seems to skirt; nonetheless, the poem shows awareness of the infidelity tale and *reenacts it* through the operations of Odysseus and Eumaeus upon Penelope. Odysseus even brings his seduction to a climax by telling Penelope a story about women gazing upon Odysseus, whose manly flesh is adorned with a tunic that glistens like the skin of an onion (19.232–235). But of course Odysseus *has* spent most of his ten-year journey sleeping with and/or firing up erotic longing in women and goddesses. Whether various goddesses or Odysseus is responsible for this, it is ill-suited to the avenger of sexual misdeeds and certifier of civilized fidelities, and the poet, true to his method of "seeing something as something else," has Odysseus take on the role of serial seducer just when he is supposed to be inspecting fidelities, thus himself *completing, with his own wife, the list of seductions* that Nauplios put in motion. In fact, he does so in the persona of Aithon, the brother of Idomeneus, left behind at the Cretan court and thus in a position to host Odysseus on his way to the war. Federico in fact links Odysseus' false name Aithon with that of Leukos, the adopted son (not, alas, brother), left in charge of Idomeneus' court, who seduces Idomeneus' wife.[173] (More on Leukos below.) I find Levaniouk's account[174] of the name Aithon more persuasive. But names aside, it does appear that Odysseus' Cretan identity converges, not quite upon Idomeneus, but upon the seducer of Idomeneus' wife, who in the tradition is called Leukos.

Those are some of the threads of this plot that surface later in the poem. We started to see these implications by noticing a convergence between Odysseus

---

[169] Might this incident be alluded to at *Iliad* 5.412–415?

[170] Apollodorus *Epitome* 6.9; Lycophron 1093–1095, 1214–1225 with Tzetzes' scholia; Hyginus 117. Sommerstein (2000:126n18) suggests that these events were referred to in Aeschylus' *Palamedes*.

[171] However, Σ Lycophron 1093, amidst the list of wives seduced, includes καὶ ἐν Ἰθάκῃ δὲ τοὺς μνηστῆρας παρεσκεύασε συναχθῆναι, "and in Ithaka he contrived that the suitors be gathered." In another version (Σ *Odyssey* 4.797; see Levaniouk 1999:126) Nauplios deals more directly with Penelope, throwing her into the sea—where she is saved by the *pēnelopes*, hence her name. (He also, according to one version, caused the suicide of Odysseus' mother by sending false news of his death: Σ *Odyssey* 11.197, 202.)

[172] Lycophron 1093–1095; 1219 "weaving hate with lying devices"; Dictys Cretensis 5.2; Hyginus 117. Gantz 1993:607.

[173] For Federico (1999:295n108), Aithon ("shining") fits with the set of names associated with the kingship of Crete that recall astral models.

[174] Levaniouk 2000.

and Idomeneus, while at the same time, Odysseus plays the role of the serial seducer. But look again at the Cloak Story itself: it may even end at the very point at which the entire Nauplios plot is set in motion. In the story, "Odysseus" says:

κλῦτε, φίλοι· θεῖός μοι ἐνύπνιον ἦλθεν ὄνειρος.
λίην γὰρ νηῶν ἑκὰς ἤλθομεν· ἀλλά τις εἴη
εἰπεῖν Ἀτρεΐδῃ Ἀγαμέμνονι, ποιμένι λαῶν,
εἰ πλέονας παρὰ ναῦφιν ἐποτρύνειε νέεσθαι ...

Hear me, friends! A divine dream came to me in my sleep:
We have come too far from the ships! Now would there be anyone
to tell Atreus' son Agamemnon, shepherd of the people,
in hopes he will order more men to come from the ships?

Odyssey 14.495–498

Why does he mention that they are "too far from the ships"? This may be a detail taken from the story of the murder of Palamedes, which, of course, prompts his father's vengeance, echoes of which we have just seen. While the accounts vary, the version reported by Hyginus bears a curious resemblance to the scene in the Cloak Story.

Ulysses, because he had been taken in by a trick of Palamedes son of Nauplius, was scheming day after day how to kill him. Finally he formed a plan and sent a soldier of his to Agamemnon to tell him that he had had a vision in his sleep[175] that they should move the camp for one day. Thinking this was true, Agamemnon ordered the camp to be moved for one day; Ulysses then alone, secretly, at night buried a great amount of gold where the tent of Palamedes had been ...

Hyginus 105

Hyginus' version of the murder of Palamedes probably derives from Euripides' *Palamedes*.[176] It could be that this plot was a specifically tragic innovation: in the *Cypria*, by contrast, Odysseus and Diomedes simply drowned Palamedes while he was fishing, rather than framing him as a traitor by burying gold under his tent.[177] Hyginus' version involves not only gold but also a letter written in "Phrygian characters," which might seem out of place in a version circulating at the time of the *Odyssey*. But it is not so far off from the story of Bellerophon (*Iliad* 6.156–202) and its mysterious tablets. And there is no reason

---

[175] Or, "in his sleep, he had seen Minerva urging him that ..." (*in quiete vidisse se Minervam suadentem ...*).

[176] Scodel 1980:53.

[177] Very brief mention at Pausanias 10.31.2 (= *Cypria* fr. 21 Allen).

to believe that the *Cypria*'s fishing version was the only one extant before the fifth century; perhaps there was a familiar story that involved a dream and the moving of the camp.[178]

If the Cloak Story does allude to the murder of Palamedes,[179] it would be using a familiar Homeric strategy. By ending with a scene very much like the beginning of the Palamedes story, the Cloak Story would use exactly the same technique as the Trojan Horse story that Odysseus requests of Demodokos in Book 8—another story of ambush and hidden identities! and one in which Thoas is sometimes found[180]—discussed in Chapter 1.[181] In both cases, the end of the story brings on another identity for Odysseus. In Book 8, when Demodokos leaves off, Odysseus weeps like the woman he jabbed with the butt of his spear in the continuing world of the story, which plays on nightmarishly in his head, while he attempts to disguise himself (with a cloak!). Here in the Cloak Story, Odysseus indicates he has taken the seed of Eumaeus' suggestion (the Aetolian messenger) and wishes to "don the cloak of the messenger." In Book 8, the character's memories "leaked" into the register of the simile, such that bard and character merged. We can now compare this effect with the effect of the Cloak Story, seen in its context *as a reaction* to Eumaeus' story of the Aetolian. Not only are the Book 8 and Book 14 stories structured similarly (breaking off at a strategic moment), but they also both make full use of bard-character dynamics, to create a slippage between bard and character.[182]

In terms of plot, both the Cloak Story and the Trojan Horse story in Book 8 are examples of *mise en abyme*: specifically of Odysseus' infiltration of his own

---

[178] Stesichorus makes Palamedes the inventor of the alphabet (fr. 213 PMG), which makes plausible that the letter version of Palamedes' death goes back to the early sixth century. In any case, a letter is not required for the gold to be planted and "discovered" under his tent.

[179] That the Cloak Story alludes to some story in the poetic repertoire would be consistent with Nagy's treatment of the Cloak Story as *ainos*, and as *epos* (cf. 14.466) in the sense of "poetic utterance" (Nagy 1979:236). Richard Sacks, in an oral presentation at the University of Chicago in 2003, made rich suggestions about how the *Odyssey* may be taking up earlier stories about the Thesprotians and about Palamedes.

[180] Virgil *Aeneid* 2.261–262; Hyginus *Fabulae* 108; Quintus Smyrnaeus 12.318. Marks (2003:212 with n10) suggests this may have been the case in the *Ilias parva* or another Cyclic epic.

[181] As noted there, this is the technique Plato imitates in his use of the *Iliad* opening.

[182] The Cloak Story and the Trojan Horse story use the beginnings and endings, or stitchings, of story in this very specific way involving performance and identity. This technique, if one may call it that, is from one point of view a species of the "topical poetic" of the poetic performances in *Odyssey* 8, discussed by Ford (1992:112–114) and also exemplified by the *Iliad*'s use of stories from the beginning and ending of the war (see especially Kullmann 1960:227–357, 365–368). Ford's suggestion that this reflects competitive performance practices is plausible. In the case of the cluster of stories worked through by Odysseus and Eumaeus, we can see the agonistic roots within the dramatic situation itself rather than in an actual poetic competition. The projection of poetic competition adds a dimension to the ongoing performance that could vary depending on how it was played by the performer. Rather than a species of the topical poetic, it is a play upon it.

household. The Trojan Horse story, for example, features a disguised Odysseus clamping down the mouth of someone crying out at a possible reunion with his wife, as in the bathing episode with Eurykleia.[183] Yet the Cloak Story is more than *mise en abyme*. The end of the Cloak Story, the fruit of the collaboration between Odysseus and Eumaeus, initiates a new role: the seducer of Penelope.

In short, the performer enacts, spreads out for view, the process of "slipping into roles." If one were to draw a table and compare the attested plots of the various unhappy Achaean homecomings to the plot of the *Odyssey*, one would see clearly the resemblance but lose sight of how the process itself—how Odysseus slips into this role—is adumbrated. In a story in which Odysseus seems to be unmasking himself recklessly to his herdsman, he is also responding to a suggestion made by Eumaeus, in his invocation of the "wandering Aetolian." In this he repeats his approach in the first Cretan Tale, where he takes a similar suggestion from Athena. Here however the stranger adopts another role on top of the Cretan one: the seducer hired by Nauplios.

This seducer, in the version followed by Lycophron, is another Cretan in the household of Idomeneus. The man who seduces Idomeneus' wife Meda is, as Lycophron puts it, a "snake" "nursed at home" named Leukos.[184] Idomeneus had adopted Leukos and eventually promised him his daughter in marriage. When Idomeneus departed for Troy, he left Leukos in charge of affairs in Idomeneus' palace, somewhat as the bard was to look after Klytemnestra. Eumaeus too is, of course, the guardian of Odysseus' possessions (13.405). The fact that Leukos was raised in the house of Idomeneus brings to mind the fact that Eumaeus was brought up by Odysseus' mother Antikleia with Odysseus' sister (15.363). Given that Eumaeus has already revealed his own role as a messenger to Penelope, and has suggested that the charming messengers he has let through to her have had a corrosive effect on her sense of reality, listeners can include Eumaeus in their developing sense of the Idomeno-Cretan subplot. This sense will be confirmed when Eumaeus encounters Penelope in 16.338, ἄγχι παραστάς, delivering his message to her so privately that there is not even direct discourse we can hear, in contrast with the herald sent by Telemachus' men, who has just blurted out his odd one-line message (16.337) in the midst of her maids. The contrast between Eumaeus' intimate, discreet relationship with Penelope and the herald's lack of tact seems to be the only reason the poet has set up this awkward simultaneous delivery of messages.

---

[183] On the detailed parallels between the Horse story and the second half of the *Odyssey*, see Andersen 1977.
[184] Lycophron 1216–1224.

Although this quality of Eumaeus is kept in the background, such that the audience never suspects he would actually betray Odysseus, the Leukos role emerges again at 16.457–459, where Athena changes Odysseus' appearance back "lest the swineherd recognize him, looking him in the face, and go to *echephrōn* Penelope, delivering a message, and lest he not keep it checked in his *phrenes*." The impact of this understated but shocking comment is kept in check by the humorous context: Eumaeus is just returning from delivering a message to Penelope, and Athena's quick maneuver with her *rhabdos* prevents him from swiveling around on his heel to deliver yet another message.[185]

The poet initiated the Idomeneus plot in Book 13 as if through an offhand suggestion of Athena. Odysseus had then taken up the thread and added to it his own anxieties in the face of someone who could have been Telemachus. The most salient part of the Idomeneus story in Book 13 was the presence of his son as the "first person he encounters" on the beach. In Book 14 the poet disguises his plot-making capacity by burying it in Eumaeus' story of the wandering, murderous Aetolian messenger. The seed from this story is in turn taken up by Odysseus in his Cloak story, which in turn may be based on the story of Palamedes' murder. All of these stories—the stories of Idomeneus' homecoming (especially the Leukos version), the story of Palamedes and the device of the plow, the murder of Palamedes, and Nauplios' revenge by having the Achaean wives seduced—are related, but they appear piecemeal, as individually improvised tales, within the Cretan Tales and in the related conversations.[186]

In other words, the poet has shared out the "seeds of the story" among Athena, Eumaeus, and Odysseus in Books 13–14. The rich stew of poetics and presence in Book 14 derives from the fact that the bard "shares out" this plotting to Eumaeus and Odysseus at the same moment that he "becomes" Eumaeus, and then suddenly Odysseus again, as discussed earlier. *His "poetic" and "presencing" functions are revealed, as it were, to stem from a deeper part of himself that we did not know existed,* as we didn't know he "had Eumaeus in him." Yet another doll emerges within this nest of presences in the performer, uncovering a richer poem than one in which this conspiratorial plotting takes place entirely within the world of the poem, leaving out the poet's plotting capacities and his activity as an act-or. This hidden core of the bard's plotting capacities having been revealed, when Eumaeus departs the scene at the end of Book 14, one can see in the retreating Eumaeus, his back to us as he heads to the pigs, the bard himself

---

[185] On the other hand, the humor of the image reinforces the idea of Eumaeus continuously filtering outside messengers through his hut and escorting them to the queen.

[186] Recall once again Ford's (1992:112–114) "topical poetic."

drily unimpressed[187] with the creative process just exposed, while Odysseus remains on the surface, buoyed by the thought of his next maneuver, as the serial seducer.[188] The fact that this is not exactly a novel role for Odysseus even within the plot of the *Odyssey* reinforces this effect. One part of the performer is pleased to be concocting the plan, while another part is unimpressed: "he was going to do that anyway. He is only *as-if* coming up with the plan." It is the illusion of splitting himself into two, of locating the capacity for plotting and the "source of action" in two different places, that justly provokes the anxieties of Platonic characters about the "manyness" of the bard.[189] The splitting even finds its way *into* the story, when the bard, as Odysseus as Cretan, casts Eumaeus as Odysseus, and addresses him in his plea for a cloak.[190] All this happens to heighten listeners' interest in Eumaeus. But one must not, in a rush to discuss character, glide over these dynamics of bard and character, plot and performance, *poiēsis* and *genesis*.

Eumaeus' Autobiography

Eumaeus and Odysseus have, wittingly/unwittingly, set in motion a subplot, that of the pan-Mediterranean seducer, which sits uneasily alongside both the plot of the returning husband and the *theoxenia* plot.[191] Odysseus was afraid he would play the role of Idomeneus, in Book 13; his identity in the Cretan Tales progressively drifts toward that of Idomeneus but veers off into that of Leukos, when he seduces his own wife, such that she has an erotic dream of the man who

---

[187] As Bowie (2013 *ad* 14.481) observes, following Minchin 2007, the Cloak Story might "win over the herdsmen, who could feel amusedly superior to this self-styled Trojan warrior who did not know how to behave in the cold in which they spent much of their lives." If the story sounds like someone who has been drinking (Bowie 2013:223), that further sets up the split. Indeed, if the last lines (503–506; see Bowie 2013 *ad loc.*) are "crude" and "spoil the effect of Odysseus' speech," it may be better not to follow the Alexandrian editors in athetizing them, so that they set up Eumaeus' response.

[188] One of several actorly alternatives; the script is a rich mine. The richness is not diminished by the fact that Eumaeus' retreat is described by the performer as narrator.

[189] Recall the discussion in the Introduction of the opening of the *Iliad* and Plato's use of that example in the *Republic*, and his use of the Theoclymenos example in the *Ion*.

[190] 14.503–506. This address of Eumaeus as Odysseus seems to be a culmination of the "musical chairs" type of play at work here between master and slave. At once Odysseus casts Eumaeus as Odysseus, the bard plays with which character he "is," and the bard casts his Odyssean identity into the audience (*his* addressee).

[191] For a different conflict of plot-types at the end of the *Odyssey*, see Felson 1994 and Felson 1996:165: the *Odyssey* assigns Penelope "roles in two incompatible types of plot: in BRIDE-CONTEST and MARRIAGE-AVOIDANCE."

is the likeness of Odysseus.[192] All of this gives the return plot a playful quality, a slight uncertainty about Penelope's faithfulness.[193]

With all of this set in motion, Eumaeus himself now redeploys to quite different effect the theme of the seductive messenger in his autobiography, where a deceptive Phoenician seduces a slave in his household, Eumaeus' nurse, and, after a year of preparing for their escape together by gathering wealth, sends her a messenger:

> ἀλλ' ὅτε δὴ κοίλη νηῦς ἤχθετο τοῖσι νέεσθαι,
> καὶ τότ' ἄρ' ἄγγελον ἧκαν, ὃς ἀγγείλειε γυναικί.

> But when at last the hollow ship was loaded for them to go,
> just then they sent a messenger, who was to bring word to the
>   woman.
>
> *Odyssey* 15.457–458

This messenger, an *anēr poluidris* (459), nods to the woman, and she bolts for the Phoenician ship, abducting Eumaeus to pay her fare.[194] This is how Eumaeus came to be in the house of Odysseus.

This disturbing tale derives part of its effect from the way it recycles the theme of the woman, the deceptive Phoenician, and the *poluidris* messenger. Yet the effect of this story is not to ring one more change upon these themes and to condemn the woman responsible. Instead, the script brilliantly interweaves story and performance, the stories exchanged within the story-world with the presences produced in the performer, to induce a severe ethical disorientation both for the audience and, as we shall see, for Odysseus. This disorientation haunts the remainder of the poem with its ostensibly triumphalist conclusion. Such haunting is on a different level from the winking hints of a centrifugal protagonist brewing in the Cretan Tales.

Eumaeus tells his story only in response to Odysseus' request. Odysseus (the stranger) has inquired about his own mother and father (15.347–350). Eumaeus tells Odysseus what he already knows from his visit to Hades. Eumaeus emphasizes Laertes' wish to die, because of his grief for his absent child (he laments him, 355, as though dead) and his dead wife—which brings Eumaeus to the story of Antikleia's own grief-induced death. This theme of parents dying out of grief for their child is important enough within Odysseus' own story. However, since

---

[192] 20.88–90. Penelope dreams of someone who is the *eikelos* of Odysseus, while the stranger himself looks just about how Odysseus must look, since misfortunes age mortals quickly (19.358–360); Eurykleia has never seen anyone who looked and sounded so much like Odysseus (19.379–381).

[193] Felson 1994; Murnaghan 1987; Katz 1991.

[194] She assures the Phoenicians the clever toddler will sell for μυρίον ὦνον, "an exorbitant price," 452.

Odysseus' return is now in progress, there is another set of parents whose grief now becomes more salient: the noble parents of the kidnapped, enslaved Eumaeus.

The shift to the matter of Eumaeus' parents is made by a series of canny, but seemingly artless, steps. After mentioning Antikleia's death, Eumaeus says that it used to be dear to him to go to *her* and "question and answer" (15.362): Antikleia played for him a role now being played by Penelope. Backing up a step in time, he reveals that Antikleia raised him together with Odysseus' sister Ktimene.[195] Since Odysseus' Cretan persona, though a bastard, was honored *no less* by his father than his legitimate children (14.203), it is awful when Eumaeus lets on that dear mistress Antikleia honored him "only a little less" (15.365) than Ktimene. Proceeding forward again in time, the two children reach *hēbē*: for Ktimene there is marriage and gifts; for Eumaeus there is a cloak, a chiton, and some clothes, to be sure; some sandals; and "fieldward she dispatched me. And/but she loved me [all the?] more in her heart." (ἀγρόνδε προίαλλε· φίλει δέ με κηρόθι μᾶλλον, 15.370). Now, via the transition through time to the current mistress, Penelope, Eumaeus layers his present lack of access to mistress and palace on top of the mild banishment he received when he reached *hēbē*. He makes the transition through the familiar theme of the gods "increasing his work" (372), which work provides a bit of solace in the form of food and drink for himself, and of "giving to revered folk" (373), an opportunity to nod to his audience. In contrast to this mutual relationship with the gods, a different situation obtains with the current mistress of the house, which Eumaeus expresses in a curious fashion.

> ἐκ δ' ἄρα δεσποίνης οὐ μείλιχον ἔστιν ἀκοῦσαι
> οὔτ' ἔπος οὔτε τι ἔργον, ἐπεὶ κακὸν ἔμπεσεν οἴκῳ,
> ἄνδρες ὑπερφίαλοι· μέγα δὲ δμῶες χατέουσιν
> ἀντία δεσποίνης φάσθαι καὶ ἕκαστα πυθέσθαι
> καὶ φαγέμεν πιέμεν τε, ἔπειτα δὲ καί τι φέρεσθαι
> ἀγρόνδ', οἷά τε θυμὸν ἀεὶ δμώεσσιν ἰαίνει.

Literally:

> And, you see, from the mistress, it is not *meilichon* [pleasant] to hear
> either word or deed, since evil has fallen on the house,
> *hyperphialoi* [haughty] men. Greatly do the domestics miss
> talking opposite the mistress and finding everything out
> and eating and drinking, and then too bringing something

---

[195] This is the only time we hear of Odysseus' sister in the poem, which otherwise emphasizes the single male line Laertes-Odysseus-Telemachus.

fieldward [cf. 370, also initial position], such as always warms the
spirit of domestics.

Odyssey 15.374–379

First of all, this lack of interaction with the queen is very odd, when we
know that Eumaeus is continuously bringing messages to Penelope. On the other
hand, he specifies elsewhere (14.378; see above) it is "no longer *philon*" to do so
for *him*—ever since the Aetolian's visit, whatever happened then! Here "it is not
meilichon," a word that in the context of messages seems to imply both that
any message he might get from the queen might not be pleasant to hear (and
meilichon itself may describe the "word or deed," rather than the "hearing"), and
that the speaker herself might no longer be "gentle," now that *hyperphialoi* men
have moved in.

Rather than take this obvious bait concerning the queen, however,[196]
Odysseus in his reply pursues instead the pitiful implications for Eumaeus
(emphasized by the repetition of ἀγρόνδ' in the concluding verse, 379). Indeed
it seems to be the first time Odysseus has ever considered the history of his
host, to whose perspective he, as the Cretan, seemed so fantastically oblivious
in Cretan Tale 2. He exclaims:

ὦ πόποι, ὡς ἄρα τυτθὸς ἐών, Εὔμαιε συβῶτα,
πολλὸν ἀπεπλάγχθης σῆς πατρίδος ἠδὲ τοκήων.
ἀλλ' ἄγε μοι τόδε εἰπὲ καὶ ἀτρεκέως κατάλεξον,
ἠὲ διεπράθετο πτόλις ἀνδρῶν εὐρυάγυια,
ἧ ἔνι ναιετάασκε πατὴρ καὶ πότνια μήτηρ,
ἦ σέ γε μουνωθέντα παρ' οἴεσιν ἢ παρὰ βουσὶν
ἄνδρες δυσμενέες νηυσὶν λάβον ἠδ' ἐπέρασσαν
τοῦδ' ἀνδρὸς πρὸς δώμαθ', ὁ δ' ἄξιον ὦνον ἔδωκε.

O popoi, how little you were, swineherd Eumaeus,
when you were driven far from your fatherland and your
parents!
But come, tell me this and tally it precisely,
was it ravaged by men—the town with wide ways,
in which your father lived and your mistress mother,

---

[196] Another moment to imagine performance. Nothing extraordinary need be done, but the
performer may pause while the audience wonders whether he, becoming Odysseus (or receding
back into Odysseus), will pursue the bait. Instead he realizes, at long last, the humanity of
his interlocutor: he has parents and a past. This through-line can be fruitful for performance
whether or not we imagine the actual Odysseus already knew (and incorporated into his own
Tale) Eumaeus' story.

or while you were alone among sheep or cattle
did hostile men take you in ships and cross you over
<u>to the house of this man, and he gave a worthy price?</u>
Odyssey 15.381–388

Once again Odysseus uses a phrase that seems to invite Eumaeus to recognize him: τοῦδ' ἀνδρὸς is "an expression often used in Greek poetry by the speaker in reference to himself."[197] Stanford *ad loc.* calls this "a daring ambiguity to make the audience gasp." How should this be played? Does Odysseus, beneath his disguise, know this story already, reaching back to his childhood?[198] What tone does the performer adopt when Odysseus *ptoliporthos* asks whether Eumaeus is here because his city was sacked? Last but not least, I note the "worthy price" that ends the speech, which occurs only here and in Eumaeus' reply, just a few lines later[199] (see below). Eumaeus will in fact "quote" this entire line.

Eumaeus begins his speech with a double move, setting the scene of his own performance and the scene of the beginning of his own story, his own life. Both are isolated places of eating, drinking, and telling tales that one finds in scenes of the afterlife and of the golden age. First he sets up the space of performance as a kind of endless night. His rhythms and repetitions make clear to his audience that they are in for a long, important tale of woe that is a break from what has gone before and settle them in comfortably. His introduction forms a ring-composition (390–402)[200] focused on the idea of sleep (394 καταλέχθαι verbally echoes 383 κατάλεξον). He invites anyone whose *thumos* so bids them to go out to sleep (396). Meanwhile "we two" will take pleasure in drinking, eating and delighting in each other's woes, remembering them: "for even among pains a man takes pleasure, who has suffered very much and wandered far (πολλὰ πάθη καὶ πόλλ' ἐπαληθῇ)" (15.400–401). Here is the second use of this pair of words that conjure up the ideas of deception and truth.[201] The νύκτες ἀθέσφατοι he refers to in line 392, like the stormy night during which Odysseus begins his cloak tale, indicate the longest nights of the year, the nights around the winter

---

[197] Ahl and Roisman 1996:185; cf. Bakker 2005:78, citing *Iliad* 19.140, and p. 82 on Hesiod *Theogony* 24 τόνδε δέ με, "this-here me."

[198] Louden (1997:101 with n42) notes that several commentators assume Odysseus' prior knowledge of Eumaeus' autobiography and even suggest that he modeled his own story, which is of course given first, upon it.

[199] 15.429; cf. *Odyssey* 20.383, ὅθεν κέ τοι ἄξιον ἄλφοι, "which would fetch a worthy sum for you."

[200] See Hoekstra in Heubeck and Hoekstra 1989 *ad loc.* A ἀνείρεαι ἠδὲ μετάλλᾳς (390) B delight (391) C drink (391) X sleep (392–396) C' drink (398) B' delight (399–401) A' ἀνείρεαι ἠδὲ μετάλλᾳς (402).

[201] Cf. above on 14.362, ὅσα δὴ πάθες ἠδ' ὅσ' ἀλήθης, "as much as you've suffered and as much as you've wandered." The pun admittedly works better in the present verse, where α precedes πάθη.

solstice. It would seem that the festival of Apollo, the *lykabas*, during which the bow-contest takes place, marks the first appearance of the moon following the solstice, or perhaps the first full moon.[202] Since Eumaeus is later emphatic that he has Odysseus for "three nights" (17.515), these are perhaps three moonless nights before the new appearance of the moon. We are now in the middle of that three-night sequence.[203]

Eumaeus' performance takes place in a winter solstice period. But Eumaeus also sets his *story* in a solstice—now conceived of as a place rather than a time.

> νῆσός τις Συρίη κικλήσκεται, εἴ που ἀκούεις,
> Ὀρτυγίης καθύπερθεν, ὅθι τροπαὶ ἠελίοιο,
> οὔ τι περιπληθὴς λίην τόσον, ἀλλ' ἀγαθὴ μέν,
> εὔβοτος, εὔμηλος, οἰνοπληθής, πολύπυρος.
> πείνη δ' οὔ ποτε δῆμον ἐσέρχεται, οὐδέ τις ἄλλη
> νοῦσος ἐπὶ στυγερὴ πέλεται δειλοῖσι βροτοῖσιν·
> ἀλλ' ὅτε γηράσκωσι πόλιν κάτα φῦλ' ἀνθρώπων,
> ἐλθὼν ἀργυρότοξος Ἀπόλλων Ἀρτέμιδι ξὺν
> οἷς ἀγανοῖς βελέεσσιν ἐποιχόμενος κατέπεφνεν.
> ἔνθα δύω πόλιες, δίχα δέ σφισι πάντα δέδασται·
> τῆσιν δ' ἀμφοτέρῃσι πατὴρ ἐμὸς ἐμβασίλευε,
> Κτήσιος Ὀρμενίδης, ἐπιείκελος ἀθανάτοισιν.

> There is a certain island called Syrie—perhaps you've heard
>   of it:
> above Ortygia, where are the turnings of the sun.
> Not at all too populous, but good:
> good for grazing, good for flocks, full of wine, lots of wheat.
> Hunger never approaches the people, nor does any other
> illness come around, chilling for poor mortals.
> But when they get old, the tribes of folks in this city,

---

[202] The essential discussion is Austin 1975:245.

[203] Cf. page 192 with Figure 14 above on the embassy occupying the calendrical center of the *Iliad*, with one month preceding and following. Taplin (1992:19, 29–30 and passim) hypothesizes that the *Iliad* was created to be performed over the course of three nights, whereas the *Odyssey* splits into two parts, which, he says, might count against his theory (p. 19). Yet this mention of three nights, in the context of telling stories, seems to fit with a three-day scheme. Simply dividing the *Odyssey* into three parts of eight books each, the Book 15 story comes near the end of the middle night. On the dovetailing between hero and bard with respect to performance time in African epic performance, see Martin 1989:234. On the "three days" motif in tragedy and ritual, see Buxton 2003:176–177.

approaching, silver-bowed Apollo, with Artemis,
with their gentle arrows plying, put to death.
There are two cities, and every thing is divided in twain:
and of them both my father was the king,
Ktesios son of Ormenos, like to the immortals.

Odyssey 15.403–414

Eumaeus' homeland, Syrie, is set at the τροπαὶ ἠελίοιο, "turnings of the sun" (15.404), that point on the eastern horizon where the sun rises at the winter solstice: where it "turns around" and comes north again.[204] The fact that, elsewhere in hexameter, τροπαὶ ἠελίοιο refers only to a time[205] makes the location all the more fantastic, as does the way it is layered on top of the current point in time: the very turning of the year itself. "I am from right now, the turning-point." This is the turning point. A setting at a point on the horizon indicates emphatically the fairy-tale nature of his home.[206] Eumaeus follows this up with golden-age imagery: the fertility and the absence of evil in Syrie, and the fact that Apollo and Artemis kill the inhabitants when they grow old with "gentle arrows." This detail will recur in what follows.[207]

The evil that descends upon this idyllic world comes in the form of ravening Phoenicians, living up to their stereotype as "gobbling" (τρῶκται, 416) merchants who deceive women by dangling trinkets in their faces. One of the Phoenicians seduces a Phoenician slave woman in Eumaeus' house. Eumaeus begins her story thus, clearly focusing our attention on her as a new starting point:

ἔσκε δὲ πατρὸς ἐμοῖο γυνὴ Φοίνισσ᾿ ἐνὶ οἴκῳ,
καλή τε μεγάλη τε καὶ ἀγλαὰ ἔργ᾿ εἰδυῖα·

There was in the house of my father a Phoenician woman,
beautiful and tall and knowing splendid works.

Odyssey 15.417–418

---

[204] So Hoekstra in Heubeck and Hoekstra 1989 *ad loc.*; Levaniouk 2011:314–315. Contra, Kirk, Raven and Schofield 1983:52–54 and n3 (citing Lorimer), who believe the phrase indicates the direction from which the sun rises at the summer solstice.

[205] *Works and Days* 564, 663 (line-end); *Works and Days* 479 (mid-line).

[206] On Syrie as a paradise, see Louden 1999:54 with n23; Segal 1994:170. Levaniouk (2011:313–315) notes the connection of "Ortygia" (15.404) with Artemis and especially her killing of Orion with "gentle arrows" (*Odyssey* 5.125–126), a passage resonating with the description of Syrie, with Artemis' killing of Eumaeus' nurse, and also with Idas' abduction of Marpessa, from (according to Simonides, *PMG* 563) Ortygia.

[207] Eumaeus' father "Ktesios Ormenides" is reminiscent of a "lord of death" figure: Heckenlively 2007. For other work on comparative mythology bearing on Eumaeus, see below.

Surprisingly, the woman receives the full-hexameter description character-istic of Athena.[208] Eumaeus does not blame her particularly,[209] except that she, as a member of the female race, has a weakness for sex:

πλυνούσῃ τις πρῶτα μίγη κοίλῃ παρὰ νηΐ
εὐνῇ καὶ φιλότητι, τά τε φρένας ἠπεροπεύει
θηλυτέρῃσι γυναιξί, καὶ ἥ κ' εὐεργὸς ἔῃσιν.

First, as she was washing, someone mingled with her by a hollow
    ship
in bed and in love, which beguile the minds
of tender women, even one ever so good at her work.

Odyssey 15.420–422

After they make love in the ship, the Phoenician asks the woman, called simply "Phoenissa," where she is from. It turns out that she, like Eumaeus, comes from a wealthy father. She became a slave when Taphian pirates abducted her while she was coming from the field. She ends her life-story thus:

ἀλλά μ' ἀνήρπαξαν Τάφιοι ληΐστορες ἄνδρες
ἀγρόθεν ἐρχομένην, πέρασαν δέ με δεῦρ' ἀγαγόντες
τοῦδ' ἀνδρὸς πρὸς δώμαθ'· ὁ δ' ἄξιον ὦνον ἔδωκε. [= 388]

But Taphian pirate-men seized me
as I was coming from the field, and sold me, bringing me here
to the house of this man: and he gave a worthy price.

Odyssey 15.427–429

When the performer-as-Eumaeus utters these lines, he is looking at his audience—at us and at Odysseus—and echoing the last line of Odysseus' inquiry: how did you come "to the house of this man, and he gave a worthy price" (line 388)? Eumaeus has fashioned a story in which he "becomes" a woman who utters the cold line of Odysseus (a line that does not appear elsewhere in Homer). The woman is either already saying this line ironically, or the Phoenician is still in the process of tapping her buried resentment, her feeling that the price was not at all what she is "worth." The performer/Eumaeus himself may or may

---

[208] 13.289, which many scholars (e.g. Stanford 1996 *ad loc.*) take to be Athena's "authentic" or "normal" appearance. It is this Athena who has sent Odysseus to Eumaeus to ask him "every-thing" (13.411). One hesitates to credit Athena with this intervention of Eumaeus, but there is the line. Eumaeus then would ventriloquize (see below) an Athena-like figure (or, perhaps, vice versa) in the course of telling Odysseus "everything." On this appearance of Athena, see Pucci 1995:105–108, with bibliography on the question of "authenticity."

[209] Cf. Segal 1994:171–172. Contrast Benardete 1997:118.

not convey that quality in the tone of his voice, but he has managed to project Odysseus' speech into the voice of someone for whom it is unsettlingly *atopon*.[210] The pointed nature of the speech is somehow enhanced by the fact that Eumaeus was obviously not present to hear it, and may seem to have contrived it for the present circumstance.

If he repeats any gesture "Odysseus" (that is, himself as Odysseus) has made to accompany the deictic τοῦδ' ἀνδρὸς, the speech suddenly collapses into a direct, pointed, indictment of "this-here man" who owns the house in which or near which we are listening to the story—a man who believes his family has paid a worthy price for a human being.[211] (Such a gesture is in fact part of Eumaeus' story: the nurse Phoenissa "points out" the house of Eumaeus' father [15.424, πατρὸς ἐπέφραδεν ὑψερεφὲς δῶ] before telling her countryman the story of her own abduction. Perhaps this makes more likely the presence of significant gestures within the story.) We recall that Eumaeus has begun by collapsing the "time" of the performance (the winter solstice) with the "place" of his story (the solstice-point). Here he has reprised and condensed this collapse into the phrase τοῦδ' ἀνδρὸς.

It is this woman who will proceed to abduct the toddler Eumaeus. The Phoenicians spend a year accumulating wealth from the people of Syrie, following an agreement between the lovers not to communicate. Finally a *polyidris* man arrives to signal to the woman that she is to come away with him at once. She whisks up Eumaeus, along with some fine tableware, as the "price" of her journey (453): Eumaeus *is* the worthy price of the woman's freedom. Because he is "so clever" (or "profitable": κερδαλέον, like Odysseus[212]), the woman suggests to the Phoenicians that they will get μυρίον ὦνον by selling him:

> κερδαλέον δὴ τοῖον, ἅμα τροχόωντα θύραζε·
> τόν κεν ἄγοιμ' ἐπὶ νηός, ὁ δ' ὑμῖν μυρίον ὦνον
> ἄλφοι, ὅπῃ περάσητε κατ' ἀλλοθρόους ἀνθρώπους.

> so clever/profitable is he, running along outside:
> him I can bring on board, and he would fetch you an exorbitant
>   price,
> wherever you sell him among foreign peoples.

Odyssey 15.451–453

---

[210] Let the reader perform the speech, with its antecedents, for an audience, and try to contain the power of Eumaeus launching Odysseus' line into the mouth of this slave woman.

[211] If the poem is performed by a bard for a wealthy patron, the screw is turned once again. Cf. the *Sirat Bani Hilal* poets focusing criticism on their despised patrons (Reynolds 1995, esp. 74–87).

[212] Cf. Louden 1997:111.

During the voyage the woman abruptly dies. Because of the insistence upon the Phoenicians' duplicitousness, the cause of the woman's death, struck by Artemis, seems like the product of Eumaeus' childish fantasy. She is dumped overboard; Eumaeus poignantly says, "then I was left alone, grieving at heart" (αὐτὰρ ἐγὼ λιπόμην ἀκαχήμενος ἦτορ, 15.481). In this affecting line (which is also the last phrase of Odysseus' Cretan Tale to Athena, 13.286), the nurse's death is seen from the perspective of a toddler who does not understand he is being abducted. Eumaeus concludes:

τοὺς δ' Ἰθάκῃ ἐπέλασσε φέρων ἄνεμός τε καὶ ὕδωρ,
ἔνθα με Λαέρτης πρίατο κτεάτεσσιν ἑοῖσιν.
οὕτω <u>τήνδε τε</u> γαῖαν ἐγὼν ἴδον ὀφθαλμοῖσι.

The wind and the water brought them near to Ithaka,
where Laertes bought me with his goods.
That is the way I came to see <u>this</u> land with my eyes.
Odyssey 15.482–484

This time Eumaeus does not include "worthy price" in the description of Laertes' transaction. "*That* is the way *I saw this land* with my eyes," he says in summary, adding a generalizing[213] τε: as any abandoned boy, on the brink of slavery, would see it. Not like you wanted it seen, one might add. The phrase "this land" (484), echoing the repeated line "to the house of this man," brings the story to a pointed close. This poignant, pregnant line (one sees Ithaka, looming on the western horizon) encompasses the insight listeners, including Odysseus, have gained into slavery, now seen as an endless cycle of "paying the price" for a human being.[214]

Eumaeus has conveyed this message by turning the tables on Odysseus, drawing on his words and projecting them into the mouth of the dead Phoenissa. At the same time, he projects the phrase "this man" onto another plane to show what "the house of this man" really is. Eumaeus has ceased to be an obstacle to be overcome, or a mere "guide to the underworld" in the manner of Circe.[215] He has passed a judgment upon Odysseus; he has shown him what he is and what manner of institution he seeks to restore.

---

[213] The phrase τήνδε τε γαῖαν does occur also at 13.238; for Hoekstra in Heubeck and Hoekstra 1989 *ad loc.* following Ruijgh the τε is a mere "metrical stop-gap."

[214] Eumaeus, whose name brings him into connection with his nurse, is structurally in the position of Leukos, who kills the wife and child of Idomeneus; meanwhile both men are anxiously awaiting the arrival of Telemachus.

[215] In Celtic tradition "the guise adopted by the Lord of the Otherworld Feast was that of a man carrying a pig, in effect a swineherd" (Chatháin 1979/1980:201 with n6).

Such a statement seems at odds with the events to follow. Eumaeus does, of course, go on to support Odysseus and is key to the restoration of the righteous king. And although he is made to seem gentler than the other "good" herdsman Philoitios, Eumaeus will taunt the goatherd Melanthios, the "bad" slave, before cruelly torturing him to death on Odysseus' instructions.[216] Eumaeus even owns a slave, Mesaulios, rendering incongruous his sophisticated "dialectical" critique of slavery.[217]

This one slave-woman's plight, her speech, and the extreme compression of this one line of hers, hangs over the scene as a troubling presence. In this she is close kin to the freshly widowed woman being led into slavery by Odysseus, whose grief bursts through Odysseus and the bard in Book 8, leaving no trace on Odysseus' subsequent speech, no ripple upon his consciousness, perhaps until he asks Eumaeus for his life story. Once we the audience have been in the "you" seat to receive Phoenissa's line, we cannot be entirely comfortable with the notion that what we are witnessing is the restoration to power of the god-blessed monarch, even though that is on the face of it how it is presented. This reaction of the audience, carefully calibrated by the poet, has not been more generally recognized because the power of the line in performance, the collapsing of spaces and times that conveys, among other things, the horrific cycle of slavery, has been overlooked, as though it were merely another repetition of a formula.[218] But, just as Odysseus constantly picks up phrases from Eumaeus and weaves

---

[216] Hankey notes (1985:32) that the last time Eumaeus is apostrophized is in the introduction to these mocking words, 22.194.

[217] There is a parallel to the "presentification" and withdrawal of Eumaeus in Thompson's (1999:190) discussion of the novels of Iris Murdoch and their similarity to Platonic dialogue: "Readers of *The Book and the Brotherhood* ... may be chastened at the eventual realization that they have cast off all of the characters they had been identifying with throughout the tale, whereas the good character perished before anyone fathomed his presence." In the *Odyssey*, the good character, Eumaeus, continues to be present while failing to evince his superior qualities. For Thompson, Murdoch "thwarts our inclination for easy identification with her characters" and "spurns the solace of the bardic poet." Plato and Murdoch provide a dialectic unavailable in Homer, who exemplifies the "easy read" (p. 196). But the present episode is not an "easy read" or an "easy listen"; I suggested in the Introduction that Plato did not hold this view of Homer either.

[218] The line is not heard outside of these two instances. Pucci's 1995 "Afterword" is a brief overview of the variety of ways Homeric repetitions are meaningful. His example of Thetis calling Achilles ὠκύμορος "swift-fated" (1.417) a few lines after Achilles' epithet πόδας ὠκύς "swift-footed" is heard can serve as an example of a formula being used for *ēthopoiia* (on which see Martin 1989). As Thetis picks up Achilles' epithet, so does Eumaeus pick up Odysseus' last line and incorporate it. A. B. Lord (2000:180) remarks that Eumaeus' story "should be part of a recognition scene between Eumaeus and Odysseus ... We have examples in the Yugoslav material in which the recounting of how someone came to know the hero ... is part of a recognition theme leading to the question, 'By what means would you recognize him if he were to appear?' Eumaeus' tale, then, may be a fragment of a recognition scene that is never completed, but is attracted to this position because such a scene is expected here."

them into his story, this is not the first time Eumaeus has strategically reused a line or phrase from Odysseus' mouth. In particular, as with "and he paid a worthy price," it is the very last word out of Odysseus' mouth (ἀλήθην, "I wandered," 14.118) that Eumaeus picks up at the beginning of their encounter, and develops a speech that uses the wordplay between wandering/wanderers (ἀλητεύων, ἀλῆται) and truth (ἀληθέα), cramming four forms of these words into five lines (14.122–126).[219] Eumaeus even goes so far as to take the idea of Odysseus' being seen in Crete at Idomeneus' palace and put it in the mouth of an Aetolian (which Aetolian is then reused by Odysseus in his Cloak Story).[220]

So Eumaeus' reuse of Odysseus' line is of a piece with their whole interaction. This interaction, then, bears some of the features, such as verse-capping, of poetic competitions of various kinds, likely including the competitions in which the Homeric poems took shape, but in any case prevalent throughout Greek poetic culture.[221] I do not suggest that Eumaeus and Odysseus were actually played by two separate rhapsodes. Like the "as-if" improvisation of the Cretan Tales, this seems to be a conversation within the world of the poem that incorporates or re-stages the practices that form it, rather than being evidence of an actual "seam" between rhapsodes. The last line of Odysseus that Eumaeus has masterfully re-cast into Phoenissa's mouth is something like the "cue" or idea (ὑποβολή) that one performer hands off for the next to do something with,[222] and indeed, to use in order to undercut the other. But I suggest the line works all the better coming out of one mouth rather than two, as the audience witnesses the transformation of the individual performer.

Somewhat similar is Antilokhos' speech to Achilles (*Iliad* 23.544–554), on which Martin comments, "As often in the *Iliad*, we get the impression that a character has heard the previous poetic narration: Antilokhos here seems to be throwing back at Achilles the latter's unique way of speaking about his possessions ..."[223] As Antilokhos plays Achilles, so too Eumaeus plays Odysseus; as Antilokhos throws Achilles' words back at him, so too Eumaeus and Odysseus.[224]

---

[219] This punning is characteristic of poetic competitions; see below.

[220] As noted above, the last phrase of Odysseus' first Cretan tale ends with the phrase αὐτὰρ ἐγὼ λιπόμην ἀκαχήμενος ἦτορ, "But I was left behind, grieving at heart," which, like the "and he paid a worthy price" line, also finds its way into Eumaeus' story (15.481) with a transformed effect. Of course, Eumaeus was not present for the first Cretan tale. But since it otherwise fits the pattern of the two men riffing off one another's speeches, it belongs somewhere along the spectrum of responsive echoes; see below n224.

[221] Collins 2004.

[222] Collins 2004, esp. 194–195.

[223] Martin 1989:188n71.

[224] Another example of one character "throwing back" another character's words at him after a long delay is Diomedes in *Iliad* 9.33 throwing Agamemnon's "as is fitting" (2.73); Martin 1989:24. Into a similar category goes Odysseus' omission of the last lines of Agamemnon's speech in his verbatim

This comparison to the "cue" used by competitive poets may ease doubts about the significance of the quoted line, and about audiences' attunement to such undermining quotation. The re-contextualizing of this line may also be compared with the passages discussed by Mark Edwards as "*Topos* and Transformation"[225]: the *topos* of "paying a worthy price" for a human being, at first a conventional motif, is transformed and expanded into a story that exposes or transforms its meaning. But noting a relationship with such transformations does not speak very precisely to the effect, or the weight, of the line. How much weight should be placed on the speech where Eumaeus "becomes" the unfortunate Phoenissa? To what can the speech be compared, in order to better assess its significance within the poem?

Eumaeus and Phoenix

An attentive reader of Chapter 2 and Interlude 1 will have realized that Eumaeus' speech bears a resemblance to the speech of Phoenix in *Iliad* 9. On the level of presence, Eumaeus becoming Phoenissa is a less histrionic (less "possessed") version of Phoenix becoming Kleopatra. Mythologically speaking (poetics/ *poiēsis*), it is also less elaborate, in that there is no intervening woman whose constellation of stories forms a bridge between the male storyteller and the sexually charged female truth-teller he ultimately vivifies, unlike the case of Phoenix and Kleopatra, whose mother Marpessa plays such a mediating role in Phoenix's "actorly" process. The speech of Eumaeus shows that Homeric poetry can deploy the same technique more subtly, confining his gestures to the

---

report to Achilles, and Achilles' suspicious response to this (9.312–313), despite not hearing Agamemnon; Nagy 1979:52. Cf. the two conversations between Athena and Zeus in Books 1 and 5 of the *Odyssey* when Athena is reminding Zeus about Odysseus, on which see Segal 1994:124. Zeus repeats a line from the earlier conversation (5.22=1.64), but omits the line that followed, about forgetting Odysseus. That line, however, is recalled by Athena, who reshapes the line, substituting memory for forgetting (5.11, 1.65). There is then a spectrum running from one speech that directly responds to another (Martin 1989:156n28, citing Lohmann 1970:131–182), to delayed responses such as Diomedes' to Agamemnon, to echoes of the last line of a speech by a character who did not witness that speech. The fact of traditional formulaic diction does not mean that we should only pay attention to echoes at the most obvious end of the spectrum, even though we will not all agree which examples belong at the other end as opposed to being insignificant (cf. the complaint of R. Friedrich [2011:279] that Achilles did not hear Agamemnon's speech). On Homeric cross-referencing more generally, see Nagy 2003:7–19, especially p. 16: any "cross-reference that we admire in our two-dimensional text did not just happen one time in performance, but presumably countless times in countless reperformances within the three-dimensional continuum of a specialized oral tradition." The capping practices discussed by Collins 2004 entail that the ancient audience would generally be more, not less, attuned to such throwing-back of words than we are. For another rich example of a responsive speech with significant variation, see Pucci 1993 on Achilles' lament as a response to Briseis'. See also Martin 2000.

[225] Edwards 1987b.

indication of "the house of this man" as opposed to Phoenix's banging of earth, grasping of knees, and the like.

Nevertheless the two speeches are intertwined in terms of their speakers, performance, underlying mythology, and their place in their respective poems.[226]

In each speech, a loyal retainer of the major hero of the poem offers a story that turns out to be more than it appears. Each speaker has served as foster-father: Phoenix of Achilles, Eumaeus[227] of Odysseus' son Telemachus. The affectionate term ἄττα, "papa, foster-father" is used only of Phoenix and Eumaeus in Homer.[228] Eumaeus' reunion with Telemachus is marked by the simile about the father reunited with his only son after a long absence (16.17–21). Later of course Odysseus' and Telemachus' shrill cries of reunion are figured as those of birds being robbed of their fledglings (16.216–219).

Each speaker is a figure of subordinate status who describes, in his lengthy speech, how he came to live in the home of the hero. In fact, Odysseus, with his notion of a "worthy price," seems to be fishing for a story along the lines of Phoenix finding sanctuary with Peleus, as though the slave Eumaeus were a kind of Phoenix, awarded an entire people to rule instead of a herd of pigs.

Each speaker "becomes" a woman who turns out to be strangely sympathetic. "Strangely" in Eumaeus' case, because it is she who abducts him, but she is only trying to undo the damage Eumaeus' family has done by purchasing her. "Strangely" in Phoenix's case, because the woman (at risk of abduction) utters a truth entirely at odds with Phoenix's purpose. The woman in each speech thus speaks a truth at odds with the rhetorical ends of a man: Kleopatra undermines Phoenix; Phoenissa undermines Odysseus.[229]

Each story takes place in a dwelling that has hints of the underworld: Eumaeus' endless night at the dead of winter solstice, Achilles' House of Hades.[230]

Each speaker presides over a turning point or threshold for the hero: Phoenix is trying to get Achilles out to the battlefield; Eumaeus provides escort for Odysseus into the palace.

Both Phoenix and Eumaeus, moreover, allude to the myth of Alkyone and Keux. The raped Marpessa used to cry like the halcyon bird. In Eumaeus' speech, the

---

[226] Scodel (2002:155–172) pairs Eumaeus and Phoenix as "outstanding instances of the rhetorics of traditionality and inclusion." The way these characters are introduced in the poem produces a puzzle for the listener, which is then solved in the course of the story and produces certain effects.

[227] Etymologically, Eumaeus' name seems to refer to this role. Cf. Peradotto 1990:107.

[228] Rose 1980:296n28, citing Chantraine 1968–1980, ἄττα: "… Le sens originel pourrait être 'père nourricier.'"

[229] Both women undermine Odysseus, since Phoenix shares the mission of the city-sacker in *Iliad* 9. And both truths concern slavery—though Kleopatra also includes the killing of men and the burning of a city.

[230] See above, page 207n39.

Phoenician sailors dump Phoenissa into the sea and she falls "like a *kēx*" (15.479), *kēx* being another word for *kēux*. This bit of allusive mythology thus falls into place in a series of other links between the two speeches involving solar myth.[231]

The myth of the married couple Alkyone and Keux is the solstice myth par excellence: Alkyone, in the form of the *alkyōn*/halcyon bird, breeds at the winter solstice, during the fourteen "halcyon days" in the middle of winter storms. Eumaeus tells his story in such an environment and situates his homeland at the solstice point; he also situates Phoenissa's death "as Zeus made the seventh day" of their voyage (15.477); her death, which is the beginning of Eumaeus' life of slavery, comes perhaps at the midpoint of the halcyon days.

Odysseus is arriving in the midst of this winter storm, from all signs the fire to light the darkness, the sun returning to restore fertility and righteousness to the kingdom, a theoxenic god come to judge the hospitality of the people during the Lykabas feast of Apollo.[232] In dramatic counterpoint to this schema is a slave woman who utters her truth and expires at the very turning point of the sun.

While Eumaeus' story, and Odysseus' return, is set at the winter solstice, and Odysseus' vengeance unfolds during a Lykabas festival for Apollo, whatever that was, the *Odyssey* itself may have been performed during a solstice as well. Erwin Cook interprets the Ithakan section of the poem against the background of the "Athenian New Year Festival," using Burkert's interpretation of the festivals surrounding the Panathenaia, where the *Odyssey* was performed. As Cook notes, there is a discrepancy with the Athenian New Year in that the *Odyssey*'s events unfold at the winter solstice, whereas the Athenian New Year begins around the summer solstice. But other cities and regions, including Delos, began their year at the winter solstice.[233] It is possible that the *Odyssey* was developed in performance at a solstice festival, and even a winter solstice festival.[234] Certainly, the

---

[231] See Chapter 2, page 139, on the version of the story in which Keux dies in a shipwreck. This simile of the *kēx* to describe Phoenissa's dying at sea and being dumped overboard perhaps refers to this version of the story. Of course, the mere reference to the *kēx* may not be enough to trigger the story; it is when we see how it falls into the overall parallel between Eumaeus and Phoenix, and the overarching patterns of Phoenix's speech, that this reference takes on meaning. Levaniouk (2011:315) mentions the *kēx* simile in the course of discussing the solar myths in the second half of the *Odyssey*; she also links it to the myth of Idas and Marpessa.

[232] Flaumenhaft 1982; Kearns 1982; Austin 1975; Frame 1978.

[233] Cook 1995:146.

[234] Levaniouk 2008, after acknowledging the theory that the festival of Apollo within the poem is a New Year festival (p. 29), cites the indications of spring noted by Austin, and mentions the return of Apollo to Delphi in early spring (p. 33). See Levaniouk's (2011:15–16) sensible discussion of the *Odyssey*'s relation to New Year and solar myth complexes. Levaniouk 2011 is focused on the mythological resonances between *Odyssey* 19–20 (along with the bird-mythology associated with Penelope) and the festival of Apollo within the poem.

Alkyone-Keux story should find a place in such a schema, yet neither Cook nor Austin note the allusion.[235]

The *Iliad*, as we saw, integrates the theme of the solstice into the structure of Phoenix's speech. The solstice is a turning point, a burst of fertility in the dead of winter: a return. Likewise, Phoenix approaches the center of a ring composition and finds there the compressed story of the rape of Marpessa, a coiled energy that springs forth later from the *phrēn* of Kleopatra. The ring composition echoes the figure of the winter solstice.

Both speeches are crucial to their poems, explicitly giving voice to what is suppressed by the reigning ideology,[236] if that is what it is, of sacking cities, using the resulting women as tokens of honor and slaves, and returning to restore order to a slave-owning society. Each poem undermines that ideology in several other ways, but in these two speeches, the performer, through a male character, gradually approaches and embodies the voice of a woman who simply tells the unadorned truth.[237] Each is the undertow of the force driving the plot of each poem.

Rendering judgment is, moreover, central to both Eumaeus and Phoenix outside of the two speeches under comparison. Both men preside over events

---

[235] The association between Odysseus and the returning sun is clear. But there may also be a connection to the phoenix-bird in particular (single male line, etc.). I do not recall an ancient text that makes the connection, but in Monteverdi's *Il ritorno d'Ulisse in patria*, Penelope calls Ulysses her Phoenix.

Illustratevi, o Cieli,
rinfioratevi, o prati!
Aure, gioite!
Gli augelletti cantando,
i rivi mormorando
or si rallegrino!
Quell'erbe verdeggianti,
quell'onde sussurranti,
or si consolino!
Già ch'è sorta felice,
dal cenere troian,
la mia Fenice!

For the analogous association between Odysseus/Penelope and Alkyone/Keux, see Levaniouk 1999 and 2011: Ch. 17.

[236] Scodel (2002:172) makes a similar point about Eumaeus, based on the puzzle created initially by his epithet and the way he is introduced. The poet "accents the disjunction between the heroic stature of Eumaeus ... and his actual social position ... The poet ... places Eumaeus firmly within the tradition. By implying that everyone knows this story already, the poet avoids responsibility for it and declines to draw any moral for the real world. By distancing the implications of the character from himself, he makes the potential message even more powerful, for its authority is not his but the tradition's. He also reduces the danger of offending elite members of the audience. The bard's work is a continual exercise in discretion."

[237] In this they are akin to Thersites ("the only person who speaks honestly in [the assembly] is Thersites, the incarnation of the ugly truth," Whitman 1958:261), who still sometimes has trouble getting heard.

in each poem's closing action. Both events are athletic contests with solar associations.[238] Phoenix is positioned by Achilles as a judge for the chariot race in the funeral games for Patroklos (23.358–361) on a lookout at the turning point "so that he might remember the runnings and report back the truth about the race." Phoenix performs the ring-compositional speech par excellence, then largely disappears, only to reemerge standing at the center of the ring-compositional race par excellence. Eumaeus is put in charge of the bow for the contest in *Odyssey* 21, finally putting it into the hands of Odysseus.

Eumaeus as Judge

It has been argued, based on comparative evidence from the Iranian and Celtic traditions, that this act of Eumaeus is part of his function of certifying the rightful king.[239] Thus Eumaeus' judging function is not merely a later development of epic, but is rooted in very ancient structures and themes.

Eumaeus' status as a judge, or overseer, comes to light when he is first introduced by Athena (13.405).[240] There he is called ὑῶν ἐπίουρος. The significance of ἐπίουρος emerges at *Iliad* 13.450, where Zeus engenders Minos as Κρήτῃ ἐπίουρον. Eumaeus guards and protects the pigs, and then "judges well the best of the swine" for the suitors every day, and having judged it, sends it away to its death (14.108 καί σφι συῶν τὸν ἄριστον ἐῢ κρίνας ἀποπέμπω). He is then a figure, for pigs, similar to the underworld judge Rhadamanthys, whom the Phaeacians once escorted to Euboia to "look over" (ἐποψόμενον 7.324) Tityus, presumably to judge him and to escort him to his death. Warning against taking "the best of the pigs" as parody, Jamison[241] notes the association of the boar with kingship in Indian tradition, and the fact that the usual word for "pig" (σῦς / ὗς) in the *Odyssey* is the same as the word for "boar." In fact, Jamison sees the large role allotted to Eumaeus "not as mere window-dressing but as a subtle underlining of the kingship theme."[242] Aside from the bow contest itself, Jamison lists many convincing parallels within Indian myth and ritual associated with kingship for many seemingly ordinary actions in the second half of the *Odyssey*, including many actions taken by Eumaeus, such his sandal-making when Odysseus first sees him (14.23). As Poli points to parallels for Eumaeus' role in the bow contest within the Iranian and Celtic traditions, so too Jamison

---

[238] See Interlude 1. A. B. Lord (2000:186) notes the parallel function of contests or games in the respective withdrawal/devastation/return plots of the two poems.

[239] Poli 1984, 1992.

[240] This line is repeated at 15.39, in the corresponding speech of Athena to Telemachus.

[241] Jamison 1999:267–268.

[242] Jamison 1999:267.

finds a precise parallel for Eumaeus' placing the bow in Odysseus' hands (*Odyssey* 21.378–379; cf. 234–235) in Sanskrit ritual texts.[243]

Although these parallels, which would have Eumaeus' role in the poem point back to a ceremonial king-certifier, are convincing, they do not encompass the entirety of his role. The figure of Eumaeus combines aspects of several roles seen elsewhere in myth. As I showed above, the paradoxical language at the beginning of Book 14, along with the solar imagery of Eumaeus' resemblance to Circe and the 360 boars who sleep outside the pens, indicate that Eumaeus in some sense has custody not only of Odysseus' livelihood but of his life: the *days* of his life. Eumaeus even tallies Odysseus' ζωή ('life') (14.96–104) in a passage that resembles Circe's description of Thrinacia with its solar herds (12.127–131). Such a speech recalls wisdom traditions in which counting out the days of a human being's life teaches about mortality, such as Solon's advice to Croesus (Herodotus 1.32) or Utnapishtim's sleep test for Gilgamesh.[244] All of this points to Eumaeus as both a judge and an allotter of *biotos*. This role extends beyond a ceremonial certifier of the rightful king, as with some of the parallel Indo-European traditions, to that of a judge and instructor.

And it is precisely about the value of a human life (cf. also the weighing of souls, *psychostasia*), about the price (ὦνος) for a human being, that Eumaeus teaches Odysseus. Eumaeus, by "becoming" the slave Phoenissa, shows Odysseus that a price paid for a human being, rather than being fair or worthy (ἄξιος), instead leads to endless attempts to right the balance. In this he is the converse of Phoenix. On the one hand, Phoenix does not want Achilles to "abandon" him by leaving Troy (cf. Eumaeus "abandoned" by Phoenissa, 15.481); on the other hand, he is attempting to stir Achilles into battle where he will risk his life. Phoenix is explicit that he would not ask Achilles to return to battle if it were not for the gifts Agamemnon is offering. The way Phoenix ends the Meleager story, papering over Meleager's death with the statement that "he didn't get the gifts," emphasizes the weighing of Achilles' life against a material value. The goods are to compensate Achilles not only for Briseis, but for risking his life. So Phoenix's speech too, although there despite its speaker, ends by exposing the folly of compensation for human life. Both speeches, then, can be thought of as counterpoints to the comic situation in the beginning of *Odyssey* 13, where Odysseus is exposed as someone for whom treasure

---

[243] "Exactly as the Adhvaryu priest hands the bow to the king at his consecration, so does the faithful acolyte of Odysseus confer his token of kingship on his still-disguised lord with a physical gesture denied to the other contenders" (Jamison 1999:262).

[244] In *Gilgamesh* Tablet 11, Gilgamesh is told he may attain immortality if he can stay awake for seven days. Instead the hero falls asleep instantly, sleeping through all seven days, and is shown loaves of bread in varying states of decay that indicate the number of days he has been asleep. Cf. Psalm 90.

weighs more heavily than even his own life. Recall that, in *Iliad* 9, it is Odysseus who meticulously itemizes what Agamemnon thinks it should take for Achilles to once again risk his life.

Thus, while the second half of the *Odyssey* unfolds as a theoxeny with Odysseus as judge, or as a re-certification of the righteous king, the poem simultaneously casts Eumaeus in the role of judge, not only supervising the *biotos* of Odysseus' kingdom in his absence, but also rendering judgment upon that kingdom, its system of slavery (of paying an ἄξιος ὦνος for human beings), and Odysseus as restorer thereof. This double plot discourages a straightforward audience response. Yet the script of the *Odyssey* unfolds in such a way that the audience sees *not two "plots" in contention, but rather the emergence of a new layer within the performer*. The bard, who has in Books 1–13 prepared us to see Odysseus himself as constituting "who he really is," has reserved for Eumaeus' speech the revelation that there was still "one more layer" deeper in his identity and produced a surprising voice that overturns Odysseus' perspective.[245] The shock of this judgment seems to produce a curious effect on Odysseus, as we shall now see.

The Apostrophes; Divine Swineherd

κατὰ τύχην δὲ τὴν Ὀδυσσέως λαχοῦσαν πασῶν ὑστάτην αἱρησομένην ἰέναι, μνήμῃ δὲ τῶν προτέρων πόνων φιλοτιμίας λελωφηκυῖαν ζητεῖν περιιοῦσαν χρόνον πολὺν βίον ἀνδρὸς ἰδιώτου ἀπράγμονος, καὶ μόγις εὑρεῖν κείμενόν που καὶ παρημελημένον ὑπὸ τῶν ἄλλων, καὶ εἰπεῖν ἰδοῦσαν ὅτι τὰ αὐτὰ ἂν ἔπραξεν καὶ πρώτη λαχοῦσα, καὶ ἀσμένην ἑλέσθαι.

The soul of Odysseus, by chance getting the last lot of all, went to choose, and in the memory of former labors, in recovery from the love of honor, went around for a long time seeking the life of a private, uninvolved man, and with effort found it lying somewhere neglected by the

---

[245] It is worth comparing the effect here to the emergence of Patroklos in *Iliad* 16, discussed in the previous chapter. Although in the case of Eumaeus there is a full emergence in speech of a new consciousness in Eumaeus, there is still a slight relationship to the case of the half-present Patroklos, haunting the gate that is the bard's body, in that the audience may think, in both cases, that they have already witnessed the emergence of the character that the performer most "is," the character really "there" in his depths—Odysseus because of *Odyssey* 9–12, and Achilles because of his speech in *Iliad* 9. The further depth revealed in Eumaeus differs from that revealed through Patroklos, of course, and these two chapters are laying out each separately lest all this be relegated to a single "technique." But the similarity should not be entirely overlooked, in case it can help see further the quality of the presence in each case.

others. And seeing it she said that she would have done the same thing if she had got the first lot, and being saved,[246] chose it.

Plato Republic 620c–d

The apostrophes to Eumaeus and his title *dios*, which as we saw at the beginning of this chapter is used in tandem with *dios* Odysseus, have received plenty of scholarly attention.[247] The reasons given for the series of apostrophes range from metrical pressures[248] to Eumaeus' "altruistic, loyal, sensible, vulnerable"[249] character and/or the poet's "affection" for him. Especially fruitful is the approach of Louden,[250] for whom the apostrophes reflect Eumaeus' role as internal audience for Odysseus. It is true that apostrophe establishes an I-thou relationship, rather than mere characterization, but there is more to be said. The apostrophes belong to the complex flow of bard-character dynamics we have been discussing; Eumaeus is more than an ideal listener. In effect, the bard as Odysseus, returning to the world of mere mortals whose perspective should be inferior, has run up against a consciousness superior to (or at least capable of judging) his own. As with our first example in Chapter 1, the apostrophes to Patroklos in *Iliad* 16, which are best heard as focalized through an Achilles who "bursts through" the persona of the observing bard,[251] the apostrophes to Eumaeus are a rupture of the space of performance. The turn to Eumaeus away from the audience is not merely a sign of the affection that either the bard or Odysseus feels for Eumaeus. Rather the bard registers the effect this character has had upon him, as it were—upon his "Odyssean" identity—by turning aside to address him when Odysseus first encounters him.

Yet that is not a complete account of these apostrophes, which are scattered so liberally throughout the entire encounter between Odysseus and Eumaeus that their effect has been thought to be dulled.[252] Are they to be

---

[246] See Frame 1978:6–12 on the connection between *asmenos* and *neomai/nostos*. I have over-translated it to suit the context.

[247] Parry 1972; Block 1982; Richardson 1990:170–174; Martin 1993:239; Kahane 1994; Louden 1997; Benardete 1997:120–124, 130; Scodel 2002:157–159.

[248] Matthews 1980; Reece 1993:152 with bibliography in n8; Mackay 2001:17.

[249] Parry 1972:21. Reece (1993:152 with n7) notes that the ancient scholia tended toward this view.

[250] Louden 1997. Louden (p. 109) notes the difference made by oral performance: "the bard's direct address to Eumaios embodies direct address to the external audience in performance"; p. 110, "We, as Eumaios, are the present hosts of Odysseus." Cf. Richardson 1990:174. Martin 1993:239 interprets the apostrophes as focalized by Telemachus, rather than Odysseus.

[251] See above, pages 55–57.

[252] After a sensitive reading of the apostrophes to Menelaos and Patroklos, Parry (1972:20–21) remarks that "there is less to say" about the apostrophes to Eumaeus; the "fact that they are used over and over" makes them seem "little more than a reflex." Cf. Mackay (2001:17–18): in the *Odyssey* "we are clearly encountering a fossilised formula which will likely have been somewhat emptied of its apostrophic impact through repetition."

heard as voiced by the bard, "becoming" Odysseus as Eumaeus is introduced? Or as voiced by Odysseus, "peeking through" the bard, even as he occasionally "peeks through" his beggar's disguise? The poem does not always use apostrophe to introduce speeches by Eumaeus; rather it alternates between apostrophe and a regular third-person introduction.[253] Does this alternation indicate an oscillation between "being" Odysseus and being the bard, or, on the contrary, is it one more indication of the fact that Odysseus has fully taken over the bard's identity, and/or that the bard has fully entered into the world of the poem? Does the poet here address us, the audience, as Eumaeus? Or does he rather lean back and address Eumaeus with eyes closed or focused in the distance? Since after all he addresses Eumaeus in the past tense ("And then you, Eumaeus, said"), this would give an impression of an aged Odysseus (or an Odysseus in the afterlife, that is, in the present *of performance* and so already dead) recalling the encounter.

The Eumaeus apostrophes are in one sense less startling than those in the *Iliad*, since Eumaeus is, as Louden emphasizes, the "you" for the speaking Odysseus; Eumaeus and Odysseus have a long encounter stretching over two books. The *Iliad* apostrophes more obviously reach across the line of death: in *Iliad* 16, to reanimate the "dead" Achilles to re-witness the death of Patroklos, or to suddenly make him present on the battlefield from his tent.[254] In fact, a uniform interpretation may not be desirable: the apostrophes' sheer frequency leaves room for them to be performed differently as the poet proceeds, giving different interpretations or "mappings" of each apostrophe.

The first apostrophe occurs the first time Eumaeus is responding to Odysseus (14.55), once the two men have settled into the hut and Eumaeus has made a makeshift seat for the stranger. The apostrophe here "locks us in" to the scene by initiating an "I-you" relationship just as the conversation indoors begins. (This effect could be accentuated by movement and gesture in performance. "Odysseus" sits, locks eyes with the audience as his now-seated-interlocutor Eumaeus [or with Eumaeus in his mind's eye], addresses him, locking in the moment, and then slips *into Eumaeus*.) Here the two men are entering into a different kind of space by entering the hut, like the ambassadors to Achilles in *Iliad* 9 or Achilles and Priam in *Iliad* 24.

There is an analogy to the use of objects in Cretan Tale 1. There the bard made a transition from his role as a bardlike Odysseus on Phaeacia to the intimate "present," concocting a tale out of objects that hovered between himself

---

[253] Cf. Russo in Russo, Fernandez-Galiano and Heubeck 1992 *ad* 17.272.

[254] Recall from Chapter 3 the concurrence between reanimating Achilles and drawing him out of his tent to re-witness the death of Patroklos; his tent is figured as a death-realm of inaction (and later, overtly, as the house of Hades) as he is already a hero of cult.

and the audience. The intimacy was a comic one. Here the apostrophes mark an increased focus not on objects or the appearance of the interlocutor but on the interlocutor's thoughts and speeches: monologue in an open space on the beach becomes dialogue in an intimate space. Not only do they mark such a focus, they themselves enact it. Odysseus "back" from the dead bursts through the presence of the bard into the now unfolding conversation, which is thereby enlivened.

The audience is free to hear all of the early apostrophes as prompted by affection, or by the pleasure of exchanging stories (cf. Eumaeus at 15.401). But sometimes the context suggests a more particular function for apostrophe: for instance, to make a transition between the space of story and that of performance. At 14.360, the apostrophe comes directly after Cretan Tale 2, where the yarn-spinning Odysseus, who has been recycling old stories (and, perhaps, anticipating or dreaming up his future adventures), comes abruptly back into "present" space and time in the swineherd's hut, with the apostrophe. At 14.507, just after the Cloak Story, the bard introduces Eumaeus' disarming revelation of the Aetolian with an apostrophe. This one thus anticipates and prepares for the "Aetolian moment." That moment was another opportunity for the performer to pause at the brink between identities: to allow the shocked Odysseus to peek through; to split himself into two parts, one of which is outdoing the other. The apostrophes are similar moments, when the performer pauses on the brink between inside and outside the story he is telling. The apostrophe introducing the "Aetolian" speech can, thus, be played as an appreciation of the fact that Odysseus is about to be "had," to be ambushed into thinking that he is only the latest in a series of men come to bring stories of Odysseus: bardlike men whose repertoire includes or exceeds that of the present performer, who may have been thought to be improvising an entirely fresh Tale of Odysseus before our eyes, but who is now revealed to be telling just another story.

The beauty in these apostrophes lies in the fact that they can be experienced as coming both from Odysseus' mouth and from that of the bard: they span the two men. They also span two time periods: the time during which Odysseus addresses Eumaeus as "you," and the time at which that encounter lies in the past. (Again, such a time period may be projected by the audience into the underworld.) Yet another way of putting this is to say that the bard here gives up his control of the narrative, ceding his identity entirely to that of his character, Odysseus. What prompts that giving over of narrative control is—is scripted as—the encounter with Eumaeus. All of this contributes to the impression of a bard who, having created a character inside of the epic for himself to become, to (together with Athena) wield his own power of narrative control and ethical superiority, has run up against another character in the fictional world who is *bardically and* ethically superior to himself. This is akin to the addresses to

Patroklos in *Iliad* 16, where the bard is "as if" grieving over an event he himself has shaped or at least is responsible for narrating, but goes beyond it.

On the other hand, we have also commented on Eumaeus' perspective as being still further "inside" the bard than Odysseus was, such that, far from being another "real presence" mysteriously encountered within a fictional world, Eumaeus was to be seen as further within the poet-performer, surprising only to the audience.

The performer not only addresses Eumaeus as "you" but also describes him as δῖος, "godlike," and as ὄρχαμος ἀνδρῶν, "leader of men."[255] Eumaeus' perspective is godlike compared with the perspective of Odysseus, and this is registered by the performer as he enters into the encounter with Eumaeus.

The apostrophes, then, encapsulate the vertigo created by the entire encounter with Eumaeus. At once further out and further in than Odysseus, this slave causes a split in the performer and in our own ability to interpret him. This is another prime example of the "manyness" of Homer indicted by Plato's characters in the *Republic*. The bard embodies the aristocrat and the slave, scripting his poem such that it is difficult to grasp which he "really" is, like a democrat. He has "entered the character" of the tyrant[256] as well as the swineherd, and weighs them against each other. Ultimately, however, the perspective of Eumaeus, like that of Kleopatra in the *Iliad*, is not one more perspective to be lined up against others, or one of many masks the protean poet adopts, but the perspective that is ignored by the plot as it is experienced on the surface (the aristocrat returning as theoxenic god) and that, once exposed, continues to overhang that plot as a shadow.

---

[255] 15.351, 15.389, 16.36, 17.184. On Plato's allusion to this phrase in the *Statesman*, in a way that "hints at Eumaeus's importance," see Benardete 1997:120–121.

[256] Cf. Plato *Republic* 577a.

Conclusion

E PIC IS NOT SIMPLY A STRIPPED-DOWN VERSION OF TRAGEDY, some sort of primitive ancestor. Instead, the "half-acting" of epic creates an *atopia*—a placelessness, an uncanniness—in which the absent and the past take over the present, along multiple paths. The performance dynamic creates separate realms of action—present, past, divine, human, living, dead—on occasion layering these on top of one another. These boundaries, once in place, can be perforated, seen through, or obliterated.

Something of what Artaud says about drama applies to epic as well:

> It is in the light of magic and sorcery that the *mise en scene* must be considered, not as the reflection of a written text, the mere projection of physical doubles that is derived from the written work, but as the burning projection of all the objective consequences of a gesture, word, sound, music, and their combinations.[1]

Performance is just as vital to the one-man show of epic as it is to multi-actor, masked, costumed, staged tragedy.

Through the script the performer can use a dialogue between two characters to modulate his relationship to the audience. He can also create the effect of merging with a given character. Here we move beyond space to factors such as ethics, awareness, reflexivity, wit, sympathy, and the various kinds of identification.

The divisions within the performer's body and the space of performance have a fructifying relationship with divisions in the realm of poetics or in the story-world. This is true for the separate realms of the living and the dead (e.g., in Phoenix's curses), or two centers of consciousness (Phoenix/Kleopatra), where performance at once gives body to these divisions in the world of the poem but also dramatizes their ruptures. Through the kinesthetics of his emotions and gestures, the performer can even make one *story*, with multiple characters, intrude into the space of another.

---

[1] Artaud 1958:73.

The Homeric performer's situation informs the themes of the poem and is informed by them. For example, Odysseus' disguise has an effect on *what is happening* (performance), but solo performance has surely shaped the theme of disguise and its use in the script. Once we have become attuned to the virtues of spaces such as Achilles' tent or Meleager's *thalamos*, we not only appreciate their effect, we may conclude that this effect is why the center of the center of the poem is set in Meleager's *thalamos*.

The interaction between poetics and performance continues on the level of structure. A technique like ring composition allows certain things to happen in the space of performance, but performance in turn affects ring composition—a structure within all kinds of media, each with its own effect. Phoenix's speech, with the Marpessa story at its center, uses ring composition not simply as a mnemonic device for the poet or a guiding thread for the audience, but to enable the bard, the audience, and their milieu to be transformed. Ring composition is crucial to the performance. But when we realize that the speech itself is seated at the core of the ring structure that is the *Iliad*,[2] it becomes difficult to divide the performative from the mnemonic or the architectonic. The same man travels the "path of song" and the embodied course of action.

The phenomenon of characters' involuntary reenactment of their own and others' actions dovetails with the performer's own "mere reenactment." The *Iliad* as a whole makes massive use of background stories, "reenacting" and "pre-enacting" them in its plot. Perhaps the *Iliad*'s strange reenactment of events from the entire war in the space of a few weeks is a product of the mode of performance. Perhaps reenactment is not simply a theme that epic inherits from hero cult; rather, both hero cult and epic bring forth the dynamics of reenactment in their own ways.

Even stories that lie in the background of the poems are interwoven with the dimension of presence. These include stories about trauma and suppressed fears, which lend themselves to actorly mediation. Stories deeper in the background concerned ghosts and resurrection. Did the bard enlist these stories because of the use he could make of them in performance, or did these inherited themes govern the kind of performance he was aiming at?

The Homeric one-man show aims at "reanimation," not only at conveying significance or meaning. While any performance traffics in the uncanniness of human action, this peculiar poetry exposes the search for the source of action. It enacts the beginning of a tale both in the sense of plot and in the sense of the source of agency; but it also conveys to us, somehow, renewed access to this source. The script throws audience, bard, and characters into a strange feedback

---

[2] See above, pages 192–193.

loop of causation, producing splits in the performer and in us. This is why Plato and Aristotle felt that it was particularly important in the case of Homer to articulate what was happening in the space of performance, because they found it disturbing and enigmatic. And that is why they resorted to mimesis.

But the play involved in Homeric performance does not entail that its meaning is slippery, that the poem is "unreadable" or carnivalesque or protean. Perhaps the playful nature of poem is ultimately like play itself: it fosters understanding, development, life, access to the source of thought and action. Acting and spectating put us behind the eyes and hands of another and expose layers of ourselves. That is why Plato only played at banning the poet, in affectionate imitation of Agamemnon's banning of Chryses.

This gives us a fresh perspective on the poems' ethical dimensions. The play of character is less protean than it is layered. The script is aimed at allowing suppressed perspectives and characters to emerge (Trojan Horse, Phoenix/Kleopatra; Eumaeus/Phoenissa), especially once and future slaves. This ethical awakening is just part of the "reanimation" that the poems convey through mimesis.

If we pay careful attention to the script,[3] and if we elevate performance to the same level as poetics, the two become intertwined, change each other, and add up to something completely new. Rather than allusions we have intrusions into body and space. Background stories foment a kind of unconscious, not an "intertextual unconscious"[4] or a psychological one imputed to a single character, but a walled-off wellspring of memory and emotion that is shared among poem, character, and the body of the bard. To entwine poetics and presence is to produce, or recover, a living thing.

---

[3] Brook (1968:13): "Some writers attempt to nail down their meaning and intentions in stage directions and explanations, yet we cannot help being struck by the fact that the best dramatists explain themselves the least. They recognize that further indications will most probably be useless. They recognize that the only way to find the true path to the speaking of a word is through a process that parallels the original creative one. This can neither be by-passed nor simplified." Aristotle would approve of this performance/script unity. Brook is discussing written drama; epic is even more unified. The script is not to be embellished but reenacted.

[4] Riffaterre 1987.

Appendix A
Rhapsodes in Vase Painting; *Rhapsōidia*

Vase painting provides evidence for the nature of Homeric performance, though not as much as might be thought, and not in as much abundance as for other musical contests held at the Panathenaia.[1] The earliest depictions of performance on vases of Panathenaic shape pre-date Plato's *Ion* by a century and a half, however, and so constitute precious evidence. Some of these have been interpreted as depicting rhapsodic performance. None of the vases are labeled "rhapsode," however, and the identification of even the most famous "rhapsode" vase is disputed. That is the Kleophrades Painter's depiction[2] shortly after 500 BCE of a bearded man standing on a platform, holding a knotted staff (a *rhabdos?*) and reciting (or singing). Beazley was confident this was a rhapsode. Herington calls this vase "the only pre-Platonic evidence for the manner in which the Greeks performed their epic poetry,"[3] and stresses that he is unable to find any other vase that "quite certainly represents an epic rhapsode." This judgment, and the widespread reproduction of the vase, is due to the words painted as coming out of the performer's mouth, ὧδε ποτ' ἐν Τίρυνθι, 'once upon a time in Tiryns': a hexameter up to the trochaic caesura, but, unfortunately, not from the *Iliad* or the *Odyssey* (or any other identifiable poem) as we know them. On the reverse is an aulos player dressed more elaborately and also on a platform. Shapiro,[4]

---

[1] Shapiro 1993:95. Victors in musical contests, unlike athletes, did not receive amphorae as prizes. Vases depicting musical contests are not prize vases but souvenirs; they are panathenaic in shape and conventions but slightly smaller, and are referred to as "pseudo-panathenaic." M. L. West's *OCD*[3] article "Rhapsodes" (unlike West 1997; see below) typifies the slippery way ceramic evidence is adduced: "Originally reciters of epic accompanied themselves on the lyre, but later they carried a staff instead ... Both are shown on vases." West does not indicate here why he does not interpret lyre-players on pots simply as lyre-players.

[2] London E270; ARV² 183, 15.

[3] Herington 1985:14.

[4] Shapiro 1993:96.

pointing to the Kleophrades Painter's practice of spreading a single scene over the two sides of the vase, suggests that the two sides depict an aulode (a singer), rather than a rhapsode, and his accompanist, a pairing which other panathenaic-shaped vases show performing together on the same platform. Shapiro, however, unlike the even more skeptical Friis Johansen,[5] does allow that other vases do depict rhapsodes.

One of Shapiro's criteria here seems to be the use of a staff: he rejects one figure previously identified as a rhapsode ostensibly because the performer is not carrying a staff. By contrast, Bundrick, while accepting that a rhapsode may be depicted with a distinctive staff, suggests two other vases as depicting rhapsodes even though they lack them.[6] The question of whether and when a rhapsode used a staff is difficult to answer on the basis of vase paintings, since sticks are held by audience members, young and old, and by figures identified as "judges" or "trainers."[7] The "judge" and/or "trainer" figures are sometimes identified by the fact that their sticks are longer and forked, but this is not always the case for figures so identified. Shapiro notes that the "rhapsode" on a panathenaic-shaped vase in Oldenburg holds a staff with a curved handle that seems to differ from that held by his standing listeners.[8] He believes another panathenaic-shaped vase from Liverpool[9] is the earliest depiction of a rhapsode, from about 540 BCE. This man leans on a staff, looking slightly down, as he stands between two seated listeners, one of whom sniffs a flower in a pose familiar from other depictions of the audience in Panathenaic musical contests.[10] Although the figure is not presented on a platform, the shape of the vase and the typical pose of Athena between two columns on the obverse indicate a musical contest, and, as Shapiro says, it is difficult to see what else this man could be if not a rhapsode.

While kitharists and auletai are easily identifiable, rhapsodes need a staff to be recognized as such. Indeed, perhaps their lack of a *distinctive* prop is linked to their relative unpopularity on pots.[11] Yet the only other vase painting Shapiro regards as indisputably rhapsodic[12] shows a performer on a bema who seems to lack a staff, all the more striking in that his two listeners have them.

[5] Friis Johansen (1967:236n324): the panathenaic-type amphorae "nowhere depict a contest between rhapsodes." It is not clear whether this comment rules out the depiction of rhapsodes who are performing, but not competing, at the Panathenaia.

[6] Bundrick 2015.

[7] Beazley 1922:72–73.

[8] Shapiro 1993:98; fig. 25. Shapiro earlier (1989:46) mooted the possibility that all three were rhapsodes, or that the figure at left, the only one with the forked staff, was a judge.

[9] Liverpool, National Gallery 56.19.18; Shapiro 1993 figs. 26–27.

[10] Shapiro 1993:100.

[11] Bundrick 2015:25.

[12] Dunedin E48.226: Shapiro 1989 pl. 22b–c; Beazley 302889.

There are, then, on vases officially commemorating the Panathenaia and on other shapes associated with such musical content, depictions of solo performers unaccompanied by a musical instrument, some of whom carry staffs. This visual evidence suggests that, at least from the second half of the sixth century, around the time of the controversial "Panathenaic rule," rhapsodes performed at the Panathenaia and, at least sometimes, used a staff. Whether Homeric performers in other locations and at earlier dates used a staff or musical accompaniment is another question.

Many discussions do not separate the depiction of Homeric performance from the depiction of "epic" (variously defined) or even more general categories. To be sure, any depiction of performance can stimulate thought: West mentions the representation (on a red-figure amphora from Vulci) of Musaeus carrying *both* a lyre *and* a tall laurel wand and relates this to Murko's 1919 report that the Serbian bard "*if necessary*, holds a staff, or the long Turkish tobacco-pipe, or some other substitute, instead of his *gusle*."[13] Two valuable points: actual performance need not conform to fixed rules, and performers like to hold things. Nevertheless, it is important to realize how scanty is the visual (and other) evidence for *Homeric* performance in proportion to the space it occupies in scholarly discourse.

Visual depictions of musicians have been enlisted to support the contention that epic performance was accompanied by a kithara. Carter, arguing that epic grew out of ancestor cult (an independently interesting hypothesis), points to depictions of lyre players from the Bronze Age and afterward, claiming that "some of these must show occasions of epic recitation."[14] But a connection between any given depiction of a lyre player and the Homeric poems is lacking. Many scholars, of course, interpret the depiction of bards within the *Odyssey* as a self-portrait of the poet-performer as someone who sings (cf. "sing, Muse ...")[15] accompanied by a stringed instrument; some would even add a particular

---

[13] West 1966 *ad Theogony* 30; emphasis mine.

[14] Carter 1995:286.

[15] But as Segal (1994:182) notes, not only do Alkinoos (11.368) and Eumaeus (17.518) compare Odysseus to a singer (*aoidos*), but the disguised Odysseus also refers to his story as singing (14.464). Nagy (1990b:21) writes: "the word *aeidō* [sing] (as in *Iliad* I 1) is a functional synonym, in contexts where the medium refers to its own performance, of the word *e(n)nepo* 'narrate, recite' (as in *Odyssey* I 1), which does not explicitly designate singing ... Self-references in Archaic Greek poetry may be diachronically valid without being synchronically true." Especially since Odysseus refers to his own narration as singing, it is not clear that Demodokos or Phemius is in any sense a self-portrait, even one that is only diachronically valid; it could be deliberately anachronistic or not referring to the current (current at any stage) poet's own modality at all. Like Taplin (1992:30), I am "driven away from the model supplied by the bards of the *Odyssey*." Cf. Collins 2004:168. But again, the answer to this question is not dispositive for the present inquiry.

melody.[16] This notion that we should base our idea of Homeric performance on Demodokos and Phemius is separate from the argument from visual evidence, but it leaks into many discussions without comment.[17]

The use of a staff has been approached from another direction, namely the origin and meaning of the word ῥαψωιδός, "rhapsode."[18] Modern discussions focus on two passages from Pindar (*Nemean* 2.2 and *Isthmian* 4.63) and their scholia. Pindar himself does not use the word "rhapsode," but his diction suggested to ancient commentators a connection to two different words, ῥάπτω, "to sew," and ῥάβδος, "staff, wand, stitch, rivet." At *Nemean* 2.2, Pindar sings of the Homeridai as ῥαπτῶν ἐπέων ... ἀοιδοί, "singers of stitched verses." In *Isthmian* 4,[19] Pindar says that Homer has honored Ajax throughout humankind: erecting Ajax's entire *aretē*, ἔφρασεν κατὰ ῥάβδον, "he pointed it out with his staff." The scholia on these passages relate both ῥαπτῶν and ῥάβδος to ῥαψωιδός and ῥαψωιδία:

τοὺς ῥαψῳδοὺς οἱ μὲν ῥαβδῳδοὺς ἐτυμολογοῦσι διὰ τὸ μετὰ ῥάβδου δηλονότι τὰ Ὁμήρου ἔπη διεξιέναι. Καλλίμαχος (fr. 138)·
   καὶ τὸν ἐπὶ ῥάβδῳ μῦθον ὑφαινόμενον
   ἠνεκὲς ἀείδω δεδεγμένος.
οἱ δέ φασι τῆς Ὁμήρου ποιήσεως μὴ ὑφ᾽ ἓν συνηγμένης, σποράδην δὲ ἄλλως καὶ κατὰ μέρη διῃρημένης, ὁπότε ῥαψῳδοῖεν αὐτήν, εἱρμῷ τινι καὶ ῥαφῇ παραπλήσιον ποιεῖν, εἰς ἓν αὐτὴν ἄγοντας.

Some etymologize "rhapsodes" as "rhabdodes" because of their going through the lines of Homer with a *rhabdos*. Callimachus: "And taking up the story on a *rhabdos*, I sing it, and it is woven continuously."[20] Others say that since the poetry of Homer was not gathered into one, but was dispersed and divided into sections, then when they would rhapsodize it, they would be making a sort of concatenation or seam [ῥαφῇ], gathering it into one.

Scholion 1d (Drachmann) ad *Nemean* 2.1

---

[16] Danek and Hagel 1995, whose reasoning, however, if applied to iambic trimeter, would show that trimeter too was sung. The movement from a Demodokos-like singer to a rhapsode as depicted on pots and in the *Ion* is a common unspoken assumption.

[17] For example, Gentili (1988:6) cites Demodokos and Phemius as evidence that "the rhapsode's mode of performance might or might not involve the use of song." Perhaps, but Demodokos and Phemius are not called rhapsodes within the poems themselves, so this is confusing.

[18] Chantraine 1968–1980 v. ῥαψωιδός; Meyer 1918; Fränkel 1925; Patzer 1952; Sealey 1957:317; Herington 1985 Appendix 2, Nos. 1, 28, 29; Gentili 1988:6–7; Ford 1988 (comprehensive discussion with bibliography); Nagy 1996a:61–76; West 1997:163–164; Collins 2004:179–184; West 2010; González 2013:§10.1.1.

[19] 4.37–38 Race; 3/4.56 S-M.

[20] Or "and the narrative woven around a staff I received and sing continuously": Collins 2004:182.

Modern scholars generally reject an etymological connection to ῥάβδος in favor of ῥάπτειν, "stitch."[21] The precise nuances of "stitching" have commanded more attention than a connection to the "staff" because of the stitching metaphor's implications for composition, whether it applies to line-by-line composition or to the stitching together of sections[22] by later rhapsodes (as in the above scholion). It is nevertheless significant that the connection with ῥάβδος seems to be more popular in ancient testimony[23] and that this is explicitly connected with the practice of carrying staffs in performance. (For example, Σ *Ion* 530a, Herington App. 2 No. 29: "They were so called because in telling the Homeric epics they held *rhabdous daphinas*.") The etymology is important, but so are folk etymologies. The scholia are late evidence, to be sure; but keep in mind Pindar's own use of the phrase κατὰ ῥάβδον in describing Homer's activity. Pindar's phrase, in the context of ἔφρασεν and ὀρθώσαις, surely refers to the ῥάβδος as staff or wand,[24] and thus is a welcome early complement to the ceramic evidence that, though earlier than Pindar, does not refer explicitly to Homer. I do not defend a derivation of "rhapsode" from "rhabdos." Nor does settling questions about this word necessarily settle issues of early Homeric performance. However, where the "stitching" interpretation of "rhapsode" has borne a heavy burden in arguments about composition, I am happy to take the folk-etymological *rhabdos* theory as emblematic of my own interpretation. Rhapsody *qua* ῥάπτειν stresses composition, and *poiēsis*; rhapsody *qua rhabdos*-wielding

---

[21] Herington (1985:167) considers the history and meaning of *rhapsode* "still unsolved." Ford (1988:300) states: "We now reject as phonologically impossible the most popular ancient derivation, from ῥάβδος." This seems likely (cf. González 2013: §10.1.1 "there is no linguistic path from ῥάβδος to ῥαψῳδός"), but the proof is not given. Ford and LSJ cite this scholion as though the *rhabdos* there is unqualifiedly a staff. But Callimachus, while he may also play on the meaning "staff," clearly has in mind the "stitching" or fabric metaphor (compare ὑφαινόμενον ἠνεκὲς with *Iliad* 12.297 ῥάψε ... ῥάβδοισι διηνεκέσιν), or even, given the word's wide application to stick-like objects, an unattested meaning such as "shuttle" or "distaff." (Cf. the statement in the *Nem.* 2 scholia that a rhapsode was called στιχαοιδός because a *rhabdos* could also be called a *stikhos*; see Collins 2004:182.) The scholiast seems to be using the passage as evidence of the derivation rhapsode < rhabdode < rhabdos, "staff" (cf. the scholiast's διεξιέναι). Fränkel 1925 suggests the origin of the term should be sought in epic usage of ῥάπτειν and leaves aside ῥάβδος, except when (as in the *Iliad* passage just cited) it means "rivet." Note that this very passage in the *Iliad* links ῥάπτειν and ῥάβδος, whether ῥάβδος means "stitch" or "rivet." This complicates things considerably, and scholars are perhaps too eager to separate these words (contrast Chantraine's more cautious ῥάπτω entry).

[22] See Burgess 2004:13n51.

[23] González 2013: §10.1.1.

[24] The entire phrase is typically cryptic. May we link ὀρθώσαις as well as ἔφρασεν with κατὰ ῥάβδον, lending the phrase a necromantic flavor (cf. Appendix B below)? Are we to render ἐπέων closely with ῥάβδον? LSJ does so, yet blandly renders ῥάβδον ἐπέων "measure of his verses," perhaps having in mind the one Pindar scholium (on *Isthmian* 4.63) explaining κατὰ ῥάβδον by κατὰ στίχον. Cf. Meyer 1918:330; Patzer 1952; Ford 1988:306; González 2013:§10.1.1.

stresses performance, and (especially in the *rhabdos'* transformative powers) presence/becoming or *genesis*.

Andrew Ford concludes that ῥαψῳδία, though etymologically connected to composition (a "stitched" verse), refers to a mode of performance: "the solo presentation, in public, of a poetic text without musical accompaniment."[25] Building on Patzer, Ford argues convincingly that the range of texts that were normally recited in this way were stichic, and so could be said to be "stitched" together line by line. ῥαψῳδία then "comprises the meters that, even when performed without musical accompaniment, remain vividly perceptible as verse."[26] Is it only coincidence that this corresponds to performers who are free to hold a *rhabdos*? Here Ford's etymological focus precludes full discussion of the staff.[27]

Ford notes that compositions normally performed as rhapsody, that is, unaccompanied, may be set to music. Since the evidence is scanty, one should admit the possibility that rhapsodes occasionally accompanied themselves, perhaps even when reciting Homer.

We have pursued the issue of the staff and musical accompaniment because for this, unlike many questions about Homeric performance, there is some evidence. But the question has implications for the interpretation of Homer. To know whether the bard held a lyre or a staff would be to know a little about his freedom of movement and his ability to gesture. This study's analysis of certain passages explores the potential of a staff-wielding performer, and suggests that the script, at least in these passages, was developed with a staff in mind (and hand). But it is important to acknowledge that other modes of performance incorporate a histrionic dimension: there is no neat equation such as staff: kithara :: histrionic: non-histrionic. One should not look at photos of seated Serbian *guslars* and listen to recordings and shudder to think of acting. This Herington makes clear in his epilogue, recreating a competition in kithaŕody of Timotheus' *Persians*. While certain gestures become impossible holding a lyre or kithara/guitar, others become possible, even inviting. Witnesses include singers who wield guitars, and, to take a modern epic example, Benjamin Bagby's twenty-first-century performances of *Beowulf*.[28]

---

[25] Ford 1988:303.
[26] Ford 1988:303.
[27] One might argue that the use of the staff *qua* prop extends beyond the range of the rhapsodic as Ford traces it, beginning with the Callimachus fragment quoted in the scholia above, such that the *rhabdos* would extend beyond the traditional range of *rhapsōidia*. But even here, the Callimachus fragment is elegiac, not strophic. If, as Ford emphasizes, traditionally "rhapsodic" (non-melic) poetry may be set to music, it may also be true that melic poetry may be rhapsodically recited. See Ford 2002:25. The *rhabdos* is, as it were, the instrument taking the place of the kithara or the aulos in the *rhapsōidia* compound: so would go the folk etymology.
[28] Failing a live performance, see Bagby 2006.

Nevertheless in our earliest (Platonic) sources, late as they are (*Laws* 658b; *Ion* 533b) *rhapsōidia* is distinguished from *kitharōidia*, and rhapsodes are linked with actors (*Ion* 536a; Aristotle *Poetics* 1462a6). Nagy argues for an increasing "theatricalization" of Homeric poetry, with the Homeristai mentioned by Athenaeus, Petronius, and other late authors[29] forming a kind of end point of this process. At least some of the Homeristai enacted scenes from Homer with multiple actors equipped with swords and shields. Nagy summarizes the thrust of Petronius' treatment: "the histrionics of these performers are being ridiculed as an abstruse exercise in art, on display for pretentious but ludicrously ignorant connoisseurs."[30]

But these performers seem to be outliers, rather than a point at the end of a historical development. Nagy's schema, whereby the Homeric poems are increasingly "theatricalized," is based in part on the existence of these Roman-period Homeristai and the fact that Plato and Aristotle portray rhapsodes as (overly) histrionic. But, granted the premise of increasing histrionics, it is not clear that the portrayal of singers *within* the Homeric poems is standing for the early end of this spectrum, a spectrum that parallels Nagy's (and others') evolutionary model for the Homeric text, whereby fixity of the text means a "script" which *in turn* entails "acting."[31]

Even if we were to grant still further that the earliest performers of the Homeric poems sang to a stringed instrument like Demodokos, we cannot infer their performance style, mode, or aim from Yugoslav *guslars*; it is as plausible that they were like Bagby doing *Beowulf* to the Anglo-Saxon harp. And although actorly technique might be perfected using a fixed text, it is not obvious that in the early stages of the development of the poems the performer would be any less histrionic. Plato and Aristotle speak of histrionic performers, but also of a variety of performances. There must have been a difference between Ion in full glory before the masses and the rhapsodes heard "almost every day" by such aristocrats as Niceratus (Xenophon *Symposium* 3.5), even if this is an

---

[29] "Theatricalization"; "ever more theatrical and mimetic over time": Nagy 1996a:162, 165; Collins 2004:203–218. On Homeristai, Nagy (pp. 158–168) discusses Athenaeus 620b–c; Achilles Tatius, *Clitophon and Leucippe* 3.20.4, 8.9.2–3; Artemidorus 4.2 ed. Pack; Petronius, *Satyricon* 59.2–6; and papyri from the second and third centuries CE. Similarly, Danek and Hagel (1995:15–17): improvised "Epengesang zur Phorminx" breaks off at a certain point, after which we see only the endpoints of two different lines of development—uncreative rhapsodes without music, and setting fixed texts to new music. For a skeptical view of Athenaeus' testimony on earlier Homeristai, see Boyd 1994, esp. 116n18.

[30] Nagy 1996a:166.

[31] González 2013 repeatedly invokes the "dramatic" or "mimetic potential" of Homeric epic. "In adopting under the influence of drama some of the accoutrements of the acting trade, he was only bringing out the extraordinary mimetic potential already inherent in the *Iliad* and the *Odyssey*" (González 2013, Conclusion). If the mimetic potential was there, and "extraordinary," what spark does either evolution or the influence of drama add?

exaggeration.[32] Nor does the rhapsodes' alleged stupidity[33] entail that the more creative poet, or monumental composer, or even "Homer," was not aware of or interested in the effect of his own presence and performance mode. The contrary is in fact the case. Throughout this study, to repeat, "script" simply refers to the words that are actualized in performance, however fixed, because there is no better word.

Having said all of this, as I have repeatedly stressed, I am not arguing in this book for a high degree of histrionics, or really any particulars at all; only in a few places is the effect of a particular gesture brought to bear, and that need not be unsubtle. (I have not, however, hidden my suspicion that there was a staff involved by siphoning off all mentions of it to these Appendices.) What is important to realize is that the evidence for the histrionic presence of the bard is not all in. The wealth of internal evidence of the poems as scripts remains untapped until one stands up and begins performing. You can sit down if you like.

[32] M. L. West 2001:19; Pelliccia (2003:111) suggests these rhapsodes were text-teachers specifically hired to teach Niceratus the text verbatim.

[33] Plato *Ion*; Xenophon *Memorabilia* 4.2.10; Xenophon *Symposium* 3.6. Cf. Redfield (1973:144): "they possessed the stupidity which is often found among, and even recommended for, actors. The performer is not a creator; he responds to another's creation ..." My point is simply that one cannot assume rhapsode: stupid: actorly :: creative bard: non-stupid: wooden. Cf. Collins 2004:135–146.

Appendix B

The Homeric Performer, the Staff, and "Becoming the Character"

The "play" between bard and character, their inner dynamics, variations, attunements, narratological ensembles and assemblies, can be brought to life by looking at a series of objects that threads through both the *Iliad* and the *Odyssey*, consisting of scepter, spear, staff, sword, etc. Within the poems, the scepter signifies that the speaker holding it has the authority, or inspiration, of the gods (cf. "scepter-bearing kings"). But let us for a moment imagine that the performer of the poems himself held in his hand such an instrument, say, a staff. It seems certain that at some stage, rhapsodes did use such an instrument to assist them with their histrionic, entrancing performances. How might this have worked?

As discussed in the Introduction, the first character the Homeric performer "becomes" (in terms of direct discourse) is Chryses, priest of Apollo, who is carrying a golden scepter, which the performer richly describes before "becoming" Chryses and voicing his speech. The performer of the poem and the priest within it share this implement: it spans the realm of the performance and the realm of the story. When the bard becomes Chryses, if that bard is holding a staff, his audience can see as well as hear that he has become Chryses; his appearance now overlaps with that of the character, and the audience is suddenly shunted to Troy, beholding the character before their eyes. The scepter then goes on to play a dramatically effective role in the beginning of the *Iliad*, where it possibly shifts hands to each speaker in the first assembly, receives a lyrical outburst as that by which Achilles swears (1.234–239), and finally is thrown down by Achilles (1.245). It is taken up again in 2.46 by the deluded Agamemnon (whose authority wielding it we now question), and receives the phrase σκῆπτρον πατρώιον, ἄφθιτον αἰεί, "his ancestral scepter, unwithering forever," fraught with dramatic possibilities; its glorious history is recited (2.101–108), and it is swiftly taken up by Odysseus (2.186) with the same ironic phrase, to drive the Achaeans back to their seats like cattle and to beat Thersites to a pulp (2.265).[1] Finally Odysseus stands up with it (2.279) to deliver his speech on the omens at Aulis, a long stretch of time during which Odysseus' physical presence pointedly overlaps with that of the performer—appropriately so, recalling the events at Aulis[2]—but after what a ride!

Now it is sometimes assumed (see Appendix A) that at the time the Homeric poems were composed, the bard would have held not a 'rhapsodic' staff, but a singer's lyre, as the singers depicted within the poems use. But perhaps the staff is not only a fifth-century phenomenon. Hesiod, after all, says that the Muses "gave me a scepter, a branch of blooming laurel, a marvel, and breathed into me a divine voice" (*Theogony* 30–32) and with it knowledge of future and past. The branch held by Hesiod, then, had a quasi-magical power to transport him to another realm: that transport (as well as 'authority,' etc.) is what it *signifies*. Similarly such implements can be used, by characters within the *Odyssey*, to effect a transformation into another realm or into another form. Circe's magic wand, with which she changes men into mute beasts and back again into speaking humans, may allude to the "bridging" quality of the performer's staff that is used to "animate" characters; see below. Immediately one also thinks of Hermes' staff. But all that is within the realm of what the stick *means, within* the poem, and how it is used by characters (including "Hesiod" as a character ["I"] represented within the poem).

Now within the space of performance the bard may have actually used such a thing, even in the era before staff-wielding rhapsodes show up in the ceramic record, as evidenced by the opportunities the *Iliad* and particularly the *Odyssey* provide for the performer to use the staff to embody his connection to a character and to play with that connection. There are many passages where we can see the possibilities for play with this "prop" fully realized. The array of uses to which the bard may put the prop can be brought to light by looking at a variety of passages that each present different performative possibilities. That variety *among* passages alerts us to a similar diversity of ways a bard could use such an object in any *single* passage. Let us consider one.

---

[1] On the ironies of the scepter's history and uses here, see for example Thalmann 1988:10–13.

[2] Cf. Bakker (1993:18), on Odysseus as a performer in the speech about Aulis, recalling a scene of which he and his audience have been eyewitnesses.

Odysseus in the Underworld

When, in Book 11, Odysseus journeys to the beyond to consult Teiresias and visit other dead souls, he does so not by crossing into a house of Hades, but by necromancy of a very particular type. He digs a ditch of a specified size, sacrifices some animals, and then wards off the approaching specters from the blood so that they drink of it (gaining the ability to speak and to recognize him) in an orderly fashion, one by one. He wards off the ghosts with his sword (11.48–50, 11.82, 11.88–89, cf. 11.147–149): we may imagine the performer here gesturing with his staff. Note the repeated description of the drawing-out of the sword from his thigh, both in order to dig the ditch and in order to ward off souls, in both Circe's instructions and in the 'actual' acts (10.535, 11.24, 11.48, cf. 11.231). The amalgamation that is the bard and Odysseus, describing Circe's instructions, gets to 'rehearse' the act, and then to carry it out. One is the preparation; the other is the animating act. Remember that it is Odysseus, sitting among the Phaeacians, narrating this scene, saying "*I held them off with my spear, etc.*" Thus, there are three parties involved so far: Odysseus-necromancer, Odysseus-storyteller, and the bard. Here is a place where there is a full flowering of the inner tensions and confluences among these three parties. As Odysseus by lowering his sword allows each departed spirit to cross toward him, toward the blood, to regain their consciousness and voice, so too does the bard (and the Odysseus who is sitting among the Phaeacians), imitating the sword action with his staff, allow each succeeding character to cross toward and "enter" *him*, and thus to speak. For since, with epic, we are dealing with a single embodier of voices, and not either a dramatic ensemble of embodiments or a page with written signs, on one level what we the audience see is Odysseus, summoning souls, and then that same person becoming each soul. As Odysseus is in the Phaiakis crossing over from hero of the *Iliad* to teller of his own tale, and into a post-heroic future where bards are already telling his story, he invokes the spirits of those who did not make that crossing with him and are left behind, needing his help to reanimate their stories.

The interpretation, the registration, of this, like any passage, is dependent on imagining it in performance: how would the performer handle his staff? Playfully? Ironically? Tentatively and with a sense of awe? Positing the use of the staff does not imply any particular tone; the bard may use it to heighten the sense of mystery of bringing the characters to light, or he may engage his audience's sense of play, as though to say, "Let's see what this thing can do ..." All possibilities are open, and these possibilities for *delivery* make all the difference for our sense of the realms "in play" and the distance or closeness between them. We would do well to imagine them all.[3]

Odysseus wards off other souls awaiting the approach of Teiresias, only possessor of *nous* in the underworld, who carries a golden scepter (11.91), as did the Chryses who stepped forth in *Iliad* 1. He asks Odysseus to step away from the trench and withdraw his sword so that he may drink. Odysseus does so, and as he does, he sheaths his sword: with this sheathing, he is literally allowing Teiresias to "speak νημέρτεα," but insofar as he dovetails with the bard, he is saying somewhat as an illocution, "I am not the speaker any more: he is." Teiresias with his scepter, and his knowledge of the plot to come, seems iconically bardic. But when he is done with his plot-revealing prophecy (at whose climax stands a very staff-like object, the planted oar), Odysseus remarks that it's all well and good, and he's sure the gods have plotted everything—but what about his mother? "Tell me, lord, how can she recognize me as I am?" (144). Teiresias gives him an answer that seems to apply equally well to the underworld situation and to the performance. "Easily shall I tell you a word and put it in your *phrenes*: Whomever you allow, of the dead who have perished, to go near the blood, he will speak unerringly to you: and whomever you begrudge this to, he will go back again" (146–149). Now, Odysseus already knows this full well, and so the effect of Teiresias' speech is that he is not talking about necromancy any more, but pointing toward something else: the animating power of the staff for the performer. Thus the speech becomes demonstrative and meditative, "trying out" the staff's powers.

The staff/sword enacts the boundary that the "beyond" characters, now cast as dead, cross to come to life through the bard. At the same time it serves as a marker of the bard's control over his narrative, as is brought out when Odysseus says (230) he got the idea to control the throngs of dead women by letting them step up to the blood one by one, as though this were a new idea and not precisely the same one that he had just used on his mother, and at once there follows a variation on the "drawing the sword from along my thigh" line. This connection of the performer's prop with the teller's control of the narrative gains further resonance during the so-called "intermezzo," when Odysseus pauses in his tale and the Phaeacians tell him what they want to hear about

---

3   The way the staff bridges realms resembles Winnicott's idea of the transitional object (e.g., Winnicott 1971). The transitional object denotes in the first place the infant's experience, "the intermediate area of experience, between the thumb and the teddy bear," but it extends into adult play and creativity. It is "the intermediate area between the subjective and that which is objectively perceived." It is not that the bard's staff *is* a transitional object. But for readers familiar with this idea, it provides an impetus toward *seeing* the poetry, experiencing it as enactment that bridges real and unreal, past and present, here and there, me and not-me, and especially, dead and alive.

next, which gives a strong impression that Odysseus is tailoring the order of events in the underworld to suit the audience.[4]

The underworld use[5] is the most explicitly 'theoretical' and at the same time the most concrete embodiment of the connection between staff and 'becoming the character.' It is the explicitness of the swordplay here that marks it out as play, as the bard's display of his own mental and physical equipment, but it highlights the fact that these elements are in play all the time. Quite possibly there is some sort of movement within the *Odyssey* in its use or neglect. The prop is always being received and put away for safekeeping. After agreeing to take Theoclymenos aboard, for example, Telemachus receives his spear (15.282) and stows it carefully. After directing Theoclymenos to the house of Peiraios, famous for his spear (15.544), removing him temporarily from the audience's purview, Telemachus picks up the spear again (15.551), only to hand it over to Eumaeus (16.40). Does this become the bow at last bestowed by Eumaeus (21.378–379)? All of this maneuvering seems to start with Odysseus throwing down his beggar's staff at the approach of the dogs (14.31). As Clay notes, the only occurrence of σκῆπτρον as a "common staff with no connection to status or authority, is (perhaps significantly?) the staff of the disguised Odysseus (13.437; 14.31; 17.199)."[6] This staff, given to him by Athena herself, is, as Nagler writes, "the predecessor of that with which Odysseus will later go to the 'assemblage' of his townsmen when Eumaeus, acting as his herald, leads him as ἄνακτα ... σκηπτόμενον, 'sceptered lord' into the city. Its power is that of illusion rather than outright authority, but that befits Odysseus, especially at this stage of his career."[7] Nagler goes on to observe that Odysseus asks Eumaeus for a ῥόπαλον (17.195) to replace the σκῆπτρον he lost, "but the poet reveals its true meaning (199)": "And [or, 'but'] Eumaeus gave him a suitable σκῆπτρον."[8] This fort-da act with the staff of authority does not simply add up to the triumphant epiphany of our hero, but works together with the bard's nuanced embodiment of Odysseus and Eumaeus in the poem's third quarter, as plumbed in Chapter 4.

The *Iliad* may use the staff differently. Consider for instance the sword-drawing line ending in ὀξὺ ἐρυσσάμενος παρὰ μηροῦ. This phrase occurs seven times in the *Odyssey*, notably in the bedroom encounter with Circe (10.321; cf.

---

[4] Doherty 1991.

[5] Some scholars find Odysseus' mode of getting to the Beyond puzzling in terms of the geography of ancient underworld belief, and in visual consistency. It is plausible that the rigging of this scenario is governed by performance considerations. See Page 1955:22–26; Kirk 1962:236–237; Heubeck in Heubeck and Hoekstra 1989:75.

[6] Clay 2003:73, within a valuable discussion of Hesiod's wielding of the σκῆπτρον in the *Works and Days* versus in the *Theogony* (pp. 73–75).

[7] Nagler 1974:123–124.

[8] Nagler 1974:125.

10.294), and seems to be a comic or Odyssean version of what is, in the *Iliad*, a precursor to a kill (*Iliad* 1.190, 21.173, both of Achilles). In *Iliad* 1.190, the bard has all sorts of possibilities while Achilles, hesitating whether to draw his sword, is visited by Athena; in line 194, when he finally draws it, Athena appears in the same line, and when he sheaths it (220), she departs. If we presume the "precursor to a kill" usage to be the primary one, the comedy of its bedroom use stands out. (Similarly at *Odyssey* 9.300 Odysseus draws his sword only to realize a trick is in order, while at 10.126 the drawn sword cuts a cable to enable Odysseus' getaway by ship.) The underworld use would add a meditative or metatheatrical note; the sword's utter uselessness in the face of shades runs up against and yet enhances its effectiveness in terms of poetic embodiment. Shall we speak of a comic and a tragic staff? This is perhaps a better dichotomy than "Odyssean versus Iliadic," for the *Iliad* does not exclude sly comedy. (I mentioned the ironic uses of the authoritative scepter, from Books 1 and 2.) At 6.318, Hektor enters Helen's bedroom with his phallic spear, and this apparatus, we might imagine, morphs into the bow fondled by the dawdling Paris (6.322). (Perhaps this in itself makes more plausible the analogous Odyssean morphing of the beggar's staff into the bow.) The intermittent presence in the *Iliad* (absent in the *Odyssey*) of the shepherd in his simile, there to observe quietly and disappear again, is another chance for variety in instantiation: perhaps the bard stands stock still and holds his shepherd's staff (like the shepherd Hesiod) while he recites the simile.[9]

The staff is an object of contemplation that allows the bard to play with varying degrees of embodiment, with a vast array of effects.[10] It is a crucial "intermediary" for *us*, helping us visualize the levels of presence and absence, and objects and personae mediating between presence and absence, involved in the performance of the *Iliad* and the *Odyssey*.

---

[9]   Cf. Lombardo on the performance of similes in the *Iliad*: "In performance, I found myself isolating the similes somewhat and marking them—pausing a little before and after, changing the voice, *dropping any percussion I may have been using*—in order to bring out their quality as poetic events distinct from the poetry of the narrative and speeches" (Lombardo 1997:x, my emphasis). Lombardo's use of italics for similes re-creates on the page the simple act that at once is a *dropping* of a mask, and yet also a transport to elsewhere, the performer's stopping to look at what he has done and what he is channeling. The shepherd who emerges out of these similes embodies the astonished quietness: the performer can *be* him, from Lombardo's testimony, by *dropping* a mask. This produces a sense of extreme penetration of the scene.

[10] To draw on the kinesthetic imagination, think of the standup comic's microphone and stool. Though the comic rarely sits on the stool, it may be essential to the performance. Likewise, microphones no longer need stands, or even need to be held, but hand-held ones are better props than clip-ons. Smokers know the usefulness of a cigarette for "becoming the character," even if it is oneself. Recall West's remark on staffs and pipes substitutes for the *gusle*, Appendix A, page 329 above. More recently solo performers use bottles of water: plastic bottles can be wielded more easily than glasses. On the deictic and symbolic aspects of the guitar or microphone, see Zumthor 1990:162.

The thinking that results from envisioning the use of this prop—or, if you would prefer, the kithara—goes beyond the immediate moment of performance. In other words, thinking through the use of the prop involves ideas that resonate with broader structural and thematic issues. It makes tangible the connection between performance and the themes of death and escort in the poem. Where the Iliadic staff often embodies the power to kill, to dispatch a hero to his death, the counterpart in the Nekyia raises the dead. Yet we can now see that the Iliadic poet performs a similar act when he "raises" each hero, *now* dead, by bringing him forth on the battlefield for a brief appearance, before his death "again" in the time of the poem. Consider further the *Iliad* performer's staff when it represents a weapon. In the space of performance, the performer, facing out toward the audience, faces what in the space of the battlefield is his (at the moment unembodied) opponent. When one dying hero after another is embodied, it is easy to see that the direction the performer faces comes to seem during certain passages like the space of death. There is a resemblance between the battle scene and *Odyssey* 11: in both cases the staff marks the border between the still-living hero and the realm of death. In the battle scenes, he may wield the staff as a weapon to ward off, usually in vain, the approach of death. In the Nekyia, the staff used by the performer-as-Odysseus both marks the border between the hero and the dead characters and can effect the crossing of that border, with the dead characters crossing *into* the body of the performer to speak. The Hermes-like role of the hero, as well as the epic performer, is given a tangible reality and substance.

Finally, the staff helps us to forge connections to another crucial theme, that of the other self, the object representing the self. Consider the oar Odysseus must plant (11.129) when he reaches the place where the natives mistake the oar for a winnowing fan. Yes, it is symbolic that the rower's work is done. But clearly here we could work with an interpretation of it as a stand-in or symbol of the man himself—a piece of wood like the oar that evokes Elpenor as it marks his grave.[11] The *dalos* (firebrand) that the lonely man buries in ash, evoked in the simile under the olive (*Odyssey* 5.488), shunts between an external object and yet the internal source of life, something the man can manipulate and something that he is. So too the epic performer in becoming a character has an external object to manipulate as well as a perspective to embody from within.

---

[11] See Nagy 1990a:214–215.

Bibliography

Adkins, Arthur W. H. 1960. *Merit and Responsibility: A Study in Greek Values.* Oxford.

Ahl, Frederick, and Hanna Roisman. 1996. *The Odyssey Re-Formed.* Ithaca.

Aitken, Ellen Bradshaw, and Jennifer K. Berenson Maclean, eds. 2004. *Philostratus's Heroikos: Religion and Cultural Identity in the Third Century C.E.* Atlanta.

Alden, Maureen. 2000. *Homer Beside Himself: Para-narratives in the Iliad.* Oxford.

Alexiou, Margaret. 2002. *The Ritual Lament in Greek Tradition.* Revised by Dimitrios Yatromanolakis and Panagiotis Roilos. Lanham, MD.

Allen, T. W., ed. 1912. *Homer Opera.* Vol. 5, *Hymni, Cycles, Fragmenta, Margites, Batrachomyomachia, Vitae.* Oxford.

Andersen, Øivind. 1977. "Odysseus and the Wooden Horse." *Symbolae Osloenses* 52:5–18.

———. 1987. "Myth, Paradigm and 'Spatial Form' in the *Iliad*." In *Homer: Beyond Oral Poetry,* ed. J. M. Bremer, I. J. F. de Jong, and J. Kalff, 1–13. Amsterdam.

Armstrong, James I. 1958. "The Arming Motif in the *Iliad*." *American Journal of Philology* 79:337–354.

Artaud, Antonin. 1958. *The Theater and Its Double.* Trans. Mary Caroline Richards. New York.

Auerbach, Erich. 1953. *Mimesis: The Representation of Reality in Western Literature.* Trans. Willard R. Trask. Princeton.

Austin, Norman. 1966. "The Function of Digressions in the *Iliad*." *Greek, Roman, and Byzantine Studies* 7:295–312.

———. 1975. *Archery at the Dark of the Moon: Poetic Problems in Homer's "Odyssey."* Berkeley.

———. 1983. "Odysseus and the Cyclops: Who Is Who." In *Approaches to Homer,* ed. Carl A. Rubino and Cynthia W. Shelmerdine, 3–37. Austin.

Bagby, Benjamin. 2006. *Beowulf* (DVD). Produced by Charles Morrow and Jon Aaron. New York.

Bakhtin, Mikhail M. 1981. *The Dialogic Imagination: Four Essays by M. M. Bakhtin.* Trans. Caryl Emerson and Michael Holquist. Austin.

Bakker, Egbert J. 1993. "Discourse and Performance: Involvement, Visualization and 'Presence' in Homeric Poetry." *Classical Antiquity* 12:1–29.

———. 1997a. *Poetry as Speech: Orality and Homeric Discourse*. Ithaca.

———. 1997b. "Storytelling in the Future: Truth, Time and Tense in Homeric Epic." In Bakker and Kahane 1997:11–36.

———. 1999. "Homeric ΟΥΤΟΣ and the Poetics of Deixis." *Classical Philology* 94:1–19.

———. 2005. *Pointing at the Past: From Formula to Performance in Homeric Poetics*. Hellenic Studies 12. Washington, DC. http://nrs.harvard.edu/urn-3:hul.ebook:CHS_BakkerE_Pointing_at_the_Past.2005.

Bakker, Egbert, and Ahuvia Kahane, eds. 1997. *Written Voices, Spoken Signs: Tradition, Performance, and the Epic Text*. Cambridge, MA.

Balty, J. 2000. "Variations autour du thème d'Hélène." In *Agathos daimon: Mythes et Cultes: Études d'iconographie en l'honneur de Lilly Kahil*, 1–7. Bulletin de correspondance hellénique, Supplément 38. Athens.

Bannert, Herbert. 1981. "Phoinix' Jugend und der Zorn des Meleagros." *Wiener Studien* N.F. 15:69–94.

Bassett, Samuel E. 1919. "Actoris in the *Odyssey*." *Classical Quarterly* 13:1–3.

———. 1933. "The Fate of the Phaeacians." *Classical Philology* 28:305–307.

———. 1938. *The Poetry of Homer*. Berkeley.

Bauman, Richard. 1984. *Verbal Art as Performance*. Orig. pub. 1977. Long Grove, IL.

Beazley, J. D. 1922. "Citharoedus." *Journal of Hellenic Studies* 42:70–98.

Becker, Andrew S. 1990. "The Shield of Achilles and the Poetics of Homeric Description." *American Journal of Philology* 111:139–153.

Beilock, Sian L., and Susan Goldin-Meadow. 2010. "Gesture Changes Thought by Grounding It in Action." *Psychological Science* 21:1605–1610.

Bellamy, Elizabeth J. 1994. "From Virgil to Tasso: The Epic Topos as an Uncanny Return." In *Desire in the Renaissance: Psychoanalysis and Literature*, ed. Valeria Finucci, 207–232. Princeton.

Benardete, Seth. 1997. *The Bow and the Lyre: A Platonic Reading of the Odyssey*. Lanham, MD.

Benveniste, Emile. 1969. *Indo-European Language and Society*. Trans. E. Palmer. London.

Bergren, Ann L. T. 1975. *The Etymology and Usage of PEIRAR in Early Greek Poetry: A Study in the Interrelationship of Metrics, Linguistics and Poetics*. State College, PA.

———. 1980a. "Allegorizing Winged Words: Simile and Symbolization in *Odyssey* V." *Classical World* 74:109–123.

———. 1980b. "Helen's Web: Time and Tableau in the *Iliad*." *Helios* 7:19–34.

———. 1981. "Helen's 'Good Drug': *Odyssey* IV 1–305." In *Contemporary Literary Hermeneutics and Interpretation of Classical Texts*, ed. S. Krésic, 201–214. Ottawa.

———. 1983. "Odyssean Temporality: Many ReTurns." In *Approaches to Homer*, ed. Carl A. Rubino and Cynthia W. Shelmerdine, 38–73. Austin.

———. 1995. "The Remarriage of Penelope and Odysseus: Architecture Gender Philosophy. A Homeric Dialogue." In Carter and Morris 1995:205–220.

Bernabé, A., ed. 1987–2007. *Poetae Epici Graeci: Testimonia et Fragmenta* I–II(1–3). Berlin.

Block, Elizabeth. 1982. "The Narrator Speaks: Apostrophe in Homer and Virgil." *Transactions of the American Philological Association* 112:7–22.

Boedeker, Deborah. 1988. "Protesilaos and the End of Herodotus' *Histories*." *Classical Antiquity* 7:30–48.

Boegehold, Alan L. 1999. *When a Gesture Was Expected*. Princeton.

Bölte, Felix. 1907. "Rhapsodische Vortragskunst: Ein Beitrag zur Technik des homerischen Epos." *Neue Jahrbücher für das klassische Altertum, Geschichte und deutsche Literatur und für Pädagogik* 19:571–581.

Bonnafé, A. 1985. "L'olivier dans l'Odyssée et le fourré du Parnasse: Reprises de termes et reprises de thèmes." *Quaderni di storia* 21:101–136.

Booth, Wayne. 1961. *The Rhetoric of Fiction*. Chicago.

Bouvier, David. 2002. *Le sceptre et la lyre: L'Iliade ou les héros de la mémoire*. Grenoble.

Bowie, A. M. 2013. *Homer: Odyssey, Books XIII and XIV*. Cambridge.

Bowra, C. M. 1964. "The Meaning of a Heroic Age." In *The Language and Background of Homer: Some Recent Studies and Controversies*, ed. G. S. Kirk, 22–47. Cambridge.

Boyd, Timothy W. 1994. "Where Ion Stood, What Ion Sang." *Harvard Studies in Classical Philology* 96:109–121.

Bremmer, Jan. 1983. *The Early Greek Concept of the Soul*. Princeton.

———. 1988. "La plasticité du mythe: Méléagre dans la poésie Homérique." In *Métamorphoses du mythe en Grèce antique*, ed. Claude Calame, 37–56. Geneva.

Brennan, T. C. 1987. "An Ethnic Joke in Homer?" *Harvard Studies in Classical Philology* 91:1–3.

Brilliant, Richard. 1984. *Visual Narratives: Storytelling in Etruscan and Roman Art*. Ithaca.

Brook, Peter. 1968. *The Empty Space*. New York.

Brooks, Peter. 1984. *Reading for the Plot: Design and Intention in Narrative*. New York.

Brügger, Claude. 2016. *Homers Ilias Gesamtkommentar*, Band IX, Sechzehnter Gesang, Faszikel 2. General ed. Anton Bierl and Joachim Latacz. Berlin.

Budick, Sanford, and Wolfgang Iser, eds. 1989. *Languages of the Unsayable: The Play of Negativity in Literature and Literary Theory*. New York.

Bundrick, Sheramy. 2015. "Recovering Rhapsodes: A New Vase by the Pantoxena Painter." *Classical Antiquity* 34:1–31.

Buranelli, Francesco, ed. 1987. *La tomba François di Vulci*. Rome.

Burgess, Jonathan. 1997. "Beyond Neo-Analysis: Problems with the Vengeance Theory." *American Journal of Philology* 118:1–19.

———. 2001. *The Tradition of the Trojan War in Homer and the Epic Cycle*. Baltimore.

———. 2004. "Performance and the Epic Cycle." *Classical Journal* 100:1–23.

———. 2017. "The Tale of Meleager in the *Iliad*." *Oral Tradition* 31:51–76.

Burkert, Walter. 1983. *Homo Necans: The Anthropology of Ancient Greek Sacrificial Ritual and Myth*. Trans. Peter Bing. Berkeley.

———. 1985. *Greek Religion*. Trans. John Raffan. Cambridge, MA. [Orig. pub. as *Griechische Religion der archaischen und klassischen Epoche*. Stuttgart, 1977.]

———. 1987. "The Making of Homer in the Sixth Century B.C.: Rhapsodes versus Stesichorus." In *Papers on the Amasis Painter and His World*, 43–62. Malibu, CA.

———. 2004. *Babylon - Memphis - Persepolis: Eastern Contexts of Greek Culture*. Cambridge, MA.

Buxton, R. G. A. 2003. "Euripides' *Alkestis*: Five Aspects of an Interpretation." In *Oxford Readings in Classical Studies: Euripides*, ed. J. Mossman, 170–186. Oxford.

Cairns, Douglas L., ed. 2001. *Oxford Readings in Homer's Iliad*. Oxford.

Carlisle, Miriam, and Olga Levaniouk, eds. 1999. *Nine Essays on Homer*. Lanham, MD.

Carpenter, Rhys. 1946. *Folk-Tale, Fiction and Saga in the Homeric Epics*. Sather Classical Lectures 20. Berkeley.

———. 1958. "Phoenicians in the West." *American Journal of Archaeology* 62:35–54.

Carter, Jane B. 1995. "Ancestor Cult and the Occasion of Homeric Performance." In Carter and Morris 1995:285–312.

Carter, Jane B., and Sarah P. Morris, eds. 1995. *The Ages of Homer*. Austin.

Cavell, Stanley. 2003. *Disowning Knowledge in Seven Plays of Shakespeare*. Cambridge.

Chantraine, Pierre. 1948. *Grammaire homérique*. Vol. 1, *Phonetique et morphologie*. Paris.

———. 1953. *Grammaire homérique*. Vol. 2, *Syntaxe*. Paris.

———. 1968–1980. *Dictionnaire étymologique de la langue grecque*. Paris.

Chatháin, Próinséas Ní. 1979/80. "Swineherds, Seers, and Druids." *Studia Celtica* 14/15:200–211.

Clark, Mark Edward. 1986. "Neoanalysis: A Bibliographic Review." *Classical World* 79:379–394.

Clay, Jenny Strauss. 1976. "The Beginning of the *Odyssey*." *American Journal of Philology* 97:313–326.

———. 1980. "Goat Island: *Od.* 9.116–141." *Classical Quarterly* 30:261–264.

———. 1983. *The Wrath of Athena: Gods and Men in the Odyssey.* Princeton.

———. 1989. *The Politics of Olympus.* Princeton.

———. 1994. "The Dais of Death." *Transactions of the American Philological Association* 124:35–40.

———. 2002. "Odyssean Animadversions." In *Omero tremila anni dopo,* ed. F. Montanari and P. Ascheri, 73–83. Rome.

———. 2003. *Hesiod's Cosmos.* Cambridge.

———. 2011. *Homer's Trojan Theater.* Cambridge.

Coarelli, Filippo. 1983. "Le pitture della Tomba François a Vulci: Una proposta di lettura." *Dialoghi di Archeologia* 3s., 1:43–69.

Coldstream, J. N. 1976. "Hero-Cults in the Age of Homer." *Journal of Hellenic Studies* 96:8–17.

Collins, Derek. 2004. *Master of the Game: Competition and Performance in Greek Poetry.* Hellenic Studies 7. Washington, DC.

Cook, Erwin. 1992. "Ferrymen of Elysium and the Homeric Phaeacians." *Journal of Indo-European Studies* 20:239–267.

———. 1995. *The Odyssey in Athens.* Ithaca.

Crane, Gregory. 1988. *Calypso: Backgrounds and Conventions of the Odyssey.* Beiträge zur klassischen Philologie 191. Frankfurt am Main.

Crotty, Kevin. 1994. *The Poetics of Supplication: Homer's Iliad and Odyssey.* Ithaca.

Currie, Bruno. 2015. "Cypria." In Fantuzzi and Tsagalis 2015:281–305.

Daitz, Stephen G. 1991. "On Reading Homer Aloud: To Pause or not to Pause." *American Journal of Philology* 112:149–160.

Dällenbach, Lucien. 1989. *The Mirror in the Text.* Trans. J. Whitely. Cambridge. [Orig. pub. as *Le Récit spéculaire. Essai sur la mise en abyme.* Paris, 1977.]

Danek, Georg. 1998. *Epos und Zitat: Studien zu den Quellen der Odyssee.* Vienna.

Danek, Georg, and Stefan Hagel. 1995. "Homer-Singen." *Wiener Humanistische Blätter* 37:5–20.

David, A. P. 2006. *Dance of the Muses: Choral Theory and Ancient Greek Poetics.* Oxford.

Detienne, Marcel. 1973. "L'olivier: Un mythe politico-religieux." In *Problèmes de la terre en Grèce ancienne,* ed. M. I. Finley, 293–306. Paris.

———. 1977. *The Gardens of Adonis: Spices in Greek Mythology.* Trans. Janet Lloyd. Atlantic Highlands, NJ.

———. 1996. *The Masters of Truth in Archaic Greece.* Foreword by P. Vidal-Naquet. Trans. Janet Lloyd. New York. [Orig. pub. as *Les Maîtres de vérité dans la grèce archaïque.* Paris, 1967.]

Detienne, Marcel, and Jean-Pierre Vernant. 1991. *Cunning Intelligence in Greek Culture and Society.* Trans. Janet Lloyd. Chicago.

Di Benedetto, Vincenzo. 1998. *Nel laboratorio di Omero.* Turin.

Diderot, Denis. 1963. *The Paradox of Acting.* Trans. Walter Herries Pollock. New York. [Orig. pub. as *Paradoxe sur le comédien.* Paris, 1830.]

Dodds, Eric R. 1967. *The Greeks and the Irrational.* Berkeley.

Doherty, Lillian E. 1991. "The Internal and Implied Audiences of *Odyssey* 11." *Arethusa* 24:145–176.

———. 1995. *Siren Songs: Gender, Audiences, and Narrators in the Odyssey.* Ann Arbor.

———. 2008. "Nausikaa and Tyro: Idylls of Courtship in the Phaiakian Episode of the *Odyssey* and the Hesiodic *Catalogue of Women.*" *Phoenix* 62:63–76.

Douglas, Mary. 1999. *Leviticus as Literature.* Oxford.

———. 2007. *Thinking in Circles: An Essay on Ring Composition.* New Haven.

Dowden, Ken. 1996. "Homer's Sense of Text." *Journal of Hellenic Studies* 116:47–61.

Dubois, Page. 2003. *Slaves and Other Objects.* Chicago.

Dué, Casey. 2002. *Homeric Variations on a Lament by Briseis.* Washington, DC. http://nrs.harvard.edu/urn-3:hul.ebook:CHS_Due.Homeric_Variations_on_a_Lament_by_Briseis.2002.

Dué, Casey, and Mary Ebbott. 2010. *Iliad 10 and the Poetics of Ambush: A Multitext Edition with Essays and Commentary.* Hellenic Studies Series 39. Washington, DC. http://nrs.harvard.edu/urn-3:hul.ebook:CHS_Due_Ebbott.Iliad_10_and_the_ Poetics_of_Ambush.2010.

Dué, Casey, and Gregory Nagy. 2004. "Illuminating the Classics with the Heroes of Philostratus." In Aitken and Maclean 2004:49–73.

Dupont-Roc, Roselyne, and Jean Lallot. 1980. *Aristote: La Poétique.* Paris.

Ebbott, Mary. 2005. "Butler's Authoress of the *Odyssey*: Gendered Readings of Homer, Then and Now." *Classics@* 3: https://chs.harvard.edu/CHS/ article/display/1313.

Ebel, Henry. 1972. *After Dionysus: An Essay on Where We Are Now.* Rutherford, NJ.

Edmunds, Lowell. 1997. "Myth in Homer." In Morris and Powell 1997:415–441.

———. 2016. "Intertextuality without Texts in Archaic Greek Verse and the Plan of Zeus." *Syllecta Classica* 27:1–27.

Edwards, Mark W. 1980. "Convention and Individuality in *Iliad* 1." *Harvard Studies in Classical Philology* 84:1–28.

———. 1987a. *Homer, Poet of the Iliad.* Baltimore.

———. 1987b. "Topos and Transformation in Homer." In *Homer: Beyond Oral Poetry,* ed. J. M. Bremer, I. J. F. de Jong, and J. Kalff, 47–60. Amsterdam.

———. 1991. *The Iliad: A Commentary,* vol. V: *Books 17-20.* Cambridge.

Else, Gerald. 1957. *Aristotle's Poetics: The Argument.* Cambridge, MA.

———. 1967. *Aristotle: Poetics.* Ann Arbor, MI.

Emlyn-Jones, Chris. 1986. "True and Lying Tales in the *Odyssey.*" *Greece and Rome* 33: 1–10.

Erbse, Hartmut, ed. 1969–1988. *Scholia graeca in Homeri Iliadem (scholia vetera).* 7 vols. Berlin.

Fajardo-Acosta, Fidel. 1990. *The Hero's Failure in the Tragedy of Odysseus: A Revisionist Analysis.* Studies in Epic and Romance Literature 3. Lewiston, NY.

Fantuzzi, Marco. 2012. *Achilles in Love: Intertextual Studies.* Oxford.

Fantuzzi, Marco, and Christos Tsagalis, eds. 2015. *The Greek Epic Cycle and Its Ancient Reception: A Companion.* Cambridge.

Farron, S. G. 1979–1980. "The *Odyssey* as an Anti-Aristocratic Statement." *Studies in Antiquity* 1:59–101.

Federico, Eduardo. 1999. *Dall'Ida al Salento: L'Itinerario mitico di Idomeneo cretese.* Atti della Accademia nazionale dei Lincei 396. Memorie (Accademia nazionale dei Lincei. Classe di scienze morali, storiche e filologiche), ser. 9, vol. 11, fasc. 2. Rome.

Feeney, D. C. 1991. *The Gods in Epic: Poets and Critics of the Classical Tradition.* Oxford.

Felman, Shoshana. 1982. *Literature and Psychoanalysis: The Question of Reading, Otherwise.* Baltimore.

Felson, Nancy. 1984. "Meleager and the Motifemic Analysis of Myth: A Response." *Arethusa* 17:211–223.

———. 1994. *Regarding Penelope: From Character to Poetics.* Princeton.

———. 1999. "Vicarious Transport: Fictive Deixis in Pindar's *Pythian Four.*" *Harvard Studies in Classical Philology* 99:1–31.

Felson, Nancy, and William Merritt Sale. 1983. "Meleager and Odysseus: A Structural and Cultural Study of the Greek Hunting-Maturation Myth." *Arethusa* 16:137–171.

Fenik, Bernard C. 1968. *Typical Battle Scenes in the Iliad.* Hermes Einzelschriften 21. Wiesbaden.

———. 1974. *Studies in the Odyssey.* Hermes Einzelschriften 30. Wiesbaden.

———, ed. 1978. *Homer: Tradition and Invention.* Leiden.

———. 1986. *Homer and the Nibelungenlied: Comparative Studies in Epic Style.* Cambridge, MA.

Fenno, Jonathan. 2007. "'Who Was the First, Who the Last?': Counting the Named Victims of Homeric Warriors." Oral presentation, Annual Meeting of the Classical Association of the Middle West and South (CAMWS), April 2007.

Fergusson, Francis. 1949. *The Idea of a Theater.* Princeton.

Ferrari, Gloria. 2004. "The 'Anodos' of the Bride." In Yatromanolakis and Roilos 2004:245–260.

Finkelberg, Margalit. 1986. "Is ΚΛΕΟΣ ΑΦΘΙΤΟΝ a Homeric Formula?" *Classical Quarterly* 36:1–5.

———. 2002. "The Sources of *Iliad* 7." *Colby Quarterly* 38:151–161.

Fish, Stanley. 1980. "Literature in the Reader: Affective Stylistics." In Tompkins 1980:70–100.

Flaumenhaft, Mera J. 1982. "The Undercover Hero: Odysseus from Dark to Daylight." *Interpretation* 10:9–41.

Flickinger, Roy C. 1936. *The Greek Theatre and Its Drama*. Chicago.

Foley, Helene P. 1978. "'Reverse Similes' and Sex Roles in the *Odyssey*." *Arethusa* 11:7–26.

Foley, John Miles. 1990. *Traditional Oral Epic: The Odyssey, Beowulf, and the Serbo-Croatian Return Song*. Bloomington, IN.

———. 2002. *How to Read an Oral Poem*. Urbana.

Ford, Andrew. 1988. "The Classical Definition of ΡΑΨΩΙΔΙΑ." *Classical Philology* 83:300–307.

———. 1992. *Homer: The Poetry of the Past*. Ithaca.

———. 1996. Review of Erwin F. Cook, *The Odyssey in Athens: Myths of Cultural Origins* (Ithaca, 1995). *Bryn Mawr Classical Review* 96.4.27.

———. 1997a. "Epic as Genre." In Morris and Powell 1997:396–414.

———. 1997b. "The Inland Ship: Problems in the Performance and Reception of Homeric Epic." In Bakker and Kahane 1997:83–109.

———. 2002. *The Origins of Criticism: Literary Culture and Poetic Theory in Classical Greece*. Princeton.

Fraiman, Susan. 1995. "Jane Austen and Edward Said: Gender, Culture and Imperialism." *Critical Inquiry* 21:805–821.

Frame, Douglas. 1978. *The Myth of Return in Early Greek Epic*. New Haven.

———. 2009. *Hippota Nestor*. Hellenic Studies 37. Washington, DC. http://nrs.harvard.edu/urn-3:hul.ebook:CHS_Frame.Hippota_Nestor.2009

Fränkel, Hermann. 1925. "Griechische Wörter." *Glotta* 14:1–13.

———. 1997. "Essence and Nature of the Homeric Similes." In *Homer: German Scholarship in Translation*, trans. G. M. Wright and P. V. Jones, 103–123. Oxford. Orig. pub. as *Die homerischen Gleichnisse*. Göttingen, 1921.

Franko, George F. 2005–2006. "The Trojan Horse at the Close of the *Iliad*." *Classical Journal* 101:121–123.

Frazer, James G., ed. 1921. *Apollodorus: The Library*. 2 vols. Cambridge, MA.

Freud, Sigmund. 1955. "The 'Uncanny.'" Trans. James Strachey. In *The Standard Edition of the Complete Psychological Works of Sigmund Freud*. Vol. 17. *An Infantile Neurosis and Other Works*, ed. J. Strachey, 217–256. London.

Friedrich, Paul. 1975. "Defilement and Honor in the *Iliad*." *Journal of Indo-European Studies* 1:119–126.

———. 1977. "Sanity and the Myth of Honor: The Problem of Achilles." *Ethos* 5:281–305.

———. 1986. *The Meaning of Aphrodite*. Chicago.

———. 2001. "Lyric Epiphany." *Language in Society* 30:217–247.

Friedrich, Paul, and James Redfield. 1978. "Speech as a Personality Symbol: The Case of Achilles." *Language* 54:263–288.

———. 1981. "Contra Messing." *Language* 57:901–903.

Friedrich, Rainer. 2011. "Odysseus and Achilles in the *Iliad*: Hidden Hermeneutic Horror in Readings of the *Presbeia*." *Hermes* 139:271–290.

Friis Johansen, Knud. 1967. *The Iliad in Early Greek Art*. Copenhagen.

Fritz, Kurt von. 1943. "*Noos* and *Noein* in the Homeric Poems." *Classical Philology* 38:79–93.

Frontisi-Ducroux, Françoise. 1986a. *La cithare d'Achille*. Rome.

———. 1986b. "La mort en face." *Metis* 1:197–217.

Frye, Northrop. 1957. *Anatomy of Criticism*. Princeton.

Fulkerson, Laurel. 2002. "(Un)Sympathetic Magic: A Study of *Heroides* 13." *American Journal of Philology* 123:61–87.

Gaca, Kathy. 2008. "Reinterpreting the Homeric Simile of *Iliad* 16.7–11: The Girl and Her Mother in Ancient Greek Warfare." *American Journal of Philology* 129:145–171.

Gadamer, Hans-Georg. 1989. *Truth and Method*. 2nd ed., trans. J. Weinsheimer and D. G. Marshall. London.

Gainsford, Peter. 2001. "Cognition and Type-Scenes: The *Aoidos* at Work." In *Homer, Tragedy and Beyond: Essays in Honour of P. E. Easterling*, ed. Felix Budelmann and Pantelis Michelakis, 3–21. London.

———. 2003. "Formal Analysis of Recognition Scenes in the *Odyssey*." *Journal of Hellenic Studies* 123:41–59.

Gaisser, Julia Haig. 1969. "A Structural Analysis of the Digressions in the *Iliad* and *Odyssey*." *Harvard Studies in Classical Philology* 73:1–43.

Gantz, Timothy. 1993. *Early Greek Myth*. 2 vols. Baltimore.

Garber, Marjorie B. 1987. *Shakespeare's Ghost Writers: Literature as Uncanny Causality*. New York.

Gentili, Bruno. 1988. *Poetry and Its Public in Ancient Greece*. Trans. A. Thomas Cole. Baltimore. Orig. pub. as *Poesia e pubblico nella Grecia antica*. Rome, 1995.

Gilbert, Stuart. 1955. *James Joyce's Ulysses: A Study*. New York.

Goffman, Erving. 1959. *The Presentation of Self in Everyday Life*. Rev. ed. New York.

———. 1974. *Frame Analysis: An Essay on the Organization of Experience*. New York.

Goldhill, Simon. 1984. "Exegesis: Oedipus (R)ex." *Arethusa* 17:177–200.

———. 1988. "Reading Differences: Juxtaposition and the *Odyssey*." *Ramus* 17: 1–31.

———. 1989. "Reading Performance Criticism." *Greece and Rome* 36: 172–182.

Goldhill, Simon. 1991. *The Poet's Voice: Essays on Poetics and Greek Literature.* Cambridge.

Goldhill, Simon, and Robin Osborne, eds. 1999. *Performance Culture and Athenian Democracy.* Cambridge/New York.

Goldin-Meadow, Susan, and Sian L. Beilock. 2010. "Action's Influence on Thought: The Case of Gesture." *Perspectives on Psychological Science* 5.6:664–674.

Goldman, Michael. 1975. *The Actor's Freedom: Toward a Theory of Drama.* New York.

———. 1985. *Acting and Action in Shakespearean Tragedy.* Princeton.

González, José M. 2013. *The Epic Rhapsode and His Craft: Homeric Performance in a Diachronic Perspective.* Hellenic Studies 47. Washington, DC. http://nrs.harvard.edu/urn-3:hul.ebook:CHS_GonzalezJ.The_Epic_Rhapsode _and_his_Craft.2013.

Goodyear, F. R. D. 1981. *The Annals of Tacitus, Books 1-6. Volume II: Annals I.55-81 and Annals 2.* Cambridge.

Gould, Thomas. 1963. "Aristotle and the Irrational." *Arion* 2:55–74.

Graf, Fritz. 1985. *Nordionische Kulte.* Rome.

———. 2014. "Derveni and Ritual." In *Poetry as Initiation: The Center for Hellenic Studies Symposium on the Derveni Papyrus,* ed. I. Papadopoulou and L. Muellner, 67–85. Washington, DC.

Gray, Vivienne. 2005. "Short Stories in Herodotus' Histories." In *Brill's Companion to Herodotus,* ed. Egbert Bakker, Irene J. F. de Jong, and Hans van Wees, 291–317. Leiden.

Gresseth, Gerald K. 1964. "The Myth of Alcyone." *Transactions of the American Philological Association* 95:88–98.

Griffin, Jasper. 1977. "The Epic Cycle and the Uniqueness of Homer." *Journal of Hellenic Studies* 97:39–53.

———. 1980. *Homer on Life and Death.* Oxford.

———. 1987. "Homer and Excess." In *Homer: Beyond Oral Poetry,* ed. J. M. Bremer, I. J. F. de Jong, and J. Kalff, 85–104. Amsterdam.

———, ed. 1995. *Homer: Iliad IX.* Oxford.

Grossardt, Peter. 2001. *Die Erzählung von Meleagros. Zur literarischen Entwicklung der kalydonischen Kultlegende.* Mnemosyne Supplement 215. Leiden.

Grossman, Allen, with Mark Halliday. 1992. *The Sighted Singer: Two Works on Poetry for Readers and Writers.* Baltimore.

Gudeman, A. 1934. *Aristoteles Peri Poiētikes.* Berlin.

Gumbrecht, H. U. 2004. *Production of Presence: What Meaning Cannot Convey.* Stanford.

Guthrie, W. K. C. 1993. *Orpheus and Greek Religion: A Study of the Orphic Movement.* Princeton.

Haft, Adele J. 1984. "Odysseus, Idomeneus and Meriones: The Cretan Lies of *Odyssey* 13–19." *Classical Journal* 79:289–306.

———. 1989. "Odysseus, Aethon, and the Trojan Horse Stratagem." *Classical Bulletin* 65:67–70.

Hainsworth, Bryan. 1993. *The Iliad, A Commentary.* Vol. 3, *Books 9–12.* General ed. G. S. Kirk. Cambridge.

Halliwell, Stephen. 1987. *The Poetics of Aristotle: Translation and Commentary.* Chapel Hill, NC.

———. 1989. "Aristotle's *Poetics.*" In Kennedy 1989:149–183.

———. 1998. *Aristotle's Poetics.* Chicago.

———. 2002. *The Aesthetics of Mimesis: Ancient Texts and Modern Problems.* Princeton.

Halliwell, Stephen, et al., eds. 1996. *Aristotle, Poetics. Longinus, On the Sublime. Demetrius, On Style.* Cambridge, MA.

Halperin, David M. 1990. *One Hundred Years of Homosexuality: And Other Essays on Greek Love.* New York.

Hankey, Robin. 1985. "Eumaeus and the Moral Design of the *Odyssey.*" In *Essays in Honour of Agathe Thornton,* ed. R. Hankey and D. Little, 26–34. Otago.

Hansen, Leigh Jellison. 1980. "Death and the Indo-Europeans: Some Traditions." *Journal of Indo-European Studies* 8:31–40.

Hansen, William F. 1977. "Odysseus' Last Journey." *Quaderni Urbinati di Cultura Classica* 24:27–48.

———. 1982. *The Conference Sequence: Patterned Narration and Narrative Inconsistency in the Odyssey.* Berkeley.

———. 1997. "Homer and the Folktale." In Morris and Powell 1997:442–462.

Haubold, Johannes. 2000. *Homer's People: Epic Poetry and Social Formation.* Cambridge.

Harriott, Rosemary. 1969. *Poetry and Criticism Before Plato.* London.

Heath, Malcolm. 1985. "Hesiod's Didactic Poetry." *Classical Quarterly* 35:245–263.

———. 1987. "Homeric Criticism." Review of F. Frontisi-Ducroux, *La Cithare d'Achille* (Rome, 1986) and F. Ferrari, *Oralita ed espressione* (Pisa, 1986). *Classical Review* n.s. 37:139–142.

Heckenlively, T. 2007. "Hesiod and the Eros of Death: the problem of Keyx." Oral presentation, Annual Meeting of the Classical Association of the Midwest and South (CAMWS), April 2007.

Hedreen, Guy. 1991. "The Cult of Achilles in the Euxine." *Hesperia* 60:313–330.

Heidegger, Martin. 2000. *Introduction to Metaphysics.* Trans. Greg Fried and Richard Polt. New Haven.

Heiden, Bruce. 1996. "The Three Movements of the *Iliad.*" *Greek, Roman, and Byzantine Studies* 37:5–22.

Heiden, Bruce. 2000. "The Placement of 'Book Divisions' in the *Odyssey*." *Classical Philology* 95:247–259.

Herington, John. 1985. *Poetry into Drama: Early Tragedy and the Greek Poetic Tradition*. Sather Classical Lectures. Berkeley.

Herzfeld, Michael. 1983. "The Excavation of Concepts: Commentary on Peradotto and Nagy." *Arethusa* 16:57–68.

Heubeck, Alfred. 1984. "Das Meleagros-Paradeigma in der *Ilias* I 529–599." In *Kleine Schriften zur griechischen Sprache und Literatur*, 128–135. Erlangen. Orig. pub. 1943, in *Neue Jahrbücher* 118:13–20.

Heubeck, Alfred, J. B. Hainsworth, et al., eds. 1988–1992. *A Commentary on Homer's Odyssey*. 3 vols. Oxford.

Heubeck, Alfred, and Arie Hoekstra, eds. 1989. *A Commentary on Homer's Odyssey, Vol. II: Books IX-XVI*. Oxford.

Heubeck, Alfred, Stephanie West, and J. B. Hainsworth, eds. 1988. *A Commentary on Homer's Odyssey*. Vol. 1, *Books I-VIII*. Oxford.

Heyne, Christian G., ed. 1834. *Homeri Ilias*. Oxford.

Hillers, Delbert R., and Marsh H. McCall, Jr. 1976. "Homeric Dictated Texts: A Reexamination of Some Near Eastern Evidence." *Harvard Studies in Classical Philology* 80:19–23.

Höckmann, Ursula. 1982. "Nestor und Phoinix in der Tomba François in Vulci." *Boreas (Münstersche Beiträge zur Archäologie)* 5:78–87.

Hoekstra, Arie. 1981. *Epic Verse before Homer: Three Studies*. Amsterdam.

Hogan, James C. 1973. "Aristotle's Criticism of Homer in the *Poetics*." *Classical Philology* 68:95–108.

Howald, Ernst. 1924. "Meleager und Achill." *Rheinisches Museum* 73:402–425.

Hubaux, Jean, and Maxime Leroy. 1939. *Le mythe du phénix dans les littératures grecque et latine*. Liège.

Irwin, Elizabeth. 2008. "Gods among Men? The Social and Political Dynamics of the Hesiodic Catalogue of Women." In *The Hesiodic Catalogue of Women: Constructions and Reconstructions*, ed. R. Hunter, 35–84. Cambridge.

Iser, Wolfgang. 1989. "The Play of the Text." In Budick and Iser 1989:325–339.

Jamison, Stephanie. 1999. "Penelope and the Pigs: Indic Perspectives on the *Odyssey*." *Classical Antiquity* 18:227–272.

Janko, Richard. 1987. *Aristotle: Poetics I*. Indianapolis.

———. 1994. *The Iliad: A Commentary, vol. IV: Books 13-16*. Cambridge.

Jauss, Hans Robert. 1974. "Levels of Identification of Hero and Audience." *New Literary History* 5:283–317.

Jensen, Minna Skafte. 2002. "Phoenix, Achilles and a Narrative Pattern." In *Noctes Atticae*, ed. Bettina Amden, et al., 159–163. Copenhagen.

Johnson, W. R. 1976. *Darkness Visible*. Berkeley.

Johnston, Sarah Iles. 1992. "Xanthus, Hera and the Erinyes, *Iliad* 19.400–418." *Transactions of the American Philological Association* 122:85–98.

Jong, Irene J. F. de. 1987. *Narrators and Focalizers: The Presentation of the Story in the Iliad.* Amsterdam.

———. 1988. "Homeric Words and Speakers: An Addendum." *Journal of Hellenic Studies* 108:188–189.

———. 1992. "The Subjective Style in Odysseus' Wanderings." *Classical Quarterly* 42:1–11.

———. 1996. "Sunsets and Sunrises in Homer and Apollonius of Rhodes: Book-Divisions and Beyond." *Dialogos* 3:20–35.

———. 2001. *A Narratological Commentary on the Odyssey.* Cambridge.

Jouan, François. 1966. *Euripide et les légendes des Chants cypriens, des origines de la guerre de Troie à l' Iliade.* Paris.

Kahane, Ahuvia. 1994. *The Interpretation of Order: A Study in the Poetics of Homeric Repetition.* Oxford.

Kakridis, Johannes T. 1949. *Homeric Researches.* Acta Reg. Societatis Humaniorum Litterarum Lundensis 45. Lund.

Katz, Marilyn. 1991. *Penelope's Renown: Meaning and Indeterminacy in the Odyssey.* Princeton.

Kearns, Emily. 1982. "The Return of Odysseus: A Homeric Theoxeny." *Classical Quarterly* 32:2–8.

Kennedy, George A., ed. 1989. *The Cambridge History of Literary Criticism.* Cambridge.

King, Ben. 1999. "The Rhetoric of the Victim: Odysseus in the Swineherd's Hut." *Classical Antiquity* 18:74–93.

King, Bruce M. Unpublished MS. "*Iliad* 11.668–762 and Beyond: The Cattle-raid and the Genre of the *Iliad.*"

Kirk, G. S. 1962. *The Songs of Homer.* Cambridge.

———, ed. 1964. *The Language and Background of Homer.* New York.

———. 1970. *Myth, Its Meaning and Functions.* Berkeley.

———, ed. 1985. *The Iliad: A Commentary.* Vol. 1, *Books 1–4.* Cambridge.

———, ed. 1990. *The Iliad: A Commentary.* Vol. 2, *Books 5–8.* Cambridge.

Kirk, G. S., J. E. Raven, and M. Schofield, eds. 1983. *The Presocratic Philosophers.* 2nd ed. Cambridge.

Knox, Peter E. 2015. "The Literary House of Mr. Octavius Quartio." *Illinois Classical Studies* 40:171–184.

Koenen, Ludwig. 1994. "Greece, the Near East, and Egypt: Cyclic Destruction in Hesiod and the Catalogue of Women." *Transactions of the American Philological Association* 124:1–34.

Kosman, Aryeh. 1992. "Acting: *Drama* as the *Mimesis* of *Praxis.*" In Rorty 1992:51–72.

Kozak, Lynn. 2017. *Experiencing Hektor: Character in the Iliad.* London.

Kretler, Katherine. 2018. "Tapping the Wellsprings of Action: Aristotle's Birth of Tragedy as a Mimesis of Poetic Practice." In *Thinking the Greeks: A Volume in Honour of James M. Redfield*, ed. Bruce M. King and Lillian Doherty, 70–90. Abingdon and New York.

Kullmann, Wolfgang. 1955. "Ein vorhomerische Motiv im Iliasproömium." *Philologus* 99:167–192.

———. 1956. "Zur ΔΙΟΣ ΒΟΥΛΗ des Iliasproömiums." *Philologus* 100:132–133.

———. 1960. *Die Quellen der Ilias*. Hermes Einzelschriften 14. Wiesbaden.

———. 1984. "Oral Poetry Theory and Neoanalysis in Homeric Research." *Greek, Roman, and Byzantine Studies* 25:307–323. Trans. Thomas Kullmann.

———. 2001. "Past and Future in the *Iliad*." In Cairns 2001:385–408. Trans. Leofranc Holford-Strevens. Orig. pub. 1968 as "Vergangenheit und Zukunkft in der Ilias." *Poetica* 2:15–37.

Lang, Mabel L. 1969. "Homer and Oral Techniques." *Hesperia* 38:159–168.

———. 1983. "Reverberation and Mythology in the *Iliad*." In *Approaches to Homer*, ed. Carl A. Rubino and Cynthia W. Shelmerdine, 140–164. Austin.

———. 1995. "War Story into Wrath Story." In Carter and Morris 1995:149–162.

Lateiner, Donald. 1995. *Sardonic Smile: Nonverbal Behavior in Homeric Epic*. Ann Arbor, MI.

Lavery, Bryony. 2004. *Frozen*. New York.

Lawrence, Marion. 1965. "The Velletri Sarcophagus." *American Journal of Archaeology* 69:207–222.

Leaf, Walter. 1900–1902. *The Iliad of Homer*. 2 vols. London.

Ledbetter, Grace. 1993. "Achilles' Self-Address: *Iliad* 16.7–19." *American Journal of Philology* 114:481–491.

Létoublon, Françoise. 1983. "Le miroir et la boucle." *Poétique* 53:19–36.

———. 2001. "The Mirror and the Loop." In Loraux, Nagy, and Slatkin 2001:375–383. New York.

Levaniouk, Olga. 1999. "Penelope and the *Pênelops*." In *Nine Essays on Homer*, ed. Miriam Carlisle and Olga Levaniouk, 95–136. Lanham, MD.

———. 2000. "*Aithôn*, Aithon and Odysseus." *Harvard Studies in Classical Philology* 100:25–51.

———. 2008. "Penelope and the Pandareids." *Phoenix* 62:5–38.

———. 2011. *Eve of the Festival: Making Myth in Odyssey 19*. Washington, DC.

———. 2012. "Οὐ χρώμεθα τοῖς ξενικοῖς ποιήμασιν: Questions about Evolution and Fluidity of the *Odyssey*." In Montanari, Rengakos, and Tsagalis 2012:369–409.

Levine, Daniel B. 1982. "Homeric Laughter and the Unsmiling Suitors." *Classical Journal* 78:97–104.

Libera, Anne, ed. 2004. *The Second City Almanac of Improvisation*. Evanston, IL.

Lloyd-Jones, H. 1983. *The Justice of Zeus.* 2nd ed. Sather Classical Lectures 41. Berkeley.

Loesch, Katharine T. 1965. "Literary Ambiguity and Oral Performance." *Quarterly Journal of Speech* 51:258–267.

Lohmann, Dieter. 1970. *Die Komposition der Reden in der Ilias.* Berlin.

Lombardo, Stanley, trans. 1997. *Iliad.* Indianapolis.

Loraux, Nicole, Gregory Nagy, and Laura Slatkin, eds. 2001. *Antiquities.* Vol. 3 of *Postwar French Thought.* New York.

Lord, Albert B. 1951. "Composition by Theme in Homer and Southslavic Epos." *Transactions of the American Philological Association* 82:71–80.

———. 1995. *The Singer Resumes the Tale.* Ithaca, NY.

———. 2000. *The Singer of Tales.* 2nd ed. Ed. S. Mitchell and G. Nagy. Cambridge, MA. First edition 1960.

Lord, Mary Louise. 1967. "Withdrawal and Return: An Epic Story Pattern in the Homeric Hymn to Demeter and in the Homeric Poems." *Classical Journal* 62:241–248.

Louden, Bruce. 1993. "An Extended Narrative Pattern in the *Odyssey.*" *Greek, Roman, and Byzantine Studies* 34:5–33.

———. 1997. "Eumaios and Alkinoos: The Audience and the *Odyssey.*" *Phoenix* 51:95–114.

———. 1999. *The Odyssey: Structure, Narration, and Meaning.* Baltimore.

Lowe, N. J. 2000. *The Classical Plot and the Invention of Western Narrative.* Cambridge.

Lowenstam, Steven. 1981. *The Death of Patroklos: A Study in Typology.* Königstein/Ts.

———. 1993. *The Scepter and the Spear: Studies on Forms of Repetition in the Homeric Poems.* Lanham, MD.

———. 1997. "Talking Vases: The Relationship between the Homeric Poems and Archaic Representations of Greek Myth." *Transactions of the American Philological Association* 127:21–76.

Lucas, D. W. 1968. *Aristotle: Poetics.* Oxford.

Lyne, R. O. A. M. 1998. "Love and Death: Laodamia and Protesilaus in Catullus, Propertius, and Others." *Classical Quarterly* 48:200–212.

Lynn-George, Michael. 1988. *Epos: Word, Narrative, and the Iliad.* Atlantic Highlands, NJ.

MacCary, W. Thomas. 1982. *Childlike Achilles: Ontogeny and Phylogeny in the Iliad.* New York.

Mackay, E. Anne. 2001. "The Frontal Face and 'You': Narrative Disjunction in Early Greek Poetry and Painting." *Acta Classica* 44:5–34.

———, ed. 2008. *Orality, Literacy, Memory in the Ancient Greek and Roman World.* Leiden.

Mackay, E. Anne, Deirdre Harrison, and Samantha Masters. 1999. "The Bystander at the Ringside: Ring-Composition in Early Greek Poetry and Athenian Black-Figure Vase Painting." In *Signs of Orality: The Oral Tradition and Its Influence in the Greek and Roman World*, ed. E. Anne Mackay, 115–142. Leiden.

Maclean, Jennifer K. Berenson, and Ellen Bradshaw Aitken, eds. and trans. 2001. *Flavius Philostratus: Heroikos*. Atlanta.

Macleod, Colin. 1982. *Iliad, Book XXIV*. Cambridge.

———. 2001. "Homer on Poetry and the Poetry of Homer." In Cairns 2001:294–310.

Maehler, Herwig, ed. 2004. *Bacchylides: A Selection*. Cambridge.

Maggiani, Adriano. 1983. "Nuovi dati per la ricostruzione del ciclo pittorico della tomba François." *Dialoghi di archeologia* 3s., 1:71–78.

Malkin, Irad. 1998. *The Returns of Odysseus: Colonization and Ethnicity*. Berkeley.

Mango, Marlia Mundell, and Anna Bennett. 1994. *The Sevso Treasure*. Ann Arbor, MI.

Marks, J. 2003. "Alternative Odysseys: The Case of Thoas and Odysseus." *Transactions of the American Philological Association* 133:209–226.

———. 2008. *Zeus in the Odyssey*. Hellenic Studies Series 31. Washington, DC. http://nrs.harvard.edu/urn-3:hul.ebook:CHS_Marks.Zeus_in_the_Odyssey.2008.

Martin, Richard. 1989. *The Language of Heroes: Speech and Performance in the Iliad*. Ithaca.

———. 1993. "Telemachus and the Last Hero Song." *Colby Quarterly* 29:222–240.

———. 1997. "Similes and Performance." In *Written Voices, Spoken Signs: Tradition, Performance, and the Epic Text*, ed. Egbert Bakker and Ahuvia Kahane, 138–166. Cambridge, MA.

———. 2000. "Synchronic Aspects of Homeric Performance: The Evidence of the Hymn to Apollo." In *Una nueva visión de la cultura griega antigua hacia el fin del milenio*, ed. A. M. González de Tobia, 403–432. La Plata.

———. 2005. "Cretan Homers: Tradition, Politics, Fieldwork." *Classics@* 3: https://chs.harvard.edu/CHS/article/display/1337.

———. 2007. "Outer Limits, Choral Space." In *Visualizing the Tragic: Drama, Myth, and Ritual in Greek Art and Literature*, ed. Chris Kraus, Simon Goldhill, Helene P. Foley, and Jaś Elsner, 35–62. New York.

Marzullo, Benedetto. 1980. "Die visuelle Dimension des Theaters bei Aristoteles." *Philologus* 124:189–200.

Matthews, V. J. 1980. "Metrical Reasons for Apostrophe in Homer." *Liverpool Classical Monthly* 5:93–99.

McCullough, Karl-Erik. 2005. "Using Gestures in Speaking: Self-Generating Indexical Fields." PhD Diss., University of Chicago, Department of Linguistics.

McNeill, David. 2005. *Gesture and Thought*. Chicago.

McNeill, David, et al. 2001. "Catchments, Prosody and Discourse." *Gesture* 1:9–33.

Meijering, Roos. 1987. *Literary and Rhetorical Theories in Greek Scholia*. Groningen.

Merkelbach, Reinhold. 1951. *Untersuchungen zur Odyssee*. Munich.

Merkelbach, Reinhold, and Martin West. 1965. "The Wedding of Ceyx." *Rheinisches Museum für Philologie* 108:300–317.

———. 1983. *Hesiodi Opera*. Ed. F. Solmsen. 2nd ed. Oxford.

Messing, Gordon M. 1981. "On Weighing Achilles' Winged Words." *Language* 57: 888–900.

Meyer, Eduard. 1918. "Die Rhapsoden und die homerischen Epen." *Hermes* 53: 330–336.

Minchin, Elizabeth. 1992. "Homer Springs a Surprise: Eumaios' Tale at *Od.* o 403–484." *Hermes* 120:259–266.

———. 1995. "Ring-Patterns and Ring-Composition: Some Observations on the Framing of Stories in Homer." *Helios* 22:23–35.

———. 2007. *Homeric Voices: Discourse, Memory, Gender*. Oxford.

———. 2008. "Spatial Memory and the Composition of the *Iliad*." In Mackay 2008:9–34.

———. 2012. "Memory and Memories: Personal, Social, and Cultural Memory in the Poems of Homer." In Montanari, Rengakos, and Tsagalis 2012:83–99.

Monro, D. B. 1901. *Homer's Odyssey, Books XIII–XXIV*. Oxford.

Montanari, Franco, Antonios Rengakos, and Christos Tsagalis, eds. 2012. *Homeric Contexts: Neoanalysis and the Interpretation of Oral Poetry*. Berlin.

Morris, Ian, and Barry Powell, eds. 1997. *A New Companion to Homer*. Mnemosyne 163. Leiden.

Morrison, James V. 1992. "Alternatives to Epic Tradition: Homer's Challenges in the *Iliad*." *Transactions of the American Philological Association* 122:61–71.

Most, Glenn. 1983. "Of Motifemes and Megatexts: Comment on Rubin/Sale and Segal." *Arethusa* 16:199–218.

———. 1989. "The Structure and Function of Odysseus' *Apologoi*." *Transactions of the American Philological Association* 119:15–30.

Moulton, Carroll W. 1974. "Similes in the *Iliad*." *Hermes* 102:381–397.

———. 1977. *Similes in the Heroic Poems*. Hypomnemata 49. Göttingen.

Muellner, Leonard. 1990. "The Simile of the Cranes and Pygmies: A Study of Homeric Metaphor." *Harvard Studies in Classical Philology* 93:59–101.

———. 1996. *The Anger of Achilles: Mênis in Greek Epic*. Ithaca, NY.

———. 2012. "Grieving Achilles." In Montanari, Rengakos, and Tsagalis 2012: 197–220.

Mühlestein, H. 1981. "Der homerische Phoinix und sein Name." *Živa Antika* 31:85–91.

———. 1987. *Homerische Namenstudien*. Frankfurt.

Mullen, William. 1982. *Choreia: Pindar and Dance*. Princeton.

Murnaghan, Sheila. 1987. *Disguise and Recognition in the Odyssey*. Princeton.

———. 1997. "Equal Honor and Future Glory: The Plan of Zeus in the *Iliad*." In *Classical Closure: Reading the End in Greek and Latin Literature*, ed. D. H. Roberts, F. M. Dunn, and D. Fowler, 23–42. Princeton.

Nagler, Michael. 1974. *Spontaneity and Tradition: A Study in the Oral Art of Homer*. Berkeley.

———. 1980. "Entretiens avec Tirésias." *Classical World* 74:89–106.

———. 1990. "Odysseus: The Proem and the Problem." *Classical Antiquity* 9: 335–356.

———. 1993. "Penelope's Male Hand: Gender and Violence in the *Odyssey*." *Colby Quarterly* 29:241–257.

———. 1996. "Dread Goddess Revisited." In Schein 1996:141–161.

Nagy, Gregory. 1974. *Comparative Studies in Greek and Indic Meter*. Cambridge, MA.

———. 1979. *The Best of the Achaeans: Concepts of the Hero in Archaic Greek Poetry*. Baltimore.

———. 1982. "Theognis of Megara: The Poet as Seer, Pilot, and Revenant." *Arethusa* 15:109–128.

———. 1987. "The Sign of Protesilaos." *MHTIΣ* 2:207–213.

———. 1990a. *Greek Mythology and Poetics*. Ithaca and London.

———. 1990b. *Pindar's Homer: The Lyric Possession of an Epic Past*. Baltimore.

———. 1996a. *Poetry as Performance: Homer and Beyond*. Cambridge.

———. 1996b. *Homeric Questions*. Austin.

———. 1997. "Homeric Scholia." In Morris and Powell 1997:101–122.

———. 2001a. "The Sign of the Hero: A Prologue." In *Flavius Philostratus: Heroikos*, ed. Jennifer K. Berenson Maclean and Ellen Bradshaw Aitken, xv–xxxv. Atlanta.

———. 2001b. "Reading Bakhtin Reading the Classics: An Epic Fate for Conveyors of the Heroic Past." In *Bakhtin and the Classics*, ed. R. Bracht Branham, 71–96. Evanston, IL.

———. 2002. *Plato's Rhapsody and Homer's Music: The Poetics of the Panathenaic Festival in Classical Athens*. Hellenic Studies 1. Washington, DC. http://nrs.harvard.edu/urn-3:hul.ebook:CHS_Nagy.Platos_Rhapsody_and_Homers_Music.2002.

———. 2003. *Homeric Responses*. Austin.

———. 2004. "Poetics of Repetition in Homer." In Yatromanolakis and Roilos 2004:139–148.

———. 2009. *Homer the Classic*. Hellenic Studies 36. Washington, DC. Orig. pub. http://nrs.harvard.edu/urn-3:hul.ebook:CHS_Nagy.Homer_the_Classic.2008.

———. 2010. *Homer the Preclassic*. Sather Classical Lectures 67. Berkeley.

———. 2013. "The Delian Maidens and Their Relevance to Choral Mimesis in Classical Drama." In *Choral Mediations in Greek Tragedy*, ed. R. Gagné and M. G. Hopman, 227–256. Cambridge.

———. 2017. "Diachronic Homer and a Cretan *Odyssey*." *Oral Tradition* 31:3–50.

Newton, Rick. 1984. "The Rebirth of Odysseus." *Greek, Roman, and Byzantine Studies* 25:5–20.

———. 2009. "Geras and Guest-Gifts in Homer." In *Reading Homer: Film and Text*, ed. K. Myrsiades, 58–88. Madison, NJ.

Nickel, Roberto. 2002. "Euphorbus and the Death of Achilles." *Phoenix* 56:215–233.

Nimis, Stephen A. 1987. *Narrative Semiotics in the Epic Tradition: The Simile*. Bloomington and Indianapolis.

———. 1999. "Ring-composition and Linearity in Homer." In *Signs of Orality: The Oral Tradition and Its Influence in the Greek and Roman World*, ed. E. Anne Mackay, 65–78. Leiden.

Nisbet, R. G. M., and Margaret Hubbard. 1970. *A Commentary on Horace: Odes, Book 1*. Oxford.

Notopoulos, James A. 1949. "Parataxis in Homer: A New Approach to Homeric Literary Criticism." *Transactions of the American Philological Association* 80:1–23.

———. 1951. "Continuity and Interconnexion in Homeric Oral Composition." *Transactions of the American Philological Association* 82:81–101.

Noy, David. 2000. "'Half-burnt on an Emergency Pyre': Roman Cremations Which Went Wrong." *Greece and Rome* 47:186–196.

Nünlist, René. 2003. "The Homeric Scholia on Focalization." *Mnemosyne* 56:61–71.

Nussbaum, Martha C. 1986. *The Fragility of Goodness: Luck and Ethics in Greek Tragedy and Philosophy*. Cambridge.

Oehler, Robert. 1925. *Mythologische Exempla in der älteren griechischen Dichtung*. Diss., Basel.

O'Sullivan, James N. 1984. "The Sign of the Bed: *Odyssey* 23.173ff." *Greek, Roman, and Byzantine Studies* 25:21–25.

Otterlo, W. A. van. 1948. *De Ringcompositie als Opbouwprincipe in de Epische Gedichten van Homerus*. Amsterdam.

Pache, Corinne Ondine. 1999. "Odysseus and the Phaeacians." In Carlisle and Levaniouk 1999:21–33.

Padel, Ruth. 1992. *In and Out of the Mind: Greek Images of the Tragic Self*. Princeton.

———. 1995. *Whom Gods Destroy: Elements of Greek and Tragic Madness*. Princeton.

Page, Denys L. 1955. *The Homeric Odyssey*. Oxford.

———. 1959. *History and the Homeric Iliad*. Berkeley and Los Angeles.

———. 1973. *Folktales in Homer's Odyssey*. Cambridge.

Papadopoulou, Ioanna. 2014. "Testing Our Tools: Open Questions on the Derveni Papyrus." In *Poetry as Initiation: The Center for Hellenic Studies Symposium on the Derveni Papyrus*, ed. I. Papadopoulou and L. Muellner, ix–xxiv. Washington, DC.

Parry, Adam. 1964. "The Language of Achilles." *Transactions of the American Philological Association* 87:1–7. Reprinted in Kirk 1964:48–54.

———. 1972. "Language and Characterization in Homer." *Harvard Studies in Classical Philology* 76:1–22.

Parry, Milman. 1971. *The Making of Homeric Verse. The Collected Papers of Milman Parry*. Ed. Adam Parry. Oxford.

Patzer, Harald. 1952. "ΡΑΨΩΙΔΟΣ." *Hermes* 80:314–325.

Pazdernik, Charles F. 1995. "Odysseus and His Audience: *Odyssey* 9.39–40 and Its Formulaic Resonances." *American Journal of Philology* 116:347–369.

Pelliccia, Hayden. 2003. "Two Points about Rhapsodes." In *Homer, the Bible, and Beyond*, ed. Margalit Finkelberg and Guy G. Stroumsa, 97–116. Leiden.

Peradotto, John. 1974. "*Odyssey* 8.564–571: Verisimilitude, Narrative Analysis, and Bricolage." *Texas Studies in Literature and Language* 15.5. Special Classics Issue 1974.

———. 1990. *Man in the Middle Voice: Name and Narration in the Odyssey*. Martin Classical Lectures, New Series 1. Princeton.

———. 1997. "Modern Theoretical Approaches to Homer." In Morris and Powell 1997:380–395.

———. 2002. "Prophecy and Persons: Reading Character in the *Odyssey*." *Arethusa* 35:3–15.

Petegorsky, Dan. 1982. "Context and Evocation: Studies in Early Greek and Sanskrit Poetry." PhD diss., University of California, Berkeley.

Petzold, K.-E. 1976. "Die Meleagros-Geschichte der Ilias." *Historia* 25:146–169.

Poli, Diego. 1984. "La Funzione del 'Mediare' in Eumeo." *Aion: Annali del Seminario di studi del mondo classico, Sezione linguistica* 6:285–312.

———. 1992. "Le Divin Porcher: Un essai de comparaison." *Études celtiques* 29:375–381.

Porter, David. 2010. "The Simile at *Iliad* 16.7–11 Once Again: Multiple Meanings." *Classical World* 103:447–454.

Porter, James I. 2008. "The Disgrace of Matter in Ancient Aesthetics." In *Kakos: Badness and Anti-Value in Classical Antiquity*, ed. Ineke Sluiter and Ralph M. Rosen, 283–318. Mnemosyne Supplements 307. Leiden.

Powell, Barry. 1977. *Composition by Theme in the Odyssey*. Beiträge zur klassischen Philologie 81. Meisenheim am Glan.

Pratt, Louise. 1994. "*Odyssey* 19.535–50: On the Interpretation of Dreams and Signs in Homer." *Classical Philology* 89:147–152.

Price, Thomas D., and A. W. Van Buren. 1935. "The House of Marcus Loreius Tiburtinus at Pompeii." *Memoirs of the American Academy in Rome* 12: 151–153.

Price, T. H. 1973. "Hero-Cult and Homer." *Historia* 22:129–144.

Pucci, Pietro. 1993. "Antiphonal Lament between Achilles and Briseis." *Colby Quarterly* 29:258–272.

———. 1995. *Odysseus Polytropos: Intertextual Readings in the* Odyssey *and the* Iliad. 2nd ed. Ithaca.

———. 1996. "The Song of the Sirens." In Schein 1996:191–199. Orig. pub. 1979. *Arethusa* 12.121–32.

Pugliese Carratelli, Giovanni. 1990. *Pompei: pitture e mosaici.* Rome.

Purves, Alex. 2019. *Homer and the Poetics of Gesture.* Oxford.

Rabel, Robert J. 1988. "Chryses and the Opening of the *Iliad.*" *American Journal of Philology* 109:473–481.

Rebuffat, D., and R. Rebuffat. 1978. "De Sidoine Apollinaire à la Tombe François." *Latomus* 37:88–104.

Redfield, James M. 1973. "The Making of the *Odyssey.*" In *Parnassus Revisited,* ed. Antony Yu, 141–154. Chicago.

———. 1979. "The Proem of the *Iliad*: Homer's Art." *Classical Philology* 74:95–110.

———. 1990. "Drama and Community: Aristophanes and Some of His Rivals." In *Nothing to Do with Dionysos?,* ed. John J. Winkler and Froma I. Zeitlin, 314–335. Princeton.

———. 1994. *Nature and Culture in the Iliad: The Tragedy of Hector.* Expanded ed. Durham.

———. 1995. "Homo Domesticus." In *The Greeks,* ed. Jean-Pierre Vernant, 153–183. Chicago.

———. n.d. "Briseis as a Speaking Sign." Unpublished MS.

Reece, Steve. 1993. *The Stranger's Welcome: Oral Theory and the Aesthetics of the Homeric Hospitality Scene.* Ann Arbor.

———. 1994. "The Cretan *Odyssey*: A Lie Truer Than Truth." *American Journal of Philology* 115:157–173.

Rehm, Rush. 2002. *The Play of Space.* Princeton.

Reinhardt, Karl. 1997. "The Telemachy, Circe and Calypso, The Phaeacians." In *Homer: German Scholarship in Translation,* trans. G. M. Wright and P. V. Jones, Introduction by P. V. Jones, 217–248. Oxford.

Rendsburg, Gary A. 2008. "The Two Screens: On Mary Douglas's Proposal for a Literary Structure to the Book of Leviticus." *Jewish Studies Quarterly* 15:175–189.

Reynolds, Dwight F. 1995. *Heroic Poets, Poetic Heroes: The Ethnography of Performance in an Arabic Oral Epic Tradition.* Ithaca.

Richardson, N. J. 1980. "Literary Criticism in the Exegetical Scholia to the *Iliad*: A Sketch." *Classical Quarterly* 30:265–287.

———. 1983. "Recognition Scenes in the *Odyssey* and Ancient Criticism." *Papers of the Liverpool Latin Seminar* 4:219–235.

———. 1993. *The Iliad: A Commentary*. Vol. 6, *Books 21–24*. Cambridge.

Richardson, Scott. 1990. *The Homeric Narrator*. Nashville.

Richter, Gisela. 1928–1929. "A Statue of Protesilaos in the Metropolitan Museum." *Metropolitan Museum Studies* 1:187–200.

Riffaterre, Michael. 1987. "The Intertextual Unconscious." *Critical Inquiry* 13: 371–385.

Ringer, Mark. 1998. *Electra and the Empty Urn: Metatheater and Role Playing in Sophocles*. Chapel Hill.

Roisman, Hanna M. 1990. "Eumaeus and Odysseus: Covert Recognition and Self-Revelation." *Illinois Classical Studies* 15:215–238.

Rorty, Amélie Oksenberg, ed. 1992. *Essays on Aristotle's Poetics*. Princeton.

Rose, Gilbert P. 1980. "The Swineherd and the Beggar." *Phoenix* 34:285–297.

Rose, Peter. 1988. "Thersites and the Plural Voices of Homer." *Arethusa* 21:5–25.

———. 1992. *Sons of the Gods, Children of Earth: Ideology and Literary Form in Ancient Greece*. Ithaca.

———. 1997. "Ideology in the *Iliad*: Polis, Basileus, Theoi." *Arethusa* 30:151–199.

Rosner, Judith A. 1976. "The Speech of Phoenix: *Iliad* 9.434–605." *Phoenix* 30:314–327.

Royle, Nicholas. 2003. *The Uncanny*. Manchester.

Russo, Joseph, Manuel Fernandez-Galiano, and Alfred Heubeck. 1992. *A Commentary on Homer's Odyssey*. Vol. III. *Books XVII–XXIV*. Oxford.

Russo, Joseph, and Bennett Simon. 1968. "Homeric Psychology and the Oral Epic Tradition." *Journal for the History of Ideas* 29:483–498.

Ryder, Frank G., trans. 1962. *The Song of the Nibelungs: A Verse Translation from the Middle High German Nibelungenlied*. Detroit.

Sachs, Eva. 1933. "Die Meleagererzählung in der *Iliad* und das mythische Paradeigma." *Philologus* 88:16–29.

Sacks, Richard. 2012. "Odysseus Traditions and the τέλος of the *Odyssey*." *Donum natalicium digitaliter confectum Gregorio Nagy septuagenario a discipulis collegis familiaribus oblatum*. Ed. V. Bers, D. Elmer, D. Frame, and L. Muellner. Washington, DC. http://chs.harvard.edu/CHS/article/display/4843.

Said, Edward. 1993. *Culture and Imperialism*. London.

Schadewaldt, Wolfgang. 1965. *Von Homers Welt und Werk. Aufsätze und Auslegungen zur Homerischen Frage*. 4th ed. Stuttgart.

Schechner, Richard. 2003. *Performance Theory*. 2nd ed. New York.

Schechner, Richard, and Willa Appel, eds. 1990. *By Means of Performance: Intercultural Studies of Theatre and Ritual.* Cambridge.

Schein, Seth L. 1984. *The Mortal Hero: An Introduction to Homer's Iliad.* Berkeley.

———, ed. 1996. *Reading the Odyssey: Selected Interpretive Essays.* Princeton.

———. 2016. *Homeric Epic and its Reception: Interpretive Essays.* Oxford.

Schibli, Hermann S. 1983. "Fragments of a Weasel and Mouse War." *Zeitschrift für Papyrologie und Epigraphik* 53:1–25.

Scodel, Ruth. 1980. *The Trojan Trilogy of Euripides.* Hypomnemata 60. Göttingen.

———. 1982a. "The Achaean Wall and the Myth of Destruction." *Harvard Studies in Classical Philology* 86:33–50.

———. 1982b. "The Autobiography of Phoenix: *Iliad* 9.444–95." *American Journal of Philology* 103:128–136.

———. 1998. "Bardic Performance and Oral Tradition in Homer." *American Journal of Philology* 119:171–194.

———. 1999. *Credible Impossibilities: Conventions and Strategies of Verisimilitude in Homer and Greek Tragedy.* Beiträge zur Altertumskunde. Stuttgart.

———. 2002. *Listening to Homer: Tradition, Narrative, and Audience.* Ann Arbor.

Scott, W. C. 1974. *The Oral Nature of the Homeric Simile.* Mnemosyne Supplement 28. Leiden.

———. 2009. *The Artistry of the Homeric Simile.* Hanover, NH.

Sealey, R. 1957. "From Phemius to Ion." *Revue des études grecques* 70:312–355.

Segal, Charles. 1962. "The Phaeacians and the Symbolism of Odysseus' Return." *Arion* 1:17–64.

———. 1967. "Transition and Ritual in Odysseus' Return." In *La Parola del Passato: Rivista di Studi Antichi* 116:321–342.

———. 1978. "'The Myth Was Saved': Reflections on Homer and the Mythology of Plato's *Republic.*" *Hermes* 106:315–336.

———. 1983. "*Kleos* and its Ironies in the *Odyssey.*" *L'Antiquité Classique* 52:22–47. Reprinted in Schein 1996:201–221.

———. 1994. *Singers, Heroes, and Gods in the Odyssey.* Ithaca.

Severyns, Albert. 1928. *Le Cycle épique dans l'école d'Aristarque.* Paris.

Shapiro, H. A. 1989. *Art and Cult under the Tyrants in Athens.* Mainz am Rhein.

———. 1993. "Hipparchos and the Rhapsodes." In *Cultural Poetics in Archaic Greece,* ed. Carol Dougherty and Leslie Kurke, 92–107. Cambridge.

Simon, Bennett. 1978. *Mind and Madness in Ancient Greece: The Classical Roots of Modern Psychiatry.* Ithaca.

Sinos, Dale S. 1980. *Achilles, Patroclus, and the Meaning of Philos.* Innsbruck.

Slatkin, Laura. 1986. "Genre and Generation in the *Odyssey.*" ΜΗΤΙΣ 1:259–268.

———. 1991. *The Power of Thetis: Allusion and Interpretation in the Iliad.* Berkeley.

Slatkin, Laura. 1996. "Composition by Theme and the *Metis* of the *Odyssey*." In Schein 1996:223–237.

———. 2007. "Notes on Tragic Visualizing in the *Iliad*." In *Visualizing the Tragic: Drama, Myth, and Ritual in Greek Art and Literature*, ed. Chris Kraus, Simon Goldhill, Helene P. Foley, and Jaś Elsner, 19–34. New York.

———. 2011. *The Power of Thetis and Selected Essays*. Washington, DC.

Smith, John D. 1991. *The Epic of Pabuji*. Cambridge.

Snell, Bruno. 1952. "Bakchylides' Marpessa-Gedicht Fr. 20A." *Hermes* 80:156–163.

Sofer, Andrew. 2003. *The Stage Life of Props*. Ann Arbor.

Sommerstein, Alan H. 2000. "The Prologue of Aeschylus' *Palamedes*." *Rheinisches Museum* 143:118–127.

Sowa, Cora. 1984. *Traditional Themes and the Homeric Hymns*. Chicago.

Stanford, W. B., ed. 1996. *The Odyssey*. Repr. of 2nd ed. London.

Stanley, Keith. 1993. *The Shield of Homer: Narrative Structure in the Iliad*. Princeton.

Starobinski, Jean. 1975. "The Inside and the Outside." Trans. Frederick Brown. *Hudson Review* 28:333–51. Orig. pub. 1974 as "'Je hais comme les portes d'Hadès.'" *Nouvelle revue de psychanalyse* 9:7–22.

———. 2002. "The Promise of *Idomeneo*." Trans. Richard Pevear. *Hudson Review* 55:15–30.

Steiner, Deborah. 2001. *Images in Mind: Statues in Archaic and Classical Greek Literature and Thought*. Princeton.

Stewart, Andrew. 1983. "Stesichoros and the François Vase." In *Ancient Greek Art and Iconography*, ed. Warren G. Moon, 53–74. Madison, WI.

Stewart, Douglas. 1976. *The Disguised Guest: Rank, Role and Identity in the Odyssey*. Lewisburg, PA.

Sullivan, Francis A. 1950. "Charon, the Ferryman of the Dead." *Classical Journal* 46:11–17.

Sun, Nilaja. 2008. *No Child ...*. New York.

Swain, S. C. R. 1988. "A Note on *Iliad* 9.524–99: The Story of Meleager." *Classical Quarterly* 38:271–276.

Taplin, Oliver. 1978. *Greek Tragedy in Action*. Berkeley.

———. 1980. "The Shield of Achilleus within the *Iliad*." *Greece and Rome* 27:1–21.

———. 1992. *Homeric Soundings: the Shaping of the Iliad*. Oxford.

Thalmann, William G. 1988. "Thersites: Comedy, Scapegoats, and Heroic Ideology in the *Iliad*." *Transactions of the American Philological Association* 118:1–28.

———. 1998. *The Swineherd and the Bow: Representations of Class in the Odyssey*. Ithaca.

Thompson, D'Arcy. 1936. *A Glossary of Greek Birds*. 2nd ed. Oxford.

Thompson, Norma. 1999. "Against Entertainment." In *Literary Imagination, Ancient and Modern: Essays in Honor of David Grene*, ed. Todd Breyfogle, 177–202. Chicago.

Thompson, Stith. 1966. *Motif-Index of Folk Literature*. 6 vols. Bloomington.

Tompkins, Jane P. 1980. *Reader-Response Criticism: From Formalism to Poststructuralism*. Baltimore.

Tran, V. Tam Tinh. 1964. *Essai sur le Culte d'Isis à Pompéi*. Paris.

Trapp, M. B. 1997. *Maximus of Tyre: The Philosophical Orations*. Oxford.

Tsagalis, Christos. 2012a. *From Listeners to Viewers: Space in the Iliad*. Hellenic Studies 53. Washington, DC. http://nrs.harvard.edu/urn-3:hul.ebook:CHS_Tsagalis C.From_Listeners_to_Viewers.2012.

———. 2012b. "Deauthorizing the Epic Cycle: Odysseus' False Tale to Eumaeus (*Od.* 14.199–359)." In Montanari, Rengakos, and Tsagalis 2012:309–345.

Turner, Jeffrey S. 1993. "ΑΤΟΠΙΑ in Plato's Gorgias." *International Studies in Philosophy* 25:69–77.

van Brock, N. 1959. "Substitution rituelle." *Revue Hittite et Asiatique* 65:117–146.

van den Broek, R. 1971. *The Myth of the Phoenix According to Classical and Early Christian Traditions*. Leiden.

van der Valk, M., ed. 1971–1987. *Eustathii archiepiscopi Thessalonicensis commentarii ad Homeri Iliadem pertinentes ad fidem codicis Laurentiani editi*. 4 vols. Leiden.

Vermeule, Emily. 1979. *Aspects of Death in Early Greek Art and Poetry*. Berkeley.

Vernant, Jean-Pierre. 1991. *Mortals and Immortals: Collected Essays*. Ed. Froma I. Zeitlin. Princeton.

———. 2006. *Myth and Thought among the Greeks*. Trans. Janet Lloyd with Jeff Fort. Paris.

Vivante, Paolo. 1982. *The Epithets in Homer: A Study in Poetic Values*. Yale.

Wace, A. J. B., and F. H. Stubbings, eds. 1962. *A Companion to Homer*. New York.

Walcot, Peter. 1977. "Odysseus and the Art of Lying." *Ancient Society* 8:1–19.

Walsh, George B. 1984. *The Varieties of Enchantment: Early Greek Views of the Nature and Function of Poetry*. Chapel Hill.

Watkins, Calvert. 1970. "Language of Gods and Language of Men: Remarks on Some Indo-European Meta-linguistic Traditions." In *Myth and Law among the Indo-Europeans*, ed. J. Puhvel, 1–17. Berkeley.

———. 1977. "On ΜΗΝΙΣ." *Indo-European Studies* 3:686–722.

———. 1995. *How to Kill a Dragon: Aspects of Indo-European Poetics*. New York.

Watrous, John. 1999. "Artemis and the Lion: Two Similes in *Odyssey* 6." In Carlisle and Levaniouk 1999:165–177.

Webber, Alice. 1989. "The Hero Tells His Name: Formula and Variation in the Phaeacian Episode of the *Odyssey*." *Transactions of the American Philological Association* 119:1–13.

Weil, Simone. 1945. "The *Iliad,* or the Poem of Force." Trans. Mary McCarthy. *Politics* (November 1945): 321–331.

West, Martin L., ed. 1966. *Hesiod: Theogony.* Oxford.

———, ed. 1978. *Hesiod: Works and Days.* Oxford.

———. 1981. "The Singing of Homer and the Modes of Early Greek Music." *Journal of Hellenic Studies* 101:113–129.

———. 1985a. *The Hesiodic Catalogue of Women.* Oxford.

———. 1985b. "The Hesiodic Catalogue: New Light on Apollo's Love-Life." *Zeitschrift für Papyrologie und Epigraphik* 61:1–7.

———. 1988. "The Rise of the Greek Epic." *Journal of Hellenic Studies* 108:151–172.

———. 1997. *The East Face of Helicon: West Asiatic Elements in Greek Poetry.* Oxford.

———. 2001. *Studies in the Text and Transmission of the Iliad.* Munich.

———, ed. and trans. 2003. *Greek Epic Fragments from the Seventh to the Fifth Centuries BC.* Loeb Classical Library. Cambridge, MA.

———. 2010. "Rhapsodes at Festivals." *Zeitschrift für Papyrologie und Epigraphik* 108:151–172.

———. 2011. *The Making of the Iliad: Disquisition and Analytical Commentary.* Oxford.

———. 2013. *The Epic Cycle: A Commentary on the Lost Troy Epics.* Oxford.

West, Stephanie R. 1981. "An Alternative Nostos for Odysseus." *Liverpool Classical Monthly* 6.7:169–175.

———. 2001. "Phoenix's Antecedents: A Note on *Iliad* 9." *Scripta Classica Israelica* 20:1–15.

Whitman, Cedric H. 1958. *Homer and the Heroic Tradition.* Cambridge, MA.

Whitman, Cedric H., and Ruth Scodel. 1981. "Sequence and Simultaneity in *Iliad* N, Ξ and O." *Harvard Studies in Classical Philology* 85:1–15.

Wilamowitz-Moellendorff, U. von. 1927. *Die Heimkehr des Odysseus: Neue Untersuchungen.* Berlin.

Wiles, David. 1987. "Reading Greek Performance." *Greece and Rome* 34:136–151.

———. 1997. *Tragedy at Athens: Performance Space and Theatrical Meaning.* Cambridge.

———. 2000. *Greek Theatre Performance: An Introduction.* Cambridge.

Willcock, Malcolm M. 1964. "Mythological Paradeigma in the *Iliad.*" *Classical Quarterly* 58 (N.S. 14):141–154.

———. 1977. "Ad Hoc Invention in the *Iliad.*" *Harvard Studies in Classical Philology* 81:41–53.

———. 1978–1984. *The Iliad of Homer.* 2 vols. New York.

Wilson, August. 1986. *Fences.* New York.

Winnicott, Donald W. 1971. *Playing and Reality.* New York.

Winter, Irene J. 1995. "Homer's Phoenicians: History, Ethnography, or Literary Trope? A Perspective on Early Orientalism." In Carter and Morris 1995: 247–271.

Woodhouse, W. J. 1930. *The Composition of Homer's Odyssey*. Oxford.

Wright, Doug. 2004. *I Am My Own Wife*. New York.

Wyatt, William F. 1989. "The Intermezzo of *Odyssey* 11 and the Poets Homer and Odysseus." In *Studi Micenei ed Egeo-Anatolici*. Fasc. 27. Incunabula Graeca 89. Rome.

Yatromanolakis, Dimitrios, and Panagiotis Roilos, eds. 2004. *Greek Ritual Poetics*. Hellenic Studies 3. Washington, DC.

Zamir, Tzachi. 2010. "Watching Actors." *Theatre Journal* 62:227–243.

Zanker, G. 1981. "Enargeia in the Ancient Criticism of Poetry." *Rheinisches Museum* 124:297–311.

Zanker, Paul, and Björn C. Ewald. 2012. *Living with Myths: The Imagery of Roman Sarcophagi*. Trans. Julia Slater. Oxford.

Zarrilli, Phillip. 1990. "What Does It Mean to 'Become the Character': Power, Presence and Transcendence in Asian In-body Disciplines of Practice." In Schechner and Appel 1990:131–148.

Zeitlin, Froma. 1996. *Playing the Other: Gender and Society in Classical Greek Literature*. Chicago.

Zumthor, Paul. 1990. *Oral Poetry: An Introduction*. Trans. Kathryn Murphy-Judy. Minneapolis.

Subject Index

Index of Homeric Passages